Daughter
OF THE REVOLUTION

mela

multi-ethnic literatures of the americas

AMRITJIT SINGH, CARLA L. PETERSON, C. LOK CHUA, SERIES EDITORS

The MELA series aims to expand and deepen our sense of American literatures as multicultural and multi-lingual and works to establish a broader understanding of "America" as a complex site for the creation of national, transnational, and global narratives. Volumes in the series focus on the recovery, consolidation, and reevaluation of literary expression in the United States, Canada, and the Caribbean as shaped by the experience of race, ethnicity, national origin, region, class, gender, and language.

Lin Yutang
CHINATOWN FAMILY
EDITED AND WITH AN INTRODUCTION BY *C. Lok Chua*

Pauline E. Hopkins
DAUGHTER OF THE REVOLUTION:
THE MAJOR NONFICTION WORKS OF PAULINE E. HOPKINS
EDITED AND WITH AN INTRODUCTION BY *Ira Dworkin*

Claude McKay
A LONG WAY FROM HOME
EDITED AND WITH AN INTRODUCTION BY *Gene Andrew Jarrett*

SHADOWED DREAMS: WOMEN'S POETRY
OF THE HARLEM RENAISSANCE
2ND EDITION, REVISED AND EXPANDED
EDITED AND WITH AN INTRODUCTION BY *Maureen Honey*

Daughter
OF THE REVOLUTION

THE MAJOR NONFICTION WORKS OF
Pauline E. Hopkins

EDITED AND WITH AN INTRODUCTION BY
Ira Dworkin

RUTGERS UNIVERSITY PRESS
NEW BRUNSWICK, NEW JERSEY, AND LONDON

Library of Congress Cataloging-in-Publication Data

Hopkins, Pauline E. (Pauline Elizabeth)
    Daughter of the revolution : the major nonfiction works of Pauline E. Hopkins ; edited and with an introduction
by Ira Dworkin.
        p. cm. — (Multi-ethnic literatures of the Americas)
    Includes bibliographical references and index.
    ISBN-13: 978-0-8135-3961-4 (hardcover : alk. paper)
    ISBN-13: 978-0-8135-3962-1 (pbk. : alk. paper)
    1. African Americans—History—1877–1964.   2. African Americans—Biography.   3. Racism—United States—
History—20th century.   4. United States—Race relations—History—20th century.   5. Racism—History—20th
century.   I. Dworkin, Ira, 1972–.   II. Title.   III. Series.
    E185.6.H7 2006
    973'.0496073—dc22

                                                                                                2006011576

A British Cataloging-in-Publication record for this book is available from the British Library.

This collection © 2007 by Rutgers, The State University
Introduction and scholarly apparatus copyright © 2007 by Ira Dworkin

Text design by Adam B. Bohannon
Visit our Web site: http://rutgerspress.rutgers.edu
Manufactured in the United States of America

Yesterday I sat in the old Joy street church and you can imagine my emotions as I remembered my great grandfather begged in England the money that helped the Negro cause, that my grandfather on my father's side, signed the papers with Garrison at Philadelphia. I remembered that at Bunker Hill my ancestors on my maternal side poured out their blood. I am a daughter of the Revolution, you do not acknowledge black daughters of the Revolution but we are going to take that right.

—PAULINE E. HOPKINS

CONTENTS

ILLUSTRATIONS

ACKNOWLEDGMENTS

Much of this work was undertaken at the University of Miami in Coral Gables, Florida. My gratitude is due to Africana Studies, American Studies, and the Office of Interdisciplinary Studies in the College of Arts and Sciences for funding several research trips and enabling me to hire an excellent research assistant, F. Hunter Carey, who spent a semester helping me to edit my transcriptions. Professor Edmund Abaka, director of Africana Studies, was a valuable mentor and colleague. Bryanna Herzog and her staff at the University of Miami Digital Media Lab patiently provided technical support. University of Miami Richter Library, in particular the Interlibrary Loan Office, was another crucial resource.

My sincere appreciation is also due to librarians at Boston University's Howard Gotlieb Archival Research Center, Brooklyn College Library, Emory University's Woodruff Library Special Collections and Archives Division, Fisk University's Franklin Library Special Collections, Howard University's Moorland-Spingarn Research Center, New York Public Library's Humanities and Social Science Library and Schomburg Center for Research in Black Culture, Rutherford B. Hayes Presidential Library, University of Pennsylvania's Van Pelt Library, and Yale University's Beinecke Rare Book and Manuscript Library and Sterling Memorial Library. Beth M. Howse, special collections librarian at Fisk, and Donna M. Wells, prints and photographs librarian at Moorland-Spingarn, provided access to rare materials that I am honored to reproduce here.

From the time when this book was only a proposal, I have been encouraged by the unflagging interest of Leslie Mitchner, editor in chief at Rutgers University Press. Everyone whom I have worked with at the press has been consistently helpful. Additional thanks are due to the editors of the Multi-Ethnic Literatures of the Americas series—Carla L. Peterson, C. Lok Chua, and Amritjit Singh—and to the press's anonymous reader. In particular, Carla Peterson's input has greatly improved the final product.

I am grateful to the extraordinary community of colleagues, students, family, and friends who have contributed to this project. I was introduced to Hopkins through her novel *Contending Forces* in an undergraduate class at Wesleyan University taught by Professor Ann duCille. A. Papatya Bucak, Terri Francis, Hollis Gentry, John Cullen Gruesser, Chris Iannini, Alisha Knight, Alan Lewis, Jessica Metzler, Stacy Morgan, Anne Rice, Ray Sapirstein, Hanna Wallinger, and Jim Zwick all graciously responded to queries related to this project. John Gruesser provided an unpublished Hopkins letter and has been a dependable resource. Hanna Wallinger deserves a wholehearted thank you for providing copies of Hopkins's speeches on the Garrison and Sumner centenaries. Terri Francis, Jeffrey Ogbonna Ogbar, Ranen Omer-Sherman, and Michele Wallace provided insightful commentary on an early version of my introduction; their contributions can be measured by the lack of resemblance between what they read and what is published here. In addition to all of the folks named above, my research has benefited from the wise counsel and encouragement of Tuzyline Allan, Houston Baker, Moustafa Bayoumi, Peter Bellis, Michael Carlebach, George Cunningham, James deJongh, Andrew Draper, Geoffrey Jacques, Jeff Kerr-Ritchie, Gordon Thompson, Lindsey Tucker, Tisha Ulmer, and many others. Terri Francis, mentioned under several categories listed above, warrants appreciation under several additional rubrics not listed here for her support as I prepared this volume.

Finally, thank you to Pauline E. Hopkins and her readers, from her day to today, for sustaining the literary communities that make this work.

CHRONOLOGY

For biographical details on Hopkins, see Ann Allen Shockley, "Pauline Elizabeth Hopkins: A Biographical Excursion into Obscurity," and Hanna Wallinger, *Pauline E. Hopkins: A Literary Biography*.

1859	Pauline Elizabeth Hopkins born in New England. John Brown leads antislavery raid on federal arsenal in Harpers Ferry, Virginia. Harriet Wilson publishes *Our Nig*, considered first published novel by an African American woman.
1861	U.S. Civil War begins.
1863	Emancipation Proclamation, issued by President Abraham Lincoln, takes effect, enabling African American soldiers to serve in the Union Army.
1865	End of Civil War. Thirteenth Amendment to the Constitution outlaws slavery.
1868	Fourteenth Amendment to the Constitution grants blacks citizenship.
1869	African Methodist Episcopal (AME) Church's *Christian Recorder* publishes Frances E. W. Harper's *Minnie's Sacrifice* serial novel.
1870	Fifteenth Amendment to the Constitution grants all male citizens the right to vote.
1874	Hopkins wins a $10 prize from the Congregational Publishing Society of Boston for her essay on "The Evils of Intemperance and Their Remedy."
1876	*Christian Recorder* begins Harper's *Sowing and Reaping: A Temperance Story* serial novel.
1877	The era of Radical Reconstruction ends with the withdrawal of federal troops from the South.
1879	Hopkins premiers her musical play *Peculiar Sam; or, The Underground Railroad* (revised as *Slaves' Escape; or, The Underground Railroad*).
1881	Tuskegee Institute in Alabama established with Booker T. Washington as first principal.
1882	Hopkins' Colored Troubadours perform a concert at Arcanum Hall in Allston, Massachusetts.
1884	Death of William Wells Brown.
1888	*Christian Recorder* begins Harper's *Trial and Triumph* serial novel.
1890	Mississippi disfranchises black citizens; by the end of the decade, all other southern states follow suit.
1892	Harper's *Iola Leroy* published. Anna Julia Cooper's *A Voice from the South* published. Hopkins works as a stenographer for Massachusetts Republican politicians.
1893	World's Columbian Exposition held in Chicago. Paul Laurence Dunbar's *Oak and Ivy* published.
1894	*The Woman's Era* begins publication.

1895   Booker T. Washington delivers address to the Atlanta Cotton States Exposition. Hopkins is hired as a stenographer for the Massachusetts census bureau.

1896   *Plessy v. Ferguson* Supreme Court decision sanctions segregation. National Association of Colored Women is organized. Ethiopian troops under Menelik II defeat Italian invaders at Aduwa. Dodd, Mead publishes Dunbar's *Lyrics of a Lowly Life*.

1898   Following an explosion that sinks the U.S.S. *Maine* in Havana Harbor, the United States enters the Cuban War of Independence and acquires Guam, Puerto Rico, and the Philippines from Spain. Anti-Imperialist League formed. Hopkins represents the Woman's Era Club at the Annual Convention of New England Federation of Woman's Clubs.

1899   Filipino rebellion against U.S. occupation begins. Houghton Mifflin publishes Charles W. Chesnutt's short story collections, *The Conjure Woman* and *The Wife of His Youth and Other Stories of the Color Line*. Hopkins completes her novel *Contending Forces*.

1900   Pan-African Conference meets in London. Houghton Mifflin publishes Chesnutt's first novel, *The House Behind the Cedars*. The Colored Co-operative Publishing Company publishes Hopkins's *Contending Forces*. *Colored American Magazine (CAM)* publishes its first issue and begins Hopkins's *Famous Men of the Negro Race* series.

1901   U.S. President William McKinley assassinated; Vice President Theodore Roosevelt inaugurated as president. Booker T. Washington's *Up From Slavery* published. Boston Literary and Historical Association formed. *Boston Guardian* publishes its first issue. *CAM* begins Hopkins's *Famous Women of the Negro Race* series and *Hagar's Daughter* serial novel.

1902   *CAM* publishes Hopkins's *Winona* serial novel and begins Hopkins's *Of One Blood* serial novel.

1903   William Monroe Trotter is arrested for leading a demonstration at a Booker T. Washington speech in Boston. W.E.B. Du Bois's *The Souls of Black Folk* published. William Dupree takes over the *CAM,* and gives Hopkins the title of "Literary Editor." *CAM* publishes Hopkins's *Furnace Blasts* series.

1904   Roosevelt elected U.S. president. John Freund becomes involved in the affairs of the *CAM*. Fred R. Moore, a Washington confidante, purchases the magazine and moves it from Boston to New York. Under Moore, Hopkins's role at the *CAM* diminishes, and she is eventually "forced to resign." *Voice of the Negro* publishes its first issue, and hires Hopkins.

1905   Niagara movement, organized by Du Bois, holds its first meeting. International Workers of the World formed in Chicago, marking the radicalization of the labor movement. *Chicago Defender* newspaper publishes its first issue. Hopkins self-publishes *A Primer of Facts Pertaining to the Early Greatness of the African Race and the Possibility of Restoration by its Descendants*. *Voice of the Negro* publishes Hopkins's *The Dark Races of the Twentieth Century* series. Hopkins addresses William Lloyd Garrison centenary in Boston.

1906	Atlanta riot forces *Voice of the Negro* to relocate to Chicago. Following the Brownsville Affair in Texas, President Roosevelt supports the dishonorable discharge of black soldiers unjustly implicated in a shooting.
1907	The relocated and renamed Chicago-based *Voice* ceases publication.
1909	National Association for the Advancement of Colored People (NAACP) is organized. The *Colored American Magazine* ceases publication.
1910	The NAACP *Crisis,* edited by Du Bois, publishes its first issue.
1911	Hopkins addresses Charles Sumner centenary in Boston.
1912	James Weldon Johnson's *The Autobiography of an Ex-Coloured Man* published anonymously.
1914	World War I begins.
1915	Death of Booker T. Washington. D. W. Griffith's film *Birth of a Nation,* based on fiction by Thomas Dixon, premiers.
1916	Marcus Garvey arrives in New York and creates U.S. branches of the Universal Negro Improvement Association. *New Era Magazine,* founded by Hopkins and Walter Wallace, publishes two issues, which feature Hopkins's *Men of Vision* series and *Topsy Templeton* serial novel.
1917	The United States enters World War I.
1918	World War I ends.
1919	The first Pan-African Congress meets in Paris. White mobs attack blacks across the United States during "Red Summer" of racist violence.
1920	Nineteenth Amendment to the Constitution grants women the right to vote.
1925	Alain Locke edits an issue of *Survey Graphic* magazine, later reissued as the *New Negro.*
1928	Nella Larsen's *Quicksand* and *Passing* published.
1930	Pauline Hopkins dies in Cambridge, Massachusetts, from burns sustained during a fire at her home.

1. Pauline E. Hopkins (1859–1930).

INTRODUCTION

Pauline E. Hopkins is most remembered for her first novel, *Contending Forces: A Romance Illustrative of Negro Life North and South*, which was published in Boston in 1900. Her publisher, the Colored Co-operative Publishing Company, vigorously used its monthly *Colored American Magazine* to promote it, and she soon became the magazine's most recognizable personality. Through its pages, which, in its first four years of publication, featured three of her serial novels and seven of her short stories, Hopkins emerged as a major literary figure whose prodigious output makes her one of the most published African American women writers of fiction prior to the 1920s.

Today, her reputation stands primarily on the quality of her fiction, which has been widely available since the late 1980s. Building on black feminist scholarship and publications by Ann Allen Shockley, Gwendolyn Brooks, Mary Helen Washington, Claudia Tate, and Hazel Carby, among others, Oxford University Press's Schomburg Library of Nineteenth-Century Black Women Writers reprinted all of her fiction from the *Colored American Magazine* in three volumes: *Contending Forces, The Magazine Novels of Pauline Hopkins,* and *Short Fiction by Black Women, 1900–1920,* which includes her stories. Other editions have followed. During the past two decades, Hopkins has quickly become recognized as one the most accomplished African American novelists of the period and is a mainstay in college classrooms, dissertations, academic journals, and scholarly monographs. In 1996, *The Unruly Voice: Rediscovering Pauline Elizabeth Hopkins,* edited by John Cullen Gruesser, showcased a range of new critical work and provided bibliographies of primary and secondary materials. A new literary biography by Hanna Wallinger (*Pauline E. Hopkins: A Literary Biography,* University of Georgia Press, 2005) and other forthcoming studies promise to open new doors on the whole of her career and life, and to ensure that this interest continues.

While readers of Hopkins's fiction may be peripherally aware of her career as an editor and essayist, the writings themselves have long been unavailable and remain largely unfamiliar despite occasional excerpts in anthologies such as the *Norton Anthology of African American Literature* and Gerald Early's notable inclusion of *The Dark Races of the Twentieth Century* in the now out-of-print second volume of *Speech and Power: The African American Essay and Its Cultural Content from Polemics to Pulpit.* While the current scarcity of her nonfiction contrasts with the widespread availability of her fiction, in a prospectus for 1901 the *Colored American Magazine* gave top billing to her nonfiction series *Famous Men of the Negro Race.*[1] This nonfiction voice, which was so central to the *Colored American Magazine,* is collected for the first time in this anthology.

As a novelist, editor, and essayist, Hopkins helped to shape a major literary periodical that, on its first anniversary in May 1901, proudly claimed 100,000 readers.[2] With a monthly circulation reaching 20,000, the *Colored American Magazine* was almost certainly the most widely read African American journal of the twentieth century's first decade, and Hopkins was its best-known personality.[3] It was not the first African American national literary magazine, but rather built on the foundations of nineteenth-century publications such as the African Methodist Episcopal Book Concern's *AME Magazine* and the still-in-existence *Christian Recorder,* and the New York-based *Anglo-African Magazine.* And although it was distinct from local newspapers that were familiar in African American communities nationwide, it remained indebted to the vibrant literary culture nurtured by the *New York Age, Indianapolis Freeman,* and hundreds of smaller publications that flourished at the end of the nineteenth century. The black press, in its various forms, was a vibrant outlet for intellectuals like Hopkins to speak out against the deterioration of black rights in the post-Reconstruction era. This period, which historian Rayford Logan famously termed the "nadir," was characterized by the rise of lynching, mass disfranchisement, legislation that restored power to the former Confederacy, and court decisions that sanctioned segregation. Yet even when white supremacist violence targeted black newspaper editors, the press remained a stalwart outlet for voices of opposition.

Pauline E. Hopkins, the Colored Co-operative Publishing Company, and the *Colored American Magazine*

The Boston-based Colored Co-operative Publishing Company was, as its name indicates, an enterprise committed to racial uplift through collective endeavor, and its first publication was Pauline Elizabeth Hopkins's novel *Contending Forces.* Hopkins, who was then in her forties, conceptualized her writing practice in collective terms, as part of her involvement in groups like the Woman's Era Club, where in 1899, "an entertaining and interesting afternoon was spent at Japanese Tea, given to Miss Pauline Hopkins, to aid her in the publication of her novel, 'Contending Forces,' portions of which she read."[4] A year earlier, she had delivered a paper as a representative of the Woman's Era Club at the Annual Convention of the New England Federation of Woman's Clubs.[5] As Elizabeth McHenry explains in *Forgotten Readers: Recovering the Lost History of African American Literary Societies,* "Hopkins's indication that she would be 'glad to give readings before women's clubs in any section of the country' suggests that she imagined African American clubwomen as a primary audience for her work."[6] These audience relationships were integral components of a public intellectual career that included magazine publishing and editing, fiction and essay writing, as well as musical theater and oratory.

Hopkins's close contact with the organized women's club movement and other vital intellectual communities fostered her development as an author. It was a somewhat different trajectory than the stereotyped solitary author in a cloistered room producing a work of individual genius. Yet contrary to the claims of Joseph R. McElrath Jr. and Robert C. Leitz III, the editors of a 1997 collection of letters by novelist and short story writer Charles W. Chesnutt, Hopkins's contributions are hardly diminished because her publishing house lacked the conventional prestige of Chesnutt's Houghton, Mifflin & Co: Chesnutt "had finally prevailed as an author, unlike the majority of black writers, who could do no better than Pauline Hopkins when she placed her 1900 novel *Contending Forces* with Boston's Colored Co-operative Publishing Company."[7] Far from a failure, Hopkins's association with the Colored Co-operative Publishing Company enabled her to engage her readers on a consistent basis not only through her novel, which was marketed to the *Colored American Magazine*'s readers and offered as a premium to subscribers, but also through other writings that appeared in the journal. McElrath and Leitz's focus on book publishing as a marker of success is odd since Chesnutt's stories in the *Atlantic Monthly* and *Puck* circulated more widely than his books. Moreover, the *Colored American Magazine* probably issued more copies per month than Houghton, Mifflin did of Chesnutt's first four books combined.[8] While the publication of Chesnutt's works by Houghton, Mifflin is a significant milestone in African American letters, Hopkins's relationship with the Colored Co-operative Publishing Company represents a signal moment in the development of black literary communities at the start of the twentieth century.

The Colored Co-operative Publishing Company was founded in Boston in 1900 by four young African American men, all under the age of thirty and born in Virginia. They envisioned Hopkins's fiction as a practical medium, which the *Colored American Magazine* characterized in terms of her rapport with her audience: "the wrongs of her race shall be so handled as to enlist the sympathy of all class of citizens, in this way reaching those who never read history or biography."[9] Her fiction, which was a unique fusion of political, historical, and sentimental themes, shared the political commitments of her nonfiction. Her historical fiction includes a novel that features abolitionist John Brown (*Winona*) and a story that recounts the rebellion aboard the *Creole* slaveship ("A Dash for Liberty"). Her serial novel *Of One Blood; or, The Hidden Self*, the story of the restoration of an African American doctor to the Ethiopian throne, deals with imperialism and colonialism, drawing on the life and writing of missionary William H. Sheppard (who appears in passing in "Mrs. Jane E. Sharp's School for African Girls").[10]

In *Reconstructing Womanhood: The Emergence of the Afro-American Woman Novelist*, a study central to the revival of interest in Hopkins, Hazel Carby explains, "The network of these relations between *Of One Blood* and other, nonfictional articles in the *Colored American Magazine* indicated the extent of an intertextual coherence, achieved under Hopkins's literary editorship, which aimed at the reconstruction of a sense of pride in an African heritage."[11] Carby's assessment suggests the importance of recognizing Hopkins not only as a writer, but also as an editor and, ultimately, as a public intellectual. With her editorial vision, Hopkins did more than create a forum for the fiction for which she is known today; she helped shape the day's most important African American forum, which during her tenure published creative works by William Stanley Braithwaite, Benjamin Brawley, James Corrothers, Daniel Webster Davis, and Angelina Grimké.

By the time that Hopkins began to write for the *Colored American Magazine*, she was an established performer and speaker in Boston, where her family moved shortly after her 1859 birth. Literary work was something of an inheritance for Hopkins, whose family tree includes poets James Monroe Whitfield, Elijah William Smith, and George Boyer Vashon.[12] Her literary career—and this anthology—begins in 1874, when she won a writing contest sponsored by the Congregational Publishing Society of Boston for "The Evils of Intemperance and Their Remedy," an essay that reveals her budding gifts and her interest in addressing social issues through writing. She received a $10 prize, an award donated by William Wells Brown, the abolitionist and author who remained a major influence throughout her career.[13] By the end of the decade, Hopkins was writing musical plays, the best known of which, *Peculiar Sam; or The Underground Railroad* (later revised and performed under the title *Slaves' Escape*), premiered in 1879 and continued to be performed for at least two more years.[14] She was herself a celebrated soprano vocalist, who performed in productions of the play, and in recitals and concerts with her family ensemble, Hopkins' Colored Troubadours.

In subsequent years, Hopkins continued to combine literature and public performance by working as a lecturer on a neo-abolitionist circuit. Her most notable presentation boldly praised Toussaint L'Ouverture, the leader of Haiti's successful revolution against slavery. As recounted in the *Colored American Magazine*, she delivered this lecture at Boston's Tremont Temple, a historic center of abolitionist organizing, where, as readers knew, black activists famously met before attempting to block the return of Anthony Burns to slavery in 1854.[15] And Hopkins later made her readers aware that Tremont Temple served as the headquarters for the New England Woman's Club and as a meeting place for the Woman's Era Club. As secretary of the Woman's Era Club and a speaker at Tremont, she actively participated in the very traditions that she celebrates.

At the end of the 1890s, as Hopkins prepared *Contending Forces* for publication, excerpts of the novel were, Shockley notes, being "read before women's clubs throughout the country."[16] After the book's release, the Colored Cooperative Publishing Company turned its attention to a monthly magazine that could reach its audience on a continuing basis (although they published at least one more book, Ellen F. Wetherell's *In Free America; or, Tales from North and South*). Significantly, the company developed an institutional practice that reflected its priorities of collective outreach and uplift. Readers of the *Colored American Magazine* were invited to purchase certificates of deposit in the cooperative and contributors were compensated with cooperative membership. The company's desire to nurture an African American literary community was expressed in an announcement that appeared regularly during the *Colored American Magazine*'s first year, eagerly soliciting readers to "separately and collectively" contribute to "the perpetuation of a history of the Negro race."[17] The first issue, published in May 1900, announced itself on its cover as "An Illustrated Monthly Devoted to Literature, Science, Music, Art, Religion, Facts, Fiction and Traditions of the Negro Race," and featured articles about an African American army regiment serving in Cuba, segregation on public transportation in Virginia, and the Burns case.

From the start, Hopkins was a central part of the venture. The sixty-four-page premier issue featured her short story "The Mystery Within Us" and announced that she would be inaugurating a "Women's Department" to cover the club movement: "While Miss Hopkins has a very happy manner of presenting any subject which she may write, she has that which is of still greater value in a department of this kind, a heartfelt desire to aid in everyway possible in uplifting the colored people of America, and through them, the world."[18] The editors clearly appreciated her multifaceted literary talents, as well as the breadth of her interests, in particular her internationalism and her focus on women's issues.

The magazine, which maintained branch offices and agents throughout the United States as well as in the West Indies and in Liberia, especially valued Hopkins's international commitment to racial uplift. Her well-known Toussaint oration manifested a strong diasporic consciousness and was the basis for her first major nonfiction publication, the 43,000+-word series *Famous Men of the Negro Race*. By inaugurating the series, which premiered in November 1900, with Toussaint, she foregrounds Haiti, which won its independence in 1804, and a black political tradition rooted in militant resistance and national independence, themes she addressed throughout her career. She concludes the installment with an explicit explanation of the relevance of the Haitian Revolution to African Americans' fight for freedom. By citing battles where African American soldiers famously fought against slavery, she declares the Civil War to be part of an international movement for black liberation. This internationalism, which would be one of the characteristic elements of her nonfiction, provided the starting point for an extremely productive period for Hopkins and the *Colored American Magazine*.

Hopkins followed *Famous Men of the Negro Race* with the 36,000+-word *Famous Women of the Negro Race*, which spotlighted another of her priorities, the active participation of women in the public sphere. While she recognized that literary work provided an outlet for women's voices, she made clear that she most admired writers who contributed more than books and articles. In the second of two installments on "Literary Workers," she praises the poet and fiction writer Frances Ellen Watkins Harper for providing emotional and financial assistance to the widow of abolitionist John Brown and to the families of his comrades following the 1859 Harpers Ferry rebellion. Harper's contributions are compatible with those of Harriet Tubman, the Underground Railroad conductor whose close relationship with John Brown she noted two months earlier. Harper's willingness to undertake "the rough work" made her a paragon of activism whose literary labors Hopkins acknowledges alongside those of reformers such as Ida B. Wells-Barnett and Mary Church Terrell. These female figures modeled the viability of literary work as a means of political activity and racial uplift, a path that Hopkins herself followed.

Most of Hopkins's nonfiction consists of biographies, which she recognized as a genre that addressed more than the life of its individual subject. As C. K. Doreski explains in a rare scholarly treatment of Hopkins's nonfiction, *Famous Men of the Negro Race* and *Famous Women of the Negro Race* shared the literary traditions of the Puritans and Ralph Waldo Emerson, but "move from the inherited rhetoric of the representative biographical sketch to a culturally defined, intertextually enriched vision of the way in which all history *is* biography."[19] By the time Hopkins wrote her two series, the use of biographical series to tell black history was already well established by authors such as William Wells Brown, James T. Haley, William Cooper Nell, William Still, and George Washington Williams, all of whom Hopkins referenced, as well as in works by H. G. Adams, Wilson Armistead, and William J. Simmons with which she was likely familiar.

Hopkins's biographical series aimed to present a course for racial advancement by summoning historical movements, most often radical abolition, in which people worked cooperatively to advance the causes of freedom. After *Famous Men* and *Famous Women* concluded, she incorporated Emerson's "Heroism" into the opening of a third series entitled *Heroes and Heroines in Black* in January 1903. Although only one article was published under that header, it reveals that Hopkins envisioned a biographical practice that placed men and women side by side. Furthermore, this promising essay uniquely joins renowned national political and military leaders like Robert Smalls with local heroes in Kentucky and Massachusetts who bravely rescued their neighbors from fires or drowning. While it is not clear why the series never developed as such, Hopkins continued to write biographies for the magazine, several of which are included along with the lone installment of *Heroes and Heroines in Black* in this volume's section on "Selected Biographies from the *Colored American Magazine.*" When read collectively, this diverse assemblage, which includes white poet-abolitionist John Greenleaf Whittier and South African journalist Alan Kirkland Soga, reveals not isolated individuals, but an inclusive historical vision that reflects Hopkins's values of antiracism, abolition, women's uplift, internationalism, cultural empowerment, and economic justice.

Hopkins's rise as a biographer occurred at a time when Booker T. Washington, the country's best known black leader, was facing increasing opposition from progressive African Americans. For the October 1901 final installment of

Famous Men of the Negro Race, Hopkins profiled Washington, and her understated jabs at her subject announce her refusal to kowtow to powerful men, a stance that would ultimately get her fired from the magazine. In the very first issue, the editors' explication of their position toward Washington indicated a delicate balance between recognizing Washington's power and addressing their northern readers' general difference of opinion: "His plans may not be yours, but I believe, if they reach the many poor boys and girls in many different sections of the South, you nor I should take exception to them. . . . We of New England can, with credit to ourselves, forbear the spirit of criticism and lend him our encouragement in every method of work he may undertake believing him as loyal to the welfare of the race as we are."[20] While judiciously warning against "misconstruing a word uttered by him in the great cause of justice that has been so clearly set forth by his manly and courageous efforts," the statements themselves presume the opposition that had been developing for several years in the magazine's hometown of Boston.[21]

Pauline E. Hopkins and the *Colored American Magazine* Controversy

The opposition at which the *Colored American Magazine* hinted in May 1900 coalesced in March 1901, with the formation of the Boston Literary and Historical Association by a group of progressive Boston intellectuals that included Hopkins. The group's "intention," according to McHenry, "was to launch a self-conscious attack on the prestige and racial policies of Booker T. Washington and his 'Tuskegee Machine.'"[22] One of the founders of the Boston Literary and Historical Association was William Monroe Trotter, who was one of Washington's less polite critics. After Trotter and George Washington Forbes began publishing the belligerently antagonistic *Boston Guardian* newspaper in November 1901, Washington responded by funding the *Advocate* and the *Enterprise,* two Boston newspapers published by Tuskegee allies associated with the National Negro Business League. When both papers failed, Washington discretely purchased another Boston newspaper, the *Colored Citizen,* which he hoped to use as a counterbalance to the *Boston Guardian.* When the *Colored Citizen* was financially fraught, the magazine's founder, a Washington crony, tried to move its plant into the *Colored American Magazine*'s office in October 1903. As Hopkins recounts in an April 16, 1905, letter to Trotter, printed in this collection in a section on "The *Colored American Magazine* Controversy," "This we refused him in very few words for we mistrusted his intentions knowing the man."

During this period, the most dramatic confrontation between Washington and his critics occurred on July 30, 1903, when a melee resulted from a protest by Trotter and some associates at a Boston speech by Washington. As a result of Washington's vindictive pursuit of criminal charges against the demonstrators for what was dubbed the "Boston Riot," Trotter served a month in jail. At the same time, Washington was instigating Yale undergraduate William Pickens to sue the *Boston Guardian* for libel after Pickens was contemptibly defamed for naively questioning Haiti's ability for self-rule. In July 1903, Hopkins pseudonymously profiled Pickens in the *Colored American Magazine*, acknowledging his "erroneous conception of the political and social conditions existing in Hayti," but generously attributing it to "the fervent zeal of youth." Like Hopkins, who saw Pickens as the victim of "wily schemes of capitalists and unprincipled territory grabbers" aiming to create divisions among black intellectuals, Forbes felt sympathy for the young student, and decided to settle the suit by printing an apology. Trotter, who was in jail at the time, disapproved of his coeditor's settlement, and as a result their partnership ended. When Washington's attorney then surreptitiously tried to purchase Forbes's share of the paper, Trotter suspected Washington's involvement and blocked him. Having failed in his attempt to take over the *Guardian*, Washington set his sights on one of its clear allies, the more established, if less hostile, Boston-based *Colored American Magazine*, whose advertisement in the *Guardian* at the height of its Boston Riot coverage prominently announced its allegiance.[23]

The advertisement in the controversial newspaper may have been a sacrifice for the *Colored American Magazine*, which was experiencing serious financial instability that made it vulnerable to Washington's machinations. No April 1903 issue was ever published. For May and June, there was a combined issue, which was the first published under a new management team led by William Dupree, a superintendent at the Boston Post Office. Dupree was well known in Boston circles dating back to his Civil War service as a commissioned officer in the Massachusetts Fifty-fifth Regiment. Another of the regiment's four African American officers was James Monroe Trotter, and the two men eventually married sisters.[24] Since James Trotter, who died in 1892, was William Monroe Trotter's father, Dupree was William's uncle and therefore, despite periods of friction between the clans, the *Colored American Magazine*'s new management was connected to the progressive Boston community through family ties that were common knowledge—a July 1901 profile of Dupree noted the families' relationship.[25] (Hopkins herself had an intellectual debt to the senior Trotter, whose book *Music and Some Highly Musical People* was one of her sources for the "Phenomenal Vocalists" installment of *Famous Women*.) As part of the new team that Dupree assembled, Hopkins was given even more prominent standing. In the masthead, there were four names listed: the three owners and Pauline E. Hopkins, "Literary Editor." Advertisements for the magazine were headed, "Established 1900/ The *Colored American Magazine*/Edited by Pauline E. Hopkins."[26]

Soon after Dupree resuscitated the magazine, John C. Freund, the white European editor of the New York-based *Music Trades*, which had a declining circulation less than one-third that of the *Colored American Magazine*, entered the picture, claiming to be a disinterested patron offering editorial and financial assistance.[27] However, Freund quickly became the agent of Washington's takeover. In January 1904, the *Colored American Magazine* declared itself "Under New Management" and offered copies of Washington's books as premiums to

2. This advertisement highlighting Hopkins's involvement appeared in the *Colored American Magazine* in March 1904.

entice new subscribers (a promotional role formerly accorded *Contending Forces*). In the same month, Freund hosted a dinner for the staff of the magazine and other prominent black Bostonians, an event that Hopkins participated in and covered in "How a New York Newspaper Man Entertained a Number of Colored Ladies and Gentlemen at Dinner in the Revere House, Boston, and How the Colored American League Was Started." In her article, which is dominated by a Freund speech that includes criticism of Hopkins for her "tendency to refer to her people as a 'proscribed race,'" he encourages the formation of the Colored American League, which was announced in a supplement to the March 1904 issue.

The March 1904 issue also represented a visual turning point for the *Colored American Magazine*. Freund's dissatisfaction with the magazine commenced with the cover photographs of young African American women, mostly representatives of women's clubs. Whereas women appeared on thirty-six of the first forty-one covers (and three of the five exceptions were in the first five issues), Freund got his wish and men took over beginning in March 1904. A new cover design even replaced long-running cameo sketches of Phillis Wheatley and Frederick Douglass (see illustration 9) with two male figures, one representing industrial labor and the other classical education. Starting in March 1904, men appeared on the cover for nine consecutive months, whereas one man had appeared in the previous two years. The next woman to appear was the Madonna in December 1904. As if to mark the declining influence and imminent departure of Hopkins, the

3. This supplementary picture of the founders of the Colored American League appeared in the March 1904 issue of the *Colored American Magazine*. The cameo of Hopkins (#12) appears on the left.

ED AMERICAN LEAGUE

August 1904 cover featured Theodore Roosevelt, who (not counting the pictures of a white-looking Madonna and baby Jesus that appeared every December) was probably the first white individual so honored.[28] At a time when black images were consistently contested, portraiture and other illustrations served the mission of the *Colored American Magazine* by venerating black women on a monthly basis. Like W.E.B. Du Bois's installation at the Negro Pavilion at the 1900 Paris Exposition and Booker T. Washington, N. B. Wood, and Fannie Barrier Williams's "magnificently illustrated" *A New Negro for a New Century* in the same year, the magazine intervened in early twentieth-century discourse around photography, visual representation, and race.

The changes to the cover reflected debates about the text. Of particular concern to Freund was the magazine's coverage of the Philippines, which, according to Hopkins's letter to Trotter, helped incite "our patron's ire and . . . Mr. Washington's wrath because" two April 1904 articles—one critiquing industrial education and the other a profile of "Filipino-martyr" José Rizal—"not only offended the South, but, also, seemingly, reflected upon President Roosevelt's Philippine policy." Hopkins directly challenged President Roosevelt more than a year earlier in her February 1903 article, "Latest Phases of the Race Problem in America," which begins the section on "The *Colored American Magazine* Controversy" because her mistrust of the president epitomizes the political attitudes that led to her ouster. Although the article begins with outwardly positive commentary on Roosevelt's foreign policies in the Philippines, Panama, Venezuela, Cuba, and Romania, Hopkins quickly moves to warn readers to beware of the "falseness of friendship." Rather than celebrating

4. Reflecting the views of the magazine's new ownership, Robert H. Terrell's August 1904 cover story on Theodore Roosevelt describes him as "one of the great 'Men of Our Times.'"

Roosevelt's seeming defense of a black postmaster, she announces skeptically, "This seems too good to be true." (Sadly, her skepticism of Roosevelt was proven warranted in 1906, when he lost most of his African American support following the dishonorable discharge of 167 African American soldiers without trial after a shooting in Brownsville, Texas. The order was reversed in 1972.) In her review of Roosevelt's appointments, she suggests that readers should not categorically celebrate the appointment of African Americans, but should look deeper at the appointee's politics. For example, Roosevelt appointee W. H. Lewis did not represent a black constituency, was part of a Cambridge, Massachusetts, party machine that other black leaders had left, and opposed a memorial to Benjamin Butler, a general who advocated emancipation early in the Civil War. Hopkins's insistence on maintaining an independent political voice elicited the criticisms of Freund and, by proxy, Washington.

As a result of writing and publishing such articles, Hopkins was eventually "frozen out" of the magazine and soon thereafter "forced to resign" (as she explains in her 1905 letter to Trotter). A series of letters that Freund sent to Hopkins and Dupree between late January 1904 and April 1904 (and which Hopkins later forwarded to Trotter) details his rising dissatisfaction with her leadership. Freund criticizes Hopkins for her antagonism, for her unwillingness to cultivate a white readership, for her excessive attention to lynching, for her lack of gratitude, for her stubbornness, for being too literary-minded, and for the internationalism of her coverage.[29] On the final point, she retorts in her letter to Trotter, "he was curtailing my work from the broad field of international union and uplift for the Blacks in all quarters of the globe, to the narrow confines of the question as affecting solely the Afro-American." Freund, Washington, and their ilk looked on her internationalism and pan-Africanism unfavorably.

For refusing to capitulate to Freund, Hopkins saw her role diminish. April 1904 was the last month she was listed as "Literary Editor." By June 1904, Washington arranged for Fred R. Moore to purchase the magazine, become its editor, and move its offices to New York. Although she relocated to New York with the magazine and worked there until September 1904, her name never again appeared in the masthead or the table of contents. Following her departure, the *Colored American Magazine* saw its circulation drop despite a one-third reduction in the price in March 1904.[30]

From the *Voice of the Negro* to the *New Era Magazine*

When her four-year association with the *Colored American Magazine* ended, Hopkins was quickly hired by the *Voice of the Negro*, which in November 1904 boasted: "MISS PAULINE E. HOPKINS is a well-known literary star among the Boston magazine writers. By any amount of coaxing and begging and paying we have been able to secure her services as one of our regular contributors."[31] In January 1905, soon after her hiring, her new employer published a column by Du Bois that refers to "$3000 of 'hush money' used to subsidize the Negro press in five leading cities," which opened his public crusade against Washington's control of the black press.[32] As part of his efforts to expose Washington's shenanigans, on March 15, 1905, Du Bois wrote to Trotter seeking "every scrap of evidence you have going to prove Washington's bribery of newspapers."[33] As literary scholar Alisha Knight points out, Trotter must have immediately turned to Hopkins for help because, one month after receiving Du Bois's query, he received her ten-page, single-spaced account of Washington's involvement in the takeover of the *Colored American Magazine*.[34] In the April 1905 letter, Hopkins told a story of her departure as a byproduct of overlapping racial, international, and gender politics, an account that differed dramatically from the magazine's claim of her "ill-health."[35] Trotter forwarded the letter to Du Bois, who cited it in a 1912 article in the *Crisis* magazine, which he edited. In the unsigned article on "The Colored Magazine in America," Du Bois soundly concluded that Hopkins was dismissed because "her attitude was not conciliatory enough."[36]

Hopkins maintained her popularity at the *Voice of the Negro,* which promoted her writings alongside Du Bois's series *The Beginnings and Endings of Slavery:* "In the July number of *The Voice of the Negro* we will have the last of two series of very valuable papers. . . . Miss Pauline E. Hopkins contributes her last paper on the *Dark Races of the Twentieth Century*. Many people have written us and spoken to us about Miss Hopkins' articles. Evidently they have awakened great interest in the history of the colored people of the world."[37] In the same month that she was being lauded in the *Voice of the Negro*, the *Colored American Magazine* reprinted, perhaps in response to readers' inquiries, its disingenuous explanation for the absence of its best-known personality.[38] Evidently her departure remained noteworthy nearly a year after she had disappeared from the pages of the magazine. Meanwhile rivalry or jealousy led to Moore's refusal to advertise the flagging *Colored American Magazine* in the *Voice of the Negro*.[39]

Even though the *Colored American Magazine* continued to publish until 1909, it never again achieved the literary quality or level of circulation that it had during Hopkins's tenure. Its decline coincided with the rise of Hopkins's new employer, which was soon recognized, according to scholar Walter C. Daniel, as "the most prestigious black periodical in the nation."[40] Even Washington privately conceded as much in a 1906 letter to Moore, "In magazine breadth, dignity and form, your best friends will tell you that it [*Colored American Magazine*] does not come up to the Voice of the Negro."[41] The *Voice of the Negro* provided a forum for Hopkins to address international topics in her five-part series, *The Dark Races of the Twentieth Century*.

As Ann duCille points out, Hopkins's farsighted international interests (along with those of Du Bois and others) were exemplary of an African American analysis "of power relations between colonizer and colonized" that is prototypical of modern intellectual analyses of postcolonialism.[42] In her own day, her values were consistent with the work of the Boston Literary and

Historical Association, which, through discussions of Cuba and China, explored "the possibility of creating a unified front with other 'darker races' throughout the world."[43] Her audience, the community of readers based at the Boston Literary and Historical Association, was, like her, committed to learning about the "dark races" of the world.

The work of early black magazines was not separate from the work of social organizations and movements. In the first issue of *Voice of the Negro*, editor J. Max Barber declared his desire for the publication "to be more than a mere magazine."[44] True to his plan, it helped to promote the inaugural meeting of the Niagara movement, which Du Bois organized the following year. The Niagara movement spawned the National Association for the Advancement of Colored People (NAACP) in 1909, and the *Voice of the Negro* "laid a basis for *Crisis*," which, according to Abby Arthur Johnson and Ronald Maberry Johnson in *Propaganda and Aesthetics: The Literary Politics of African-American Magazines in the Twentieth Century*, "Du Bois considered a successor."[45] With Du Bois as editor, the *Crisis*, which put out its first issue in November 1910 as the organ of the NAACP, quickly became a widely read, politically progressive national journal in the mold that Hopkins helped to develop at the *Colored American Magazine*.

The success of the *Voice of the Negro*—its peak circulation of 15,000 copies per month approached that of the *Colored American Magazine* at its height—was cut short by racist violence. Following September 1906 riots in Atlanta, the magazine and Barber were forced to leave the city after he was exposed as the author of an anonymous letter to the *New York World* that was critical of the white press and leading figures in Georgia. Although Barber quickly reestablished the renamed *Voice* in Chicago, it ceased publication one year later.

The *Voice of the Negro* was a victim of the attacks on the independent black press that Hopkins ominously foresaw in 1905 when her pamphlet *A Primer of Facts Pertaining to the Early Greatness of the African Race and the Possibility of Restoration by its Descendants* endorsed Du Bois's "hush money" claim: "The Propaganda of Silence is in full force. Newspapers and magazines have been subsidized or destroyed if the editors fearlessly advocated the cause of humanity." The title page of the self-published, Cambridge, Massachusetts, volume was headed "Black Classics Series . . . . Number One," suggesting that she projected an (apparently unrealized) ongoing sequence of tracts that would attract readers by promoting Hopkins as "Author of 'Contending Forces,' 'Hagar's Daughter,' 'Winona,' 'Talma Gordon,' 'Famous Men of the Negro Race,' 'Famous Women of the Negro Race,' Etc." (See illustration 11.)

A Primer of Facts opens with a familiar discussion of monogenesis, which echoes many of the ideas at the center of Hopkins's serial novel, *Of One Blood*. In her lexicon, "blood" had several layers of meaning. Most prophetically, she described the flow of blood in terms of economic progress: "Blood will flow, but not by the seeking of the Black, and he will only participate in the fight when the government places in his hands arms for its protection. . . . When labor and capital become contending forces, the Black will float into the full enjoyment of citizenship. Blood will flow, for humanity sweeps onward, and God's purposes never fail." She references the title of her first novel, *Contending Forces,* to suggest that blood is not only a marker of racial unity, but also a product of struggle, which was part of the historical lens through which she viewed the world. Like Thomas Carlyle, whose ideas about heroism resurrected Oliver Cromwell for nineteenth-century readers, Hopkins considered political violence, particularly when it bore the imprimatur of religious justification, to be a viable strategy.

With her increasing focus on the connections between racial justice and class struggle, a position she impressively asserted in her 1902 profile of Munroe Rogers, Hopkins found it difficult to be a female public intellectual. In a 1906 letter to author John E. Bruce, she acknowledges that her ideas on political economy were not taken as seriously as they deserved: "I have argued the union of the Negro with labor for a number of years, but being only a woman have received very small notice; however, it matters not who moves the sun as long as we are convinced that 'she do move.'"[46] Despite her invisibility, she remained committed to the cause of racial and economic justice, and never lamented her lack of personal acclaim. During the decade following the letter, Hopkins was not employed as a full-time journalist and earned her income as a stenographer.

In a speech celebrating the 1905 centenary of abolitionist William Lloyd Garrison, Hopkins introduced herself forcefully: "you do not acknowledge black daughters of the Revolution but we are going to take that right." In her address to the audience of Boston liberals, she insistently assumed for African American women a political lineage that included the American Revolution, the radical abolitionist movement, and the Civil War. As "a daughter of the Revolution," a political stage was her birthright and she intended to claim her heritage. In 1911, at a Charles Sumner centenary program that Trotter organized, she continued to promote an international agenda: "now is the psychological moment for the forward movement of the dark races upon the world's arena." Like the abolitionists in the multiracial fight against slavery, she envisions a movement "side by side with all other downtrodden people clasp[ing] hands in the good fight of all races up and no race down." In the face of obstacles, she maintained her principled commitment to equality.

Throughout this period, Hopkins remained active in the Boston progressive community and in 1916 reentered magazine publishing. With Walter Wallace, the first president of the Colored Co-operative Publishing Company, she started the *New Era Magazine,* a journal explicitly modeled on their previous collaboration. A picture of William Stanley Braithwaite, whose poetry appeared in the *Colored American Magazine,* adorned the cover, which announces its subtitle: "An Illustrated Monthly Devoted to the World-Wide Interests of the Colored Race." (See illustration 12.) The first sentence of the prospectus reiterates its commitment "to the best interests of the colored race, not alone in this country, but throughout the world."[47] Articles in the inaugural issue covered Liberia, Haiti, Jamaica, and Puerto Rico. Hopkins was still allied with Trotter, whose *Guardian* advertised in the fledgling magazine. Even George Forbes, Trotter's onetime coeditor, wrote an obituary. Although a portrait of the recently deceased Washington was offered as a premium for an annual subscription, its inaugural "Editorial and Publisher's Announcements" forcefully advocated agitation for the ballot and equality: "We disapprove the doctrine of silence under the injustice of disfranchisement, segregation, restricted education and restricted employment for the sake of peace between the races."[48] The concluding appeal was for an interracial alliance to achieve "Political freedom, social freedom, economic freedom."[49]

Hopkins, the magazine's most prominent personality, was represented by new fiction and essays, which consciously continued the *Colored American Magazine*'s mantle. Her biographical series, *Men of Vision,* was advertised as a sequel to *Famous Men of the Negro Race* and *Famous Women of the Negro Race.* A prospectus announced the intention to reprint *A Primer of Facts* as a serial. However, the *New Era Magazine* only put out two issues, and the company never reached its "ultimate aim of establishing in Boston, not alone a strong and helpful magazine, but a *Race Publishing House,* that shall stand as a permanent and lasting monument of race progress."[50]

Recovering Pauline E. Hopkins

While the *New Era Magazine* was unable to achieve its aim, Hopkins's oeuvre is a lasting monument of the sort she imagined. Although her work and the Boston-era *Colored American Magazine* continue to receive "very small notice" in discussions of the period's political discourse, a new generation of readers now have access to a widening body of her writings and can assess her legacy for themselves. It will be more difficult for future scholars to overlook her as historian August Meier did in his 1953 examination of Washington and the *Colored American Magazine,* which never mentions Hopkins or her *Famous Men* biography of Washington, focusing instead on "a vigorous attack on Washington and his philosophy written by George Washington Forbes, coeditor of the Boston *Guardian* (Washington's most bitter newspaper critic)."[51] Meier's interpretation of Forbes's article, which never mentions Washington by name, is based primarily on its author's eventual reputation since Forbes's article "The Last Act" appeared in June 1900, more than a year before the *Guardian* put out its first issue, let alone became anyone's "most bitter newspaper critic."

Even Hopkins scholars have followed Meier's lead; Jill Bergman acknowledges Hopkins's "support—if guarded at times" for Washington, finding that her biography of him "celebrated his contributions to the race."[52] The misreading of Hopkins's attitude toward Washington alters the complexion of early twentieth-century intellectual culture, which is typically personified by the Washington/Du Bois rift. In his analysis of the Boston Riot, Washington biographer Louis R. Harlan concludes that the decision to press charges against Trotter hastened "what was slowly evolving anyhow, the polarization of black leadership into two warring camps, one led by Washington and the other led not by Trotter but by Du Bois, the most distinguished intellectual and champion of higher education among blacks."[53] Harlan squeezes out not only Trotter, but the Boston Literary and Historical Association and the *Colored American Magazine,* which Washington himself considered significant enough to undermine in the wake of the Boston Riot. Hopkins garners no mention in Harlan's biography of Washington, effectively erasing her from the canon of his critics, and she fares no better in Stephen R. Fox's biography of Trotter. Nonetheless, on her death in a tragic fire at her home in August 1930, the national edition of the *Chicago Defender,* one of a new breed of African American newspapers, remembered her on the front page as "a writer and orator of high recognition, especially in New England."[54]

Full recognition of Hopkins's importance requires the ongoing recovery of the political, institutional, and cultural contexts in which she lived and worked. What Carby terms "intertextual coherence" can be found throughout the broader intellectual culture of the period, enabling the writings and editorial work of Hopkins to be situated in a variety of institutional sites such as the black press, the club women's movement, and literary societies. She was active with organizations like the Woman's Era Club and the Boston Literary and Historical Association, and inspired and promoted the work of smaller groups like the Putnam, Connecticut-based *Colored American Magazine* Club, which read the magazine and had "general discussions, and by this means not only the members but the families which they represent benefited."[55]

By 1904, when the *Voice of the Negro* put out its first issue, Barber could proudly proclaim the journal as "an indication that our people are becoming an educated, a reading people."[56] Hopkins sought to cultivate and nurture these kinds of "reading people" through intellectual networks of women's groups, churches, literary societies, newspapers, and journals like the *Colored American Magazine,* through which she helped to define the direction of the black press in the twentieth century. The magazine itself proved to be a forum for African Americans to debate issues of concern and to intervene on matters of historical representation, and her nonfiction reflects the collaborative nature of black leadership which, like the reading practice brilliantly documented by McHenry in *Forgotten Readers,* takes place in communities.

Literary Strategies and Intertextuality

As an essayist, Hopkins consciously participated in these literary communities through frequent citations of the familiar voices of prominent abolitionists, most notably Parker Pillsbury, Wendell Phillips, and William Wells Brown. Her reliance on the work of Brown, who was instrumental in her ear-

5. On its first anniversary in May 1901, the *Colored American Magazine* published this portrait of the "active members" of the *Colored American Magazine* Club, which had been "organized in Putnam, Conn., several months ago by Miss Josephine Hall, for the literary and social advancement of its members. . . . Miss Winney Bates acts as President and Miss Grace Leathers fills the office of Secretary. . . . Miss Cora Spalding is a dressmaker, and not only the colored people are served by her, but many whites. Other members are equally successful in their several vocations." See Elliott, "The Story of Our Magazine," 77.

liest extant writings, provides an ongoing tribute that is at the very least equal to her profile of him in *Famous Men of the Negro Race*. Hopkins does more than write about Brown; she writes from him, and in the process inscribes herself in the abolitionist/intellectual tradition that he represents. She is committed to the recovery of this history because it provides a model for the abolition of Jim Crow, which the Boston Suffrage League's Garrison centenary pamphlet called the "anti-slavery cause of today." That the pamphlet excised the entire "daughter of the Revolution" passage in its reproduction of her address only confirms her assertion that she needed "to take that right" even as she shared the platform with Albert E. Pillsbury, a founding member of the Boston NAACP and the nephew of Parker Pillsbury.

In addition to citing abolitionist sources, Hopkins sometimes incorporated their voices without acknowledgment. Many passages that appear under Hopkins's byline are culled directly from other writers. The voice that emerges is not strictly that of an essayist, but also that of an editor, compiler, and arranger as she credited herself on the title page of her 1905 pamphlet. While she usually mentioned her source intratextually and occasionally appended a note, she often copied passages without quotation marks or direct attribution. Hopkins was aware of her own era's protocols (which were markedly different than those of today), as her self-conscious "compiled and arranged" attribution in *A Primer of Facts* indicates. The evidence suggests that she was motivated by a desire to claim a particular mantle, not to mislead her readers, since most of her sources were readily identifiable to her contemporaries and nearly all are mentioned somewhere in her oeuvre. Abolitionist authors were political and literary icons for Hopkins, and her relationship to these writers remains significant even though twenty-first-century readers might consider her questionable handling of their words to be plagiarism.

As a compiler and arranger, Hopkins was not alone. An 1895 *Afro-American Encyclopaedia*, which she certainly knew, was "Compiled and Arranged by James T. Haley." Hopkins's use of outside sources, particularly newspaper accounts, employed a method that, according to historian John Hope Franklin, was pioneered in the 1880s by African American historian George Washington Williams, whose contributions Hopkins mentioned in *A Primer of Facts*.[57] Franklin's description of Williams's problems incorporating historical documents could be applied to Hopkins. Her prodigious output in the early 1900s, like that of Williams twenty years earlier, raises the possibility that her nonfiction was also "hastily written," resulting in a product that may appear to be "a documentary history," but which "also suggested improperly digested material."[58] In a section of his *History of the Negro Race in America* on "Representative Colored Men" (and women), Williams presented a series of historical biographies. A similar approach to history was also prominent in works by Brown, Haley, William Ferris, and Still that Hopkins used.

Hopkins's brand of documentary biography was based on a desire to portray the lives of public figures. Her decision to use published, and therefore already-public, materials is consistent with her belief in representative and collective biography. Indeed, one could argue that much of the material she used was made available for such a purpose. Besides, there is no record of anyone—even her critics like Washington, who no doubt recognized her extensive use of his book *The Story of My Life and Work*—commenting, disapprovingly or otherwise, on her methods of incorporation. The *Colored American Magazine*'s desire to use her fiction to get through to "those who never read history or biography" implies a preference for using narrative rather than conventional historical apparatus (such as citation) to communicate effectively with its readers. If the incorporation practiced by Hopkins was not planned, it certainly suited her aims.

More generally, intertextuality was common among nineteenth-century writers of African American history and biography. For example, a racial description that Hopkins uses at the end of chapter three of *A Primer of Facts* appears in Brown's *Rising Son*, a volume that she frequently used. For the passage in question, Brown cites Samuel Stanhope Smith and James Cowles Prichard (whom Hopkins does not mention), though his direct source was probably Wilson Armistead's *A Tribute for the Negro* (1848). Furthermore, Haley used the same material in *Afro-American Encyclopaedia* (1895), without citing Armistead or Brown (or Smith or Prichard). While this complex genealogy indicates that Hopkins was not alone in her incorporation of outside sources, it nonetheless complicates the task of reconstructing precise annotations for Hopkins's text.

As revealing as they are, Hopkins's heavy reliance on other writers creates one of my biggest editorial challenges. My priority has been to present her texts comprehensively in ways faithful to their original publication. I have sought to maintain this integrity by leaving those sources that Hopkins did not acknowledge unacknowledged in the body of the text, while adding footnotes to enable all readers to easily identify them. By annotating many of her uncited sources, the footnotes to this edition begin to reconstruct Hopkins's library and to identify the periodicals she read, which will prove valuable to students of the period. However, identification is only the first step because Hopkins changed verb tenses, omitted passages without using ellipses, and altered points of view. Her editorial liberties, such as her adoption of the collective first-person plural point of view, inflect meaning. Unlike biographies, which tell a third party's story, Hopkins's nonfiction often facilitates her subjects' speaking on their own behalf. In her adaptation of John Mercer Langston's peculiar third-person autobiography, for example, Hopkins takes the liberty of restoring his first-person voice. In her Frederick Douglass profile, she changes a *Century Illustrated Magazine* reference from "darky" to the somewhat more dignified "Negro boy," and elsewhere she capitalized "Negro" when citing Jeannette Robinson Murphy, an author committed to white supremacy. The revised citations bear the mark of her unique hand and must be considered a complicated form of authorship.

Hopkins's reliance on the words of others does not render the works in this collection unoriginal. While not a traditional journalist, there is evidence that she conducted interviews and undertook firsthand reporting. And when she incorporates the prose of others, she does so in highly original frames, with introductions and conclusions that provide innovative interpretations. By presenting this material as Hopkins originally did with the addition of footnotes, this anthology seeks a balance between preserving Hopkins's deliberate incorporation of outside sources and crediting those sources in a fashion that is usefully transparent. Readers of this collection have the opportunity to engage the material comprehensively and consider its relationship to Hopkins and, with the help of footnotes, as part of a particular intellectual milieu.

Daughter of the Revolution: The Major Nonfiction Works of Pauline E. Hopkins collects Hopkins's major known nonfiction writings, which she wrote under her name, as Sarah Allen, her mother's maiden name, as J. Shirley Shadrach, a pseudonym, and in the case of a juvenile piece as Pauline E. Allen. The sources include the *Colored American Magazine, Voice of the Negro, New Era Magazine, Boston Guardian,* pamphlets, and manuscript items from Fisk University Franklin Library Special Collections. The major works are *Famous Men of the Negro Race, Famous Women of the Negro Race, Furnace Blasts, The Dark Races of the Twentieth Century, A Primer of Facts Pertaining to the Early Greatness of the African Race and the Possibility of Restoration by its Descendants,* and *Men of Vision.* Additional sections include "Juvenilia" from the 1870s, "The *Colored American Magazine* Controversy," "Selected Biographies from the *Colored American Magazine,*" and "Published Orations."

Due to considerations of space, I have excluded a handful of essays from this collection. First, a three-part series, "Reminiscences of the Life and Times of Lydia Maria Child," is a selection of Child's published letters, with minimal intervention by Hopkins. Second, "A New Profession: The First Colored Graduate of the Y.M.C.A. Training School, Springfield, Mass." offers commentary on African American education and Booker T. Washington in the context of a biography of a local (rather than "famous") figure, David Wilder. Third, "Echoes from the Annual Convention of Northeastern Federation of Colored Women's Clubs" reprints some material that she published in the "Club Life among Colored Women" segment of *Famous Women,* and echoes the *Boston Guardian's* August 15, 1903, report on the meeting (thereby providing further evidence of Hopkins's connection to Trotter).[59] Fourth, "Mr. M. Hamilton Hodges," a short profile of the singer, was one among her latest signed pieces for the *Colored American Magazine.* Fifth and finally, "The New York Subway," a unique topic for Hopkins, marks the December 1904 beginning of her relationship with the *Voice of the Negro,* and quotes Samuel Smiles's *Self Help,* a book she received as a gift from Freund. I intend to make these essays available in an alternative format, and their absence here should not be interpreted as a commentary on their quality or significance, but rather as a result of the practical contingencies of publishing.

With the exception of the letter to Trotter that provides a crucial account of Hopkins's experiences at the *Colored American Magazine,* I have elected to exclude her letters (including one to Cornelia Condict, which appeared in the *Colored American Magazine* and is reprinted in the *Norton Anthology of African American Literature*). While my research has not uncovered many letters by Hopkins, that project deserves to be undertaken systematically and comprehensively. The same may be said for her speeches, additional examples of which may remain to be found; both of the items included in the section on "Orations" were published soon after she delivered them.

This volume contains only work with Hopkins's byline, excluding unsigned material and editorials. Although she certainly wrote substantial sections of the *Colored American Magazine* during much of her tenure (as she did at the *New Era Magazine* more than a decade later), these unsigned pieces are excluded for consistency and due to the difficulties of confirming authorship. The June 1900 "Women's Department," which she "edited" from reports of women's clubs, is in this same category, though it includes thoughtful prose probably written by Hopkins. She also probably contributed to "Here and Now," a regular feature that included short profiles of contributors, clubwomen, and others that bear consideration as works of biography. Her frequent anonymous publications suggest another form of collective authorship. Just as she did not always fully credit others, she did not demand it for herself. Authorship, particularly in light of the issues discussed in this introduction, cannot always be definitely demarcated. Indeed, as editor, she had a hand in all of the pieces published in the *Colored American Magazine*. Therefore, for those interested in Hopkins and the literary culture of her era, the best supplement to this material is a full reading of the *Colored American Magazine*, which this volume cannot replace. Moreover, the visual significance of the magazine deserves additional attention that requires a return to the source since the illustrations reproduced here do not even skim the surface of a rich, unexplored archive.

During her time at the *Colored American Magazine*, Hopkins often published under her mother's maiden name, Sarah Allen. This matrilineal tribute prevented her own name from dominating the table of contents. However, in March 1902, after the "wonderful success" of her serial novel *Hagar's Daughter*, the magazine revealed the identity of "Sarah A. Allen" in an effort to promote sales of *Contending Forces*.[60]

The August 1902 issue advertised that Sarah Allen would be writing a biography of Professor Charles Winter Wood for the September issue. When the article on Wood appeared as promised, Allen was not listed as the author. Instead the byline credited "J. Shirley Shadrach." The magazine does not offer any biographical information on Shadrach, which is certainly another pseudonym for Hopkins. Six articles were attributed to Shadrach between September 1902 and March 1904, including two installments of *Furnace Blasts*, which takes its title from a John Greenleaf Whittier poem that Hopkins cited in her September 1901 profile of him and used as the epigraph for the first chapter of *Contending Forces*. The portrait of Wood has the markings of Hopkins's brand of biography, which here, as in *Famous Men* and *Famous Women*, is a forum to discuss the larger social and political issues of the day. Her comments on the potential for a "Negro" president in the Wood profile appear among several paragraphs from Shadrach that appeared nearly verbatim in *A Primer of Facts*. The appropriation runs both ways. Not only does Hopkins's 1905 pamphlet use the same language that "Shadrach" used in 1902 and 1903, but in a July 1903 profile of William Pickens, "Shadrach" uses the same language that Hopkins used in her 1900 Toussaint profile: "We feel with the late Frederick Douglass that, as the north star is eternal in the heavens, so will Hayti remain forever in the firmament of nations." Therefore, the essays attributed to J. Shirley Shadrach include both previously published and not yet published work by Hopkins.

Hopkins likely adopted the Shadrach pseudonym in part so that she would not be listed as the author of three articles in a single issue. The first two issues in which she used this moniker included installments of both *Famous Women of the Negro Race* and her serial novel *Winona*. In certain instances, the pseudonym may have been an attempt to distance herself from the more controversial topics addressed and frank language used in discussions of prostitution, amalgamation, interracial marriage, and Pickens's speech on Haiti.

As for Hopkins's choice of name, English Renaissance poet and playwright James Shirley is listed as "J. Shirley" in Francis Turner Palgrave's enormously popular *The Golden Treasury of the Best Songs and Lyrical Poems in the English Language,* which was available in several late nineteenth-century editions. Anti-imperial sentiments such as "Victorious men of earth, no more/ Proclaim how wide your empires are" from "The Last Conqueror" and "The glories of our blood and state/Are shadows, not substantial things" and "Only the actions of the just/Smell sweet, and blossom in their dust" from "Death the Leveller" understandably appealed to Hopkins. If "J. Shirley" represents her literary inclinations, Shadrach represents the political tradition that Hopkins sought to recover. Shadrach Minkins, who was arrested in Massachusetts under the 1850 Fugitive Slave Act, appears in her *Famous Men* profiles of Lewis Hayden and Robert Morris, both of whom aided his dramatic escape from a Boston courthouse. Unlike Anthony Burns and Thomas Sims, two other prominent "fugitives" who she often invoked, Shadrach, whose biblical namesake survived the wrath of Nebuchadnezzar and his furnace, successfully escaped to Canada with the help of abolitionists.

Notes

1. "A Few of the Good Things," [ii].
2. Elliott, "The Story of Our Magazine," 43.
3. The *Colored American Magazine*'s "sworn statement of circulation" in its 1902 advertisement in Rowell's *American Newspaper Directory* gives its December 1901 circulation at 20,170 copies, and its 1901 monthly average at 17,840. See *American Newspaper Directory* (1902), 1509.
4. "Report of the Woman's Era Club," 1.
5. "Annual Convention," 4.
6. McHenry, *Forgotten Readers,* 231.
7. McElrath and Leitz, *"To Be an Author,"* 9.
8. For sales information on Chesnutt, see Andrews, *The Literary Career of Charles W. Chesnutt,* 69n30, 117, 124, 127.
9. "Pauline E. Hopkins," 219. The identical phrase from this unsigned article is used to describe Hopkins in Elliott, "The Story of Our Magazine," 47.
10. For more on the connection between *Of One Blood* and Sheppard, see Dworkin, "American Hearts," 154–197.
11. Carby, *Reconstructing Womanhood,* 159–160.

12. For details on Hopkins's family background, see Wallinger, *Pauline E. Hopkins*, 20–23.

13. Shockley, "Pauline Elizabeth Hopkins," 22.

14. A facsimile of *Peculiar Sam; or, The Underground Railroad* with music is reproduced in Southern, *African American Theater*, 119–205. The text of the musical, without the score, is reprinted in Hamalian and Hatch, *The Roots of African American Drama*, 100–123.

15. Hall, "The Funeral of Liberty," 51.

16. Shockley, "Pauline Elizabeth Hopkins," 25.

17. "Announcement," 197.

18. "Editorial and Publishers' Announcements" (*CAM*, May 1900), 64.

19. Doreski, "Inherited Rhetoric," 75.

20. "Editorial and Publishers' Announcements" (*CAM*, May 1900), 61–62.

21. Ibid., 61.

22. McHenry, *Forgotten Readers*, 166.

23. A *Colored American Magazine* advertisement appeared in the August 8, 1903, issue of the *Boston Guardian*.

24. Fox, *The Guardian of Boston*, 5, 14.

25. "Col. William H. Dupree," 229.

26. The advertisement appeared in the March 1904 issue of the *Colored American Magazine*.

27. For circulation statistics of the *Music Trades*, see *American Newspaper Directory* (1902), 672; *American Newspaper Directory* (1904), 695.

28. I have been unable to locate three covers from the first five years of the magazine.

29. Twenty-four letters that Freund sent to Hopkins and Dupree between November 1903 and April 1904 are in the Pauline E. Hopkins Papers, Fisk University Franklin Library Special Collections.

30. Bullock, *The Afro-American Periodical Press*, 236.

31. "Our Christmas Number," 501.

32. Du Bois, "Debit and Credit," 677.

33. Du Bois to Trotter, 97.

34. Knight, "Furnace Blasts for the Tuskegee Wizard." Thank you to Alisha Knight for sharing her forthcoming article manuscript.

35. "Publishers' Announcements," 700.

36. [Du Bois], "Colored Magazine in America," 33.

37. "The *Voice of the Negro* for July 1905," 364.

38. Fred Moore, "Retrospection of a Year," 342.

39. Harlan, "Booker T. Washington and the *Voice of the Negro*," 55.

40. Daniel, *Black Journals of the United States*, 369.

41. Booker T. Washington, quoted in Johnson and Johnson, *Propaganda and Aesthetics*, 14.

42. duCille, "Discourse and Dat Course," 124.

43. McHenry, *Forgotten Readers*, 171.

44. Barber, "The Morning Cometh," 38.

45. Johnson and Johnson, *Propaganda and Aesthetics*, 24.

46. Hopkins to John E. Bruce. Thank you to John Cullen Gruesser for sharing his transcription of the letter.

47. "Announcement and Prospectus of the *New Era Magazine*," 1. The "Announcement and Prospectus" that begins the first issue of the magazine is numbered separately from the magazine proper, which also starts with page 1.

48. "Editorial and Publisher's Announcements" (*New Era*, Feb. 1916), 60.

49. Ibid.

50. "Announcement and Prospectus of the *New Era Magazine*," 1.

51. Meier, "Booker T. Washington and the Negro Press," 69.

52. Bergman, "'Everything we hoped she'd be,'" 188.

53. Harlan, *Booker T. Washington*, 53.

54. "Aged Writer Dies," *Chicago Defender*, August 23, 1930, 1.

55. Elliott, "The Story of Our Magazine," 77.

56. Barber, "The Morning Cometh," 38.

57. Franklin, *George Washington Williams*, 104–105.

58. Ibid., 112.

59. See "In Annual Convention," *Boston Guardian*, August 15, 1903, 1. The report concludes, "In our next the Friday's session and echoes of the convention will be published." I have not located a copy of the August 22, 1903, *Boston Guardian*, which seems like a probable source for Hopkins's "Echoes from the Annual Convention of Northeastern Federation of Colored Women's Clubs."

60. "Editorial and Publishers' Announcements" (*CAM*, Mar. 1902), 335.

A NOTE ON THE TEXT

All of Hopkins's sources are reprinted as they appeared when originally published with the exceptions of evident typographical errors or factual inaccuracies. I have maintained her occasionally idiosyncratic punctuation except in those rare instances where I believe it significantly impedes clarity. Incidental misspellings of well-known proper names have been silently corrected; when names are consistently misspelled, such as Robert "Browne" Elliott, the first occurrence is noted and, whenever possible, explained in the footnotes. I have maintained Hopkins's spelling of "Hayti," as it was an elective reference to the island's indigenous name, "Ayti." In the case of names that were misspelled in her sources, I have offered explanatory notes. She sometimes capitalized *Black* and sometimes did not; I have abided by the original publications. Hopkins significantly made a point to capitalize *Negro*, so in those few instances when *negro* appears in lowercase, I have marked the text "[*sic*]." (In some of these cases, such as her transcription of Freund's speech, there are provocative interpretations of her intent.) [Square brackets], which I have kept to a minimum, are always mine; (round parentheses) belong to Hopkins. I have not added ellipses; all of those that appear belong to Hopkins.

In accordance with modern typesetting, the names of newspapers, books, or other complete works appear in italics, though Hopkins inconsistently preferred quotation marks. Also in accordance with modern style, extended citations have been offset; however, I have only offset those quotations that Hopkins identifies as quotations. Unacknowledged quotations are presented as Hopkins chose to present them; I have added footnotes to identify her sources.

In the cases of widely available and frequently reprinted works by Carlyle, Emerson, Milton, Shakespeare, Whittier, Wordsworth, and others, it is impossible to confirm the editions that Hopkins used. For poems that she doesn't identify, I have given the author, title, and year of original publication. Oftentimes, she cited a source second- or third-hand. Furthermore, many of her sources were themselves derivative of other texts, creating a complex genealogy. My priority has been to identify, as best as possible, her direct sources. Scholars should consider the possibility of an alternate source text as a potential explanation for variations between her essays and those cited in the footnotes. There are many additional difficulties in this process, including the near impossibility of recovering many local press accounts and organizational publications. As one example, there are large gaps in surviving copies of the *Boston Guardian*, a newspaper that Hopkins read and used as the basis for several articles. It is plausible that additional sources could be identified in these gaps.

Overall, I have tried to minimize the number of footnotes. I identify only those sources that have a specific and direct correlation to Hopkins's essays. They either serve an explanatory purpose or identify a source that she definitively used. In the case of the latter, the keys to corroborating positive identification are phrasing and language, not probability, content, or philosophical confluence alone. The footnotes provide the range of pages that she referenced, but do not account for paraphrase or other editorial changes. Some of the things that appear to be changes might indicate that Hopkins used a different edition than what I have identified. If I were to annotate her changes intratextually, the manuscript would be decidedly less legible and, furthermore, would undermine Hopkins's quite methodical process of incorporation.

Readers are encouraged to refer to Hopkins's sources, many of which are available in the microfilm set associated with Randall K. Burkett and Nancy Hall Burkett's *Black Biography, 1790–1950: A Cumulative Index,* which has been an indispensable resource for me. In addition, some of her sources are available online through resources like Documenting the American South (University of North Carolina at Chapel Hill), Making of America (University of Michigan), and Project Gutenberg (Project Gutenberg Literary Archive Foundation). See the works cited section for full publication information for footnoted sources, including online addresses. Finally, the index is a resource to help readers identify and cross-reference sources and names (often abbreviated or only a surname) that may be explicated at their first occurrence.

PART I

Juvenilia (c. 1870s)

The two essays in this section are Hopkins's earliest known writings. Both were tran-
scribed from handwritten manuscripts in the Pauline E. Hopkins Papers in Franklin
Library Special Collections, Fisk University. "The Evils of Intemperance and Their Remedy" won a Congregational Publishing Society essay contest sponsored by William Wells
Brown in 1874. The incomplete manuscript ends abruptly mid-sentence on its eleventh
page. The concluding page or pages do not appear to have survived and the manuscript
is unsigned. "One Scene from the Drama of Early Days" was signed "Pauline E. Allen,"
which indicates that Hopkins used her mother's maiden name as a youth. (William A.
Hopkins, whose last name Pauline later took, may have been her stepfather.) While "One
Scene" is sometimes identified as a play, it opens with a narrative survey of theater and
concludes with a prose description of a dramatic rendering of Daniel in the lions' den.
Taken together, these juvenile writings reveal Hopkins's interest from an early age in
participating in public debates about social issues and in thinking seriously about how
to communicate with an audience.

The Evils of Intemperance and Their Remedy.

As I rest my upon the subject which I have written at the top of my page, I feel it to be the task of a Hercules, to endeavor to en—umerate, the sin, and the depths of degredation to which, man has been reduced; by the demon of excess; not only in strong drink, but in all the train of evils which it entails.

If we consider the evils of taxation, we find that their great foundation is is strong drink, if we say our politics are impure, the question naturally arises what makes them so? and we have the same an—swer; strong drink.

If we look at our statistics for crime, of whatever character, we find the cause is Intemperance, we take up the daily papers and read that a father has killed his child or a husband brutally beaten his wife; we see a fair, promising youth brought low

6. The first page of the manuscript for "The Evils of Intemperance and Their Remedy" (c.1874) is written in the hand of Pauline Hopkins. The essay won a contest sponsored by the Congregational Publishing Society of Boston for which she received $10, an award donated by William Wells Brown. Courtesy of Fisk University Franklin Library Special Collections.

The Evils of Intemperance
and Their Remedy

*A*s I rest my upon the subject which I have written at the top of my page, I feel it to be the task of a Hercules, to endeavor to enumerate, the sin, and the depths of degredation to which, man has been reduced, by the demon of excess; not only in strong drink, but in all the train of evils which it entails.

If we consider the evils of taxation, we find that their great foundation is strong drink, if we say our politics are impure, the question naturally arises what makes them so? and we have the same answer; strong drink.

If we look at our statistics for crime, of whatever character, we find the cause is Intemperance, we take up the daily papers and read that a father has killed his child or a husband brutally beaten his wife; we see a fair, promising youth brought low to death by disease, we see a beautiful girl shunned by her former companions; and if we ask the cause of all this misery, the answer is universal, and we can safely say, rum did it.

When we think of these things, when we see the blight which they bring upon noble men and fair women, we can but pray God, to send those who, with the eloquence of men and angels and the strength of many Samsons, shall lend every effort to bring about their complete annihilation.

Let us now, for one moment, look about us, and see how Intemperance is progressing; on every hand we see happy homes, with fine intellectual children, promising in their maturer years to be statesmen, orators and fathers of whom the nation shall be proud, and tender mothers, to whom, little ones shall look up and reverence.

A few years pass away, and these same children, with bright hopes, brilliant intellects and happy hearts, go forth from their homes, to test that bright meteor which we call life; they enter society, and taste there, the gilded pleasures which will perhaps be their ruin and if they do not then, fall to the lowest depths the imperishable seed has been implanted which affects <u>them</u> in later years or which is reproduced in their children; The brain, that great organ of the mind and soul, is shipwrecked and stranded on the shoals of Intemperance, all its bright faculties of imagination, its resources of thought and fancy, its most tender human instincts, are completed, and nothing remains but the most abject wretchedness.

In a great many the physical and moral endurance is weak, and in a very short time we have a body wrecked, a mind in which all pure purposes have disappeared or been perverted, every bright hope gone drowned, beneath the waves of excess and Intemperance.

If we should ask these unfortunates how they fell, their answers would be varied, and taken in their crudest form, show us only too well, the fearful inroad which Intemperance, and immorality has made in our midst; in high places and in low places, in the palace and in the cot, they show us that the serpent's sting is there, no matter how well disguised one will say, "I held an important trust position and with others of the same vocation, I attended and gave champagne suppers," another "My friend was a wine merchant, and I frequently tested his stock," another "I was always allowed to taste my father's wine at dinner, when I was a little fellow," and very frequently the answer is given in the sorrowful words "I loved her and she tempted me."

Come with me my friends, for one moment to a neighboring city, in one of the dirtiest and most squalid side streets we pause before a miserable hovel, the dwelling is entered by a long flight of steps, which reach from the street to the front door, follow me closely and see what a sight you will look upon, in one corner of a room dimly lighted by a broken window, we can distinguish a bed and on it, is a woman, clothed in dirt and rags, a mere apology for her sex, in the last stages of intoxification, and as you look, picture <u>her</u>, if you can, a gifted beautiful girl, the pet of a cherished circle of friends on either side of a fireless stove two men are sitting scarcely able to uphold their drunken weight, every part of the room bears evidence of the most abject poverty, misery meets you whichever way you turn, do you see that bent old man sitting in the farther corner of the room? he escaped our notice when we entered, he is the father of the family, his form is bent with age and his hair white with the snows of many winters, he also is steeped in liquor, O, what a sight, so near the grave and eternity, a feeling of awe and dread like a heavy cloud is upon us, and we shudder as we turn away sick at heart.

I can see in your faces a desire to know their past history, and as we are returning I will tell it to you, in a few words it is this, the family consists of four sons, two of whom you have seen, and for the other two, ask the keeper of yonder jail, one daughter and the father and mother, all of whom are confirmed drunkards with the exception of the mother, they once held a position of wealth and respectability in society, and the father proud of his sons and their fine intellects, sent the two eldest to college, where they received fine classical educations, one of them while away fell in love and became engaged to a young lady, who, without apparent cause forsook him and married another, upon his return home the greatest alteration was visible in him, his haggard face told only too well of dissipation and excess, the bottle was seldom absent from his side, and from him the little sister and younger brothers learned to drink; the old father saw his hopes blasted, his old age desolate, and his noble children a mark of scorn and contempt, he could not survive the ruin of his loved ones, and at sixty years of age became a confirmed drunkard.

O, fathers, mothers, friends, sweethearts, beware, remember you are not only degrading society, but sinning against yourselves, for it is "woe unto him who giveth his neighbor strong drink." Young men, old men, and all who indulge in Intemperance of whatever form, <u>beware</u>, beware its results, does the wine cup glow, and sparkle, does it warm, and exhilarate, be wise, and touch not, taste not, for beneath its sparkle and glow listen to what the coiled demon is saying, he says: Come one, come all yes, I will make you weep, I will excite you to deeds of riot, robbery and bloodshed, I will take away your reason and place you in Asylums where you shall be chained like wild beasts, I will place you in poor houses and prisons and if you follow me faithfully, I will bring you to the gallows.

Fathers, I will make you fiends; wives and children, I will make you widows and orphans. Christians and ministers of the gospel I will defile the church, and make your christian character, a byword and a reproach. Statesmen senators, legislators, I will defile the government and agree to bring you to a spiritual, temporal and eternal death.

Thus saith the spirit of the wine, as it sparkles and bubbles in the glass, and is there one among us who looking these horrors squarely in the face will not say that our greatest curse is Intemperance! it is like the many headed serpent, whose poison fangs none can escape if once they become entangled. It is putting our glorious country in jeopardy, it is taking the last cent from our proud treasuries, making man lower than the brute, taking from grief stricken Virtue her proudest treasure and soiling the fair finger of truth, it is peopling the army of the Evil One and leading him on to sure victory faster than anything else we can name, sapping the life blood of our national and moral institutions, blotting happiness from the face of the earth, and sinking families and relatives in the depths of despair, indeed there can be no one who will not acknowledge in his inmost soul, that Intemperance is the great root of all evils, in whatever form they may appear, either social or national.

The greatest handiwork of God is man, created in the great Master's own image and endowed with mind, reason, and an immortal soul, and with all the faculties for distinguishing and understanding both good and evil. How great therefore is the responsibility which rests upon us, shall we in our blind perverseness rush headlong to destruction, thinking nothing of the great and awful punishment that the misuse of our more Godlike faculties will bring upon us.

We cannot look unappalled from the sublime height to which man may rise; and see the rapid descent, <u>down</u>, <u>down</u>, <u>down</u> into the slime of hopeless iniquity.

Having now been duly impressed with these <u>evils of Intemperance</u>, we most naturally look about us, and carefully calculate what the remedies shall be, and where they may be applied with the greatest success.

In the first place to strike a sure blow at the root of the matter, we must begin with abstinence in the parents. It is the duty of all parents to carefully inform themselves of their own liabilities to evil, and as carefully to <u>extinguish</u> these passions, lest they be reproduced to a stronger and more harmful degree in their offspring.

Truly great men have ever been temperate men; to be sure there has been some brilliant meteors flashing in our midst, but their glory founded on the quick-sands of <u>immorality</u>, has soon dimmed and faded, beside the sure and steady light, of honest and sincere morality and temperance; every parent therefore, who has the real interest of his children, and the community at heart, will be careful of the formation of both mind and body in his posterity.

Having thus provided for the hereditary germs in the constitution of the children, we are better prepared to apply the influence of parents and home, on the tender and easily moulded mind of childhood.

The parents of children have a great responsibility resting upon them, not only giving their own characters as a good example, but in making the home atmosphere pure and exhilarating.

They should carefully implant in tender infancy a trusting love and reverence for God, and by this means, implant at the same time, a love for all that is pure and elevating, pleasant and innocent amusements should be eagerly sought for, in order to, thus early, chord the youthful desires and requirements with the sweet home life. Wine however mild, should be strictly shunned and quiet home talks on the evils of drink, with the pledge present as a family picture, will help on the <u>future</u> cause of temperance beyond anything else.

It is easier to keep little sinless children pure, to make temperate men and women, than to reform <u>one</u>, fallen in the arms of Bacchus. Much of the character of the child rests with the father, and it behooves him to be upright, and <u>honest</u> in every sense of the word, thus giving to his little ones a <u>home standard</u> of merit, excellence, and true manliness.

But by far the greater duty lies with the mother; back to her in after years, if she has been true, when cares and temptations assail them, the heart of the stern man of business and of frivolous youth, will turn, with loving remembrances of <u>mother</u>, and home for mother's gentle, holy spirit, the holiest room of their hearts will be kept swept and garnished and her early precepts and admonishes, to avoid evil, will be found cut in the walls of that room, as a monument of woman's holiest mission, motherhood, and as a monitor, ever to urge her children on, to the goal of rest and peace.

The means which a mother may use to bring about these results, are too numerous to be here detailed; but fervent prayer, and a careful [. . .]

SOURCE "The Evils of Intemperance and Their Remedy" (c. 1874) is published courtesy of Fisk University Franklin Library Special Collections.

One Scene from the Drama
of Early Days

Pauline E. Allen

The world is but a stage, and the men and women merely actors.[1]

So says Shakespeare, the great delineator of the passions of the human heart; and the record of the world as historically compiled fully attests the truth of the poet. No writer has yet been able to create such dramatic situations and soul stirring events; such heroes, sublime and god-like, in the sacrifice of all earthly joys, for the glory of their God, as the study of biblical history reveals.

The creation, the various lapses of time, with their attendant progression, the rise and fall of nations, the rise and fall of religious creeds, form the most powerful drama of any age.

The enterprising dramatist might divide these events into three main parts: Ancient or Early days, Mediaeval, and Modern days and these three into suitable scenes and [*illegible*] plays.

If this could be done, how majestic and grand, would the presentation be; the martyrs of other days, those lowly in spirit, but high in heart, would cluster around and draw inspiration from the hero, who uplifted on the cross, breathed His blessing upon us, and ascended into heaven, to comfort and encourage His own; and finally reappear in the last scene, and establish upon earth the kingdom of the true and tried.

But while we soliloquize, sweet weird music steals over our senses; a blending of the passions: duplicity, discord and evil triumph. But above these, clear and sweet, rises a strain that must be trustfulness and resignation. We bend eagerly forward, as the curtain of the past rises, and reveals a scene of unequalled splendor. Before us lies a magnificent city, built upon a plain; palaces, gardens and beautiful villas dot the landscape; on our right rises a massive structure, terrace above terrace, each almost buried in a luxuriant wilderness of flowers, trees and shrubs; up and up it seems to rise, until we rest our eyes on the last terrace, which seems a garden suspended in the air; gleams of statuary and the mists of fountains complete the enchanting picture. On the left, the river winds gracefully in and out the trees, the sun casts

1. Shakespeare, *As You Like It*, 2.7.147–148.

its last rays over all, in a sudden glory, previous to departure; while soft music lulls us, as if a "Hand unseen, filled the symphony between."[2]

But hark! a flourish of trumpets, and a long procession of courtiers and soldiers, headed by King Darius, enters, followed by an immense concourse of people; how strange it all seems to nineteenth century eyes, the ancient armor of the warriors, mingled with the oriental garb of the people and silk and jewelled apparel of the courtiers. The king speaks: "Let Daniel be brought before me." And from the left surrounded by a guard, Daniel slowly advances and stands before Darius.

He heeds not the looks of malice, the dark smiles of triumph, which rest upon the faces of his enemies; but with form erect, his venerable head raised and his eyes filled with the light on infinite peace, he receives his sentence from Darius, "To be cast into the den of lions."

And now at the hour of sunset the decree is fulfilled and Daniel is led away, followed by the remorseful voice of the king who finding himself bound by his own laws, unconsciously yields to Supreme Power, as he comforts Daniel in these words: "Thy God whom thou servest continually, he will deliver thee!"

Up and down the monarch paces, like one of his own lions, wrathful with himself and his subjects; torn by contending emotions, he looks upon those who have counselled this deed, with an eye that foretells evil, and they tremble lest they be involved in the ruin, of their own creation. And now the music which has been sad and mournful, changes to a paean of victory, as the rosy face of morning chases away the shadows of night; louder it swells, as the scene slowly changes to the lions' den, the king is there with his subjects, and as morning breaks fully Darius calls aloud "Daniel come forth." And lo, a mighty shout bursts from the assembled multitude, as the beloved of the Lord steps forth, unharmed, bearing witness that his God is <u>able</u> and willing to save those who love and serve Him.

We hear the decree for the evil counsellors to be thrown to the lions for punishment; and the curtain slowly descends, the music grows softer and softer, until finally nothing remains but the remembrance of what has been. We feel what a blessing prayer should be to us, who are allowed its full enjoyment, and how great a privilege it is to live and sustain a character in the drama of life and how glorious will be the result if we "Act well our part," and "Dare to be a Daniel."

Pauline E. Allen
#15 State St.
City

SOURCE Pauline E. Allen, "One Scene from the Drama of Early Days" (c. 1870s) is published courtesy of Fisk University Franklin Library Special Collections.

2. Walter Scott, *The Lady of the Lake; A Poem* (1810), canto 1, verses 30–31.

PART II

Famous Men of the Negro Race *(1900–1901)*

Famous Men of the Negro Race was published in the *Colored American Magazine* in twelve monthly installments from November 1900 to October 1901. Its opening profile of Toussaint L'Ouverture begins centuries before the birth of the Haitian leader with the arrival of Christopher Columbus on the island of Hispaniola and the subsequent abuse and exploitation of the aboriginal Indian population, "who were driven into a cruel and barbarous servitude." This start signals that Hopkins's perspective is historical, hemispheric, and alert to the violence of European imperialism. Furthermore, as she declares in the essay's final sentence, Haiti's anti-colonial history is directly tied to U.S. abolition: "For the Republic of Hayti, whose freedom was cemented by the martyred blood of this soldier and statesman, we feel with the late Frederick Douglass, that as the north star is eternal in the heavens, so will Hayti remain forever in the firmament of nations." This conclusion segues to the second installment's subject, Douglass, who is recognized not only as an abolitionist, but also as a diplomat who served in Haiti. Throughout *Famous Men*, Hopkins profiles figures who represent militant and diplomatic traditions, namely abolitionists, Civil War veterans, and postbellum politicians.

One seeming anomaly in the *Famous Men* cast is educator Booker T. Washington, who appears in the final installment. Washington is not the epitome of Hopkins's leadership model, but a cautionary epilogue whose ascension is a cause for concern. Her opinion of Washington's philosophy of industrial education was no secret to readers of the series profile of former U.S. Representative and attorney Robert Brown Elliott, whose "achievements . . . prove that it is possible for a Negro to rise to great political eminence as well as a white man, if the desire for his 'industrial development' does not blind our eyes to other advantages in life." Readers of the full series also will recognize that when she compares Washington's "motives" to those of Napoleon, "whether for good or evil," the comparison is substantially less ambivalent than it might appear were the Washington portrait read independently. Napoleon was, according to Hopkins's profile of Toussaint, a leader of "scheming brain and boundless ambition" who was "determined to crush the spirit of liberty in the blacks of St. Domingo." The intertextuality between the installments enables *Famous Men* to cohere as the unified series that is presented in its entirety for the first time here.

7. (ABOVE) The November 1900 *Colored American Magazine* advertised "Toussaint L'Overture," the first installment of *Famous Men of the Negro Race*, on its cover. Miss M. Eulalia Reid, pictured here, was a vocalist and teacher who opened a music school in Baltimore.

8. (RIGHT) The *Colored American Magazine*'s illustrated first page of "Toussaint L'Overture" is shown here.

I.

Toussaint L'Ouverture

(The extraordinary fortunes of Toussaint L'Ouverture bespeak for him more than the passing interest of a dry biography, yet how few the words, how stifled must be the feelings of the heart when we endeavor to cramp the passionate flow of holy emotion aroused by studious contemplation of the character of our hero, within the narrow limits of a magazine article.[1] To fully understand the position of Toussaint and his relations with France—the brilliant sanguinary France of Napoleon Bonaparte—we must give a cursory glance at the history of the beautiful isle which once held the "Paris of America.")

The Republic of Hayti is situated on the island of Santo Domingo, which is one of a cluster known to students as the Greater Antilles; interesting on account of their situation under tropical changes and influences, and because they form, as one writer aptly claims, stepping-stones from the Old World to the New.[2]

Dec. 6, 1492, Columbus, then derided as a fanatic, landed on a beautiful island which he called Hispaniola, but in honor of a saint renamed St. Domingo. It lies in the Atlantic Ocean at the entrance to the Gulf of Mexico, is second in size to Cuba, but ranks first of the Antilles in beauty and fertility. Columbus describes the country thus: "In these delightful vales all the sweets of spring are enjoyed without winter or summer. There are but two seasons, and they are equally fine; the ground always laden with fruit and covered with flowers, realizes the delights and riches of poetical descriptions." Gold, silver and copper mines abound. Many species of valuable wood are found there, and growing side by side in the same field, cabbage, bananas, potatoes, plantains. Indian corn and sugar-cane may be seen. The island is divided, politically, into the Republic of Santo Domingo, occupying the eastern two-thirds, and the Republic of Hayti, occupying the remaining one-third.

The rapid decrease of the Indian population, the aborigines found on the island by Columbus, who were driven into a cruel and barbarous servitude by the Spanish adventurers who flocked from the Old World to the new Eldorado, demanded another source of supply to obtain laborers for the mines,

---

1. I have changed the spelling of "L'Overture" to "L'Ouverture" throughout the essay. Hopkins followed a spelling occasionally used at the time, as in D. Augustus Straker's *Reflections on the Life and Times of Toussaint L'Overture* [sic], *the Negro Haytien, Commander-in-Chief of the Army, Ruler under the Dominion of France, and Author of The Independence of Hayti* (Columbia, S.C.: Charles A. Calvo Jr., 1886).
2. Although "Haiti" was commonly used at the time, Hopkins chose the spelling that more closely approximates the indigenous name for the island, derived from the Arawak word *Ayti*, meaning "mountainous land."

and to cultivate the sugar-cane. All eyes then turned toward Africa, and thus came into regular form the commerce for slaves between Africa and America. The slaves increased on the island until in 1790 they numbered five hundred thousand to thirty thousand whites. Slavery is a many-headed monster; and from the mingling of the whites and blacks the mulattoes had sprung, and at this time numbered thirty thousand.

In contemplating the positions held by different races in the world in point of intelligence, integrity, the capability of receiving culture and becoming useful members of society, the mind, with lightning-like rapidity, passes from the altitude reached by the Anglo-Saxon to the end of the list, and rests upon the record or non-record which indicates the supposed inferiority of the Negro, and groping blindly in the darkness that envelops all that pertains to him, seeks for the ray of light in history that reveals the God in man; the divine attribute that must exist in the Negro as well as in other races, or he sinks to the level of the brute creation. In the history of this island—the sole possession of the Negro race in America—we find what we seek: the point of interest for all Negroes, whether Frenchmen, Spaniards, Americans or Africans—the point of interest for all students of the black race. The voice of history is the voice of God.

The subject of this sketch was one of the most remarkable men of the period in which he lived. That was the period of great popular upheaval in Europe, when the social and (in some measure) political aspect of Christian civilization was changed, introducing as it did the French Revolution, with its deluge of blood and reign of terror, and culminating in the person of Napoleon Bonaparte, with his scheming brain and boundless ambition to subdue the governments of the world. That was the day of Robespierre, Washington, Danton, Adams, Lafayette, Jefferson and Mirabeau.[3] That was the time when new Republican ideas as embodied in the new government of the United States was engaging the minds of the common people, and the First Continental Congress made its initial bow to civilization. But prominent among men of colossal brain, who made and unmade kings and formed governments anew, we find no worthier candidate for honors than Napoleon's black shadow—Toussaint L'Ouverture.

Races should be judged by the great men they produce, and by the average value of the masses. Races are tested by their courage, by the justice which underlies all their purposes, by their power and endurance—the determination to die for the right, if need be. If the Negro race were judged by the achievements and courage in war of this one man, by his purity of purpose and justice in times of peace, we should be entitled to as high a place in the world's relation of facts respecting races, as any other blood in the annals of history.

3. Maximilien Robespierre (1758–1794), Georges Jacques Danton (1759–1794), and Honoré Gabriel Riqueti, Comte de Mirabeau (1749–1791), were French Revolutionary leaders. George Washington (1732–1799), John Adams (1734–1826), and Thomas Jefferson (1743–1826) were the first three presidents of the United States, all considered founders of the nation. Marie Joseph Paul Yves Roch Gilbert du Motier, Marquis de Lafayette (1757–1834), was a French soldier who fought against the British in the American Revolution and drafted France's *Declaration of the Rights of Man and Citizen* (1789).

The rise of the blacks under Toussaint was in reality the culmination of a series of altercations between the Home government and the whites and mulattoes of the colony. To fully appreciate the advent of this man we must consider the surroundings that demanded such a character.

The French Revolution burst upon the world in 1789; it found the slaves sullen and indifferent, the mulattoes alert and eager for an opportunity to throw off their galling bonds. "The mulattoes as with us," says Wendell Phillips,

> were children of the slaveholders, but, unlike us, the French slaveholder never forgot his child by a bondwoman. He gave him everything but his name,—wealth, rich plantations, gangs of slaves; sent him to Paris for his education; so that in 1790 the mulatto race held one-third of the real estate and one-quarter of the personal estate of the island. But though educated and rich, he bowed under the same yoke as with us. Subjected to special taxes, he could hold no public office, and if convicted of any crime, was punished with double severity. His son might not sit on the same seat at school with a white boy; he might not enter a church where a white man was worshipping, and when he died, even his dust could not rest in the same soil with a white body. Such was the white race and the mulatto,—the thin film of civilization beneath which surged the dark mass of five hundred thousand slaves.[4]

When the National Convention in Paris at the commencement of the Reign of Terror issued its famous declaration,—"Liberty, Equality,"—the mulattoes in the colony of St. Domingo immediately contributed six million francs to its support, and asked in return that they be recognized socially and civilly. The Assembly acknowledged the munificent gift with a decree: "All free-born Frenchmen are equal before the law."

James Oge, the son of a wealthy mulatto woman, educated at Paris and well known there in all political circles, was selected to carry the decree to the island. When it was laid before the General Assembly there the enraged planters tore it in pieces, seized Oge, broke him upon the wheel, quartered the yet palpitating body, and sent a part to be hung up in each of the four principal cities of the island, reviving a custom that had been dead since the suppression of the Spanish Inquisition. Oge was a martyr; so was John Brown a few years later at Harper's Ferry.[5] Every great movement in the name of right demands its innocent victim. The death of Oge sowed the seed which caused the blacks to rise and free themselves in St. Domingo. The spirit of John Brown marched on and on until it swept this country like an avalanche, and freed six millions from oppression.

---

4. Wendell Phillips, "Toussaint L'Ouverture" (1861), in *Speeches, Lectures, and Letters* (Boston: Lee and Shepard, 1872), 470.

5. Hopkins wrote "Harper's Ferry" with an apostrophe, following a common spelling for Harpers Ferry that was used by Wendell Phillips and William Still, among others.

News of the death of Oge reached Paris. Robespierre rushed to the *Tribune* and shouted: "Perish the colonies rather than sacrifice one iota of our principles!" The Convention reaffirmed the decree, and returned it to the island for execution.

Part of the Colonists wished annexation to the United States. Others, loyalists in principle, appealed to George III of England. Governor Blancheland found himself deposed, and fled from the capital. He appealed to the mulattoes who had fled to the mornes, but having experienced his bad faith, they refused to help him. Remembering that the blacks were grateful to Louis XIV for his "Black Code," the first movement made by any power in their behalf, he appealed to them through agents; and so successful was he, that on Aug. 21, 1791, fifteen thousand blacks, equipped from the arsenal, appeared in the midst of the colony. In this movement Toussaint Breda first appeared.[6]

Such was the beginning of a revolt that ought to have a world-wide fame. It stands without a parallel in history,—the successful uprising of slaves against their masters, and the final establishment of their independence. This fact is doubtless due in great measure to the physical features of the island, as well as to the fierce spirit that demanded liberty or extermination.

The Historical Society of Pennsylvania possesses an authentic list in manuscript of the French officers who came to aid the Americans during the Revolutionary War: among them was the Vicomte de Fontagnes, major-general at the siege of Savannah, who commanded a legion of free Negroes and mulattoes from St. Domingo; their officers were Andre, Rigaud, Beauvais, and Beauregarde, all men of color, who afterwards became generals under the Republic; and also Henri Christophe, who later was king of Hayti. From the rise of the blacks, the history of the island seems merged in the exploits of one man—L'Ouverture.

This Negro left hardly a line for history to feed upon. We have but the reluctant testimony of his enemies. They all pronounce him to have been brave, sagacious, and endowed with wonderful powers for war and government,—attributes which history says were prostituted from noble ends by savagery in battle and hypocrisy in religion. But we are happy to know that these views do not accord with the known facts of his life, with the tenderness that enwraps his memory among his native Haytians whom he delivered from bondage, nor with the story contained in the Haytian state papers.

Toussaint was a Negro of unmixed blood. There is a mysterious significance in the diversity of races. The mission of the white man is quite different, probably, from that for which the black man was destined. How puerile and insignificant the theories which are advanced against the black man by men of thought and education who should know better. Until both these races have worked out the destiny for which they were created, judgment must be held in abeyance. Probably Toussaint was of the Senegal African race, who

6. Prior to adopting the surname L'Ouverture, Toussaint sometimes went by "Breda," the surname of the man who owned him.

most nearly resembled the whites in character and features, and were distinguished from other tribes by their intellectual superiority and warlike disposition. While yet a slave Toussaint learned to read, and some light may be thrown upon his intellectual capacity when we examine the list of books which engrossed his mind during the years of his leisure upon the plantation before he was called to be a leader of men. These favorite works were: Caesar's *Commentaries, History of Alexander the Great,* D'Orléans' *History of Revolutions in England and Spain,* Marshal Saxe's *Military Reveries,* Herodotus, Lloyd's *Military and Political Memoirs,* English Socrates, Plutarch, Cornelius Nepos, etc.[7] He knew something of herbs, too, and first joined the army as a physician.

As a soldier, we find him in 1800 after seven years of war, at the head of the newly freed, leading them from victory to victory for France under Bonaparte. The Spaniard was driven back into his own cities and there conquered, and for the first time in years the island obeyed one law under one flag. His reward was the name of General-in-chief, and for his phenomenal success in overcoming difficulties the army gave him the name L'Ouverture: the opening. As a ruler, Carlyle's words best describe him: "The natural king is one who melts all wills into his own."[8] In 1800 Toussaint issued a proclamation: "Sons of St. Domingo, come home. We never meant to take your houses or your lands. The Negro only asks the liberty which God gave him. Your houses wait for you; your lands are ready; come and cultivate them."[9] The exiled planters returned on the word of this black. One thing is very clear: that the ruin of Toussaint was due in great measure to his loyalty to France and his filial feeling for Bonaparte. He did not make himself a king, as he might have done, while France was engaged in European warfare. He did not urge his people to resist the mother-country when she should wish to reclaim her colonies; instead, he taught his people sincere love for all that was for the glory of France. Under his paternal administration, law, morals, religion, education and industry were in full force, while commerce and agriculture flourished.[10] *No retaliation* was the command of this ex-slave to his generals; and no one was so severely dealt with as those who infringed upon this order. The wars in the unhappy island were waged in the most barbarous fashion before Toussaint's elevation to power and after his betrayal. In the interval that had ensued, all his influence was on the side of mercy. The ferocity of his followers was but a copy of the conduct of the whites who had invented the most fearful punishments for the unfortunate blacks taken in battle, or even

---

7. Harriet Martineau, *The Hour and the Man* (1841; repr., New York: AMS Press, 1974), 3:254–255. The full titles (in English for translated titles) of the books that Martineau lists in her Appendix are Julius Caesar's *Commentaries,* Des Claison's *History of Alexander and Caesar,* Pierre Joseph d'Orléans's *The History of the Revolutions in England Under the Family of the Stuarts, from the Year 1603 to 1690* and *Histoire des révolutions d'Espagne,* Comte de Maurice Saxe's *Reveries; or, Memoirs Upon the Art of War,* and Henry Lloyd's *A Political and Military Rhapsody, on the Invasion and Defence of Great Britain and Ireland.*
8. Thomas Carlyle, quoted in Phillips, "Toussaint L'Ouverture," in *Speeches,* 479.
9. Phillips, "Toussaint L'Ouverture," in *Speeches,* 479.
10. Martineau, *The Hour and the Man,* 3:252–253.

when basely betrayed into their hands under the protection of a flag of truce. It is no small evidence of Toussaint's greatness, then, that he enforced during such times such a principle as *no retaliation*.[11] He was often reproached with having more love for the whites than for his own people; nor was this accusation without some foundation, for a few months before the arrival of General LeClerc he sacrificed his own nephew, General Moyse, for disregard of orders for the protection of the Colonists.[12] General Moyse was the betrothed husband of his daughter Genefrede, and his death caused a breach in the family that was never healed. Harriet Martineau has most beautifully pictured General Moyse's death in her celebrated novel *The Hour and the Man*. The following is an extract:

Therese was struck with awe as she stood, from time to time, beside the bed on which lay Genefrede. She heard at intervals the tap of a distant drum, and, she was certain, a discharge of firearms. The door from the corridor presently opened and closed again, before she could throw back the shawl from her face. She flew to the door to see if any one was there who could give her news. M. Pascal was walking away toward the farther end. When she issued forth he turned and apologized for having interrupted her, believing that the salon would be unoccupied at this early hour.

"Tell me—only tell me," said she, "whether it is over."

"Not the principal execution—I came away; I saw what melted my soul, and I could endure no more."

"You saw L'Ouverture?" said Madame Dessalines, anxiously.

"I have seen man as a god among his fellowmen."

A gleam of satisfaction lighted up Madame Dessalines' face through its agony.

"It was too touching, too mournful to be endured," resumed M. Pascal. "Never was man idolized like L'Ouverture. For him men go willingly to their deaths without protest, without supplication."

"I do not know—I do not understand what has been done," said Therese. "But does not every black know that L'Ouverture has no private interests; nothing at heart but the good of us all?"

"That is the spell," replied Pascal. "This sacrifice of his nephew will confirm it with my countrymen, as well as with yours, forever. L'Ouverture walked slowly along each line of the soldiery; and I declare to you, that though all knew that he was selecting victims for instant death, there was passionate love in every face."

"I believe it," said Therese. "And he?"

"He was calm; but a face of deeper sorrow never did I see. I did not, however, stay to see General Moyse brought out."

11. Ibid., 3:249.
12. Ibid., 3:253.

As he was speaking there was heard the heavy roll of drums at a distance, followed by a volley of musketry.

"That is it!" cried M. Pascal; and he was gone. Therese drew her shawl over her head. She desired in the sickness of her heart never to see the daylight more. She did not move, but she presently heard Father Laxabon's soft voice saying:

"Pardon, madame; but I am compelled to ask where is Mademoiselle L'Ouverture?"

"She is asleep," said Therese, rousing herself; "asleep, if she be not dead. If this last sound did not rouse her, I think the trump of doom will hardly reach her soul."

This last sound had roused Genefrede. She started up, supposing it night, but felt so oppressed that she sprang from bed with a confused wonder at finding herself dressed, and threw open the door to the salon.

"My daughter"—said Father Laxabon. She came forward with a docile and wistful look. "My daughter," he continued, "I bring you some comfort."

"Comfort?" she repeated doubtingly.

"Not now, Father," interposed Therese. "Spare her."

"Spare me?" repeated Genefrede, in the same tone.

"His conflict is over, my daughter," continued the Father, advancing toward Genefrede. "His last moments were composed; and as for his state of mind in confession"—

He was stopped by a shriek so appalling that he recoiled as if shot, and supported himself against the wall. Genefrede rushed back to the chamber and drove something heavy against the door.

"The windows!" exclaimed Therese. She stepped out upon the balcony. No one was there.

"The reservoir!" thought Therese in despair.

She was not mistaken. Genefrede stood on the brink of the deep and brimming reservoir; her hands were clasped above her head for the plunge when a strong hand seized her arm and drew her irresistibly back. In ungovernable rage she turned and saw her father.

"They say!" she screamed, "that everyone worships you! Not true now! Never true more! I hate—I curse"—

He held up his right hand with the action of authority which had awed her childhood. It awed her now. Her voice sank into a low shuddering and muttering.[13]

---

13. Ibid., 2:189–197. Part of Harriet Martineau's *The Hour and the Man* was serialized in the *Colored American Magazine* from February 1904 until August 1904. The serial commenced when Hopkins was editor and continued as long as she worked with the new owners in New York. The magazine's publication of Martineau suggests that Hopkins's influence remained even after her name stopped appearing in the magazine.

While we admire the grandeur of a great moral heroism as exhibited in the abnegation which led this man, for the sake of what he called justice, to destroy his nephew—the betrothed of his daughter—the only child of a wifeless brother, still we feel that such a course would have been beyond us of the present day and generation; nor do we feel shame in making such a confession when we consider the treachery of the whites, who even then contemplated L'Ouverture's destruction.

So great was Toussaint's determination that the whites should acknowledge the good faith of the blacks, that he disbanded his army and sent his men back to cultivate the very estates where they had formerly lived as slaves. Too late he saw the folly of his act when the armament which came to re-establish slavery appeared off Samana.[14] But unfortunately all these acts had had the effect of weakening the resistance of the blacks to France, and we presume must have been the cause of the insertion of that remarkable clause in the Constitution of the Haytian Republic after the final establishment of the freedom and independence of Hayti: "No white man, whatever be his nationality, shall be permitted to land on the Haytian territory with the title of master or proprietor; nor shall he be able, in future, to acquire there either real estate or the rights of a Haytian."

Toussaint's bitterest enemies have never charged him with sensuality, love of money, or wanton cruelty. He loved his God first, as became a man; next to his God he placed his race and the mother country; last, his family absorbed all the great tenderness of a heart too pure for the machinations of wily strategists. Again we quote from Martineau to illustrate the perfect purity of the love which existed between Toussaint and his wife:

"Yet I look upon Genefrede as perhaps the most favored of our children. It is so great a thing to be so beloved!"

"It is indeed the greatest thing." Margot stopped as a turn in the walk brought them in view of the house. The long ranges of veranda stood in the moonlight, checkered with the still shadows of the neighboring trees. Every window of the large white mansion gave out a stream of yellow light, to contrast with the silvery shining of the moon. "This is very unlike the hut we went to when we were married, Toussaint. Yet I was quite happy and contented. It is, indeed, the greatest thing to be loved."

"And have you not the greatest thing here, too? Do I not love you, my Margot?"

"Oh, yes! Yes, indeed, we love each other as much as we did then—in that single room, with its earthen floor, and its cribs against the wall, and the iron pot in the fireplace, and the hen pecking before the door. But, Toussaint, look at the difference now! Look at this beautiful house, and all the gardens and cane-pieces—and think of our palace at Port au Prince—and think of the girls as they look at church, or in the boat today—and

14. Samana Peninsula is located in the northeastern Dominican Republic.

how the country is up rejoicing wherever you go—and how the Assembly consider you—think of all that has happened since that wedding-day of ours at Breda! It is so fine, so wonderful, that you shall not frighten me about anything that can happen. I am sure the blessing of God is upon you, my husband, and you shall not make me afraid."[15]

George III offered him any title, any revenue, to hold the island under the British crown. He refused.

Once his carriage was riddled with bullets; but luckily, he was on horseback on the other side. The seven Frenchmen concerned in the attempt were arrested, and expected to be shot. The next day was a saint's day, and Toussaint had them placed before the altar. When the priest reached the prayer for forgiveness, Toussaint repeated it with him, and the offenders were allowed to go unpunished. His Christianity was broad. In 1800 admission to the House of Commons required that the candidate first should partake of the Episcopal communion. In 1800 religious bigotry in the United States was intense, and at that time this Catholic ex-slave ordered as the first line of his Constitution: "I make no difference between religious beliefs."

When it at last became evident that Napoleon was determined to crush the spirit of liberty in the blacks of St. Domingo, Toussaint became the intrepid leader who obeyed to the letter the stern mandates of war. Day after day he, with Christophe, looked out across the waters of Cap Samana for the expected French fleet. He looked on a sight no native had ever seen before. Sixty ships of the line, crowded by the best soldiers of Europe, rounded the point. He counted the flotilla, let the reins fall on the neck of his horse, and turning to Christophe said: "All France is come to Hayti; they come to make us slaves, and we are lost!" He then recognized the only mistake of his life—his confidence in Bonaparte, which had led him to disband his army.

Returning to the hills he issued the only proclamation which bears his name and breathes of vengeance: "My children, France comes to make us slaves. God gave us liberty; France has no right to take it away. Burn the cities, destroy the harvests, tear up the roads with cannon, poison the wells, show the white man the hell he comes to make!" And he was obeyed.

When William of Orange saw Louis XIV cover Holland with troops, he said: "Break down the dikes, give Holland back to ocean!" And Europe said: "Sublime!" When Alexander saw the armies of France descend upon Moscow, he said: "Burn Moscow, starve back the invaders!" And Europe said: "Sublime!"

This black saw all Europe marshalled to crush him, and gave to his people the same heroic example of defiance.

15. Martineau, *The Hour and the Man*, 2:107–108.

Beaten in the field, the French then took to lies. They cheated every one of his officers except Christophe, Dessalines, and his own brother Pierre, and finally these, too, deserted him and he was left alone. He then sent to LeClerc: "I will submit."

He went down to his house in peace; it was summer. LeClerc remembered that the fever months were coming on, when one wave of that royal hand would sweep his troops into the sea. He was too dangerous to be left at large. So they summoned him to a council;—and here is the only charge made against him: they say he was fool enough to go. But he was not cheated. He was under espionage. He probably reasoned thus: "If I go quietly I shall be treated accordingly." And he went. The moment he entered the room the officers drew their swords and told him he was a prisoner; he was not at all surprised, but seemed very sad. They put him on shipboard and weighed anchor for France. As the island faded from his sight he turned to the captain and said: "You think you have rooted up the tree of liberty, but I am only a branch; I have planted that tree so deep that all France can never root it up." From the moment he was betrayed the Negroes began to doubt the French, and rushed to arms. Then flashed forth that defying courage which shows how alike all races are when tried in the same furnace. The war went on. Napoleon sent over thirty thousand more troops, but disaster followed all his efforts. What the sword did not devour the fever ate up. LeClerc died, and Pauline carried his body back to France.[16]

Toussaint's death is shrouded in mystery. He was at first confined in the Temple, until Napoleon gave up hoping to extort from him the secret of buried treasures which it was erroneously reported that he possessed. We know not the exact manner of his taking off, but that he was cruelly murdered there is no doubt. It is commonly accepted as a truth, however, that while Toussaint was very ill the commandant left the fortress for two or three days, with the key of Toussaint's cell in his pocket. When he returned the prisoner was dead.

Our hero had the pity and sympathy of all generous spirits of the time during his disappearance. Wordsworth's sonnet is particularly delightful:

> Toussaint, the most unhappy man of men!
> Whether the whistling rustic tend his plow
> Within thy hearing, or thy head be now
> Pillow'd in some deep dungeon's earless den:
> O miserable chieftain! where and when
> Wilt thou find patience? Yet die not: do thou
> Wear rather in thy bonds a cheerful brow:

16. Phillips, "Toussaint L'Ouverture," in *Speeches*, 485–491.

Though fallen thyself, never to rise again,
Live and take comfort. Thou hast left behind
Powers that will work for thee: air, earth and skies.
There's not a breathing of the common wind
That will forget thee: thou hast great allies;
Thy friends are exultations, agonies,
And love, and man's unconquerable mind.[17]

The family of Toussaint was first sent to Bayonne, and afterward to Agen, where one of the sons died of a decline. The two elder ones endeavoring to escape from the surveillance under which they lived, were embarked for Belle Isle and imprisoned in the citadel, where they were seen in 1803. On the restoration of the Bourbons not only were they released, but a pension was settled on the family. Madame L'Ouverture died in the south of France in 1816 in the arms of Placide and Isaac.

Placide espoused Josephine de Lascase, the daughter of a nobleman, in 1821. When he died, in 1841, he left his widow with a daughter, Rose Toussaint L'Ouverture. This woman was living in 1892, at the advanced age of sixty-nine years, in the retired village of Dordogne, at Siorac, where she was universally esteemed. She received at that time a pension of 1,552 francs from the French government.

Unroll the scroll that records wonderful achievements, and among the thousands there your eye will linger upon Thermopylae and Marathon and Plataea.[18] Later you will point with pride to the Americans in the Revolutionary War; still later you will admire the brilliancy of the mind that accomplished its own aggrandizement in the person of Napoleon Bonaparte.

All these things were done by men of education capable of thinking and acting for themselves; with a long line of ancestry, perhaps, which transmitted to its later offspring the power to command armies and hold the reins of government. But think of the rise of the Haytian slaves under a slave! armed with nothing but their implements of toil and their own brave hearts, who out of their mountains and running streams forged the arms that drove back the conqueror of the world; and clasping Freedom to her breast, Hayti crowned herself with the cap of liberty.

History has recorded these deeds, and they shall be known; God intends it so! Therefore the history of the Island of St. Domingo is interesting to the Negroes of the United States; brothers in blood, though speaking different languages, we should clasp our hands in friendship when we look back upon our past, when we, too, though unaccustomed to the sound or use of arms, marched to Fort Wagner and to Fort Pillow, and there raised our bethel

---

17. William Wordsworth, "To Toussaint L'Ouverture" (1802), quoted in Martineau, *The Hour and the Man*, 3:263.

18. Thermopylae, Marathon, and Plataea were battles of the Greco-Persian Wars (492–449 BC).

consecrated by the life-blood of the brave black man. History has recorded that, also, and it shall be known; God intends it so![19]

Let us not fear for the future of Hayti or for the future of the whole race; the same God rules today who ruled in ages past. As a race we shall be preserved, although annihilation sometimes seems very near. For the Republic of Hayti, whose freedom was cemented by the martyred blood of this soldier and statesman, we feel with the late Frederick Douglass, that as the north star is eternal in the heavens, so will Hayti remain forever in the firmament of nations.[20]

SOURCE "Famous Men of the Negro Race: Toussaint L'Ouverture," *Colored American Magazine* 2.1 (Nov. 1900): 9–24.

19. Fort Wagner and Fort Pillow were Civil War battles in which African American troops played a central role. On July 18, 1863, white Colonel Robert Gould Shaw led the black soldiers of the famed Massachusetts Fifty-fourth Regiment in a failed assault on Fort Wagner at Morris Island, South Carolina. The Fifty-fourth suffered heavy casualties, which included the death of Shaw. On April 12, 1864, at Fort Pillow, Tennessee, Confederate troops, refusing to treat African American soldiers as prisoners of war, murdered more than three hundred people following Union surrender. "Remember Fort Pillow" became a battle-cry for African American soldiers. Hopkins repeatedly invokes other Civil War campaigns in which U.S. Colored Troops were prominent, including Fort Fisher, Olustee, and Honey Hill. In January 1865, after one failed attempt, Union troops successfully took Fort Fisher, which protected the Confederate port of Wilmington, North Carolina. In February 1864, at Olustee, west of Jacksonville, Florida, Confederate troops repelled a Union assault. In the Confederate victory at the November 1864 battle of Honey Hill, South Carolina, U.S. Colored Troops served valiantly. These battles figured prominently in African American writing about the Civil War.

20. Hopkins repeats this sentence in her profile of William Pickens.

II.

Hon. Frederick Douglass

One of the most remarkable things in the curriculum of life is the birth and growth of a great mind. In times of social or political changes the upheaval of civil strife bringing in its train the death of old institutions and ideas, changes in government and in religion, the passing of mighty nations or races to the rear while new leaders are destined to press onward with the standard of advancement, then, when God stands with one foot on the sea and one on the shore leading the march of human progress toward the perfection that shall usher in the millennium on earth—at such times great men are born; in obscurity, in degradation, under the law it may be, that ever in our earthly pilgrimage the life of our dear Redeemer shall be reproduced while time still holds—at such periods a hero comes unheralded and unsung in the solitude of poverty and communes with nature. No books, no teaching, no interchange of thought with cultured mentality, alone with the skies, the sea, the earth and his inner consciousness—the essence of the spirit, "a man of genius, heaven's perfect gift" is given to humanity.

So came into being the gift of God to the Black race in the United States at the darkest hour in its history. Suddenly, as the heavens hung in sullen blackness, from out the gloom of the south a star shot forth celestial radiance—Frederick Douglass was born.

Whatever man has accomplished in the plan of civilization is but a story of the lives of the great leaders of men, the creators of whatsoever the general mass of men contrive to do; the outer material result, the practical realization and embodiment of thoughts that dwelt in the great ones sent into the world as messengers of God. "The soul of the whole world's history is the history of these."[21]

We can imagine the slave child Fred rolling and tumbling over the grass with other slave children each in his tow shirt, fed on ash-cake, and in spite of bad treatment and frequent whippings, thriving under the beating so freely administered by "old Aunt Kate," who was the foster mother of the small army of plantation pickaninnies on the Lloyd plantation.

The Lloyd plantation deserves more than a passing tribute. This home where Frederick Douglass was born was founded by Edward Lloyd, the Puritan, in 1668. Maryland's bluest blood and most aristocratic family was found in this home. It had furnished at least one governor for the state.

---

21. Thomas Carlyle, "Lecture I (Tuesday, 5th May, 1840): The Hero as Divinity," in *On Heroes, Hero-Worship, and the Heroic in History* (1840; Project Gutenberg, 1997), http://www.gutenberg.org/dirs/etext97/heros10.txt.

In this, Governor Lloyd's time, there was a certain bailiff, at Wye, one Captain Anthony of St. Michael's, at one time master of a bay craft in the service of the governor, also a relative of the Lloyd's. This man was the owner of a likely Negro who escaped from bondage, and by his remarkable powers, acquirements, and address became known to the world as Frederick Douglass. In 1881 Mr. Douglass being then marshall of the District of Columbia, was moved to re-visit the scenes of his childhood and thrall, and one day found himself on the porch of Wye House, where he was received by the sons of Colonel Lloyd, their father being absent, with that courtesy which is extended to every stranger who finds his way thither. When he made known the motive of his visit, he was conducted over the estate, from spot to spot that he remembered and described with all their childish association; here a spring, there a hedge, a lane, a field, a tree. He called them by their names, or recalled them by some simple incident, and all the glowing heart of the man seemed to go out to the place as he passed from ghost to ghost as in a dream. And then a strange thing happened; standing mute and musing for a while, he said slowly and low, as one who talks in his sleep. "Over in dem woods was whar me and Mar's Dan uster trap rabbits." "Mars Dan" was the governor's son, Was it the man's half-playful, half-pathetic sense of the grotesque in congruity of the situation? Or was it glamour?—all the tremendous significance of a phenomenal life compacted into the homely reflection and phrase of a barefoot Negro boy.

He plucked flowers from the graves of dead Lloyds he had known, and at the table drank to the health of the master of the house and of his children, "that they and their descendants may worthily maintain the character and the fame of their ancestors."[22]

"Grotesque incongruity" indeed when we think of the great man's past— playing, laughing, chattering, shouting in glee, no anxious dreams of the future, and even the present suffering causing but a transient grief, and compare it with that grand and dazzling future of idolatry when the world paused to listen to Frederick Douglass's words.

For ten years the child Fred lived this life, seeing the separation of families, listening to the shrieks and cries of men and women flogged at the quarters, hearing the prayer, "Oh, Lord, how long?" Until that age, though a remarkably bright boy, he had probably had no ambitious dreams, but in his mind

22. John Williamson Palmer, "Old Maryland Homes and Ways," *Century Illustrated Magazine* 49.2 (Dec. 1894): 246. Hopkins here replaced the word *darky* that appeared in the *Century* with *Negro boy*. In a footnote, Palmer cites "Hon. John L. Thomas, in the *Baltimore American*, June, 1881." Hopkins acknowledges her use of Palmer; William Wells Brown, *The Rising Son; or, The Antecedents and Advancement of the Colored Race* (1874; rev. ed., Boston: A. G. Brown, 1876); and Parker Pillsbury, *Acts of the Anti-Slavery Apostles* (1883; repr., Freeport, N.Y.: Books for Libraries Press, 1970) in a note at the end of her essay.

uneasiness began to take the place of endurance as he asked himself "Why is it thus with my people alone?" "Is there no help?"

Then he was sent to Baltimore to his young mistress who was also a member of the influential Lloyd family. She taught him to read the Bible, and the first rays of knowledge illuminated his mind. He taught himself to write by the models in his young master's copy-book. Then came that mental thirst which must be quenched and he soon secured the speeches of Sheridan, Lord Chatham William Pitt and Fox.[23] His wonderful mental powers were awakened, his superior natural gifts began to reveal themselves. We can easily believe that in the veins of this man ran the best blood of old Maryland families mingled with the noble blood of African princes.

With enlightenment came dissatisfaction. He grew morose and gloomy; voices and beckoning hands called him and pointed to freedom's land. He determined to escape from thralldom. How he accomplished this is too well-known to rehearse it here. He chose New Bedford for his home, and there continued his studies, applying himself closely to mastering all the branches of education which slavery had robbed him of in early youth. At this time, too, he adopted the name of Douglass, after reading the *Lady of the Lake*.[24]

How surprised and delighted the illustrious author would have been could he have foreseen to what use the name Douglass would come through the medium of his famous poem. While he was acquiring knowledge, he was engaged in the humblest toil to provide his daily bread.

He learned something outside of books in New Bedford; there he saw the colored people owning their comfortable little homes and farms, schooling their children and transacting their own business. A wonderful new world of thought and action stretched before his startled gaze. Then and there he resolved to conquer it.

His advent as a lecturer was as remarkable as any event in his history. The following description of the scene is from Parker Pillsbury's *Anti-Slavery Apostles*.

Several of our speakers were colored, of whom New Bedford at that time had many (1841). I think there were two religious societies of colored people there, each with meeting-house and minister. . . .

One of them spoke so effectively at our meetings that he was invited to go with us to Nantucket, with promise of expenses paid. Not much was required for fare, for he and his wife were allowed only on the forward

---

23. Douglass learned to read and developed his literary skills by using Caleb Bingham, *The Columbian Orator: Containing a Variety of Original and Selected Pieces, Together with Rules, Calculated to Improve Youth and Others in the Ornamental and Useful Art of Eloquence* (1810), which included writings by Irish playwright Richard Brinsley Sheridan (1751–1816) and British politicians William Pitt, First Earl of Chatham (1708–1778), and Charles James Fox (1749–1806).

24. Walter Scott, *The Lady of the Lake; A Poem* (1810).

deck, where they suffered from both sun and rain, especially on our return, by rain. Our company, of course, protested, but the rule was imperious.

A young New Bedford barber, slightly colored, named Sanderson, never a slave, tall, handsome, made one of the finest addresses I had then heard on the subject of slavery, Edmund Quincy, who sat by me, remarked, and truly, as the young man sat down. "There was not an error of grammar in that speech." And it was more than half an hour in delivery.

Later in the evening our invited friend from New Bedford, the fugitive slave (Frederick Douglass), came to the platform. The house was crowded in every part, and he evidently began to speak under much embarrassment. To that time the meeting had advanced with increasing fervor, and, as this was the last session, I began to fear a decline for the close. But the young man soon gained self-possession, and gradually rose to the importance of the occasion and the dignity of his theme. In the course of his remarks he gave a most side-splitting specimen of a slave-holding minister's sermon, both as to delivery and doctrine, the text being: "Servants, obey in all things your masters." . . .

When the young man closed, late in the evening, though none seemed to know nor care for the hour, Mr. Garrison arose to make the concluding address. The crowded congregation had been wrought up almost to enchantment—particularly by some of the utterances of the last speaker, as he turned over the terrible Apocalypse of his experiences in slavery.

Mr. Garrison rose to make the concluding address. He was singularly serene and calm. He only asked a few simple, direct questions. The first was: "Have we been listening to a thing, a piece of property, or a man?" "A man! A man!" shouted fully five hundred voices of women and men.

"And should such a man be held a slave in a republican and Christian land?" was another question. "No, no! Never, never!" again swelled from the same voices, like the billows of the deep. But the last was this: "Shall such a man ever be sent back to slavery from the soil of old Massachusetts?" this time uttered with all the power of voice of which Garrison was then capable, now more than forty years ago. Almost the whole assembly sprang with one accord to their feet and the walls and the roof of the Athenaeum seemed to shudder with the "No, no!" loud and long continued in the wild enthusiasm of the scene. As soon as Garrison could be heard, he caught up the acclaim, and superadded: "No! a thousand times no! Sooner the lightnings of heaven blast Bunker Hill monument till not one stone shall be left standing on another!"

The whole can be better imagined than described by pen of mine.

Before us stood one trophy, self-delivered, self-redeemed from our chattel slavery system, then seething with all the terrors of the second death. And why should we not have rejoiced then and there? For that proved none other than the baptismal, the consecrating service of Frederick Douglass into the life-work and ministry which he has since so wonderously fulfilled.[25]

White men and black men had spoken on slavery but never like Frederick Douglass. The newspapers were filled with sayings of the "eloquent fugitive." He made his audiences weep, laugh, swear. He opened the hearts of thousands to mercy and pity for the slave by his eloquence and pathos. Many kept away from his lectures lest they be converted against their will. He knew the gamut of the human heart and swept the strings with a master hand.

In 1841 he accepted an agency as lecturer for the anti-slavery society and became at once invaluable to its promoters.

He visited Europe in 1845. In that same year he published the story of his life by this act giving a forward movement to the progress of the black race.[26] This book was a soul-stirring and thrilling memoir of his slave life and the heartrending scenes with which he was so closely connected. He was most kindly received abroad and he traveled the length and breadth of England advocating the cause of his brother in chains in such powerful and eloquent language that the very heart of the people was stirred to its secret depths. He spoke as one with authority—as one into whose soul the iron of unutterable sorrow had entered.

It is argued by some that Frederick Douglass's ability as an editor and publisher did more than all his platform eloquence to compass the freedom of his people; that, of course, is a question.

Previous to 1848 the colored people of this country had no literature. The *National Reformer,* the *Mirror of Liberty,* the *Colored American, The Mystery,* the *Disfranchised American,* the *Ram's Horn,* and other papers of smaller magnitude, had been in existence, and ceased to live. All of these journals had done something towards raising the black man's standard, but literary work of colored men was received with great allowance by the whites and they were considered out of their sphere when they meddled with journalism. But Mr. Douglass's well-earned fame gave his paper at once a standing with the first journals in the country; and he drew around him a score of contributors and correspondents from Europe, as well as all parts of America and the West Indies, that made its columns rich with the current news of the world.

In appearance Mr. Douglass was tall and well-made with a grandly developed head stamped with the sign-manual of intellectual superiority—a head that delighted phrenologists. His voice was full round, rich, clear, and his enunciation perfect. I remember well the sensations which filled my own breast the first time it was my privilege to listen to the "grand old man." Child as I was, I felt that I could listen to the mellow richness of those sonorous accents forever. His bearing full of simplicity, was the dignified bearing of a

25. Pillsbury, *Acts of the Anti-Slavery Apostles,* 325–328.
26. Frederick Douglass published his first autobiography, *Narrative of the Life of Frederick Douglass, an American Slave; Written by Himself,* in 1845.

wealthy cosmopolitan, sure of himself and of the world's homage, master of himself, unpretentious yet brilliant as a star.

He handled his subject well, with that soulful eloquence which like a pure spring issued from the spirit of the God-head within him, coming in a flood, sweeping away every obstacle of contradiction, overwhelming and swallowing every adversary. With these god-like gifts it is not a matter of wonder that he should have assumed first rank upon the lyceum platform as a lecturer, a peer of Wendell Phillips, and like him having many imitators.[27]

What were the times and conditions which tended to produce this inspired enthusiast and to place the slave-holder's chattel before the world on the same platform with Phillips, engaged in the same mission, the confidante of Wm. Lloyd Garrison, Parker Pillsbury and others?

The introduction of the cotton-gin into the South enhanced the value of slave-property and there seemed no immediate prospect of the gradual emancipation of the slaves, which question had begun to be agitated in several states. Then came the formation of the Anti-slavery society in 1832, one year after the publication of *The Liberator,* in Boston. The agitation of the question in Congress, the mobbing of Wm. Lloyd Garrison who was driven from the Anti-slavery platform in Boston by the cultured, rich Puritan patriots of the great commonwealth. They laid hands on Garrison with cries of violence, put a rope about his waist, and dragged him to imprisonment! Mobs quickly followed this act of Massachusetts, in Utica, New York, and in New York City. The experience of Rev. Elijah P. Lovejoy, a native of Maine, who in St. Louis edited the *St. Louis Times* and advocated through its columns justice to the enslaved Negro, recalls the story of Ida Wells Barnett, colored journalist and lecturer, in these more recent years. Lovejoy was murdered; Mrs. Barnett lost all her property but escaped with her life. In New York colored people were hunted like wild beasts, their churches and homes burned, with no attempt at protection.

It was suggested to the Legislature of one of the Southern States, that a large reward be offered for the head of a citizen of Massachusetts who was the pioneer in the anti-slavery movement. A similar reward was offered for the head of a citizen of New York. This insult was not received in either State. The position of the American churches on the question of slavery did great damage to the cause of Christianity. Christmas [*sic*] defended slavery out of the Bible.

The enactment by Congress of the Fugitive Slave Law caused the friends of freedom to feel that the General Government was fast becoming the bulwark of slavery. The rendition of Thomas Sims, and later that of Anthony Burns, was humiliating to the friends of the Blacks.[28]

27. William Wells Brown, *Rising Son*, 437–440.

28. The Fugitive Slave Act of 1850, a draconian law whose provisions included the criminalization of any person accused of aiding escaped former slaves, was approved by Congress on September 18, 1850. Thomas Sims and Anthony Burns were residents of Massachusetts who were infamously enslaved under the Fugitive Slave Act. Their cases were rallying points for the antislavery movement.

The "Dred Scott Decision" added to the smouldering fire.[29] By this decision in the highest court of American law, it was affirmed that no free Negro could claim to be a citizen of the United States, but was only under the jurisdiction of the separate State in which he resided; that the prohibition of slavery in any Territory of the Union was unconstitutional; and that the slave-owner might go where he pleased with his property, throughout the United States, and retain his right. This decision created much discussion, both in America and in Europe, and injured the good name of the country abroad.

The Constitution thus interpreted by Judge Taney, became the winding sheet of liberty, and gave boldness to the Southerners. The slave-holders in the cotton, sugar and rice growing states began to urge the re-opening of the slave-trade, and the driving out of all free colored people from Southern States. In the Southern Rights' Convention, Baltimore, June 8, 1860, a resolution was adopted calling on the Legislature to pass a law to that effect. Every speaker took the ground that such a law was necessary to preserve the obedience of the slaves. Judge Catron of the Supreme Court of the United States, opposed the law. He said the free colored people were among the best mechanics, artisans, and most industrious laborers in the States, and that to drive them out would be an injury to the State itself. (The governments of the Southern States in 1900, will please take notice.)

Yet these free colored people were driven out in many States, and those unable to go, were reduced to slavery. These free people had never been permitted by law to school their children, or to read books that treated against the institution of slavery. The Rev. Samuel Green, a colored Methodist preacher, was convicted and sent to the Maryland penitentiary, in 1858, for the offence of being found reading *Uncle Tom's Cabin*. The growth of the "Free-Soil" party, which had taken the place of the "Liberty" party; the struggle in Kansas; the "Oberlin Rescue Trials"; and, lastly, the "John Brown Raid," carried the question of slavery to the highest point.[30] All efforts,—in Congress, in the pro-slavery political conventions, and in the churches, added fuel to the flame that was making rapid inroads upon the inhuman monster. The hour struck upon the horologe of eternity; the Negro was destined to be free.

Progress follows upon the heels of discontent. Discontent is abroad and people open their eyes to the wickedness going on about them. Knowledge

29. On March 6, 1857, the U.S. Supreme Court remanded Dred Scott to slavery. In his infamous decision, Supreme Court Chief Justice Roger Brooke Taney (1777–1864) overstepped the parameters of the case to proclaim that African Americans had "no rights which any white man was bound to respect."

30. The Free Soil Party (1848–1854) opposed the expansion of slavery under the motto, "free soil, free speech, free labor, and free men." Among its founding members were veterans of the abolitionist Liberty Party (1840–1848). A civil war was fought in Kansas to determine whether or not the state would permit slavery following the Kansas-Nebraska Act of 1854. Thirty-seven rescuers from Oberlin, Ohio, were arrested for violating the Fugitive Slave Law in September 1858 after successfully liberating John Price to Canada. They were released in July 1859. John Brown, an antislavery veteran of the Kansas battles, led a group of abolitionists on a raid of the U.S. armory at Harpers Ferry, Virginia (in what is now West Virginia), on October 16, 1859. Brown was captured and on December 2, 1859, he was hanged.

brought discontent to the slave Fred, and with it the grand resolve—liberty or death. God had need of workers in the vineyard and he called also another—a young white man whose inheritance was universal liberty from ancestors remote—he saw "pregnant liberty heaving in the qualms" the day Garrison was mobbed, then and there the abolitionist Wendell Phillips was born with a purpose divinely conceived, to be the companion of the self-emancipated slave. Event succeeded event in Frederick Douglass's life; opportunity embraced brought to the "sage of Anacostia" honor and renown.[31] Though a slave in the South, we must conclude that he knew something of the great events recorded here. The development of the natural cunning and the keen wit of the slave compassed all difficulties in the way of obtaining news of all current events pertaining to the Negro.

Douglass was present, practically, at the birth of aggressive anti-slavery agitation; he watched with interest the birth of the "Free Soil" party, and when the "Republican party" first saw the light of day, with its face set firmly against the further extension of slave territory and the insolent domination of the slave power, he clapped his hands for joy.

Those old days seem far away to us of the present generation; some of us may even wish to never recall the horrors of our past. But is there not cause for anxiety? Are things, in the main, very much different at this hour?

To-day we have again the rise of the slave-power, for the old spirit is not dead; the serpent was scorched, not killed; so we have lynch-law and a black Postmaster Baker murdered in cold blood and neither redress nor protection from the Federal Government.[32] We have the Convict-lease system and the word of influential Southerners that in it they have "a better thing than slavery, for them."

Frederick Douglass lived long enough to feel anxiety concerning the political and social status of his people from the vacillating policy of politicians in the power of the "machine."

Speaking of an article written by Mr. T. Thomas Fortune on "Southern Home Rule," he said:

It is thoroughly comprehensive in its treatment, and will strike the true patriots of the country with no little alarm at the condition that seems to surround us. The nation should find a remedy for all this wrong. Unless it does this, it cannot be regarded otherwise than as a foul curse upon the age in which we live—a sham, a delusion and a snare. The situation is full of argument. It is like Mr. Lincoln's favorite method. He simply made a

---

31. Anacostia is the southeastern Washington, D.C., neighborhood where Douglass lived at 14th and W streets.

32. On February 22, 1898, three months after he was appointed postmaster of majority-white Lake City, South Carolina, Frazier B. Baker and his infant daughter were brutally murdered. His wife and their other children were seriously injured in the attack on the family.

statement of facts, and they in themselves constituted a sufficient argument. The bare statement of our wrongs is really the best argument that can be made. They exist. There is no denial of them, nor any palliation.

In the treatment of this great question we have all been fools, and the Republican party has been the biggest fool of all during a period covering sixteen years. They have pursued a course of folly and adopted a policy of fire. It was the same during the war that threatened to tear asunder the Union. Mr. Lincoln fought the war with only one hand. His white hand was used in front, while his black hand was tied behind him. The Republican party has not been able to advance far from this policy even unto this day.

I want the Negro question kept uppermost in the public mind. There is a disposition now to relegate it to the rear, as there was in 1884, when the Blaine idea dominated the Republican party. In that campaign they undertook to tie my tongue. They did not try to define the limits of my argument, but I could feel their purpose and desire in the drift of their discussions.

I hope that we shall be able to stay in the Republican party, but it must be true to us. The Negro is to-day the soul of the Republican party. He is its life, its energy, that mighty force that gave impulse to its birth and existence. I believe that this is to be ultimately a composite nation. There will eventually come in this country a dictatorship. There is a growing demand for a strong government, that will be able to protect all of its citizens—rich and poor, white and black—alike.

The election of Cleveland eight years ago turned loose arrogance and assumption everywhere. The country was gradually growing worse and worse and more intolerant in its hearing of all questions relating to the Negro. I don't see anything for us to do but to make sentiment favorable to the race; and let us make it aggressively.[33]

O, venerable and historic sage!

> 'Twas the sunset of life gave thee mystical lore,
> And coming events cast their shadows before.[34]

33. Timothy Thomas Fortune (1856–1928) was a journalist who published the *New York Globe*, *New York Freeman*, and, from 1887 to 1907, the *New York Age*. For about a decade beginning in the mid-1890s, Fortune and the *Age* were closely allied with Booker T. Washington. In the 1880s, Fortune criticized Douglass's loyalty to the Republican Party as strategically ineffective. Douglass backed 1884 Republican presidential nominee James Gillespie Blaine (1839–1893) of Maine, who advocated the enforcement of Section 2 of the Fourteenth Amendment, which provided for the reduction of congressional representation for states that denied the franchise to African American men. Douglass supported Blaine's campaign position, which Fortune, according to his biographer Emma Lou Thornbrough, believed "amounted to acquiescence in disfranchisement." See Emma Lou Thornbrough, *T. Thomas Fortune: Militant Journalist* (Chicago: University of Chicago Press, 1972), 85.

34. Thomas Campbell, "Lochiel's Warning" (1802).

As a freeman and a citizen the respect of mankind has been heaped upon his head, and trusts of great honor have been laid in his lap by a great nation. In 1881 he was Marshal of the District of Columbia; was Recorder of Deeds, and later Minister-Resident and Consul-General to Hayti.

While holding the latter office an effort was made by the United States Government to obtain a naval station at Môle St. Nicolas. The charge was made against Mr. Douglass that he was the means of defeating the acquisition of an important station at the Môle. It was said that he wasted his first year in Hayti in needless parley and delay, and finally reduced the chances of getting the Môle to such a narrow margin as to make it necessary for the government to send Rear-Admiral Gherardi as a special commissioner to Hayti and take the matter out of his hands.

As soon as Mr. Douglass's term of office expired he made a gallant defense of his actions, which were grossly misrepresented, in the *North American Review*, to the entire satisfaction of his friends and the discomfiture of his enemies.[35]

The government has not yet acquired the Môle St. Nicolas from Hayti, and it is doubtful if it ever does.

In his old age, with his wife and children and grandchildren about him, he rested in the evening of his life from his labors. His villa was one of the finest and most desirable in the Republic, whose original proprietor stipulated in the deed of transfer that the property should never be owned by a descendant of the African race. This estate is situated just beyond the eastern branch on the outskirts of Washington, embowered in oaks, commanding a view of the Navy Yard and the shaft of the Washington Monument. It gives a magnificent view of the most magnificent city on this continent. Such was Cedar Hill, where Douglass closed his eyes in sleep after life's fitful fever in 1895.

He had lived in Washington over twenty years, fifteen at Cedar Hill; before that time he lived at New Bedford three years; at Lynn, five; at Rochester, N.Y., twenty-five. He twice married.

Mr. Douglass loved music, and played the violin. When the young people of Washington visited him at the Cedar Hill home, he frequently accompanied some expert pianist among them with the violin. His grandson, Joseph, inherits Mr. Douglass's musical gifts, and is not only a professional violinist, but has written some excellent scores. Joseph was Mr. Douglass's favorite grandchild. He had a large and extensive library, where one might see splendid busts of Feuerbach and Strauss.[36] Fine engravings adorned the walls, a bas relief of Dante overlooking the pictures on the wall.

Mr. Douglass may have had his faults; who on this earthly planet has not? But they were not such as would dim one page of his great career.

---

35. Frederick Douglass, "Haiti and the United States: Inside History and the Negotiations for the Môle St. Nicolas" (Pts. 1 and 2), *North American Review* 153 (Sept. 1891): 337–345; 153 (Oct. 1891): 450–459.
36. Ludwig Feuerbach (1804–1872) and David Friedrich Strauss (1808–1874) were German philosophers.

He presents to us in his life an example of possibilities which may be within the reach of many young men of the rising generation—a mission divinely given, grandly accomplished. An honored name is his bequest to the Negro of the United States.

Note.—The author has used for books of reference Dr. Brown's *Rising Son*, and extracts from John Williamson Palmer in the *Century Magazine* for 1894, and Parker Pillsbury's *Anti-Slavery Apostles*.

SOURCE "Famous Men of the Negro Race: Hon. Frederick Douglass," *Colored American Magazine* 2.2 (Dec. 1900): 121–132.

III.

William Wells Brown

*T*he subject of this memoir, William Wells Brown, was widely known both at home and abroad. He was no ordinary man. Like other Negroes who have left us the example of noble lives, he accomplished an almost impossible task in surmounting the training received in slavery. In himself he was a refutation of the charge of the inferiority of the Negro. Doctor Brown's belief was that we ourselves possess the elements of successful development, but that we need live men and women to make the development. His claim was that the struggle for our rights, the last great battle-royal, is with ourselves, and the problem can be solved by us alone.

William Wells Brown was born in Lexington, Ky., in the year 1816. His mother was a slave, his father a slaveholder. The child was taken to Missouri in his infancy, and his boyhood was passed in St. Louis.

At ten years of age he was hired out to a captain of a steamboat running between St. Louis and New Orleans. He remained there a year or two, and was then employed as office-boy by Elijah P. Lovejoy, then editor of the *St. Louis Times,* in his printing-office. He spent one year there, and no doubt there imbibed the thirst for knowledge that led to his adoption of a career of letters.

After this he was again let out to a steamboat captain, and in 1834 the young man made his escape and came North.

Fortunate as usual, he obtained a situation as steward of a Lake Erie steamer, and while there was able to do much good for fugitive slaves, giving free passage to sixty-five in one year. He organized an association to help the fleeing bondmen. This association had a fund, employed counsel, furnished clothing and whatever else was needed by the fugitives. Meantime he devoted his nights to study at evening schools and under private instruction.

A man of deep convictions and unquenchable resolves, he could not remain idle. The motive power of his nature forced him into fresh fields of labor.

In the autumn of 1843 the great anti-slavery movement absorbed the self-emancipated slave. While connected with this movement Doctor Brown passed through many stirring scenes, among which may be mentioned the riot at Harwich, Mass., in 1848, when Parker Pillsbury, S. S. Foster, Lucy Stone and others were beaten with kicks and blows, the clothing torn from their persons, pitched over platforms and trampled by an infuriated mob. Doctor Brown nobly bore his part in this scene. Of him Mr. Pillsbury says: "William Wells Brown was among the earliest and most eminent fugitives to appear on our platforms. And what had these men out of which to create a self-made manhood, or any manhood? But whoever thinks of how scant material our codes, customs, constitutions, schools and churches permitted the colored people a half century ago to set up the business of self-made men making!"[37]

In 1849 Doctor Brown accepted an invitation to visit Europe, and he was immediately accepted by the American Peace Society to represent them at the Peace Congress at Paris. Under such auspices, with letters of recommendation from leading white citizens to influential Britons, and followed by the best wishes of the colored citizens, who held a mass meeting the evening previous to his departure, commending him to the care and confidence of all lovers of liberty in England, he sailed the 18th of July, 1849.

In the Old World Doctor Brown's reception was most flattering. A large and enthusiastic meeting held in the Rotunda at Dublin, and presided over by James Haughton, Esq., was the scene of his first introduction. After spending twenty days in Ireland, Doctor Brown started for Paris. The members of the Peace Congress were somewhat surprised on the last day of the session when the American ex-slave made a speech. His reception was most flattering; his address created a profound sensation. At its conclusion the speaker was warmly greeted by Victor Hugo, president of the Congress, and many other distinguished men.

Upon his return to England, George Thompson, Esq., was among the first to greet him; and at a very large meeting held in Music Hall, Bedford Square, and presided over by Sir Francis Knowles, Bart., many distinguished public men spoke. This was a most flattering reception. While abroad Doctor Brown published his first book, *Three Years in Europe*, a work which at once placed him high as an author; this was followed by *Clotelle* in 1853; in 1854, *Sketches of Places and People Abroad*; in 1863, *The Black Man*; *The Negro in the Rebellion*, 1866; *The Rising Son* in 1885; and *My Southern Home*.[38]

Doctor Brown was the recipient of many congratulations on his work as an author, and the British press vied with their American brothers in doing honor to this new star in the world of letters.

Besides writing his books, Doctor Brown was a regular contributor to the columns of the London *Daily News*, *The Liberator*, *Frederick Douglass's Paper*, and the *National Anti-Slavery Standard*. In addition to his literary labors, he was busily engaged in the study of medicine.

After travelling extensively for six years, Doctor Brown returned to the United States in 1854; and a welcome meeting was held in Tremont Temple, with Francis Jackson, Esq., in the chair, and at which Wendell Phillips said:

37. Pillsbury, *Acts of the Anti-Slavery Apostles*, 482.

38. *Rising Son* was first published in 1874. Also, see William Wells Brown, *Three Years in Europe; or, Places I Have Seen and People I Have Met* (1852); *Clotel; or, The President's Daughter, a Narrative of Slave Life in the United States* (1853); *Sketches of Places and People Abroad; the American Fugitive in Europe* (1855); *The Black Man: His Antecedents, His Genius, and His Achievements* (1863); *The Negro in the American Rebellion, His Heroism and His Fidelity* (1867); *My Southern Home; or, The South and its People* (1880).

I rejoice that our friend Brown went abroad; I rejoice still more that he has returned. The black man comes home to no liberty but the liberty of suffering—to struggle in fetters for the welfare of his race. It is a magnanimous sympathy with his blood that brings him back. I honor it. We meet to do it honor. Franklin's motto was, "*Ubi libertas, ubi patria,*"— "Where liberty is, there is my country." Had our friend adopted that for his rule, he would have stayed in Europe. Liberty for him is there. The colored man who returns, like our friend, to labor, crushed and despised, for his race, sails under a higher flag. His motto is: "Where my country is, there will I bring liberty."[39]

Doctor Brown did not enter immediately upon the practice of his profession, but continued with renewed vigor in the fight for the freedom of his race. In traveling through his native country he felt keenly the difference between this country and Europe in its treatment of the colored man. He gives an amusing account of his passage on the steamer between Ithaca and Cayuga Bridge:

When the bell rang for breakfast I went to the table, where I found some twenty or thirty persons. I had scarcely taken my seat when a rather snobby-appearing man of dark complexion began rubbing his hands, and, turning up his nose, called the steward and said to him: "Is it the custom on this boat to put niggers at the table with white people?"

The servant stood for a moment as if uncertain what reply to make, when the passenger continued: "Go tell the captain that I want him." Away went the steward. I knew well for what the captain was wanted. However, as I was hungry I commenced helping myself to what I saw before me, though keeping an eye on the door through which the captain was soon to make his appearance. As the steward returned and I heard the heavy boots of the commander on the stairs, a happy thought struck me, and I eagerly watched for the coming in of the officer. A moment more and a strong voice called out:

"Who wants me?"

I answered at once, "I, sir."

"What do you wish?" asked the captain.

"I want you to take this man from the table," said I.

At this unexpected turn of affairs the whole cabin broke out into roars of laughter, while my rival on the opposite side of the table seemed bursting with rage. The captain, who had joined in the merriment, said:

"Why do you want him taken from the table?"

"Is it your custom, captain," said I, "to let niggers sit at table with white folks on your boat?"

39. Josephine Brown, *Biography of an American Bondman, by his Daughter* (1856; repr., New York: Oxford University Press, 1991), 104.

This question, together with the fact that the other passenger had sent for the officer, and that I had stolen his thunder, appeared to please the company very much, who gave themselves up to laughter, while the Southern-looking man left the cabin with the exclamation, "Damn fools!"[40]

Doctor Brown was long connected with the temperance cause in Massachusetts. The Grand Division of the Sons of Temperance of Massachusetts elected him Grand Worthy Associate of that body, thus giving him a seat in the National Division of the Sons of Temperance of North America, where, at its meeting in Boston in 1871 his speech in behalf of admission of colored delegates from Maryland, will long be remembered.

Doctor Brown was ably seconded in all his efforts by his lovely and estimable wife, formerly Miss Annie Gray of Cambridge, Mass. Mrs. Brown came from a well-known Massachusetts family, and is a sister of Horace J. Gray, Esq., of Cambridge, for many years deputy collector of the Internal Revenue under Charles W. Slack, Esq., at Boston, Mass. Mrs. Brown was noted for her beauty, when as Miss Annie Gray she won the heart of the talented doctor; she was of great value to her illustrious husband in his literary work, and became closely identified with him in all his labors. Their joint efforts for the spread of temperance among the colored people of Boston deserve the highest praise.

While in discharge of his duties as organizer for "The National Association for the Spread of Temperance and Night Schools Among the Freed People at the South," in 1871, in the state of Kentucky, he became a victim of the Ku-Klux, and only his ready wit and knowledge of medicine saved his life.

Another incident that was always told by the doctor with great pride, and which showed his keen appreciation of humor, self-possession and fertility of resource in an emergency, occurred in the winter of 1844 at Aurora, New York:

Doctor Brown was advertised to speak in the old church, which was filled to overflowing with an audience made up mostly of men who had previously determined that the meeting should not be held. The time for opening the meeting had already arrived, and the speaker was introduced by my father, as chairman.

The coughing, whistling, stamping of feet, and other noises made by the assemblage, showed the prejudice existing against the anti-slavery cause, the doctrines of which the speaker was there to advocate. This tumult lasted for half an hour or more, during which time unsalable eggs, peas and other missiles were liberally thrown at the speaker. One of the eggs took effect on the doctor's face, spattering over his nicely

40. Alonzo Moore, "Memoir of the Author," in *Rising Son*, by William Wells Brown, 21–23.

ironed shirt bosom, and giving him a somewhat ungainly appearance, which kept the audience in roars of laughter at the expense of our fugitive friend.

Becoming tired of this sort of fun, and getting his Southern blood fairly roused, Doctor Brown, who, driven from the pulpit, was standing in front of the altar, nerved himself up, assumed a dramatic air, and said: "I shall not attempt to address you; no, I would not speak to you if you wanted me to. However, let me tell you one thing; and that is, if you had been in the South a slave as I was, none of you would ever have had the courage to escape; none but cowards would do as you have done here tonight."

Doctor Brown gradually proceeded into a narrative of his own life and escape from the South. The intense interest connected with the various incidents, as he related them, chained the audience to their seats, and for an hour and a half he spoke, making one of the most eloquent appeals ever heard in that section in behalf of his race. I have often heard my father speak of it as an effort worthy of our greatest statesmen.

Before the commencement of the meeting the mob had obtained a bag of flour, taking it up into the belfry of the church, directly over the entrance door, with the intention of throwing it over the speaker as he should pass out. One of the mob had been sent in with orders to keep as close to the doctor as he could, and who was to give the signal for the throwing of the flour.

So great was the influence of the speaker on this man that his opinions were changed; and instead of giving the word, he warned the doctor of the impending danger, saying, "When you hear the cry of 'Let it slide!' look out for the flour." The fugitive had no sooner learned these facts than he determined to have a little fun at the expense of others.

Pressing his way forward, and getting near a group of the most respectable of the company, including two clergymen, a physician, and a justice of the peace, he moved along with them, and as they passed under the belfry the doctor cried out at the top of his voice, "Let it slide!" when down came the flour upon the heads of some of our best citizens, which created the wildest excitement, and caused the arrest of those engaged in the disturbance.

Everybody regarded Doctor Brown's aptness in this matter as a splendid joke; and for many days after the watchword of the boys was, "Let it slide!"

(Extract from "Moore's Memoirs of Doctor Brown.")[41]

Doctor Brown was a handsome, well-formed man, somewhat above middle height. He had a pleasing countenance. As a man of letters he won the

41. Ibid., 33–35.

brightest laurels of his riper years, although he was very successful in his chosen profession of medicine.

No eulogy of Doctor Brown is needed. The speeches delivered and books written by him exhibit depth of thought, flights of eloquence, and a conception of statesmanship calculated to throw the haughty master of such a man far in the background. His work speaks for itself.

It is well for us of this generation, removed by thirty-seven years from the maelstrom of slavery in which such men struggled, it is well for us to ponder the history of these self-made men of our race, and mark the progress they made with nothing but the husks of living to stimulate the soul thirsting for the springs of knowledge.

How many of us today can occupy and fill their vacant places? Not alone *occupy*, but *fill* them. Alas! how few, when we consider our advantages. If much is given, much is required. An ignorant man will trust to luck for success; an educated man will *make* success. God helps those who help themselves.

SOURCE "Famous Men of the Negro Race: William Wells Brown," *Colored American Magazine* 2.3 (Jan. 1901): 232–236.

IV.

Robert Brown Elliott

Circumstances are arising every hour in these momentous times, when the Negro is making wonderful and lasting history through the medium of the very oppression placed upon him, designed to force him into unredeemable inefficiency, which make the life-story of such a man as Robert Brown Elliott of inestimable value to the rising generation.[42]

He is said to have been born in Boston, Mass., Aug. 11, 1842, of West Indian parentage. Some time afterwards he was sent to relatives living in Jamaica, where he received a liberal education in the common school. He then went to England, and in 1853 entered High Holborn Academy, London, and in 1855 was admitted to Eton College.

While in England he commenced the study of law with Sargeant Fitzherbert of the London bar. After he completed his law course he traveled and saw Ireland, Scotland, the West Indies, and South America. His early training then was such as produces a man of resolute character, knowing no fear of man, and bending the knee to God alone,—a man, too, of profound thought and learning. He had within him the genius which constitutes a man of letters; the energy without which judgment is cold and knowledge inert. We can scarcely conceive at this day the feelings which must have overwhelmed him when he had exchanged the free air of Europe for the vitiated civil and political atmosphere of the United States. But here was his home, his birthplace; here dwelt more than four millions of unhappy beings, related to him by racial ties, living in

> Doleful shades, where peace
> And rest never dwelt, hope never came.[43]

So he returned resolved to do what he could for his unhappy race. His first care must have been to familiarize himself with the laws which riveted the chains about his people. He was here through all the exciting times which preceded the Rebellion; and when the war became an actual fact, entered the United States navy as a sailor, served until its close, bearing upon his body the scars of wounds received in battle.

---

42. Following D. Augustus Straker's misspelling, Hopkins consistently wrote "Robert Browne Elliott"; I have silently corrected the spelling to "Brown." See Straker, *Euology* [sic] *on the Life, Character and Public Services of Robert Browne* [sic] *Elliott, Ex-Member of Congress and Speaker of the House of Representatives of South Carolina* (Columbia, S.C.: William Sloane, 1884).

43. Milton, *Paradise Lost*, bk. 1, lines 65–66.

In 1867 Mr. Elliott went to Charleston, S.C., and entered the office of the Charleston *Leader,* afterwards the *Missionary Record,* as a printer. He soon became one of the editors, and from this we may date his remarkable career as a statesman.

The war was over; the status of the Negro decided; he was a free man and a citizen. The states lately in rebellion must be handled by Congress, and the new element in the Southern problem (the free Negro) was a great embarrassment to the powers at Washington. "What shall we do with the Southern States?" Charles Sumner answered the question easily when he said: "They are now a clean slate on which Congress may write laws." Today the answer is as easily given as then the path is as clear for the settlement of all difficulties if Congress were disposed to exercise the power won for it by the sacrifice of much blood and treasure.

The work of reconstruction then began, and in 1868 the people of South Carolina assembled in what is known as the "Constitutional Convention," for the purpose of framing a new constitution for that state. Mr. Elliott was a delegate to this convention; he was barely twenty-five.

The convention was in session for nearly fourteen days; Mr. Elliott was very modest in speech and bearing until Feb. 3, when in a speech a member favored the payment of the former slaveholder for the slave. This was the long-expected opportunity, and Mr. Elliott made a telling speech, full of zeal and patriotism. From that hour he was known as a powerful leader of the race.

At the close of the convention, Mr. Elliott was chosen by the voters of Barnwell County a member of the House of Representatives in 1868, where he served until Oct. 23, 1870. In this new position he soon made himself felt, by reason of his skill as a parliamentarian and his knowledge of law, easily becoming the leader in the House, members and large audiences listening to his words in debate with great admiration.

March 25, 1869, he was appointed State Assistant Adjutant General. At this time Republican politics were in a tottering condition in South Carolina. Desire for office, love of money, the ignorance of the voting population, gave unbounded opportunity for dishonest gains. In the different state legislatures the battle was fought. These bodies were composed almost entirely of Negroes. The few whites were no help to them, and in most cases it would have been better for the whole country if those same whites had been in some state prison. This was a trying position for the newly enfranchised blacks, but they did their work nobly; they gave the South the first system of free schools that had ever existed in the land of King Cotton. In the ten years of Negro legislation in the South there is enough of good, sound wisdom to arrest the favorable attention of all close students of human nature. At this time, then, when the power of the party trembled in the balance, Robert Brown Elliott, as chairman of the State Executive Committee, by his superior political skill, led the party to victory until 1876, when the Democratic party fraudulently usurped the government.

For his devotion to party, as well as his well-known ability, he was chosen a member of the Forty-second Congress in 1881, and was re-elected to the

Forty-third Congress, the first Negro of unmixed blood to sit in the halls of Congress in the United States of America. In connection with this event there were many peculiar coincidences, and none is more so than the fact that Robert Brown Elliott took the seat once filled by Preston Brooks. Perhaps a rehearsal of a few of the main features of Brooks' attack on Senator Sumner will be interesting to many young readers:

On the 19th and 20th of May, 1856, Senator Sumner delivered a speech in the Senate which described what he called "the crime against Kansas"; and the excuses for the crime he denominated the apology tyrannical, the apology imbecile, the apology absurd, and the apology infamous. In the course of this speech he indulged in caustic personal criticism against Senator Butler of South Carolina. Butler was not present.

On the 22d of May, two days after the speech, Preston S. Brooks, a nephew of Senator Butler, entered the Senate chamber to retaliate by violence. The session was short, and after adjournment Senator Sumner remained at his desk, writing. Occupied with his work, the Senator did not notice Brooks sitting across the aisle to his left, where in conversation with a friend he was manifesting his impatience that a lady seated near Mr. Sumner did not take her departure from the chamber. Almost at that moment she arose and went out, for quickly afterwards Brooks got up and advanced to the front of the Senator's desk. Leaning upon the desk, and addressing Mr. Sumner with a rapid sentence or two, to the effect that he had read his speech, and it was a libel upon his absent relative, and that he had come to punish him for it, Brooks began striking him on the head with a gutta-percha walking-cane of ordinary length, and about an inch in diameter.

Surprised, blinded and stunned by the blows, Mr. Sumner's first instinct was to grapple with his assailant. The effort was futile; the desk was between them, and being by his sitting posture partially under it, Mr. Sumner was prevented from rising fully to his feet until he had by main strength in his struggles, wrenched it from its fastenings on the floor. In his attempt to follow Brooks they became turned, and from between the desks moved out into the main aisle. By this time through the repetition of the heavy blows and loss of blood Mr. Sumner became unconscious. Brooks seizing him by the coat-collar, continued his murderous attack, till Sumner reeling in utter helplessness, sank upon the floor beside the desk nearest the aisle, one row nearer the center of the chamber than his own. The witnesses variously estimated the number of blows given at from ten to thirty. Two principal wounds, two inches long and one inch deep, had been cut on the back of Mr. Sumner's head; near the end of the attack Brooks' cane was shivered to splinters.[44]

44. John G. Nicolay and John Hay, "Abraham Lincoln: A History. The Attack on Sumner, and the Dred Scott Case," *Century Illustrated Monthly* 34.2 (June 1887): 203–204. Nicolay and Hay's *Century* serial on Lincoln was published by the Century Company in book form as *Abraham Lincoln: A History* in 1890.

The shock of the attack and the serious wounds Senator Sumner received produced a spinal malady, from which he rallied with great difficulty, and only after severe medical treatment and years of enforced abstinence from work. It was on the 4th of June, 1860, that he again raised his voice in debate. Both Butler and Brooks were dead, but in the main the personnel and the spirit of the pro-slavery party still confronted him.[45]

Under the reign of misrule in the Republican party at the South extravagance, high taxes, the filling of State offices by men unfitted for such trusts, made the whites feel themselves degraded in the eyes of the world. Northern sympathy emboldened them, resulting in the Ku-Klux organization and a reign of terror which still curses that section. Mr. Elliott delivered a famous speech in this connection in Congress on the Bill to Enforce the Provisions of the Fourteenth Amendment,—the Ku-Klux Bill. He portrayed a horrible condition in the state of South Carolina, women and children not escaping the fate of husband and father. On May 30, 1872, Messrs. Voorhees of Indiana and Beck of Kentucky made the initial denunciation of Republicanism in the South.[46]

But his greatest glory lies in his speech on the Civil Rights Bill.

Hon. Charles Sumner introduced this bill in the Senate, designed to give equal political rights and privileges to all citizens, without regard to color or previous condition of servitude, by all inn keepers, common carriers and the like. The bill met with strong opposition even from the Negro's friends. Mr. Sumner declared that "rights were not based on expediency, but were founded in justice."

The bill passed the Senate, and went to the House for debate. Among its opponents were the Hon. Alexander Stephens of Georgia, ex-vice-president of the late confederacy. On the Republican side were Hon. Ben Butler and James G. Blaine; but the opportunity to show that the Negro was entitled to his rights because of his worth as a man was not to be lost, and Robert Brown Elliott was chosen as the one best fitted for the task. Prof. D. Augustus Straker, LL.B., thus describes the scene:

Mr. Stephens was brought into the House in the accustomed manner—in his chair. He severely arraigned the constitutionality of the Civil Rights Bill and its policy, as did Mr. Beck of Kentucky and Mr. Harris of Virginia. At the close of Mr. Stephens' speech the House of Representatives, now filled in every possible manner with United States senators who had suspended their labors to witness this sight; foreign ministers, judges, lawyers, clergymen, scientists, authors, and the laity innumerable, all were

45. Ibid., 207.
46. In 1872, Daniel Wolsey Voorhees (1827–1897), of Indiana, U.S. representative (1861–1866, 1869–1873), U.S. senator (1877–1897), and James Burnie Beck (1822–1890), of Kentucky, U.S. representative (1867–1875), U.S. senator (1877–1890), were Democratic representatives. They were allied with John Thomas Harris (1823–1899), of Virginia, U.S. representative (1859–1861, 1871–1881).

there to witness the political miracle, and if God was God to worship him, and if Baal was God to worship *him*. At last Mr. Elliott in reply to Mr. Stephens said:

> Mr. Speaker: While I am sincerely grateful for the high mark of courtesy that has been accorded me by this House, it is a matter of regret to me that it is necessary at this day that I should rise in an American Congress to advocate a bill which simply asserts rights and equal public privileges for all classes of American citizens. I regret, sir, that the dark hue of my skin may lend color to the imputation that I am controlled by motives personal to myself in my advocacy of this great measure of natural justice. Sir, the motive that impels me is restricted by no such narrow boundary, but is as broad as your Constitution. The bill, however, not only appeals to your justice but it demands a response from your gratitude. In the events that led to the achievement of American independence, the Negro was not an inactive or unconcerned spectator. He bore his part bravely upon many battlefields, although uncheered by that certain hope of political elevation which victory would secure to the white man. The tall granite shaft which a gratified state has reared above its sons who fell in defending Fort Griswold against the attack of Benedict Arnold, bears the name of John Freeman and others of the African race, who then cemented with their blood the cornerstone of your Republic.

Mr. Elliott then considered the bill in its legal, constitutional, political and social aspect, showing himself a lawyer able to stand with honor among his peers in Congress. Replying to Mr. Stephens directly, he said:

> I meet him only as an adversary; nor shall age or any other consideration restrain me from saying that he now offers this government, which he has done his utmost to destroy, a very poor return for its magnimous treatment, to come here and seek to continue, by the assertion of doctrines obnoxious to the true principles of our government, the burdens and oppressions which rest upon five millions of his countrymen who never failed to lift their earnest prayers for the success of this government, when the gentleman was seeking to break up the union of these states, and to blot the American republic from the galaxy of nations.

After listening to these awful and potent truths, Mr. Stephens ordered himself to be taken to his committee-room.

Mr. Elliott then directed his attention to Mr. Beck of Kentucky, who had vaunted the chivalry of his own state. Mr. Elliott reminded him that in the second war of American independence General Jackson reported of the white Kentucky soldiers that "at the very moment when the entire discomfiture of the enemy was looked for, with a confidence amounting almost to certainty, the Kentucky reinforcements, in whom so much reliance had been placed, ingloriously fled." In quoting this indisputable piece of history, I do so only by way of admonition, and not to question the well-attested gallantry of the true Kentuckian, and to suggest to the gentleman that it would be well that he should not flaunt his heraldry so proudly while he bears this bar-sinister on the military escutcheon of his state,—a state which answered the call of the Republic in 1861 when treason thundered at the very gates of the capital, by coldly declaring her neutrality in the impending struggle.

He then closed his wonderful effort with these significant words:

Notwithstanding long years of oppression and suffering, the colored citizen has a filial affection for his white brethren, and as Ruth of old, so say they to those who would treat them as outcasts: "Entreat me not to leave thee, or return from following thee; for whithersoever thou goest I will go, and where thou lodgest I will lodge; thy people shall be my people and thy God my God; where thou diest I will die, and there will I be buried; the Lord do so to me and more if aught but death part thee and me."[47]

Today the Civil Rights Bill passed by Congress is almost a dead letter, and the Southern States are quietly and persistently robbing the Negro population of all rights of citizenship. The blacks cannot look for justice or toleration from late slaveholders and their descendants. If a man has no right to vote for men and measures which tax himself and his property, that man is a slave. We are told that the elective franchise is not a *right,* but a privilege; something to be allowed a man as a reward of merit for good conduct continued for so long a time. In a republican government of *the people* like ours, the franchise is not a privilege, but a *right,*—a right belonging to every man who has not forfeited it by crime. The signs of the times point to the commitment of a heinous crime against the Negro, in which the North won by fair and plausible words from its Southern brother, is willfully quiescent. The shame and folly of deserting the Negro are only equalled by the wisdom of recognizing and protecting their power in the first years of the emancipation.

Wendell Phillips said once:

We are accustomed to use the words North and South familiarly. By the North I mean the civilization of the nineteenth century,—I mean that

---

47. Straker, *Euology* [sic], 12–15. Straker delivered his eulogy on Robert Brown Elliott at Bethel AME Church in Columbia, South Carolina, on September 24, 1884. Elliott delivered his famous civil rights speech to the Forty-third Congress, on January 6, 1874.

equal and recognized manhood up to which the race has struggled by the toils and battles of nineteen centuries,—I mean free speech, *the welcome rule of the majority*—I mean the Declaration of Independence!

By the South I mean likewise a principle. I mean an element which, like the days of Queen Mary and the Inquisition, *cannot tolerate free speech,* and punishes it with the stake; the aristocracy of the skin, which considers the Declaration of Independence a sham,—which believes that one-third of the race was born booted and spurred, and the other two-thirds ready saddled for that third to ride,—I mean the thing that manifests itself by barbarism and the bowie-knife, by bullying and lynch law.[48]

These words were spoken on a New York platform in 1863, and describe the situation today to the very life. Last week an eminent Southerner (F. Hopkinson Smith), sixty-two years old, eminent as a writer and lecturer, on a Newton, Mass., platform, at an evening's entertainment, attacked the great work of Harriet Beecher Stowe.

If the illustrations chosen by Mrs. Stowe as models for her characters in *Uncle Tom's Cabin* were only types, and not generalities, why does the South still persist in wanton cruelties toward its Negro population? Years and experience have not, we fear, brought feelings of toleration into very many Southern hearts. The old virus of slavery which resented Northern intervention in any form still exists in the passions of all Southern society in spite of his plea thrown to the white citizen: "The people of this country are all alike. They are all Americans."

If the slaveholders ever cared for the crippled, the old, the sick, under slavery, still the question arises: Where was the glory to them in this act? If the slave had received compensation for his labor in the service of these men, he could have cared for himself without the aid of that charity that would not see a "yellow dog hurt."

Dropping the Negro from the discussion, we ask: If Harriet Beecher Stowe's work caused the war, what good was there in it for all humanity? We know that she indirectly raised the status of white Southern womanhood, giving it a pure, moral atmosphere in the home life; healed the cankering sore of domestic infidelity in the husband and of immorality in the son, as exemplified in the children of two races,—unlawful product of the crime of bondage and plantation sensuality. Many a planter's wife has dragged out a miserable existence with an aching heart, at seeing her place in her husband's affections usurped by her beautiful mulatto maid.

On the same platform and in the same year Mr. Phillips also said: "Today the question is not merely whether the Negro shall be free, but whether this great free, model state, the hope of the nations and their polar star, this experiment of self-government, this normal school of God for the education of the masses,

48. Phillips, "The State of the Country" (1863), in *Speeches,* 534.

shall survive, free, just, entire, *able not only to free the slave,* but to pay the further *debt it owes him,—protection as he rises into liberty, and a share in the great State he aided to found.*[49] What answer can we make in the face of existing conditions? Mr. Phillips continued: "We have a state of mind to annihilate.[50] *To bar out ideas* is the plan of the South, to cripple, confine, break down the free discussion of these Northern States. Unless he can do that he is not safe; to *mould Massachusetts into a silent, unprotesting* Commonwealth."[51] And we may now add to this illustrious man's prophecy, Mr. F. Hopkinson Smith's own words: "What the Negro people really need is *to go way back and begin all over again where they started in their freedom,* at industrial development."[52]

The phrase "industrial development" is greatly misunderstood by our white friends. To them it means an excuse, gladly hailed, to force the Negro to retrograde. To us it means, education of head and hand, not confining the Negro to any particular line of employment, certainly with no intention of curtailing his efforts to raise himself into any business, profession or social condition that intrinsic worth and fitness may warrant him in seeking.

Soon after making his great civil rights speech, Mr. Elliott resigned his seat in Congress and returned to South Carolina. He was elected a member of the House of Representatives from Aiken County and was chosen Speaker of the House. The question has often been asked: Why did General Elliott abandon a high office for one lower in rank, casting aside honor, fame, and a large salary. From what motive? *Fidelity to the Republican party.*

Corruption was at the heart of Republicanism. In this time of trouble party managers sought General Elliott's aid and counsel. Pride of party doubtless made him seek to stem the torrent about to sweep over the entire state. In 1876 General Elliott was elected to the office of attorney-general of South Carolina, the first Negro in the United States ever elected attorney-general. He entered upon the discharge of his duties, but the end of the power of Republicanism had come in that state, and by force and fraud political power was wrested from the party. All Republicans were driven from office by the decision of the Supreme Court. The accounts of the high-handed proceedings of the Court are close in analogy to the late embroilment in Kentucky down to the most trifling incident. No prominent Republican was safe, and criminal charges were preferred against most of them. The pet scheme of the Democrats was to drive Robert Brown Elliott from the state; but so bravely did he bear himself, and so unimpeachable had his conduct been that he passed unstained and untouched through the trying ordeal. In 1880 General Elliott was appointed by Hon. John Sherman United States treasurer at

49. Ibid., 542.
50. Ibid., 543.
51. Ibid., 539.
52. For an excerpt of F. Hopkinson Smith's speech, see "Two Views of *Uncle Tom's Cabin,*" *Outlook* 67.4 (Jan. 26, 1901): 236.

Charleston, S.C. In 1879 he was a delegate to the National Convention at Chicago from South Carolina. He distinguished himself there by rising in the convention and seconding the nomination of Hon. John Sherman for President of the United States. His speech was brilliant and able, and immediately gave the Negro voter a new standing in the councils of the nation; he became a factor, and not a mendicant begging for crumbs of political comfort. Upon the death of President Garfield he was relieved of his office, after which he recommenced the practice of law at New Orleans, where he died suddenly Aug. 9, 1884, lamented by white and black alike.

Today we cannot point to one man who has reached the dizzy heights of superiority occupied by General Elliott. By his achievements we prove that it is possible for a Negro to rise to great political eminence as well as a white man, if the desire for his "industrial development" does not blind our eyes to other advantages in life. Robert Elliott's life story is interwoven inseparably with the political history of the United States in the most critical period of its existence. His death was a great loss to his race and to his country.

The story of this man's life should be an incentive to the young men of the present. Step by step he accomplished many ambitions, leaving a shining trail of light behind him.

SOURCE "Famous Men of the Negro Race: Robert Brown Elliott," *Colored American Magazine* 2.4 (Feb. 1901): 294–301.

V.

Edwin Garrison Walker
Born in Charlestown, Mass., Sept. 28, 1835;
died in Boston, Mass., Jan. 13, 1901

The Dead March wails in the people's ears;
The dark crowd moves, there are sobs and tears;
The black earth yawns; the mortal disappears;
Ashes to ashes, dust to dust:
He is gone who seemed so great,—
Gone; but nothing can bereave him
Of the force he made his own
Being here;
And he wears a truer crown
Than any wreath that man can weave him.
God accept him! Christ receive him![53]

*I*t is decreed all men must die. Men who have died are as the sands by the sea, but those who have left footprints on the sands are few indeed. Although we are descended from the same parent stock, yet are we different. One man excels another as one sun differeth from another in its celestial glory. So if a man's life—his good deeds, acts of kindness, of philanthropy toward his fellows—be like a sun of greatest magnitude in this short span allotted to us, his death creates a void; his loss seems irreparable.

All history of the great deeds or wonderful achievements of man is but biography. Each man's experiences or acts are but a repetition of the same deeds in others, perhaps—a reflection of that mind which is the common property of all humanity. Herein lies the common brotherhood of man.

We applaud these great acts because we ourselves would have acted as he did had the opportunity been ours. The exploits, the sacrifices of these men who have toiled for the development of this same common brotherhood, were performed for the education and advancement of ages yet unborn, as well as for the benefit of the present generation.

To the superficial observer, the life of Queen Victoria, her long and prosperous reign, her grace, grandeur, riches and power, presents nothing in common with this representative of a humble race; but if we overlook this superficial difference and seek the relationship of souls—the divine attribute by which alone we may claim kindred with all human life, they were kindred spirits. The

---

53. Alfred Tennyson, "Ode on the Death of the Duke of Wellington" (1852).

soul of Victoria melted within her at the cry of the bondman, and she was moved to have compassion upon his utter helplessness. Her welcoming hand carried on its outstretched palm peace and security within her Canadian domains. The same spirit stirred in Judge Walker's heart as he thrilled with indignation at the Negro's wrongs, and sought by the fiery eloquence of his oratory to arouse men to a realization of the enormity of the crime they were perpetrating against an innocent and inoffensive people. And not by words alone but by deeds, by every honest action that might create favorable sentiment.

The late queen and Edwin G. Walker were as far apart as the east is from the west, but within their hearts was unity of thought and action. "Nature is an endless combination of a few laws; she is full of a sublime family likeness in all her works."[54]

Edwin Garrison Walker, the eminent Negro barrister, was known to all his friends as "Judge" Walker. His father was a colored preacher, David Walker, himself a fugitive slave from North Carolina; his mother was also a prominent figure in the fugitive slave period.

The first prominence given to the name of Walker was in 1827, when David Walker issued his famous pamphlet, *Walker's Appeal.*[55] Right here we have the most interesting fact in the history of the abolition movement: this appeal was *the very first step taken in the attempt to arouse the people of the United States to the enormity of the crime of slavery* and the deep disgrace it was bringing upon the country. This paper was strong in sentiment, cogent in its reasonings, and breathed the thoughts of a man of powerful mind; it was hard to believe that it was written by a man but recently free. The entire country was aroused wherever it appeared; the attention of men richly endowed with intellectual gifts was attracted, and they were soon absorbed in the study of the Negro question. Fact piled on fact met them at every point of argument, and a cloud of witnesses bearing on their bodies evidence in the shape of wounds and scars revolting and horrible. These men could not withstand the evidence, and soon the very lives of the brightest ornaments of American thought and culture were absorbed in the warfare against slavery. The appeal gave us *The Liberator* and William Lloyd Garrison. The first issue of the paper was made on Jan. 1, 1831. "It was a most humble and unpretentious little sheet of four pages, about fourteen inches by nine in size, but charged with the destiny of a race of human beings whose redemption from chattel, brutal bondage was one day to shake to its foundations the mightiest republic ever yet existing on the globe."[56] The movement grew amazingly after its first inception, and soon drew to its support Nathaniel P. Rogers, S. S. Foster,

54. Ralph Waldo Emerson, "History," in *Essays: First and Second Series* (1841–1844; *Making of America,* 2005), 1:20.

55. David Walker began writing for *Freedom's Journal* in 1827, and self-published his pamphlet *Walker's Appeal, in Four Articles; Together with a Preamble, to the Coloured Citizens of the World, but in Particular, and Very Expressly, to Those of the United States of America* in 1829.

56. Pillsbury, *Acts of the Anti-Slavery Apostles,* 10.

Parker Pillsbury, Lucy Stone, Lucretia Mott, Wendell Phillips, Charles Sumner, George Thompson of England, James Buffum, Abby Foster, the Burleigh brothers and a host of others.

Such was the stock from which "Judge" Walker sprang, and such the movement into which he was born. He lived on Belmont street in Charlestown, very near to the old Catholic cemetery, after his family moved from Boston. He was well and favorably known in the city, receiving more notice because of his intelligence and race than a white lad. He was educated in the public schools, and at the close of his youthful school days learned the trade of morocco dresser. As soon as he had mastered this trade he entered business for himself on Prince street, employing three men to help him. He prospered in his work, but the young aspiring mind was not satisfied. With his first earnings he bought a copy of Blackstone, and devoted his entire attention to the study of law.[57] He was a brilliant student, and in 1864 successfully passed his examination and was admitted to the bar. At this time he had made the acquaintance of Robert Brown Elliott, and the two were fast friends, the house on Belmont street being the home of Elliott as well. Both of these men had a taste for politics; both saw and recognized the importance to the Negro that like the Irishman, he became a factor in the governing power of the land. Sitting in the gallery of the hall of the Massachusetts Legislature, these men took lessons in debate and parliamentary usage. "Bob," said Mr. Walker to his friend one day, as they leaned over the gallery railing and gazed down upon the assemblage of lawmakers, "Bob, some day I shall sit there, and help make the laws of this Commonwealth."

"All right Ned," replied Mr. Elliott; "when you do that I shall go to Congress and help make the laws for the United States."

In a very short time after that Mr. Walker *did* have the honor of representing Charlestown in the Massachusetts Legislature. He was materially aided in the accomplishment of this event by his friend, Elliott. And in 1881, as we know, Mr. Elliott was a Congressman, casting the lustre of his genius as a Negro over the entire continent.

Lawyer Walker opened his first law office in Charlestown, Mass. He was an able and eloquent advocate, much liked by his brothers in the profession, black and white, and was a great friend of Robert Morris. He was frequently assigned by judges to conduct the defence in important criminal cases, and always acquitted himself with credit. But it was upon the platform, with his race as his theme, that one enjoyed to the full his fiery and eloquent oratory, which was not only eloquent but at times sublime.

Archibald Grimké, ex-consul to San Domingo, in an eloquent address on Mr. Walker, says:

"Edwin Garrison Walker was built out of the staunchest sort of race material. His father was so built before him. Neither of them had a drop of blood

---

57. William Blackstone (1723–1780) was a British legal writer.

in his body or a single thought in his mind which was traitor to the cause of his race."[58]

And this was so because of early training in the hard school of adversity, which was the portion of the Negro in Massachusetts at the time of his birth. Few of us realize the situation or the feeling of the time. With the exception of a few staunch white friends, every hand was against us, every door closed. We cannot in these days truthfully picture the events which transpired in the development of the greatest evolution in human destiny known to modern times. Nor has justice ever been done in telling of these thrilling occurrences, to the sacrifices made of money and of personal safety by the colored men of New York and New England for the amelioration of their race. He who would be free must himself strike the first blow, some one has told us. Surely the Negro has followed that advice to the letter. Most of these colored men were stern and determined actors; not gifted with eloquent speech that fitted them for the public platform, but their zeal never slept. Within humble homes and in unpretentious churches plans were concocted for the overthrow of the slave power, and fugitive slaves were given aid and comfort and helped to places of safety. Many times the fugitive was seated in church, surrounded by a dense mass of black humanity. Outside the master, in company with the sheriff, walked up and down, ready to identify and seize his property. A carriage would drive up, and covered by the crowd, the Negro entered the carriage and was driven to a place of safety. Even in New York City they did not dare attack that crowd of desperate blacks, ready to sell life dearly.

In Boston we are told of Jacob Moore's tailor-shop in Spring Lane. There, when night shades had fallen, the shutters were carefully adjusted and doors securely locked. In the profound stillness that followed the activity of the day in this business locality, men might have been seen, singly, never together, approaching the tiny shop; the door would open silently, the figures would disappear. Phillips, Foster, Garrison—any one of these names might have been given with truth to the figures that disappeared in the darkness of Spring Lane, for all those intellectual giants were familiar visitors to Moore's tailor-shop. So it was with Peter Howard's barber-shop, situated at the corner of Irving and Cambridge streets—the same men visited his place secretly, to consult with the colored men, and to view the fugitive in concealment and devise means for his comfort and safety, while they listened to his tale of horror, and shuddered at the signs of physical torture indelibly stamped upon his quivering flesh. After these meetings the country would be startled by some new effective and daring act of the Abolitionists. In some of these scenes Walker participated in his youth.

We can imagine him as a child in his trundle-bed drawn out before the glowing log fire in the humble living room, listening, when he should have

58. Archibald Henry Grimké (1849–1930) was an attorney, activist, editor, and author. In 1894, President Grover Cleveland appointed him consul to Santo Domingo, a position he held until 1898.

been sleeping, to the serious talk of his father, neighbors and fugitive slaves—for that home sheltered many a man fleeing from oppression—listening to the stories of the wrongs of his race until his young heart was on fire with indignation. His father died when he was quite young, but the son never forgot his teaching. We see him as a youth when Anthony Burns is to be remanded to slavery. All day the streets of Boston were filled with knots of excited men, at last awakened to the strength of the slave power.

Boston was almost suburban in its character. Dover street was way out of town. Charlestown was a separate city, not yet encircled by the arms of modern expansion.

It was rumored abroad that rescue bands were forming to resist the intrusion of Dixie laws in Puritan Boston. "Clang! clang! clang!" The hoarse voice of the bells in every steeple gave the signal for opening the draws upon all the bridges leading into the city, to prevent white men and black men violating the new United States law for the rendition of slaves. Parties of men built rafts and ferried themselves across the Charles to the other shore. Probably Walker was among them.

State street was densely packed with men whose stern faces were ominous of thoughts within. The Boston Courthouse was in chains, two hundred rowdies and thieves sworn in as special policemen, respectable citizens shoved off the sidewalks by the slave-catchers. Was it for this they had resisted a paltry tax on tea, at the cannon's mouth, and were basely submitting to an imposition tenfold greater simply to brutalize their fellowmen? Silent the great crowd stood, while down the historic street swung the marines in hollow square within which walked the prisoner—one helpless Negro, whose chains clanked at every step, and whose manacled hands were useless to their owner. A sigh came from the crowd in one long-drawn breath, then was hushed again into unbroken silence. Suddenly on the left from the Commonwealth building slowly descended a coffin, across whose black surface was traced in white letters the one word "*Liberty.*" On the instant the suppressed feelings of the crowd broke forth in cries, groans, hisses, then they swayed in the direction of the soldiers hustling them for a moment. Weapons were drawn and gleamed and flashed for an instant about the prisoner, and answering flashes came from the men within the crowd. It was a crucial moment, when but for the fact that it was a Massachusetts crowd, mob violence would have defied the Federal government. Amid such scenes as this Lawyer Walker was trained to fidelity to his race along with Robert Morris, Charles Lenox Remond, William C. Nell, Lewis Hayden, John J. Smith, George T. Downing, Mark R. De Mortie, J. Sella Martin, and many others whom we do not now recall.

With such scenes indelibly stamped upon his mind, Lawyer Walker could not brook the crack of the party whip when it commanded him to do violence to his own best promptings in the interest of his race. In 1867 he made a speech on the Fourteenth Amendment that practically severed his connection with the Republican party. He refused to obey his political bosses, and lost the chance of re-election to the Massachusetts legislature. Then, too, he was a leal [sic] follower of Benjamin F. Butler, always stumping the state in his interest when the general was a candidate. Such things operated against his worldly advancement; and when we add to that the bitter disappointment that came to him in a cherished ambition, we cannot wonder that he felt his cup of bitterness was overflowing.

Mr. Walker relied upon himself; spoke his open convictions. He was a non-conformist to the doctrines of the Republican party, because he was a man free in body and thought. For this non-conformity he had the displeasure of the world about him, white and black.

Believing that the conservatism of the Northern Republican counts the Negro vote as always solid and reliable in the interest of one political body, he saw that a change would be beneficial. He saw, too, that to conserve the white Southern Republicans and eliminate the value of political patronage from the calculations of the black Republicans, without the loss of a single vote, was the daring scheme of the party bosses. With the experience gained in two eventful epochs in the history of this country, Lawyer Walker saw the black man's opportunity if, as a race they would only come together without regard to personal ambition; he trimmed his own sails to catch the favoring wind that greets the freelance politician, but found himself alone and unsupported. Mr. Grimké's language is very clear and forcible in stating Mr. Walker's position:

He was among the first of the colored leaders of the country to perceive clearly the folly of political solidity for the race. For no one needs to penetrate very deeply into the hidden nature of things political to discern in the peculiar circumstances of our lot in America that union among ourselves for the good of the race makes for its political strength, while, on the other hand, union for the good of a party organization is undoubtedly well for that particular party organization, but bad for ourselves, must inevitably ultimate in our growing political weakness, in our diminishing political importance as wielders of the ballot, that right preservative of all other rights and liberties in an industrial republic.

He knew enough respecting the history of political parties in America and the real motives which have ever influenced their action on the Negro question, to understand how little can be obtained from them by slavish devotion to either the one or the other at the polls. He knew that party slaves get absolutely nothing from party masters but fair promises before election and broken ones afterward; that in the United States voters realize their expectations in exact proportion to their ability to dictate terms before election day, and to their determination to mete out condign punishment to traitors later; that the only thing party managers dread is a loaded ballot leveled straight at the head and front of their power, and a finger on the trigger, which means your political life or my political rights.

Like all honest, intelligent and self-respecting leaders among us he had but one real dread, and that was of ourselves, when moving in the field of politics like dumb-driven cattle toward the goal of any party. This was why he wrote as his watchword the inspiring and invincible legend: "Union among ourselves, division between the two great political parties." He was never truer to your interests than when he conceived such a wise course of action for the race, never braver than when he endeavored through good and evil report to follow without flinching, the way thus pointed out, steep and rugged as it was, to its logical issue; though in doing so he had to part company with old party associates, and with old and tried race associates also, though he became an object of suspicion among you as a target for unjust and harsh criticism and contumely, as of one who had been false to your rights, to the best interests of the race. You knew many years before he died that he was not false to your rights.

Where today are the party leaders and representatives in Congress who log-roll for freedom, for a larger infusion of impartial justice into the laws of the land, for equal rights for the poor oppressed Negro? Are they Senator Hoar or Senator Lodge? The first is too busy opposing, and the second too much engrossed in engineering, through Congress measures for the subjugation of the Filipinos to spare a thought for the redress of the wrongs of nine million people lying beaten and bleeding at their very doors, in their very midst.

It is a curious fact, and significant that the bravest words yet spoken in our defence in the present session of Congress came not from either Senator Hoar or Lodge or Hanna, not from Republican senators and Congressmen, but from a Massachusetts Democrat, from an Irish-American Democrat of Boston, the Hon. John F. Fitzgerald. This brave man was a friend of Edwin Garrison Walker, whose brave sympathy for the Irish race quickened in turn sympathy for us in the breasts of many a true man of Irish blood in Boston.

Lawyer Walker honored the Irish voter, and was a member of a secret order of Irishmen, himself the only black man in it. He honored them because he saw in their acts the lesson of example for the blacks.

Fifty years ago an Irishman could not obtain employment in many of these old Puritan cities. His hopes were centered in the corner grocery, where rum was the staple article on sale, or in gathering rags. But the judicious use of the ballot has placed Pat in the front ranks of the prosperous men of America's business world. He controls ward politics in most of our large cities, and is gradually but surely making inroads toward the possession of state politics in Massachusetts; and he will tell you it has all been done by strict devotion to his race in the political arena; ready to accept any proposition, no matter what, that promises another mount on the rungs of ambition's ladder. He is the most venal of all politicians—a trickster and ward-heeler of the most pronounced type, in comparison with whom the Negro politician, whose black deeds are flaunted in our faces as proof of our utter unworthiness to possess the ballot, is an angel of light or a babe in the woods.

All these things "Judge" Walker knew; and although he felt keenly the harsh criticism on his acts, still he never wavered. He remarked to us many times: "Faithfulness to the race will prove to most of us the graveyard of our hopes and aspirations, for the white man will not forgive the Negro who paints his people as they are, and works devotedly for their elevation. But with this knowledge I accept the alternative gladly. I will never cease fighting our false friends until death seals my lips eternally." And he never did.

He knew that our destruction lay in our facile obedience to one party at all hazards. He saw that the Republican party is not what it was; the old ideas which gave it birth; the inalienable right of man to liberty of person, mind, education and religion, have changed under the management of the present generation and the infusion of young republicanism, to a commercial and financial basis; a subserviency which has reduced all things to a dollars-and-cents basis without regard to the ethical standpoint. He held that such being the situation, we must change to meet the times. Neither did he tolerate the new school of action which calls for a line of demarkation in the education of the Negro. Education is our security for freedom; no race could have been held in bondage as was ours save for our ignorance.

For three years he was president of the Colored National League, and at the time of his death was president of the Equal Rights Association. He was also Past Grand Master of the Order of Love and Charity.

His obsequies were held in Charles-street A.M.E. Church, Boston, and were attended by delegates from all over New England, representatives of all classes and conditions of men—white and black. Reverend Thomas, pastor of the church, was in charge, and many noted speakers paid him tribute; among them the most touching were the farewell words of the venerable Geo. T. Downing of Newport, R.I. The representatives of Suffolk bar attended in a body. On Feb. 12 a memorial meeting was held at the Charles-street A.M.E. Church, under the auspices of the Colored National League. The president of the league, I. D. Barnett, opened the meeting; prayer was offered by the Rev. Dr. William H. Thomas. Judge Pettingill of Malden was the presiding officer of the meeting.

Interesting remarks were made by Judge Pettingill, Geo. W. Forbes, who gave an extended account of his life, Mark R. De Mortie, J. S. Gaines, Hon. Archibald Grimké, Hon. Clement G. Morgan, Edward Everett Brown and others. Sympathetic resolutions were adopted.

And now having finished this brief sketch of his career, we may ask: What was his character?

Let us not confound character with reputation. Reputation is what others think or speak of one, but character is implanted by Divinity; and in "Judge" Walker was an unswerving brotherly love for his race,—a love that was all-suffering, all-absorbing, all-abstaining, all-inspiring, that had vowed never to soil its hands by any compliance that would betray a brother. That was his character.

> Farewell!
> And though the ways of Zion mourn
> When her strong ones are called away,
> Who like thyself have calmly borne
> The heat and burden of the day,
> Yet He who slumbereth not nor sleepeth
> His ancient watch around us keepeth;
> Still, sent from his creating hand,
> New witnesses for truth shall stand.[59]

SOURCE "Famous Men of the Negro Race: Edwin Garrison Walker," *Colored American Magazine* 2.5 (Mar. 1901): 358–366.

59. John Greenleaf Whittier, "To Daniel Wheeler" (1847).

VI.

Lewis Hayden

The life of Lewis Hayden is not the record of one great as a scholar, nor of one gifted with eloquent speech fitting him to grace a public platform as an orator, but of one who did well the work that the Lord provided for his hand. To this work he consecrated all that he had, and all that the future might give him, thereby fulfilling the law—Love one another.

He was endowed with a great mind although lacking the training of cultivation. But what of that? We have lived to prove the truth of the aphorism: Great minds are not made in schools. Numbers of men have studied professions, and only two or three out of a dozen have become great in their chosen calling; this is easily explained—they had not the necessary genius. We are all endowed with certain gifts at birth, and these gifts should be cultivated. Many fail in life because of covetousness,—Robert Elliott was a great orator, and they feel that they may become the same, not seeming to realize the fact that they do not possess the necessary qualifications to produce such a man as Elliott. This was never the case with Lewis Hayden; he coveted no man's genius, but did the best that he could with his own special gifts, and at his death held the respect of all persons—white and black—from the governor down to the lowliest citizen of the grand old commonwealth of Massachusetts.

Mr. Hayden was born in Kentucky, but the date is lost in the dark annals of slavery. He escaped with his wife, Harriet, when quite a young man. It was the usual thrilling story of hiding in barns, swamps and forests by day, and travelling by night ever toward the North Star, then the beacon-light in the travail that preceded the birth of liberty.

From our knowledge of Mr. Hayden's character we feel assured that his master must have held him as a very valuable possession. He was a noble specimen of the Negro, finely featured, tall and of splendid muscular development. He was probably absolutely necessary to the success of his master's business interests. But the vigorous body held a bright, shrewd mind—a mind strong to think and reason. One fine morning Lewis and his wife were missing from their usual haunts; by night travel, through watching and fasting, and by the divine aid of Providence their escape was accomplished.

The fugitives reached Oberlin, Ohio, pursued by their master and his friends, after many hairbreadth escapes, and from that city they went to Canada by way of Detroit, Mich.

The adventures of this worthy couple would fill a large pamphlet. Often their pursuers seemed right upon them, but the danger would pass, and friendly hands would succor them in the hour of dire distress. Among these friends Mr. Hayden esteemed very highly Calvin Fairbanks and Delia Webster, both white, who were stripped of their property and finally imprisoned in the Maryland State Prison for helping fugitive slaves. When these misfortunes came upon these good people, Mr. Hayden was in a position to liquidate, in part, the heavy debt of gratitude which he owed this man and woman. Through his efforts friends were induced to interest themselves in the prisoners, and they were finally released.

After settling in Boston Mr. Hayden engaged in the business of tailoring, having a store on Cambridge street, just above North Anderson street (then known as Bridge street).

Mr. Hayden's influence grew, and in the latter part of the 60's he was chosen a member of the Massachusetts Legislature from old Ward Six. At the close of his political career he was appointed to a position in the office of the Secretary of State, where he served until his death, April 8, 1889.

The funeral exercises of Lewis Hayden were attended by the governor and council, and the department of the Secretary of State was closed, all the employees joining with the colored population in mourning the loss of this man to the world.

Lewis Hayden's greatness came from his love of his race and the sacrifices he made of money, of time and of physical comfort for the redemption of a people from chattel bondage. His life was passed amid scenes of moral agitation which convulsed the mightiest republic the world has ever known, when Christ's words were fulfilled literally: I came not to send peace but a sword on earth. At that time pro-slavery men of the North were constantly sending forth poisonous vapors whose noxious fumes stifled the heart and conscience of the nation. The writings of President Lord of Dartmouth College on slavery and the abolitionists were fearful, says Pillsbury.[60] In the light of "The Golden Rule," of Confucius, and of the Sermon on the Mount, centuries after, they were infamous. Amid the blazing terrors of Fort Wagner and Port Hudson, the torments of Andersonville and Libby prisons, they are truly diabolical.[61] Andover Latin Academy and Lane Theological Seminary had driven away large numbers of their high-minded students by downright pro-slavery intolerance. Canaan (New Hampshire) Academy had been broken up for the unpardonable sin of admitting a few colored pupils on equal terms with the white, by vote of the people in legal town meeting assembled. A committee was appointed for the business, and, as officially reported in the *New Hampshire Patriot*, the edifice was lifted from its foundations, and by three hundred men and a hundred yoke of oxen was hauled out of town.

60. Pillsbury, *Acts of the Anti-Slavery Apostles*, 217.
61. In July 1863, Port Hudson, Louisiana, was the site of a crucial Union victory during the Civil War. Andersonville in southwestern Georgia, and Libby Prison in Richmond, Virginia, were two of the most notorious Confederate military prisons of the Civil War.

Well does Senator Wilson in his history, ask in his account of it: "Could the fanaticism of slavery go farther than that?"[62]

In all of these wonderful events which were then happening we find Lewis Hayden bearing a prominent part. His house sheltered the fugitives in many a dark hour. At the time that William and Ellen Craft escaped by the Underground Railroad, Hayden's home was their secure retreat. There they were absolutely safe. It is told that at any time one entering the house in the evening would have found the table surrounded by men engaged in earnest study, one hand holding the spelling-book, or writing in the copybook, the other resting upon pistol or knife ready to seize them, if necessary, and sell life dearly. The outer door leading into the house was always securely fastened by a bolt and chain. One night a man in slouch hat and long black cloak knocked for admission; Mrs. Hayden answered the call, and for a few moments a wordy warfare ensued; the gentleman then revealed his identity in the words: "Why, Mrs. Hayden, don't you know me?" It was Wendell Phillips.

It was surmised among the authorities that in this house William and Ellen Craft would be found. The marshal of the city was approached for aid in taking the fugitives from the building.

"So you think they are in Hayden's house, do you? Well, I know Hayden, and no money will induce me to try to make an arrest from his place."

It was a wise conclusion, for in the basement of that residence stood a keg of powder ready to be ignited.

"Before a fugitive slave shall be taken from under my roof, we will all go together, pursuers and pursued. I do not value life myself, and would count such a death glorious!" said the sturdy patriot.

In the case of the slave Shadrach, Mr. Hayden and Mr. John J. Smith worked together to effect his safe arrival in Canada.[63] His master was in Boston searching for him and accidentally met him. Shadrach was arrested, but with Hayden's help got away and hid himself at Mr. Gardner's, who lived then near the corner of Hampshire and Prospect streets, Cambridge, Mass. Miss Eliza Gardner tells an interesting story of the affair. She says: "We were busily engaged in household duties when Shadrach, who had slept there the night before, rushed in from the street and cried out in an excited tone of voice: 'They had me, ma'am, they had me! See! look! there they go now!'"

Sure enough; we rushed to the window and saw across the street a typical swarthy Southerner in a slouch hat well pulled down over his eyes, and a large cloak. He was watching the house next to ours, doubtless thinking Shadrach

---

62. Henry Wilson (1812–1875), author of *History of the Rise and Fall of the Slave Power in America* (1873–1877), was a Massachusetts Free Soil/Know-Nothing/Republican politician, who served in the U.S. Senate (1855–1873) and as U.S. vice president (1873–1875). After his death, Samuel Hunt completed the third and final volume of Wilson's *History*.

63. Following his arrest under the 1850 Fugitive Slave Act, Shadrach Minkins (c. 1814–1875) was dramatically rescued from a Boston courthouse on February 15, 1851. Following his escape, abolitionists safely shuttled him to Canada.

was there. You can imagine how frightened we all felt, for my father was away, no one but women in the house. Just then we saw on the opposite side of the street the well-known form of Mr. Hayden. Apparently he was not looking toward our house, but traveling from it as fast as possible. Presently far up the street on the other side we espied Mr. John J. Smith. Then we knew we were safe. These friends stayed in Cambridge all day in the vicinity of the house, but not near enough to awaken suspicion. After nightfall Shadrach was smuggled out of the house by the back way, and Mr. Hayden and Mr. Smith drove with him all night, never leaving him until he was in St. Albans, Vt., en route for Canada.

One point alone in Lewis Hayden's history would ennoble him and endear him to posterity,—his connection with John Brown!

The blow John Brown struck at Harper's Ferry was like the first shot fired at Lexington, which was "heard around the world." "Slavery is sin! Come all true men, help pull it down." Thus spoke John Brown.

In this wonderful happening Lewis Hayden played a conspicuous part. What were the plans and purposes of the noble old man is not precisely known, and never will be; but whatever they were, they were a long time maturing. Very nearly all, we may say all, the funds used in that memorable attempt, were raised in Boston. It was in Lewis Hayden's care, and was sewed all about the edges of the carpet in the back parlor of the Hayden house, so well known to many of us, North as well as South. John Brown himself stopped there with Hayden for weeks, just before he left Boston for the last time.

The whole movement, though premature in its commencement, struck a sounding blow on the fetters of the slaves throughout the South, and caused the master to tremble for his own safety, as well as for the safety of the institution.

In such movements as this Mr. Hayden spent much money. He might have been wealthy, for he possessed the faculty of making money, but he scattered it broadcast to help those poorer than himself. When it at last became known that the Hayden property was involved, rich philanthropists made up a purse and redeemed the property.

At the time of Mrs. Hayden's death there was some dissatisfaction felt by warm personal friends with the way in which the estate was left. We are informed that such was the understanding at the time the estate was redeemed. Harvard College is very rich, it is true, but it does not seem out of place that the name of Hayden, rich in the lore that gives life to the history of romantic old Boston, should live again in the Hayden scholarship within the walls of Harvard.

The deeds of men of a past generation are the beacon lights along the shore for the youth of today. We do not rehearse deeds of riot or bloodshed from a desire to fire anew the public mind, but because our traditions and history must be kept alive if we hope ever to become a people worthy to be named with others. We must pause sometimes in the busy whirl of daily life and think of the past, and from an intelligent comprehension of these facts read the present signs of the times.

We do not desire to abuse the whites of this country, thinking by so doing to cover up our own shortcomings, but we feel that the truth must be told though the heavens fall. It is an unfortunate fact that the Negro is a great imitator. It seems to us, then, that the only solution of this problem lies in the *uplifting of the moral life of our white population, first of all*. When the Negro no longer sees vice applauded and virtue degraded, the thief a capitalist, and the honest man a pauper, then the efforts that are being put forth to enlighten the dense ignorance of large masses of Negroes, will bear fruit.

These old fathers, like Lewis Hayden, thought the question of the rights of the black man settled when slavery was abolished. But again we have the same old question in a new dress,—the depravity of the Negro; and with this for a shield, every right, human and divine, is to be taken from us. The question then was: Has the Negro a right to resist his master? We settled that in the Civil War. The question now is: Has the Negro a right to citizenship? This last question cannot be settled by strife. Carrie E. Busby, the young colored woman of St. Joseph, Mich., who has started on a lecture tour, in which she will publicly urge all Negroes to rise in arms against the whites, says: "We love peace, but if we can't get it without war, then I say to arms!"

We are non-resistants. We are not with her in her movement. Not because we do not believe in war, but because war means extermination, and that is not what we are here for. We are in this fight to stay, and we can only come out victorious by using methods that are proof against failure.

There is nothing stronger than human prejudice, nothing more dangerous than public opinion. We must convert the prejudiced and change public opinion.

They have put wickedness into the statute-book, and its destruction is just as certain as if they had put gunpowder under the capitol. That is our faith. That it is which turns our eyes from ten thousand newspapers, from thousands of pulpits, from millions of Republicans and Democrats, from the government, from the army, from the navy, from all that we are accustomed to deem great and potent,—turns it back to the first murmured protest that is heard against bad laws. We recognize in it the great future, the first rumbling of that volcano destined to overthrow these mighty preparations, and bury all this laughing prosperity which now rests so secure on its side.

Each man holds his property and his life dependent on a constant agitation like that which originated in the anti-slavery cause. Eternal vigilance is the price of liberty; power is ever stealing from the many to the few. Only by unintermitted agitation can a people be kept sufficiently awake to principle not to let liberty be smothered in material prosperity.

SOURCE "Famous Men of the Negro Race: Lewis Hayden," *Colored American Magazine* 2.6 (Apr. 1901): 473–477.

VII.

Charles Lenox Remond

*T*he idea of a great political or social reform is first conceived by an individual brain. Invisible forces nurse the thought-germ, and at maturity we may have a brilliant genius like William Lloyd Garrison influencing men's minds in the direction of right action, the propagandist of a great movement encircling the civilized world, and drawing all men to its support. Wonderful indeed is the plan of Almighty God, for the amelioration of mankind, and the consummation of universal salvation. Opposition and persecution there may be, but the onward march of a reform is as resistless as the flood that sweeps all before it.

Christ said: If I be lifted up I will draw all men unto me. And so, in every generation there are those born who are willing to be "lifted up" for the redemption of mankind. Thus by constant example we have come to know that all the benefits this life can give us in the mysterious future toward which we are all journeying, proceed from the sacrifices made and sufferings endured by us for the good of others,—from birth through life even unto the resurrection, when we enter into the rest reserved for those who do His will, love, or the common brotherhood of man, is the magic key that gives us Christ. It knows not sex, nor person, nor partiality, but seeketh virtue and wisdom everywhere, to the end of increasing virtue and wisdom.

The abolitionists, from William Lloyd Garrison down to the humblest coworker in the movement, were all men endowed with that power which might be called psychic magnetism coming directly from the essence of the God-head dwelling within them. Charles Lenox Remond was the first Negro to enter the abolitionist movement as a regular lecturer in the anti-slavery cause, and was, no doubt, the ablest representative the race had till the appearance of Frederick Douglass, in 1842.

Ordinarily a biography is expected to begin with some genealogical narrative, intended to show that the person presented to the reader was descended from ancestors of renown. They boast in England of a descent from William the Conqueror. In our own country, New Englanders date from the landing of the Pilgrim Fathers, while the boast of the South is from the colonization in the time of Queen Bess. But these men of the Negro race whom we delight to honor, had no ancestors. "Self-made," they traced their lineage from the common ancestor, Adam. Their patent of nobility is found in the sacrifices that they made to lift the yoke of human bondage from their over-burdened, downtrodden race; their crown of glory was the victory that crowned their efforts.

Charles Lenox Remond, like many other illustrious personages, had no ancestry to boast of. He was born at the historic city, Salem, Massachusetts, on the first of February, 1810; died at Reading, Mass., on December 22, 1873. Mr. Remond, by virtue of his birth in a free state, was able to obtain early training in the best of schools. In 1838, he took the field as a lecturer, under the auspices of the American Anti-Slavery Society, and, in company with the Rev. Ichabod Codding, canvassed the States of Massachusetts, Rhode Island and Maine. In 1840, he visited England as a delegate to the first "World's Anti-slavery Convention," held in London. He remained abroad two years, lecturing in the various towns of the united kingdom. The series of resolutions offered by David Lee Child are interesting to the present generation because of their immediate bearing upon the subject of this sketch. They are found in Vol. 2 of the life of William Lloyd Garrison:

> Resolved, That the American Anti-Slavery Society regard with heartfelt interest the design of the World's Convention, about to assemble in London; and anticipate from its labors a powerful and blessed influence upon the condition and prospects of the victims of slavery and prejudice, wherever they are found.
>
> Resolved, That our beloved friends, William Lloyd Garrison, Nathaniel Peabody Rogers, Charles Lenox Remond and Lucretia Mott be and they hereby are appointed Delegates, to represent this Society in the said Convention, and we heartily commend them to the confidence and love of the universal abolition fraternity.
>
> Resolved, That the anti-slavery enterprise is the cause of universal humanity, and as such calls together the World's Convention; and that this Society trusts that that Convention will fully and practically recognize, in its organization and movements, the EQUAL BROTHER-HOOD of the entire HUMAN FAMILY, without distinction of color, sex, or clime.[64]

The delegates to the Convention took passage on the "Columbus," which put to sea on May 22, 1840, after a very stormy time in New York, where they had attended a National meeting, where much excitement was aroused, in consequence of so many of the "Garrison party" mixing with their colored friends on terms of equality. The same trouble pursued the party on board ship. The captain was a Virginian, but did not discriminate against his white abolition passengers. Remond, however, on account of his color, was compelled to go in the steerage; and the second mate, who began by striking William Adams on account of a remonstrance against his cruelty to a sailor,

64. Wendell Phillips Garrison and Francis Jackson Garrison, *William Lloyd Garrison, 1805–1879: The Story of His Life, Told by His Children* (New York: Century Company, 1885–1889), 2:351–352. William Lloyd Garrison's children prepared their father's papers, correspondence, speeches, and newspaper clippings for publication in four volumes.

on finding that Remond was to be the Rhode Island delegate's companion, caused a narrow bed, two feet wide, to be put up, and said Adams might sleep there with his "nigger," and assigned his berth to other parties.[65] At this Convention all women delegates were excluded. In condemnation of this act, Garrison, Rogers, Remond and Adams refused to become members of the body, and seated themselves in the small gallery of the house, where they were welcomed and visited by the most distinguished men and women of the united kingdom. Lady Byron sat there with them conversing with Garrison and Remond. She afterwards became a warm friend and patron of the latter.

On June 24, 1840, a public meeting was held in Exeter Hall, which is described by Mr. Garrison in a letter to his wife:

"The assembly was immense, and the various speakers were received in the most enthusiastic manner. When O'Connell made his appearance, the applause was absolutely deafening. He made a speech of great power and denounced American slaveholders in blistering language—at the same time paying the highest compliments to American abolitionists. No invitation was given to Thompson, Phillips, or myself, to speak; Remond stepped forward of his own accord and was repeatedly cheered by the audience. He took them by surprise and acquitted himself very creditably. Prejudice against color is unknown here."[66]

We gain some idea of the treatment accorded Remond socially while abroad from another letter written by Mr. Garrison:

The hospitality of our English friend is unbounded. Several splendid entertainments have been given to us—one, by the celebrated Mrs. Opie, and another by the rich Quaker banker, Samuel Gurney. He sent seven barouches to convey us to his residence (one of the most beautiful in the world), a few miles from the city; and a great sensation did we produce as we paraded through the streets of London. The dinner was magnificent, and all the arrangements on the most liberal and elegant scale.

After the banquet was over we had several speeches. The Duchess of Sutherland (who ranks next to the Queen, and is celebrated for her beauty), accompanied by her daughter and Lord Morpeth, honored us with their presence. The Duchess came in a splendid barouche, drawn by four fine horses, with postillions, etc. Her husband is the richest man in the kingdom, and she is noted for her liberality. I have seen Lady Byron repeatedly, and the day before yesterday took dinner and tea with her at the house of Mrs. Reid, an opulent Unitarian lady.

I would just add that our colored friend, Remond, invariably accompanies us, and is a great favorite in every circle. Surely, if dukes, lords,

65. Ibid., 2:361.
66. Ibid., 2:382–383.

duchesses, and the like, are not ashamed to eat, sit, walk and talk with colored Americans, the democrats of our country need not deem it a vulgar or odious thing to do likewise. Charles made a short but good speech in Exeter Hall the other day. The Duchess of Sutherland has signified her wish to see him also at her palace. You see how abolitionism is rising in the world![67]

In the *Herald of Freedom* we find more of Remond. From this we learn that "about the middle of July, 1840, Garrison, Rogers, Remond, and Thompson began by rail their pilgrimage to 'the gray metropolis of the North.' The first stopping-place was Sheffield, where the hospitality of the Rawsons was enjoyed. Thence the route led to York and to Newcastle-on-Tyne, for the sake of visiting Harriet Martineau, then writing the *Hour and the Man,* at Tynemouth."[68]

At ten o'clock on the morning of July 28, Garrison and Rogers bade goodbye to Glasgow, and shortly afterward to Thompson, Remond, and others who accompanied them to Greenock.

Mr. Remond was warmly welcomed upon his return home, and resumed his vocation as a lecturer, which he continued until the breaking out of the Civil War; then he became a recruiting officer for the colored regiments. At the close of the struggle he was appointed to a responsible position on the clerical force of the Custom House at Boston. He occupied this position until his death, literary work receiving all the attention that his spare time permitted.

In stature Mr. Remond was small, of spare make, neat, wiry in build, very elegant in appearance, well-bred, had a pleasing voice, and was graceful in his platform manners. Those who knew him trace a great resemblance in Dr. Lorimer, pastor of Tremont Temple church. Parker Pillsbury thus describes him as he appeared on the lecture platform:

Charles Lenox Remond earned a place in anti-slavery history worthy a monument, as well as extended biography. Salem, the place of his birth and residence during most of his life, never knew him, never will do any justice to his memory and worth. But he achieved a reputation both in his own country and Great Britain that might well be coveted, and doubtless was, by thousands who knew him in Salem, and all over Massachusetts and New England; but who scorned him and his race, not more for their color than condition in slavery, down to which so many of them were consigned by the republicanism, the religion and the unhallowed prejudice and hatred of the nation. Many times I have myself gazed on him with admiration when before the best Boston audiences, he acquitted himself with a power of speech, argument and eloquence, which rarely, if

67. Ibid., 2:387–388.
68. Ibid., 2:395.

ever, thrilled a house of congress or legislative hall. And I would often wonder how many young men of Salem, how many in Massachusetts, who had enjoyed all the advantages of grammar school, high school or academy, from which his color drove him away could come there and occupy and fill his place. In England, where he spent nearly two years, he vindicated the cause of the oppressed and won the confidence and applause of British abolitionists. He was everywhere hailed as the champion of his race, and treated with the most friendly and respectful attention. He bore from England the warmest sympathies and best wishes of the friends of emancipation. He was commissioned to bear the address of sixty thousand Irishmen to their countrymen in America, headed by the names of O'Connell and Father Mathew.[69]

Arriving in Boston, he went to the Eastern railroad station to take passage for his home in Salem. He was not allowed to take his seat with other passengers, but was compelled to occupy what was called the "Jim Crow" car. Several of his white friends, wishing to welcome him on his return, met him at the station and took seats with him. They were ordered by the conductor to leave the "Jim Crow" car, voluntarily, or to be removed by force! Thus was this gentleman of character and culture, fresh from his travels and the hospitalities of the best families of England, rudely and roughly treated on his arrival in his native state.[70]

His reply to the charges made against the abolitionists and his eulogy of Mr. Garrison, as the hero and champion of the anti-slavery enterprise and faithful friend of the colored race everywhere, North as well as South, was one of the most earnest, eloquent and impressive utterances I had ever heard from human lips, no matter of what color or race.[71]

Mr. Pillsbury goes on to say: "Sarah P. Remond, sister of Charles Lenox Remond, went to the West and, with her brother, did service above all praise—removing prejudice against their complexion and winning fast friends wherever they came. Sarah subsequently went to England, studied medicine in London, went to Italy, married, and settled in a large medical practice in Florence. These it was my privilege to meet as best of friends, as well as coworkers in that mighty, moral and peaceful struggle for humanity and liberty which made the middle of the nineteenth century memorable amid the ages."[72]

Mr. Remond was, undoubtedly, a man of great talent, possessed of a brilliant genius. The practical spirit he endeavored to inculcate was that of comprehensive Christianity. His personal character was in accordance with his teaching—charitable, kind-hearted, affectionate, temperate in living, doing

69. Pillsbury, *Acts of the Anti-Slavery Apostles*, 481–482.

70. Ibid., 239–240.

71. Ibid., 335.

72. Ibid., 487.

his work as if he felt it a pleasure; even when loaded with injustice and contumely, there was a daily beauty in his life, in its earnestness and simplicity, in its purity, which was an example in itself.

No breath of scandal ever touched this man; his life-course flowed on along devious paths, touching closely, at times, sin and degradation, but still the stream was as sweet and pure as when it left the fountain-head of life.

We learn the lesson from this life that "no man liveth to himself alone." It is of the vast outlying mass of human suffering that we need constantly to be reminded. It is the contrast between things as they are in the sight of God and things as they seem in the sight of man, that escapes the human eye in our busy civilization. God raised up these old fathers when he brought about the emancipation of the American slave, and shall we doubt Him now? What though the way be long and dark, the same farseeing glance that then saw our need and provided for the want, is piercing the gloom of the present situation, and understands the complications of our present surroundings. The abolitionists made their appearance at the right time, and our present want of strong incorruptible defenders of the right will be filled. Many will come forward gladly to be "lifted up" for those who cannot demand their own rights, set forth their own wrongs, or portray their own sufferings. Of such men was Remond. He helped to tear the veil asunder, which parted the whites and blacks, striking with his own hand a blow to help shatter the cruel fetters which bound his race. And his influence is with us today, ruling us by example from beyond the grave.

Slavery is no more, but there still remains a tremendous amount of work to be done before the race will stand on a sound, progressive basis. In these days of many national problems there is no more serious question than that which concerns the American Negro. For the good of all, we invite suggestions and help from impartial, well-informed observers of the signs of the times. Just now the fad of the hour is to find evidence to sustain certain men in their grave apprehensions as to the fitness of the Negro for citizenship, and a final home in this his native land. We contend that a true investigation into the merits of this newly enfranchised race has never been made. Undoubtedly, there may be some facts connected with the illiterate masses of the Black Belt that might give slight color to the false, black-hearted and revolting crimes of which we are accused in a wholesale manner by the Judas Iscariots that have been vomited forth from among us the last few months, but with all our faults we are no different from any other race of people who go to make up the heterogeneous mass called "Americans"; "we are no better, and we are no worse than they."

The writer of a book is a preacher who reaches all men, whose influence cannot be gauged. Surely, it is of the first importance that he do his work faithfully and honestly; that he be true in his written precepts, lest he lead his readers astray. There may be some excuse for the attitude of the Southern whites toward us; they have been trained for generations to believe the Negro a curse to the country; but the position they occupy is not a finality, it will change with time, and under the pressure of the advancement that the Negro is bound to make despite all obstacles or new theories, and the change in public opinion that their advancement is bound to bring about.

But what shall we say of the colored American who, having talent and opportunity to help build up, strengthen and succor us on our wearisome journey, deliberately adopts a policy of despair that will bind us down in a meaner bondage than that we have just escaped! For such a one there seems no atonement unless, like Judas of old, he be moved to acknowledge his sin and go out and hang himself.

Let us take courage in the face of slander and opprobrium. Never were the principles of a liberty-loving people put to so severe a test as those of this Republic. Believing in God, as the ruler of mankind, and in the inalienable rights of "all" men, this government was established by the people, for the people.

Necessarily, mistakes have been made, yet we know that, under God, in spite of all difficulties, there must finally be developed a democratic government, powerful, safe, grand through its regard for the rights of others and its practice of justice toward all citizens. All the good things that these old fathers hoped for and worked for will yet be ours, and other advocates shall be raised up fit for the times, and as grand as was Remond and his associates.

> Therefore not unconsoled we wait in hope,
> To see the moment when the righteous cause
> Shall gain defenders zealous and devout,
> As they who have opposed us.[73]

SOURCE "Famous Men of the Negro Race: Charles Lenox Remond," *Colored American Magazine* 3.1 (May 1901): 34–39.

73. William Wordsworth, "The Excursion. Book Fourth: Despondency Corrected" (1814).

VIII.

Sergeant William H. Carney

While *The Colored American Magazine* for June is in press, the whole of this great nation, as one man, will perform the solemn duties of Memorial Day.

It is a pleasant task—that of commemorating and revering once each year, the memory of those men who have laid upon the altar of Liberty the most precious of earthly possessions—life. Greater love than this hath no man. It is fitting then, that from among our famous men, we select for this issue the story of the life of Sergeant Carney, still living in New Bedford, Mass.

The Civil War is counted one of the greatest epochs of the nineteenth century, and the history of the Union army the most romantic in the military history of the world. The fame of Grecian valor stirs the blood, and in fancy one realizes, as if by participation, the youth going forth to his first experience of battle; the mother giving him his shield; her perfect forgetfulness of mother-love or mother-fear expressed in her parting words: "With your shield, or on it."

We turn to Rome, at whose shrine the military hero bows the knee in homage and in awe; her romantic history, intrepid valor and mighty prowess fills the world with admiration; her influence broods and casts it shadow over the scholar and soldier today as freshly as it did centuries ago. She stands unrivalled in her grim glory, and there she will stand for ages to come.

Adown the aisles of Time the fame of Charles the Great has marched triumphantly from the middle ages. A man of vast ideas, brilliant statesmanship and knightly courage, he has left an indelible impression on the pages of history. In the eighteenth century Napoleon passed meteor-like across the horizon in his wonderful career. Up they go! Pelion on Ossa piled![74] Brilliancy on top of brilliancy; great leaders with great minds; far-reaching and grasping ambition, one on the other. The desire for self-aggrandizement which pervades the careers of these Titans of supremacy, is too apparent for us to feel more than a cold admiration forced upon us by greatness. But when we at last reach the great war of the Rebellion, we have sympathy and admiration combined: sympathy for its motive which in its holiness was almost God-like; admiration for courage never surpassed.

The soldiers of the Army of the Republic! What historian, however brilliant, can ever do them justice! This is a fitting time to look backward and think of their incomparable deeds of valor: Fort Wagner, Fort Fisher, Fort

---

74. In Greek mythology, when Otus and Ephialtes wanted to overthrow the gods, the twin giants attempted to pile Mount Pelion on Mount Ossa, but were killed by Apollo and condemned.

Pillow, Olustee and many others indelibly stamped upon the hearts of the American people.

There is in this country today a band of patriots whose achievements in, and connection with the war, are deserving of separate mention—the black contingent of the Grand Army of the Republic.

On July 21, 1861, occurred the memorable battle of Bull Run. The two great armies met, fought, and finally one fled to Washington, the other to Richmond.

Governor Andrew had offered to President Lincoln colored troops. "Mr. Andrew," said the President, "you are ahead of time."

Time and again the strength of the two armies was tried on many a bloody field; time and again defeat desolated the Federal forces. Man said: This is a white man's war, but God said otherwise.

Sorrow sat enthroned in every household at the North. Despair stalked abroad. Here comes in the Negro. This was the position: The government trembling on the edge of an abyss; order fled, terror reigned.

"Will the Negro fight?" "Try him and see," said Governor Andrew. Then the Governor's proposition was accepted, and in a night, as it were, warriors grim and implacable sprang from the peaceful occupations of civil life armed to the teeth. The 200,000 black troops who marched into the thick of the fray brought hope in their shining countenances, "good luck" in their iron frames and brawny sinews. Then, indeed, as in old Bible days, the sun stood still, that the tide of victory might not be stayed by night.

The Fifty-fourth Regiment of Massachusetts Volunteer Infantry was called into the service of the United States by the President under the Act of Congress, passed January 26, 1863.[75] Recruiting began February 9, 1863, in Boston. A camp of rendezvous was opened at "Camp Meigs," Readville, Mass., on February 21, with a squad of twenty-seven men; and by the end of March, five companies were recruited, comprising four hundred and fourteen men. This number was doubled during April; and, on May 12, the regiment was full. Every State in the United States was represented in this celebrated regiment, and almost every nation on the globe contributed colored men to help found it. Interest in the Fifty-fourth is world-wide and not confined to one section. Among the recruits was William H. Carney.

Orders were received for it to proceed to the Department of the South, and the regiment broke camp on May 28, and landed in Boston to receive the colors which were to be presented by the Governor on the Common.

The regiment formed in hollow square, distinguished persons occupying the centre. The flags were four in number,—a national flag, presented by

---

75. Hopkins gave this date as July 21, 1861 (the date of the First Battle of Bull Run), repeating an obvious error of William Wells Brown, *The Negro in the American Rebellion: His Heroism and His Fidelity* (Boston: Lee and Shepard, 1867), 147. I have changed the date to January 26, 1863, which is when the secretary of war authorized the enlistment of African American soldiers.

young colored ladies of Boston; a national ensign, presented by the "Colored Ladies' Relief Society"; an emblematic banner, presented by ladies and gentlemen of Boston, friends of the regiment; and a flag presented by relatives and friends of the late Lieutenant Putnam.[76] The emblematic flag was of white silk, handsomely embroidered, having on one side a figure of the Goddess of Justice, with the words, "Liberty, Loyalty and Unity" around it. Lieutenant Putnam's flag bore a cross with a blue field, surmounted with the motto, "In hoc signo vinces."[77] All were of finest quality and workmanship. In presenting the flags the Governor said:

I shall follow you, Mr. Commander, your officers, and your men, with a friendly and personal solicitude, to say nothing of official care. My own personal honor, if I have any, is identified with yours. I stand or fall as a man and a magistrate, with the rise or fall in the history of the Fifty-fourth Massachusetts Regiment.[78]

I have also the honor, Mr. Commander, to present to you the State colors of Massachusetts,—the State colors of the old Bay State, borne already by fifty-three regiments of Massachusetts soldiers, white men thus far, now to be borne by the Fifty-fourth Regiment of soldiers, not less of Massachusetts than the others. Whatever may be said, Mr. Commander, of any other flag which has ever kissed the sunlight, or been borne on any field, I have the pride and honor to be able to declare before you, your regiment, and these witnesses, that, from the beginning up till now, the State colors of Massachusetts have never been surrendered to any foe. You will never part with that flag so long as a splinter of the staff or a thread of its web remains within your grasp.[79]

To the Governor's remarks Colonel Shaw replied briefly:

Your Excellency:—We accept these flags with feelings of deep gratitude. They will remind us not only of the cause we are fighting for, and of our country, but of the friends we have left behind us, who have thus far taken so much interest in this regiment, and who, we know, will follow us in our career. Though the greater number of men in this regiment are not Massachusetts men, I know there is not one who will not be proud to fight and serve under our flag. We may have an opportunity to show that you have not made a mistake in intrusting the honor

---

76. Haldimand Sumner Putnam (1835–1863), Union Army soldier, Seventh Regiment, New Hampshire Volunteers, was killed in the assault on Fort Wagner.

77. "In this sign, thou shall conquer."

78. William G. Hawkins, *Lunsford Lane; or, Another Helper from North Carolina* (Boston: Crosby and Nichols, 1863), 222–223.

79. Ibid., 225.

of the State to a colored regiment!—the first State that has sent one to the war.[80]

These words were indelibly stamped upon the hearts of those Negro soldiers. Times of heroism are times of danger, but with that knowledge came an utter contempt for safety. Many of them had once been slaves at the South; some had been free for years; others had escaped after the breaking out of the war. Most of them had relatives still in bondage, and had a double object in joining the regiment. They were willing to risk their lives for the freedom of those left behind; and if they failed in that, they might, at least, have an opportunity of settling with the old boss for past cruelties. Each man, therefore, registered a vow in heaven that day to conquer or die.

On July 16, 1863, the Fifty-fourth Regiment was attacked by the enemy, on James Island, in which a fight of two hours' duration took place, the Rebels greatly outnumbering the Union forces. The Fifty-fourth, however, drove the enemy before them. About ten o'clock in the evening of the next day Colonel Shaw received orders to report to General George C. Strong, at Morris Island, to whose brigade the regiment was transferred.

On July 18, about four P.M., they began their march for Fort Wagner, without food or rest. They reached General Strong's headquarters about six and a half o'clock, and halted for five minutes. The General expressed a great desire to give them food and stimulants; but it was too late, as they had to lead the charge. They had been without tents during the pelting rains of Thursday and Friday nights. General Strong was impressed with the high character of the regiment and its officers; he wished to assign them to the post where the most severe work was to be done and the highest honors won.

When they had come within six hundred yards of Fort Wagner, they formed in line of battle, the colonel heading the first, and the major the second battalion. This was within musket-shot of the enemy. There was little firing from the enemy; a solid shot falling between the battalion, and another to the right, but no musketry. The regiment was addressed by General Strong and by Colonel Shaw. Officer of the Day, John Brown, R. A. Bell Post 134, reports Colonel Shaw's words to have been: "Men, yonder lies the fort. You are the first black men of Massachusetts; the eyes of the world are upon you. You are novices yet in the art of war, but at such a time as this age is nothing, but blood is what tells."

At seven and a half o'clock the order for the charge was given. They advanced at quick time, changed to double-quick when at some distance on.

When about one hundred yards from the fort the rebel musketry opened with such terrible effect, that for an instant the first battalion hesitated,—but only for an instant; for Colonel Shaw, springing to the front and waving his sword, shouted, "Forward, my brave boys!" and with a cheer and a shout they

80. Ibid., 227–228.

rushed through the ditch, gained the parapet on the right, and were soon engaged in a hand to hand conflict with the enemy. Colonel Shaw was one of the first to scale the walls. He stood erect to urge forward his men, and while shouting for them to press on, was pulled by a hook over the fort, down upon the cruel points of sharpened sticks and other materials which formed the stockade. If any life remained when his body finally touched the ground, it was probably most cruelly extinguished.

The Fifty-fourth were intrepid soldiers; only the fall of Colonel Shaw prevented their entering the fort. Before the war ended the Rebels offered fifty thousand dollars in gold for the colonel and soldiers of the Fifty-fourth!

Before the regiment reached the parapet of the fort the color-sergeant was wounded; and, while in the act of falling, the colors were seized by Sergeant William H. Carney, who bore them up, and mounted the parapet, where, he, too, received four severe wounds. But, on orders being given to retire, the color-bearer, though almost disabled, still held the emblem of liberty in the air, and followed his regiment by the aid of his comrades, and succeeded in reaching the hospital, where he fell exhausted and almost lifeless on the floor, saying,—"The old flag never touched the ground, boys!"

Surely the honor of Massachusetts was safe in such hands!

The following correspondence tells its own story:

NEW YORK, 596 BROADWAY, ROOM 10.
DECEMBER 13, 1865.
TO ADJUTANT-GENERAL OF MASSACHUSETTS, BOSTON:

Sir—Will you please give me the name of some officers of the Fifty-fourth Massachusetts colored regiment, so that I can obtain information concerning the famous assault that regiment made on Fort Wagner? I wish to learn the facts relating to the wounded color-bearer, who, though severely wounded, bore the flag heroically while crawling from the parapet to his retreating or repulsed regiment. It would make a splendid subject for a statuette.

RESPECTFULLY,
T. H. BARTLETT,
"SCULPTOR."

BOSTON, DECEMBER 18, 1865.
WILLIAM SCHOULER, ADJUTANT-GENERAL:

Dear Sir—Your letter of the 15th to my brother, enclosing one from Mr. Bartlett, and requesting me to furnish a statement of facts relating to Sergeant Carney, of the Fifty-fourth Massachusetts Volunteers, is received. The following statement is, to the best of my knowledge and belief, correct. During the assault upon Fort Wagner, July 18, 1863, the sergeant, carrying the national colors of the Fifty-fourth Massachusetts Volunteers, fell; but, before the colors reached the ground, Sergeant Carney of Company C grasped them and bore them to the parapet of the fort, where he received wounds in both legs, in the breast, and in the right arm; he, however, refused to give up his trust. When the regiment retired from the fort, Sergeant Carney, by the aid of his comrades, succeeded in reaching the hospital, still holding on to the flag, where he fell, exhausted and almost lifeless, on the floor, saying, "The old flag never touched the ground, boys."

Sergeant Carney is an African of, I should think, full blood; of very limited education, but very intelligent; bright face, lips and nose finely cut, head rather round, skin very dark, height about five feet eight inches; not very athletic or muscular; has lived in New Bedford, Mass., for many years.

E. N. HALLOWELL,
"LATE COLONEL, ETC."

We will add that Sergeant Carney was born about 1840, being twenty-two years of age at time of enlistment, March, 1863. He is living still in New Bedford, following the business of letter-carrier. He is highly respected by all citizens.

When inquiry was made at Fort Wagner, under flag of truce, for the body of Colonel Shaw, the answer was: "We have buried him with his niggers! Neither death nor the grave has divided the young martyr and hero from the race for which he died; and a people will remember in the coming centuries, when it plays its part in history, that 'he was buried with his niggers!'"

"They buried him with his niggers!"
    Together they fought and died.
There was room for them all where they laid him,
    (The grave was deep and wide),
For his beauty and youth and valor,
    Their patience and love and pain;
And at the last day together
    They shall all be found again.

"They buried him with his niggers!"
    A wide grave should it be.
They buried more in that shallow trench
    Than human eye could see.
Ay! all the shames and sorrows
    Of more than a hundred years
Lie under the weight of that Southern soil
    Despite those cruel sneers.

"They buried him with his niggers!"
   But the glorious souls set free
Are leading the van of the army
   That fights for liberty
Brothers in death, in glory
   The same palm-branches bear;
And the crown is as bright o'er the sable brows
   As over the golden hair.

The Negro soldier went to war to fight for sacred Liberty; for half rations and half pay, for no quarter from a venomous foe. The brilliancy of their victories followed close upon each other; their gallantry and noble deed will live as long as history lives. "Oh, the wild charge they made, all the world wondered!"

Today we have a right to mourn doubly, to remember the sufferings and sacrifices of the past, to remember the sufferings and sacrifices of the present, and in anxious dread, await the future. Compromise and political necessity forced the war. Compromise and political necessity are showing their false, smiling faces all over the country. Compromise and political necessity hope to force us away from this country, or else grind our ambitious advance down to serfdom. But not yet, friends; the same God lives and is supreme today that lived in '60, '61, '62, '63 and '64, and has ruled this country up to 1901, and intends to make the black people a race without fear or reproach. Never did the Negro prove recreant to his trust,—at home with his master's family or on the field of battle he was faithful to his duty and to the flag. The South has that against us. The Negro represented great money investments, unbounded wealth. Rebellion lost the Southern gentleman his capital, his living; he has that against us. Without the Negro the war would probably have ended differently. They have that against us. And so, as the weakest object, the South today takes out of the Negro its losses and its revenge.

Our fate on this continent hangs tremblingly in the balance, but we still have faith in Divine love and pity. The past of the Negro has proved him a warrior, strong and intrepid; the present, a scholar capable of the closest application to his books and of accomplishing all that any student can hope to accomplish. The future is a fair unwritten page which we can make what we choose. In years to come the Negro youth will gather on Memorial Day to live over the story of the deeds of the brave; and some will say: "Grandfather fought at Wagner, or Great-grandfather fell at Fort Fisher."

May that future Afro-American realize the benefits of sacrifices, hopes and prayers.

Almighty and Omnipotent God, in Thee we trust! Into Thy hands we give ourselves and our race!

SOURCE "Famous Men of the Negro Race: Sergeant William H. Carney," *Colored American Magazine* 3.2 (June 1901): 84–89.

IX.

John Mercer Langston

A great English writer tells us: Unquestionably, the greatest thing that can be said of a man is, that he had no father; that he sprang from nothing, and made himself; that he was born mud and died marble; but the next best thing is, that having something, he made it more; being given the fulcrum, he invented his machines, and wrought his engines, till he made conquests that gave lustre to his name. These words are particularly applicable to the subject of this biography. His career was phenomenal. His individuality and personal force intense.

There is no part of the United States where the name of the late John M. Langston is unknown, where his brilliant career is not pointed to with pride by the Afro-American, for he loved his friends, his country, and his race.

His books, his speeches, his professional career as a lawyer and as an educator, his last and most conspicuous efforts as a statesman, endear him to the lowliest in the walks of life as well as to the highest in culture and social prominence. The history of the race is brighter, our position loftier for the example of his life and work.

The story of his life reads like a fairytale, and strengthens us in our opinion, that the true romance of American life and customs is to be found in the history of the Negro upon this continent.

John Mercer Langston was born upon a plantation in Louisa County, Virginia, December 14, 1829, in the home of the favored slave of the place, for his owner, Captain Ralph Quarles, was his father.

Captain Quarles was a man of wealth, owning many slaves; a person of culture, and with peculiar and unusual views with regard to slavery. He believed that slavery ought to be abolished. Naturally, his views attracted attention and met with severe condemnation from the families composing the social system of Louisa County. Finally, he found himself ostracized, and he was forced to live his life exclusively among his slaves. Thus situated, he chose his life-companion Lucy Langston, a slave-girl, held by him in pledge for money borrowed by her former owner. Of Indian extraction, she possessed but a slight proportion of Negro blood. This woman accepted her lot with resignation, and Captain Quarles made her the mother of his four children, one daughter and three sons. She always exhibited earnest solicitude and deepest affection for their welfare. The mother and children were emancipated, and by will Captain Quarles did all that he could for them, appointing judicious executors, providing well for the education of his sons, and making due allowance for their favorable settlement in business life.

After the death of his parents, in 1834, Mr. Langston, then five years old, removed to Chillicothe, Ohio, to the home of Colonel Gooch, his first guardian. At ten years of age he passed into the care of Mr. Richard Long, who was originally from New England. Severe in his management of boys, his idea of the highest style of boyhood was realized when it could be said of one that he was a good worker. Of the discipline he received while with this man, Mr. Langston says: "On the whole, by reason of the excellent association enjoyed with the children, of the family, the moral and religious training given, in the ways of industry and self-reliance, I lost nothing by the change into this family, where strict and severe discipline of life prevailed. The treatment received was calculated to improve my condition, while fitting me mentally and morally for the taxing duties soon to come upon me."[81] Upon leaving Mr. Long, the lad was sent to Cincinnati to school. At this time, in the State of Ohio, there were no school opportunities for colored youth. Educational advantages were offered in a private school kept by two white men, scholarly and well-disposed to the colored race.

Late in the fall of 1840 Mr. Langston received his first introduction to mob-violence, and which made a lasting impression on his mind.

For several weeks feeling against the Abolitionists and the colored people in Cincinnati had run high; there were reasons for grave apprehensions of an attack upon the two classes, and such fear proved well-grounded, for about nine o'clock one Friday night a deadly attack was made upon the colored people, which lasted three days. The mob reached the highest pitch of fury and seized the press of Dr. Gamaliel Bailey, editor and publisher of the *Philanthropist*, and threw it into the Ohio river. The record of deaths, among both white and colored people, can never be made. Says Mr. Langston: "Those were dark days; and they who still survive them may never forget the circumstances of their occurrence, and the public sentiment which made them possible at that time!"[82]

About this time Mr. Langston was placed under the tutelage of Mr. George B. Vashon, who was a member of the Junior Class at Oberlin College, and Mr. William C. Whitehorn, also at Oberlin. Both of these men were colored and favorably known scholars as teachers and orators. They were the first colored graduates of Oberlin—one taking the degree, Bachelor-of-Arts, in August, 1844; the other, in the following August, 1845.

Under these young men Mr. Langston was discovered to possess high elements of scholarly power. There is no doubt that but for them the lad would,

81. John Mercer Langston, *From Virginia Plantation to the National Capitol; or, The First and Only Negro Representative in Congress from the Old Dominion* (1894; repr., New York: Arno Press, 1969), 58. Although Langston wrote his autobiography in the third-person voice, Hopkins rewrote quoted passages in the first-person point of view, thereby asserting Langston's authority in her biography in a way that he did not in his own text.

82. Ibid., 67.

in all probability, never have attempted a collegiate and professional course of study.

The town of Oberlin was founded by Messrs. Philo P. Stewart and John J. Shipherd in 1833. Mr. Langston tells us: These men were controlled in their purposes; by the religious idea. They would build a city, a community and a college, upon their Christian faith, as embodied in the saying, "They knew Christ only and Him crucified."[83]

In 1835 Lane Theological Seminary interdicted the discussion of slavery, and thus drove two-thirds of its best students away. Oberlin school was the gainer thereby. Messrs. Asa Mahan and John Morgan, respectively, trustee and professor, left Lane Seminary and went to Oberlin. The school became a college with Mr. Mahan as its first president and Mr. Morgan a leading professor.

The "Oberlin Movement," headed by the men named, and the "Abolition Movement," led by William Lloyd Garrison, had their origin the same year. As early as 1835 the question of the coeducation of white and colored students was broached. The debate was exciting; the board stood equally divided, one half for, and the other half against the proposition. The president of the Board of Trustees held the casting vote, and Rev. John Keep voted for the admission of colored students to Oberlin College. The real spirit and metal of Oberlin was not tested until 1858, however, when the "Oberlin Wellington Rescue Case," the succor of a fugitive slave, became famous. In this case the men and women deserted the town to rescue the black boy, John Price, from a United States deputy marshal, who had arrested him and attempted to return him into bondage.[84]

In such a community the boy Langston was educated and trained.

When Mr. Langston had completed his academic and collegiate course, he was just entering manhood. Immediately an important question presented itself to him: What shall I do? What business shall I pursue? The answer came instantly: I will practice law. But where could a colored man find a place to study law? Who would take him as a student, and give him the instruction he would require?[85]

Mr. Langston's own account of the humiliations he suffered and difficulties which he overcame is most interesting. Finally perseverance brought reward. Professor John Morgan, the friend of the Negro race, advised him to return to Oberlin, pursue the regular course of theology as preparatory to his study and practice of law. The course covered three years; the studies developed the highest order of scientific, metaphysical, logical, linguistic and literary power. Thus Mr. Langston became the first colored student to enter a theological school in the United States. It was held by many white students

---

83. Ibid., 97.

84. In the "Oberlin Rescue Trials," John Price was captured and taken to Wellington, Ohio, where residents of Oberlin, Ohio, rescued him in September 1858.

85. Langston, *From Virginia Plantation*, 104–105.

that theological and metaphysical science was too intricate for the Negro intellect; a great many are of the same opinion still. Such persons attending the recitations of Mr. Langston's classes, would express surprise at the case with which he handled the most difficult subjects.

He completed the theological course brilliantly, August, 1853, and went immediately to study for admission to the Bar, with Judge Philemon Bliss, at Elyria, Lorain County, Ohio. At the end of two years Judge Bliss gave Mr. Langston the usual certificate, and moved the court to appoint a special committee to examine him for admission to practice as an attorney and counsellor-at-law and solicitor in chancery, September 13, 1854, which was done, and he became the first colored lawyer of Ohio. Within less than one year after his admission to the bar, his practice had become lucrative; his clients were all white. They sought him and his services as if they had full confidence in his ability. As to his standing as a lawyer, the following testimony is interesting:

> Being at Oberlin a few years since and learning that a suit was to be tried in which Langston was counsel for the defence, I attended. Two white lawyers were for the plaintiff. One day was consumed in the examination and cross-questioning of witnesses, in which the colored lawyer showed himself more than a match for his antagonists. The plaintiff's counsel moved an adjournment to the next day. The following morning the court-room was full before the arrival of the presiding justice and much interest was manifested. Langston's oratory was a model for the students at the college, and all who could leave their recitations were present. When the trial commenced, it was observed that the plaintiff had introduced a third lawyer on their side. This was an exhibition of weakness on his part, and proved the power of the black lawyer, who stood single-handed and alone. The pleading commenced and consumed the forenoon, the plaintiff only being heard. An adjournment for an hour occurred, and then began one of the most powerful addresses that I had heard for a long time. In vigor of thought, in imagery of style, in logical connection, in vehemence, in depth, in point and beauty of language, Langston surpassed his opponents, won the admiration of the jury and the audience; and what is still better, he gained the suit. Mr. Langston's practice extends to Columbus, the capital of the State, and he is considered the most successful man at the bar. (Dr. Brown, in *The Black Man*.)[86]

About this time occurred his marriage with Miss Caroline M. Wall, born in Richmond County, North Carolina, and reared in Harveysburg, Ohio.

Mr. Langston now settled down to systematic lines of advancement. His remarkable powers and wonderfully fertile mind, his genius accompanied by

---

86. William Wells Brown, *The Black Man: His Antecedents, His Genius, and His Achievements* (New York: Thomas Hamilton, 1863), 236–237.

skill, good sense, a well-balanced mind and a strong purpose to achieve a place in the world by overcoming all obstacles, brought him increase of power and influence upon the public mind; he believed more than ever that abuses to his race were to be laid bare, their wrongs righted, and reforms effected in the State laws as affecting the Negro. With this end in view he mastered politics in the early days of his professional career. He was nominated for town clerk of Brownhelm Township, Ohio, March, 1855, and by his election had the honor of being the first colored man in the United States ever elected to an office by a popular vote. This achievement gave him name and fame all over the country, and he was immediately invited by the American Anti-Slavery Society to address a meeting at the Metropolitan Theatre, New York City. He was to speak thirty minutes, and receive fifty dollars and expenses.

It was a most important occasion. On the first day Hon. Charles Sumner and Hon. Henry Wilson were the speakers. Mr. Langston spoke on "Anniversary Day" proper, with Messrs. William Lloyd Garrison, Theodore Parker, Wendell Phillips and Miss Antoinette Brown, before such men as Henry Ward Beecher, Dr. E. H. Chapin, Dr. Cheever, James Mott, Gerrit Smith, Henry H. Garnet, Dr. W. W. Brown, Stephen Foster, Henry B. Stanton, Charles L. Remond, Robert Purvis, Dr. James McCune Smith.[87]

His speech was novel in its general features. Up to this time no such anti-slavery meeting had been held in the United States, one which brought together so many distinguished persons, where such impressive and commanding utterances were heard. The whole country was favorably impressed, and the abolition party gained new life and hope.

Upon Mr. Langston's removal to Oberlin, in 1857, he was made a member of the City Council, and in 1860 of the Board of Education, serving in this capacity for ten consecutive years.

In 1866 Mr. Langston visited Washington on a mission to the President, in behalf of a client. Among the interesting incidents of the trip was his admission to the Supreme Court of the United States. General James A. Garfield had known Mr. Langston as an Ohio lawyer for many years. The General was a member of the court, conspicuous for his large ability and professional success. Accompanying Mr. Langston to the court, vouching for his learning, his experience and character as a practicing attorney and counsellor-at-law and solicitor in chancery of Ohio, moved his admission to that court,—and Mr. Langston's certificate of admission bears date of January 17, 1867.

With the election of Abraham Lincoln for president of the United States, the overthrow of slavery seemed at hand. And so it proved, for soon the War of the Rebellion was upon the nation. At its beginning there was the strongest feeling in all parts of the country against taking colored men as soldiers. Mr. Langston says: It was not until after the famous meeting of loyal governors at Altoona, Pennsylvania, the early part of 1863, that the purpose was expressed by John A.

---

87. For the text of Langston's speech, see Langston, *From Virginia Plantation*, 151–155.

Andrew, governor of Massachusetts, as permitted by his colleagues and authorized by the general government, to organize regiments of such persons. Governor Andrew assigned the work to Mr. George L. Stearns, a loyal friend of John Brown, and a Boston merchant; New England could not produce a man of higher social position, anti-slavery fame and general influence than Mr. Stearns. As his chief recruiting agent for the western part of the country, Mr. Stearns selected and employed Mr. John M. Langston. Mr. Langston relates many interesting stories and gives many valuable facts in relation to his connection with the recruiting service, which lack of space will not allow us to record.

At close of war Mr. Langston labored assiduously among the freed people during the period of reconstruction. The manner in which he was regarded is clearly shown in the newspapers of the period. The *Daily Courier* of Hannibal, Missouri, December 18, 1865, after Mr. Langston had spoken upon "Education, Money and Character," contained an article, from which the following is quoted:

> We could not help wondering as we listened to the eloquent utterances of John M. Langston, where was that terrific heel of pro-slavery despotism that five years ago would have crushed in its incipiency as if it had been an egg-shell, such a demonstration. Gone down with the institution which it supported and which supported it. . . . Consumed— perished ingloriously and ignominiously and forever.
>
> We cannot attempt to follow the eloquent speaker in his train of remarks. Those who did not hear him could gain no adequate idea of the rare excellence of the address from our poor and meager jottings. Suffice it to say, that his words were full of oppositeness to the audience and the occasion. To the colored men he said: Above all things, GET EDUCATION! GET MONEY! GET CHARACTER! May God speed and bless his noble efforts.[88]

Mr. Langston was appointed General Inspector of the Bureau of Refugees, Freedmen and Abandoned Lands, April, 1867, under General O. O. Howard. Mr. Langston says: "Among the most agreeable things connected with my tours, labors and experiences under the Freedmen's Bureau in the South, was the cordial welcome I received from the devoted, laborious, self-sacrificing workers, mostly white, who, having left pleasant Northern homes, had gone among the emancipated classes, where they gave their services upon the most limited remuneration to the education and elevation of the ex-slaves. But above all other consideration the greatest satisfaction in connection with my labors is found in the fact that so many boys and girls in the schools of the freed people of the South, have since, by diligence, perseverance, industry and good conduct, won for themselves respectability, influence and usefulness in

88. Langston, *From Virginia Plantation*, 245–246.

the community. As an educational instrumentality, Howard University was located at Washington for the benefit of the freed people through the Freedmen's Bureau, of which General O. O. Howard was commissioner. October 12, 1868, Mr. Langston was made a professor of Howard University, and he immediately set about the establishment of the law department. Such was the good understanding between Professor Langston and President Grant, that the former was able to secure for his students of the law department, clerical and other positions under the government. At times there were as many as a hundred persons, male and female, colored and white, thus located while pursuing their studies as his law students.

It was in the law department of Howard University that the first class [of] colored law students ever known in the United States was organized, and for the first time in the history of the world a young lady was found in the class, who graduated with her associates in June, 1872. Miss Charlotte B. Ray of New York graduated with high honor.

As the name and character of the law department of the university became known, and the results of its training were made manifest, an increasing number of white students joined it, and pursued, with their colored associates, its regular course of study, many of them graduating with honor.

Mr. Langston resigned his position in 1876, having served the institution as professor of law for seven full years, the last two as acting president and vice.

Upon his election and inauguration, President Hayes tendered Mr. Langston the office of minister-resident and consul-general to the historic Haytian Republic, September 28, 1877. Of his services and achievements while holding this high office, we quote briefly from an article written in 1879 by Bishop James Theodore Holly, Episcopal bishop of Hayti, and one of the most distinguished colored men of the nineteenth century:

"Mr. Langston is a philanthropist combining the broad and liberal views of true and progressive American republicanism. The starting-point of his life necessarily gave his character this bent in the most pronounced manner. Hence he arrived in Hayti with open and undisguised sympathies for them as a people whose national starting-point was so similar to his own as an individual."[89]

Aside from his official duties, Mr. Langston, as the chief representative of the United States in Hayti, is so imbued with the spirit of American institutions, that a personal influence goes out from him that is producing a salutary effect on the Haytian people and government to the endless credit of the American nation and people, who have found in him such a worthy, high-toned and faithful exponent of their liberty-loving principles.

Upon the election of Hon. Grover Cleveland president of the United States, Mr. Langston tendered his resignation from the office he had so nobly filled.

89. Ibid., 400.

In 1885 Mr. Langston accepted the presidency of the Virginia Normal Institute, which he held two years.

We come now to the last and greatest event in this grand man's history—his nomination in 1888 to the Fifty-first Congress, representing the Fourth Congressional District of Virginia. He was first brought forward as a candidate for election as a delegate to the National Convention by the District Congressional Convention.

The campaign of 1888, in the district when one considers the peculiar division of parties, the issues presented to the people, the manner in which it was conducted, Mr. Langston's treatment by the Democratic party and a powerful faction of the Republican party, its final results, closing in his complete vindication, must stand as among the most remarkable ones of American politics. There is no record of the nomination of any other man to Congress in the face of such defiant opposition as that which confronted Mr. Langston.

The Fourth Congressional District of Virginia consists of eleven well-populated counties in the "Black Belt of Virginia," where the colored voters outnumber the whites, two to one.

Mr. Langston soon found that the Democratic theory against Negro domination in any form was justified on the plea that ignorance and poverty should not dominate intelligence and wealth. They were opposed to him, and ready to adopt any method to compass their purposes, although Mr. Langston's nomination had been dependent upon the high qualifications ascribed to him, which attested his fitness for Congressional honors far beyond the most talented white men of the district.

The white Republicans generally employed every means against him, for directly after the Chicago convention in 1888, the proclamation was made against Mr. Langston by General Mahone, chairman of the State Republican Executive Committee, followed by white Republicans, and a few colored over whom he had control, that NO COLORED MAN WOULD BE ALLOWED to represent the Fourth Congressional District of Virginia in the Congress of the United States. It was, indeed, a formidable and seemingly invincible conspiracy.

In due time Mr. Langston was asked to submit the legality of his nomination to the National Republican Committee. This he refused to do, claiming that the Republicans of the district in regular convention assembled, by unanimous vote, had put him in nomination for Congress, and there was no power under accepted regulations of the party competent to call their action in question.

This stand taken by him threw the expense of the campaign upon his own private resources. Thereupon, Mr. Langston bought a place in the heart of the city of Petersburg, with a large, convenient hall suitable for all purposes and called "Langston Hall." This hall is famous in connection with the organization and prosecution of his work in the voting precincts of the district.

It was a most important campaign to the nation. Great consequences depended upon the success of the election to the party which saved the Union and represented free institutions. Through the neglect and bad management of the State Committee, in its desire to defeat Langston, the State was lost to Harrison and Morton, going over to the Democracy by a plurality of only 1,600 votes.[90] By fraud at the polls Mr. Langston was defeated, of course; appreciating this fact, he determined to contest the election. Then he realized that the case was almost hopeless, for no leading lawyer was willing to accept his retainer of a thousand dollars. He found all agencies working against him —fraud, intimidation, obstruction, hindrance of voters, foul manipulation of ballots—and, greater of all, the social influences were in full operation.

After a hard fight he succeeded in getting a hearing. Testimony was taken and transmitted for consideration by the committee on contested elections, appointed by the House of Representatives. In spite of all hostile influence brought to bear upon the committee, the facts of the case were so clearly brought out in the evidence submitted that all saw the merits of Mr. Langston's claim, and it was settled in his favor. But even after this favorable report, the opposition of every Democrat in the House was so unyielding that they notified the Republican members that they never would consent to the seating of Mr. Langston; that they would obstruct business by not maintaining a quorum in the House.

The Hon. Thomas B. Reed of Maine, then Speaker, and other leaders of the House realized the duty confronting them, and rose equal to the occasion. It was determined to secure the quorum necessary for action: the rules of the House were amended to facilitate business and prevent filibustering. The Speaker was authorized thereby, when members were present and refrained from voting on a call of the roll, to count them as present, if necessary to make a quorum.

These new provisions, defended by one party and assailed by the other, were rigidly enforced by the Speaker, whom his opponents called "Czar Reed."

The Fifty-first Congress was noted for important measures: the McKinley Bill, with Mr. Blaine's "reciprocity policy"; the Sherman Law, a new pension bill.[91] But of greatest interest to the colored Americans was the so-called

90. Benjamin Harrison (1833–1901) and Levi Parsons Morton (1824–1920) made up the Republican Party presidential ticket in 1888. Harrison was an Indiana Republican, who served in the U.S. Senate (1881–1887) and as president (1889–1893). Morton was a New York Republican who served as U.S. representative (1879–1881), vice president (1889–1893), and New York governor (1895–1897).

91. The Fifty-first Congress met in 1890 with Republican control of both houses. The Republicans passed the McKinley Tariff Bill, which raised import tariffs. Resulting higher consumer prices hurt them with the electorate. As secretary of state in the cabinet of President Benjamin Harrison, James G. Blaine was the commissioner of the First International Conference of American States (also known as the Pan-American Conference), where he negotiated reciprocal trade agreements with other nations. John Sherman (1823–1900), Ohio Republican politician, U.S. representative (1855–1861), U.S. senator (1861–1877, 1881–1897), sponsored two of the session's most prominent bills: the Anti-Trust Act of 1890, which was designed to limit industrial monopolies, and the Silver Purchase Act, which increased government purchases of silver. The Dependent Pensions Act of 1890 expanded benefit coverage for military veterans and their widows.

"Force Bill," passed by the House and lost by the defection of Republicans in the Senate.[92] But for those men the vexed question of the Negro franchise would have been settled years ago, in our favor, beyond a peradventure. Mr. Langston was enthusiastically received in the House and cordially treated while there.

The Cleveland Leader, January 17, 1891, comments on Mr. Langston's speech in the House:

> Mr. Langston made a speech which was eloquent and effective. No higher compliment can be paid him than to state that he commanded the close attention of all in the chamber. There are not five men in the House who can talk as well as Langston. He speaks without notes and his command of language is masterly. No doubt there are scores of Democrats in that body who would give a YEAR'S SALARY FOR HALF AS GOOD A GIFT OF ORATORY. It is scarcely credible, but it is true that he caused the eyes of some of these case-hardened Democrats to moisten by his impassioned appeals for justice to the black men and to the white men of the South, who are proscribed because they are Republicans.[93]

From the time John Mercer Langston entered the arena of life as a man he was recognized as an intrepid leader, and he was a powerful and dominant figure in American life at home and abroad.

For us it is no unimportant inquiry to make, after reviewing the beginning and close of such a career, "How was it that such ends were accomplished and brought forth from such unpromising a dawn?"

Mr. Langston accomplished his own success in life. His determination was supreme. His motto, "SELF-RELIANCE THE SECRET OF SUCCESS."[94] His perseverance, self-trust, were as great as the decision of his will. He was indebted to his training in the hard school of adverse feeling for the Negro in this country for the development of all that was best within him. In these elements of firmness and unswerving resolution lie the essential principles of success, in every arduous undertaking for all men of all races.

SOURCE "Famous Men of the Negro Race: John Mercer Langston," *Colored American Magazine* 3.3 (July 1901): 177–184.

92. The Lodge Force Bill, as the Federal Elections Bill of 1890 was known, was a Republican attempt to enforce the Fifteenth Amendment to the Constitution's promise of the franchise for African Americans. The bill was named for its House sponsor, Massachusetts Republican Henry Cabot Lodge (1850–1924), U.S. representative (1887–1893), U.S. senator (1893–1924).

93. Langston, *From Virginia Plantation,* 514–515.

94. Langston's motto appears on the title page of *From Virginia Plantation.*

X.

Senator Blanche K. Bruce

*T*he spring of 1864 saw a great change in the status of the American Negro. Many events had contributed to this result: Slavery no longer existed in the District of Columbia, the honor of its abolishment belonging to Henry Wilson, Senator from Massachusetts. The States of Maryland and Missouri also proclaimed emancipation. Representatives of Hayti and Liberia, whom the slave power had kept out, were admitted by the government at Washington and received with the representatives of other nations. But more than anything else, the unsurpassed bravery of the colored troops at Fort Wagner, Port Hudson, Olustee, and Honey Hill, had fired the Northern heart with enthusiasm for these chattels of the South.

We of this day do not realize that the African slave-trade was still in operation as late as the year 1862, but it was even so. Nathaniel Gordon was convicted of piracy in the United States District Court in the city of New York, for having fitted out a slaver, and shipped nine hundred Africans at Congo with a view of selling them as slaves. Every effort was made to save him from the consequences of his violation of the act of prohibition made by Congress hitherto a dead letter on the statute books, but money and ingenuity were alike in vain; President Lincoln refused to interfere, and Gordon was executed on February 7, 1862.

While colored men were fighting for the Union without the sanction of the government, their families in the South, if free, were sold into slavery; and if already in that sad condition, were driven into harder bondage. But with all, the nation was steadily moving toward freedom.

The gallant deeds of the black contingent were tinged with no hope of reward. Their efforts were worth to the government only half rations and half pay. It is a matter of history that the Fifty-fourth Massachusetts went into the battle of Olustee with "Three cheers for Massachusetts, and seven dollars a month."[95] Although these men had not been paid off, refusing to accept less than the amount allowed white soldiers, and their families at home were in want, they were as obedient and brave as any men in the army. The influence of their acts can never be estimated nor the gain to the race gauged.

The gratitude of the North to the Negro soldier found expression in 1864 in the appointment of Dr. A. T. Augusta, a colored man, as surgeon of colored volunteers, with the rank of major. M. R. Delany, M.D., was soon after appointed a major of volunteers.

95. Brown, *Rising Son*, 368–369.

The steamer *Planter,* brought out of Charleston by Robert Smalls was placed in his command.

John S. Rock was admitted to practice law within all counties of the United States: this was an acknowledgment of the civil rights of the Negro.

James Monroe Trotter, a native of Grand Gulf, Mississippi, educated in Ohio, was made a lieutenant.

William H. Dupree, a native of Virginia, also educated in Ohio, was made a lieutenant.

Charles L. Mitchell, a native of Connecticut, employed as a printer by William Lloyd Garrison on the *Liberator* became a lieutenant also.

Hon. John M. Langston was appointed to a position in the Freeman Bureau.

Ebenezer D. Bassett about this time was selected for Minister and Consul-General to Hayti.[96]

All these wonderful happenings in the life of the Negro were astonishing when compared with his past experiences and history. Colored men, indeed, held honorable situations in the Custom Houses of the various States, in the Post Office and Revenue Department. The air of progress was all about the Negro and he made rapid strides in education and the accumulation of wealth. The time was ripe for the advancement of colored youth, and many availed themselves of the opportunity; among the number was Blanche K. Bruce.

Mr. Bruce was born March 1, 1841, in Prince Edward County, Virginia. He was of African descent and a slave. He received the rudiments of an education from the tutor of his master's son. We judge, therefore, that his servitude was tempered with mercy, and that the natural intelligence of the bond boy was appreciated by his master.

After emancipation Mr. Bruce obeyed the call for education to the Negro and taught school in Hannibal, Missouri, for a time. The thirst for knowledge would not be appeased, however, and his longings soon turned his footsteps toward Oberlin College, the intellectual nurse of so many black men of eminence and renown.

When about twenty-five years of age, he concluded to adopt Mississippi for his home, and it is in connection with the history of that State that we find the story of this illustrious man's public life. Mississippi absorbed his talents and made him Sergeant-at-arms of the Legislature, a member of the Mississippi Levee Board, Sheriff of Bolivar County in 1871–4, County Superintendent of Education, 1872–3, United States Senator on February 3, 1875, as a Republican, taking his seat on March 4, 1875, and serving till March 3, 1881.

On May 19, 1881, he entered upon the office of Register of the Treasury, to which he was appointed by President Garfield, the friend of Hon. John M. Langston and many struggling black men.

96. Ibid., 390–392.

In 1886 Senator Bruce delivered a lecture on the condition of his race entitled "The Race Problem," and another on "Popular Tendencies." He was a strong advocate of the Blair Educational Bill which was the chief measure under consideration by the National Convention of Colored Men held at Washington, D.C., in 1889.

The end of the war brought a new era in the Negro's history. Slavery's chains were broken, but he had not yet received all his rights of citizenship. With the work of reconstruction, however, this question was forced upon the attention of the whole country, and brought with it all the virus of Negro hate that could be thought of. Writing of this time in the *Rising Son*, Dr. Brown says:

> President Andrew Johnson threw the weight of his official influence into the scales against the newly-liberated people, which for a time cast a dark shadow over the cause of justice and freedom. Congress, however, by its Constitutional amendments, settled the question, and clothed the blacks with the powers of citizenship; and with their white fellow citizens they entered the reconstruction conventions, and commenced the work of bringing their States back into the Union. This was a trying position for the recently enfranchised blacks; for slavery had bequeathed them nothing but poverty, ignorance, and dependence upon their former owners for employment and the means of sustaining themselves and their families.
>
> In the work of reconstruction, the colored men had the advantage of being honest and sincere in what they undertook, and labored industriously for the good of the country.
>
> The speeches delivered by some of these men in the conventions and State legislatures exhibit a depth of thought, flights of eloquence, and civilized statesmanship, that throw their former masters far in the background.
>
> The riots in various Southern states, following the enfranchising of the men of color, attest the deep-rooted prejudice existing with the men who once so misruled the rebellious states. Outbursts of ill feelings caused the loss of many lives, and the destruction of much property. No true Union man, white or black, was safe. The constitutional amendment, which gave the ballot to the black men of the North in common with their brethren of the South, aroused the old pro-slavery feeling in the free states, which made it scarcely safe for the newly enfranchised to venture to the polls on the day of election in some of the Northern cities. The cry that this was a "white man's government," was raised from one end of the country to the other by the Democratic press, and the Taney theory that "black men had no rights that white men were bound to respect," was revived with all its Negro hate. Military occupation of the South was all that saved the freedmen from destruction.

The expulsion of the ex-rebels from the Georgia Legislature in 1867, and the admission of the loyal colored men, whose seats had been forcibly taken from them, had a good effect upon all the Southern States, for it showed that the national administration was determined that justice should be done.[97]

In spite of all efforts on the part of the government, the Southern prejudice grew and manifested itself in deeds of violence against the Negro population. Organizations of white men were formed known as "White Caps," "Ku Klux," etc. Years have in no way mitigated the hatred of the South. The men of that section have not relented in their purpose of utter annihilation of the Negro's civil rights—the equality of all men before human tribunals, as they are all equal before the Divine tribunal and laws, the only mark of high civilization which distinguishes freedom from barbarism.

In 1875 occurred the gigantic frauds of the Mississippi elections. These wrongs were against loyal whites and Negroes. So violent an outbreak could not be allowed to pass unnoticed, and the Senate passed resolutions and ordered an investigation by five Senators.

On that memorable occasion, Senator Bruce made a speech which for breadth of thought and expression of wise statesmanlike sentiments placed him among the Solons of the Republic.[98] Delivered twenty-five years ago, it describes accurately the present condition of the black man. It is at once suppliant, prophetic and manly in its appeal to the better nature of all citizens. Such literature from the best thought of our self-made men should be preserved among us, a part and parcel (side by side with our Bible teaching) of the common necessary things that make up our daily life. We give an extract:

> I had hoped that no occasion would arise to make it necessary for me again to claim the attention of the Senate until I had acquired a fuller acquaintance with its methods; but silence at this time would be infidelity to my senatorial trust and unjust to both the people and State whom I have the Honor to represent.
>
> The conduct of the late election in Mississippi affected not merely the fortunes of partisans but put in jeopardy the sacred rights of the citizen. The truth of the allegations relative to fraud and violence is strongly suggested by the very success claimed by the democracy. In 1873 the republicans carried the State by 20,000 majority; in November last the opposition claimed to have carried it by 30,000; thus a democratic gain of more than 50,000. Now, by what miraculous or extraordi-

97. Ibid., 413–416.
98. Greek politician and poet Solon (c. 630 BC–c. 560 BC) was known as one of the "Seven Wise Men of Greece."

nary interposition was this brought about? Under the most active and friendly canvass, the voting masses could not have been so rapidly and thoroughly reached as to have rendered this result probable.

The republicans—nineteen-twentieths of whom are colored—were not brought, through the press or public discussions, in contact with democratic influences to such an extent as would produce a change to their political convictions.

To the spirit that prevailed in that section, I read from the *Yazoo Democratic,* an influential paper published at its county seat:

> Let unanimity of sentiment pervade the minds of men. Let invincible determination be depicted on every countenance. Send forth from our deliberative assembly of the eighteenth the soul-stirring announcement that Mississippians shall rule Mississippi though the heavens fall. Then will woe, irretrievable woe, betide the radical tatterdemalion. Hit them hips and thigh, everywhere and at all times.
>
> Carry the elections peaceably if we can, forcibly if we must.

Lawless outbreaks have not been confined to any particular section of the country, but have prevailed in nearly every State at some period of its history. But the violence complained of and exhibited in Mississippi and other Southern States, pending a political canvass, is exceptional and peculiar; * * it is the attack by an aggressive, intelligent, white political organization upon inoffensive, law-abiding fellow-citizen; a violent method for political supremacy, that seeks not the protection of the rights of the aggressor, but the destruction of the rights of the party assailed.

Violence so unprovoked, inspired by such motives, looking to such ends is a spectacle dangerous to our free institutions.

It will not accord with the laws of nature or history to brand the colored people as a race of cowards. * * * I ask Senators to believe that no consideration of fear or personal danger has kept its quiet under provocations and wrongs that have sorely tried our souls. But feeling kindly toward our white fellow-citizens, appreciating the good purposes and offices of the better classes, and, above all, abhorring a war of races, we determined to wait until such time as an appeal to the good sense and justice of the American people could be made.

We began our political career under the disadvantage of inexperience in public affairs that generations of enforced bondage had entailed upon our race. We suffered from vicious leadership. The States of the South were impoverished and in a semi-revolutionary condition—society demoralized, industries prostrated, the people sore, morbid and turbulent.

Despite these drawbacks, the constitutions formed under colored majorities, whatever their defects may be, were improvements of the instruments they were designed to supersede.

We want peace and good order at the South; but it can only come by the fullest recognition of the rights of all classes. The sober American judgment must obtain in the South as elsewhere in the Republic, that the only distinctions upon which parties can be safely organized and in harmony with our institutions, are differences of opinions relative to principles and policy of government, and that differences of religion, nationality, or race can neither with safety nor propriety be permitted for a moment to enter into the party contests of the day.

They (the Negroes) deprecate the establishment of the color line by the opposition, not only because the act is unwise, but because it isolates them from the white men of the South, and forces them, in sheer self-protection and against their inclination, to act seemingly upon the basis of a race prejudice that they neither respect nor entertain. Withal, as they progress in intelligence and appreciation of the dignity of their prerogative as citizens, thus as an evidence of growth, beginning to realize the significance of the proverb: "When thou doest well for thyself, men shall praise thee," are disposed to exact the same protection and concession of rights that are conferred upon other citizens by the Constitution, and that too without the humiliation involved in the enforced abandonment of their political convictions.

Underlying the ideas that form the foundation of the Republic, deep in the hearts of the patriotic millions of the country there is a conviction that the laws must be enforced, and life, liberty, and property must, alike to all and for all, be protected.

Mr. President, I represent the interest of nearly a million voters. They number more than a million producers, who, since their emancipation and outside of their contributions to the production of sugar, rice and tobacco, cereals and the mechanical industries of the country, have furnished nearly 40,000,000 bales of cotton, which at the ruling price of the world's market have yielded $2,000,000,000, a sum nearly equal to the national debt; producers who, at the accepted ratio that an able-bodied laborer earns, on an average $800 per year, annually bring to the aggregate of the nation's great bulk of values more than $800,000,000.

I have confidence not only in my country and her institutions but in the endurance, capacity, and destiny of my people. Whatever our ultimate position in the composite civilization of the Republic, and whatever varying fortunes attend our career, we will not forget our instincts for freedom nor our love of country.[99]

99. The text of Bruce's famous March 31, 1876, Senate speech was published as a pamphlet and otherwise circulated widely. See Blanche Kelso Bruce, *The Mississippi Election: Speech in the United States Senate, March 31, 1876* (Washington, 1876).

The Negro question is the great problem before the American people. The South must be regenerated. We thought this had been done, but awaken in the dawn of the twentieth century, alas, to mourn our error. In the words of the silver-tongued orator, Wendell Phillips: "We must take up the South and organize it anew. It is not the men we must fight,—it is the state of society that produces them. But when we have done it, there remains behind the still greater and more momentous problem, whether we have the strength, the balance, the virtue, the civilization to absorb millions of ignorant, embittered, bedeviled Southerners, and transmute them into honest, educated, well-behaved, Christian mechanics, worthy to be the brothers of New England Yankees. That is the real problem. To that this generation should address itself."[100]

SOURCE "Famous Men of the Negro Race: Senator Blanche K. Bruce," *Colored American Magazine* 3.4 (Aug. 1901): 257–261.

100. Phillips, "The State of the Country," in *Speeches*, 547–548.

XI.

Robert Morris

*T*ruly it is a great thing for a race that it get an articulate voice; that it produce a man who will speak forth melodiously what the heart of the people feels," says Carlyle.[101] We delight to honor the great men of our race because the lives of these noble Negroes are tongues of living flame speaking in the powerful silence of example, and sent to baptize the race with heaven's holy fire into the noble heritage of perfected manhood. The contemplation of the life-work of these men is about all that we have to cheer and encourage us in our strivings after high ideals, and to appease our longings for the perfect day of our true emancipation,—the black man's sweet but ever-vanishing vision of the Holy Grail.

Shall we not prize these great men of ours, and crown them? Do they not reflect upon us the radiant light of nobility? Are they not centers about which we may rally, these standard-bearers, in our hard struggle against the adverse winds and tides of life? They are about all that we can claim as absolutely our own; we are of one blood, and of one kind with them.

The life and character of Robert Morris demand our reverence. His life comes to us as a lesson of accomplishment from the barest possibilities. Born amidst environments of liberty, intimately associated with the descendants of Revolutionary Puritans, Robert Morris found himself an alien in his birth-place. The air, the birds, the streams, the winds spoke to him of freedom,—of thought, religion and action. To him alone liberty was denied. Early in youth, the lad whose only crime was the African blood that flowed in his veins, learned the sad lessons of humiliation and endurance; he learned, too, to strive for freedom of being and action.

It is our aim in this brief sketch to view him as a youth, jurist, man, a Negro, and a Christian; and to interweave the loftier features of one with the lovelier traits of the other. We paint him as known in life to many of his friends who still live,—full of benevolence, zeal and fearlessness; uniting the warm heart and the open hand, with the kind manners of a humble, cheerful Christian, with the dauntless spirit and the uncompromising love of truth which should distinguish him who is called to govern or teach.

Cumono Morris was the first member of the Morris family in America. He was a native African, and was carried to Ipswich, Mass., when very young. We are told that the lad grew to manhood and won the respect of the community

101. Carlyle, "Lecture III (Tuesday, 12th May, 1840): The Hero As Poet," in *On Heroes*, http://www.gutenberg.org/dirs/etext97/heros10.txt.

in which he lived, so much so that a byway of the town was called for him Cumono Lane. He was taught the trade of a carpenter, and built the first church erected in the town.

This man had a son, York Morris; and in him we find again a man respected by the people where he dwelt. In due time York Morris grew to man's estate, moved to Salem, Mass., and married Miss Nancy Thomas. He lived in Salem, doing well whatever work his hands found to do.

Colored people, then as now, were compelled to do whatever they could to gain a living. Lowly occupations were followed, called by some people "menial"; it is not the word to use in conjunction with virtuous toil; honest labor is always noble. York Morris was a waiter in the most exclusive families of Salem, and he soon acquired property and made a comfortable home for his wife and eleven children of whom Robert Morris was one.

It is a pleasure to trace the experiences of this typical family of New England Negroes, as told by our esteemed friend and honored citizen, Mr. Emory T. Morris, a direct descendant of the family and nephew of the late barrister Robert Morris.

In listening to his interesting stories of old days as told him by his parents, we, too, experience the injustice, persecution, and proscription that once made even free Massachusetts an odious place for the hunted Negro. At that time the common titles for our sacred abolitionists were "fanatics," "enthusiasts," "disorganizers," "scorners of the pulpit," "traitors." In the words of Mr. Phillips: "When the pulpit preached slave-hunting, and the law bound the victim, and society said 'Amen!'"[102]

Robert Morris was born June 8, 1823; he died December 12, 1882. He went to Master Dodge's school, and helped his family about the home until he was thirteen years of age.

About this time, we are told that Mrs. Ellis Gray Loring, of Mount Vernon Street, Boston, wife of a famous abolitionist, often visited relatives in Salem. On one of these visits, her husband, who accompanied her, was greatly pleased with the slender brown lad who waited at table, and as he desired to have a boy about Robert's age, he quickly made arrangements with the lad's parents that he should go to Boston and live in his family. The lad began his duties in a few days after this chance meeting, as a servant in Mr. Loring's house. And at the same time he took the first step in that eventful career which was to testify to the origin of the Negro from the common father Adam; the voice of God rebuking the wickedness of the times and saying to the world, "Behold, of one blood have I made all nations of men."[103]

Mr. Loring was a lawyer and employed a clerk for copying who neglected his duties, and so the colored lad, being a good penman, helped out by doing copying at the office, and for a time he was servant, office-boy and clerk.

---

102. Phillips, "Sims Anniversary" (1852), in *Speeches*, 75.
103. Acts 17:26. This biblical verse is among the most frequently cited by Hopkins.

Mr. Loring was greatly pleased with the manner in which the lad discharged all duties assigned him, and one day said to him: "Robert, when you get through with your work, spend your time in a useful way; go down to the office and study." Mr. Morris availed himself of the privilege with alacrity, and Mr. Loring would tell him when to go home. One day he again spoke to the young man: "Robert, you are capable of making something of yourself. Do you wish to learn a trade, or do you wish to study law?" The lad chose the law, and the second step was taken in the mighty sequence of events destined to give the world its first practicing colored lawyer. Geo. W. Searle, Esq., speaking of his career says: "He was doubtless much indebted to the friendship of his patron, Ellis Gray Loring, and coming to the bar under his wing he was respected as he otherwise might not have been. I do not purpose to say a word against the bar of that day. It was a splendid fraternity, with Webster at its head, and Choate and Loring and Bartlett.[104] But the advent of a Negro lawyer was an experiment, and open to the natural repugnance of a conservative profession."

For several years Mr. Morris remained in Mr. Loring's office as clerk and student, and he was true to his manhood. He was well-known about the business centers of Boston and bore the reputation that for energy, perseverance and shrewdness in advancing the business interests of his employer, he could not be excelled.

The late Edwin G. Walker said of him in an eulogy pronounced in 1883, after Mr. Morris's decease:

Looking at the people of this country as I have in the past, and as I see them now, I do not believe that nearly fifty years ago there was any other colored man living in this land, who had a taste for, and an ambition to study law and practise law, that could have done so and met with a success as brilliant and real as that which witnessed the close of Mr. Morris's career. I am speaking of him as the little humble colored boy who laughed at obstacles while he was undermining the walls that closed out from the young of his race, opportunities to enter a profession that would afford them many chances to grapple, hand to hand with the most desperate and shameful prejudice that ever disgraced a Christian people.[105]

Mr. Morris was married, soon after coming of age, to Miss Catherine Mason, a highly respected Boston woman, who made him a devoted wife. Mr.

---

104. Daniel Webster (1872–1852), Anti-Jacksonian/Whig politician, U.S. representative (1813–1817 [N.H.]; 1823–1827 [Mass.]), U.S. senator (1827–1841, 1845–1850 [Mass.]), U.S. secretary of state (1841–1843, 1850–1852); Rufus Choate (1799–1859), Massachusetts Whig politician, U.S. representative (1831–1834), U.S. senator (1841–1845); and Ichabod Bartlett (1786–1853), New Hampshire Republican politician and attorney, U.S. representative (1823–1829) were prominent New England attorneys and politicians.

105. Edwin G. Walker, "Eulogy," in *In Memoriam: Robert Morris, Sr.* (Boston, 1883), 30. This memorial pamphlet is the main source for Hopkins's profile of Morris.

Loring was still the good angel of the Morris house, and the young couple were united in the parlors of the mansion on Mt. Vernon Street.

On February 2, 1847, the third step was taken by the young colored man, and Robert Morris was admitted to the Suffolk bar. It is generally believed that Mr. Macon B. Allen was the first Negro to pass the bar examination, in May, 1845, and to him doubtless belongs the honor; but we have heard so little of the gentleman, that we always think of Mr. Morris as the first colored lawyer to make himself felt at the American bar.

Mr. Morris realized fully the difficulties which beset his path in his chosen profession. For him there was no hope of favor; he must be prepared to endure insult heaped on insult with sphinx-like patience resolved to die and make no sign. The trial of his first case made it quite clear to friend and foe that the young advocate was built on heroic lines of the material that gives to the world heroes. There was no mistake in his calling; he possessed all the requisites of a successful attorney.

His first case was an action brought by a colored man for services rendered. Entering the office of the opposing attorney to consult about matters pertaining to the case, Mr. Morris addressed him in his usual genial and taking way and was received with cutting insolence. The lawyer started from his chair, and shaking his fist in our friend's face said:

"Are you going to try that case?"

"I am," replied Mr. Morris.

"Then I will give you the devil!" shouted the white man fairly boiling over in his wrath.

We can imagine that Mr. Morris left the office with a heavy heart, doubting for the moment his courage to face and overcome such obstacles. Telling the story in his own words, Mr. Morris was wont to say:

"I went to my office. I sat down and cried. I thought of the mighty odds against which I must contend, and then it was that I made the vow I have never broken. It was this: I would prove myself to be a man and a gentleman, and succeed in the practice of law, or I would die."[106]

What a sermon for the youth of today lies in this simple picture!

On the day of the trial the court room was crowded with colored people, their countenances filled with anxiety and hope for Mr. Morris's success. Again we quote his words:

"I felt like a giant, and when my case was called, I tried it for all it was worth; and until the evidence was all in, the arguments on both sides made, the judge's charge concluded and the case given to the jury, I spared no pains to win. The jury after being out a short time returned, and when the foreman, in reply to the clerk, answered that the jury had found for the plaintiff, my heart bounded up, and my people in the court room acted as if they would shout for joy."[107]

106. Ibid., 32–33.
107. Ibid., 33.

Boston's Negro lawyer after this was continually in the public eye, and soon had as many criminal cases upon his docket as any other attorney in the county. He was, in fact, the favorite criminal lawyer of Suffolk bar. His clients were from the humble walks of life, white and colored, by far the greater number being white, and Irishmen. It is strange but true that Mr. Morris's financial success as a lawyer was due to the earnest efforts and true hearts of his Irish clients who admired and implicitly trusted their friend "Mr. Morrissey."

His standing as a lawyer and a man is clearly defined in the speeches made by eminent Massachusetts lawyers at the bar meeting in Boston, called to commemorate the life and death of this eminent man. Speaking of Mr. Morris, Mr. George W. Searle said:

We, the compeers of the deceased, are rightly held as attesting witnesses of the career now closed and the life lived. I knew Robert Morris from the outset to the close and knew him well. I bear witness to the high standing of the first practising American colored lawyer whose name and fame will be long treasured in the annals of Suffolk bar. His career is a type of American civilization. Neither the English nor the French bar has, to my knowledge, ever had a colored lawyer in its ranks.

Robert Morris was certainly a successful lawyer. Business was his forte and delight. He was a man of eminent sense, sound judgment, ripe discretion, and dexterous movement in the conduct of a case. He had the remarkable faculty of thinking while on his feet. He was ingenious in planning, and artistic in filling up the outline of a defence. He was skilful, discreet and judicious in cross-examination. And in the jury address he was persuasive and plausible. His moral standing was of the highest, his integrity unquestioned, and he was an honorable practitioner in the best sense of the term. He looked out for himself, indeed, but he also looked out for his clients. He was true as steel and as brave as a lion. He treasured no animosities. The result was that he had many friends and few or no enemies.[108]

Judge Russell said:

The man who triumphs over adverse circumstances is always worthy of respect. We love to repeat the poet's tribute to him:

Who breaks his birth's invidious bar
And grasps the skirts of happy chance,
And breasts the blows of circumstance,
And grapples with his evil star.[109]

108. "Meeting of the Members of the Suffolk Bar," in *In Memoriam: Robert Morris, Sr.*, 15–19.
109. Alfred Tennyson, "In Memoriam A.H.H." (1850).

It is often said that Mr. Morris deserves credit for what he did for his race. I thank him for what he did for ours. While it is sad to be the victim of low prejudice, it is worse to be its slave; and Robert Morris did a man's work toward emancipating the white men of this community from that yoke.[110]

Honorable Patrick A. Collins said: "I have known Robert Morris for twenty-six years. I was office-boy in his office; I can say that I owe my success in life to Mr. Morris. He went through life like a man, faithful to all his duties, and generous to all his kind."[111]

Such was Robert Morris as a jurist and a man. Let us for a brief space contemplate him as a Negro.

Born at the beginning of the great transition period in the history of the United States, when the exciting events and important happenings of the times all pertained to the Negro, he had rare opportunities in early manhood and maturity to distinguish himself as a champion of his race.

The Mexican War, the annexation of Texas, the rescinding of the Missouri Compromise, the passage of the fugitive-slave act, Brooks's assault on Sumner in the Senate chamber, the execution of John Brown, the firing on Sumter, he saw and worked to avert. At that time the "Jim Crow" car existed in Massachusetts. Those were the days when Sarah Remond, refined, elegant and polished, fresh from sharing the advantages of travel abroad in company with her talented brother, fought with the conductor who attempted to eject her from the regular passenger coach bound for Salem, until her clothing was torn from her and hung in shreds, and even then he was forced to lift the daring woman bodily from the car to the platform.

Robert Morris no less brave than Miss Remond, struck terrible blows at the exclusive school system for Negroes in Boston. He availed himself also of every opportunity that offered to annoy the railroad companies. He would go in person to theatres, lecture rooms, churches, and other public places, buy his ticket and force the employees to eject him, then he would carry the matter into the courts.

In this way Mr. Morris succeeded in breaking up a barbarous custom of exclusion on account of color.

The free people of the whole North—principally of Boston, New York and Philadelphia—were alive to their rights, held conventions yearly, recounted their grievances and pressed their claims to citizenship. These meetings, speeches and appeals raised the Negro in the estimation of the whites, and constantly added new friends to help the cause.

His attitude on the Negro solder in the Civil War is often questioned. The truth is that when the war broke out, he, with other colored men, went to the

---

110. "Meeting of the Members of the Suffolk Bar," in *In Memoriam: Robert Morris, Sr.*, 21–22.
111. Ibid., 22–23.

State House and offered to raise a regiment of Negroes, which could have been done in three days. He asked for these men colored officers, the same pay and that they be given the same chance with other men who would help defend the Federal Government. We know that this offer was rejected, for it was "a white man's war," and "niggers" didn't count then any more than they do today in some quarters. Mr. Morris said to Governor Andrew, "Perhaps when you want us we won't go; I think I shall work to that end."

For these "disloyal" words they threatened to send him to Fort Warren.[112]

Strange reasoning that which at one moment declares a Negro to be a living witness of Darwin's theory of the missing link, and incapable of thought above a monkey, and that the signers of the Declaration of Independence did not consider that the words "all men" described or included Negroes, and the next moment holds him responsible for disloyalty which can only be an attribute of a citizen and a man.

The most heroic proof of his devotion to his race, was given during the trying time of the operation of the fugitive-slave law. Mr. Morris threw hope, ambition and discretion to the winds, he offered life itself for the rescue of his fugitive black brother.

On the night of April 3, 1851, Thomas Sims was arrested, and returned into slavery. Morris was at the Boston Court House to encourage and sustain. Next came the rendition of Anthony Burns. There, too, was the young black advocate. (See James Freeman Clarke's "Discourse on Christian Politics."[113]) Then came the crucial test. A colored man, Shadrach, was claimed as a slave; he was arrested and thrown into prison. The commissioners of the United States Court rendered the decree that remanded Shadrach to bondage. Thomas S. Harlow, Esq., has described the scene thus:

> Scarcely was the decision announced when the court-room door was opened by Mr. Morris and a signal given to the crowd of white and colored men who filled the corridor, anxiously waiting the result of the hearing. The uncontrollable mass swarmed in, heedless of all attempts of the officers to keep them back; the genial deputy marshal took refuge under the table, and with a suddenness and a fervor which might almost be compared to the chariot of fire that swept away the Prophet Elijah, Shadrach, enveloped in the cloud which darkened the whole room, disappeared from the view of those who claimed to own him, and was next heard of in Canada.[114]

112. Fort Warren, in Boston Harbor, served as a Union prison during the Civil War.
113. See James Freeman Clarke, *The Rendition of Anthony Burns: Its Causes and Consequences; A Discourse on Christian Politics, Delivered in Williams Hall, Boston, on Whitsunday, June 4, 1854* (Boston: Crosby, Nichols, 1854).
114. "Meeting of the Members of the Suffolk Bar," in *In Memoriam: Robert Morris, Sr.*, 13.

For his share in this breach of law Morris was indicted in the Circuit court, along with Lewis Hayden, Richard Dana, Jr., Charles Sumner, Theodore Parker, Deacon Scott (of the old St. Paul church on Smith Court) and others. The trial was before Judge Curtis. The ablest member of Essex bar assisted the District Attorney in the prosecution, but without success. Mr. Morris and his assistants were triumphantly acquitted.

In politics, Mr. Morris was an independent. He appreciated the Negro's strength in politics and felt that prejudice should not be allowed to affect his standing as an American citizen. The Negro question was paramount in his mind to all others among the American people. He knew the importance of the work to be done to repair the damage done by slavery to an innocent people, and the mighty task confronting the whole nation to raise the race out of its helpless condition. He knew, too, that our future in this country depends more upon individuals than upon parties. To quote his own words:

> We must hammer away upon the meanness that is practised by those who assume to be the leaders of the people of this country. Slavery is gone; one of our hands is at liberty. What we want is to have both hands free, and that equal rights shall prevail; but until then we have no time for the discussion of any other question in American politics. People lecture us upon the constant cry we have kept up about the rights of the black man. They say that we are wrong and injuring our cause: don't you believe it! Our position now is like that of the Abolitionist in days gone by. We are taking up this work just where many of them left it. Unless we stand out as did these same Abolitionists, we shall never succeed in making party leaders concede to us, that which is our due and which they so persistently withhold.[115]

Prophetic words! We bear testimony today to their truth.

The life of this man was a grand test of the Negro's ability and manhood. He became influential at the time, when, with Rev. Henry Highland Garnet of New York, Charles Lenox Remond, Father Beman and Father Snowden, he helped form the advance guard to do battle for the race. Douglass, Grimes, W. W. Brown and other eminent pleaders were then unknown, and Robert Morris dared to do deeds from which even the boldest of these men shrank when their time of prominence came.

Mr. Morris embraced the Catholic religion in his maturer years, and was a faithful and honored member of that Church. His daily life was an exemplification of the command: Love one another.

Mr. Morris had one son, Robert Morris, Jr., who survived his father's death but two weeks. This young man was profoundly educated. He had studied at

---

115. Walker, "Eulogy," in *In Memoriam: Robert Morris, Sr.*, 41.

Oxford, England, in France, in Rome, and at the Harvard Law School. For a long time he was French interpreter at the Suffolk bar.

Solitary and alone Robert Morris went forward to wrest honors from fickle Fortune. His life is a rich legacy to point the young Negro to the heights of manhood. His greatness consisted in his sublime persistence and wonderful courage under difficulties, and his devotion to a high ideal. Nobly patient, his enthusiasm never flagged; he clutched his ideal blindly.

"Such a man is what we call an original man. A messenger he, sent from the Infinite Unknown with tidings to us."[116]

SOURCE "Famous Men of the Negro Race: Robert Morris," *Colored American Magazine* 3.5 (Sept. 1901): 337–342.

116. Carlyle, "Lecture III (Friday, 8th May, 1840): The Hero as Prophet," in *On Heroes*, http://www.gutenberg.org/dirs/etext97/heros10.txt.

XII.

Booker T. Washington

The subject of this sketch is probably the most talked of Afro-American in the civilized world today, and the influence of his words and acts on the future history of the Negro race will be carefully scrutinized by future generations.

Dr. Washington's life-story has been rehearsed so frequently by writers of both races, that it has become familiar in the households of the land.

We all know that he was born a slave on a plantation in Franklin County, Virginia, in 1858 or 1859. He describes Hale's Ford, near his birthplace, as a town with one house and a post-office. His master's name was John Burroughs, for whose family his mother cooked.

Dr. Washington's early life and struggles are stories common to thousands of Negroes,—freedom, poverty, a desire for education, the hardships encountered to compass the coveted end, his admission to Hampton and his final graduation from that college, a year at Wayland Seminary, Washington, D.C., and his "slumbering ambition" to become a lawyer.[117] We read with pleasure the account of his life as a teacher at Malden, West Virginia, where he had received his first training in the three r's "reading, 'riting and 'rithmetic." His own description of his work there is highly entertaining:

> I not only taught school in the day, but for a great portion of the time taught night school. In addition to this I had two Sunday schools: the average attendance in my day school was, I think, between 80 and 90. As I had no assistant it was a very difficult task to keep all the pupils interested and to see that they made progress in their work.
>
> One thing that gave me great satisfaction and pleasure in teaching this school was the conducting of a debating society, which met weekly and was largely attended by the young and older people.[118]

After an interval of successful work in this field, Dr. Washington tells of his work as a teacher at Hampton. He says:

> I was surprised by being asked by Gen. Armstrong to return to Hampton Institute and take a position, partly as a teacher and partly as a

---

117. Booker T. Washington, *The Story of My Life and Work* (1900; repr., New York: Negro Universities Press, 1969), 70.
118. Ibid., 67–68.

post-graduate student. This, I gladly consented to do. Gen. Armstrong had decided to start a night class at Hampton for students who wanted to work all day and study for two hours at night. He asked me to organize and teach this class. At first there were only about a half dozen students, but the number soon grew to about thirty. The night class at Hampton has since grown to the point where it numbers six or seven hundred.

At the end of my second year at Hampton as a teacher, in 1881, there came a call from the little town of Tuskegee, Alabama, to Gen. Armstrong for some one to organize and become the Principal of a Normal School, which the people wanted to start in that town. Gen. Armstrong asked me to give up my work at Hampton and go to Tuskegee in answer to this call. I decided to undertake the work, and after spending a few days at my old home in Malden, West Virginia, I proceeded to the town of Tuskegee.[119]

No one will question the assertion that Dr. Washington and Tuskegee are one.

Tuskegee Institute is the soul of the man outlined in wood, in brick and stone, pulsating with the life of the human hive within on whom he has stamped his individuality.

As the absorbing topic of two continents, wherever the Negro is discussed, is the "Washington Industrial Propaganda," which has gained proselytes in every section of our country among influential and wealthy citizens, we shall trace the growth of the Institute from its inception, quoting from the founder's story as given in his book, *The Story of My Life and Work.*

When I reached Tuskegee, the only thing that had been done toward starting the school was the securing of $2,000. There was no land, building, or apparatus. I opened the school on July 4, 1881, in an old church and a shanty that was almost ready to fall down from decay. On the first day there was an attendance of thirty students, mainly those engaged in teaching in the public schools of the vicinity. I remember that, during the first months I taught in this little shanty, it was in such a dilapidated condition that, when it rained, one of the larger pupils would cease his lessons and hold the umbrella over me while I heard the recitation. After the school had been in session for several months, I began to see the necessity of having a permanent location for the institution, where we could have the students not only in their class rooms, but get hold of them in their home life, and teach them how to take care of their bodies in the matter of general cleanliness. It was rather noticeable that, notwithstanding the poverty of most of the students who came to us in the earlier months of

119. Ibid., 71–72.

the institution, most of them had the idea of getting an education in order that they might find some method of living without manual labor; that is, they had the feeling that to work with the hands was not conducive to being of the highest type of lady or gentleman.[120]

We can well believe this prejudice against labor was true of the Negro, and we ought to expect nothing different from a class so long accustomed to see nought but excellence in the behavior of the white race. "Massa Charles" lolled in his hammock while the slave worked. All the training of the Negro was in the direction that despised labor and made it a crime for a gentleman to labor.

Irony of fate! that sees the Southern gentleman adopting today, for the salvation of his section, the despised tactics of the "greasy Northern mechanic."

Feeling that it was necessary to make a great effort to improve the school, Dr. Washington secured a loan of $500 from Gen. J.F.B. Marshall, treasurer of Hampton Institute, and with this money bought an abandoned farm of 100 acres. Purchases of adjacent land and gifts of the same have increased the site to 2,460 acres.

Speaking of the great amount of assistance given him by the white inhabitants of the town, Dr. Washington says:

"I have been in a good many Southern towns, but I think I have never seen one where the general average of culture and intelligence is so high as that of the people of Tuskegee. We have in this town and its surroundings a good example of the friendly relations that exist between the two races when both races are enlightened and educated."[121]

Through the efforts of Miss Davidson, Dr. Washington's first assistant teacher at Tuskegee in the North, money enough was secured to repay Gen. Marshall's loan and build Porter Hall, the first building on the grounds, which was dedicated on Thanksgiving Day, 1882. From this time on the school's reputation grew, and it soon became a problem what to do with the increasing number of applicants, anxious to secure an education.

In May, 1882, Dr. Washington had married Miss Fannie N. Smith of Malden, W. Virginia; she died in 1884, leaving one child, Miss Portia Washington, recently graduated from the Normal School at Framingham, Mass. In 1885, Miss Olivia Davidson became Mrs. Washington; this estimable woman died in 1889. Two sons survive her—Baker Taliaferro and Ernest Davidson.

In 1893, Dr. Washington married Miss Maggie James Murray, a graduate of Fisk University, who is well known to the public in all sections of the country.

In February, 1883, the State Legislature of Alabama was so impressed with the excellent character of the school that they voted to increase the annual appropriation from two to three thousand dollars. That summer a four-room

---

120. Ibid., 79–82.
121. Ibid., 87.

cottage was put up to hold sixteen young men, and three board shanties were rented which would accommodate thirty-six additional students.

"In September, 1883, $1,100 was secured through Rev. R. C. Bedford from the Trustees of the Slater Fund. I might add right here that the interest of the Trustees of the Slater Fund, now under the control of Dr. J.L.M. Curry, special agent, has continued from that time until this, so that now the institution receives $11,000 from the Fund," says Dr. Washington; also: "With this impetus a carpenter shop was built, a windmill set up to pump water into the school building, a sewing machine bought for girls' industrial room, mules and wagons for the farm, and work on the new buildings, Alabama Hall, was vigorously pushed."[122]

In March, 1884, through influence of Gen. Armstrong, meetings were held in Baltimore, Philadelphia, New York and Boston, having for their object the completion of Alabama Hall, and by much hard work funds were secured, $10,000 in all.

In the spring of same year Dr. Washington was invited by Hon. Thomas W. Bicknall, of Boston, President of the National Educational Association, to address that body at its session during the summer at Madison, Wisconsin. At that assembly there were at least five thousand teachers present, representing every State in the Union. This was the first great meeting, national in character, at which the doctor had had an opportunity of presenting his work.

Between 1884 and 1894, the hardest work was done in securing money for Tuskegee. This was the period of growth. In 1884, the enrollment was 169. In 1894 the enrollment had increased to 712, and 54 officers and teachers employed, and 30 buildings practically all built by the labor of the students.

In 1883, they received their first donation of $500 from the Peabody Fund through Dr. J.L.M. Curry, general agent. This amount has been increased to twelve or fifteen hundred dollars each year.

In 1895, Dr. Washington lectured on "Industrial Education," under the auspices of the Students' Lecture Bureau of Fisk University. We give two extracts from the speech: "Despite all our disadvantages and hardships ever since our forefathers set foot upon the American soil as slaves, our pathway has been marked by progress. Think of it: We went into slavery pagans; we came out Christians. We went into slavery pieces of property; we came out American citizens. We went into slavery without a language; we came out speaking the proud Anglo-Saxon tongue. We went into slavery with slave chains clanking about our wrists; we came out with the American ballot in our hands." Continuing his speech, he said:

> As a race there are two things we must learn to do—one is to put brains into the common occupations of life, and the other is to dignify common labor. Twenty years ago every large and paying barber shop was in

122. Ibid., 105.

the hands of black men; today in all the large cities you cannot find a single large or first-class barber shop operated by colored men. The black man had had a monopoly of that industry, but had gone on from day to day in the same old monotonous way without improving anything about the industry. As a result, the white man has taken it up, put brains into it, watched all the fine points, improved and progressed, until his shop today is not known as a barber shop, but as a tonsorial parlor, and he is no longer called a barber, but a tonsorial artist.[123]

In the spring of 1895 he accompanied a committee of Atlanta, Ga., people to Washington to appear before the Committee on Appropriation for the purpose of inducing Congress to help forward the Exposition which the citizens of Atlanta were planning to have. The bill passed with little opposition.

Dr. Washington was proposed for chief commissioner, but declined to serve, accepting instead the position of commissioner for the State of Alabama, and was also made one of the judges of award in the Department of Education. Tuskegee Normal and Industrial Institute prepared a large and creditable exhibit, having with one exception (Hampton Institute) the largest exhibit in the Negro building. Three gold medals were awarded to institutions of learning, and Tuskegee got one of them.

On September 18, Dr. Washington made his great speech, tendering the Negro exhibit of which the *New York World* said that it was one of the most notable speeches, both as to character and the warmth of its reception, ever delivered to a Southern audience.[124] For this address Dr. Washington received many flattering encomiums from leading men all over the country.

In 1896, Harvard College conferred the honorary degree of Master of Arts upon him. Mr. Washington is the first of his race to receive an honorary degree from a New England University.

In 1897 occurred the dedication of the Robert Gould Shaw monument in Boston. The dedicatory exercises were held in Music Hall, Boston, which was packed from top to bottom with a distinguished audience. Many old anti-slavery men were there. Hon. Roger Wolcott, Governor of Massachusetts, presided. Again Mr. Washington's address was the feature of the occasion, and he scored another great hit.[125]

By dint of hard work and much persuasive eloquence, Dr. Washington secured the honor of a visit from President McKinley to Tuskegee, at the time of the Atlanta Peace Jubilee, December 14 and 15, 1898. On the morning of

---

123. Ibid., 142–144.

124. On September 18, 1895, Washington delivered his famed address to the Atlanta Cotton States Exposition. The text of the speech, later dubbed the "Atlanta Compromise" by its critics, circulated widely and is included in Washington, *The Story of My Life and Work*, 165–171.

125. For the text of his speech at the dedication of Saint Gaudens's Shaw Memorial, see Washington, *The Story of My Life and Work*, 236–242.

December 16, at eight o'clock, the President, Mrs. McKinley, with his cabinet, their families and distinguished generals, including Generals Shafter, Joseph Wheeler, Lawton, etc., were met by Governor Joseph F. Johnston of Alabama, and his staff and the Alabama Legislature, at Tuskegee. The morning was spent in a parade and inspection of the grounds, all of which were witnessed by more than six thousand visitors. After this they retired to the large chapel, where the President and others made addresses.

Dr. Washington's public career as a speaker is full of interest; we can, of course, in an article like this, give but a bare outline of many brilliant occasions in which he has participated as the central figure. His speeches on the Negro problem, and in behalf of the Institute, are able and teem with humor, and they possess also the essential property of attracting the attention of the monied element, for Dr. Washington is without a peer in this particular line, and as a result Tuskegee is the richest Negro educational plant in the world.

Immediately after the public meeting held at the Hollis Street Theatre in 1899, friends quietly started a movement to raise a certain sum of money, to be used in sending Dr. and Mrs. Washington to Europe. They remained abroad from May 10 until August 5, gaining much needed rest. While abroad lynching was especially frequent in the South, and Mr. Washington addressed a letter to the Southern people through the medium of the press. We give an excerpt:

> With all the earnestness of my heart I want to appeal, not to the President of the United States, Mr. McKinley, not to the people of New York nor of the New England States, but to the citizens of our Southern States, to assist in creating a public sentiment such as will make human life here just as safe and sacred as it is anywhere else in the world.
>
> For a number of years the South has appealed to the North and to Federal authorities, through the public press, from the public platform and most eloquently through the late Henry W. Grady, to leave the whole matter of the rights and protection of the Negro to the South, declaring that it would see to it that the Negro would be made secure in his citizenship.[126] During the last half dozen years the whole country, from the President down, has been inclined more than ever to pursue this policy, leaving the whole matter of the destiny of the Negro to the Negro himself and to the Southern white people among whom the great bulk of the Negroes live.
>
> By the present policy of non-interference on the part of the North and the Federal Government, the South is given a sacred trust. How will she execute this trust?[127]

126. Henry Woodfin Grady (1850–1899) was a Georgia journalist and orator known for his 1886 address on "The New South." See Henry Woodfin Grady and Oliver Dyer, *The New South* (New York: Robert Bonner's Sons, 1890).

127. Washington, *The Story of My Life and Work*, 336–337.

It is all very well to talk of the Negro's immorality and illiteracy, and that raising him out of the Slough of Despond will benefit the South and remove
unpleasantness between the races, but until the same course is pursued with
the immoral and illiterate *white* Southerner that is pursued with the Negro,
there will in no peace in that section. Ignorance is as harmful in one race as in
another. The South keeps on in her mad carnage of blood: she refuses to be
conciliated. The influence and wealth which have flowed into Hampton and
Tuskegee have awakened jealous spite. She doesn't care a rap for the "sacred
trust" of Grady or any other man. We hear a lot of talk against the methods of
the anti-slavery leaders, but no abolitionist ever used stronger language than
the Rev. Quincy Ewing of Mississippi, in his recent great speech against
lynching. We wonder how they like it down that way? Will they hang him or
burn him?

The effect of that speech has been as electrical as was the first gun from
Sumter. We could shout for joy over the words: "I have always been and am
now a States-right Democrat; but I say with no sort of hesitation that if Mississippi cannot put a stop to the lynching of Negroes within her borders—
Negroes, let us remember, who are citizens of the United States as well as of
Mississippi—then the Federal Government ought to take a hand in this business!"[128] The reverend gentleman does not believe in treating a cancer with
rose water.

Through the generosity of wealthy friends, Tuskegee has now an endowment fund of $150,000, from which the school is receiving interest.

The site of the Institute is now 835 acres. The other large tract is about four
miles southeast of the Institute and is composed of 800 acres and known as
"Marshall farm." Upon the home farm is located forty-two buildings. Of
these, Alabama, Davidson, Huntington, Cassidy and Science Halls, the Agricultural Trades and Laundry Buildings, and the chapel are built of brick.
There are also two large frame halls—Porter and Phelps Halls, small frame
buildings and cottages used for commissary storerooms, recitation rooms,
dormitories and teachers' residences. There are also the shop and saw-mill,
with engine rooms and dynamo in conjunction. The brickyard, where the
bricks needed in the construction of all brick buildings are made by pupils,
turned out 1,500,000 bricks in 1899.

The Agricultural Department, Prof. G. W. Carver, of the Iowa State University, in charge, attracts much attention on account of changes wrought in

---

128. Quincy Ewing, *A Sermon on Lynching by the Rev. Quincy Ewing in St. James Episcopal Church,
Greenville, Miss., August 11th, 1901* (New Orleans: Women's Christian Temperance Union of Louisiana,
1901), 14. This pamphlet edition of Ewing's sermon was reprinted from "The Lynching of Negroes in Mississippi," which appeared in the September 21, 1901, edition of the *Chicago Public*. Earlier the sermon
appeared in the August 27, 1901, edition of the *Boston Herald*, which is most likely where Hopkins read it.
Washington quoted from it in "Lynch Law and Anarchy" (1901), repr. in *The Booker T. Washington Papers*,
edited by Louis R. Harlan and Raymond W. Smock (Urbana: University of Illinois Press, 1972–1989),
13:500–504.

old methods by scientific agriculture.[129] The building is well-equipped at a cost of $10,000, and contains a fine chemical laboratory. Agriculture is an important feature in the life of the school. 135 acres of the home farm are devoted to raising vegetables, strawberries, grapes and other fruits. The Marshall farm is worked by student labor, keeping from thirty to forty-five boys on it constantly. It produces a large amount of the farm products used by the school and 800 head of live stock.

The Mechanical Department is in the Slater-Armstrong Memorial Trades' Building, dedicated in 1900. It is built entirely of brick, and contains twenty-seven rooms. The bricks were made by student labor. The building contains directors' office, reading room, exhibit room, wheelwright shop, blacksmith shop, tin shop, printing office, carpenter shop, repair shop, wood-working machine room, iron-working machine room, foundry, brick-making and plastering rooms, general stock and supply room, and a boiler and engine room. The second floor contains the mechanical drawing room, harness shop, paint shop, tailor shop, shoe shop, and electrical laboratory, and a room for carriage trimming and upholstering.

The Department of Domestic Science is directed by Mrs. Booker T. Washington, and embraces laundering, cooking, dressmaking, plain sewing, millinery and mattress making. A training school for nurses has for instructors the resident physician and a competent trained nurse.[130]

There is also a division of music, a Bible training department and an academic department, all of which are carried on extensively with elaborate equipments.

From this brief review of the life of the founder of Tuskegee Institute and the prodigious growth of the work there we can but conclude that this is a phenomenal age in which we are living, and one of the most remarkable features of this age is Booker T. Washington,—his humble birth and rise to eminence and wealth.

View his career in whatever light we may, be we for or against his theories, his personality is striking, his life uncommon, and the magnetic influence which radiates from him in all direction, bending and swaying great minds and pointing the ultimate conclusion of colossal schemes as the wind the leaves of the trees, is stupendous. When the happenings of the Twentieth Century have become matters of history, Dr. Washington's motives will be open to as many constructions and discussions as are those of Napoleon today, or of other men of extraordinary ability, whether for good or evil, who have had like phenomenal careers.

SOURCE "Famous Men of the Negro Race: Booker T. Washington," *Colored American Magazine* 3.6 (Oct. 1901): 436–441.

129. Tuskegee scientist, agronomist, and teacher George Washington Carver (c. 1865–1943) received his B.A. (1894) and M.S. (1896) from Iowa State.
130. Washington, *The Story of My Life and Work*, 406–412.

PART III

Famous Women of the Negro Race *(1901–1902)*

*F**amous Women of the Negro Race* appeared in the *Colored American Magazine* from November 1901 to October 1902. Due to a combined January—February 1902 number, the complete series consists of eleven installments even though the October 1902 conclusion "Higher Education of Colored Women in White Schools and Colleges" was labeled "XII."

Hopkins's biographical voice further develops over the course of *Famous Women*, which begins with a section on "Phenomenal Vocalists." While the series does devote early installments to Sojourner Truth and Harriet Tubman, thereby giving women abolitionists the same standing she gave men in *Famous Men,* Hopkins shifts her orientation toward collective biography with installments on "Literary Workers," "Educators," and "Artists." In the concluding segment, Hopkins articulates "the right of the woman of color to live in the world on the same terms as a white woman does." As for the belief that education makes women less desirable, Hopkins, who herself never married, explains that marriage is a partnership in which activist women are the best companions. In its entirety, this series articulates a fundamental component of Hopkins's literary and political vision, namely her feminist insistence on the full and active participation of women in all aspects of the public sphere.

I.

Phenomenal Vocalists

*W*hat a beneficent art is music. So deeply impressed was one celebrated man of the immense importance and influence of music that he is said to have exclaimed, "Let who will make the laws of the people, but let me make their songs."

Many of the ancients considered music as an accidental discovery of the Egyptians, while listening to the whistling of the wind through the reeds on the banks of the river Nile.

The existence of music is coeval with the creation of man. If we were competent to analyze the music of all nations, civilized or uncivilized, we should find that they bear a great resemblance to each other. We should find that the melodies of Scotland, Ireland, France, Hindostan and China, all please us, and are formed on a scale founded on an original law of nature, and we should find also, that this scale is substantially the same as that upon which our modern music of today is founded, albeit the music of the present day is a complicated and difficult art requiring profound study and great concentration of energy to acquire proficiency.

The Bible furnishes us with the most ancient references, and from it we learn much of the musical proclivities of the Hebrews. From hieroglyphics on works of art in Egypt we read how highly music had been cultivated by the inhabitants; even the Greeks learned of the Egyptians. In Rome music, as an art, was borrowed from the Greeks, and while she stood in the pride of superiority as the conqueror of the world, music was carried to excess. After Nero, however, it declined, and small wonder when we contemplate the horrible vividness of Sienkiewicz's picture of Nero fiddling over the ruins of burning Rome.[1] From the earliest ages of the Christian church music has been employed in conducting religious exercises. What the first music was we can but conjecture as nothing definite is known, but in the beginning of the fourth century, regular choirs were introduced divided into two parts and required to sing alternately at a higher or a lower pitch, and this accumulation of sound into a grand whole, produced the most startling effects of which music is capable; therefore, we have now the succession or repetition of parts in a musical composition called a fugue.

The idols of one generation make way for the little gods of the next. "It is only here and there that a commanding genius stands on a pinnacle so high

---

1. Polish novelist Henryk Sienkiewicz (1846–1916) published *Quo Vadis: A Narrative of the Time of Nero* in 1897.

that its divine light shines upon remote ages which point to it as a distinct landmark in its own sphere." The human voice echoes and re-echoes in our hearts long after the strains which held us spellbound have died away. The magnificent voices of Malibran, Alboni, Parepa-Rosa, Titiens, Jenny Lind, Nilsson, Lucca, Kellogg and Cary need no monuments to preserve their memories to humanity.[2] The great artist belongs to God, and is imperishable. Like Moses, he stands upon the mount and receives the eternal laws of art. He forgets his inner life, joy and sorrow disappear; he ascends on the wings of his beloved art, and brushing the gates of Paradise translates into his earthly work some of the entrancing melody of the heavenly choirs.

The Negro's right to be classed as a man among men, has been openly doubted, nor do we find this doubt removed in the dawn of the Twentieth Century; rather is it now a popular fad to regard the Negro as hopelessly incompetent and immoral, doomed to years of self-abasement and appren-. ticeship before he will be worthy to be classed among the men of civilization. But in the hours of the blackest despair that may come to humanity the silent forces of divinity are working for the amelioration of the oppressed and unfortunate ones of earth. The genius of music, supposed to be the gift of only the most refined and intellectual of the human family, sprang into active life among the lowly tillers of the soil and laborers in the rice swamps of the South. The distinguishing feature of Negro song is its pathos and trueness to nature. It is the only original music of America, and since emancipation has become a part of the classical music of the century.

The story of the Negro musician is fraught with intense interest for us. Wherever God dwells he leaves a token of His presence, and he steeped the American serf to the lips in divine harmony. Music is one of the very elements of the soul and voice, implanted by an all-wise Creator, part of our God-given nature—sign—manual of the universal kinship of all races. Who can measure God's methods? Be a man black or white is insignificant. In the intellect lies the miracle. What a grand thought it is that a higher law than our will regulates events; that our labors to degrade or elevate an individual or a race are altogether vain for God exists. "There is a soul at the centre of nature and over the will of every man, so that none of us can wrong the universe." In giving the life-stories of five great artists it is pleasant to worship before these half-deserted shrines and drink in the beauty and inexhaustible charm of these singers, two of whom are of a past generation. It is profitable, too, for us to appreciate the fact that the women of the race have always kept pace with

2. Her international list of female vocalists names Maria Malibran (1801–1836), Spanish mezzo-soprano vocalist, composer, instrumentalist; Marietta Alboni (1823–1894), Italian contralto vocalist; Euphrosyne Parepa-Rosa (1836–1874), Scottish soprano vocalist; Therese Titiens [Titjens] (1831–1877), Hungarian-German soprano vocalist; Johanna Maria Lind (1820–1887), Swedish soprano vocalist; Christine Nilsson (1843–1921), Swedish soprano vocalist; Giovannina (Strazza) Lucca (1814–1894), Italian soprano vocalist and music publisher; Clara Louise Kellogg (1842–1916), U.S. soprano vocalist; and Annie Louise Cary (1841–1921), U.S. contralto vocalist.

every advance made, often leading the upward flight. The work accomplished by these artists was more sacred than the exquisite subtleness of their art, for to them it was given to help create a manhood for their despised race.

In writing of the attainments of a people it is important that the position of its women be carefully defined—whether endowed with traits of character fit for cultivation, bright intellects and broad humanitarianism, virtuous in all things, tender, loving and of deep religious convictions. Given these attributes in its women and a race has already conquered the world and its best gifts.

Maligned and misunderstood, the Afro-American woman is falsely judged by other races. Nowhere on God's green earth are there nobler women, more self-sacrificing tender mothers, more gifted women in their chosen fields of work than among the millions of Negroes in the United States. The opening of the same scenes, the same pursuits and interests, with the same opportunity for education as is enjoyed by more favored people, have brought out the noblest and best in the women of our race. But an assertion is of no value unless proven. To this end we give the achievements of Negro women who were beacon lights along the shore in the days of our darkest history.

ELIZABETH TAYLOR GREENFIELD, known as the "Black Swan," was born a slave in Natchez, Miss., in 1809. When but a year old she went to Philadelphia under the care of the Quaker lady, who was her owner. A warm affection existed between them, so much so, that discovering her talent she gave Elizabeth a good education, and when Mrs. Greenfield died, in 1844 she left Elizabeth Taylor a substantial bequest which was never received by the beneficiary.

Miss Taylor finally added the name of Greenfield to her own.

Upon the death of her owner, finding herself thrown upon her own endeavors to obtain a livelihood, Miss Greenfield having previously acquired some knowledge of musical culture, and being encouraged thereto by philanthropists who had learned her simple story, decided to put her wonderful vocal powers to the test, and in October, 1851, she sang before the Buffalo Musical Association, representing the best musical talent in the city, and her fame as a phenomenal vocalist was assured. "Give the 'Black Swan' the cultivation and experience of Jenny Lind or Mlle. Parodi and she will rank favorably with those great artistes."[3]

It was found that her voice was of immense compass. She struck every note in a clear and well-defined manner, and reached the highest capacity of the human voice with great ease. Beginning with G in the *bass clef,* she ran up the scale to E in the *treble clef,* giving to each note its full power and tone.

While in Albany, January 19, 1852, *The Daily State Register* said of her:

"The concert was a complete success. The compass of her wonderful voice embraces twenty-seven notes, reaching from the sonorous bass of a baritone

3. James M. Trotter, *Music and Some Highly Musical People* (1881; repr., New York: Johnson Reprint Corporation, 1968), 71. Teresa Parodi (1827–1878) was an Italian soprano vocalist.

to a few notes above Jenny Lind's highest. She plays with ability upon the piano, harp and guitar. In her deportment she bears herself well, and, we are told, converses with much intelligence. We noticed among the audience Governor Hunt and family, both Houses of the Legislature, State officers, and a large number of our leading citizens."[4]

And so we might go on quoting praises and plaudits for this black prodigy *ad infinitum.* We can but stand in awe before the wonderful planning of God's issues: In the midst of the darkest happenings in the Negro's history upon this continent, in a slave-holding republic. He sent an angel's voice to dwell within a casket ebony-bound, with the peculiarly carved features of racial development indelibly stamped upon it, to confound the scepticism of those who doubted his handiwork.

After singing in nearly all the free States, she resolved to visit Europe for purposes of study. She embarked from New York, April 6, 1853; arrived in Liverpool, April 16. Arrived at London a painful surprise awaited her—her manager had abandoned her and she found herself in a strange land, penniless and without friends.

She had been told of Lord Shaftesbury's goodness, and she resolved to call upon him. The nobleman immediately granted her an interview and gave her a letter of introduction to his lawyer.

At this time Harriet Beecher Stowe was in London, and speaking of Miss Greenfield, she says:

> Today the Duchess of Sutherland called with the Duchess of Argyle. Miss Greenfield happened to be present, and I begged leave to present her, giving a slight sketch of her history. I was pleased with the kind and easy affability with which these great ladies conversed with her. The Duchess of Sutherland seemed much pleased with her singing and remarked that she would be happy to give her an opportunity of performing in Stafford House.
>
> "I never so fully realized," continues Mrs. Stowe, "that there really is no natural prejudice against color in the human mind. Miss Greenfield is a dark mulattress, of a pleasing and gentle face, though by no means handsome. She is short and thick set, with a chest of great amplitude, as one would think on hearing her tenor. I have never seen, in any of the persons to whom I have presented her, the least indications of suppressed surprise or disgust, any more than we should exhibit on the reception of a dark-complexioned Spaniard or Portuguese."[5]

Describing the concert at the Stafford House, Mrs. Stowe says:

---

4. Ibid., 75–76.

5. Harriet Beecher Stowe, *Sunny Memories of Foreign Lands* (Boston: Phillips, Sampson, 1854), 1:319–320, quoted in Trotter, *Music*, 81.

The concert room looked more picturesque and dreamy than ever. The piano was on the flat stairway just below the broad central landing. It was a grand piano standing end outward, and banked among hot-house flowers, so that only the gilded top was visible. Sir George Smart presided. Miss Greenfield stood among the singers on the stairway. She wore a black velvet head-dress and white carnelian earrings, a black moire-antique silk made high in the neck, with white lace falling sleeves and white gloves. There was profound attention when her turn came to sing. Her voice, with its keen, searching fire, its penetrating vibrant quality, its *timbre*, cut its way like a Damascus blade to the heart. She sang the ballad "Old Folks at Home," giving one verse in the soprano and one in the tenor voice. As she stood partially concealed by the piano, it was thought that the tenor part was performed by one of the gentlemen. She was rapturously encored. Between the parts Sir George took her to the piano and tried her voice by skips, striking notes here and there at random, without connection, from D in alto to A first space in bass clef. She followed with unerring precision, striking the sound nearly at the same instant his finger touched the key. This brought out a burst of applause.

Lord Shaftesbury was present. He said, "I consider the use of these halls for the encouragement of an outcast race a consecration. This is the true use of wealth and splendor when they are employed to raise up and encourage the despised and forgotten."[6]

As our space is limited we can give but the scantiest outline of this wonderful woman's career while abroad. We can judge what it must have been from the character of the certificates appended:

Sir George Smart has the pleasure to state that her Majesty Queen Victoria commanded Miss Greenfield to attend at Buckingham Palace on May 10, 1854, when she had the honor of singing several songs.

————

To Miss Greenfield, from Sir George Smart, Kt., Organist and Composer to Her Majesty's Chapel Royal.
No. 91, Gr. Portland St., London.
June 24, 1854.[7]

This is to certify that Miss Greenfield had the honor of singing before Her Majesty the Queen at Buckingham Palace. By Her Majesty's command.

6. Stowe, *Sunny Memories*, 2:103–105, quoted in Trotter, *Music*, 82–83.
7. Trotter, *Music*, 86.

C. B. Phipps.
Buckingham Palace, July 22, 1854, London.[8]

Miss Greenfield's return from abroad was the signal for brilliant receptions, all over the North, in her honor. At the Meionian, Boston, the elite of the city crowded the hall to overflowing at five dollars a ticket.

But Miss Greenfield always remained the same. Her head was not turned by flattery. She was ever brave, patient, noble, ambitious, charitable to all, remembering her own hard struggles. She died in Philadelphia, Penn., in 1876.

MADAME ANNIE PAULINE PINDELL was born in Exeter, N.H., 1834.[9] When an infant the sound of a musical instrument would cause the most intense excitement in the child, and as she grew older it was discovered that she possessed a remarkable organ in height, depth and sweetness.

In those days the free colored people gave small thought to the cultivation of any talent that they might possess, so nothing was done to develop the girl's great gift.

At nineteen the young girl married Joseph Pindell, a brother of the Baltimore Pindells, so well known in that city, and later in Boston. Proud of his wife's talent he encouraged her to study and improve, and soon Mrs. Pindell became a familiar figure among musical circles in Boston.

In those days there were no great music schools and so Mrs. Pindell studied first with a celebrated German professor and later was under the tuition of Wyzeman Marshall in elocution, and of his brother in music—vocal and instrumental. Indefatigable in her desire to acquire knowledge and improve in her art, the singer added to her vocal work the study of German, French and Italian, and she also made herself an expert performer on the piano, harp and guitar. She also delighted in original composition and Ditson's house published her songs, of which "Seek the Lodge Where the Red Men Dwell," was the most widely known, becoming a popular "hit" of the day.

Mrs. Pindell went to California in 1860, and for thirty years her magnificent organ was celebrated on the Pacific coast. On the occasion of a visit to the Hawaiian Islands during Queen Emma's reign, Mrs. Pindell was presented with a diamond necklace worth fifteen hundred dollars. The compass of this singer's voice was the same as the "Black Swan's," embracing twenty-seven notes, from G in bass clef to E in treble clef. Musical critics compared her to Madame Alboni.

Madame Pindell died at Los Angeles, Cal., May 1, 1901.

---

8. Ibid.

9. Annie Pauline Pindell may have been Hopkins's aunt. See Hanna Wallinger, *Pauline E. Hopkins: A Literary Biography* (Athens: University of Georgia Press, 2005), 21.

ANNA MADAH and EMMA LOUISE HYERS are natives of California.[10] They early showed signs of musical precociousness and were placed under the tuition of Professor Hugo Sank, and later were taught by Madame Josephine D'Ormy. They made their debut at the Metropolitan Theatre, Sacramento, California, April 22, 1867.

Of this debut *The San Francisco Chronicle* said:

Their musical power is acknowledged. Miss Anna Madah has a pure, sweet soprano voice, very true, even and flexible, of remarkable compass and smoothness. Her rendition of "Casta Diva," and her soprano in the tower scene from "Il Trovatore," and Verdi's "Forse è lui che l'anima," as also in the ballad "The Rhine Maidens," was almost faultless, and thoroughly established her claims to the universal commendations she has received from all the connoisseurs in melody who have heard her.

Miss Louise is a natural wonder, being a fine alto singer, and also the possessor of a pure tenor-voice. It is of wonderful range, and in listening to her singing it is difficult to believe that one is not hearing a talented young man instead of the voice of a young girl. Her character song was one of the greatest "hits" ever made; and henceforth her position as a favorite with an audience is assured.[11]

After this debut the young women retired for study, but in a short time moved East, singing to enthusiastic audiences in Western towns and cities. In Chicago their reception was most flattering, their remarkable musical gifts created intense excitement among people of high musical culture.

About this time Mr. Wallace King, a tenor singer of great ability, a native of Camden, New Jersey, joined the famous sisters; Mr. John Luca, of the Luca family, a cultured baritone, completed a quartette which became well known from Maine to California. Mr. A. C. Taylor, New York, was the pianist.

The Hyers sisters appeared at the Peace Jubilee concerts, Boston, Mass., under P. S. Gilmore, before an audience of fifty thousand people, supported by a chorus of twenty thousand voices.

In 1875 Mr. Napier Lothian and his orchestra gave a series of Sunday night concerts at the Boston Theatre, at all of which the Hyers sisters were the attraction.

They next appeared in *Out of Bondage,* a four-act musical comedy, written for the sisters by Mr. Joseph B. Bradford, of Boston, under the management of Redpath's Bureau.[12] This play was but a skeleton sketch, designed to show off

10. The Hyers sisters performed in several productions of Hopkins's musical *Peculiar Sam; or, The Underground Railroad* in the early 1880s.

11. Trotter, *Music,* 162–163.

12. Joseph Bradford's *Out of Bondage* (1876) is published in Eileen Southern, ed., *African American Theater* (New York: Garland, 1994). In this volume, Southern pairs Bradford's musical with Hopkins's *Peculiar Sam; or, The Underground Railroad.*

the musical ability of the performers. But it served its purpose, and gave impetus to study and careful cultivation of the musical gifts of talented musicians who desired to adopt the lyric stage as a profession. The introduction of this drama, in which, for the first time, all the characters were represented by colored people, marks an era in the progress of the race. Never, until undertaken by these ladies, was it thought possible for Negroes to appear in the legitimate drama, albeit soubrette parts were the characters portrayed.

Emma Louise Hyers is dead; Anna Madah is now travelling with Isham's Colored Comedy Company.

MADAME MARIE SELIKA, prima donna soprano, "The Queen of Staccato."

This lady is a native of Cincinnati, Ohio. Her wonderful talent as a vocalist was discovered and given to the world by Max Strakosch of opera fame, some twenty years ago. Soon after her debut Madame Selika found her way to Boston, where she spent three years in assiduous study at the best music schools. Desiring to attain the highest perfection in her art, however, she determined to go abroad.

Madame Selika's reception into exclusive musical circles had been flattering, and when her visit to Europe was announced a testimonial concert was arranged by Boston's most influential citizens. The following correspondence is self-explanatory:

    BOSTON, MARCH 30, 1882.
    TO MADAME MARIE SELIKA, BOSTON, MASS.

Being informed of your intended early departure for study abroad, we beg to tender you a testimonial concert, to be given at a time and place suitable to your convenience, in token of our appreciation of your attainments and promise in your profession, and of our cordial interest in your behalf.

    VERY TRULY YOURS,
    JOHN D. LONG, SAMUEL A. GREEN, HENRY B. PIERCE, EBEN D. JORDAN, B. J. LANG, WHITE, SMITH & CO., WENDELL PHILLIPS, OLIVER DITSON, AND OTHERS.

    BOSTON, APRIL 8, 1882.
    HIS EXCELLENCY GOVERNOR JOHN D. LONG, HIS HONOR MAYOR SAMUEL A. GREEN, HON. HENRY B. PIERCE, DR. S. W. LANGMAID, GENERAL A. P. MARTIN, WENDELL PHILLIPS, ESQ., EBEN D. JORDAN, ESQ., B. J. LANG, ESQ., AND OTHERS.

Gentlemen:—I am in receipt of your kind letter of the 30th ult., couched in most friendly terms, tendering me a testimonial concert prior to my intended departure abroad to complete my musical studies. Deeply sensible of the honor you do me, I gratefully accept your proffer and would suggest that the concert be given at Music Hall, on Thursday evening, April 20th.

I AM, GENTLEMEN, RESPECTFULLY YOURS,
MARIE SELIKA.

Her first concert abroad was given at St. James Hall, London, England, Saturday, October 14, 1882, under the immediate patronage of his excellency the Spanish minister, the Marquis De Casa Laiglesia.

VOCALISTS:
Madame Carlotta Patti, Madame Evans Warwick, Madame Marie Selika, Mr. Percy Blandford, Mr. Joseph Lynde and Signor Vergara.

INSTRUMENTALISTS:
Car Tito Mattel, Pianist: Signor Papina, Solo Violin; Monsieur Ernest De Munck, Violoncelliste Solo, de S.A.R. Le Grand Duc De Saxe.

CONDUCTORS:
Sir Julius Benedict and Signor Tito Mattel.

It is needless to say that the artiste was grandly successful in her venture, and studied under the most famous vocal teachers in Europe. We append a few extracts from the European press:

"Madame Selika, with her coal-black hair, possesses an uncommonly rich and beautiful soprano voice, and sings with an ease and correctness which shows careful training. She sang the 'Fior de Margueritta Polka,' by Arditti, in which she used an exquisite staccato."—*Dresden Nachrichten.*

"Mme. Selika, a soft soprano voice, which reaches without effort the three-lined octave. She renders trills and cadenzas with a clearness and purity which shows careful study. In the Cavatina from Traviatta, she displayed all these qualities in the most remarkable manner, and also sang with genuine musical feeling. In response to enthusiastic applause, she sang the Echo-song by Echart."—*Berliner Fremdenblatt.*

Referring to Mme. Selika's début in that city, the *Schweinfur Anzieger* of February 26, 1884, says:

The audience was literally carried away with enthusiasm by the singing of this wonderful woman. Only once before has the city of Schweinfur been favored with so rare an opportunity of listening to so bewitching a voice as that possessed by this American lady, and that was on the occasion of the concert of the celebrated contest of Totto Luger, the opera singer of the Royal Court of Prussia. With a well-trained voice, her

admirable colorature and her perfect intonations, she not only capti-
vates the amateur listener, who, in his sympathy, becomes electrified by
the singer, and feels himself drawn irresistibly towards her, but she also
becomes the cynosure of attention to every connoisseur of the divine
art, who may happen to hear her, and who takes pleasure in availing
himself of every opportunity of lavishing upon her such plaudits as the
harmony and melody of her magnetic voice so richly deserve.

Upon her return from Europe, Mme. Selika toured the country, under the
patronage and management of Lieut. W. H. Dupree, of Boston. She resides at
Baltimore, Md., where she is established as a singer and vocal teacher.

SOURCE "Famous Women of the Negro Race I: Phenomenal Vocalists," *Colored American Magazine* 4.1 (Nov. 1901): 45–53.

II.

Sojourner Truth
A Northern Slave Emancipated by the State of New York, 1828

*A*ll our ideas of slavery are connected with the South. Very few people of this generation realize that slavery actually existed in all its horrors, within the very cities where, perhaps, we enjoy the fullest liberty today; but so it was. The details of the life of one who experienced all the horrors of Northern servitude are peculiarly interesting.

Negro slavery was in reality forced upon the country under the colonial systems of Holland and Great Britain. It developed injustice, dread suspicion and cruelty attendant upon the peculiar institution. By the Assiento Treaty with Spain, at the peace of Utrecht, 1713, England, in the words of Bancroft (Vol. III, 411), "extorting the privilege of filling the New World with Negroes," had secured with the Spanish colonies a monopoly of the trade in slaves, to the extent of bringing from the African coast an average of 30,000 a year to be sold in the American market.[13] Of these but a small proportion came to New York. In 1741, at the date of the famous "Negro plot" in New York city, there were about 1,500 slaves located there out of a population of about 8,000 souls. During the time of the excitement attendant upon the discovery of the plot thirteen Negroes were publicly burned to death over a slow fire. The legislature of the State also declared at that time that "all encouragement should be given to the direct importation of slaves; that all *smuggling* of slaves should be condemned as *an eminent discouragement to the fair trader*."[14]

It is also interesting to note that in 1807, no less than fifty-nine of the vessels engaged in that trade were sent out from the State of Rhode Island, which then could boast of but 70,000 inhabitants.

The history of slavery and slave trading in Massachusetts is one of the most surprising volumes ever issued by the American press. New Hampshire, too, held slaves. General Washington himself, while President of the United States, hunted a slave woman and her child all the way into that State. Vermont had a fugitive case in 1808. But the brave Judge Harrington stunned the

13. George Bancroft's (1800–1891) ten-volume *History of the United States from the Discovery of the American Continent* (1856–1874) was published in several revised editions. Volume 3 addresses slavery and the slave trade in the British colonies in the Americas.

14. Olive Gilbert, *Narrative of Sojourner Truth, a Northern Slave, Emancipated from Bodily Servitude by the State of New York, in 1828* (Boston: J. B. Yerrinton and Son, 1850), 138.

remorseless claimant with his decision that "nothing less than a bill of sale from the Almighty could establish ownership" in his victim. Thus we see that slavery was a sin and crime of both North and South. It was sustained by the government, it was sanctioned by almost the whole religious world of the United States, and this crime of slavery became the "sum of all villainies."

Sojourner Truth's life is remarkable because she experienced that Northern slavery of which we know so little at present. When well advanced in years she became a great worker in the anti-slavery cause. Parker Pillsbury says:

> In the New Testament "Acts of the Apostles," mention is made of "honorable women, not a few," who went everywhere preaching the anti-slavery word. Sarah and Angelina Grimké, who emancipated their slaves in South Carolina, abandoned affluence and gave the remainder of their lives to the cause of freedom and humanity. Sallie Holley, daughter of Hon. Myron Holley, of New York, graduate with Lucy Stone, of Oberlin College, who, after freedom was established, became a teacher among the freed people. Susan B. Anthony, Sarah P. Remond, sister of Charles Lenox Remond. But most wondrous of all was the Ethiopian Sybil, Sojourner Truth, still living (1883), a centenarian and more.[15]

We append certificate of character given Sojourner Truth by men whose signatures are valuable, not only as a guarantee of the authenticity of this woman's statements, but also because of their own remarkable life stories.

NEW PALTZ, ULSTER CO., OCT. 13, 1834.

This is to certify that Isabella, this colored woman, lived with me since the year 1810, and that she has always been a good and faithful servant; and the eighteen years that she was with me, I always found her to be perfectly honest. I have always heard her well spoken of by everyone that has employed her.

JOHN J. DUMONT.[16]

BOSTON, MARCH, 1850.

My acquaintance with the subject of the accompanying narrative, Sojourner Truth, for several years past, has led me to form a very high appreciation of her understanding, moral integrity, disinterested kind-

15. Parker Pillsbury, *Acts of the Anti-Slavery Apostles* (1883; repr., Freeport, N.Y.: Books for Libraries Press, 1970), 486–487.
16. Gilbert, *Narrative of Sojourner Truth*, 144.

ness, and religious sincerity and enlightenment. Any assistance or co-operation that she may receive in the sale of her narrative, or in any other manner, I am sure will be meritoriously bestowed.

WM. LLOYD GARRISON.[17]

The subject of this biography, Sojourner Truth, as she called herself—but whose name was originally Isabella—was born between the years 1797 and 1800. She was the daughter of James and Betsey, slaves of Colonel Ardinburgh, Hurley, Ulster County, New York.[18]

Colonel Ardinburgh was of the class known as Low Dutch. Isabella was an infant when her master died, and with other chattels became the property of his son Charles. Her earliest recollections of this master was his removal to a new house which he had built as an hotel, and living in the cellar under the house which was assigned the slaves as their sleeping apartment,—women and men sleeping in the same room. She described this room as a dismal chamber, its only lights a few panes of glass through which the sun never shone; the space between the loose boards of the floor, and the uneven earth below, was often filled with mud and water giving forth noxious vapors chilling and fatal to health. All sexes and all ages slept on those damp boards, like the horse, with a little straw and a blanket.

On the death of Charles Ardinburgh Isabella's family were again to change owners.

Isabella's father, who, when young, was tall and straight, was called "Bomefree." Her mother was named "Mau-mau Bett."[19]

When this sale was about to take place the question arose as to what should be done with the faithful, diligent Bomefree, now grown infirm from exposure and hardship, when separated from his wife. After some contention it was finally agreed, as most expedient for the heirs, that Mau-mau Bett receive her freedom, on condition that she support her husband. This decision was received joyfully by the objects of it. The privilege was also granted them of remaining in the cellar before described. Several years after this Mau-mau

---

17. Ibid.

18. In this biography, Hopkins follows Gilbert's spellings of "Ardinburgh," "Scriver," and "Van Wagener," which Nell Irvin Painter identifies as the family names Hardenbergh, Schriver, and Van Wagenen. When Hopkins is faithful to her source (in this case Gilbert), I have maintained her intended spelling because the figures are preeminently characters in Truth's narrative, rather than historical figures like Toussaint, Robert Brown Elliott, or Truth herself. See Nell Irvin Painter, *Sojourner Truth: A Life, A Symbol* (New York: Norton, 1996), 11, 14, 25.

19. Hopkins writes "Bromefree" instead of Bomefree, and "Man-man" instead of Mau-mau. Since her spellings diverge from those of Gilbert, I have changed what appear to be errors back to how they appeared in Gilbert (whose spellings are confirmed by Painter). Nonetheless, there are intriguing possible interpretations of Hopkins's consistent use of "Man-man." Painter explains that Truth's mother Elizabeth, "Betsy," was known as "Mau Mau," which means "Mama" in Dutch. See Painter, *Sojourner Truth*, 11.

Bett died, and Bomefree was left alone—penniless, weak, lame and nearly blind.[20]

Isabella and her brother Peter were allowed to attend the funeral of their mother and pay their father a short visit. She described her father's state in most pitiful terms: "'Oh,' he would exclaim, 'I had thought God would take me first,—Mau-mau was so much smarter than I, and could get about and take care of herself; and I am *so old*, and *so helpless*. What *is* to become of me? I can't do anything more—my children are all gone, and here I am left helpless and alone.' And then, when I was leaving him," continued Isabella, "he raised his voice, and cried aloud like a child—*Oh, how he did cry*! I hear it now—and remember it as well as if it were but yesterday—*poor old man!!!*"[21]

After this the Ardinburghs "took turns about" in keeping him—permitting him to stay a few weeks at one house, and then a time at another. But the old man's constitution did not yield to age, exposure, or a desire to die. Again the Ardinburghs tired of him, and offered freedom to two old slaves—Caesar, brother of Mau-mau Bett, and his wife Betsey—on condition that they take care of James. A cabin in the woods far from neighbor or friends became the home of these three decrepit old people, no one of whom was in a condition to render much assistance to the other. In a short time Caesar and Betsey died, and again Bomefree was left desolate. But shortly after this, however, this deserted wreck of humanity was found on his miserable pallet, frozen and stiff in death. The news of his death reached John Ardinburgh, who declared that "Bomefree, who had ever been a kind and faithful slave, should have a good funeral." This "good funeral" consisted of a jug of ardent spirits, and some black paint for a coffin!

We have given this reminiscence as an example of that kind and generous treatment accorded slaves that many leading Southerners are proclaiming today. What a compensation for a life of toil, submission, and neglect! We, in our pleasant homes surrounded by kind friends, can try in vain to picture the dark and desolate state of that poor old man. But such was slavery, and such would be our fate today, could the South but force her principles upon the government. When sold at the death of her master, Charles Ardinburgh, Isabella was struck off for one hundred dollars to one John Nealy, of Ulster County, New York; and she had the impression that in this sale she was connected with a lot of sheep.[22]

This was true, for Negroes were sold along with domestic animals and in the same inventory. We give an advertisement from *Anti-Slavery Apostles* which illustrates this fact.

"On the first Monday of February next will be put up at public auction, before the court house, the following property, belonging to the estate of the

---

20. Gilbert, *Narrative of Sojourner Truth*, 13–21.
21. Ibid., 21–22.
22. Ibid., 22–26.

late Rev. Dr. Furman, viz.: A plantation or tract of land, on and in the Wateree swamp. A tract of the first quality of fine land, on the waters of Black river. A lot of land in the town of Camden. A library of a miscellaneous character, chiefly theological. *Twenty-seven Negroes, some of them very prime. Two mules, one horse, and an old wagon.*"[23]

It is only by gauging the tremendous meaning of the last sentence that we realize the depths from which such men as Douglass, Toussaint L'Ouverture, Langston, Bruce, Washington and Elliott have sprung—from the level of *mules, horses, sheep, and old wagons!*

When sold to Mr. Nealy, Isabella was nine years old. She could only speak Dutch, and the Nealys only English. For some time, owing to this unfortunate circumstance, there was dissatisfaction on the part of her owners and much suffering to herself. She suffered terribly with the cold and in the winter her feet were frozen for want of shoes. One Sunday morning she was sent to the barn, where her master awaited her, with a bundle of rods, prepared in the embers, and bound together with cords. He tied her hands together before her, and whipped her cruelly. He whipped her till the flesh was deeply lacerated and the blood streamed from her wounds. The scars from this whipping remained on her body when she was 108 years old. She said, "When I hear 'em tell of whipping women on the bare flesh, it makes my flesh crawl, and my very hair rise on my head! Oh! my God! what a way is this of treating human beings." In a short time Isabella was bought by a Mr. Scriver, a fisherman, who also kept a tavern. Here she led a wild, out-of-door life. She carried fish, hoed corn, dug roots and herbs for beer and did errands. But she felt that her morals suffered, if a slave may be allowed those attributes. Here she learned to curse, which was against the teachings of her poor slave-mother. Happily, she was sold in about a year, in 1810, to Mr. Dumont, with whom she remained till a short time before her emancipation by the State, in 1828. Subsequently Isabella was married to a fellow-slave, named Thomas, who had previously had two wives, both of whom had been taken from him and sold far away. This marriage was after the fashion of slavery, one of the slaves performing the ceremony for them. No true minister could perform a mock marriage, unrecognized by any civil law, and liable to be annulled at any moment, at the caprice of the master.

Southerners talk much of their horror of amalgamation. It is not a desire of the Negro race as a whole. Such marriages have occurred and probably will occur in isolated cases, but they will not become universal. But with all the protests that the South may utter against such marriages, we know that they calmly and quietly contemplate a state of licentiousness which their wicked laws have created, not only enforcing crime upon the Negro, but also upon

---

23. Pillsbury, *Acts of the Anti-Slavery Apostles*, 483.

the privileged portion of the South—the whites themselves, the same, very nearly, as the laws of slavery days.

When Isabella found herself the mother of five children, she rejoiced to think that she had increased her master's property. In her account of her life she says that she looked back upon that time with horror at her ignorance and degradation. After emancipation had been decreed by the State, some years before the time fixed for its consummation, Isabella's master told her that if she would do well, and be faithful, he would give her free papers one year before she was legally free by statue. On the arrival of July 4, 1827, the time specified for her to receive her papers, she urged her master to fulfill his promise; but he refused. Her very faithfulness had probably operated against her, and he found it hard to give up his faithful Bell. She resolved to escape. One morning, just before daybreak, she crept out the back entrance, her infant on one arm and her wardrobe on the other. Then she prayed for help and guidance and, rising, made her way to the house of one Levi Rowe, whose wife showed her a place where she might find help. She went to the house and was kindly received by Mr. and Mrs. Van Wagener, and after learning her story they employed her.

One very interesting point in the history of Sojourner Truth is the rescue of her son. Mr. Dumont sold her son, a child five years old, to a Dr. Gedney. This man disposed of him to his sister's husband, who took the child to Alabama.

This was a fraudulent and illegal transaction, the law expressly prohibiting the sale of any slave out of the State,—and all minors were to be free at twenty-one years of age; the child had been sold with the understanding that he was to be emancipated at the specified time.

When Isabella heard of the sale of her son she immediately started, alone and friendless, to expose the transaction and force them to return the boy.

Unencumbered by stockings, shoes, or any heavy article of clothing, she started on her journey to find the court. She first sought the help of the friendly Quakers by whom she was taken to Kingston to the Court House, where, after many experiences, she reached the Grand Jurors and made her complaint. A writ was given her to have served on the culprit, and she walked some eight or nine miles to serve it, only to find that Gedney had escaped across North River.

He consulted a lawyer, who advised him to go to Alabama and bring the boy back. Soon after this Gedney went to Kingston and gave bonds for his appearance at the next session of the court. When Isabella heard that she must wait six months longer before she could receive satisfaction, she was distracted with grief.

"What! wait another court! wait months? Why, long before that time, he can go clean off, and take my child with him—no one knows where."

A benevolent person directed her to see a Lawyer Demain. She went to him, told her story in her impassioned way and enlisted his sympathy. He told her to get him five dollars and he would get her son for her in twenty-four hours.

"Why," she replied, "I have no money and never had a dollar in my life!"

He replied, "If you will go to those Quakers who carried you to court, they will help you to five dollars, I have no doubt."

This she did; collected considerable more than the money specified, and carried the lawyer more money than he had asked for. When asked why she did not buy shoes and clothing with the over-plus, she replied: "Oh, I do not want money or clothes now, I only want my son; and if five dollars will get him, more will *surely* get him."

The next day her son was given her by the court. Upon examination the child's back from head to foot was found covered with indurations most frightful to behold. She exclaimed:

"Oh, Lord Jesus, look! see my poor child! Oh, Lord render unto them double for all this! Pete, how did you bear it?"

"Oh, this is nothing, mammy—if you should see Phillis, I guess you's *scare!* She had a little baby, and Fowler cut her till the milk as well as blood ran down *her* body. You would *scare* to see *Phillis*, mammy."[24]

Isabella went to reside in New York about a year after this, and became a member of the Methodist Church in John Street. From there she took her letter to the Zion's Church, in Church Street, composed entirely of colored people, where she remained until she went to reside with Mr. Pierson, after which she as drawn into the "kingdom" set up by the prophet Matthias: This was a religious delusion, the most extraordinary of modern times. A full description of this sect is found in a work published in 1835, entitled *Fanaticism; its Source and Influence; illustrated by the simple narrative of Isabella, in the case of Matthias, etc.*[25]

Many of the terrible happenings in the life of this woman, she would not publish, the most potent reason which she gave for withholding such tales being that, were she to tell all that transpired to her as a slave it would seem so unnatural that she would not be believed.[26] It is a curious study—the religious development of the slaves. How, when and where did they receive their ideas of religion and religious duties? The question of the Negro's claim to manhood was settled by God himself when He implanted the divine, unquenchable spark within the black man's lowly breast; and, tacitly, it has always been admitted by a slave-holding community when with gigantic inconsistency they expected willing and intelligent obedience from the slave because *he was a man*—at the same time by a soul-harrowing system crushed the last vestige of manhood in him.[27]

24. Gilbert, *Narrative of Sojourner Truth*, 44–54.

25. Gilbert Vale published *Fanaticism; Its Source and Influence, Illustrated by the Simple Narrative of Isabella, in the Case of Matthias, Mr. and Mrs. B. Folger, Mr. Pierson, Mr. Mills, Catherine, Isabella, &c. &c. A Reply to W. L. Stone, with the Descriptive Portraits of All the Parties, While at Sing-Sing and at Third Street* in 1835.

26. Gilbert, *Narrative of Sojourner Truth*, 81–82.

27. Ibid., 15.

We find then, in Isabella, a great phenomenon. Her religious experience is surprising. To note the workings of a powerful mind through the trials and mysteries of life until it is able to receive and assimilate that divine "light, that lighteth every man that cometh into the world," is astonishing.[28]

Isabella's mother talked to her of God. She knew that God was "a great man"; she believed that he noted all her actions in a big book. But she knew not that God knew a thought of hers until she uttered it aloud. Truth and error were strangely mixed in her mind. She prayed under the open canopy of heaven, and speaking in a loud tone commanded God to hear her.[29] In adversity she would promise God obedience, but when ease came her thoughts turned from Him whom she only knew as a help in trouble. If she had no trouble, she felt no need of prayer.[30]

But one day, she tells us, He revealed himself to her as He is—that he was *all over*, pervading the universe, and that there was no place where God was not. Her unfulfilled promises arose before her; she saw herself as she was.[31] She describes the character of Christ as revealed to her, most beautifully:

"I did not see him to be God; else how could he stand between me and God? I saw him as a friend, standing between me and God, through whom love flowed as from a fountain."

She believed Jesus to be the same spirit that was in our parents, Adam and Eve, in the beginning, when they came from the hand of their Creator. When they sinned through disobedience, this pure spirit forsook them, and fled to heaven; that there it remained, until it returned again in the person of Jesus; and that, *previous to a personal union with him, man is but a brute, possessing only the spirit of an animal.*[32]

Let us remember that these words came from a woman who could neither read nor write, and who knew religion only by revelation!

Isabella left New York after she lost her savings which she had placed in the bank. Mr. Pierson, before spoken of, induced her to invest her funds in a common fund which he established to be drawn from by all the faithful. At the breaking up of the "kingdom" she lost her little all.[33]

Disgusted with the wickedness just escaped, she left the city on June 1, 1843, telling no one where she was bound. Upon reaching Berlin, Conn., she sent her children word of her whereabouts.

In Hartford, she became acquainted with the Second Advent doctrines. Not believing in noise and confusion when worshipping God, she rebuked the confusion that prevailed at the meetings of this sect. She assured them:

28. Ibid., 59.
29. Ibid., 59–60.
30. Ibid., 63.
31. Ibid., 65.
32. Ibid., 69.
33. Ibid., 97.

"The Lord comes still and quiet. Here you are talking about being changed in the twinkling of an eye. If the Lord should come, he'd change you to *nothing!* for there is nothing in you." Ministers were taken aback at so unexpected an opposer, and they commenced a discussion with her, asking her questions, and quoting scripture to her; concluding finally that she knew much that man had never taught her.

From Hartford she journeyed to Enfield and to Springfield, lecturing, preaching and working by the day. At Springfield she was regarded as a wonder. Describing her, a friend says: "People listened eagerly to Sojourner and drank in all that she said. When she arose to speak in our assemblies, her commanding figure and dignified manner hushed triflers into silence, and her singular and sometimes uncouth modes of expression never provoked a laugh, but often whole audiences melted into tears by her touching stories. She had a remarkable gift in prayer and great talent in singing."[34]

She finally cast her lot with the Northampton Association. This community was composed of some of the choicest spirits of the age, where all was characterized by an equality of feeling, a liberty of thought and speech, and a largeness of soul, she could not have before met with, in any of her wanderings. In this brief article we cannot hope to give more than a skeleton sketch of the life and good works of Sojourner Truth. Through all the scenes of an eventful life one traces the workings of a great mind. She was endowed with fearlessness and child-like simplicity, *purity of character, unflinching adherence to principle,* and enthusiasm, attributes which under different circumstances have produced the most wonderful characters that the world has ever known.[35]

SOURCE "Famous Women of the Negro Race II: Sojourner Truth," *Colored American Magazine* 4.2 (Dec. 1901): 124–132.

34. Ibid., 109–114.
35. Ibid., 120–122.

III.

Harriet Tubman ("Moses")

*T*oo legibly are the characters written on our hearts and the world—"All seek their own!" Selfishness is the great law of our degenerated nature. When the love of God is unthroned in the heart, then self vaults into the vacant seat, and there, in some shape, continues to reign.

The life of Jesus stands out for our imitation as the one solitary exception in a world of selfishness. His entire life was one abnegation of self; a beautiful living picture of that "charity that seeketh not her own." During His forty days' temptation, He spread no table for himself, He reared no covering for his shelterless head. But how different is the spirit abroad today in this old sinful world! We go on day after day pouring out oblations to the idol of self; envying and grieving at the good of a neighbor; unable to brook the praise of a rival; establishing a reputation on the ruins of another, fostering jealousy, discontent, and every kindred passion. "But *we* have not so learned Christ!"

Not many of us are animated with the idea which seems to have possessed Harriet Tubman throughout her eventful life—to lay out time, talents, and opportunities for God's glory, and the good of our fellow-men, taking a generous interest in the welfare and pursuits of others, and engaging in schemes for the mitigation of human misery. This woman deserves all the good that can be said of her, all the publicity that can be given her past deeds, all the financial aid that a generous public can bestow.

In looking back over the strange Providences which have befallen us as a race, in the light of today's sociological changes, we can but feel that the same reasons exist at present, and quite as potent, for the preservation of all records pertaining to persons or events connected with our remarkable history, as existed before emancipation.

William Still says in his remarkable work:

These facts must never be lost sight of. The race must not forget the rock from which they were hewn, nor the pit from whence they were digged. Like other races, this newly emancipated people will need all the knowledge of their past condition which they can get.

The bondage and deliverance of the children of Israel will never be allowed to sink into oblivion while the world stands. Those scenes of suffering and martyrdom that millions of Christians were called upon to pass through in the days of the inquisition are still subjects of study, and have unabated interest for all enlightened minds.

The same is true of the history of this country. The struggles of the pioneer fathers are preserved, produced and re-produced, and cherished with undying interest by all Americans, and the day will not arrive while the Republic exists, when this history will not be found in every library.

The heroism of the fugitive slave encouraged the abolitionist fathers as nothing else did in the dark old days. Every step they took to rid themselves of their fetters gave unmistakable evidence that the race had no more eloquent advocates than its own self-emancipated champions.

We of today are as imperatively required *now* to furnish the same manly testimony in support of the ability of the race to *surmount the remaining obstacles* growing out of *oppression, ignorance* and *poverty*.

In the political struggle the hopes of the race have been sadly disappointed. From this direction no lasting advantage is likely to arise very soon. Well-conducted shops and stores; lands acquired and good farms managed in a manner to compete with other races; valuable books produced and published on important subjects, are some of the fruits which a race is expected to exhibit from newly gained privileges.

"How?" through extra endeavor and determination as shown in hundreds of cases of the struggles of such women and men as "Moses" to obtain freedom, education and property.[36]

In giving a sketch of the life of Harriet Tubman we find that this woman, though one of earth's lowliest ones has shown an amount of heroism in her character rarely possessed by those of any station of life. Her name deserves to be handed down to posterity side by side with those of Grace Darling, Joan of Arc and Florence Nightingale; for none one of them has shown more courage and power of endurance in facing danger and death to relieve human suffering than has this woman in her heroic and successful endeavors to reach and save all whom she might of her oppressed and suffering race, and pilot them from the land of bondage to the promised land of Liberty. She is still working for them although worn out by sufferings and fatigue, broken in health by the cruelties to which she has been subjected. "A few years more and there will be a gathering in the place where all wrongs are to be righted, and Justice will assert itself and perform its office. Then not a few of those who have esteemed themselves the wise and noble of this world, will take the lowest places while upon Harriet Tubman's head a kind hand will be placed, and in her ear a gentle voice will sound, saying: 'Friend! come up higher.' "[37]

Harriet Tubman known at various times and in various places by many different names, such as "Moses," in allusion to her being the leader of her people in their exodus from the land of bondage; the conductor of the

36. William Still, *The Underground Railroad: A Record of Facts, Authentic Narratives, Letters, Narrating the Hardships, Hair-Breadth Escapes and Death Struggles of the Slaves in their Efforts for Freedom* (1871; rev. ed., Philadelphia: People's Publishing Company, [1878]), 6.
37. Sarah H. Bradford, *Scenes in the Life of Harriet Tubman* (Auburn, N.Y.: W. J. Moses, 1869), 1–4.

Underground Railroad; and "Moll Pitcher," for the energy and daring by which she delivered fugitive slaves from the South, was called Araminta Ross when she was born in 1820, in Dorchester County, Eastern Shore, Maryland. Her parents were Benjamin Ross and Harriet Green, both slaves. Harriet had ten brothers and sisters all rescued by her before the war. She married John Tubman, a free colored man, in 1844. Harriet's master was a very cruel man, and he hired her out when six years of age to others as cruel and tyrannical as himself. Her experience with her first mistress is distressing and fills the heart with bitterness towards those who could so unsex themselves by descending to the level of brutes. After she entered her teens she worked as a field hand for many years, following the oxen, loading and handling wood and carrying heavy burdens, by which her muscle was developed so that her feats of strength have even called forth the wonder of strong men.[38]

Indeed, her plantation life was cruelly interesting all through. Her back and shoulders are marked by the biting lash, and bear witness to the inhumanity of the institution from which she fled. A cruel blow upon the head with a weight from the scales inflicted a lifetime injury which causes her to fall into a state of somnolency from which it is almost impossible to arouse her. Moses has no education, yet the most refined persons would listen for hours to her strange and eventful stories.

Her last master was Dr. Thompson who died in 1849. At his death the slaves were to be sold and Moses in dread of future, determined to leave for freedom. So one day she started out singing as she walked the country roads:

> When dat ole chariot comes,
>   I'm gwine to lebe you;
> I'm boun' for de promised land,
>   I'm gwine to lebe you.[39]

Which meant something more than a journey to Canaan. By night cunningly feeling her way, and finding out who were friends, until after a long and painful journey she found, in answer to careful inquiries, that she had at last crossed the imaginary line that separated her from liberty. This was in President Jas. K. Polk's administration.

"Soon as I foun' I had crossed de line," she said, "I looked at my hands to see if I was de same person. There was such a glow over everything; the sun came like glory through de trees and over the fields, an' I felt like I was in heaven."[40]

But this strange woman was lonely and unhappy when she thought of her relatives and friends languishing in slavery and groaning beneath the lash.

38. Ibid., 9–10.
39. Ibid., 17.
40. Ibid., 19.

She determined that they, too, should taste the sweets of liberty. She went to Philadelphia and worked in hotels and clubhouses, and Cape May. When she had made money enough to pay expenses, she made her way back, hid herself, and gave notice to those who were ready to strike for freedom. When her party was made up, she would start always on Saturday night, because advertisements could not be sent out on Sunday, which gave them one day in advance. When pursued, advertisements were posted everywhere. A reward of $40,000 was offered for the head of the woman who was constantly inducing slaves to flee from their masters. She travelled in cars when these posters were above her head, and she heard them read by those about her—being unable to read herself. But she went on trusting in the Lord. She said, "I started with this idea in my head, that there's two things I've got a right to, and these are Death or Liberty—one or tother I mean to have. No one will take me alive; I shall fight for my liberty, and when de time is come for me to go, de Lord will let them kill me." And with this faith she went back and forth nineteen times. Eleven times from Canada.[41]

Men from Canada who had made their escape years before, and whose families were still in bondage, sought Moses, and got her to bring their dear ones away. This woman—one of the most ordinary looking of her race; unlettered; no idea of geography! asleep half the time—would penetrate the interior slave States, hide in the woods during the day, feed on homely fare at night, bring off whole families of slaves, and pilot them to Canada, after running the gauntlet of the most difficult parts of the Southern country. No captures were ever made from Moses. The fugitives believed that she had supernatural powers, and indeed her spiritual development was wonderful. Her dreams, visions and impressions were credited by the most refined and educated whites. Her vision of John Brown, before she had met him, and her recognition of him and his sons from her dreams was enough to carry conviction to the most bigoted antagonist of supernatural phenomena. One man was asked: "Were you not afraid of being caught?"

"O, no," said he. "Moses is got de charm."

"What do you mean?"

"De white can't catch Moses, kase you see she's born wid de charm. De Lord has given Moses de power."[42]

She travelled on foot over mountains, through forests, across rivers, meeting perils by land, perils by water, perils from enemies, perils among false brethren. Sometimes her party would be foot-sore and bleeding, and declare they could not go on, they must stay where they were and die; others thought a voluntary return to slavery better than being overtaken and carried back, and would insist upon returning; then there was no remedy but force; the

41. Ibid., 20–21.
42. William Wells Brown, *The Rising Son; or, The Antecedents and Advancement of the Colored Race* (1874; rev. ed., Boston: A. G. Brown, 1876), 538.

revolver carried by this bold and intrepid pioneer would be pointed at their heads. "*Dead niggers tell no tales,*" said Harriet; "go on or die"; and so she compelled them to drag their weary limbs on their northward journey.[43]

At one time she left her party in the woods, and went to one of the stations of the Underground railroad, and got food for the famishing people. She dared not return until night for fear of being watched; after nightfall the sound of a hymn came to the ears of the concealed fugitives, and they knew that their deliverer was at hand:

> Hail, oh hail, ye happy spirits,
> Death no more shall make you fear:
> No grief, nor sorrow, pain nor ang (anguish),
> Shall no more distress you there.
>
> Dark and thorny is the desert,
> Through de pilgrim makes his ways,
> Yet beyon' dis vale of sorrow,
> Lies the fiel's of endless days.[44]

Said Harriet:

The firs' time I come by singing dis hymn, they don' come out to me till I listen if de coas' is clear; then when I go by an' sing it agin, they come out. But if I sing:

> Moses, go down in Egypt,
> Till ole Pharo' let me go;
> Hadn't been fo Adam's fall,
> Shouldn't hab to die at all.

Then they don' come out, fer dar's danger in the way.[45]

Harriet was one of the individual rescuers of Charles Nalle, at Troy, N.Y., April 1859. When he was brought before the commissioner, Harriet rushed in and running one of her arms around his mangled arm held on to him without losing her hold though the struggle to drag him to Judge Gould's office continued for hours. Moses fought like a man.

When the war broke out, Moses went into active service, and at once left for the South. Long before Butler's "contraband of war" doctrine was recog-

---

43. Bradford, *Scenes*, 24–25.
44. Ibid., 25–26.
45. Ibid., 26–27.

nized by the government, says Dr. Brown, Moses was hanging upon the skirts of the Union Army, and doing good service for her race that sought protection in the lines.[46] When the Negro put on the "blue," Moses was in her glory, and travelled from camp to camp, being always treated in the most respectful manner. The black men would have died for this woman.

Moses followed Sherman in his march "From Atlanta to the Sea," and witnessed the attack of Petersburg.[47] She nursed sick soldiers, and assisted Gen. Hunter when he sent an expedition up Combahee River with several gunboats.[48] She was sent into rebel lines as a spy, and brought back valuable information as to the position of armies and batteries. On her way home from these labors, while on a car passing from New Jersey, the conductor forced her out of the car with such violence that she was unable to work for a long time, and in fact has never fully recovered. Mr. Wendell Phillips sent her sixty dollars which kept her and her old father and mother from freezing and starving that winter.[49]

We append letters endorsing Harriet Tubman, written by men of note who were associated with her in her adventurous life. Sent to Mrs. Bradford who issued a pamphlet on Harriet Tubman's life.[50]

———

PETERBORO, JUNE 13, 1868.

My Dear Madam:—I am happy to learn that you are to speak to the public of Mrs. Harriet Tubman. Of the remarkable facts in her life I have no personal knowledge, but of the truth of them as she describes them I have no doubt. I have often listened to her, in her visits to my family, and I am confident that she has a rare discernment, and a deep and sublime philanthropy. With great respect, your friend,

GERRIT SMITH.[51]

46. Brown, *Rising Son*, 538. In 1861, Benjamin Franklin Butler (1818–1893), Union general in the Civil War, and later U.S. representative (Republican, 1867–1875, 1877–1879) and Massachusetts governor (Democrat, 1883–1884), declared that escaped former slaves were "contraband of war" and should not be returned to the South.

47. Brown, *Rising Son*, 538–539.

48. David Hunter (1802–1886), Union general in the Civil War, led the 1st South Carolina, an early African American regiment, in a campaign on the Combahee River in South Carolina.

49. Bradford, *Scenes*, 23–24.

50. Tubman's biographer Sarah H. Bradford (b. 1818), a New York abolitionist, wrote *Scenes in the Life of Harriet Tubman* (1869) and *Harriet: The Moses of Her People* (New York: Geo. R. Lockwood and Son, 1886). Textual evidence suggests that Hopkins primarily used the earlier *Scenes* as her main source.

51. Bradford, *Scenes*, 5.

JUNE 16, 1868.

My Dear Madam:—The last time I ever saw John Brown was under my roof, as he brought Harriet Tubman to me, saying: "Mr. Phillips, I bring you one of the bravest and best persons on this continent—General Tubman, as we call her."

He then went on to recount her labors and sacrifices in behalf of her race. After that Harriet spent some time in Boston, winning the confidence and admiration of all those who were working for freedom. With their aid she went to the South more than once, returning always with a squad of self-emancipated men, women and children, for whom her marvellous skill had opened a way of escape. After the war broke out, she was sent with endorsements from Governor Andrew and his friends to South Carolina, where in the service of the Union, she rendered most important and efficient aid to our army.

In my opinion there are few captains, perhaps few colonels, who have done more for the loyal cause since the war began, and few men who did more before that time for the colored people; than our fearless and most sagacious friend, Harriet.

FAITHFULLY YOURS,
WENDELL PHILLIPS.[52]

My Dear Madam:—Mr. Phillips has sent me your note asking for reminiscences of Harriet Tubman, and testimonials of her extraordinary story. I have never had reason to doubt the truth of what Harriet said in regard to her career. Her dreams, visions and warnings should not be omitted in any life of her, particularly those relating to John Brown. She was in his confidence in 1858–9, and he had a great regard for her which he often expressed to me. She aided him in his affairs, and expected to do so still further, when his career was closed by that wonderful campaign at Virginia.

She has often been in Concord, where she resided at the house of Emerson, Alcott, the Whitneys, the Brooks family, Mrs. Horace Mann, and other well-known people. They all admired and respected her, and nobody doubted the reality of her adventures.

In 1862 she went from Boston to Port Royal under the advice and management of Mr. Garrison, Gov. Andrew, Dr. Howe, and other leading people. Her career in South Carolina is well-known to some of our officers, and I think to Col. Higginson, now of Rhode Island, and Col. James Montgomery, of Kansas. I regard her as the *most extraordinary person of her race* I have ever seen. She is a Negro of almost pure blood, can neither read nor

52. Ibid., 5–6.

write, and has the characteristics of her race and condition. But she has done what can scarcely be credited on the best authority, and she has accomplished her purpose with a coolness, foresight and patience which in a *white man would have raised her to the highest* pitch of reputation. I am, dear madam, very truly your servant,

F. B. SANBORN.
SEC. MASS. BOARD OF STATE CHARITIES.[53]

———

WASHINGTON, JULY 25, 1868.
MAJ. GEN. HUNTER.

My Dear Sir: Harriet Tubman, a colored woman, has been nursing our soldiers during nearly all the war. She believes she has a claim for faithful services to the command in South Carolina with which you are connected, and she thinks that you would be disposed to see her claim justly settled. I have known her long, and a nobler spirit, and a truer, seldom dwells is the human form. I commend her to your kind and best attention.

WM. H. SEWARD.[54]

The government has never assisted Mrs. Tubman in any way. Are Republics ungrateful?

SOURCE "Famous Women of the Negro Race III: Harriet Tubman ('Moses')," *Colored American Magazine* 4.3 (Jan.–Feb. 1902): 210–223.

53. Ibid., 53–55.
54. Ibid., 65.

IV.

Some Literary Workers

*T*he great struggle of humanity which at present convulses the entire world, and of which race and color are but incidental factors, is a stupendous problem for scholars to solve as to its final issue.

This human striving for supremacy is the primary movement of the age in which we live. The observant eye can trace the impress of Divinity on sea and shore as He, in mighty majesty, protects the weak in the great battle that is now on between the Anglo-Saxon and the dark-skinned races of the earth. Nature is apt in devising compensations. The increasing gravity of our situation in relation to the body politic, and the introduction of new peoples who must live under the same ban of color that we are forced to endure, may operate to our advantage by bringing about desirable changes in the future of our race. The victory of England over the Boers would be the triumph of the black. The subjugation of Cuba, Porto Rico and the Philippines, the purchase of the Danish West Indies—all is but the death knell of prejudice, for the natural outcome of the close association that must follow the reception of these peoples within our Union, will be the downfall of cruel discrimination solely because of color. In this way malice defeats itself.

We maintain these sentiments in spite of the fact that hateful feelings against the Negro are brought into the North by the influence of the South, no stone being left unturned to foist upon the northern Negro the galling chains of the most bitter southern caste prejudice which is widening the circle of its operations day by day.

It was a criminal omission on the part of those statesmen, who, having the power vested in them to enact laws to protect an innocent, helpless people in the rights which the outcome of an arduous and bloody war had conferred upon them, yet shirked their responsibilities for a nauseous sentimentality, leaving to this generation a heritage of woe. They knew then as we do now, that "unsettled questions have no pity for the repose of nations," and like Banquo's ghost, they are unbidden guests at every feast and will not down.

Unsettled questions have brought us the happenings of the past few months—sociological whirlwinds—the martyrdom of President McKinley, the Washington episode at the dining table of the White House, the Tillman-McLaurin's incident in Congress and mob law triumphant in the appointment of Mr. Geo. R. Koester as collector of internal revenue for South Carolina.[55]

---

55. President William McKinley (1843–1901) was assassinated in September 1901. On October 16, 1901, his successor, Theodore Roosevelt, hosted Booker T. Washington for dinner at the White House. This

Agitation of the vexed question is condemned by a majority of the Caucasian race, and many leading men and women of color deprecate any harsh allusions in the meetings of clubs and societies, to the all important "race question." Yet, can we be silent? Some person says "Unpleasant contention is sure to follow any such allusion." No matter, let us do our duty and meet the issue boldly.

"Gag law" is nothing new; but it is unique to see its enforcement attempted by intelligence in the race. It was early adopted by Southern leaders way back in 1840, whereby all petitions on the subject of slavery were "tabled" without discussion, and free speech was abolished. History but repeats itself in 1902.

Said Mr. Phillips in 1860, on the platform of Music Hall, Boston:

Some of you may think that everybody talks now of slavery, free speech, and the Negro. That is true; and I am not certain that the longest liver of you all will ever see the day when it will not be so. The Negro for fifty or thirty years, has been the basis of our commerce, the root of our politics, the pivot of our pulpit, the inspiration of almost all that is destined to live in our literature. For a hundred years, at least, our history will probably be a record of the struggles of a proud and selfish race to do justice to one that circumstances have thrown into its power. The effects of slavery will not vanish in one generation, or even in two. It were a very slight evil, if they could be done away with more quickly.

It will probably be a long while, a very long while, before the needle of our politics will float free from this disturbance, before trade will cease to feel the shock of this agitation, before the pulpit can throw off vassalage to their prejudice and property, before letters take heart and dare to speak the truth.

A bitter prejudice must be soothed, a bloody code repealed, a huckstering constitution amended or made way with, social and industrial life re-arranged, and ministers allowed to take the Bible, instead of the Stock List, as the basis of their sermons.[56]

Were not his words prophetic? Are they not as true to-day as when he gave them life on that Sunday in December so many years ago?

When Mr. Phillips left Music Hall at the conclusion of the exercises, he was met by a mob on Winter street, with cries of "There he is!" "Crush him out!" "Down with the Abolitionist!" "Bite his head off!" "All up!" etc. They gave

episode, which came to symbolize Washington's power, brought the new president a maelstrom of criticism. John McLaurin (1860–1934) and Benjamin Tillman (1847–1918), South Carolina's two Democratic senators, had a fistfight on the U.S. Senate floor on February 22, 1902. Despite evidence of George R. Koester's involvement in an 1893 lynching in South Carolina, President Roosevelt appointed him to a government post in that state.

56. Wendell Phillips, "Mobs and Education" (1860), in *Speeches, Lectures, and Letters* (Boston: Lee and Shepard, 1872), 319–320.

vent to their impotent rage in yells and hisses, following him to the door of his house. Such is the tax that evil levies on virtue.

We know that it is not "popular" for a woman to speak or write in plain terms against political brutalities, that a woman should confine her efforts to woman's work in the home and church.

The colored woman holds a unique position in the economy of the world's advancement in 1902.

Beyond the common duties peculiar to woman's sphere, the colored woman must have an intimate knowledge of every question that agitates the councils of the world; she must understand the solution of problems that involve the alteration of the boundaries of countries, and which make and unmake governments.

A famous woman of the favored race has said that she did not wish her work to be judged with reference to her sex; that she feared that women workers were praised unduly. Yet it seems difficult to escape entirely from this evil. Women are so active in advancing the cause not only of women, but of men, and in fact of the entire human family. Women who have enjoyed the "higher education" with its broadening culture, esthetic influence and the pure desire inculcated to uplift humanity, are doing much for the masses among their own people.

Upon the Negro woman lies a great responsibility,—the broadening and deepening of her race, the teaching of youth to grasp present opportunities, and, greater than all, to help clear the moral atmosphere by inculcating a clearer appreciation of the Holy Word and its application to every day living. The Negro woman will learn—is learning—many things she has not been fully aware of concerning human nature in general, and philanthropic and political methods in particular. The more clearly she understands the governing principles of the government under which she lives and rears her children, the surer will be an honorable future for the whole race.

From the time that the first importation of Africans began to add comfort and wealth to the existence of the New World community, the Negro woman has been constantly proving the intellectual character of her race in unexpected directions; indeed, her success has been significant.

From the foregoing we conclude that it is the duty of the true race-woman to study and discuss all phases of the race question.

Emerson tells us that "the civility of no race is perfect whilst another race is degraded."[57] We love this country, we adore the form of government under

---

57. Ralph Waldo Emerson, *An Address Delivered in the Court-House in Concord, Massachusetts on 1st August, 1844, on the Anniversary of the Emancipation of the Negroes in the British West Indies* (Boston: J. Munroe, 1844), 32–33. Hopkins uses this quote in her essay on "The New York Subway" as well as on the title page and in the text of *Contending Forces*. See Pauline E. Hopkins, "The New York Subway," *Voice of the Negro* 1.12 (Dec. 1904): 612; and Pauline E. Hopkins, *Contending Forces: A Romance Illustrative of Negro Life North and South* (1900; repr., New York: Oxford University Press, 1988), [5], 20, 150.

which we live; we want to feel that it will exist through ages yet to come. We know that it cannot stand if the vile passions which are convulsing the people at the present time are allowed to continue. Let the women then, without adverse criticism, continue to help raise the race by every means in their power, and at the same time raise our common country from the mire of barbarism.

It was a curious phenomenon, in the midst of oppression and wrong, the discovery of so great a genius in the guise of a fragile child of a despised race.

The story of Phillis Wheatley's life is common history with all classes of people, yet, we love to rehearse it, renewing our courage, as it were, for the struggle of life, with live coals from the altar of her genius. To quote Carlyle, it was: "Like a little well in the rocky desert places, like a sudden splendor of heaven! People knew not what to make of it."[58]

She was brought from Africa to America in 1761, when between seven and eight years of age.

Mrs. John Wheatley went into the Boston slave market one day to purchase a girl for her own use. Mrs. Wheatley's heart was touched by a good looking child just imported from the African coast, and who appeared to be suffering from the effects of the sea-voyage and the rigorous climate. The lady bought the child and called her Phillis. Struck with her uncommon brightness of the intellect of her new purchase, the mistress taught the child to read and in about fifteen months after her arrival in this country little Phillis had attained the English language to such a degree that she could read the most difficult portions of the Scripture to the great astonishment of all who knew her.

At the age of twelve this intellectual prodigy could write letters and sustain a correspondence that would have been a credit to one twice her age, writing in 1765 a letter to Rev. Mr. Occom, the Indian minister while in England. In the family the little negress [sic] met with the kindest treatment, her genius demanding that she be treated as an equal and a companion. Indeed, she was an object of attraction, astonishment and attention with all refined and highly-cultured society at the home of the Wheatley's and abroad. Scholars, divines and literary characters vied with each other in supplying her with books and helping to develop her wonderful intellectual powers. She studied Latin and translated one of Ovid's tales which was published in America and England. In 1773 a small volume of her poems was published in London, dedicated to the Countess of Huntingdon.

At the age of twenty-one, Phillis was emancipated by her master, and on account of failing health took a sea-voyage to England. While there she was received with flattering attention in the first circles of society. In the midst of

---

58. Thomas Carlyle, "Lecture V (Tuesday, 19th May, 1840): The Hero as Man Of Letters," in *On Heroes, Hero-Worship, and the Heroic in History* (1840; Project Gutenberg, 1997), http://www.gutenberg.org/dirs/ etext97/heros10.txt.

her social and literary triumphs Mrs. Wheatley who was very ill, sent for her to return, and so strong was the love between mistress and maid that Phillis cheerfully gave up the affluence surrounding her to return to her benefactress.

Phillis married Dr. Peters, a man of her own race, described by some as having considerable talents, and by others as of a mean nature that envied the achievements of the cultured woman he had married. Be this as it may, she did not long survive, her health declined rapidly, and she died in 1780, at the age of twenty-six.

The style of her writings is pure; her verses full of beauty and sublimity; her language chaste and elegant. Could she have lived a few years longer she would have been renowned as a poet. Still she accomplished her destiny which was by the development of her genius to show to the world the injustice done her race.

Among the women of the race blessed by Divinity with an extraordinary portion of His pure spirit, it gives us pleasure to record the name of Mrs. Francis Grimké, formerly Miss Gertrude L. Fortune, of Philadelphia. In 1854 Miss Fortune entered the Higginson Grammar School at Salem, Mass., where she won the reputation of being an apt pupil. Entering the high school, she graduated from that institution with honor, having received a premium for "A Parting Hymn," sung at graduation. This composition gave evidence that Miss Fortune was a literary genius. She became a correspondent of the *National Anti-Slavery Standard,* and wrote a series of spicy letters that attracted attention from many white journals. Her poem, "The Angel's Visit," is not surpassed by anything in the English language.

Miss Fortune (Mrs. Grimké) stands between the Anglo-Saxon and the African, with fine features, well-developed forehead, and an intellectual countenance, her gifted mind is well stored with gleanings from the works of the best authors. For many years her writings were published in the *Atlantic Monthly,* during the time that she taught in the Southern States, where she was well known and highly appreciated.

Among the Reformers of the nineteenth century none stands more powerful than Mrs. Ida B. Wells-Barnett. Her story is romantic. Everybody has heard of this fearless woman. She stirred Europe with her eloquent appeals until Parliament and crowned heads delighted to honor her. The press of her own country, governors, senators, representatives, heard her with pleasure and profit. She is without doubt the first authority among Afro-Americans on lynching and mob violence.

Ida B. Wells was born in Holly Springs, Miss., and was left an orphan when a little girl of fourteen years. For six years she had attended Rusk University, the college founded by the Freedmen's Bureau, her tuition paid by her parents. Their death charged her with the support of six little brothers and sisters, a task which she bravely assumed.

At fourteen she was teaching a district school, studying herself, and attending the college when unemployed. In 1889 she went to Memphis, where she was first employed as a teacher, and then as a journalist, editing, and finally controlling the *Free Speech,* a paper published in the interests of the colored race. For three years she met with unbounded success. Miss Wells developed great talent as a public speaker, and was in great demand among her people. In 1892 the crisis came that materially changed the course of her life. The unprovoked and cruel murder of three innocent black men in a suburb of Memphis aroused the girl-editor. She knew the men personally, and the shock of their awful death gave her a fierce courage. She published the true story of the crime. The result we all know. Her office was raided by a mob, her presses destroyed, she was driven from Memphis on pain of death if she returned.

She found a refuge in New York, and from there, when her story became known, she went by invitation to England, where her extreme youth, her earnestness and simple eloquence, her magnetic personality opened a way for her everywhere. Columns of praise were lavished upon her, and upon her return to New York she received an ovation as the champion of her race and an acknowledged power upon the public platform.

Miss Wells married Lawyer Barnett, a prominent advocate of Chicago and a well-known editor and newspaper man.[59]

We append interesting testimonials of Mrs. Barnett's work abroad:

"Miss Ida B. Wells, an American colored lady from Tennessee, pleaded the cause of her race on Tuesday evening last, in the Friends' Meeting House, Glasgow, before a large audience. The graphic picture she gave of the persecution and brutal tyranny to which the colored people of the Southern States are subjected by the whites, was listened to with rapt attention. Nothing more harrowing has been for years related from a Glasgow platform than the narrative she gave of the cruelties and outrages perpetrated upon her people."— *The Scottish Pulpit.*

Those who heard Miss Wells may be interested in her labors in Great Britain. After lecturing successfully in Edinburgh and Glasgow, she passed on to the chief English provincial towns, and then to London. Special interest attaches to her last public appearance in London, which was at the World's Women's Temperance Union at St. James' Hall, Piccadilly. She was placed immediately on the left of Lady Henry Somerset, Miss Frances Willard being on the right. When Lady Somerset invited Miss Wells to speak on temperance subjects, Miss Wells replied that she had only one excuse for being before the British public, and that was to protest against "lynch law," and expressed her desire that the association that works for "God, home, and every land" would use its influence against

---

59. Wells married Ferdinand Lee Barnett in 1895.

this evil. Thereupon Lady Somerset introduced Miss Wells and allowed her to make this appeal.—*Aberdeen Evening Gazette*, June 28, 1893.

After hearing Miss Wells an Aberdeen journalist wrote:

That the habit of treating persons with Negro blood in their veins with social contempt, bringing against the race monstrous accusations without evidence, and carrying reckless vengeance the length of wrecking property and destroying human life by the process of lynching is a disgrace to America, is clear. The only wise and safe way to remove a foul blot from the scutcheon of the greatest republic on earth is for Americans, from the most prominent statesman to the meanest citizen, to give practical effect to their professed Christianity by a frank and honest recognition of the fact—which, indeed, ought to be their pride—that all citizens of that republic are on one and an equal footing in respect of social rights as well as the protection of the law; and that so long as the conditions of good citizenship are respected, neither race nor color can form any disqualification where true freedom reigns.

SOURCE "Famous Women of the Negro Race IV: Some Literary Workers," *Colored American Magazine* 4.4 (Mar. 1902): 276–280.

V.

Literary Workers *(Concluded)*

*I*n presenting to our readers a short sketch of the labors of Frances Ellen Watkins Harper we feel more than glad of an opportunity to add our mead of praise to the just encomiums of many other writers for the noble deeds of an eminent Christian woman. We need give but the simple facts of the many acts that composed her life work, but these speak in trumpet tones, louder than extravagant praise or fulsome compliment.

Mrs. Harper was born in Baltimore, Maryland, in 1825; freeborn she yet partook of the cup of woe under the oppressive influence which was heritage of bond and free alike under slave laws. She was an only child and was left an orphan at the tender age of three years. Happily an aunt took charge of her, and until she was thirteen she was sent to a private school for free colored children in Baltimore kept by an uncle, the Rev. William Watkins. At the conclusion of this period the little girl was deemed fit for labor and was put out to work in order that she might earn her own living. She endured many trials, but in the midst of the most trying ordeals preserved her desire for knowledge. She posed a remarkable talent for composition, and when but fourteen wrote an article which attracted the attention of the lady for whom she was working. To the honor of this woman be it said that she appreciated the girl's extraordinary talent, and while she was zealously taught sewing, housework and the care of children, books were furnished her and many leisure hours were permitted her in which she was able to indulge her longing for intellectual food.

At eighteen the young girl published her first volume, called "Forest Leaves."[60] Some of her productions were also published in the newspapers, attracting much attention.

In 1851 she left Baltimore and resided a short time in Ohio, where she was engaged in teaching. Becoming dissatisfied with her surroundings, she removed to Little York, Penn., and engaged in teaching again. While there she saw much of the underground railroad and her mind became imbued with the desire to help her people in some way. About this time Maryland enacted a law forbidding free people of color from the North from coming into the State on pain of being imprisoned and sold into slavery. A free man violated this law and was sold to Georgia; he escaped, was discovered and remanded to slavery.

---

60. Although biographies of Harper mention *Forest Leaves*, according to Frances Smith Foster, there are no known extant copies. See Frances Smith Foster, ed., *A Brighter Coming Day* (New York: Feminist Press, 1990), 8.

He died soon after from the effects of exposure and suffering. In a letter to a friend, referring to this outrage, Mrs. Harper wrote: "Upon that grave I pledged myself to the Anti-Slavery cause." In another letter she wrote: "It may be that God himself has written upon both my heart and brain a commission to use time, talent and energy in the cause of freedom."[61] In this faith she began the study of Anti-Slavery methods and documents, finally visiting Boston, where she was received with great kindness by the Anti-Slavery people. From there she proceeded to New Bedford, where she addressed a public meeting on the "Education and Elevation of the Colored Race." The following month she was engaged by the State Anti-Slavery Society of Maine, with what success is shown from one of her letters:

BUCKSPORT CENTRE,
SEPT. 28, 1854.

The agent of the State Anti-Slavery Society travels with me, and she is a pleasant, sweet lady. I do like her so. We eat together, sleep together. (She is a white woman.) In fact, I have not been in one colored person's house since I left Massachusetts; but I have a pleasant time. My life reminds me of a beautiful dream. What a difference between this and York! I have lectured three times this week. I have met with some of the kindest treatment I have ever received.[62]

Her ability and labors were everywhere appreciated, and her meetings largely attended. She breakfasted with the Governor of Maine.

For a year and a half she continued speaking in the Eastern States with marked success; the papers commending her efforts highly. The following extract is from the *Portland Daily Press* respecting a lecture delivered after the war:

"She spoke for nearly an hour and a half, her subject being 'The Mission of the War, and the Demands of the Colored Race in the Work of Reconstruction.' Mrs. Harper has a splendid articulation, uses chaste, pure language, has a pleasant voice, and allows no one to tire of hearing her. We shall attempt no abstract of her address; none that we could make would do her justice. It was one of which any lecturer might feel proud, and her reception by a Portland audience was all that could be desired. We have seen no praises of her that were overdrawn. We have heard Miss Dickinson, and do not hesitate to award the palm to her darker colored sister."[63]

In 1856, desiring to see the fugitives in Canada, she visited the Upper Province. While in Toronto she lectured, where she was well received and lis-

61. Still, *Underground Railroad,* 758.
62. Ibid., 758–759.
63. Ibid., 760.

tened to with great interest. We give an extract from a letter unfolding her mind and showing her impressions of the land where her race found a refuge:

> Well, I have gazed for the first time upon Free Land, and, would you believe it, tears sprang to my eyes, and I wept. Oh, it was a glorious sight to gaze for the first time on a land where a poor slave flying from our glorious land of liberty would in a moment find his fetters broken, his shackles loosed, and whatever he was in the land of Washington, beneath the shadow of Bunker Hill Monument or even Plymouth Rock, "here he becomes a man and a brother." I have gazed on Harper's Ferry, or rather the rock at the Ferry; I have seen it towering up in simple grandeur, with the gentle Potomac gliding peacefully at its feet, and felt that it was God's masonry, and my soul had expanded in gazing on its sublimity. I have seen the ocean singing its wild chorus of sounding waves, and ecstacy has thrilled upon the living chords of my heart. I have since then seen the rainbow crowned Niagara chanting the choral hymn of Omnipotence, girdled with grandeur and robed with glory; but none of these things have melted me as the first sight of Free Land. Towering mountains lifting their hoary summits to catch the first faint flush of day when the sunbeams kiss the shadows from morning's drowsy face may expand and exalt your soul. The first view of the ocean may fill you with strange delight. Niagara—the great, the glorious Niagara—may hush your spirit with its ceaseless thunder; it may charm you with its robe of crested spray and rainbow crown; but the Land of Freedom was a lesson of deeper significance than foaming waves or towering mounts.[64]

Mrs. Harper was not contented to make speeches and receive plaudits, but was ready to do the rough work, and gave freely of all the moneys that her literary labors brought her. Indeed, it was often found necessary to restrain her open hand and to counsel her to be more careful of her hard-earned income.

When the John Brown episode was agitating the nation, no one was more deeply affected than Mrs. Harper. To John Brown's wife she sent a letter saying: "May God, our God, sustain you in the hour of trial. If there is one thing on earth I can do for you or yours, let me be apprized. I am at your service."[65]

Not forgetting Brown's comrades, then in prison under sentence of death, true to the impulses of her generous heart, she wrote to their relations offering financial aid—sending clothing and money. "Spare no expense," she says, "to make their last hours as bright as possible. Now, my friend, fulfil this to the letter. Oh, is it not a privilege, if you are sisterless and lonely, to be a sister to the human race and to place your heart where it may throb close to

64. Ibid., 760–761.
65. Ibid., 762.

down-trodden humanity?"[66] In the fall of 1860, in Cincinnati, O., Mrs. Harper married Fenton Harper, a widower. She then retired to a small farm bought from the accumulated sales of her books, etc., and for a time was absorbed by the cares of married life. Mr. Harper died May 23, 1864.

After this event Mrs. Harper again appeared as an advocate for her race. She had battled for freedom under slavery and through the war. She now began laboring as earnestly for equality before the law—education, and a higher manhood, especially in the South.

She traveled for several years, extensively through Southern cities, visiting the plantations and lowly cabin homes, addressing schools, churches, meetings in Court Houses and Legislative Halls, under most trying conditions.

Her private lectures to freedwomen are particularly worthy of notice. Desiring to speak to women, along the objects of wrong and abuse under slavery, and whom emancipation found in deepest ignorance, Mrs. Harper made it her business to talk to them of their morals and general improvement, giving them the wisest counsel in her possession. For all this work she made no charge, working and preaching as did the Master—for the love of humanity.

After her labors in the South ceased, Mrs. Harper returned to Philadelphia and began active work in the Sabbath schools. Her work in the temperance field must also be noticed.

Mrs. Harper has always read the best magazines and ablest weeklies published; she is familiar with the best authors, including De Tocqueville, Mill, Ruskin, Buckle, Guizot, etc.[67]

Before the learned and unlearned Mrs. Harper has spoken in behalf of her race; during seventeen years of public speaking she has never once been other than successful in delivering thousands of speeches. By personal effort alone she has removed mountains of prejudice. At least we may be allowed to hope that the rising generation will be encouraged by her example to renewed courage in surmounting prejudice and racial difficulties. Fifty thousand copies of her four books have been sold. They have been used to entertain and delight hundreds of audiences.

Grace Greenwood, in noticing a course of lectures in which Mrs. Harper spoke, pays her this tribute:

> Next on the course was Mrs. Harper, a colored woman; about as colored as some of the Cuban belles I have met at Saratoga. She has a noble head,

---

66. Ibid., 763.

67. Still, *Underground Railroad*, 778. Still lists writers Alexis de Tocqueville (1805–1859), French politician and author of *Democracy in America* (1835); John Stuart Mill (1806–1873), Scottish philosopher, economist, and author of many books, including *A System of Logic* (1843), *On Liberty* (1859), *The Subjection of Women* (1869); John Ruskin (1819–1900), British art historian and author; Henry Thomas Buckle (1821–1862), British historian and author of *History of Civilization in England* (1857, 1861); and François Pierre Guillaume Guizot (1787–1874), French historian, educator, and politician.

this bronze muse; a strong face, with a shadowed glow upon it, indicative of thoughtful fervor, and of a nature most femininely sensitive, but not in the least morbid. Her form is delicate, her hands daintily small. She stands quietly beside her desk, and speaks without notes, with gestures few and fitting. Her manner is marked by dignity and composure. She is never assuming, never theatrical. Every glance of her sad eyes was a mournful remonstrance against injustice and wrong. Feeling in her soul, as she must have felt it, the chilling weight of caste, she seemed to say:

> I lift my heart up solemnly,
> As once Electra her sepulchral urn.[68]

As I listened to her there swept over me a chill wave of horror, the realization that this noble woman, had she not been rescued from her mother's condition, might have been sold on the auction block to the highest bidder—her intellect, fancy, eloquence, the flashing wit that might make the delight of a Parisian salon, and her pure, Christian character all thrown in—the recollection that women like her could be dragged out of public conveyances in our own city, so frowned out of fashionable churches by Anglo-Saxon saints.[69]

Mrs. Harper is still living in Philadelphia; she is eighty odd years old, and is lovingly spoken of and known to her friends and acquaintances as "Mother Harper."

We append her poem published in 1871, "Words for the Hour," because it fits the times and our present needs:

> Men of the North! it is no time
>   To quit the battle-field;
> When danger fronts your rear and van
>   It is no time to yield.
>
> No time to bend the battle's crest
>   Before the wily foe,
> And, ostrich-like, to hide your heads
>   From the impending blow.
>
> The minions of a baffled wrong
>   Are marshalling their clan;
> Rise up! rise up enchanted North!
>   And strike for God and man.

---

68. Elizabeth Barrett Browning, *Sonnets from the Portuguese* 5 (1845–1846).
69. Still, *Underground Railroad*, 779–780.

This is no time for careless ease;
    No time for idle sleep;
Go light the fires in every camp,
    And solemn sentries keep.

The foe you foiled upon the field
    Has only changed his base;
New dangers crowd around you
    And stare you in the face.

O Northern men! within your hands
    Is held no common trust;
Secure the victories won by blood
    When treason bit the dust.

'Tis yours to banish from the land
    Oppression's iron rule;
And o'er the ruined auction block
    Erect the common school.

To wipe from labor's branded brow
    The curse that shamed the land,
And teach the Freedman how to wield
    The ballot in his hand.

This is the nation's golden hour,
    Nerve every heart and hand,
To build on Justice as a rock,
    The future of the land.

True to your trust, oh, never yield
    One citadel of right!
With Truth and Justice clasping hands
    Ye yet shall win the fight![70]

Among the present generation of famous women of the colored race Mrs. Mary Church Terrell holds a prominent place. Possessed of youth, education, ability and great personal charms, the future promises much to the race who are anxiously watching her progress.

70. Foster notes that "Words for the Hour" was published "in *Poems* (1871), but was obviously written during the Civil War." See Foster, *A Brighter Coming Day*, 185n.

In the fall of 1891 society was electrified by a notable event—the marriage of Mr. Robert H. Terrell (now Judge Terrell) of Washington, D.C., to Miss Mary Eliza Church, only daughter of Mr. R. R. Church of Memphis, Tenn.

Judge Terrell was then popularly known in Boston as "our Bob." He had endeared himself by his genial, unassuming manners during his stay at Harvard College, to all our citizens, and New England people felt that they had a personal interest in his welfare along with the Washingtonians. Of course the news of his marriage created much comment.

A brief account of that wedding may interest the feminine portion of our readers.

The ceremony was performed in the parlors of Mr. Church's residence, on Lunderdale street. Rev. William Klinedean of St. Mary's Cathedral officiated. The bride wore a costume of white French faille and orange blossoms and lace bridal veil. There were no bridesmaids. Nannette, the four-year-old sister of the bride, handed the wedding ring to the priest on a silver dish.

Among the guests were Hon. Blanche K. Bruce, Hon. T. F. Cassels, Prof. B. K. Sampson, ex-Gov. P.B.S. Pinchback of Louisiana, Hon. J. R. Lynch, U. A. Ridley of Boston, and many others. Costly presents testified to the esteem and good wishes of friends all over the country.

Mr. and Mrs. Terrell visited Philadelphia, New York and Boston before going to Washington, their future home. The arrival of the young couple in Boston was attended with many festivities. They reached Auburndale on Sunday and received old friends all day. Receptions were tendered them by Mr. and Mrs. Joseph Lee, Mr. and Mrs. J. H. Lewis, Mr. and Mrs. U. A. Ridley and many others. Mrs. Terrell was graduated from Oberlin College and enjoyed the rare privilege of a supplementary course in music, art and science in the conservatories of Paris, Berlin, Lausanne and Florence.

Mrs. Terrell had the honor of serving as President of the National Association of Colored Women's Clubs for two terms. So highly is she thought of as a public speaker on race questions and women's work that at a recent meeting of the National Woman's Suffrage Association, at the First Presbyterian Church, Washington, Mrs. Terrell had the distinction of representing the Equal Suffrage Association of Washington (white), composed of sub-organizations of noted membership. Mrs. Terrell was chosen on the first ballot. Mrs. Terrell was also enrolled as a life member of the National American Woman's Suffrage Association upon the motion of Mrs. E. A. Russell, a wealthy white lady of Minneapolis, Minn. The fee of fifty dollars was paid by Mrs. Russell.

Surely there is a silver lining to the sable cloud that envelops us as a race when we know of such generous acts being done to one of our own people.

Recently Mrs. Terrell has made a highly successful tour of several large New England cities. She was everywhere warmly received, addressing a brilliant audience Sunday afternoon, February 2, in Court Square Theatre, Springfield, Mass., under the auspices of the Y.M.C.A (white). Her subject was "The Bright Side of a Dark Subject," a happy presentation of the much-discussed race question. Her effort was spoken of by the daily press as the finest heard in that section for years.

Mrs. Terrell was presented to Prince Henry at the Waldorf-Astoria, and speaks warmly of the kindness shown her by the royal visitor and his guests.

No record of the fruitful work of colored women would be complete without the name of Mary Shadd Cary.[71]

She was a native of Delaware and resided for years in Canada. Tall and slim, with a fine head, good features, intellectual countenance, bright eyes, she held a foremost place among the brave-hearted, daring women of the race who stood shoulder to shoulder with the men in the times, not so long ago, that tried men's souls.

Mrs. Cary received a better education than usually fell to colored women, even though free, and this privilege she improved. She early took an interest in all measures tending to elevate the race, and at various times filled the positions of school teacher, school superintendent, publisher, editor, lecturer, etc. She was a brilliant speaker, ready and witty in debate. Mrs. Cary had a strong determined will and could not be checked in doing what she conceived to be her duty. When the government determined to put colored men in the field to aid in suppressing the Rebellion, this woman raised recruits in the West and brought them to Boston with as much skill and order as any recruiting officer under the government. Her men were considered the best lot brought to headquarters.

Few persons did more for the moral, social and political elevation of the Negro than Mrs. Cary.

In the lives of these women are seen signs of progress. Some of us tremble for the future; God knows it is dark enough at present. But brightness is all about us. There are silver linings to the sable clouds. Dissatisfaction and restlessness, even cruel wrong, are but hastening on the day of jubilee.

Thomas Jefferson said: "It is unfortunate that the efforts of mankind to recover the freedom of which they have been deprived should be accompanied with violence, with errors, and even with crime. But while we weep over the means, we must pray for the end."[72]

Why is the present bright? Because, for the first time, we stand face to face, as a race, with life as it is. Because we are at the parting of the ways and must choose true morality, true spirituality and the firm basis of all prosperity in races or nations—honest toil in field and shop, doing away with all superficial

---

71. Following William Wells Brown, Hopkins misspells Cary as "Carey," which I have corrected. See Brown, *Rising Son*, 539.

72. Thomas Jefferson to Francois D'Ivernois (1795), in *The Writings of Thomas Jefferson*, edited by Paul Leicester Ford (New York: G. P. Putnam, 1892–99), 7:5.

assumption in education and business. Under the healthful regime that wrong and outrage have imposed upon us, we can see the rise of a sturdy, determined people; a true and ennobling church composed of men and women truly spiritualized, and a ministry fit to lead a people. All this the race that builds well on the solid rock of common sense, conscience and loyalty to man and God, will demand from its leaders and will obtain.

> One adequate support
> For the calamities of mortal life
> Exists; one only,—an assured belief
> That the procession of our fate, howe'er
> Sad or disturbed, is ordered by a Being
> Of infinite benevolence and power,
> Whose everlasting purpose embrace
> All accidents, converting them to good.[73]

SOURCE "Famous Women of the Negro Race V: Literary Workers (Concluded)," *Colored American Magazine* 4.5 (Apr. 1902): 366–371.

73. William Wordsworth, "The Excursion. Book Fourth: Despondency Corrected" (1814).

VI.

Educators

*B*y the toleration of slavery, the great American government lowered its high standard and sullied its fair fame among other nations. Though slaves were introduced by the fathers across the seas, this was not accepted as an apology for crimes worse than murder. Great minds of every clime condemned American slavery. It was felt that no possible excuse could be offered for the crime of chattel bondage being fostered by a government so proudly heralding its championship of human liberty and equality.

Slavery was the sum of all villainies, and the slave-holder the greatest of villains.

It may be truly said that through the intellect speaks the soul, proving man's kinship with God and his heirship to immortality. Nature gives to the immature mind and unseeing eye matter already formed and boundaries set which are accepted blindly until the intellect, aroused by cultivation, penetrates the form and passes the boundaries seeking the First Principle of these things. Before the resistless restlessness of this cultured intellect, the intricate laws of Nature become but accessories to aid man in his search for the how and why of his own existence and of the entire universe. By it he adds fullness and richness to life; and if he pursue the development of the mind along the lines which bring nearness to Divinity, then he soars above the sordidness of earth and exemplifies in body and mind those characteristics resembling our Creator which we are taught should be the end of every well-directed life. All this a state of servitude denies to man.

For the elevation of humanity, and that man may begin here that primary development of the soul to be continued beyond the grave, let us hope, the common school was founded. In ancient times, Aristotle held and taught that "the most effective way of preserving a State, is to bring up the citizens in the spirit of the Government; to fashion, and as it were, cast them in the mould of the Constitution." Indeed, all thinkers agree that principles of right, equity, and justice must underlie all ideas of progressive civilization; and that a true conception of individual and mutual rights of property, contract, and government can never be successfully propagated except through the medium of the public school.

The slave-holder of the South early saw and appreciated the power of the God-given maxim "Mind is the glory of man"; he knew the power of a general diffusion of knowledge by the common school. What would become of this institution if the manhood of the Negro were not denied? He had read, too, the Declaration of Independence: "All men are created equal." So, to logically follow the Declaration it was necessary to prove the Negro a brute, that it might not be said that the government was based or the social, educational, moral and religious extinction of the rights of millions of immortal beings.

With the subtleness of Satan they proclaimed the inferiority of the Negro intellect, and to prove their reasoning correct began to bring about the state they desired by special enactment of laws which should sufficiently degrade the helpless beings in their control. The mind befogged and mentality contracted was more effectual than manacles and scourges in giving safety to the "peculiar institution," and would furnish ample excuse for all atrocities.

To the Negro then, bond or free, all school privileges were denied. At the opening of the war between the States, Mr. Phillips agitated disunion as the only road to abolition. To him, the Constitution that in a measure protected, even partially, the master who held property in human beings, was but a "covenant with death and an agreement with hell," and, as such, the constitution became odious in his eyes.[74] When, however, the first gun was fired at Fort Sumter, he changed his condemnation of the Union to support of it, and accepted war as a means to the end he had in view. In 1863–64, he advocated the arming, educating and enfranchising the freedman. Then came into life the colored school-mistress, and of her heroic efforts to lighten the intellectual darkness which enveloped the ex-slave, no eulogy that we can write would half tell the story of her influence upon her race in building character, inculcating great principles, patiently toiling amidst the greatest privations far from home and pleasant surroundings. The colored teacher grasped the situation in its entirety,—that education is the only interest worthy the deep, controlling anxiety of the thoughtful man. The struggle that these women made for an independent, self-respecting manhood for their race was against desperate odds.

The ex-slave was totally unfit to cope with life's emergencies. The first necessity of human endeavor—a true home—simply did not exist. There was no room in that desert of mental blackness for the practice of even the common arts of life.

To these people, erstwhile counted as the beasts of the field, the colored teacher gave an awakened intelligence with which to secure their further education along industrial lines and the art of right living; fostered a delight in duty which gave them the habit of sustained endeavor; stability of character; warmth of heart to keep them true to family and social pieties; a sense of obligation which made them good citizens; an awakening to joy in their birthright of universal liberty. It was providential that previous to the war, private schools were established in all the large Northern cities; and under the most stringent laws in slaveholding States, the ambitious Negro would somehow contrive to learn to read and write; consequently, when the call came for colored teachers many were found sufficiently well-equipped. It is instructive as well as interesting to study the laws affecting the education of the Negro as

74. Phillips, "Harper's Ferry" (1859), in *Speeches*, 282. Also see Isaiah 28:18.

applied in each State, and how bravely the struggle for learning was waged in the very teeth of oppression.

In Alabama, 1832: "Any person or persons who shall attempt to teach any free person of color or slave to spell, read, or write, shall upon conviction thereof be fined a sum not less than $250, nor more than $500."

In Arkansas instruction was practically denied.

Connecticut's history tells a sad tale of New England prejudice against the Negro. Outrage was sanctioned in that State, sanctified and supported by laymen and churchmen of great but warped intellectuality. What wonder that slavery with all its attendant horrors continued so long to curse the land!

The well-known devotion of New England to popular education encouraged a hope that a collegiate school on the manual-labor plan might be established in New Haven, but the cruel prejudice of Connecticut people defeated the plan September 8, 1831, at a public meeting, it was resolved by the mayor, common council, and legal voters to resist the establishment of such a school by every legal means.

Miss Prudence Crandall, a member of the Society of Friends, established a school for young ladies in Canterbury, Conn., in the autumn of 1832. A few months after her school opened, she admitted Sarah Harris, a colored girl, a member of the village church. This young woman attended the district school and desired to become better educated in order to teach among the children of her race. Although a classmate of some of Miss Crandall's pupils, objections were immediately raised to her remaining in the school.

All Miss Crandall's property was invested in the building, and the alternative of dismissing the colored girl or losing her white pupils was a bitter trial, but she met the issue grandly, rising above all personal interest in devotion to principle.

Having determined upon her course, she advertised at the beginning of her next term, her school would be opened to young ladies and misses of color, and others who might wish to attend. The people of Canterbury, greatly enraged, called a town meeting to abate the threatened "nuisance." Notwithstanding all opposition the school opened with fifteen or twenty pupils, but they were insulted upon the streets, the stores closed against them and her, their well filled with filth and the house assailed. The Legislature passed an act making the establishment of schools for colored youth illegal, and this act was received by the citizens of Canterbury with firing of cannon, ringing of bells, and demonstration of great rejoicing. Physicians refused to attend the sick of her family. The Trustees forbade her to come with them into the house of God. Miss Crandall was finally arrested for the crime of teaching colored girls, but in July, 1834, after many trials, the case was quashed, the court declaring it "unnecessary to come to any decision on the question as to the constitutionality of the law."

Soon after this an attempt was made to burn Miss Crandall's house. In spite of all difficulties, however, she continued to struggle on in her work of benevolence. But her enemies were determined and implacable, and on September 9, 1834, assaulted her house with clubs, rendering it untenantable, and then acting upon the advice of friends, the project was abandoned.

How great must have been the degradation of New England when upon this delicate, lovely woman the torture was inflicted of social ostracism, insult, exclusion from God's house, a criminal trial, and confinement in a murderer's cell,—all inflicted by the church, the county, the State!

Delaware taxed free colored persons for the fund to educate white children, but in 1840 the Society of Friends formed the African School Association, at Wilmington, and established two schools for boys and girls of color.

In the District of Columbia prejudice was rampant, and the laws very stringent against the education of Negroes, for slaves formed a large part of the population of the capital. But the colored people of the District were eminently progressive; they determined to have schools and to educate their children, and in the face of persecution that might well have daunted the most daring, instituted private schools where the children were taught the rudiments of learning. Among the many energetic women who opened these schools we mention Mrs. Anne Maria Hall, Anne Eliza Cook, Nannie Waugh, Louisa Parke Costin, Martha Costin, Martha Becraft, and the members of the Wormley family.

One of the most successful schools was operated by Miss Myrtilla Miner, for four years. She received applications from more pupils than she could admit. Her work was done in a quiet, unostentatious manner, but she possessed a rare union of qualifications,—good sense, tact, industry, energy—all of which wait upon successful ventures. Her school attracted the attention of philanthropists everywhere and finally led to the establishment of the Normal School for Colored Female Teachers under the care of the "Washington Association for the Education of Free Colored Youth." We append an extract from the appeal for aid which Miss Miner sent out to the friends of the oppressed.

While good men send forth shiploads of bread to feed the famishing of other lands, and the country sends free equipments of ships, money and men to bear home the oppressed of other nations; why not remember the suffering at home, who suffer for want of soul-food; for enlightenment of mind, such as a Christian nation should be careful to bestow.

Shall the colored people of Washington be allowed the instruction necessary to enlighten their minds, awaken their consciences, and purify their lives? We fear some will answer "No," but there are others who will say "Yes," and to these we earnestly look for aid.

We would at this time considerately inquire, can we be sustained in our own efforts to perfect an Institution of learning here, adequate to the wants of the people, worthy the spirit of the age, and embodying those religious principles and moral teachings which, by their fruits shall be found to purify the heart, rendering it "first pure, then peaceable"?

We earnestly urge this appeal. We entreat all ministers of Christ to care for these lost sheep; we entreat the women of our country to aid in rescuing their sex from the extremity of ignorance, dishonor and suffering; we entreat the happy mothers of our land to pity and relieve the sorrows of mothers compelled to see their children growing up in ignorance and degradation.[75]

In Florida and Georgia white children alone were educated. Georgia was very strict in establishing a penal code in 1833, against persons employing any slave or free person of color to set type or perform any other labor about a printing office, requiring knowledge of reading, writing, etc.

The laws of Illinois and Indiana were cruel in relation to the education of Negroes; a free mission institute at Quincy, Ill., was mobbed because a few colored persons were admitted to the classes.

In Kentucky and Louisiana the laws provided imprisonment for all persons teaching Negroes. The close of the war found the ex-slaves of New Orleans in a lamentable condition, and among those who were moved to tender their services to ameliorate this situation the name of Mrs. Louisa De Mortie ranks deservedly high.

She came to Boston in 1853, we believe, from Norfolk, Va., where she was born free. In 1862 she began as a public reader in Boston, where her rare ability gained her many admirers and friends among leading men and women of the country, and a successful public career seemed to be before her.

About this time hearing of the distress amongst the colored children of New Orleans, left orphans by the war, she resolved to go there and devote her life to their welfare. While there the yellow fever broke out, and although urged by relatives and friends to return to the North until it had abated somewhat, she refused to desert her post of duty among the helpless little ones.

In 1867 Mrs. De Mortie succeeded in raising enough money to erect a building for an orphans' home; but her useful career was cut short at last by yellow fever, and she died October 10, 1867, in her thirty-fourth year.

The news of her death created profound regret among all classes at the North where her name was a household word, and the newspapers of New Orleans spoke of her in the most eulogistic terms.

Mrs. De Mortie was a remarkably brilliant and gifted woman. Richly endowed by nature with the qualities that please and fascinate, it may be said with truth that she was one of the most beautiful women of her day.[76]

Negro children were excluded from the benefits of school training in Maryland, but God opened a way.

St. Frances Academy for colored girls was founded in connection with the Oblate Sisters of Providence Convent, in Baltimore, June 5, 1829, receiving the sanction of the Holy See, October 2, 1831. The convent originated with

75. Myrtilla Miner, *The School for Colored Girls, Washington, D.C.* (1854; repr., New York: Arno Press, 1969), 5–8.
76. Brown, *Rising Son*, 496–497.

the French Fathers, who came to Baltimore as refugees fleeing from the revolution in San Domingo. The colored women who formed the original society which founded the convent and seminary, were from San Domingo, though some of them had been educated in France.

The Sisters of Providence renounce the world to consecrate themselves to the Christian education of colored girls. This school under their control has developed in importance until the good it has accomplished can hardly be estimated. Teaching as the Sisters do the solid principles of domestic virtues and pure religion, a legacy is passed on of inestimable value to the unborn thousands yet to come.

Miss Fanny M. Jackson (wife of Bishop Levi B. Coppin) was born in Washington, D.C., about 1837, and was left an orphan at an early age. She was brought up by her aunt, Mrs. Sarah Clark, but the opportunities for acquiring education were limited in the District, and she went to New Bedford with her aunt Mrs. Orr. When Mrs. Orr removed to Newport, R.I., Miss Jackson took up her residence with the family of Mayor Caldwell. At this time Miss Jackson had begun to give her friends glimpses of her rare gifts of mind which have since ripened into scholarship of the most profound nature. When we consider Miss Jackson's early struggles for education and the high position she occupies to-day in educational circles, we must acknowledge her to be one of the most remarkable women of the century just closed.

Her rare genius attracted the attention of ripe scholars everywhere, and it is interesting to hear Hon. Geo. Downing, of Newport, tell of his first meeting with the lady, when they crossed swords in public debate at a citizens' meeting to consider the question of colored schools.

Mayor Caldwell was so strongly impressed by her ability that by his aid she was able to enter the school at Bristol, R.I., and begin the study of the higher branches. After preparation here, Miss Jackson went to Oberlin College, where she soon took the highest rank with other progressive students. To assist her in meeting the bills for tuition, she taught music in families in the village, and also was entrusted with the musical training of the children of the professors at the college. Miss Jackson is a fine performer on the piano, harp, guitar and organ, often serving as organist in her vacation time in the church where Minister Van Horn was so long the pastor.

Irreproachable in reputation, with rare gifts and great moral aspirations, Miss Jackson was and always has been of untold value and benefit to her race. She easily won the highest respect and sympathy from her Oberlin teachers, and she was selected as a teacher for the Institute at Philadelphia, long before graduation.[77]

The Institute for Colored Youth was founded by Richard Humphrey, of Philadelphia, a member of the Society of Friends; a people whose sympathy

---

77. Ibid., 508–510.

and charity for the oppressed Negro are proverbial, and who have earned our heartfelt gratitude and respect.

Mr. Humphrey left a fund of ten thousand dollars; a legacy coming under the guidance of the Society amounted to sixteen thousand two hundred and ninety dollars in 1838. With this sum a charter was secured from the Legislature of Pennsylvania in 1842. Its object the education of colored youth, male and female, "to act as teachers and instructors in the different branches of school learning, or in the mechanical arts and agriculture."

The Institute was permanently located on Lombard street, in 1851.

Graduating with honors, Miss Jackson at once took her position in this school, where she was principal until she resigned in 1902. Her ability in governing this institution of learning has given her world-wide fame; she is respected by parents and guardians, and loved by her pupils.

Miss Jackson has appeared on the platform where her rhetoric has dazzled the listener. As a writer she is a keen reasoner and a deep thinker, handling live issues in a masterly manner.

We would compare her to Madame De Stael, but that cultured woman was the product of centuries of education and refinement.[78] Miss Jackson is a unique figure among women of all nationalities,—a standing monument of the handiwork of the Great Architect, whose masterly creations man can never hope to approach.

SOURCE "Famous Women of the Negro Race VI: Educators," *Colored American Magazine* 5.1 (May 1902): 41–46.

---

78. Anne Louise Germaine Necker, Baroness of Stael (1766–1817), was a French novelist and philosopher, most notably interested in international and post-Revolutionary French literature.

VII.

Educators *(Continued)*

(NOTE.—See July issue of *Colored American Magazine* for life-sketch of Miss J. Imogen Howard, for thirty years a leading female educator in the New York schools.)[79]

As we have said, one necessary condition of American slavery was ignorance. By the inexorable laws of Mississippi and South Carolina the Negro was doomed to hopeless moral and mental abasement.

In 1843, Mississippi ordered all free persons of color to remove from the State. There was, of course, no provisions allowed for the education of the Negro.

North Carolina allowed free persons of color school privileges until 1835, when they were abolished by law.

South Carolina allowed privileges of no kind, and only the most rigid and extreme laws prevailed; owing to the great demand for slave labor, thousands of unhappy blacks were imported, and the slave code reached the maximum of cruelty in that State.

On the contrary, in the Northern New England States—Maine and Vermont—slavery never existed at any time, and Negroes enjoyed the same privileges as did the Anglo-Saxon. New Hampshire possessed very few slaves at any time, and at an early period passed laws against their importation. There, also, education was free to all regardless of color.

Outside of this small section, efforts were made to establish institutions for the culture of colored youth, for years they failed signally; the tree of slavery "overshadowed the whole land, shedding its blighting influence on Northern as well as Southern hearts."

The condition of the Negroes in New York was about the same as in Virginia, although their privileges were more. They were admitted to membership in the churches, and no law was passed against educational methods.

A school for Negro slaves was opened in New York in 1704, by Elias Neau, a native of France. The New York African Free School was founded in 1786, located between Beekman and Ferry Streets. After many struggles and vicissitudes, in 1815 a commodious brick building was erected, large enough to accommodate 200 pupils, and Miss Lucy Turpin took charge of the sewing with other branches. She was followed by Miss Mary Lincrum, Miss Eliza J.

---

79. Joan Imogen Howard is profiled in the "Educators (Concluded)" installment of *Famous Women of the Negro Race*.

Cox, Miss Mary Ann Cox and Miss Caroline Roe, all of whom sustained the high character of the enterprise.

When General Lafayette visited the United States, he visited this school and examined the children in geography and other studies. He professed himself much pleased with the progress the children had made.

The New York schools advanced steadily, and in 1853 the colored schools of the Board of Education of New York City and County were established. The schools were graded, and Miss Caroline W. Simpson was made principal of Colored Grammar School, No. 3, and Miss Nancy Thomas principal of No. 4 (in Harlem).

From that time until the present, the advancement of the race in New York has been inspiring. The business men of the State are second to none in the country, leading the race in many instances. Along the lines of social and educational life we find the same cheering aspect. The social life is enjoyable and refining; the schools among the best in the United States, embracing teachers honored and respected for faithfulness and ability, culture and refinement.

In Puritan Massachusetts, a traffic in human beings was carried on for over a century. Thousands were sold; and the profit accruing from the sale of Negroes in all parts of the country laid the foundation of the wealth of many an old Massachusetts family. Slaves were classed as property, being valued as "horses and hogs." They were not allowed to bear arms nor be educated. The church, too, discriminated against them in every way.

But, although Massachusetts may commit a wrong, she is not persistent in evil when the public conscience is once aroused.

It was Judge Sewall, who delivered his warning words in 1700, to the New England colonies, cautioning them against slavery and the ill-treatment of Negroes in these words: "Forasmuch as Liberty is in real value next unto Life, none ought to part with it, but upon most mature consideration."[80] People and slaves were aroused by this speech; sermons and essays continually excited the inhabitants. When the Revolution broke out and the war with England was on, the slaves fought in defence of the colonies, and thus by courage and patriotism loosened the chains of bondage in the North.

The first colored school in Boston was held in the house of Primus Hall; the second, in the basement of the Belknap-Street church (St. Paul's Baptist church), and in 1835 a school-house was erected known as "Smith School-house" from the name of Abdiel Smith, who left a fund for that purpose. Added to this fund the city of Boston allowed two hundred dollars annually, and parents were charged twelve and one-half cents per week for each child.

William C. Nell, a well-known Negro agitator of Massachusetts, was instrumental in opening Boston schools to the Race, and in 1855, after a hard

---

80. Edward A. Johnson, *A School History of the Negro Race in America, from 1619 to 1890* (Raleigh, N.C.: Edwards and Broughton, 1890), 23.

fight, in accordance with a law passed by the Legislature, colored schools were abolished.

The first colored teacher appointed in the mixed schools of Boston was Miss Elizabeth Smith, daughter of Hon. J. J. Smith,—well-known as an abolitionist, and closely associated with Messrs. Garrison, Phillips, Sumner, Hayden, Nell and E. G. Walker.

Miss Smith was born in Boston on the old historic "hill," and educated at the "old Bowdoin school" on Myrtle St., graduating from the famous Girls' High School, of Boston. The Smith family is well and favorably known all over the country, having a large circle of friends and admirers in every city. One sister, Mrs. Adelaide Terry, is a well-known vocalist and teacher of music; another sister, Miss Florence Smith, is a successful teacher in the schools of Washington, D.C. Miss Harriet Smith, the youngest, is a valuable assistant of the Bowdoin school, Boston, Mass. The only brother is Mr. Hamilton Smith, of Washington, D.C. Miss Elizabeth was the eldest living child of this interesting family.

After graduation, Miss Smith taught in the South for a time, but was appointed to the Joy-Street school in 1870, where she remained four years. Retiring from this position, she was employed in the evening schools for a number of years, being re-appointed, finally, to a permanent position in the Sharpe school. While in the active performance of her duties there, looking forward hopefully, to holding the position of principal, by promotion, she died in the latter part of 1899, deeply regretted by friends and associates.

Miss Smith was a remarkably good woman, who easily won the love and respect of her associates—teachers, pupils and companions, by her quiet, unostentatious manner, and who used her wide influence among the young of both races for their elevation and advancement.

Most men and women of the African race who have become famous because of a talent above the ordinary, are content to draw their ancestry from our common father Adam, and their talent from the bestower of all good things—our Creator. So it is with the subject of this school.

Miss Maria Louise Baldwin was born in Cambridge, Mass. Her parents were well-known and highly respected citizens of the "city across the Charles," who, like many other parents struggled hard to give their children all the advantages which parental love could bestow.

Miss Baldwin is the eldest of three children,—Miss Gertrude, her sister, has been for years a teacher in the public schools of Wilmington, Delaware; the only brother, Louis, is engaged in the real estate business at Cambridge, and has been very successful. He is a genial, popular man, much liked by his associates and business friends. Miss Baldwin's early education embraced the plain, straightforward curriculum of the New England public school,— passing from primary grade to grammar, to high, to training, imbibing grace of mind and body together with comprehensive Christianity and orderly deportment from her cultured teachers, many of them descendants of the best New England stock; acquiring depth of thought, activity in business and the value of method in all life's duties from this association.

Leaving a happy childhood behind her, the young girl entered upon the serious work of bread-winning very soon after graduation, at Chester County, Maryland, teaching there two terms. Active in mind and body, possessing great energy and executive ability, Miss Baldwin, in this probationary stage of her work, developed into a successful teacher.

In 1882 came the turning point in her life-work—she was appointed a teacher in the Cambridge public schools. This gave her the fulcrum, the one thing demanded by humanity—opportunity. Without this, aspiration and ability may be said to resemble "silent thunder"; youthful and unknown, deprived of opportunity, genius is baffled and sinks to earth never to realize its "noble aspirations." But upon her favorites Fortune is wont to smile and give first place.

We give the story of Miss Baldwin's appointment as nearly as possible in her own words:

> I was given at first an "overflow" class to teach, with the assurance that I would be kept while that class continued to be a necessity; I was, in short, a temporary teacher. Mr. Francis Coggswell, superintendent of schools, said he could not tell how long I would stay, but the next year I was called to the same place, and was confirmed in my position by the Board.
>
> The Louis Agassiz school is on Sacramento St., corner of Oxford St., and not far from the Agassiz Museum; it is in an aristocratic corner of Old Cambridge, and beneath the shadow of "Fair Harvard's" wings.
>
> For seven years I taught in all the lower grades of the school, gaining thereby invaluable experience. In 1889, Miss Ewell, then the principal of the school, and greatly beloved, resigned in June, the resignation being kept secret until after vacation, and the school opened in September without a head, remaining so until the middle of October.
>
> One Friday Mr. Coggswell asked me how I would like the position of principal. I immediately answered, "Not at all." "Why?" he inquired. I replied, "I am happier with the little children, and prefer to remain where I am. If I failed in the position you mention, it would be a conspicuous failure."
>
> Saturday morning, Mr. Coggswell called at my home, and sitting in this room where we are now, said, "Miss Baldwin, you are neglecting an opportunity to show to Cambridge more than you have already done." He added, "The committee have every confidence in your executive ability and desire you to accept the place."
>
> I was confused and somewhat dazed, and begged that he would give me until afternoon to decide. Directly he was gone I hastened to Miss Ewell's house and asked her advice. She said, "I knew you would be asked and I want you to take it."

That afternoon I told Mr. Coggswell that I would accept for two weeks, and for thirteen years I have been principal of the school, being appointed in October, 1889. There are eight assistants and three hundred and fifteen pupils. In October, 1902, I round out twenty happy years spent in teaching in the public schools of Cambridge.

As a woman of letters, Miss Baldwin's career is full of interest. She is distinctly a product of to-day, in this pursuit.

The entire colored population was happily surprised and greatly cheered when it was announced that she was chosen to deliver the address on Harriet Beecher Stowe before the Brooklyn Institute of Arts and Sciences, February 22, 1897. It was a distinctive triumph, in which Miss Baldwin stood alone beneath the searching light of public curiosity, and, in some instances, we doubt not, incredulity, among the educated whites unacquainted with her ability. She arose to the occasion grandly and fulfilled our fondest hopes, covering herself and us with new honors. We do not hesitate to say that if she had distinguished herself in no other way save in compiling and delivering this lecture, her name would have gone down to posterity as a literary genius.

Brooklyn Institute of Arts and Sciences originated as far back as 1823; it early assumed a notable place in the intellectual life of Brooklyn. In 1888, it was re-organized under Prof. Franklin W. Hooper, as director, and its past history, almost phenomenal in its brilliancy, is due to the tact and foresight of that gentleman.

It has to-day a splendid new Museum Building, 600 yearly lectures, 3,000 yearly classes and special meetings; its extension courses, its schools of art, its summer biological schools, its library, and its collections. Members of the Institute enjoy the precious privileges, and in addition to ordinary lectures, the Institute conducts special courses and entertainments. Thus, for example, the Boston Symphony concerts in Brooklyn are conducted under the auspices of its department of music at low cost to the members. The Institute has twenty-seven departments, including anthropology, archaeology, architecture, astronomy, botany, chemistry, domestic science, electricity, engineering, entomology, fine arts, geography, geology, law, mathematics, microscopy, mineralogy, music, painting, pedagogy, philology, photography, physics, political science, psychology, sculpture, and zoology.

Augustus Graham, benefactor of the Institute, provided the fund that pays for the "Washington Anniversary," February 22, being set aside to commemorate the life of some great American. Washington, Garrison, Sumner, Curtis, Lowell, and others had been taken. The February following Mrs. Stowe's death she was the subject of commemoration,—the first woman to be so distinguished. The committee wrote to Miss Baldwin, and in "fear and trembling" she accepted the honor. For this lecture Miss Baldwin was paid one hundred dollars. Among the noted men who have been called to address the members of this Institute we mention a few: Mr. Russell Sturgis; Dr. Burt G.

Wilder, of Cornell; Col. Thos. W. Higginson; Charles Kendall Adams, LL.D., of the University of Wisconsin; Hon. Charles A. Boutelle, of Maine.

Prof. Booker T. Washington lectures there in 1902.

The popularity of Miss Baldwin's lecture has been unparalleled from its first delivery. It has been repeatedly given by its talented author before associations and clubs of the highest literary repute; among them we may mention the Brooklyn Institute of Arts and Sciences; Cantabrigia Club, Cambridge; the Old South Course of historic lectures; the Municipal Lecture Course, Boston.

In complexion, Miss Baldwin is a dark mulatto; features well-defined, and an intelligent and refined countenance; her figure is well developed, inclined to embonpoint; her head is round, the organs well-balanced, and about it is coiled black, silky hair, clustering in waves over the thoughtful brow. Upon the platform she is a pleasant picture, dignified in her carriage and polished in her address; her full, softly modulated, contralto voice easily reaching the most distant corners of a hall.

We do not claim to number among our men of letters and public speakers a Tennyson or a Dickens, a Carlyle or a Hume, nor subtle diplomats of the Disraeli school, but by the lives of those men and women who have shown the slightest spark of the divine fire in the color of their life-work, we have proved our origin.

To the favored few among us who have enjoyed exceptional advantages of obtaining knowledge, and thereby cultivation, together with that nice perception which distinguishes easily between the polished achievements of inherited scholarly traits as defined by the masterpieces of fiction, scientific work or exquisite art creations of the Anglo-Saxon, and the ambitious strivings of our own people toward the same goals,—to this class our efforts may seem pathetic, and altogether vain, but let us remember,—whether the window through which the glory of sunlight comes to us is circular, square or oval, or whether it be set in the Egyptian, the Grecian, the Gothic or the architecture of the lowly cabin of the South with its mud flooring, the form of the medium does not concern us, it is the light itself,

> As sunshine broken in the rill,
> Though turned aside, is sunshine still.[81]

The Anglo-Saxon came not to his present state of perfection fully equipped; he is the product of centuries of constant practice in the arts and graces of educated civilization. If we go back a few centuries we find his ancestors described by Caesar and Tacitus. Caesar, writing home, said of the Britons, "They are the most degraded people I ever conquered." Cicero

---

81. Thomas Moore, "The Fire-Worshippers" (1817), in *The Complete Poems of Thomas Moore* (Project Gutenberg, 2005), http://www.gutenberg.org/dirs/etext05/8cptm10.txt.

advised Atticus not to purchase slaves from Briton, "because," said he, "they cannot be taught music, and are the ugliest people I ever saw."[82]

Macaulay says: "When the Britons first became known to the Tyrian mariners, they were little superior to the Sandwich Islanders" (meaning, of course, their most savage state).[83]

Rome got her civilization from Greece; Greece borrowed hers from Egypt, thence she derived her science and beautiful mythology. Civilization descended the Nile and spread over the delta, as it came down from Thebes. Thebes was built and settled by the Ethiopians. As we ascend the Nile we come to Meroe the queen city of Ethiopia and the cradle of learning into which all Africa poured its caravans. So we trace the light of civilization from Ethiopia to Egypt, to Greece, to Rome, and thence diffusing its radiance over the entire world.

The query:—What is the best course for the Negro in education to mould him into a useful self-supporting citizen? has as many sides as a chameleon has shades—in whatever light we view it, fresh complications arise, and because of these very complications we ought not to utter a wholesale condemnation of our leaders and their opinions, neither should we utter harsh words of censure against the patriotic band of thinkers who stand jealously guarding the rights of the race from dangerous encroachment.

Twenty years hence we can better judge the motives of our leaders, for Time is a true leveller; twenty years hence we can applaud with fervor the iron-hearted men who bar Oppression's way. Until then, let us exercise the virtue of charity that suffereth long and is kind; that beareth all things, believeth all things, hopeth all things, endureth all things. More and more are we led to say: "Events are God's, let Him sit at His own helm, that moderateth all."

In the careers of Miss Baldwin and our other New England teachers, the section has sustained its reputation.

Miss Baldwin is honored, respected and loved by all who know her. From pupils and parents she has always received the treatment that we delight to lavish upon those whom we love.

Intermarriage between Northern and Southern white families, the introduction of Southern teachers into the schools, and a natural feeling of kinship between the Northern and Southern Anglo-Saxon, may cause happenings in New England which smack of prejudice towards us as a race. But such things are as nothing when we remember that New England principles gave us a free Kansas way back in 1857; that New England blood was first shed in the streets of Baltimore when the tocsin of war sounded the call to save the Union; that New England cemented the Proclamation of Emancipation in the death of

82. William Wells Brown, *The Black Man: His Antecedents, His Genius, and His Achievements* (New York: Thomas Hamilton, 1863), 34.

83. Thomas Babington Macaulay, quoted in Brown, *Black Man*, 33. British politician Macaulay (1800–1859) was the author of *History of England* (1849–1861).

Col. Shaw; and, greater than all, stern New England Puritanism in the persons of Garrison, Sumner, Phillips, Stearns, Whittier, Francis Jackson, and others, gave the black man the liberty that the South would deny even to-day, if possible; gave to the Negro all over this broad land his present prosperity, no matter how inconsiderable it may appear to us; gave us Douglass and Langston, Robert Elliott and Bruce, and Booker T. Washington, with his world-famous Tuskegee Institute.

May my tongue cleave to the roof of my mouth and my right hand forget its cunning when I forget the benefits bestowed upon my persecuted race by noble-hearted New England.[84]

SOURCE "Famous Women of the Negro Race VII: Educators (Continued)," *Colored American Magazine* 5.2 (June 1902): 125–130.

84. See Psalms 137:5–6. Frederick Douglass used this verse in his famous July 5, 1852, oration, "What to the Slave Is the Fourth of July?"

VIII.

Educators *(Concluded)*

*A*half-century or more ago among the earnest workers of the great city of Boston, counted with those of prominence and refinement, of open hospitality and culture, was the family of the Howards.

For many years they lived at the homestead on Poplar St., in the then aristocratic quarter of the old West End. The house, a four-story brick edifice, was well-kept, and differed in no one particular from its flourishing neighbors, albeit its owners were colored, and it was a most unusual thing to find a Negro family so charmingly located as were the Howards, in those days when the trials endured by the race to-day were but child's play by comparison with the terrible sufferings then imposed upon the entire race.

One of the sons of this family, Edwin Frederick, brought to his home as his loving wife, Joan Louise Turpin of New York. By her genial manners and sympathetic heart this lady soon made herself a valued member of the household, and a valued friend to a large circle among members of her own race, as well as that class of broad, liberal-minded lovers of humanity among whom may be numbered such revered names as Garrison, Sumner, Wilson, Phillips, Higginson, and Lydia Maria Child, for the Howard family was identified closely with the anti-slavery movement from its inception. Married in New York, the eldest daughter of Edwin and Joan Howard, Adeline Turpin, was born in that city, and claims it as her birthplace; while Dr. Edwin Clarence and Joan Imogen are a son and daughter who delight ever that almost under the shadow of the "gilded dome" of Massachusetts' capitol building, their infancy and early youth were passed.

All three, reared under the finest moral influences, amid surroundings tended to foster a taste for literature, science, and that which is in the highest degree aesthetic, it is not surprising that we find these representatives of an honest mother and a universally beloved father, shedding sunshine and light through a long experience of private and public usefulness, in a service for the betterment of the children of our race, and for the alleviation of the sufferings of mankind.

As a physician, a graduate of Harvard Medical School, Dr. Howard is known as the senior and among the most skilful of the doctors of Philadelphia, Pa., a city where he has won his enviable professional reputation, and among whose people he is ever accorded every honor by the citizens at large and by the highest officials who administer the affairs of the Quaker city.

In early life, during a residence of five years on the "Dark Continent" he first evinced his tendency towards the medical profession. As an observer, and a student, a season was passed in the hospitals and institutions of a kindred nature in England and France. He is a valued member of the Philadelphia County Medical Society, the Pennsylvania Medical Society, and the American Medical Association, frequently being a delegate chosen to represent the first in the State and National Societies. Not among the least of the many services rendered to his adopted city is that which for eleven years was given as a member of the Board of Education.

Miss Adeline Turpin Howard, early in life offered herself as an instructor in that field of educational work where the torch frequently followed closely upon the opening of a school for that class among us then known as "Freed-men." In Virginia, that State of whose historic name every white American is proud; in Maryland's remote country hamlets; and in far away Louisiana along the banks of the Red River, unselfishly, with patience, perseverance and that spirit of self-renunciation that many have known in their efforts to lift to better lives those from whom slavery had taken God's greatest blessings, she labored for years. That many among the young and the vigorous, the old and down-trodden, long looked up to and honored her must, in these years, be a choice memory. To-day we find her active, progressive and most capable as the highly esteemed principal of the Wormley Building in West Washington, D.C., where, as the administrative head and the practical teacher, she has under her charge and that of able assistants, over six hundred girls and boys who rank well in their literary subjects, as well as in those branches of domestic art, and moral and aesthetic training which lead to good citizenship.

Joan Imogen Howard was the first colored pupil of the grammar schools of Boston to graduate and then knock at the door of the Girls' High and Normal School (then located on Mason St.) for entrance. This was accomplished without "conditions" as to her examinations; but since, hitherto, no dark-hued student had ever been seated in its halls, some apprehension was felt as to the effect on the classes. To the honor of the head-master, Mr. Seavey, and the grandly broad-minded Miss Temple, nothing of this objection was ever known or felt during the three years' course. Graduating with honor, an opening presented itself in New York City, and there until the close of the year 1901, we knew her, ever striving to take a step higher in her profession as a teacher. Knowing "The mill will never grind with the water that has passed," courses in "Methods of Teaching" were taken at short intervals at institutions of the first rank, and in 1892, she was graduated from New York University receiving a diploma and the well-earned degree of "Master of Pedagogy."

The University of the State of New York is an innovation in educational circles, embracing, as it does, all the chartered colleges and secondary schools in the State; it is an institution unique in its organization and its methods of work.

There has been scarcely any educational reform in the State of which the University has not been the promoter. In the training of teachers it has been especially active. Its field has so been extended to include the charterings of high schools, academies, and colleges and also of libraries, museums, summer schools, corresponding schools, permanent lecture courses, and all other institutions for promoting higher education.

When one considers that political issues have become in these years mainly economic, the merits of a general education of the people in the scientific aspects of their individual life becomes clear. When we consider the fact that all classes and all races in a cosmopolitan population such as ours must understand the effect that a change of governmental policy may have upon the commercial life of our Republic, it becomes plain to the dullest intellect that our future legislation, executives, and judicial officers, must have always before them the economic welfare of the people, white and black; it is, therefore, necessary that all education, professional as well as business, shall embrace a clear understanding of the relations between the industrial life of the people and the laws and policy of the government.

More and more must women enter into a knowledge of all these questions in order to be fitted to teach the embryo man the duties of good citizenship. Recognizing this need, the sociological student must bow to the increasing demands of higher education. Under the broadening influence of such educational methods, Miss Howard has developed into a perfect womanhood.

In 1892, Governor Flower of New York, through the enthusiastic advocacy of Judge Jas. C. Matthews (one of the most prominent in the legal fraternity of Albany) appointed her a member of the Board of Women Managers of the State of New York, for the Columbian Exposition. Far from being a place of embarrassment on account of its being without a parallel on any other State Board for the same grand event, Miss Howard's experiences were made a joy to her by the Governor of the State, the Mayor of Albany, and by the choice specimens of New York's most liberal-minded and aristocratic gentlewomen who formed the Board. As a result of her efforts and of the untiring, painstaking and executive sub-committee that were formed throughout the State, statistics of women's work were tabulated, exhibits gathered, and the literary works of Lydia Maria Child—almost a martyr in the cause of abolition— were gathered nearly in their entirety. These became a valued part of the rare collection of books in the artistic library of the Woman's Building in the dreamily beautiful "White City" at Chicago in 1892 and 1893. Now, they and an exhaustive account of the "Distinguished Work of the Colored Women of America" are among the treasures in the "many-millioned-dollared" capitol at Albany.

Miss Howard feels herself one with the many in this vast country, for she frequently says that she never could and never can know sectional differences. That she never could, she owes to the teachings of a revered mother; that she never can, is but a return for the spirit of loyal support, of indomitable energy, enthusiastic outpouring of money, and above all, the unanimity of effort which placed ballot after ballot to her credit, until a shower, which knew no ceasing, poured votes into the New York Telegram Office in the "Trip to Paris Contest" for sixteen months, until when the announcement of the five successful candidates was made in June, 1900, her name was the third, and the trip to France and Belgium was the result.

This she considers the crowning event in a career in which only a little has been done by her, but that little she hopes is a part of "God's great plan."

After teaching every grade required by the curriculum in the grammar departments of New York's schools, an indisposition of a serious nature, compelled her to resign her position as the teacher of the graduating class of Public School No. 80, Manhattan, and reluctantly retire from active service.

Now, as a companion to her deceased mother's sister, Mrs. Bowers, and of her esteemed brother, Dr. Howard, she resides in Philadelphia, where it is hoped a complete family circle will be formed by the addition, at no future day, of the sister who is still claimed by our old Bay State as one of its honored daughters.

Apropos of the fact that numbers of famous Negro women have been signally honored by white institutions of renown in various communities, it is profitable to pause a moment and consider the position taken by the General Federation of Women's Clubs in its recent convention at Los Angeles, Cal.

The application of the Woman's Era Club, Boston, for admission to the General Federation, was made at a time when a club could only be admitted by a majority vote of the Board of Directors. The dues were sent to the Treasurer, and Mrs. Ruffin was in Milwaukee expecting to be seated in the convention.[85] June 4, 1900, a motion was made to admit the club to membership.

The fact that the admission of a colored club would establish a precedent, made the Board unwilling to act, and the dues were returned to Mrs. Ruffin, and a motion to lay it on the table was made and carried.

During the two years which have elapsed since then there has been constant agitation over the "color question." Political "wire-pulling" of every sort has been resorted to by the Southern women and their Northern sympathizers to keep out the colored sisters, and at last success has crowned their efforts.

Mrs. Dimies T. Denison of New York placed herself on record by making the following statement to the reporter of the *Los Angeles Times*:

> The newspapers seeking for "copy" have magnified the matter. It really is only a side issue although it is important. I am sure the delegates will act wisely. The Civil War is past; the old wounds have been healed; the North and the South are re-united, and we cannot afford to take any action that will lead to more bitter feeling. The South is represented strongly in the federation, and the effect on those members is obvious if

85. U.S. reformer and clubwoman Josephine St. Pierre Ruffin (1842–1924) was a founder of the National Association of Colored Women (1896).

colored women are admitted on a social equality with white members. We must not, and I feel that the delegates will not, do anything that threatens disruption of the federation of which we are all so proud.

As a result of a vote taken on May 5, 1902, by the General Federation of Women's Clubs, it became practically impossible for colored clubs to get into the federation. The decision was for the Massachusetts-Georgia compromise, by which State rights are maintained, in that no restrictions are placed upon State Federations; but the way to membership in the General Federation is blocked by the necessity of passing two boards and the Membership Committee of the General Federation, the unanimous vote of which last committee is required for admission. The victory is thus to the South.[86]

In the discussion preceding the casting of ballots, Mrs. Gallagher of Ohio, said:

This is not a question of color, it is a question of an embryonic race, not yet strong enough to stand with us. . . . The Negroes are by nature imitators. If we admit them to associations with us, they will lose their power of independent development and become merely followers of the whites. They have not yet reached a plane on which they can compete with us and maintain their own independence. The best thing we can do for them is to let them go on developing along their own lines. Then, when they have fought their fight and won their way up, where they can stand on an equal footing with us, let us consider their admission.

In the discussion of the color question, Miss Jane Addams (Hull House, Chicago) aroused the most interest by declaring herself a partisan of colored clubs and holding the opinion that "no race can uphold a race integrity apart from other races, and that it lies with the stronger people to stand with the weaker." The final call for the previous question carried the amendment by an overwhelming vote.

The power of organization among women is a sociological study. Women were narrow mentally; it is supposed that they have been broadened by their educational opportunities and their growing influence which has, hitherto, commanded the respect of the world. We had hoped that as a race, we should receive the fair treatment, the sympathy, the loyalty, that their reputation guaranteed, but the Biennial at Los Angeles has given us a rude awakening.

They find their fellows guilty of a skin
Not colored like their own, and having power

---

86. The convention, including the debate regarding the admission of African American clubs, is covered from the perspective of the General Federation of Women's Clubs in "The Sixth Biennial," *The Clubwoman* 9.9 (June 1902): 324–325.

To enforce the wrong, for such a worthy cause
Doom and devote them as their lawful prey.[87]

At the World's Congress of Representative Women from all Lands, in 1892–3, under the superintendence of such women as Mrs. Potter Palmer, Mrs. Charles Henrotin, Mrs. May Wright Sewall, Mrs. Avery, Miss Frances E. Willard, and others, such notable women of color as Frances Ellen Harper, Fanny Jackson-Coppin, Annie J. Cooper, Fanny Barrier Williams, and Hallie Q. Brown, delivered addresses which drew the eyes of the entire world upon them and their race.

In connection with the same great Exposition, Miss Imogen Howard, as we have stated in the above sketch, was signally honored by being appointed a member of the Board of Women Managers of the State of New York, for the Columbian Exposition, the only Negro so honored by any other State. Miss Howard's peculiar fitness for the position to which she was called, added additional lustre to her fame, and her race stepped up a rung on Ambition's ladder.

In Massachusetts, we may mention that, added to her fame as a teacher and lecturer, Miss Maria L. Baldwin has for many years been a member of the Cantabrigia Club of Cambridge, than which no wealthier, no more highly cultured, no club of wider fame exists in the entire country. No token of esteem has been too high for this club of noble-minded women to bestow on their admired colored member.

In connection with the famous Boston Political class under its president, the great parliamentarian, Mrs. Harriet P. Shattuck, we may mention the fact that Mrs. Mary J. Buchanan, a beautiful and cultured woman of color, has been a member for years; has filled every office, and was for a number of seasons honored as the vice-president of the club.

Mrs. J. St. Pierre Ruffin's career as a club woman is too well known to need rehearsal, and we doubt not that many other colored women, of whom we have no knowledge, are connected with similar white institutions of wealth and influence.

In the face of this testimony to the superior work being done by all classes of Negro women, in every State in the Union where their ability has been given an opportunity to materialize, we are justly indignant that our women are branded as the intellectual inferiors of the whites in such words as were used by Mrs. Gallagher: "When they have fought their fight and won their way up where they can stand on an equal footing with us, let us consider their admission."

We know that we shall be pardoned the assertion that jealousy has something to do with the decision of the great Biennial Convention of 1902.

---

87. William Cowper, "The Task, Book II: The Timepiece" (1784). Cowper's poem appears as the epigraph to Emily Catharine Pierson, *Jamie Parker, The Fugitive* (Hartford, Conn.: Brockett, Fuller, 1851), [i]. Hopkins cites this poem in *Contending Forces*, 255.

We have felt and argued always, against unrestricted and universal suffrage, feeling that mentally woman is as narrow to-day as ever, that behind windy, grandiloquent speeches of belief in the equality of the human species, dwelt a spirit of perverseness that might at any moment break forth to our undoing.

So must Mrs. Harper have felt when during her speech at the Women's Congress, 1892, she uttered the following words, which implied a doubt of the temper of the great majority of our white female population toward the Negro.

Political life in our country is plowed in muddy channels, and needs the infusion of cleaner and clearer waters. I am not sure that women are naturally so much better than men that they will clear the stream by the virtue of their womanhood; it is not through sex, but through character that the best influence of woman upon the life of the Nation must be exerted.

I do not believe in unrestricted and universal suffrage for either men or women. I believe in moral and educational tests. I do not believe that the most ignorant and brutal man is better prepared to add value to the strength and durability of the government than the most cultured and upright woman. I do not think that willful ignorance should swamp earnest intelligence at the ballot box, nor that educated arrogance, violence and fraud should cancel the votes of honest men. The hands of lynchers are too red with blood to determine the political character of the government for even four short years.

The ballot in the hands of woman means power added to influence. How well she will use that power I cannot foretell. Great evils stare us in the face that need to be throttled by the combined power of an upright manhood and an enlightened womanhood.

American women! What a sublime opportunity to create healthy public sentiment for justice, and to brand lawless cowardice that lynches, burns and tortures humanity! To grapple the evils which threaten the strength and progress of the United States! Have they the grand and holy purpose of uplifting humanity?[88]

SOURCE "Famous Women of the Negro Race VIII: Educators (Concluded)," *Colored American Magazine* 5.3 (July 1902): 206–213.

88. Frances Ellen Watkins Harper, "Woman's Political Future," in *The World's Congress of Representative Women: A Historical Résumé for Popular Circulation of the World's Congress of Representative Women, Convened in Chicago on May 15, and Adjourned on May 22, 1893; Under the Auspices of the Woman's Branch of the World's Congress Auxiliary*, edited by May Wright Sewall (Chicago: Rand McNally, 1894), 1:435–437.

Club Life among Colored Women

> What is a woman's club? The fabric of a dream
> Touched with an altar coal and made alive,
> Instinct with hope for those who toil and strive,
> And wait to catch that joyous day's first gleam
> That ushers in a better, freer age,
> When right for one shall be for all the right;
> When all together in life's moil and fight,
> The war for right and truth shall bravely wage.[89]

While women have by individual effort done much for the progress of society, and the names of illustrious women adorn the pages of literature, art and science; and while their work of moral education has been displayed in the life of schools and colleges, and in the province of loving service upon the battle field and in the hospitals, yet it was felt that these personal efforts could best be centralized by co-operation in the form of clubs, thus giving to causes dear and vital to humanity the valuable aid of organized intelligence.

In 1868 the first movement in the great innovation was made, and shortly after "Sorosis" was formed in New York, mothered by Mrs. Croly (Jennie June), and the "New England Woman's Club" of Boston, with Mrs. Caroline M. Severance as the fostering power that gave being to this, then, remarkable organization.

New England women of any race are quick to catch inspiration from environment, and the fever of the club life soon infected the leading women of color in Massachusetts. Touched by a live coal from the altar of Progress, in 1873 the "Woman's Era Club" was formed.

The club took its name from a paper called the *Woman's Era*. This publication was devoted to the interests of colored women, and Mrs. Ruffin was its editor. It was because of the work done by this paper that the first organization of colored women was formed in 1873 and meeting held in Boston, and the following year in Washington.

This club, which is the only colored club in Massachusetts belonging to the State Federation, was started in this way:

---

89. Hopkins reprinted this poem and incorporated substantial portions of this article into her account of the Northeastern Federation of Colored Women's Clubs' 1903 convention. See Pauline E. Hopkins, "Echoes from the Annual Convention of Northeastern Federation of Colored Women's Clubs," *Colored American Magazine* 6.10 (Oct. 1903): 709–713.

Mrs. Ruffin was a member of the New England Woman's Club, whose president was Mrs. Julia Ward Howe, and which is claimed to antedate the so-called "Mother of Clubs," Sorosis, of New York. Occasionally Mrs. Ruffin would invite friends to attend these meetings, and thus interest was aroused which resulted in a formation of a new club, which was not intended necessarily to be a colored club, as it had three or four white women as members.

The club now has one hundred members. Two meetings are held each month, one of which is devoted to business and the other to literary pursuits, lectures and similar educational features. The club headquarters are in the Blue Room of Tremont Temple. Lucy Stone spoke to the club at the last meeting she ever addressed, and her words, "Help to make the world better," have been taken as the club motto.

The object of the club as laid down in its constitution is:

"The furtherance of the interests of the race generally and of our women particularly; not only through the collecting of facts which shall show our true position to the world, by endeavoring to create sentiment against the proscription under which we suffer, and by co-operating to aid in our general advancement, but also to awaken in our women an active interest in the events of the day, and giving to them through such an organization an opportunity of hearing and participating in the discussion of current topics."

The success of the club has been encouraging. The National Federation of Afro-American Women, known now as the National Association of Colored Women's Clubs, was organized in Boston, July 31, 1895, under the auspices of the Woman's Era. The first convention was held at Washington, D.C., July 20, 21 and 22, 1896, at the Nineteenth-Street Baptist Church. This great Association is now of powerful growth, adding yearly to its roll of membership Federations from every Southern State.

Many events have contributed to keeping the club in the public eye; notably the Baker episode and the opposition of the club to Miss Lillian Clayton Jewett posing as the Harriet Beecher Stowe of the race.[90]

So, through the example of a few public-spirited women, the Negro woman has become ubiquitous in club life, overflowing into all the avenues of self-help that are adopted by her white sisters as a means to the end of rising herself and "lifting others as she climbs."

This short resumé brings us to the high-water mark of the race battle in women's clubs—the Sixth Biennial of the General Federation of Women's Clubs at Los Angeles, Cal.

90. Following the lynching of Postmaster Frazier Baker in South Carolina, Lillian Clayton Jewett, a twenty-four-year-old white woman, organized a northern tour for Baker's widow Lavinia and their surviving children in July 1899. Many African Americans were critical of Jewett, her seeming profiteering, and her public display of the Bakers, who soon broke off ties with Jewett. For more on Jewett, see Roger K. Hux, "Lillian Clayton Jewett and the Rescue of the Baker Family, 1899–1900," *Historical Journal of Massachusetts* 19 (Winter 1991): 13–23.

Never in the West was there assembled from among the women of the United States, a gathering at once so large and aristocratic as filled Simpson auditorium at the Convention opening. An audience made up of nearly fifteen hundred women is well worth seeing; and when made up of bright women from representative homes the sight is unusual and interesting. The hall was decked with calla lilies; it banked the stage and was everywhere in evidence along with the lily of the valley. The arrangement of these flowers with smilax and fern was very beautiful. On either side the great organ stood immense palms, lifting their arms aloft. Fronds filled the embrasures high up in the walls banked by clusters of lilies and maidenhair. The Stars and Stripes curtained two upper windows and formed a glorious background.

Ten thousand callas transformed the choir loft into a green and white and old gold hedge. Ten thousand other lilies made into circular bands decorated the balcony faces.

Just before the opening of the convention birch-bark baskets of lilies of the valley and orange blossoms were brought into the hall in armfuls, and one was given to each of the club presidents.

Mrs. Rebecca D. Lowe, of Georgia, sat at a polished oak table on the platform, and at twelve minutes past two o'clock rose and struck the table four times sharply with the gavel. After the usual preliminaries the president declared the convention in order, and called on Mrs. Chester P. Dorland to make the opening prayer.

"Lord, from the four corners of the world we have come to this convention, as representing the homes of the world. It is to these homes the effects of this meeting, for good or for evil, will go. May many homes be made stronger and sweeter, may many crooked ways be made straight, by what we shall do and say here."

What a mockery such a prayer must have seemed to the Almighty Father as he looked into the secret hearts of a majority of the members of that convention and saw their determined denial of the fatherhood of God and the brotherhood of man!

In response to the address of welcome made by the president of the biennial local board, Mrs. Lowe said in part:

"We have come to Los Angeles with that courage and enthusiasm which ensures the accomplishment of greater things than have ever been chronicled at any previous meeting."

Verily, she spoke truly; "greater things" were done there for the betrayal of law, order and peaceful government, not to speak of the degradation of a race of people, than have been attempted since the Missouri compromise.

The question of admitting colored women's clubs to the General Federation came up on Friday morning, May 2, but it failed to disturb the serenity of the convention. In her report as Recording Secretary, Mrs. Emma A. Fox gave the main facts concerning the application of the Woman's Era Club for representation in the federation, and many of her statements were misleading and full of antipathy toward the colored sister.

On Monday, May 5, '02, a vote was taken on the great color question, the result of which practically closes the federation to colored clubs.

The debate on proposed amendments to the by-laws, including the color line, began with the motion of Mrs. Granger, of Georgia, to take up the amendment of Article II, Section 2, adopted by Massachusetts and Georgia, as a compromise on the color line dispute. It is as follows:

"Sec. 2. From a State where a club is a member of the State Federation, it would also be eligible to the General Federation if recommended to its executive board by the executive board of the State Federation; the power of admission to remain as given in Article II of the by-laws, as follows."

The motion was carried.

The fight was now on in earnest and all over the house interest deepened as delegate after delegate rose for recognition and to state her views on the great question. Mrs. Shields, of the Wednesday Morning Club of St. Louis, offered a substitute amendment which gave the assembly a distinct shock:

"Resolved: That clubs containing colored women shall be eligible to the General Federation in those States and Territories in which they are eligible to membership in their State or Territorial Federation, and that, where these organizations do not exist, race eligibility shall be declared by a three-fifths vote of the clubs."

The Missouri delegation expressed its strong disapproval of Mrs. Shields.

Next came the famous Mrs. Gallagher, of Ohio:

This is not a question of color, it is a question of an embryonic race, not yet strong enough to stand with us. Booker Washington says that greater harm would be done to the colored race than to the white by admission of the colored clubs to the federation. (Mr. Washington denies this statement.) The Negroes are by nature imitators. If we admit them to associations with us, they will lose their power of independent development and become merely followers of the whites.

They have not yet reached a plane on which they can compete with us and maintain their own independence. The best thing we can do for them is to let them go on developing along their own lines. Then, when they have fought their fight and won their way up where they can stand on an equal footing with us, let us consider their admission. But in God's name let us not hinder their independent progress by admitting them at this time.

Miss Jane Addams was the feature of the discussion which followed, and aroused great interest by declaring herself the partisan of colored clubs. She was intense.

The final call for the previous question carried the amendment by an overwhelming vote.

Mrs. Dimies T. Denison, of New York, new President of the Federation, expressed herself on the color line as follows:

"The Civil War is past; the old wounds have been healed; the North and the South have been reunited, and we cannot afford to take any action that will lead to more bitter feeling. The South is represented strongly in the Federation, and the effect on those members is obvious if colored women are admitted on a social equality with white members. We must not, and I feel that the delegates will not, do anything that threatens disruption of the Federation, of which we are all so proud."

On Monday afternoon, June 30, the Woman's Era Club held a call meeting in the Blue Room, Tremont Temple, Boston, Mass., to listen to the report of Mrs. Kate Lyon Brown, of Waltham, Mass., who went to Los Angeles to represent her own club and kindly offered to represent the Era club, when she found that Mrs. Ruffin had given up the idea of attending the Biennial convention.

It was a representative audience of Boston people that listened intently to the chief speaker, augmented by well-known men and women of color from every part of the Union. Mrs. Ruffin opened the meeting with a short account of the circumstances which led up to the trouble in clubdom some two years back. Among interesting relics shown the audience was the certificate of membership given the club at the Milwaukee convention and other souvenirs which she declared may form the basis of a law suit against the General Federation of Women's Clubs. This alone was exciting news.

Mrs. Brown, of Waltham, is a slender woman of the Anglo-Saxon race, possessed of an earnest manner and honest face which won her favor instantly with her audience. She interested her hearers from the moment she opened her mouth and began to recount her experiences from Boston to Los Angeles. The little woman swallowed insults and bore harsh criticism with the fortitude of a martyr or, what is synonymous, an old-time abolitionist.

Mrs. Brown, not knowing the strong feeling against the Era club in the Massachusetts delegation, called a meeting in the observation car to discuss the best method of getting the question before the convention. This meeting was poorly attended, and the remark was made: "We don't see why the niggers want to force themselves upon us. We think Mrs. Brown very unwise to offer herself as a delegate for the Era club. The question must not be brought up." Mrs. Brown finally promised not to be the first one to advance the color line. This happened at Springfield, Mass. Mrs. Brown was invited to breakfast at Salt Lake City with Mrs. Ward, president of Massachusetts Federation, and Mrs. West, a member of the Board of Directors of the General Federation; of course the case of the Era club came up for discussion; but Mrs. Brown got no sympathy but was told that "it cannot be."

At Los Angeles, the lady was invited to dine with Mrs. J. R. Clark, whose husband is a brother to Senator Clark. Many of the guests were strangers to one another, and Mrs. Brown heard one lady remark to another:

"Do you know whether or not that Mrs. Ruffin is coming to the convention?"

"No; I heard she wasn't here," came the reply. "But there is another strong woman from Massachusetts coming as a champion delegate for the Era club, but they have arranged it to shut her off every time she gets up."

Mrs. Brown then joined in the conversation:

"Pardon me, Mrs. Cunningham, but what did you say about that delegate?"

"I heard she was coming."

"Well," said Mrs. Brown, "I am that strong woman."

After hearing the true story of the treatment the Era club had received, every guest at the dinner became its friend.

Upon entering the convention hall Monday morning Mrs. Brown met the announcement that Mrs. Julia Ward Howe, Senator Hoar and Mr. Booker Washington had all sent telegrams warning the delegates not to bring up the color question. This was false; and all the parties accused positively deny that any such telegrams were sent.

After many trials, Mrs. Brown finally wormed her way to the front of the vast hall and addressed the chair, claiming the promise of the last meeting to be allowed to make a statement, in this way:

"'Madame President, the delegate from Massachusetts to be heard later.' Mrs. Lowe turned around and began to expostulate. I then said, 'I will appeal to the open convention.' Mrs. West stepped up and said, 'Mrs. President, this is not a question from Massachusetts, it is a personal question.' Mrs. Lowe then said, 'The delegate from Massachusetts is out of order; proceed with the morning business.'"

This was the insulting treatment given to a noble woman who had had compassion on the weak and lowly ones. Mrs. Brown says that she brings her charge against the State Federation of Massachusetts clubs. The first great wrong was perpetrated by Massachusetts sacrificing principle for policy at the Milwaukee convention. There is one thing sure, the end of all this is not yet; and it will be interesting to watch future developments.

At the close of the address, short speeches were made by Mrs. Robert Terrell of Washington, D.C., Mrs. Bruce of Tuskegee, Ala., Major R. R. Wright of Georgia, C. G. Morgan, Esq., Butler R. Wilson, Esq., G. W. Forbes, Esq., and Mrs. Agnes Adams and Miss Eliza Gardiner.

All this is but renewing the old conflict. Thrice before in the history of our country the "spaniel" North has grovelled before the South, but, thank God, the time came when the old New England spirit of Puritanism arose and shook its mane and flung off the shackles of conservatism. So it will be this time. Where we have found one Kate Lyon Brown we shall find more because God lives, and we trust Him.

The claim of the North to govern has been in the past that civilization here is nobler than in the South, and we believe this to be still an axiom.

There has always been an element at the North that never had a logic that knew neither white nor black; and has always been too conservative to recognize its duties. This is true of the pulpit and civil life.

Freedom and serfdom are at war today. The perpetuity of the Union demands a right settlement of this struggle. The Missouri compromise was the first protest of civilization against barbarism. It was unsuccessful, but the South did not succeed in killing the spirit of Freedom there aroused.

We grant that the Southern woman has given us a terrible blow and in a vital part, because woman is the natural social leader; she is responsible in great measure for society's deeds; but we have known for years where to seek our enemy; it is not the man so much as the environments of his social system. Granted that the conditions are hard for a certain class of Southern white women; but the results of profligacy are the same in any case no matter whether white or black are the partners. Certainly the rapid life of society everywhere at present, among white and black, is not suggestive of absolute purity, and the black is no worse than his environment; he follows the fashions as set by his white superior.

But if this thing be true, and pity 'tis 'tis true, it is but the result of conditions forced upon a helpless people, and not their choice; we reap the whirlwind from sowing the wind.

Meanwhile, tears and sorrow and heart-burning are the Southern white woman's portion and like Sarah of old, she wreaks her vengeance on helpless Hagar. Club life has but rendered her disposition more intolerable toward the victims of her husband's and son's evil passions.

Spite of these sad short-comings, let us hope. Never until we welcome the Negro, the foreigner, all races as equals, and welded together in a common nationality, will we deserve prosperity and peace.

SOURCE "Famous Women of the Negro Race IX: Club Life among Colored Women," *Colored American Magazine* 5.4 (Aug. 1902): 273–277.

X.

Artists

With the exception of Music, knowledge and practice of the Arts—Liberal or Mechanic—have been very limited among the Negroes of the United States. But today, when the world is moving forward by leaps and bounds, all men move with it, and in the eager search for new outlets to develop the native genius of the Negro race, and new avenues to employment for the less liberally endowed, we eagerly avail ourselves of all knowledge that will help lead us into undiscovered worlds of industrial achievement and brain development.

There seems to be ample proof to sustain the theory that the Negro under favorable circumstances can achieve remarkable results in art, literature and music. In his case there is racial temperament, intellectual and emotional, of tropical Africa, tempered by centuries of such American civilization as might come to a race in bondage; but he undoubtedly has the artistic temperament largely developed along with the genius of industry.

The conception of art among Negro students is of high order. They feel a sanctity and responsibility attached to the profession which they strive to preserve.

There is a sort of moral education in such life work. Certain corresponding characteristics grow and develop in the artist as his fingers day by day, hour by hour, create with brush and color, mallet and chisel, bud and leaf and flower, delicate tracery of vine and cloud and lineaments of face and figure, out from the unresponsive block of marble, oak or cedar, or on the dull gray canvass.

All that is valuable in the universe is brought before our eyes by painting. The true artist expresses the grandeur of hidden thought in his work, thus by inspiration giving us the full spirit and splendor of landscapes, battle scenes and brave deeds, by suggestions from his hidden self. It is, in short, the office of art to educate the perception of beauty, and to develop our dormant taste.

It would be interesting to trace the progressive steps of painting, to mark its improvement from the first rude attempt of the untutored savage to the high state of refinement it attained under the most celebrated masters. But much of its history is involved in obscurity. Like every other human invention it probably owed its origin to chance. The earliest actual account that we have of painting is in the reign of Semiramis, king of Assyria, about 200 years before the Christian Era.

We are told by Diodorus Siculus that Semiramis, having thrown a bridge over the Euphrates at Babylon, built a castle at each end of it, and enclosed them by three high walls, with terraces upon them, made of brick decorated with paintings and burnt. Egyptian painting did not reach true excellence. The best specimens, as seen in the frescos in the interiors of the sepulchers, display brilliancy of coloring, and frequently great spirit and vivacity; but the drawing is inaccurate, displaying no observance of perspective or even the simplest laws of vision.

Among female painters of the race we mention Mrs. Lottie E. Wilson, Washington, D.C., portrait artist working in oils; also, Mrs. Martha Roberts Nutter, of Boston, Mass., who has done some very successful work in landscapes as well as portraits.

Sculpture—the art of cutting or carving wood and stone into images—is a very ancient art. There is reason to believe that it is more ancient than painting, and that it stood higher in public esteem also; since ancient painters appear to have imitated the statuaries; and their works have not that freedom of style, especially with respect to the drapery, which the pencil might easily have acquired to a greater degree than the chisel.

The sacred writings mention sculpture in several places: as in the case of Laban's idols taken away by Rachel, the brazen serpent made by Moses, and the golden calf by the people of Israel.

In sculpture the Egyptians aimed at the colossal and never attained the beautiful. A remarkable peculiarity of Egyptian sculpture is, that though the earliest monuments reveal a considerable degree of artistic skill, this skill never advanced.

Painting has a greater number of requisites than sculpture; but, at the same time, its expedients are more numerous; and we may therefore affirm that sculpture is a much more difficult art. To be successful it is absolutely necessary that one acquire all the knowledge possible of Geometry, Mechanics and Anatomy, together with a knowledge of the human mind.

The annals of statuary record few artists of the fair sex, but it is pleasant to learn that a taste for this art is developing among women; and numbered among the few there is one who has made famous not only her race, but the American people, over the entire globe:

Miss Edmonia Lewis, the colored American artist, was born near Albany, New York, July 4, 1845. She is of mingled African and Indian descent, her father being a full-blooded African, and her mother a Chippewa Indian. Both parents died young, leaving the orphan girl at the age of three, and her brother, to be brought up by the Indians. Her opportunities for an education were very meagre, but she was sent to school by her brother, finally entering Oberlin College contemporary with Mrs. Fanny Jackson Coppin.

Miss Lewis is below the medium height; her complexion and features betray her African origin; but her hair is more of the Indian type, being black, straight and abundant. Her head is well-balanced, exhibiting a large, well-developed brain. Her manners are unassuming, and most winning and pleasing; her character displays all the proud spirit of her Indian ancestors.

On her first visit to Boston she saw a statue of Benjamin Franklin. She was filled with amazement and delight. The "stone image" was magical in her sight, and new powers stirred within her. "I, too, can make a stone man," she told herself, and she went at once to visit William Lloyd Garrison, and told him her desires, and asked him how she could best set about accomplishing her wishes.

Infused by her enthusiasm, Mr. Garrison gave her a note of introduction to Mr. Brackett, the Boston sculptor, and after talking with her, he gave her a piece of clay and the mould of a human foot as a study. "Go home and make that," said he; "if there is anything in you, it will come out."

The young girl went home and toiled at the piece of clay with all the stoical determination of her Indian ancestors not to be defeated in her purpose, and when it was finished, she carried it to the sculptor. He looked at her model, broke it up, and said, "Try again." She tried again, modelling this time feet and hands, and finally attempted a medallion of the head of John Brown, which was pronounced excellent.

Her next essay was the bust of Colonel Robert G. Shaw. The family of the young hero heard of the bust which Miss Lewis was making as a work of love, and went to see it, and were delighted with the portrait which she had taken from a few poor photographs. Of this bust she sold one hundred copies, and with the money she set out for Europe, full of hope and courage, in 1865.

Arrived at Rome, Miss Lewis took a studio, and devoted herself to hard study and hard work, and there she made her first statue—a figure of Hagar in her despair in the wilderness. It is a work full of feeling, for, as she says, "I have a strong sympathy for all women who have struggled and suffered. For this reason the Virgin Mary is very dear to me." And we may believe this, for Miss Lewis had suffered, almost to the last extremity, from the baleful influence of slavery and caste prejudice.

The first copy of Hagar was purchased by a gentleman from Chicago. A fine group of the Madonna with the infant Christ in her arms, and two adoring angels at her feet, was purchased by the young Marquis of Bute, Lord Beaconfield's (Disraeli) Lothair, for an altarpiece.

In 1867, she gave the world "The Freedwoman." "The Death of Cleopatra," a vividly realistic work, was sent to the Centennial Exhibition of 1876; she has also given us "The Old Arrow-Maker and His Daughter," "Rebecca at the Well," and portrait busts of Henry W. Longfellow, Charles Sumner and Abraham Lincoln. The last mentioned work in is the San José library, California.

Among Miss Lewis' other work are two small groups, illustrating Longfellow's poem of Hiawatha. Her first, "Hiawatha's Wooing," represents Minnehaha seated, making a pair of moccasins, and Hiawatha by her side with a world of love-longing in his eyes. In the "Marriage," they stand side by side with clasped hands. In both, the Indian type of features is carefully preserved, and every detail of dress, etc., is true to nature. The sentiment is equal to the execution. They are charming hits, poetic, simple, natural; and no happier illustrations of Longfellow's poem were ever made than those by Miss Lewis. A fine marble bust of Longfellow was ordered from Miss Lewis by Harvard College.

At Rome this talented woman is visited by strangers from all nations, who visit the "Eternal City," and everyone admires her great genius. Her works show great ideality, a pure heart and an awakened mind. She has, of course, found her chief patronage abroad, where her ability has removed all barriers to association with the most aristocratic leaders, and communion with the greatest minds of the age.[91]

In wood carving remarkable talent has been displayed by Miss Adina White, a young Negro woman.

Wood carving is indeed a rare gift, and one that appeals to the best traits in the artist—patience, perseverance, stability of effort—for wood is not plastic and it requires a strong imagination to evolve dainty fancies out of its hard, unyielding substance—strong imagination and firm, steady fingers.

Miss White was born in New Richmond, Ohio, a mile and a half from Gen. Grant's birthplace, but her family removed to Cincinnati when she was an infant. Here is something to think of. Not from the picturesque South nor from the cultured North have our specimens of Negro artistic talent come, but from the vigorous West.

Adina White came to Cambridge in 1900, and since that time has been studying art in the Boston art schools. This young artist tells a pathetic story of hardship borne for the sake of this work of unremitting toil and effort, and of an indomitable courage.

"If only I could make enough to study here and then go abroad," was the cry of the girl artist as she spoke of her future. Miss Richards, who was her teacher, was making every possible effort to accomplish this end for her pupil. As Adina White stood over her work, with uplifted face and looking outward as if to catch some fleeting inspiration, the idealizing influence of her work was revealed.

The pieces of carving, from her own original designs, showed such skill and ability that it was quite surprising to learn how little of real instruction the girl had had. Upon asking her when the artistic instinct came to her, she answered: "O, I don't know. I used to cut figures on everything that came in my way when I was a very small child. It always seemed natural for me to do this since I used to make toy tea cups and miniature baskets out of peach stones."

"And could you draw, too, when you were a child?"

"Yes; that was how I came to take lessons. Miss Christine Sullivan, who was the supervisor of drawing in the public schools of Cincinnati, where I was educated, noticed my drawing one day and insisted upon my studying at the Cincinnati Art Academy.

---

91. Brown, *Rising Son*, 465–468.

"The wood carving department was then under Mr. Ben Pitman, and I worked there for some time."

Miss White's work is of far more than ordinary value and quality, for she has been employed in factories where hand carving has an important place, and was intrusted by one firm to execute a piece of work for the Columbian Exposition. This must have been a proud moment for the little artist, for although the firm had all the credit (her name not appearing), the work was so exquisitely finished and the design so charming that she gained great local fame.

This carving was a table top, which represented all the wild flowers of Tennessee in a large bouquet in its centre. Miss White carved the wooden petals and stamens and stems from living flowers, and as the table was to be presented in the Tennessee Exposition Building, the design was particularly pretty and appropriate.

Of her work in the West, the most striking, perhaps, is that in the pulpit in the Bethel Church, Indianapolis. The central figure or panel represents a cross, about which a passion flower vine is entwined. At the base of the cross lies a weary-looking lamb. There is poetic instinct in the design, while the gothic treatment of the side panels and borders shows skilful handling.

A box of highly polished wood, the lid a mass of ox-eyed daisies, each leaf and each mossy center standing distinctly from the surface of the wood, was sold to a Boston patron. Beside the box were mirror frames, picture frames, wall panels and other bits, all showing the same skill in design and finish.

Interest in the artist's fortunes from the point of view of hereditary talent prompted the question:

"Did any of your parents or grandparents draw or carve?"

"No," she replied. "I don't know how I came to do it. My father is a steamboat cook, and I never heard of any of my relatives caring much for this sort of thing."

This seems a case of sporadic Negro talent, until we remember that in Miss White there is a strain of Indian blood, and when we remember also that Miss Lewis is of the same extraction—African and Indian with no white blood filtering on through the two—the coincidence is remarkable, to say the least.

As representatives of a despised people, the genius of the women we have just described is too great to be hidden from the public, while the world asks us scornfully what we have done to be classed among intellectual races, and at the same time tells us in derision that when we have proved our ability, then we shall be admitted to the brotherhood of men on an equal footing with other races.

We have been proving our ability since the days of Phillis Wheatley and Benjamin Banneker; but it is a hopeless task to undertake to convince a wilfully blind and perverse generation. There is but one thing to do for those who have this God-given genius—seek other lands and there accomplish their manhood and womanhood far removed from the blighting influences from which we suffer in this caste-ridden and prejudice-cursed land of our birth.

This is a practical age—an age in which we are beginning to view every question of labor from its industrial side. If we possess any particular talent (for we cannot all be geniuses with vivid intellectual conceptions), the first question which presents itself to the practical mind is, how this talent can best serve us as a pivot for wage-earning? This is a momentous question for the Negro race at this stage of our progress, when avenues for gathering cold American dollars are gradually lessening for us.

For self-preservation the cosmopolitan citizens of this Republic must manufacture; they must have skilled labor. The rapid increase of scientific knowledge makes art a necessity. As science throws men out of employment, art must provide employment. The scientist and artist must walk hand in hand. The invention of labor-saving machinery for the farmer, enabling one man to do the work that formerly required ten, is rapidly driving men from the country to the cities. The invention of other machinery is rapidly throwing large masses of workmen out of employment. Political causes are adding to this evil. How to put the unemployed millions to work is the problem of the day. The salvation of all our citizens depends upon its solution. Skilled labor is the answer.

It takes but a few men to fashion a ton of iron watch bar, but a thousand to work it into watch springs. Five men can make all the coarse pottery in use in a district, but it takes five hundred to make decorated ware and porcelain.

In France a large city is supported by the manufacture of watches; in Germany the rural population of the district near the Industrial Art School of Nuremberg live in comfort by the manufacture of toys, which are exported to all parts of the world. This is owing to the taste and knowledge diffused abroad by the Art School.

The demand for skilled labor is greater than ever, both to manage machinery and to take the product where machinery has left it and fashion it into value by the art of the decorator. Such a workman plies his handiwork at his own house and teaches the secrets of his trade to his family.

We look forward to the time when America shall rival other nations in Industrial Art—domestic architecture and decorative skill, and above all in all departments of painting.

The English were long held to be a people hopelessly inartistic and devoid of art possibilities; their wonderful development since 1851 challenges investigation. This is true also of America, only tenfold greater.

The Puritan immigrants of New England had an abhorrence of art which marked the followers of the Reformation, and for two centuries the bare whitewashed walls of the plain meetinghouse were in eloquent appeal against art adornment of ancient church or chapel. Such was the situation alike in England and the United States during the first half of the 19th century.

Drawing has lost its first definition as belonging to the realm of picture-making, and the movement for its general introduction into the public schools, and of definite endeavors to promote art decoration to develop and improve the art industries of the people seemed alike sudden in England and the United States. In England it was apparently the definite result of the humiliation that came to England as the result of the first world's fair held in London, in 1851.

In the United States it had its origin in Boston in 1870, where it was the direct outcome of the English movement.

American architects and their employers are awakening to a practical recognition of the value of art in the decoration of interior wall surfaces of public buildings. The value of a thorough training in industrial art drawing has at last become so generally recognized as to call for little argument.

To what does all this tend? To new avenues of employment and an awakening of all our faculties to the beauty and glory of the material world through art.

Here the Negro stands as fair a chance as any other people if he possesses the requisite skill; and for the young element there is every incentive to rise in a profession not yet overcrowded.

In all our large towns and cities we find ladies applying themselves to decorative art—on metals, ceramics and fabrics.

Mrs. Robert Ransom, well known in Boston's social life, is a most accomplished worker in decorative art. Her exquisite work on satin and china has been greatly admired at the Mechanic fairs, where she has been a regular exhibitor for years.

The philosophy of Sam Walter Foss is particularly applicable to our young people:

> The path that leads to a loaf of bread
>   Winds through the swamps of toil,
> And the path that leads to a suit of clothes
>   Goes through a flowerless soil,
> And the paths that lead to a loaf of bread
>   And the suit of clothes are hard to tread.
>
> And the path that leads to a house of your own
>   Climbs over the bowldered hills,
> And the path that leads to a bank account
>   Is swept by the blast that kills;
> But the men who start in the paths to-day
>   In the Lazy Hills may go astray.
>
> In the Lazy Hills are trees of shade,
>   By the dreamy brooks of Sleep,
> And the rollicking river of Pleasure laughs,
>   And gambols down the steep;
> But, when the blasts of winter come,
>   The brooks and rivers are frozen dumb.

Then woe to those in the Lazy Hills
    When the blasts of winter moan,
Who strayed from the path to a bank account
    And the path to a house of their own.
These paths are hard in the summer heat,
    But in winter they lead to a snug retreat.[92]

SOURCE "Famous Women of the Negro Race X: Artists," *Colored American Magazine* 5.5 (Sept. 1902): 362–367.[93]

---

92. Sam Walter Foss (1858–1911) was a newspaper editor, poet, and librarian, who was born in New Hampshire and worked in Massachusetts. His humorous verse appeared frequently in local newspapers and national magazines.

93. *Famous Women of the Negro Race* progresses from installment X in September 1902 to installment XII in October 1902. There was no installment XI.

XII.

Higher Education of Colored Women in White Schools and Colleges

Can the Negro woman learn anything? Is she capable of the highest mental culture? are questions which have been conclusively answered in the series of articles closing with this number.

We have seen that every slave State had laws against the education of the Blacks, and that the present régime of State government in the South land is in opposition to the highest educational development for the race.

We have seen, too, that the Anglo-Saxon woman, in convention assembled, has sought to place the indelible stamp of hopeless intellectual inferiority upon the Negro race in spite of voluminous testimony to the contrary. There is none so blind as they who will not see; none so hard to convince as they who wish to believe the worst of their fellow-beings.

Is the course adopted toward the unfortunate Negroes of this country according to the teaching and spirit of the Gospel which is so proudly and austerely heralded to heathen nations at an annual cost of millions? We look in vain for a trace of the graciousness attributed to the female character or the meek gentleness of Christ, in the position assumed by the Anglo-Saxon woman toward her dark-skinned sister. In the struggle for supremacy now going on in the world of women, the first principles of development are lost sight of. Whatever is divine in ourselves is most fully developed by the endeavor to make it beneficial to our neighbor. Herein is scope, and motive, and reward for the most patient effort of self-culture. In the wonderful scheme of God's earthly government, the doing of good to others is the direct means of achieving success in life for ourselves. All science, commerce, industry, spread blessings abroad, leading to fame and fortune if pursued for the benefits spread abroad. Women's education and work are no exception to this rule. For the sake of our country and its future dearest interests women of every nationality should be encouraged and invited to bear a part in the Christian duty of doing good to our neighbor, and should be trained to understand that duty and to do it.

In denying the intellectual capacity of the Negro woman, our fair-skinned sisters have forgotten that they themselves have but just gained intellectual equality in the great world of endeavor.

The condition of woman in antediluvian times was that of a drudge, and in all the higher relations of life, an inferior being.

The condition of woman in Palestine and the European states before the Christian era, was that of ignorance and imprisonment. Roman nations were distinguished for their virtue and dignity, but the law gave the husband the same absolute right to the services and even the life of his wife, as he had to those of his slaves. But the later history of pagan Rome is a terrible one, warning all peoples of the necessity of the high principles being instilled into the heart of womankind, for the fall of Rome was due as much to the wantonness and wickedness of its women as to the demoralization of its men.

The Jews attempted to preserve female purity, and the law placed women in the absolute control of parents and husbands.

The advent of Christianity exerted a favorable influence on the condition of women throughout all countries. And in the whole life of the Redeemer there was a compassionate thoughtfulness for women, an evident desire to raise her from her lowly condition, and to confer upon her some relief from the severity of the sentence pronounced in Eden. From that time until now we date her elevation. For the first six hundred years of the Christian era, the Christian woman was practically free from the subjection under which she was formerly bound. It is to the honor of the sex that in every century of the Dark Ages, there were women who sought to raise their sex from degradation; women who established schools and institutions of learning, and thus attempted to turn the attention of their sisters from frivolity and dissipation.

In the century which followed the Reformation, more than half the thrones of Europe were occupied by queens, some illustrious for their virtues, other equally conspicuous for their vices. Isabella of Spain, Catherine de Medicis, of France, Mary and Elizabeth of England, Elizabeth of Hungary, Mary, Queen of Scots, were remarkable female rulers, and their reigns compare favorably with those of the kings who preceded or succeeded them.

The eighteenth century was also remarkable for its intellectual women, some of whom were never surpassed for the vigor of their style, while others exhibited a grasp of intellect and a power of grappling with important questions of finance and political economy hitherto supposed to be beyond the ability of the sex. It was reserved, however, for the nineteenth century to witness the higher and much fuller development of the female intellect. This century gave the world Queen Victoria who may be considered the leading figure in the advancement of all womanly excellence. In literature woman has achieved a high position. In science a few great names demonstrate the capacity of the sex for high attainments in astronomy, mathematics, political economy, psychology and moral philosophy.

In mechanic arts they have exhibited skill in manipulation; in trade and commerce trained women have exhibited decided abilities. But in the Crimean War, the Civil War and the war in Germany, the remarkable executive ability of woman was fully demonstrated on the battlefield and in hospitals.

The Negro woman having risen from no greater depths, though enslaved, than the Anglo-Saxon woman, feels her womanhood stir within her and boldly advances to scale the heights of intellectual advancement, feeling that the door has been opened for her to take an active, intelligent and resolute part in the march of human progress. It seems almost as if the inspiration of the times had created a new race of colored women, a new tide set in, new forces called into play, a new era in the world's history and through all this the moral and social regeneration of a race. The command of God to the woman of color is: "Behold, I have set before thee an open door, and no man can shut it." So, let us press forward in faith believing.

If we look closely into the mass of all that has been lately written and spoken against us, it resolves itself into two main heads: first, the question as to the right of the woman of color to live in the world on the same terms as a white woman does—to work as she does, to be paid as she is, to elevate herself, intellectually and socially as she does—to make use, in short, of all that is elevating in life; and, second, the question as to the colored woman's competency so to do.

As to the first question, we do not discuss a right. We assume it. Assertion would weaken our position. That we have the right is a self-evident truth. It rests with our enemies to prove why we should not enjoy the privileges we claim. "The burden of proof," says Mill, "is supposed to be with those who are against liberty; who contend for any restriction or prohibition, either any limitation of the general freedom of human action, or any disqualification or disparity of privilege, affecting one person or kind of persons, as compared with others. The *a priori* presumption is in favor of freedom and impartiality."[94]

As to the question of competence, it must be settled by the law of natural selection and the application of the same practical tests that settle this question for the Anglo-Saxon woman. The only proof of competence is performance. The world belongs to them who take it, black or white.

The great advantage in co-education of the races lies in the self-reliance engendered in students of the weaker race, the perfect development of a manly or womanly spirit, and, in women more particularly, refinement of manner and the inculcation of the highest ideals in morality—in social life and in the home.

Most of the institutions for the higher education of women have a corps of teachers endowed with rare attainments and possessed of the purest principles of Christian womanhood. The benign influence poured upon susceptible youth by the close association between teachers and pupils in four years of academical life can hardly be estimated, especially for a race where every effort has been made to degrade its womanhood. We are happy to record that undaunted by the cruelty of caste prejudice, many young colored women have entered the sacred precincts of celebrated institutions of letters, and successfully combatting great obstacles have demonstrated to the world their peculiar fitness for service in the sacred inner courts of intellectual preeminence, regardless of race. In these schools our women have occupied unique positions, the great searchlight of publicity being constantly cast upon their every action. Thus they

94. John Stuart Mill, *The Subjection of Women* (1869).

have become pioneers in the field of letters; indeed, in every field of human life where great personal effort rebounds to the good of humanity.

We do not wish to be misunderstood; we do not imply that our race schools are not doing excellent work; it is the great opportunity of presenting an object lesson to the on-looking world, which lies within the grasp of the colored student in white institutions.

In 1860 we may well imagine that the United States was scarcely the place where one would seek colored students in white academies. But there was one such miracle in the then city of Charlestown, Mass.

The Charlestown Female Seminary was and is an institution of learning, patronized by exclusive and aristocratic circles for the education of their young females. Fifty years ago the cream of the South was gathered within its walls, and also many daughters of West Indian planters received instruction there. Mrs. Mary Livermore was graduated from the Charlestown Female Seminary many years ago, and other illustrious white women claim the institution as their alma mater.

In 1860 Miss Hattie H. Allen was graduated from the Charlestown grammar schools, and because of her Negro blood was denied admission to the high school. Being a bright, intelligent girl, and well known and liked by the white citizens, an effort was made to have her admitted to the Seminary. Miss Badger—since then well known as a teacher in the Boston Girls' High School—was the preceptress of the school; she offered no objection to receiving a colored girl.

Miss Allen was received at first as a special pupil, and gradually worked her way into the different classes, no opposition being expressed; she was finally admitted to the full curriculum of the school. On the day of graduation, three years from the time of entrance, Miss Allen was one of eight to receive a diploma, and as a special mark of favor, the colored girl was the valedictorian of her class.

After this Miss Allen taught penmanship for a while in the seminary, leaving to accept a position to teach in a private academy in Canada, where her color was no bar.

There was a profound sensation in educational circles when it was announced that a colored girl, Miss Alberta Scott, a native of Cambridge, Mass., and a product of the school system of that famous city, was about to enter Radcliffe College, and compete for honors there with the highly cultured white of American society; but so it was. Miss Scott's proudest hopes were realized and she was graduated with distinguished honors.

Since then a number of other young colored women have entered this university and among them is Miss Burrill who is a student at the present time. Among the young matrons of Boston, we record with much pleasure the name of Mrs. George W. Forbes. Mrs. Forbes was Miss Marie Elizabeth Harley, of Kingston, New York, an historic city on-the-Hudson, nestling at the foot of the Catskill Mountains. Miss Harley married Mr. Forbes of the West End branch of the Boston Public Library, November 29, 1900.

Mrs. Forbes finished her education at Kingston Academy, which ranks with the highest institutions of learning in New York State. Mrs. Forbes was the only colored graduate and remembers her alma mater with pride and pleasure. She is a very clever young woman; she is a stenographer of ability and is well up in newspaper work, being one of the staff of city reporters for the *Boston Guardian* in which her husband is interested. Added to all this, Mrs. Forbes is a cultivated musician and a pianist of ability; while Mrs. Azalia Hackley was in Boston on her concert tour, Mrs. Forbes was her accompanist on a number of occasions.

Mr. Forbes is a graduate of Amherst and has been connected with the West End branch of the Boston Public Library for years; in fact, since it was first opened to the public. No other colored man in Massachusetts has been selected for library work by the city government. Mr. Forbes is an interesting figure in the public eye; from the fearless position he has assumed in race matters, he is being felt in all race questions.

Wellesley College, too, was destined to received a representative of our race in the person of Miss Elizabeth Baker, of Cambridge, Mass., now Mrs. William H. Lewis.

Mrs. Lewis is the mother of two sturdy sons, and is absorbed in plans for the education of her children on the strict lines of solid moral and intellectual training that shall advance the race through individual effort.

This young woman is particularly interesting to us by reason of the fame that has come to her husband. W. H. Lewis is a well known Harvard athlete, having played on the football team while at Harvard Law school, and later becoming a trainer of the undergraduate. He entered upon the practice of his profession in Boston, living in Cambridge; he gained the confidence of all citizens by his strict attention to business. In 1901 he was elected to the Massachusetts Legislature from Ward 5 of Cambridge, solely by the white voters. He is the first colored man to go to the general court in five years. Colored citizens of Boston cannot gain a seat in the House. Mr. Lewis has built a fine home on Upland road in the beautiful suburb, North Cambridge; his summers are spent at Nahant where the home of Senator Lodge is located.

We have been represented at Vassar College by Miss Anita Hemmings who was born in Boston and educated in the public schools of that city. None of us will soon forget the wave of excitement which swept over the country when Miss Hemmings was graduated. Being a very beautiful girl, her connection with the race was denied by many current publications. Miss Hemmings is now employed at the Boston Public Library. Dr. Clark, who is at the head of Guilbert Academy in Winsted, Connecticut, had for a pupil in his school Miss Estelle Hill, a colored young woman. She was graduated from the academy June 6, 1897, and Dr. Clark was so thoroughly convinced of her intellectual ability that he urged her to enter Boston University and make the most of all opportunities offered her. Nothing daunted by the thought of obstacles, Miss Hill presented herself at the university and was received without hesitation. Miss Hill was not the first colored girl to enter Boston University; in 1891

Miss Anna May Barbadoes of the Haverhill High School entered Boston University and remained two years. Both of these ladies tell the same story of a cordial welcome being extended to them by teachers and pupils.

Miss Hill was graduated in 1901; since then she has married the Rev. W. H. Lucas, a cousin of Dr. Booker T. Washington.

In reviewing the careers of these young women we must not fail to note one important fact: three of them have become the wives of progressive college men. Education has not caused these women to shirk the cares and responsibilities of private life; rather, we believe, each feels the blessing which her example must be to the entire race. Education, with us, does not encourage celibacy but is developing pleasant homes and beautiful families.

The highest degree of moral culture is necessary between a wedded pair for the care of those Christian virtues which make home most like heaven in its serenity, unselfishness and attractiveness. No true man can object to thus developing the higher nature of women; we all have the happiness of knowing a far greater number of examples of women, intelligent and cultivated, active in good work, interested in all that is worthy of interest, who by the development of their faculties have added grace and luster to their natural attractions. Even men who look only for agreeable companions, acknowledge that they are to be found rather among the educated than the uneducated.

And the world has need for all the higher work of which woman is capable. In cities, villages, prisons, workhouses, in art galleries and in letters, in all branches of industry, the world is the debtor of the woman of any race who can do it service.

We who are near to the heart of the Negro—we know that a wonderful transformation is going on within the secret forces of his being. We do not fear the future, but we look forward with confidence to the time when Phoenix-like, he shall arise from the ashes of his past and become the wonder of ages yet unborn. The current of human progress is slow, sometimes apparently backward, but never permanently checked.

> The firmament breaks up. In black eclipse
> Light after light goes out. One evil star,
> Luridly glaring through the smoke of war,
> As in the dream of the apocalypse,
> Drags others down. Let us not weakly weep
> Nor rashly threaten. Give us grave [*sic*] to keep
> Our faith and patience.[95]

SOURCE "Famous Women of the Negro Race XII: Higher Education of Colored Women in White Schools and Colleges," *Colored American Magazine* 5.6 (Oct. 1902): 445–450.

95. John Greenleaf Whittier, "A Word for the Hour" (1861).

PART IV

Furnace Blasts, *by J. Shirley Shadrach (1903)*

*F*urnace Blasts consists of two installments that Hopkins published under the pseudonym J. Shirley Shadrach in the *Colored American Magazine* in February and March
1903. The title comes from John Greenleaf Whittier's poem "Furnace Blast," which
appears in her profile of Whittier (included in the "Selected Biographies" section of this
volume) and as the epigraph to the first chapter of *Contending Forces*.[1] The unambigu-
ously issue-oriented nonfiction model that Hopkins uses in the two articles in *Furnace
Blasts* differs from her biographical approach in *Famous Men* and *Famous Women*. Writing at a moment of significant change for the *Colored American Magazine,* she adopts a
more strident approach and is rewarded with an increasingly prominent role by William
Dupree's new management team. The focal points of the two wide-ranging installments
are prostitution and interracial relationships. Hopkins may have elected a pseudonym
so as not to be directly identified with the sexual subjects she addresses in the short-
lived series.

1. Pauline E. Hopkins, *Contending Forces: A Romance Illustrative of Negro Life North and South* (1900; repr.,
New York: Oxford University Press, 1988), 17. The first chapter of *Contending Forces*, "A Retrospect of the
Past," appeared in the *Colored American Magazine* in November 1900, the month that *Famous Men of the
Negro Race* premiered.

The Growth of the Social Evil
among All Classes and Races in America

Nineteen hundred and three. Our days are gliding swiftly by; let us resolve to do what we can the coming year for the substantial up-building of the race while time remains. Today is ours; tomorrow is uncertain.

As we look over the record of the year just closed we note with pain the growth of crime. Thugs galore; "cold-fingered" girls plying their nefarious calling in every large city of the Union. Once the time was that Chicago had a virtual monopoly of the street highway business, but New York and Boston are pushing Chicago to the rear. And the haunt of the strange woman, a veritable mouth of hell to the multitude. What infamy, disease, degradation and death these vices inflict upon us! How they blight and curse the lives of the innocent and helpless! What a load of shame they place upon a community!

How the changes have been rung upon the depravity of the Negro since the entrance of the twentieth century, and the charge has been boldly made by the great majority, including a respectable showing among his own race, that he is the most depraved of criminals. The females of our race, in particular, suffer from the most malicious slander, and none protest against the outrage upon a worthy class of citizens. How much we suffer through the tyranny of prejudice. How much more we suffer through the force of example. How much we suffer through the power of bad counsel coming from those virtually above us.

They who hang their heads in shame, in view of the advancing demoralization of modern civilized life, and turn away with horror-struck faces, look back to social caste prejudice which has closed the avenues of profitable employment in the face of certain races and reconsider the conclusions made against the Negro.[2]

God knows the Negro is guilty of many sins, and has contributed his share to the world's misery, for, being human, he is susceptible to the same temptations that beset the rest of the human family, but many of his moral lapses are the result of inherited traits inbred by slavery. Out of that dreadful condition there was no escape for the female slave but into the cold embraces of death; and the victims were born into that condition; they did not enter into it voluntarily, as do the wretched inmates the dens of infamy in our great cities.

---

2. Wendell Phillips, "Woman's Rights" (1851), in *Speeches, Lectures, and Letters* (Boston: Lee and Shepard, 1872), 32.

It took years to force this condition of immorality upon a helpless sex, but to their everlasting honor, be it said, they have passed from vice to virtue with a rapidity that is amazing.

The solution of this, the social problem, is a national affair. No one race is responsible for the vice of the country; no one race can produce a clear virtuous atmosphere in a cosmopolitan population like us.

It is a sad and terrible thought that, in our great cities, our manufacturing towns and villages, our sea-ports, and our manufacturing centers, of the women between the ages of fifteen and thirty, one out of every twelve is a thing of shame! The proportion is as great among young men who prefer a dissolute life to a virtuous one. To what causes shall we attribute a state of things so deplorable? The question is a difficult one, yet, it admits of an answer which will indicate most of the influences which induce immorality.

We may say in the beginning, though it is small consolation, that this vice is more prevalent in Great Britain than in America. In the continental States, especially the South of Europe, among the lower classes, chastity is the rare exception, therefore the great influx of immigration has left lasting ill effects upon the families of the poorer classes in our large cities. Voluminous testimony also proves that one great source of this evil is also found in the corruption of the youthful mind by the reading of vile literature circulated through the medium of association in schools (public and private) and by emissaries of wicked men engaged in a nefarious business. But aside from these minor sources the more prominent causes are not far to seek.

The fashionable mode of education has developed the love of display and sumptuous living as the chief end to be desired in life, teaching indirectly the practice of deception, and stimulating the love of admiration among women and an inordinate desire for the excitement of the life of a man about town, among young men.

Young women of all classes feel that they must have an easy life, costly apparel, gems and ornaments in profusion. Pressed by temptation at every point where they are weakest, they yield, after a brief struggle, and enter, covertly at first, perhaps, on a life of sin.

Young men must have fashionable clothing, cigars, wine, cards, the theatre, betting, boating, gambling. A modest position and corresponding income fail to support them; result, defalcations, petty thefts, professional burglary, an influx of snatch-thiefs, thugs, murderers, and the graves of persons crowding Potter's Field.

Thus we have it: First step,—the infelicities of our American divorce series of systems. Single young women and men see, hear and imitate. I often wonder how certain social lights can look each other in the face. Husbands and wives separated for cause, married to the causer, sit beside each other in the opera houses and churches and other public places, looked at, sneered at, gossiped about, and never turn a hair. Vice legalized. Second step,—Too much "bridge whist," too much of the social glass. Too much attention to other men's dashing wives. Too much attention from other women's husbands. Too much betting on fast horses, prize fights, and keeping up with the crowd generally. But while the ranks of fashionable vice are largely recruited from the graduates of a false system of education, the country girl and boy who have become residents of a great city, come hither on the promise of employment, with fresh, young and handsome faces, are cast among associates of doubtful or evil character, and if they love display and dress, with a corresponding dislike for hard work, the girl soon hears how "a single smile may bring her better fare and finer dresses than a month's wages," and though, at first, her soul revolts, yet she begins to parley with temptation and hesitating is lost. The boy learns from his associates how to tamper with the cash of the "old man" who is his employer or how to cast a "marked" card that shall win the coveted dollars to be expended in questionable pleasure. This is but the beginning.

There are some doubtless who yield to temptation under pressure of starvation. Many, very many beautiful girls and young men have been lured to ruin by the advice of seeming friends who have cautioned them against being "too scrupulous" as to the means taken to gain a living. This we know to be the case with many lovely young colored people. The advice and example of white friends have caused their downfall. We will not go further into the horrible details of this loathsome subject which is eating its way into the very heart of the homelife of this Republic. It is not within the power of human legislation to change the human heart, or to suppress the fires of passion and sin in the human heart; but much good might be done by judicious legislation to diminish an evil which threatens to destroy our nation.

Charles Dudley Warner once worked up an article that did the Negro great harm.[3] Others have been in the same business. He brought statistics to prove the increase of Negro criminality. Statistics may be made to prove anything under the sun. The number of Negro criminals in jails and prisons counts for nothing. In answering Mr. Warner, Mr. Paul Laurence Dunbar said some good things:

> Taking into account that some of the offenses for which a white boy would be reprimanded and released, would send a Negro to the chain gang in the South, it is easy to see how the percentage of criminals is raised. A fight upon the street, picking up coal with the accusation of throwing it off the cars, brawling generally, land the black boy in jail.

3. Charles Dudley Warner, "Education of the Negro," in *Fashions in Literature, and Other Literary and Social Essays and Addresses* (New York: Dodd, Mead, 1902), 193–224. Warner's presidential address to the American Social Science Association in Washington, D.C., on May 7, 1900, was published as a pamphlet under the title *The Education of the Negro.*

Criminals, yes, but how many of the Southern cities have reformatories for youthful offenders and for the punishment of youthful offences? I know of one case in a city not so far south of Mason and Dixon's line, where a boy ten years old was accused of throwing coal off the cars, arrested, convicted, and instead of being sent to a reformatory, was placed in jail with the lowest type of felons and with insane people. It happened that he was placed in the cell with a mad man. During the night screams were heard from the cell, but for a time were unnoticed. After awhile the keeper took his way leisurely through, and found the child horribly mutilated by the maniac. Ruined for life physically, and brutalized mentally.[4]

Here is another. An Anglo-Saxon specialty.

In January, 1901, the female house of refuge, Baltimore, in which there were several hundred young girls, was declared by the grand jury in its report to be a house of horrors, and the prosecution of its woman superintendent and the utter abolition of the institution were recommended. The report caused a tremendous sensation. We give one clause:

Heinous as are these corporal punishments, they are not more to be deplored than is the total absence of an ennobling moral atmosphere.

We had before us one witness, not an inmate, who was once connected with this institution in a professional capacity, and who resigned her position because she could not countenance the physical barbarities practiced.

This witness testified that at the time of their reception fifty per cent of the girls and young women committed to the refuge are virtuous. Then in response to a question as to the proportion of virtuous at the time of release this witness said: "There are practically none. The associations are such that during detention every moral or virtuous instinct is destroyed and the girls go straight from the refuge to lead dissolute lives."

What more terrible fate can be imagined for these involuntary recruits to the ranks of vice! Yet if these unfortunates had been Negroes, the railers against the race would have set them down as natural examples of depravity without considering the circumstances of the case.

In one of his annual reports, Rev. J. W. Hamilton, secretary of the Freedmen's Aid Society, spoke of his recent visit to the South. He visited Key West, with its 25,000 inhabitants, and said: "It has not one hundred pure Anglo-Saxon

---

4. Paul Laurence Dunbar, "Is Higher Education for the Negro Hopeless?" (1900), in *The Paul Laurence Dunbar Reader*, edited by Jay Martin and Gossie H. Hudson (New York: Dodd, Mead, 1975), 47.

Americans. One-third or one-fourth of the people of the United States are of mixed blood. Some of these pass for white, *so slightly are they mixed with Negro blood.*"

To show how the South helps to frown down the social evil and to raise the morality of the immoral (?) Negro, we quote the following:

> Columbia, S.C., Oct. 3, 1895.—Section 34 of the proposed ordinance on the legislative department was called up for consideration in the constitutional convention today. The section as reported from the committee and passed, read: "The marriage of a white person with a Negro or Mulatto, or a person with one-eighth or more Negro blood, shall be unlawful and void."

Wigg, a corpulent delegate from Beaufort, of the color of well-baked gingerbread said:

> Mr. President: We have asked the convention to be logical in their opposition to us. You have reported a section aiming at the Negro for no other purpose than to humiliate and insult us. We accept it, and ask in return that as you seem very anxious to keep the races separate, and make it unlawful for a Negro and a white person to enter into the holy bonds of matrimony, that you will at least give us protection for our girls, and punish the white men who seek to lead them from the paths of virtue. ***
>
> Is it possible that you who boast so loudly of being the proud sons of Carolina, peers of the noblest on earth, are afraid to meet this issue like men? It has gone out to the world that you have forbidden intermarriage of the races. You have made an institution ordained by our Creator, unlawful. We demand that the act you make unlawful be punishable. Dare you refuse it, and if you do what construction will public opinion place upon your refusal? Is it possible that you are guilty? Surely it cannot be.[5]

The miscegenation act was passed as amended, and all the amendments forbidding unlawful association between the races were lost.

In the face of all this, ministers preach of the immorality of the Negro and the blot that the mulatto is on the virtue of the country. Lecturers discourse on the hopeless depravity of the Negro. Authors, Southern authors mainly, write books to prove the Negro's viciousness. But a little interested research brings the truth to light.

We do things better in Boston. It won't do to judge the Negro's moral depravity by the number of mulattoes one passes on the streets here. Most of

5. James Wigg, an African American legislator from Beaufort, South Carolina, participated in the 1895 South Carolina Constitutional Convention. On October 25, 1895, he delivered a speech in defense of African American suffrage that was later published as a pamphlet and distributed in New England.

them get their white blood from their *white mothers*. And these legitimate off-springs of miscegenation form a large and increasing portion of the population of Massachusetts. It's a hard pill to swallow, but if you go at it right it is warranted not to cause instant death.

Rise and fall. Of what?

We are all familiar with the rise and fall of Rome, and could probably talk more or less of the rise and fall of Babylon. Ancient history is suggestive. Take Rome for instance. We read of its supremacy, of the splendor of its feasts, the pride of its patricians, the prodigality of its rich, the humility of its slaves, the profligacy and degeneracy of its zenith when beastly orgies, bloody slaughters in the ring and an utter disregard of personal purity hastened on decay. She rose to the apex of grandeur—and fell. Why?

We read the pathetic story of Virginia with a thrill of the heart strings that defies expression. There we behold the picture of virtue's sacrifice of life for the preservation of sacred honor.

Catiline's superb scathing of the aristocracy who scorned those beneath them and ground the face of the despairing poor while they scarred the writhing bodies of their slaves for pastime, comes down to us from the pages of history.[6] He warned them that as evil was in their hearts so evil times were in store for them. They banished him, but with terrible intuition he had read their fate. The American people are not less brutal and unjust to the Negro than was the Roman patrician to the common people of his day.

Malice defeats itself.

It is not sensible to place the blame for social impurity in a population of 80,000,000 upon one race or class alone. Criminals themselves prove this.

Since Thomas Dixon's book saw the light along with that of Col. Thomas, we have had a Jane Toppan up here in Massachusetts, whom Thomas might have taken for a model so perfectly does her case represent, in some of its details, the depraved picture he drew of crime among his own people.[7]

The Negro has met with a hundred instances to social purity, and prejudice is one of them. The white man, we believe, hardly realizes how great his prejudice is. Prejudice has impeded the progress of the new emancipation. It has injured the white man and black man alike, and still keeps on its road of

6. Catiline, Lucius Sergius Catilina (c. 108 BC–62 BC) was a Roman aristocrat who attempted to overthrow Cicero's Republic.

7. Thomas Dixon (1864–1946), white supremacist novelist from North Carolina, published *The Leopard's Spots* in 1902. It was the first volume in a fiction trilogy whose second installment, *The Clansman* (1905), was the basis for D. W. Griffith's film *Birth of a Nation* (1915). William Hannibal Thomas (1843–1935), a conservative African American commentator, included a chapter on "Criminal Instincts" in William Hannibal Thomas, *The American Negro: What He Was, What He Is, and What He May Become; A Critical and Practical Discussion* (New York: Macmillan, 1901), 208–236. Jane Toppan (1854–1938) was an infamous white serial killer who worked as a nurse in Massachusetts before her 1902 murder trial.

destruction, holding the black man down by degradation within and prejudice without. What nonsense to preach evangelization in a country where the people glory in injustice and cruelty to a portion of its population!

Rome fell. Why?

Because Omnipotence was wearied by the injustice of man. History repeats itself.

For God will visit us in judgment; and in the last hour, when He seems to have left nothing undone that he could do for His vineyard, we still forget justice and judgment; none calling for justice, nor any in the high places of government pleading the cause of the poor, the very poorest of the poor, the despised and humiliated Negro.

Rome conquered the world, and was finally swallowed up by the world which it conquered![8]

As we remarked in the opening lines of this article, the social evil is a *national* sin. The remedy lies in a thorough cleansing of the body politic and a prayer to God in the language of the ritual: "Lord have mercy upon us and incline our hearts to keep thy laws."

SOURCE J. Shirley Shadrach, "Furnace Blasts I: The Growth of the Social Evil among All Classes and Races in America," *Colored American Magazine* 6.4 (Feb. 1903): 259–263.

8. Hopkins repeats this passage near the conclusion of *A Primer of Facts.*

II.

Black or White—Which Should Be the Young Afro-American's Choice in Marriage

We have no desire to eulogize the Negro in treating this subject. As a class, Negroes are what any other people would be so long subjected to the terrorism of tyranny which blurred the relation of the sexes and thereby weakened the physical, intellectual and moral forces of an entire race. Let us also take into calculation another fact,—this was done under the domination of a people, many of whom were themselves of the most indifferent morals, to speak lightly.

The purpose of every race lover should be to familiarize the public mind with the fact that the Negro is a *human being*, amenable to every law, human and divine, that can affect any other race upon the footstool. The greatest objection to Negro enfranchisement is found in the menace of social equality which it is contended will inevitably lead to amalgamation.

The Anglo-Saxon argues that no fouler blight can fall upon his race than the curse of intermarriage with former slaves, forgetting that the "shaded Afghan" which represents the present conglomeration, once pure African, was contributed by the blood of the Southern whites.

In the fear of social equality, no allowance is made for the chance that the Negro may not care for the joys (?) of such association; it is taken for granted that he will jump at the opportunity of pushing himself into a circle where he is not wanted. The truth is, the intelligent, self-respecting Afro-American finds every intellectual and social want more than filled among his associates of his own class. Among them he finds all the refinements of life which enhance the beauty of home and woman, with that freedom of association in which is a certain cordial exhilaration only found in social equality. There vulgarity, ignorance, coarseness, do not exist, but pleasant jets of affection, delicious fountains of association metamorphose the earth, and in this happy social affinity he forgets that there is a world where prejudice bars the door of pleasure for Negroes.

But the question of marriage is one of three about which no man can speak with certainty; it defies all laws and bows only to the will of Infinity.

We are born; we marry; we die; and no power on earth can change the circumstances under which these vital happenings occur; had we such power, then would Infinity cease to be Infinity.

Shall the Anglo-Saxon and the Afro-American mix?
    They have mixed.
    Shall they continue to mix?

This is the question which underlies all personal and public prejudice and legislation against the Negro.

Every soul is a celestial Venus to every other soul. Love is omnipresent. . . . Love is our highest word and the synonym of God.

Thus sings Emerson, subtle philosopher and keen analyzer of human affairs.

Love is the bridge to close personal relations which are the foundations of social intercourse. Our interest is aroused by the sight of a couple under the magic influence of Cupid's spell. Novels which portray the tender passion with truth produce a glow in the heart that time cannot efface. No truer line was ever penned than that which says, "All mankind loves a lover."[9]

A youth and a maiden meet at a crowded reception, a glance is exchanged full of the fire of magnetism. The mischief is done. Glances are merged in courteous acts until the crisis or culmination; marriage is the result. As life wears on in the dual relation, the youth and maiden find that they have been in training for that future love which knows not sex, nor person, nor passion, but seeketh only virtue and wisdom, "for it is the nature and end of the marriage relation that the actors represent the human race to each other." Observers by nature and therefore learners, the youth and maiden soon feel that their affections are but tents of a night, and that this beautiful relation must be supplanted by that heavenly relation which is more beautiful still. Thus do we progress step by step toward a future life. And if this be the true plan of salvation, by which the ends of Infinity are to be compassed, what availeth man's puerile efforts or his petty malice, against Divine power? Be sure the plan of salvation will be accomplished if every idol of prejudice is forced upon the fiery altar of purification.

"From ebony to alabaster!"

It was the privilege of the writer to listen to the eloquent and scholarly Prof. Price, in Tremont Temple, Boston, shortly before his death.

In speaking of the wide range of choice spread out before our youth he said that there was no call for a man or woman of color to marry outside racial lines, for there was every color necessary for choice ranging from ebony to alabaster. But in spite of the variety, many Negroes are availing themselves of the privileges granted by our Northern States, to unite themselves with the Caucasian race; and this is more prevalent among men than among women.

We find no fault in this if the Negro unites himself to one who is in all things his equal—morally and intellectually. But we are sorry to say, the reverse often happens, and no men entail upon themselves and their children the deadly association of a nature vile, miasmatic and filthy, dealing death to all hope of moral cleanliness.

There is still another point to consider.

9. Ralph Waldo Emerson, "Love," in *Essays: First and Second Series* (1841–1844; *Making of America*, 2005), 1:164.

The Negro woman is not tolerated by the Anglo-Saxon; he can stand the black man but not the black woman save in the menial position of a servant or the degraded one of a concubine. Positions calling for refined service are barred to the female Afro-American, generally speaking, and the hatred of the white sister is so implacable as to become revolting.

If, then, the male of our race contracts alliance with the dominant race, by preference, what becomes of his sisters and the other female members of his family when the time comes for them to select life-partners? The sequence is inevitable under certain circumstances: an alliance of shame or the lonely celibacy from which nature revolts.

It is a situation giving food for serious reflection. Yet no human foresight can alter these evils; we must await with what patience we can, the will of Omnipotence. Legislation against the God-given institution of marriage would engender evils that we know not of.

For all the benefits then, that we dream of enjoying through the propagation of civilization, we must depend upon science and evolution.

Society and moral practices are growths, not manufactures, and improvement must come to us through the laws of social growth.

Spencer tells us, "The end which the statesman should keep in view as higher than all other ends is the formation of character."[10]

In the study of the cause and effect reaching into all departments of human life, we find "Combe's Constitution" indispensable, and would recommend it to all young people seeking for light in the darkness of the present.[11] While marriage is founded on love, that love must be controlled and guided by the fundamental moral laws. The future of the Negro as an individual and as a race lies within the hand of science, and by a just regard for the natural laws we can defy the specious reasoning which now argues so successfully against Negro manhood and womanhood.

Life brings responsibilities which may not be shirked, and it rests with ourselves to have the blessings on curses of futurity. No man liveth to himself alone. Social miseries obviously spring from a neglect of, or opposition to, the organic laws. It is now generally conceded that religion can never become thoroughly practical, nor be wholly beneficial for human improvement, until wedded to philosophy. In proportion as the study of the Great Book goes hand in hand with a study of the natural laws—both becoming familiar even to the children of the home—in just such proportion will a race be lifted permanently out of the slough of ignorance, vice, and superstition.

A fertile source of unhappiness arises from persons uniting in marriage, whose tempers, talents and dispositions do not harmonize.

10. Herbert Spencer, *The Principles of Ethics* (New York: D. Appelton, 1897), 2:380.

11. George Combe published the first of several editions of *The Constitution of Man Considered in Relation to External Objects* in 1828. Hopkins uses chapter five, "To What Extent are the Miseries of Mankind Referable to Infringement of the Laws of Nature?" at length in this essay.

"If it be true," says Combe, "that natural talents and dispositions are connected by the Creator with particular configurations of the brain, then it is obviously one of his institutions that, in forming a compact for life, these should be attended to. . . . [12] It is God who speaks from Nature in all her departments; and the brain is his workmanship as much as the Milky-Way, with its myriads of suns."[13]

If every faculty is, then, good in itself, and the folly and crime which disgrace society spring from the abuse of these faculties, and that the tendency to abuse the best portion of our mechanism, arises from moral and intellectual ignorance, how completely do these considerations go to the very root of theology and morals.

Says one celebrated author writing upon this subject:

By a proper attention we can improve and preserve the breed of horses, dogs, cattle, and indeed all other animals. Yet it is amazing that this observation operates so seldom in the human species, where it is so vitally essential. How a certain character or constitution of mind can be transmitted from parent to child, is a question of more difficulty than importance. It is equally difficult to account for the external resemblance of features, or for bodily diseases being transmitted from parent to child. But we never dream of a difficulty in explaining any appearance of nature which is exhibited to us every day. A proper attention to this subject would enable us to improve, not only the constitutions, but the characters of our posterity.[14]

We every day see sensible people who attend anxiously to the improvement of the breed of their horses, tainting the blood of their children with disease, madness, folly, dishonesty, crime the most revolting and unworthy dispositions, all through the lust of the eyes, after the flesh-pots of Egypt, meshed in the gleam of floating golden hair and the glint of ethereal blue in the orbs of the Anglo-Saxon female.[15]

Physical organization of which moral is the offspring, transmits the germs of character from parent to child. The Apii were always haughty and inflexible, the Catos always severe. The whole line of Guises were bold, rash, factious.[16]

In Persia it is said that the custom has existed for ages among the nobles, of purchasing beautiful female Circassian captives, and forming alliances with

12. George Combe, *The Constitution of Man Considered in Relation to External Objects* (1847, 8th ed.; *The History of Phrenology on the Web*, 2002), http://pages.britishlibrary.net/phrenology/constitution/chapter05.html, 177–178.

13. Ibid., 185.

14. Professor John Gregory, quoted in Combe, *Constitution of Man*, 189.

15. Professor John Gregory, quoted in Combe, *Constitution of Man*, 189–190.

16. Voltaire, *Philosophical Dictionary* (1764), quoted in Combe, *Constitution of Man*, 190.

them as wives. It is ascertained that the Circassian form of brain stands comparatively high in the development of the moral and intellectual organs. It is mentioned by some travellers, that the race of nobles in Persia is the most gifted in natural qualities, bodily and mental, of any class of that people; a fact diametrically opposite to that which has taken place in Spain and many other European countries, where the nobles intermarry constantly with each other, and set the organic laws at defiance.

The degeneracy and even idiocy of some of the noble and royal families of Spain and Portugal, from marriage with nieces, and other near relatives, is well known.[17] The father of Napoleon Bonaparte possessed a handsome person, a talent for eloquence, and a bright intellect, which he transmitted to his son. He married Laetitia Ramolini, a beautiful woman possessed of great firmness of character, in the midst of civil discord, fights, and skirmishes. Madame Bonaparte partook of all the dangers of years of civil war, accompanying her husband on horseback in many hasty flights just before the birth of the future great Emperor.[18]

David Rizzio was murdered with many circumstances of violence and terror, in the presence of Mary, Queen of Scots, shortly before the birth of James the First of England.

Napoleon and James form striking contrasts; one can draw but one conclusion. Napoleon's mother arose to the dangers of her position, and braved them; Mary was inspired by fear alone.[19]

If it be true that this lower world is arranged in harmony with the supremacy of the higher faculties, what a noble prospect is opened up by man's placing himself more fully in accord with divine institutions; and, in consequence, reaping numberless enjoyments destined for him by the Creator in Eden's first happy estate, but since lost by folly, and abiding the thousands of miseries that now render life scarcely endurable by reason of that same folly committed by our common parents.[20] The Eden of futurity, it seems, can only be regained by the development of that wisdom, and the knowledge for which Adam and Eve perilled the salvation of humanity in payment.

The worship of Mammon excites men to investigate the Natural Laws, while moral and rational consideration exert small influence in leading them to do so. Before an insurance company will take a risk of $150 on the death of an individual, they require certain answers to be sworn to by credible witnesses.[21]

A man and a woman about to marry, have, in the generality of cases, the health and happiness of many human beings depending upon their attention

17. Combe, *Constitution of Man*, 195.

18. Walter Scott, *The Life of Napoleon Buonaparte* (1827), quoted in Combe, *Constitution of Man*, 204.

19. Combe, *Constitution of Man*, 204.

20. Ibid., 209–210.

21. Ibid., 211.

to considerations as essential as those of mere speculation in money.[22] These laws are not only applicable to the domestic relations, but they are the foundation stones of the ordinary relations of society.

If we obey the moral law, we enjoy the highest gratification of which our nature is susceptible, in the activity of our noblest faculties which so nearly approach the nature of Divinity. We become objects of esteem to our fellow-men, and enjoy exalted social privileges. Our undertakings, being projected in harmony with nature, will prosper. We enjoy health of body and buoyancy of mind. We place ourselves in the best condition for observing the physical laws, and thereby reap countless blessings.

If we reverse the picture we perceive the penalties by which our Creator punishes infringements of the moral law.

The whole scheme of creation is constituted for the purpose of enforcing obedience to the moral law. Virtue, religion, happiness are founded in the constitution of human faculties, and are not dependent upon the fancies, the desires, or the mere will of man.

To what does all this tend?

To show to us,—a people long educated to measure life's responsibilities by a false standard—that we are no longer sinks for the filtration of the moral rottenness of other races, but rational beings upon whom it is now incumbent to seek the highest development in life that can come to man. That we are not to accept anything short of the best in life; and that we must impress this principle upon the tender mind of childhood. That the lust of the eyes after the flesh-pots of Egypt meshed in the gleam of floating golden hair and the glint of ethereal blue in the orbs of the Anglo-Saxon, must be suppressed.

The discovery of America created a new era in the world's history. Out of the heterogeneous mass of humanity drawn to the new land from the deteriorating countries and governments was evolved a nation, the shrewd, intelligent, hustling, and now opulent nation known from continent to continent as "Americans," unique in character, unique in government.

Within the circle of American influence, infinite forces have conspired to produce infinite varieties of the genus homo. The relation of individuals to the State—lesser lights revolving about the great centers of political, economic and social life—produced the greatest evolution in humanity ever presented by the pages of history.

In this great drama the Negro has sustained a leading part. If we catch the thread of argument the rest is easy; Representatives of African tribes have been brought to this Western El Dorado; the Northern, Central, Western and Eastern Africans, all are here commingled, thus forming a new genus of the Negro. Tribal relations have disappeared. The *Afric*-American has arisen, essentially American in every characteristic, in whom the blood of the Southern white

22. Ibid., 212.

has been contributed as the cement which binds these African tribes as one in the new genus homo.

These happenings were fore-ordained, we believe, by Infinity, long before the fall of Ethiopia from her pristine splendor. Gradually the Negro is rising; each revolution of the wheel of Destiny but brings him nearer to the end of his long probation.

The grand finale of this racial drama is about to begin, the key-note of which lies in the affirmation: "Of one blood have I made all nations of men." Today we can say how wonderfully the law of evolution is fulfilling old Bible prophecies!

To the young Afro-American who hesitates between black or white in his choice of a life partner, I say "Don't!" The time for amalgamation is not yet. In the company of the beautiful, virtuous and intellectual of your own race, lie health, happiness and prosperity.

SOURCE J. Shirley Shadrach, "Furnace Blasts II: Black or White—Which Should Be the Young Afro-American's Choice in Marriage," *Colored American Magazine* 6.5 (Mar. 1903): 348–352.

PART V

The Colored American Magazine Controversy (1903–1905)

Like *Furnace Blasts,* Hopkins's February 1903 article "Latest Phases of the Race Problem in America" was published under a pseudonym and represents her more directly political nonfiction voice. Whereas most of the figures in *Famous Men* were deceased, the figures whom Hopkins challenges here, including President Theodore Roosevelt, were very much alive. While Dupree and the new management of the *Colored American Magazine* seemed to support Hopkins through 1903, John Freund's escalating involvement culminated with the January 1904 event that Hopkins documented in "How a New York Newspaper Man Entertained a Number of Colored Ladies and Gentlemen at Dinner in the Revere House, Boston, and How the Colored American League Was Started." In this report, Freund's speech criticizing Hopkins's leadership of the magazine appears under her own byline, indicating her ironic ability to maintain some modicum of authority and editorial control while under attack. However, her refusal to capitulate to Freund sent her career at the *Colored American Magazine* on a downward spiral, which she describes in detail in her 1905 letter to William Monroe Trotter, published here from a typescript in the Pauline E. Hopkins Papers in Franklin Library Special Collections, Fisk University. The letter was written at a time when W.E.B. Du Bois asked Trotter to provide information on Washington's control of the black press. Du Bois, in turn, later referenced Hopkins's letter in the *Crisis*. Due to gaps in surviving issues of the *Boston Guardian*, I am unable to ascertain if Trotter ever published any part of Hopkins's letter in his own paper.

9. The cover of the February 1903 *Colored American Magazine* advertised "Latest Phases of the Race Problem in America" by Sarah A. Allen. Hopkins sometimes used her mother's maiden name as a pseudonym. Miss Josie R. Crump, pictured here, was a beauty contest winner and nursing student from Richmond, Virginia.

Latest Phases of
the Race Problem in America

Sarah A. Allen

Once to every man and nation comes the moment to decide,
In the strife of Truth with Falsehood for the good or evil side.

Lo! humanity sweeps onward: where to-day the martyr stands,
On the morrow crouches Judas with the silver in his hands.

New occasions teach new duties. Time makes ancient good uncouth.
They must upward still and onward who would keep abreast of Truth.
—Lowell[1]

Tyler, Fillmore, Johnson and Arthur—President Roosevelt is the fifth executive sent to this nation by the awful and inscrutable ways of Providence.

No President, since the days of Gen. U. S. Grant in 1869, has awakened the degree of interest that he has in foreign countries from the first moment that he assumed his high office. It is declared by the press that President Roosevelt and Emperor William are the two most interesting men on the world's stage today.

In Grant's time the patriotism which now appears to be on the decline, was at its height. A bloody conflict was just ended and four million slaves were free. By daring deeds of valor on many a sanguinary field of battle the Negro had demonstrated his fitness for liberty and the pursuit of happiness. Respect and friendship for the loyal and honest black face went hand in hand at home and abroad; suffrage was his.

President Grant in his first message to Congress recommended and urged the adoption of an amendment to the Constitution to make the right of franchise independent of race, color or previous condition of servitude, and the people and Congress obeyed the call and gave us the Fifteenth Amendment. Thus the Negro became a factor in the politics of the country—a bone of contention since the death of our intellectual giants in politics, and the advent of mental dwarfs.

---

1. James Russell Lowell, "The Present Crisis" (1884). Hopkins frequently cited Lowell's poem in her own writings well before it inspired the name of the NAACP's *Crisis* magazine.

Grant and his men and the Negro had been comrades-in-arms, they had tramped through swamps, waded through gore, been sorely wounded in the same battles, suffered in the same hospital tent, and the Black man had fed the starving wearer of the Union blue many a time and oft. Grant and his men knew the beat of the white heart under the black skin!

Grant knew the temper, too, of the South, and with wisdom and foresight gave us the Fifteenth Amendment that the principles for which the war was waged on many a Southern field,—the principle of national supremacy,—might be forever maintained.

Gen. Grant accepted the Negro at his par value, and never had cause to regret his action. Under his administration the colored citizen rose rapidly in the social scale. Competent men of the race were not wanting under President Grant in both houses of Congress, ministers in foreign service, consuls to European governments, cadets in military and naval academies, collectors of internal revenue, and as postmasters in large Southern cities. The Negro's political troubles began under Hayes in 1877. The rights then surrendered can never be regained. From that period on the colored citizen has lost all that he holds dear in freedom—the right to vote.

We are told that the elective franchise is not a right, but a privilege. This is not true. In a government of the people, the elective franchise is an actual, absolute right,—a right belonging to every citizen who is free from crime. Any proposal to submit the question of the political or civil rights of the Negro to the arbitrament of the whites is as absurd as to submit the question of the political rights of the whites to the arbitrament of the Negroes, with one difference,—the Negroes are loyal to the Government. They have a deep interest in the continued supremacy of the United States, and the National Government should see that the Negro is placed in a position to assist it as well as himself. The ballot commands respect and holds more strength than a standing army.

After President Hayes, the Republican party of William McKinley has done the colored man the greatest harm. Under him we lost all the political preference we had gained by President Grant's protection. The great party retrograded, and the spirit of commercialism consumed the time which should have been devoted to the upholding of the great moral principles which in the time of Sumner, Stevens, Phillips, Garrison, Lovejoy and Roscoe Conkling had placed the party and the country in the forefront of political ethics.

This hasty resumé brings us down to President Roosevelt, who found us standing on the ragged edge of despair. In sixteen months Mr. Roosevelt has done much to strengthen the moral possibilities of his office both at home and abroad. In the great questions of the hour,—those that commend the deep interest of statesmen, scholars and rulers, he has shown himself a tower of resource and efficiency, and he is more and more coming to be regarded as a factor to be reckoned with in any great question of commerce or politics.

When Mr. Roosevelt came into executive being, the shadow of the Philippine war was over the country. In a few months the cloud floated out of sight; hostilities were quickly terminated. A great diplomatic victory followed in the abrogation of the Clayton-Bulwer treaty with Great Britain.[2]

Another most notable happening was the negotiation for the purchase of the Panama canal at a reasonable figure, and the agreement of Congress upon that route across the isthmus, which if finally ratified by the necessary agreements with the Colombian government, will redound to the credit of this administration.

The administration won a success in the recent Venezuelan diplomacy. Within a week or ten days a subscription was started in Paris for a testimonial to Mr. Roosevelt, in appreciation of his successful services in promoting the principles of arbitration and the recognition of The Hague peace commission in the Anglo-German quarrel with Venezuela.

The reciprocity treaty with Cuba is said to be in fair way for a settlement which will leave the victory with the President.

Europe is impressed by the effective intervention of our Executive in the great coal strike. It is admitted abroad, too, that the remonstrance of the American government against the unjust treatment of the Jews in Roumania has been beneficial to that persecuted people.

Mr. McKinley was powerless to settle the Sampson-Schley controversy; not so President Roosevelt.[3] All the facts that we have summarized in a short executive career serves to show the remarkable ease with which this man has wielded public opinion; in all his political battles he has come out first and best. It is a significant test. There are no narrow bounds to his possibilities.

We come now to the matter of Negro appointments. The great questions so successfully undertaken are as nothing to the "family jar" now waging, ever growing hotter and hotter from the "Washington dinner" at the White House to the last great sin committed by President Roosevelt in the appointment of Mr. Lewis as assistant district attorney for Massachusetts.

President Roosevelt has said with the courage of his convictions:

I cannot consent to take the position that the door of hope—the door of opportunity—is to be shut upon any man, no matter how worthy, purely on the grounds of race and color. Such an attitude would,

---

2. In 1850, U.S. Secretary of State John M. Clayton and British Minister Sir Henry Bulwer signed a treaty agreeing to joint control of a prospective Central American canal. The Clayton-Bulwer Treaty was superseded by the 1901 Hay-Pauncefote Treaty in which Britain agreed to U.S. control of the Panama Canal.

3. A conflict between naval officers William Thomas Sampson and Winfield Scott Schley erupted during the Spanish-American War, with each questioning the other's valor for actions in combat in May and June 1898. In 1901, there was an official government inquiry into the controversy. For details on the affair, see *Record of Proceedings of a Court of Inquiry in the Case of Rear Admiral Winfield S. Schley, U.S. Navy, Convened at the Navy Yard, Washington, D.C., September 12, 1901* (Washington, D.C.: U.S. Government Printing Office, 1901–1902).

according to my convictions, be fundamentally wrong. It seems to me that it is a good thing from every standpoint to let the colored man know that if he shows in marked degree, qualities of citizenship—qualities which in a white man we feel entirely right to reward—then he will not be cut off from all hope of similar reward.[4]

These words are full of hope for the Negro and deadly miasma for the Southern whites. If Mr. Roosevelt lives up to his own utterances his life bids fair to be more strenuous than he has ever found it to be even when as a Rough Rider he engaged in many dangerous pursuits, worse than fighting on San Juan hill, and requiring more diplomacy than all his foreign policy has yet demanded.

But they who weigh well the signs of the times as they bear on the fate of the Negro, may well be pardoned if they hesitate to endorse without due calculation even the most dazzling whispers of hope borne to us on the breeze of presidential favors to black men. We trust, we hope, that the flattering tale is true, but how often have we proved the falseness of friendship.

Not long ago President Roosevelt appointed Dr. W. H. Crum of Charleston, South Carolina, to the collectorship of that city. Dr. Crum is a man of integrity who holds a leading position among his people by right of merit, and moreover, he is a shining light in his profession.

The South Carolina Legislature requested both Senator Tillman ("Bloody Ben") and Senator McLaurin to oppose this appointment on mere racial lines. Let us not forget that this is the same Legislature that indorsed the President's appointment of Koester, who with a lynching party had murdered a native-born American citizen on American soil.

With these facts in view we have waited breathlessly the next move in the game by the schemers who prefer that the federal offices in the South shall go to white Democrats rather than to colored Republicans and thus build up a white Republican party in the Southland. In the months that have passed it looked as if the President was to be a party to the conspiracy.

Scarcely had the shock of Dr. Crum's appointment passed over the country, when we were again aroused by the closing of the postoffice at Indianola, Mississippi, by order of the President.

Mrs. Cox was re-appointed by President Roosevelt as postmistress at Indianola. She is an estimable woman who is highly esteemed by the citizens of the town; her husband has been in the postal service for many years. Firmly believing that they would be supported in any violent outbreak against a Negro office-holder, the whites of Indianola—about 85 persons, or one-

---

4. Theodore Roosevelt to Hon. ___ (November 26, 1902), in *Addresses and Presidential Messages of Theodore Roosevelt, 1902–1904* (New York: G. P. Putnam, 1904), 268–269. Roosevelt used similar language in a letter to the mayor of Charleston earlier in the month. See Roosevelt to Robert Goodwyn Rhett (November 10, 1902), in *Theodore Roosevelt and His Time: Shown in His Own Letters*, edited by Joseph Bucklin Bishop (New York: Charles Scribner's Sons, 1920), 1:168–169.

fourth the population of the town—held a mass meeting and demanded Mrs. Cox's resignation. Mindful of the fate of Mr. and Mrs. Baker in the ever-memorable Baker episode, Mrs. Cox retired without protest from the contested ground. President Roosevelt is thoroughly aroused over the incident. The case was brought up at the Cabinet meeting, and Mr. Payne, the postmaster-general, at the President's request, went to the White House to continue the discussion. At the close of the conference a statement embodying the ideas of the Administration, and the determination to divert all mail for the time being to Greenville, Miss., was given out by Secretary Cortelyou.

By this heroic treatment it seems that the President has broken loose from all restraint and declared war on the "lily white" Republicans of the South, and that he intends to protect Negro federal office holders in the South. This seems too good to be true.

This brings us down to the latest act in the drama of American politics,— the appointment of Hon. W. H. Lewis as assistant district attorney, at Boston. In speaking of this appointment the *Boston Transcript*'s special says:

> Taken with a recent similar appointment in Pennsylvania, it affords some food for reflection in connection with the Crum case. The colored people represent not far from one per cent of the population of Massachusetts, while they number more than sixty per cent of the population of South Carolina, and furnish somewhere near ninety-nine per cent of its Republicans. President Roosevelt, thus far in his Administration, has appointed between sixty and seventy office-holders for South Carolina, including presidential postmasters, and Crum is the only colored one among them. This disposes of the idea that there is any intention on his part of overriding roughshod the feelings and sensibilities of the Southern whites. The appointment of Lewis to an office in Massachusetts which is more more [sic] important and much more lucrative, answers the query so frequently raised in Southern circles as to why Negro appointments are not made in the North, where the color prejudice has not assumed set forms of expression.
>
> It is also notable that President Roosevelt has been especially careful of Southern sensibilities as to the class of offices to which he has appointed colored men. *** It has been impressed upon him that what the whites particularly objected to was colored postmasters; many Southern women will not take mail from a Negro. *** He has appointed no new colored postmasters, though he has renewed the term of several to whom there was no particular objection, and has taken decided objection to the running out by violence of a mulatto woman who was serving in this capacity in Mississippi.
>
> The next class of offices in which the Southern people said they could not stand Negroes were those pertaining to the administration of justice. *** It was repugnant to Caucasian feelings to have any member of

the race brought to justice by a Negro, or for other whites to be asked to assist Negroes in doing this. ***

Then came the collectorships, particularly of internal revenue. These offices were not open to the objections raised to either of the others, as few persons in any community had to do business with the collector directly, and these were men not women. When the President suggested Negroes for such places in the South, a new objection from white sources appeared to the effect that these offices paid too much money for Negroes; that it was repugnant to Southern feelings to see so lucrative a place going to a member of the inferior race. This was a consideration the President decided he could not entertain, and so he has appointed colored internal revenue collectors in Mississippi, Georgia and elsewhere.

William Henry Lewis, Esq., recently nominated assistant United States district attorney for Boston, and appointed by Henry P. Moulton, Esq., the United States district attorney, was born in Berkeley, Virginia, Nov. 28, 1868. Both his parents were former slaves, and his father, the late Rev. Ashley Lewis, was a Baptist clergyman. Mr. Lewis's education began in the common schools of Portsmouth, where his father's church was located. After attending there he went to the State normal school at Petersburgh, where he was prepared for college. In 1888 Mr. Lewis came to New England and entered Amherst College, from which he was graduated in the class of 1892. While in college he entered actively into athletics and became captain of the football team. In his senior year he was class orator and won the Hardy prize debate and the Hyde prize oration.

In the fall of 1892 Mr. Lewis entered the Harvard Law School, and at the same time became a candidate for the Harvard foot-ball eleven, which was that year captained by Waters. Lewis soon proved himself an excellent player and won the position of center. He held the same position in the eleven under Trafford the next year, and by introducing new tactics and a new method of play made the position more important than it had ever been before. He did not play in the '94 eleven, owing to the eligibility rule, but was of great assistance in coaching the eleven. Every year since Mr. Lewis has been a prominent factor in the development of Harvard foot-ball, and has given much time and study to coaching.

Graduating from the Harvard Law School in 1895, Mr. Lewis passed his examinations and was admitted to the Bar. He made his home in Cambridge and now resides there at 226 Upland road. In 1896 he married Miss Elizabeth Baker of the class of 1898, Wellesley, and they have three children. In 1899 Mr. Lewis became prominent in Cambridge city politics and was elected to the common council that year. He was re-elected in 1900 and 1901, and in 1902 went to the Legislature, the first colored man to sit in that body since 1896. He was appointed to the Committee of Judiciary and was prominent in debates.

He made a speech against the bill for a statue of General B. F. Butler, and introduced a resolve for an investigation of the administration of justice by the courts. Mr. Lewis was well liked by his white associates in the House and was honored by being called to the chair by the presiding officer during his absence. Since he began practicing, Mr. Lewis has met with flattering success. On one case in which he was before the Supreme Court, Chief Justice Holmes complimented him for his argument in the official report of the case.

Mr. Lewis was president of the Amherst General Alumni Association, and is a member of the Middlesex club and the Cambridge Republican club. His law office is at 804 Barristers Hall, Pemberton square.

President Roosevelt knew Mr. Lewis well through his connection with Harvard athletics, and Mr. Lewis visited at Oyster Bay several years ago, stopping over night with the President. He is also well-known to Senators Lodge and Hoar, both of whom endorsed him for the position. A large number of the justices of the supreme court and the most able lawyers in the State endorsed him, as well as Governor Crane. He was a candidate for the same position under President McKinley.

The salary of the position is but $1,500 per annum, and as the *Springfield Republican* says, "does not measure up to desires recently expressed for appointments of colored men to federal office in the North."[5] We do not, however, forget that Lieutenant William H. Dupree is, and has been for years, at the head of affairs at Station A, Boston, which is an important position carrying with it a large salary. Captain Charles L. Mitchell at the custom house overlooks as much business as enters the port of Charleston, South Carolina.

The game of politics is a Chinese puzzle.

We would like to believe that the President's appointment of Mr. Lewis is an upward trend in political ethics, but, alas! how little confidence one can have in any public deed in this age of commercialism and lax morals.

Currents and counter-currents of political life in the University city are illustrated in the recent defeat of Mr. Lewis for a second term in the Legislature and his appointment to a high office following closely upon it. When Mr. Lewis was elected to the Legislature in 1902, it was well understood that he was in no wise indebted to colored voters for his election, he going from the richest and most aristocratic district of Cambridge, where very few Negroes resided, and he, of course, did not consider them his constituents. Naturally racial feeling ran high among the voters, and his speech in the House against the Butler monument augmented this feeling, and added to his foes the Grand Army men and the Sons of Veterans. Leading local politicians were scalp hunting most of the year against the machine, and a gallant fight was waged for the recognition of Negro manhood and equality before the law.

5. The *Springfield Republican* was a regular advertiser in the *Boston Guardian*. The *Guardian* also reprinted some articles from the *Republican*.

And Cambridge state and city elections were striking illustrations of the Negro's political relations in the entire country.

Among these strong men was Rev. S. T. Tice, D.D., pastor of the St. Paul A.M.E. church, Cambridge. Dr. Tice was appointed by Bishop Derrick, D.D., to do something in Cambridge for God and suffering humanity.

Dr. Tice is an able and eloquent speaker, finely educated. Under him the church entered upon a new and important work. A "social settlement" was formed for colored people of both sexes.

Ten years ago there were less than one thousand colored people in Cambridge. Today there are five thousand, and still they come from the rural Southern districts. They must be cared for and rescued from the vice of the great city, and for this the settlement was founded in the "black belt" district of Cambridge, the Castle Garden across the Charles. It is needless to say that Dr. Tice has met with unprecedented success, and in a political battle is a force to be reckoned with.

About this same time Rev. J. Henry Duckrey, M.A., pastor of Mt. Olive Baptist church thought that his people should have some representation on the school board. The Republican committee was asked to consider his name for the school committee and he was unanimously turned down by the machine.

Dr. Duckrey is another well known, influential and well-educated minister of the race; Cambridge is blessed with a number of fine colored theologians. Dr. Duckrey is a graduate of Lincoln University. He came to Cambridge ten years ago and assumed the pastorate of a mere handful of people. In that time he has increased his flock from twenty-five to over four hundred in membership, and built a handsome brick edifice on a fashionable thoroughfare in a desirable district where property is on the rise. Indignant at his treatment by the Republicans, Dr. Duckrey accepted the Democratic offer to run on their ticket for the school board. He was defeated for the position along with the other Democrats for the board on the ticket because of the women voters. The women turned out in force and defeated the Democratic ticket. But the value of the Negro vote was shown in the defeat of Mr. Lewis, Republican, on the State ticket and the re-election of Mayor McNamee, Democrat, city election, by a handsome majority. The colored vote did it. Mayor McNamee then tendered Dr. Duckrey the position of trustee of the Public Library for three years, and Dr. Duckrey has been officially notified of his confirmation by the board of aldermen.

Then came Mr. Lewis's appointment by President Roosevelt, advised by Senators Hoar and Lodge. Was it a political necessity?

Dr. Tice and Dr. Duckrey deserve the hearty thanks of the entire community for demonstrating to the world that a man is a man whether white or black, and that the right of franchise alone gives a race civil manhood. In the doubtful Northern States the Negro is a factor, and Republican leaders may well view with alarm the present evidence of his disgruntlement.

We hope and trust that President Roosevelt has met with a permanent change of heart, and that threats of social ostracism will not turn him from the path of duty. His appointments so far among Negroes have all been good. Mr. Lewis may be conservative, but he is a gentleman who will do us credit in whatever position he finds himself. Let the good work go on, and may Theodore Roosevelt be able to quote the words of noble John A. Andrew, with perfect truth, when he retires to private life.

"I know not what record may await me in another world, but this I know, that I was never mean enough to despise a man because he was poor, because he was ignorant, or because he was black."[6]

SOURCE Sarah A. Allen, "Latest Phases of the Race Problem in America," *Colored American Magazine* 6.4 (Feb. 1903): 244–251.

6. John Albion Andrew (1818–1867) served as governor of Massachusetts during the Civil War. This quotation appears frequently in discussions of his career, and was often cited. See, for example, Edwin Percy Whipple, *Eulogy on John Albion Andrew* (Boston: Alfred Mudge and Son, 1867), 21.

How a New York Newspaper Man Entertained a Number of Colored Ladies and Gentlemen at Dinner in the Revere House, Boston, and How the Colored American League Was Started

Pauline E. Hopkins

*A*n event took place at the old Revere House, Boston, celebrated in the annals of the abolition movement—on Sunday afternoon, January 24th, which is destined to have an important bearing upon the future progress of the colored race, as a movement was inaugurated for the establishment of a "Colored American League" upon so simple but exalted a plane that it can but commend itself to broadminded men and women, whatever their race or color.

On this occasion some twenty or more representative ladies and gentlemen of the colored citizens of Boston were entertained at dinner by John C. Freund of New York, a well known newspaper editor, who for over thirty years has been connected with the musical interests and industries of the country.

The purpose of the meeting was to devise plans to sustain *The Colored American Magazine*, to broaden its scope and thus increase its usefulness.

Among the guests present were: Colonel and Mrs. W. H. Dupree; Mr. and Mrs. Joseph H. Lee; Mr. and Mrs. William O. West; Captain and Mrs. Charles L. Mitchell; Mr. and Mrs. Edward Everett Brown; Mrs. Mattie A. McAdoo; Miss Pauline E. Hopkins, the editress of *The Colored American Magazine*; Mr. J. Wallace Buchanan; Mr. and Mrs. Butler R. Wilson; Mr. and Mrs. Walter Sampson; Mr. and Mrs. J. W. Watkins and Mr. and Mrs. James H. Wolff.

An excellent dinner was served by the host of the Revere House. With the coffee and cigars, Col. Dupree, president of the Colored Co-operative Publishing Co., rose and said:

What Colonel Dupree Said

As you all know, some of us have been endeavoring for several years to sustain a monthly publication known as *The Colored American Magazine*. It is published, as you also know, by the Colored Co-operative Publishing Company, an organization founded by Colored men and women, who put into it what money they could spare because they believed the time had come for the publication of a high class magazine, which should take up and discuss the great questions that interest the colored people, and which should give the world some idea of the progress we have made in the generation that has passed since the abolition of slavery. The magazine was also intended to show that the colored people can advance on all the lines of progress known to other races, that they can be more than tillers of the soil, hewers of wood and drawers of water—that they can attain to eminence (both the men and women among them) as thinkers, as writers, as doctors, as lawyers, as clergymen, as singers, musicians, artists, actors, and also as successful business men, in the conduct of enterprises of importance.

From the start the magazine attracted attention, and was fairly supported, though its business management was not all that could be desired, so that, as you know, a reorganization of the company became necessary not long ago. Such an undertaking involved, as its friends found out, a larger capital than the company had at its disposal. So the projectors of the enterprise went through distressing experiences, and there are some of us who suffered greatly in our heroic endeavor to keep the magazine alive. But we never despaired. We felt that we had so noble a cause that if we only were loyal to it, the time must come when we would have our reward.

Some months ago, Mr. Barker, ex-Paymaster in the Navy, and Superintendent of Delivery in the Boston Post Office, a man of noble character, called my attention to a series of articles which had been printed in a New York paper on the condition of the Negroes in the Island of Jamaica, in the British West Indies. These articles, with illustrations by their author, had been written by the editor of that paper. Through Mr. Barker's courtesy, I was enabled to obtain them and read them through. In Jamaica, as you know, there are some seven hundred thousand colored people and, in all, about fourteen to fifteen thousand whites. These articles, written by Mr. John C. Freund, described the life of our colored brethren in this paradise of the tropics, and took so kindly, yet just, a view of the colored race that I thought it would be a good thing if we could induce Mr. Freund to permit us to republish them in our magazine.

Thereupon, I wrote to Mr. Freund and received from him permission to republish the articles, accompanied by a promise of material help to testify to his good will towards our enterprise. In the correspondence that ensued between us and also between Mr. Freund and the editor of our magazine, Miss Hopkins, he said he would be glad to be of service to us and expressed a desire to meet some of the representative colored people of Boston, so we might lay out some comprehensive plan of action. For that purpose, he suggested that we be his guests at a dinner that we might meet in social intercourse and discuss ways and means for extending the usefulness of our magazine.

That is why we are here. That is Why Mr. Freund is our host.

Let me say that Mr. Freund was born in London of German parents, that he received his education at Oxford and London Universities, and soon after, came to this country where he has been continually at work as newspaper editor and writer ever since. He is the oldest publisher of a musical paper in this country. He is also known as a playwright, as a writer on politics and social economics. Mr. Freund has always been a friend of our race and taken an interest in our progress. For that reason, we may be glad as well as proud to have him as our host on this occasion.

What John C. Freund Said

Mr. Freund, who was accorded a generous reception, spoke as follows:

My friend, Colonel Dupree, has been so good as to tell you why we have assembled here and he has been so amiable as to refer, in kindly terms, to me personally.

That you may fully understand my position, let me say, in advance, and before we come to discuss the questions in which we are interested and the best means to further the interests of the magazine, and extend its usefulness—that I have absolutely no interest in the publishing company—hold no stock in it—and, indeed, only recently became aware of the existence of the enterprise through my friend, Mr. Barker of the Post Office, and my subsequent correspondence with Colonel Dupree. I have not come here to say pleasant things to you, nor did I make the journey from New York because I have political aspirations. I am not after the colored vote.

In a long and somewhat arduous newspaper career, with all the ups and downs, failures and successes that come to a man who has struggled for over a third of a century, there were some things which impressed themselves upon me, as worthy of my interest. Indeed, I may say that in large measure, they were the reasons why I emigrated to this new world, where I had been told there was neither prejudice of caste nor prejudice of religion, nor prejudice of race, but where a man could make himself what his ability, his industry and his courage entitled him to be. From my school days, I myself had felt the prejudice that existed at that time in England, and particularly in the English schools and universities, against the man with a foreign name, who had anything but orthodox, Protestant-Episcopal blood in his veins. As I grew older and gained experience, as I began to better understand the institutions of this country and the aspiration of its people, I took an ever increasing interest in what is called the colored race problem, not because, let me be frank, I have any particular interest in the colored people as such, but because of the principles which had appealed to me, and because I believed that a man should be what he makes himself, whether his face be white or black, his hair straight or kinky, his eyes blue or brown, whether his nose curves one way or the other.

So, having seen your magazine, and having learned something of the struggle certain of your people are making to uphold a most worthy endeavor, I have come among you to see in how far such experience as I have as a publisher, editor and writer may be of service to you—to discuss with you ways and means for carrying on the magazine—in a word, to give you, such aid as I can, and to add to it at least an effort to induce some of my friends to do likewise.

We have been told by many, even by some distinguished writers and thinkers among your own people, that the problems involved in this race issue are so complex as to be almost beyond the grasp and certainly beyond the power of solution of the most enlightened minds.

Believe me, my friends, the problems may be fully as complex as they have been described, but the principles that must guide us in every effort to solve them, are not complex. They are extremely simple.

Where shall we find these principles?

We shall find them in the Declaration of Independence, in the Constitution of the United States, and we shall also find them in the teaching of the Christian religion. It is by understanding what these principles are, it is by plainly insisting that they shall be upheld and it is by living up to them ourselves that we shall go very far to put this whole, grave question upon a very different basis to that upon which it rests to-day. The basic thought which underlies these principles may be summed up in one word—Justice!

I will scarcely even touch upon the distressing situation in which many of your people find themselves in the Southern States to-day. To understand that, a man must have the ability to place himself not only in your position, but in the position of the Southern people who emerged from a terrible war, ruined, and with that legacy which war always leaves and which it will take more than one generation to obliterate.

I do not believe that force settles anything in life, except that one individual or a nation is stronger than another. I do not believe that great questions have ever been settled by force or will be. The appeal for justice or fair play for your people in the South and even in the North, must be made without even a suspicion that you have any intention to have recourse to elements which can only aggravate the trouble and put its solution further off.

What you have to do is to put up such a proposition to the heart, the conscience, the chivalry, not only of the South, but of the people of the whole United States, that justice must—and will be done you. You have to show that you are worthy of citizenship by your ability, by your industry, by your high purpose. You must show that you can achieve success in all the walks of life, not alone as farmers and tillers of the soil.

And when you do this, you must take steps to make what you have done, known.

There are before you, therefore, two educational propositions. The colored people have to be educated, and, as has been repeatedly said by that noble apostle of justice, *The New York Evening Post,* the public must be educated to the fact that you have already risen and that you are using brave efforts to uplift your race and bring it to a higher plane.

With regard to the work to be done in raising the general condition of the colored people, let us not forget that while slavery as an institution is detestable the history of the world shows us that it has served as the stepping stone from barbarism to civilization.

Now, there are two methods to secure what is called "uplifting" a people. One, in which, many believe, is the paternal, legislative method. By this, men are taught by politicians and newspaper writers to look to the government for help, to expect laws to be passed for their benefit, which shall give them something for nothing.

I am not of these. I believe that the great thinker who said the best governed country is the least governed country was right, and that the function of government is rather to provide and guard opportunity than to pass a mass of legislation which, as we all know, generally ends in benefit to the privileged few. You cannot make men honest or industrious by act of Congress or state legislature. Neither can you confer upon them an education by any similar method.

We have, therefore, to look to the other method, which is that to-day approved by advanced thinkers, and this method is to perfect an educational organization of schools, of newspapers, of museums, trade schools, by which you can reach the individual, for a race is, after all, composed of individuals, and right here it is that your magazine, which you have struggled so bravely to keep alive for these three or four years, can do great work.

Your magazine can appeal to the individual member of your race, inspire him with hope for the future, with confidence, raise his aspiration and give him much valuable knowledge. It can do as much also by informing the people of this country, the whites, as to what you have already done, as to what you all purpose to do, in the future. Thus it will serve a double purpose. It will afford a forum to your own people, be an element of instruction to them, and it will at the same time open the eyes of your detractors and slanderers to the fact that you have already, in a single generation produced writers, thinkers, even statesmen,— produced clergymen, farmers, singers, artists, successful business men, —that you have already accumulated in the Southern States alone over five hundred millions of taxable property; so that making full allowance for the advantages you have enjoyed by living in the age of the telephone and telegraph, you have made a greater advance in a third of a century than any other race I ever knew anything about or have read anything about, did in anything like the same time.

As some of you, no doubt, have heard, there are men in the South so narrow-minded, so mistaken, that they are endeavoring to take away from you, by legislative action, the rights guaranteed to you under the Constitution.

Personally, I would abolish the right of the ignorant negro [*sic*] to vote, but only for the reason that I would abolish the right of every ignorant man to vote. I do not believe in manhood suffrage, especially when we deny the suffrage to the noblest of our mothers.

One of those who has maligned your race is Governor Vardaman of Mississippi, who in one of his recent public utterances, declared that the Negro never could rise above the level of the brute, that at best, he could be nothing but a human machine, toiling for his bread in the fields, and that education encouraged his natural criminal instincts. When the Governor of a great state stands up and says this, I feel that I must stand up on the other side and say as plainly as I can that in this declaration he has wronged himself more than the Negro, and that if he will reflect, he will see that in denying the colored people a capacity to rise he has not insulted them, but the human race, and blasphemed its Creator. For, my friends, if there are people born on this earth incapable of advancement, who never can rise above the brute, upon whom education can only have a damning influence, then I, for one, refuse to believe in a Divine Mind, in a Divine Purpose, in a Divine Creator, who could permit such an atrocity.

It is because I believe that there is no child, man or woman born on the earth who is beyond the power of love and justice, that I am here among you.

I notice, in one of the articles written by your worthy, most talented and self-sacrificing editress, Miss Hopkins, a tendency to refer to her people as a "proscribed race."

You must cease to speak of yourselves as a proscribed people. You must cease to dwell upon your wrongs in the past, however bitter, however cruel.

How shall the barriers that hold you in be broken down, if you insist upon living behind them? Your duty is to forget the past, at least, to put it behind you and to advance bravely, with your faces to the dawn and the light.

This is not a fight for the colored people. This is a fight "for humanity." It is only one more phase of the old fight against prejudice and privilege which has been going on ever since man was born.

Do you believe that you have a monopoly of prejudice? That you colored people are the only ones who have suffered at the hands of the ignorant and unenlightened? Think of the poor Jews outraged and slaughtered in Russia! Remember that it is only a few years ago that a Catholic or a Hebrew could not sit in the English House of Commons. I can go back to my boyhood days in London, and recall that every other advertisement for help in the daily papers contained the announcement: "No Irish need apply."

You yourselves, therefore, must not sustain the idea of exclusiveness. You must, as I said, no longer think of your wrongs, you must cease to think of those who speak ill of you, who take isolated cases of horror as the basis of an indictment against you all. And, indeed, is it not just that you should do so?

Have you forgotten the tens of thousands who died that you might be free? Have you forgotten the martyred Lincoln? Is it not more becoming that, instead of being exercised by the position taken by a Vardaman, you should remember and be sustained by these words of Lincoln in his Gettysburg address:

"It is rather for us to be here dedicated to the great task remaining before us—that from these honored dead, we take increased devotion to that cause for which they gave the last full measure of devotion, that we here highly resolve that these dead shall not have died in vain, that this nation, under God shall have a new birth of freedom, so that government of the people, by the people, for the people shall not perish from the earth."

I told you, a minute ago, that one of the great purposes of this, your magazine, will be to acquaint the white people with what you have already done, with the marvelous advance you have already made, with the institutions of learning that you are supporting and with the magnificent effort that you are making all over the country to uplift yourselves. But just as the whites have almost everything to learn about you, so you yourselves have almost everything to learn as to what some of our most noble-minded women as well as men are doing in your interest or rather in the cause of liberty, truth and justice.

I have already referred to *The New York Evening Post*, a paper of high standing and large influence, which I always carefully read, though I sometimes disagree with it. But there is one feature of its policy, which raises it to the highest plane, and that is, the broad, human, fearless and absolutely just position it takes with regard to this so-called race problem. There is scarcely a week, my friends, that this prominent journal does not devote some portion of its space, in its editorial and other columns, to an exposition of what the public attitude should be to your people, not alone because of your rights, but because of the work you are doing, because so many of you are winning your way to a place beside the best of us.

In this connection, I could quote you many an able writer and thinker who has stood up in your cause, or, as I would prefer to call it, in the cause of humanity. Only this month, I find in *McClure's Magazine* a magnificent article by Carl Schurz on the question, "Can the South Solve the Negro Problem?" Most of you, no doubt, have heard of Carl Schurz as a distinguished man of German birth, as a man who was a member of the Government at one time, but few of you know of the great service that this man, now advanced in age, has rendered the country. He has had, to quote the eloquent words of the editor of *McClure's*: "an active share in settling each successive phase of the Negro question since the repeal of the Missouri Compromise. He was one of the founders of the Republican party. He helped elect Lincoln to the Presidency. He fought through the Civil War. He studied the condition on the ground after hostilities ceased, and was influential in ending military rule in 1872."

Mr. Schurz' article has, to again quote the editor of *McClure's*: "The moral authority which comes only from a man who has never allowed any consideration of policy to obscure the ethical meaning of the question with which he dealt."[7]

I will quote you only a few sentences from Mr. Schurz' article. They will give you, as I said, at least some idea of the brave fight that is being made on the other side:

"Can it be said by way of moral justification," he writes,

that the colored people have deserved to be deprived of their rights as a punishment for something they have done? It is an undisputed matter of history that they came to this country not of their own volition—that they were not intruders, but that they were brought here by force to serve the selfishness of white men, that they did such service as slaves, patiently and submissively for two and a half centuries, that even during a war which was waged incidentally, if not directly for their deliverance, a large majority of them faithfully continued to serve their masters while these were fighting to keep them in slavery; that they were emancipated not by any insurrectionary act of theirs, but by the act of the government; that when after their emancipation they confronted their old masters as free men, they did not, so far as known, commit a single act of vengeance for cruelties they may have suffered while in slavery; that the right of suffrage was given to them not in obedience to any irresistible urgency on their part, but by the national power wielded by white men, to enable the emancipated colored people to protect their own rights, and that when their exercise of the suffrage brought forth, in some states, foolish extravagance and corrupt government, it was again particu-

---

7. Freund quotes the editor's unsigned headnote to Schurz's article. See Carl Schurz, "Can the South Solve the Negro Problem?" *McClure's Magazine* 22.3 (Jan. 1904): 259.

larly owing to the leadership of white men who worked themselves into their confidence and for their own profit, led them astray.[8]

Further on in his article, Mr. Schurz says:

"Here is the crucial point: There will be a movement, either in the direction of reducing the Negroes to a permanent condition of serf-dom—the condition of mere plantation hands, alongside of the mule, practically without any rights of citizenship—or a movement in the direction of recognizing him as a citizen in the true sense of the term. One or the other will prevail."[9]

You and I need not discuss which of these directions named by Mr. Schurz appeal to us, which of these directions must be taken.

No reference to those who are fighting prejudice, from which you suffer, would be complete without a tribute to our brave President, Theodore Roosevelt, who has shown, again and again, that he stands for all the people, black as well as white.

Let us also not forget the disinterested aid being given so lavishly by noble white women and men to Tuskegee and other similar institutions established for the education of the colored race.

We now come to consider what is the best plan of action.

In the first place, you must learn to help yourselves. All the help, whether it come from individuals of limited resources like myself, or from some great millionaire, will mean nothing unless you can put it to wise use and learn to become absolutely independent. You must conduct your magazine on business principles. You must get out and hustle for subscribers and advertisements. The *Magazine* must be attractive. It must stand on its own basis as worth the ten cents you charge for it. It must be conducted on a high plane so that it shall appeal to the good will and sympathy of the broadminded, so they may, of their own volition, feel an irresistible impulse to come to your aid and the aid of those principles, to maintain which you have struggled and suffered.

Before coming here, I discussed with Colonel Dupree, Mr. Watkins, the energetic treasurer of the *Magazine*, who has stood by the institution so bravely and with such tremendous self-sacrifice; with Mr. West, the business manager, with Miss Hopkins and with others of their friends, the advisability of starting a "Colored American League," whose motto shall be: "For Humanity"; which shall have no political purpose whatever, but whose one aim shall be to encourage virtue, industry and patience among the colored people, to the end that they may serve as an example to the oppressed and to those who suffer from prejudice, at the hands of their fellow men, from whatever cause, the world over.

---

8. Schurz, "Can the South Solve the Negro Problem?" 268.
9. Ibid., 270.

I would suggest to you that membership in the league be fixed at the modest sum of one dollar, which shall include a subscription for a year to the *Magazine* and also a badge or button. In this way, the thousands of subscribers and readers of the *Magazine* will at once become one family. The *Magazine* will be recognized not only among its colored friends, but among the whites, as the highest literary expression of your race. As such, it will undoubtedly receive consideration at the hands of the more enlightened editors in the country, who will be glad to take it up and review it on its merits, and certainly give it a helping hand if it deserves it.

I am glad to be with you. If you can learn a little from me, I feel and know that I shall learn much from you. The great curse of the world is ignorance. It is when we get to know one another; when we get to understand one another better; when man meets man, that we find that three-fourths of all the prejudice and three-fourths of all the wrong and three-fourths of all the misery of the world can be done away with.

When we understand one another we get right down to the great basic truth, that we are, after all, members of one human family, whatever our color or our race.

Remember always that every race has had to struggle; that every race has had its period where it suffered from prejudice and from wrong, and that it was its ability to rise and overcome every obstacle before it, that finally developed its strength and so determined its right to live.

Formation of the Colored American League

Mr. Freund's speech, which was cordially received, was followed by a general discussion, at the end of which those present formed themselves into a committee to organize "The Colored American League" on the lines suggested, to make *The Colored American Magazine* the exponent of the League's work, and to do everything in their power to aid the work by personal efforts for subscription and business.

In the discussion, some brilliant speeches were made, among others by Mr. Butler R. Wilson, a lawyer, who said that it gave him great pleasure to be present, and while he would not agree with all that had been said, he readily admitted that there was much food for thought. Even among the colored people themselves, there was large diversity of opinion as to the best way to solve the Negro problem. He said he thoroughly agreed with Mr. Freund's plea that the colored people should cease to regard themselves with the eyes of black men and black women. They should get on a broader plane—the plane of humanity.

Mr. Wolff, Vice-Commander of the Grand Army of the Republic, expressed himself eloquently and forcibly on the situation, and said he congratulated himself that his people, in Boston at least, had overcome prejudice, and that in Boston, every man had an opportunity to make his own place in the community, without regard to race or color.

Mr. Wolff paid a great compliment to the honorable life of Colonel Dupree, who had lived in the midst of the colored community for years. He also spoke of Mr. Mitchell, who has a prominent position in the Custom House, and is a veteran of the war, as a type of the best element of the colored people, as a man who did good all the time, quietly, and made no fuss or noise about it.

Miss Pauline E. Hopkins, the editress of the *Magazine,* gave a most eloquent and touching account of the struggles of the magazine, with which she has been connected almost from its inception. She said that there were times when there was not a dollar in the treasury, and when the darkness of despair settled upon the little band of men and women who had devoted themselves to the cause, but even in the worst days, when everything seemed to have gone against them, they never despaired.

Mr. Joseph Lee said that it was appropriate that the dinner and the meeting had been held in the old Revere House in Boston, the scene of so many noble efforts in the old Abolition Days. He said he thought the white man had become tired of the Negro question, and that their hope lay in the leadership of their own men and women. He asked the detractors of his race to remember that with freedom and opportunity, the South was producing to-day eleven millions of bales of cotton where, under slavery, it only produced four millions.

Mr. Edward E. Brown said:

"'Justice—Freedom—Equality!' These are the watchwords of the present day." Mr. Brown said further that he could not help being reminded of the words of John Andrew, the War Governor of Massachusetts, who, when the soldiers went to the front, said:

"I know not what record of sin there may be against me, but I do know that I was never mean enough to despise a man because he was poor, because he was ignorant, or because he was black."

Mr. Brown told how he had been born in New Hampshire, had come to Boston poor, to struggle for a living, and could say, with pride, of the Boston schools, that no white boy had ever called him "nigger," or called him "coon." He had learned his lessons on the same bench with the white boy.

"Any man," said Mr. Brown, "who withholds from us our rights, who denies us opportunity for advancement, does an act of injustice, the wickedness and cruelty of which are beyond all power of estimation. Let us never forget that we shall win, not because we are colored men, but because we have perseverance, because we have grit, because we develop ability."

At this point of the proceedings, Mrs. Mitchell, the well-known artiste, wife of Capt. Chas. L. Mitchell, sang Kipling's "Recessional," and an encore, in the most delightful manner. The discussion was closed by Mr. Buchanan, who said that while he was not a man of education, he was glad to work along the line of humanity. As far as he himself was concerned, he could as little encourage prejudice against one race as another, for did not the blood of both races flow in his veins, and how could he ask his right hand to strike his left cheek?

Mr. Sampson was the last speaker. He said that what the colored people must do to win success was to go about their work in a straightforward, practical, business way, and then the result would come.

Since the meeting was held, considerable work has been done by the promoters of the League. A large number of new subscribers have been received for the magazine. Some very distinguished men and women, both in Boston and New York, have become interested in the cause, and there is every reason to believe that within a year or more, the League will have tens of thousands of members, who will be working for the noble purpose announced by its founders.

SOURCE "How a New York Newspaper Man Entertained a Number of Colored Ladies and Gentlemen at Dinner in the Revere House, Boston, and How the Colored American League Was Started," *Colored American Magazine* 7.3 (Mar. 1904): 151–160.

Letter to William Monroe Trotter, April 16, 1905

From Pauline E. Hopkins

53 Clifton St., No. Cambridge, Mass.,
 April 16, '05.

Mr. W. M. Trotter,
 Boston, Mass.

My dear Mr. Trotter:—

Herewith I send you a detailed account of my experiences with the *Colored American Magazine* as its editor and, incidentally, with Mr. Booker T. Washington in the taking over of the magazine to New York by his agents. It is necessarily long and perhaps tedious at the outset, but I trust that you will peruse it to the end. I have held these facts for a year, but as my rights are ignored in my own property, and I am persistently hedged about by the revengeful tactics of Mr. Washington's men, I feel that I must ask the advice of some one who will give me a respectful hearing and judgment as to the best way to deal with this complicated case. I hope that you will do what you can for me.

In May, 1903, *The Colored American Magazine,* a well-known and powerful Negro organ, was sold by its creditors to the highest bidders,—Messrs. W. H. Dupree, Wm. O. West and Jesse Watkins of Boston, and I was engaged as literary editor because I was well-known as a race writer, had gained the confidence of my people, and also because there seemed to be at that time, no one else as well qualified to fill the position, for as yet the editing of a high-class magazine was puzzling work even to our best scholars.

From the start it was a struggle for us to keep our heads above water because of the financial crisis just passed and the strain that had been placed upon the confidence and purses of our people. I received a salary of $7 per week and the type-writer $3, while the owners, of course, received nothing. Mr. Dupree made up a deficit each month and becoming discouraged he notified me in August that he would close up the business as he was running behind and could not stand the strain. Mr. Watkins, however, protested, and his brother James H. Watkins thinking that under his more experienced business management matters could be improved, offered to take the business and keep us going for what he might make out of it until March 11, 1904. The firm accepted his proposition, discharged the typewriter, raised my salary to $8 per week, I doing her work of correspondence and my own editorial work, and we jogged along until November.

In November the "Announcements" were due for the ensuing year and I began to look about me for material from writers of prominence and influence. There was no money with which to pay contributors so I planned a circular which I knew would touch the people in a kindly vein asking for articles on "INDUSTRIAL EDUCATION; WILL IT SOLVE THE NEGRO PROBLEM?" These articles were to be contributed without charge. I also asked for any other matter that writers were willing to give us. A copy of this letter was sent to Hon. William Lloyd Garrison, Rev. Edward A. Horton, Mrs. Ella Wheeler Wilcox, Mrs. John A. Logan, Prof. W.E.B. Du Bois, Prof. B. T. Washington, Editor T. Thomas Fortune, Roscoe Conkling Bruce, Prof. Kelly Miller, Editor A. Kirkland Soga (East London, South Africa), and a number of other writers of prominence.[10] Every one approached responded with a free contribution except Prof. Miller who charged $5. (See accompanying copy of magazine, December 1903.)

Mr. Dupree was greatly pleased with my success and told me that he thought he could help too by soliciting Mr. John C. Freund, Editor of *The Music Trades*, New York, for permission to reproduce his series of articles on Jamaica which had appeared in his paper. We examined the articles and finding them exceptionally interesting and instructive, urged Mr. Dupree to secure them if possible. This he accomplished through the intervention of Mr. Barker of the Boston General Post Office. For full account see Mr. Dupree's own narrative in accompanying marked March number, 1904.[11] In November, 1903, Mr. Dupree received a letter from Mr. Freund promising us the articles on the Island of Jamaica in these words:—"It will give me sincere pleasure to prepare them for your magazine, and also to accompany them with such cuts as may be desirable." (See accompanying letter marked "1.")[12]

Previous to this event, in the last of October, we had received a call and a proposition from Mr. Peter Smith, founder of *The Boston Colored Citizen*, an employee and intimate friend of Mr. B. T. Washington, asking us to allow him to remove his plant to our office at 82 West Concord St. as his quarters on Charles St. were too cramped. This we refused him in very few words for we mistrusted his intentions knowing the man.

Our correspondence with Mr. Freund was of the most satisfactory kind. He gave us the articles, furnished cuts of a size suitable for our magazine and

10. The "Hon. William Lloyd Garrison" whom Hopkins mentions in this letter is William Lloyd Garrison Jr. (1838–1909), the son of the renowned abolitionist, who contributed an article to the *Colored American Magazine*.

11. See "How a New York Newspaper Man Entertained a Number of Colored Ladies and Gentlemen at Dinner in the Revere House, Boston, and How the Colored American League Was Started" in this volume.

12. All of the accompanying letters that Hopkins cites parenthetically are in the Pauline Hopkins Papers, Franklin Library Special Collections, Fisk University.

gave us $15 per month toward defraying the expense of manufacturing same. So genial, so kind, so disinterested did he appear that he very soon won our entire confidence. (He repeatedly assured us that "<u>I have no axe to grind</u>.") No mention was made of Mr. B. T. Washington to me and I thought it a case of pure philanthropy, one of those rare cases which are sometimes found among wealthy, generous and eccentric white men. About January 1, 1904, he wrote us that he would entertain 20 leading colored ladies and gentlemen, including our staff, at any hotel in Boston that Mr. Dupree might select at a cost of $2 per plate, in order to meet us all and become better acquainted than we could by letter, and also, to further the interests of the magazine by personal effort thinking that the knowledge that an influential white man was interested in our enterprise would tend to stimulate the colored people themselves to greater effort. We were greatly surprised not to say overwhelmed at the honor thrust upon us, but Mr. Dupree set about working up the dinner in a style worthy of the giver, and he succeeded admirably. (For full account see accompanying March, 1904-number.)

The dinner was given at the Revere House, Boston, and some interesting things which were said and done there have never been recorded. Among them was the opposition of Commander Wolff, Commander Massachusetts Department, G.A.R., who spoke decidedly against our accepting any overtures leading to a removal to New York before the close of the Presidential campaign, and he concluded by predicting that such a move would involve the loss of the magazine. I was called upon to offset the speech made by Mr. Wolff by detailing our hardships and financial difficulties. I learned that Mr. Freund was greatly incensed over Mr. Wolff's remarks; I could not understand his enmity but have concluded since that Mr. Wolff was on the right track in his prediction. On Monday morning following the dinner, Mr. Dupree asked me what I thought of it all and I said "it is a political move, but if you can get back your money why, we can say nothing as long as we keep the magazine afloat." The others agreed with me.

Mr. Freund took hold of our business ostensibly to correct our errors made in ignorance of the needs of a successful publication. We had been late in the month in getting out and he strove hard to have us out on time. He criticised our work harshly and nothing we did would please him, but we cared not for that as we were bent on keeping his friendship and profiting by his experience and ripe judgment. He proposed that the March number should be a great boom, sensational in character, forming the diners of January 24th into a society for the support of the magazine and having branches of the same in all sections of the country, and taking for its motto "For humanity." The badge of the order was to be a red, white and blue button with those words on the margin. This was to be given to each subscriber together with a receipt printed in three colors. 5,000 buttons were ordered and 2,500 receipts. The price of the magazine was changed, and single copies sold at 10 cents per copy instead of the former price 15 cents; yearly subscriptions fell from $1.50

to $1. All this was for the good of the cause, but made a marked shortage in our receipts which he generously made up from his private purse. (See accompanying letters marked "2," "2a," "3," "3a" and "4" which I enclose in order to show you more clearly Mr. Freund's mode of action, and to give you a slight idea of the amount of money he expended.)

Early in February, 1904, Mr. Freund sent me a bouquet of Russian violets by his Boston representative, Mr. Adelbert Loomis; the book *Self-Help* by Smiles, an expensive set of furs, a $25-check and a book *Eternalism*.[13] I had seemed to be a favorite with our benefactor and these special attentions made my position in the office very uncomfortable. As I am not a woman who attracts the attention of the opposite sex in any way, Mr. Freund's philanthropy with regard to myself puzzled me, but knowing that he was aware of my burdens at home, I thought that he was trying to help me in his way. I was so dense that I did not for a moment suspect that I was being politely bribed to give up my race work and principles and adopt the plans of the South for the domination of the Blacks.

Mr. Freund had interviewed our creditors, examined our books, knew our weakest as well as our strongest points, and held with each one of us the patriarchal relation of ancient days. He was spoken of by us in our conversations together as "Papa Freund." The following extract shows how familiar he was with my business:—

> The *Colored American Magazine,* No. 82 West Concord St., Boston, is a good periodical for the price—a dollar a year; ten cents a copy—as good as any except the *Strand,* of London. It contains interesting articles and stories and is brightly illustrated. The editress is a colored woman; a company of colored men are the publishers. John C. Freund, of *Music Trades,* is enthusiastic about their work. "What do you think," he writes me, "of a colored editress, whose salary is eight dollars a week when she gets it—with a bedridden mother to support? What do you think of a backer of the magazine, a coalblack Negro, who has put the savings of his life, from day's labor, to help it along, because he thinks it may give people a better idea of his race? What do you think of a grizzled veteran, who came out of the War an emancipated slave, unable to read or write, but has educated himself until he is the superintendent of the second largest branch of the Boston postoffice?" It is a far cry for Mr. Freund of Oxford University and the society of distinguished authors, actors and musicians to the association with Negroes, but he throws his whole heart into every philanthropic mission.
>
> —Stephen Fiske in "Sports of the Times," New York.

13. See Samuel Smiles, *Self-Help; With Illustrations of Conduct and Perseverance* (1859; Project Gutenberg, 1997), http://www.gutenberg.org/dirs/etext97/selfh10h.htm; and Orlando J. Smith, *Eternalism: A Theory of Infinite Justice* (Boston: Houghton, Mifflin, 1902).

Mr. Freund caused my salary to be raised. (See accompanying letter marked "4.") Little by little he opened his views to me and I found that he was curtailing my work from the broad field of <u>international</u> union and <u>uplift</u> for the Blacks in all quarters of the globe, to the narrow confines of the question as affecting solely the Afro-American. (See accompanying letter marked "5.")

In February another dinner was given the staff at the Revere House, Boston. Plans were laid for storming Boston by giving a grand reception in the name of the magazine, to Mr. Freund on March 19th at which 200 guests would be entertained. He seemed pleased with the fact that the league was doing good work for us and said:—

"There will be three Leagues in the field—

1. <u>The Business League</u> with <u>Booker Washington</u> at the head.
2. <u>The Colored American League</u> with <u>Col. W. H. Dupree</u> at the head.
3. <u>The Political League</u> with <u>Fortune</u> at the head. (See letters marked "6" and "7.")

Mr. Freund's letters contained many compliments on my editorial ability. (See letter marked "8.") But sometimes there was a note of alarm which puzzled me. He told me that there must not be a word on lynching, no mention of our wrongs as a race, nothing that would be offensive to the South. He wrote:—"If you are going to take up the wrongs of your race, then you must depend for support absolutely upon your own race. For the colored man today to attempt to stand up to fight would be like a canary bird to face a bulldog, and an angry one at that. The whole line of work must be conciliatory, constructive, and that is where Booker Washington is showing himself to be such a giant."

None of our efforts as a force pleased our patron; the manufacturing of the magazine he treated with contempt, and constantly bewailed the fact that he had not removed the magazine to New York where he could have supervised it personally. This, however, Mr. Dupree had flatly refused to allow until his interests were fully protected. Mr. Freund gracefully waived the point. (See letters marked "9," "10," "11," "12.") (Also programme of reception.) Mr. Dupree's confidence did not extend to allowing Mr. Freund to take the magazine to New York without the passing of legal papers which he attempted to do.

After the reception Mr. Freund began to show little by little, his true errand; he began a Washington campaign as shown by letter dated "March 24th," where he says:—

The work itself is to me so exhilarating that if I have any regret it is that my face is not black and that with such education and force as I have, I cannot go right out into the open and battle for justice alongside Booker T. Washington.

Colonel Dupree has an excellent idea—that the magazine will soon be able to get some ads from the various colored universities and high schools. I agree with him thoroughly. I shall personally go to Tuskegee after I have met Booker Washington, and give him a write-up that will make his hair stand on end. <u>You need his support</u>.

(See letter marked "13.")

The next day I received a telegram. (See copy marked "13a.") In this telegram I was asked to write a letter of introduction; I was to introduce <u>Mr. Freund to Mr. Washington!</u> Mr. Dupree and the staff requested me to comply strictly with Mr. Freund's request, so, although I had <u>NO PERSONAL ACQUAINTANCE WITH MR. WASHINGTON</u>, I wrote a letter to him detailing our situation, recounting Mr. Freund's kind acts and craving Mr. Washington's good offices as a race man in our favor. I regret that I did not preserve a copy of this letter which to say the least was unique in its character and mission. (See letter marked "14.")

Received letter marked "15" stating that MR. WASHINGTON WOULD CALL UPON HIM. (See letter marked "15.")

Received another letter dated "March 31," stating that MR. WASHING-TON HAD CALLED UPON HIM. (See letter marked "16a.")

Mr. Dupree received one also dated "March 31," which we call "THE WASHINGTON LETTER," and which is especially interesting as it details Mr. Washington's opinions regarding the magazine and its work. (See letter marked "16.")

Mr. Dupree received a letter dated "April 6," which threw a firebrand into the office and made my position unbearable. (See letter marked "17.") In this letter we note the following:—

There is, however, one rock right squarely ahead of us. That is the persistence with which matter is put into the magazine, which has no live interest, and furthermore, is likely to alienate the very few friends who might help us. Now, I have spoken on the subject already more than I care to. Either Miss Hopkins will follow our suggestion in this matter and put live matter into the magazine, eliminating anything which may create offense; stop talking about wrongs and a proscribed race, or you must count me out absolutely from this day forth. I will neither personally endorse nor help a business proposition which my common sense tells me is foredoomed to failure. Every person that I have spoken to on the subject is with me. <u>IT IS MR. BOOKER WASHINGTON'S IDEA</u>.

If you people, therefore, want to get out a literary magazine, with article [*sic*] ON THE FILIPINO, I refuse to work one minute longer with you. That is my ultimatum and I shall say no more on the subject.

To explain my position I will refer the reader to the fact that I had begged for help from many noted people, and had announced the articles which would appear during the year. Our subscribers would hold us to our promises and expect the articles offered them as inducements for their subscriptions. Among these writers were Hon. Wm. Lloyd Garrison, Rev. Edward A. Horton, Editor A. K. Soga, and a paid contributor, Prof. Hamedoe.

Prof. Hamedoe is a colored linguist who has mastered seven modern languages and thirteen Chinese dialects. He is a man well-versed in history, a traveler who has visited every corner of the globe; his work is instructive and greatly admired by colored readers.

I could not cut the articles contributed by these authors without giving great offense and alienating true friends, some of whom had gone to great expense to get matter for and to me from a distance; all were chivalrous in their desires to help the woman editor maintain her unique position with credit to the race.

A "literary magazine" applied to the articles of Editor Soga who was the corner stone of my "international policy," and whose "glittering generalities" were shown in the gracefulness of his diction and the power of his thought on race matters. He is a friend and correspondent of Editor Morales of *The West African Mail.* "Proscribed race," was a hit at my book *Contending Forces* and my serial story *Hagar's Daughter* both of which had aroused the ire of the white South, male and female, against me many of whom had paid me their compliments in newspaper squibs and insulting personal letters sent to the old management of the magazine. But Mr. Garrison's article on "Industrial Education," and Prof. Hamedoe's on "El Sr. Jose Rizal" the Filipino martyr, were the arousers of our patron's ire and of Mr. Washington's wrath because they not only offended the South, but, also, seemingly, reflected upon President Roosevelt's Philippine policy. (See accompanying April magazine for the articles of Mr. Garrison, Mr. Soga and Prof. Hamedoe.)[14]

Messrs. Dupree, West and Watkins were influenced by Mr. Freund's threat of withdrawal, and matters grew unbearable for me at the office; I was absent for a number of days. During this absence I wrote to Mr. Freund outlining to him some of the difficulties I was encountering not knowing that they were caused by him. (See letter marked "18.")

In letter "19" he virtually gives up the enterprise and tells me of the unflattering comments made upon my work (the work so recently eulogized by himself) by Boston people. (See letters marked "19" and "20.")

My Boston critics were all men working for and under Mr. Washington. $150 promised us by Mr. Freund was given right after the reception in March, to Mr. Charles Alexander, Editor of *The Boston Colored Citizen* a paper publicly believed to have been born at Mr. Washington's suggestion for the express purpose of putting *The Boston Guardian* out of business.

---

14. See William Lloyd Garrison Jr., "Industrial Education—Will it Solve the Negro Problem," *Colored American Magazine* 7.4 (Apr. 1904): 247–249; Alan Kirkland Soga, "Call the Black Man to Conference VI," *Colored American Magazine* 7.4 (Apr. 1904): 250–252; S.E.F.C.C. Hamedoe, "El Sr. Don Jose Rizal," *Colored American Magazine* 7.4 (Apr. 1904): 253–257. All three articles appeared on consecutive pages in the April 1904 issue of the *Colored American Magazine.*

About the last of April or the first of May, 1904, negotiations were opened with Mr. Dupree by Mr. Fred R. Moore, National Organizer of the Business League, looking to the purchase of the *Colored American Magazine*. It was planned to remove this plant to New York and have T. Thomas Fortune as the Editor and Pauline E. Hopkins as Associate Editor. It was understood by the force that Mr. Moore represented and <u>covered</u> Mr. B. T. Washington. I was offered $12 per week which I decided to accept having determined that I would accept the situation as I found it, succumb to the powers that were, and do all I could to keep the magazine alive unless they asked me to publicly renounce the rights of my people. They held, also, the plates of my book *Contending Forces*, and 500 bound and unbound copies of the same. The book had been sold to the former management on the monthly installment plan, and when the company failed they still owed me $175. So, being a creditor and a shareholder and a member of the Board of Directors, I had a deep interest in the business of the corporation.

After I was settled in New York, Mr. Freund wrote me a letter congratulating me on my earnest and faithful work for the purchaser of the magazine. Many promises were made me, but I soon found that I was being "frozen out" for Mr. Roscoe Conkling SIMMONS a <u>nephew</u> of MRS. B. T. WASHINGTON who now holds the position which I was forced to resign last September.

I learned much in New York. I learned that to gain full control of the *New York Age*, Mr. Peterson had received the consulship to Venezuela.[15] I learned from the lips of Mr. and Mrs. Fortune that Mr. Fortune wrote *Up From Slavery* and the famous Atlanta speech "separate as the fingers of the hand"; Mr. Fortune complains that he writes many of Mr. Washington's magazine articles at a great sacrifice to himself, financially, as to do this he has had to give up his work on white organs that netted him a good monthly income. Dr. Wheatland, of Newport, R.I., I am told on good authority, was told by Mr. Fortune that he (Fortune) wrote *Up From Slavery*.[16]

I learned that the first mortgage on Mr. Fortune's home at Red Bank, N. Jersey, is held by the Afro-American Investment Company, 14 Douglass St., Brooklyn, N.Y., Mr. Fred R. Moore, President, and that Mr. Fortune owes Mr. B. T. Washington $2500. This money was borrowed by Mr. Fortune, I am told, to help him out on his trip to the Philippines he (Fortune) intending to repay the same upon receipt of his salary for that work. He has never received a cent (or had not up to last September) his salary being held up at Washington, D.C. by the Government.

In dictating a letter to me for Mr. Washington, Mr. Moore said,—

---

15. Jerome Bowers Peterson (1860–1943), an editor of T. Thomas Fortune's *New York Age*, served as consul to Venezuela from 1904 to 1905. He returned to the *Age* following his brief diplomatic career.

16. Marcus Fitzherbert Wheatland (1868–1934) was a physician and an innovator in the field of medical radiology.

"I was more fortunate than you for I got my $400 from Fortune, but you have not yet received a dollar."

All of these facts go to show that the *New York Age* is a subsidized sheet for its editor is under money obligations to Mr. Washington, and a man so situated is not a free agent by any means. Mr. R. L. Stokes formerly Mr. Washington's secretary at Tuskegee was placed in the *Age* office last September to assist Mr. Fortune.

Mr. Washington's active agents and trusted allies are Mr. Wilford H. Smith, Counsellor-at-law, 115 Broadway, New York; Mr. Charles Anderson, recently appointed inspector Port of New York; Mr. T. Thomas Fortune, editor of the *New York Age*; Mr. Fred R. Moore, National Organizer of the Business League. Meetings are held frequently at the Stevens House, Broadway, New York, and after one of these meetings one may look out for startling occurrences. Plans are laid for "downing" opposing Negroes, wires are pulled for paying political jobs, and "ward-heeling" schemes are constantly resorted to.

Stranger than all is the fact that these men do not represent the majority of the best Negroes in the city, but are representative of the sporting Negroes alone. None of these men affiliate with the church; they are decidedly in the minority, but they are all Mr. Washington's intimate friends.

A new magazine has been started since the *Colored American* became defunct, so to speak—*The Voice of the Negro*, published at Atlanta, Georgia. This organ has offended Mr. Washington deeply by adopting an independent course. The *Voice* has caught the New York trade and Mr. Moore is swearing vengeance. He is planning to drive the *Voice* out of the field by closing the doors of the convention hall of the Negro Business League which meets in New York in August, against the representatives of the *Voice* thus placing them publicly under the ban of Mr. Washington's displeasure.

Formerly the agents of the *Colored American Magazine* sold from 800 to 1500 copies of the magazine in New York each month, now its sale averages 200 a month. Agents are urging Mr. Washington to come out in the open and acknowledge that he is the real owner of the magazine as that would make their work lighter in selling the *Colored American*. These facts were given me by a trusted agent.

Recapitulation

The *Colored American Magazine* was the strongest Negro organ put upon the market since the days of Frederick Douglass. It caught and held the attention of the colored reading public because of its strong essays on race matters and its race serial stories. Pauline E. Hopkins was a leading writer, and considered a mischievous person by the South.

The policy of the South is non-agitation of the Negro question.

Messrs. Freund and Washington are men with large business interests in the South, and, naturally, are dominated by Southern opinion.

The financial disasters which overtook the magazine were sufficient to kill the enterprise if no helping hand were extended. The white creditors approached Mr. Washington, Mr. R. C. Bruce, Mr. J. H. Lewis, of Boston, and prayed them to buy the magazine. All of these men said,—"No, let it die." Mr. Dupree then stepped into the gap moved by the tears and entreaties of Jesse W. Watkins, one of the founders, and myself.

It was unexpected and unpleasant news to the opposition when they learned that the magazine was once more being issued at Boston.

The new management maintained a respectful and conservative attitude towards Mr. Washington's policy, but held firmly to race fealty. The articles referred to on "Industrial Education" created consternation in the ranks of the Southern supporters because they were written by writers of so high a standing in the literary world as to prove that the policy of industrial education solely for the Negro was not popular, and was doomed to failure in the end. Then it must have been that the plot was formed to get possession of the magazine and turn its course into the desired channel.

We needed money. Mr. Freund assumed the character of the disinterested philanthropist with "no axe to grind." Dissensions entered into the little business family. The editor and writer was maligned and "turned down." The rest was easy.

The great question is,—Did Mr. Freund intend to help the enterprise when he took it up at the beginning and was he turned from his purpose by the influence of Mr. Washington's expressed views and desires, or was it a mutual understanding between these gentlemen from the beginning?

The letter of introduction was a curiosity. Was it possible that Mr. Freund had not met Mr. Washington? Why, if so, did he not avail himself of the help of many mutual influential white acquaintances among the white business men of great New York, anyone of whom would have performed the necessary social requirement gladly?

Another incident is the fact that he would write to Mr. Dupree and me on the same day; the letter to me would be conciliatory and complimentary to a degree; the letter to Mr. Dupree would condemn me and my methods wholesale, and its tone would be threatening in character.

It is interesting to note, after the passage of one year, that Mr. Freund's policy of "not a word of complaint," no "literary" efforts, "no talk of wrongs," or of "a proscribed race," no "glittering generalities," no "international aspect" of the Negro question, no talk of "Filipinos," has been in full swing under the rule of the purchasers who took the magazine over to New York.

What was the result? A rain of dollars into the treasury? Far from it.

The agents in every city have complained bitterly of the change of policy; it has hurt their sales; many of them have given the book up. In New York city we sold from 800 to 1500 per month; under the new policy the sales have shrunk to <u>200</u> per month and the magazine would be out of business were it not for the fact that it is supported from Mr. Washington's private purse. Nor did the whites rally to the support of the pitiful rag issued each month which was but a shadow of its former self. Numbers of agents, in disgust, have taken up the sale of the *Voice of the Negro*, the new colored organ published at Atlanta, Ga.

It is curious to note that with his usual ease, Mr. Washington has changed his tactics as to the magazine's policy and is creeping back, gradually to the position of the old management in Boston. His men are, also, planning the overthrow of the *Voice*, which has refused to adopt partisan lines.

Witnesses to the truth of the facts I have laid down in these pages are the following gentlemen:—

Mr. Wm. H. Dupree, Superintendent Station A, Boston.
Jesse W. Watkins, 439 W. 35th St., New York City.
Wm. O. West, 528 Columbus Ave., Boston, Mass.
Mrs. Jesse W. Watkins, New York City.

Mr. Dupree, of course knows more of the facts than I do, and I have no doubt would be willing to tell all that he knows if he were guaranteed protection from the malice of Mr. Washington's friends.

With the knowledge which we possess, can we be expected to worship Mr. Washington as a pure and noble soul?

Can we be expected to join in paeans of praise to his spotless character and high principles?

One cannot help a feeling of honest indignation and contempt for a man who would be a party to defraud a helpless race of an organ of free speech, a band of men of their legal property and a woman of her means of earning a living.

Sincerely yours,
Pauline E. Hopkins

N. B. This is necessarily personal in its character as I was forced to detail events just as they occurred.

SOURCE Letter to William Monroe Trotter, April 16, 1905, is published courtesy of Fisk University Franklin Library Special Collections.

PART VI

Selected Biographies from the Colored American Magazine *(September 1901–March 1904)*

S elected Biographies from the *Colored American Magazine*" includes works that Hopkins published as Sarah Allen, as J. Shirley Shadrach, and under her own name. With the exception of "Heroes and Heroines in Black," whose subtitle "1" indicates that it may have been conceived originally as part of a series, the works here stand alone, albeit within the framework of the *Colored American Magazine*, where they were published between September 1901 and March 1904. Her subjects include writers, reformers, politicians, and teachers, among others. Her biographical practice was not limited by race or nation, as evident by her profiles of John Greenleaf Whittier and Alan Kirkland Soga. As in her series, her individual profiles are typically wide-ranging forums to address important political and social issues. Her comments on Munroe Rogers recall the fugitive slave cases of the 1850s in terms of twentieth-century economic struggles in which "great masses are being enslaved by the power of gold, and crushed in the great folds of gigantic monopolies." Her insistence, in her piece on the controversial William Pickens, that the United States owes African Americans reparations—"This country owes us compound interest on the toil of our ancestors invested as capital stock in the upbuilding of this opulent and powerful Republic"—remains resonant more than a century later. Three profiles that were, like the Pickens article, published under the Shadrach pseudonym use biography to bring attention to the possibility of a black president (Charles Winter Wood), the scourge of lynching (John Henry Dorsey), and transatlantic collaboration between African Americans and Africa (Jane Sharp). Together, the biographies selected for this section represent Hopkins's political, literary, and internationalist concerns.

Whittier, The Friend of the Negro

Pauline E. Hopkins

EDITOR'S NOTE—J. W. Washington, a colored penman of Salem, Mass., copied the tribute given to Whittier upon his eightieth birthday by the Essex Club. This token contained the signatures of all the Governors of Massachusetts, Senators and Representatives; Members of the Supreme Court; Cabinet under Cleveland and many other prominent personages. This is now religiously treasured by Mrs. Pickard—the niece of Whittier.

The members of the now famous Woman's Era Club, Boston, had contemplated making a pilgrimage to Amesbury, Mass., the home of the late John G. Whittier, "High Priest of the Anti-Slavery Party," and the Walter Scott of this legendary section of New England, for some time. By invitation of Mrs. S. T. Pickard, the poet's niece, and the Whittier Home Association, July 4th was fixed upon as an appropriate season.

Amesbury is a prosperous manufacturing town which may be reached from Newburyport by electrics, if one prefers them to a trip by rail. It is a beautiful ride through historic and picturesque scenes. One passes the home of Harriet Prescott Spofford, on Deer Island, where she wrote one of her finest stories, "The South Breaker," and the poem "Inside Plum Island." As we pass over the graceful and lofty suspension-bridge, we catch tantalizing glimpses of the beautiful Merrimac which wanders through this enchanted region. This is the place to read Whittier's "The Merrimac," which begins:

> Stream of my fathers! sweetly still
> The sunset rays thy valley fill;
> Poured slantwise down the long defile,
> Wave, wood, and spire beneath them smile.[1]

Near here is Salisbury Beach, made memorable as the scene of "The Tent on the Beach" in which James T. Fields, Bayard Taylor, and Mr. Whittier are imagined to have encamped one summer.

From the hills around Amesbury, in clear weather, one may catch fine views of the mountains across the border in New Hampshire. Thus with

---

1. John Greenleaf Whittier, "The Merrimac" (1841).

scenes of beauty on every side, haunted by the legends of New England, we came at length to the famous Whittier homestead on Friend St.

An Association of Amesbury women has leased the house from the owner, Mrs. S. T. Pickard, of Boston. This lady has loaned many articles of interest assisting in the restoration of the house to its former appearance. The Association desires to raise a monument to Mr. Whittier and to this end are soliciting help from women's clubs or individuals everywhere. Any sum, however small, will be acknowledged and credited to the donor.

Among the names of the Associate members of this Association are those of President and Mrs. Wm. McKinley, Rt. Rev. Wm. Lawrence, D.D., Rev. Lyman Abbott, D.D., Hon. John Hay, President Charles W. Eliot, Hon. W. Murray Crane, Mr. Edmund Clarence Stedman, Col. Thos. W. Higginson, Mrs. Mary S. Logan, and Mrs. Mary A. Livermore.

Nothing would delight us more than to be able to take our readers into the spacious, rambling old house so quaint and comfortable, filled with reminiscences of a good, great man; the furnishings preserved and arranged in their accustomed places the same as when the master lived and moved among them.

The spirit of the poet was upon us from the moment we entered the "garden room" at once sitting-room and study, looking upon the garden; the chief treasure of the room is the old-fashioned mahogany desk where he wrote many anti-slavery poems, the War poems, "Barbara Frietchie," "Maud Muller," "The Barefoot Boy," "In School-Days" and "Snow-Bound."

It has been said that Barbara Frietchie was a fictitious character; this is not true. Barbara lived and enacted the story of the poem very much as it is written. We saw there among the treasures of that historical storehouse, pieces of the dress worn by the heroine, a portion of the flag waved by her when

> Quick, as it fell, from the broken staff
> Dame Barbara snatched the silken scarf;
>
> She leaned far out on the window sill,
> And shook it forth with a royal will.
>
> "Shoot, if you must, this old gray head,
> But spare your country's flag," she said.[2]

Above the garden room is the poet's bed-room; this, too, is the same as he used it and left it.

On the walls of the parlor one views the family portraits, noticing in each the same perfection of feature and delicate contour of head and face that is seen in Mr. Whittier's pictures, bearing testimony to generations of intellectual and spiritual development. Here hangs, also, a fine group-portrait of the

2. Whittier, "Barbara Frietchie" (1863).

original Fisk Jubilee Singers, recalling instantly memories of the wonderful vocal organs of Jennie Jackson and Mr. Loudin. Beneath this portrait stands a statuette. It represents a fugitive slave holding her infant in her arms. She stands in front of the desk at which Mr. Garrison is seated, at whose right stands Rev. Henry Ward Beecher and Mr. Whittier. The scene evidently represents the office of *The Liberator*. There is perfection of detail in every line, and the various expressions of righteous indignation excited by the fugitive story are depicted with startling vividness in the faces of the group.

The picture of the singers with the statuette beneath it, awaken powerful emotions when we think over what we owe to these men, who with keen insight, sagacity and marvellous display of statesmanship "took this country by the four corners and shook it until you could hear nothing but slavery."

How overwhelming must have been Mr. Whittier's feelings, when upon the lawn these sweet singers of an emancipated race after singing their peculiar songs of triumph and praise to God, for their true and tried champion, formed about him, and with hands upraised in benediction above his silvered head, breathed the blessings of millions of people in sweet sonorous tones of divine harmony.

> Loud and long
> Lift the old exulting song;
> Sing with Miriam by the sea
> He has cast the mighty down;
> Horse and rider sink and drown,
> He hath triumphed gloriously!
> (From "Laus Deo!")[3]

The spirit of the hour was still strong upon us, pressing down upon the soul as we stood on the greensward of the garden, and sat beneath the old apple trees where Mr. Whittier was wont to sit with Charles Sumner and Mr. Garrison planning measures which should sway a nation. Here, too, came celebrated men of every clime, pausing for a space to refresh themselves in sweet converse with the white-souled genius, John Greenleaf Whittier. We are told that every man and woman of note for fifty years, has made a pilgrimage to the home of the venerable poet.

As is customary, the Woman's Era Club held exercises in the garden as follows:

Remarks by Mrs. J. St. P. Ruffin, president of the club; an historical sketch of Mr. Whittier's life, by Pauline E. Hopkins; reading of "Barbara Frietchie," by Mrs. Ellen M. Taylor; eulogy of Mr. Whittier, by Mrs. Agnes Adams, and closing remarks by Mrs. Hannah Smith.

---

3. Whittier, "Laus Deo!" (1865).

We left the homestead reluctantly. We had come in close communion with the spirit of one of our great American heroes, who have filled the pages of history with their renown, and all demonstration was hushed into silent reverence.

A short distance up Friend Street and we came to the plain house of worship for the Friends of this section, and sat in the seat occupied by the venerable poet from early childhood. Leaving the meeting-house, we found our way to the old burial ground upon the hillside, where full of years and honors the poet was borne to rest after impressive funeral services in the garden of the homestead, September 10, 1892.

The family lot is beautiful in its simplicity, enclosed on all sides by a luxuriant evergreen hedge. Low headstones mark the resting places of all but Mr. Whittier; here the stone is slightly taller and larger. Thus there is nothing to distract the pilgrim's thoughts from the central object—the poet's grave. Here we laid our tributes of flowers; Mrs. Coleman, a teacher of Richmond, Va., spoke eloquently, and music was furnished, led by Mrs. Agnes Adams.

Deeply impressed by all we had seen and heard, we turned our faces homeward.

(EDITOR'S NOTE.—Originally there were four cedar trees, one at each corner of the burial plot; three have been destroyed to save the growth of the remaining. The surrounding hedge is of cedar, with granite border. The tombstone and hedge suffer from the desecration of devout pilgrims. We are indebted to Mrs. Pickard, the niece of Whittier, who has given aid is procuring data and illustrations.)

John Greenleaf Whittier was born in Haverhill, Mass., December 17, 1807.

The first American ancestor of the poet (his grandfather Thomas Whittier) came to America in 1638, and became a convert to Quakerism at a time when the sect was sternly persecuted. The story of their early sufferings at the hands of the Puritans must have been a tradition in the Whittier family, and in this fact we find the secret chord of sympathy which bound him to the hated Abolitionists. No poet has spoken with tenderness for humanity, or waged war more constantly and more defiantly with error and oppression. His intense hatred of wrong, and inexhaustible sympathy for struggling manhood, are expressed with remarkable force and beauty in all his work.

Born on a farm, his life was that of the ordinary farmer's boy, and thus he drew his love of nature from direct "communion with her visible forms," and her beauty and purity impregnate his poems.

Intensely American in feeling, he preserved New England customs and traditions in legendary poems such as "Mogg Megone," "Snow-Bound," and many shorter productions. In these we live again the early Puritans days.

Mr. Whittier's opportunities for acquiring an education were scanty, being limited to the winter months when farmwork was dull; but the flower of genius nestled in the brain of the youth and must find suitable expression—burning thoughts must be clothed in suitable language. The youth found a way.

His elder sister knew of his hopes and encouraged him in his aspirations. Incited by her, in his nineteenth year he contributed verse to the *Free Press*, a journal edited by William Lloyd Garrison. The story runs that Mr. Whittier sent his first poem in fear and trembling. One morning, sometime after, while at work in the fields with his father, he saw the news-carrier coming along the road. The man stopped his horse, opened the bag he carried and drew out a paper, which he gave to the anxious lad. In it Mr. Whittier found his poem in the "Poet's Corner."

Soon after this Mr. Garrison called on the lad and his parents, urging the latter to send the boy to school and thus foster his budding talent; but the rule of the day did not tend to encourage the spending of money on useless things (and too much learning was so considered) and, as the boy could read and write, it was thought no more was needed. With this idea the lad did not agree, however; his New England ambition was aroused; he determined to educate himself the best within his power.

On the farm there was a laborer who made ladies' shoes during the winter season, this being a common employment at that period. This man willingly taught the youth the trade, and by this means Mr. Whittier earned enough to warrant a term at the Haverhill Academy for six months, his board and a suit of clothes, and Dr. Elias Weld gave him the freedom of his library. The following winter he taught the district school at West Amesbury. We may well believe that a lasting friendship was established between Whittier the youth, and the master of the anti-slavery propaganda.

The death of Mr. Whittier, senior, placed the burden of the conduct of the farm upon the son. He thus became a substantial citizen, and in 1835 was sent by his constituents to the general court at Haverhill. Meantime he contributed to numerous magazines, and also occupied the editor's chair for *The American Manufacturer, The Haverhill Gazette*, and *The New England Weekly Review*.

In 1833 he openly allied himself with the anti-slavery cause, going as a delegate to Philadelphia, at the formation of the Anti-Slavery Society. He was a member of the committee on declaration of principles. Of him Mr. Garrison said: "I have no words to express my sense of the value of his services."

Mr. Whittier said of his association with this movement to ameliorate the sufferings of millions of blacks: "I set a higher value on my name as appended to the Anti-Slavery Declaration of 1833, than on the title-page of any book."[4]

---

4. John Greenleaf Whittier to William Lloyd Garrison (November 24, 1863), in Wendell Phillips Garrison and Francis Jackson Garrison, *William Lloyd Garrison, 1805–1879: The Story of His Life, Told by His Children* (New York: Century Company, 1885–1889), 4:89. The letter also appears under the title, "Formation of the American Antislavery Society," in John Greenleaf Whittier, *The Works of John Greenleaf Whittier* (Boston: Houghton, Mifflin, 1892), 7:147.

His efforts in the anti-slavery cause endear him to the Negro, and they gave to him his everlasting crown of glory.

With the appearance of the *Liberator,* Mr. Whittier issued a pamphlet called *Justice and Expediency; or Slavery considered with a view to its rightful and effectual remedy, Abolition.*

Voices of Freedom sounded the duty-call.[5] He joined forces with the great Englishman, George Thompson, M.P., and was mobbed in company with him.

In 1836, Mr. Whittier became secretary of the Anti-Slavery Society, and removing to Philadelphia (1838–9) edited the *Pennsylvania Freeman* with such vigor that a mob attacked and burned the printing office. This quiet Quaker with his inherited hatred of war and violence, faced many a brutal mob with unyielding composure. Among the treasures of the Whittier homestead is a cane, made from fragments of the wood of the burned building. There are also pictures of the building in flames.

In 1836 Mr. Whittier took up his abode in Amesbury where he lived in peaceful, dignified independence.

From 1847 to 1859 he contributed editorially to the *National Era,* an anti-slavery newspaper published at Washington, in which *Uncle Tom's Cabin* first appeared. In 1859 he was on the staff of the *Atlantic Monthly* with Holmes, Prescott, Emerson, Longfellow, Rose Terry Cooke and Mrs. Stowe. His 70th birthday occurring on December 17, 1877, was kept with honor in Boston. His publishers gave him a banquet and invited seventy guests to meet him. Mark Twain and Mrs. Stowe gave sketches of his life and work. Other great writers also contributed articles in his honor.

Pre-eminently the poet of the anti-slavery conflict, there was no phase of the great wrong and almost no episode in the struggle for its abolition which was not the subject for some burning poem. There were nearly one hundred anti-slavery poems in editions of his works, while his prose writings on the same subject were numerous. We can appreciate slightly the effect of his poems on the public mind from an anecdote given by the venerable anti-slavery singer, John W. Hutchinson, of the famous Hutchinson family. In reading this anecdote we must remember that the Civil War was "a white man's war," and even the worshipped Lincoln had said "I will save the Union with slavery if possible"; the soldiers, too, were indignant that anyone should think they were fighting to "free niggers."

Mr. Hutchinson says:

One of the most interesting episodes of our career happened during the war. In 1861 we went to Washington. I knew there was a very strong pro-slavery feeling existing in the army encamped near the capital. I felt it my duty to do what I could to reverse this sentiment, so I applied to Secretary Chase for permission to enter the federal lines and give a series of

5. See Whittier, *Justice and Expediency* (1833), in Whittier, *Works,* 7:9–57; John Greenleaf Whittier, *Voices of Freedom* (Philadelphia: Thomas S. Cavender, 1846).

concerts, indicating the object I had in view—that I wished to sing for the soldiers. I was given a pass good for fifteen days.

The army was encamped around Fairfax Seminary, and numbered 30,000 men. Our coming had been announced by letters and circulars. The church was crowded with soldiers long before the hour for beginning the exercises had arrived.

Everything passed off quietly and to the entire satisfaction of my auditors until I began singing Whittier's "Furnace Blast." ("Ein Feste Burg Ist Unser Gott," which begins:

We wait beneath the furnace-blast
   The pangs of transformation;
Not painlessly doth God recast
   And mould anew the nation.
O North and South,
   Its victims both,
      Can ye not cry,
"Let slavery die!"
And union find in freedom?)

This was too much for a portion of them. There was a hiss, followed by an interruption of the song. The officer in command of the soldiers arose and said, "If I hear a repetition of that noise, I will eject the offender." Then followed a retort, "you had better commence on me."

In an instant one-half the people were on their feet, and great confusion prevailed. Shouts of "Put out the Abolitionists," and kindred proslavery sentiments came from every part of the church. I then came down to the platform and sang a quieting song.

Word was sent to General Franklin informing him of the disturbance of the night before. He ordered the songs we had sung to be sent to him. I showed him a copy of the "Furnace Blast." He took it, read it over carefully, and then laying it upon the table, turned to a number of his staff officers, saying: "If these people are allowed to sing songs of this character, they will disorganize the army." He then hastily indited an order for our removal outside the lines.

I forthwith proceeded to Washington, obtained an audience with Secretary Chase and showed him a copy of the objectionable poem. He said it was all right, and was at a loss to understand why it had created so much trouble.

President Lincoln's attention was also called to the matter, and upon my asking if he had any objection to continuing the concerts said: "You can go wherever you are invited."[6]

---

6. A version of this anecdote is recounted in John Wallace Hutchinson, *Story of the Hutchinsons (Tribe of Jesse)* (Boston: Lee and Shepard, 1896), 1:379–391.

We, of this generation, cannot realize the difficulty and dangers encountered by the men identified with the anti-slavery struggle. Many of these men were poor or had sacrificed their fortune to their principles. In penury and want they wrought. Oftentimes their home was an attic, a cot their bed. They had bread for breakfast, bread and water for dinner, water and bread for supper, varied by the contempt of all mankind. But, withal, their treatises on slavery, written often by the feeble light of a tallow candle, were masterpieces of literature, for the Abolitionists embraced the flower of American intellectuality.

SOURCE "Whittier, The Friend of the Negro," *Colored American Magazine* 3.5 (Sept. 1901): 324–330.

Charles Winter Wood; or,
From Bootblack to Professor

J. Shirley Shadrach

Great oaks from little acorns spring," so runs the old adage; and we might fittingly place beside it another trite saying, "One must excel to win renown." Both are applicable to the career of Charles Winter Wood.

It is likely that the remarkable rise of this talented elocutionist and orator is in great measure due to what was intended for a joke.

Born in Nashville, Tenn., in 1871, he lived until nine years old in the sunny South; but circumstances—those forces over which we have no control, and which carve out our destiny from the cradle to the grave—caused him to emigrate to the great city of Chicago, where he appeared upon the streets doing business as a bootblack and newsboy. Is there a more touching sight, or one that appeals more strongly to the sympathetic soul, than that of a little child, claiming kindred with none, going about the business of bread-winning at an age when a loving mother trembles to have her darling exposed to the perils of the busy streets without the support of a strong guiding hand?

> Made to tread the mills of toil,
> Up and down in ceaseless moil;
> . . .
> Happy if they sink not in
> Quick and treacherous sands of sin.[7]

All the capital of the street child lies in his precocious brain, and his keen analysis of human nature which enables him to charm the coin from the pockets of the passing throng by any means most favorable.

Such conditions are hard for a white child to overcome; many succumb and are overcome. How much harder are the same conditions when faced by one covered with the dark skin of the despised Negro!

Well, the Negro is used to hard conditions; he will come out all right if he has patience and endurance—and doesn't starve while waiting for Americans to arouse themselves to a full perception of the wrongs inflicted on the most inoffensive class of citizens in the Republic.

---

7. Whittier, "The Barefoot Boy" (1855).

Happily for the subject of this sketch his story wears a bright and encouraging aspect.

It was his custom to visit the Old Unity Building, Dearborn street, Chicago, and solicit work from the lawyers, and very soon the polite and good-natured, ragged "shiner" attracted Justice Jarvis Blume's attention. Learning that the boy was a constant attendant at the city theatres and fond of Shakespearean tragedies, Lawyer Blume made him a proposition to recite a part of the ghost scene from *Hamlet*, the reward to be a dollar. In three days young Wood appeared and announced that he was ready for the trial. Among the audience assembled to have a "good laugh" at the boy's efforts were Senator Mason, Judge Blume, Judge Collins, Judge Wallace, State's Attorney Longenecker, Mayor Washburne.

The little bootblack gave an excellent rendition of Hamlet's long speech. The delighted audience "passed the hat," and the black tragedian pocketed about five dollars. That was in 1882, and the boy was twelve years old.

Mr. Blume arranged to have him recite before various small private companies, and then took him to Professor Walter C. Lyman, a teacher of elocution. A test showed that the lad possessed remarkable oratorical powers, and the professor not only engaged him as an office boy at four dollars per week, but agreed to give him daily lessons. At the end of the year, Wood was the star performer in the professor's annual entertainment at Central Music Hall. His greatest hit was in the scene from *The Bells*. He had heard Irving render it once and gave a clever imitation of the great English actor.[8] All these happenings aroused the attention of influential citizens, among whom we may mention Mayor Carter Harrison, of Chicago, Mr. Luther Laflin Mills and Wm. Sutherland.

In 1886 Judge Blume, who had proved himself the young man's staunch friend, took him to the house of Mr. Frank S. Hanson, owner of the New England flouring mills. The boy's reading pleased the company and led to a second engagement. As a result Mr. Hanson sent the young genius to Beloit College, where he remained eight years and graduated in the classical course. He was the only Negro in the school.

Mr. Wood stood well in his studies, but he gained many honors in oratorical contests. He created the role of Oedipus Rex, a Greek tragedy, which was produced at Beloit College and in Chicago. He won first honors at Beloit and in the contest of the State of Wisconsin. Won the interstate college contest at Galesburg, Ill., in 1895, at which time the Hon. Wm. J. Bryan acted as judge and marked Mr. Wood 100 on delivery, pronouncing it the best undergraduate oration he had ever heard. That contest represented ten States and 60,000 students. The judges were William Jennings Bryan, John J. Ingalls and Gov. Frank D. Jackson of Iowa.

On graduating from Beloit in 1895, Mr. Wood entered the Chicago Theo-

8. Beginning in 1871, British actor Henry Irving (1838–1905) performed the role of Mathias in Leopold Lewis's play *The Bells* (New York: Samuel French, 1871).

logical Seminary, and graduated three years later. In 1898 he was made pastor of a church at Warren, Ill., but was called from that position to the head of the English department at Tuskegee, which he still holds. Mr. Washington selected Mr. Wood for the John Crosby Brown scholarship at Columbia University, New York city; he is studying at this institution now in the graduate department, and is candidate for the M.A. and Ph.D. degrees.

Twenty years ago Mr. Wood was a poor bootblack, almost friendless, wholly uneducated, in the Chicago streets. Today, barely thirty years old, he is an influential man, admired, respected and greatly beloved by his people.

Anything strange in this young man's career?

Oh, yes; he is a Negro!

Well, it ought not to be so. Human nature is the same in white or black. The woods are full of just such bright, talented young colored fellows as Charles Winter Wood has demonstrated himself to be.

Do not let us forget Prof. R. T. Greener, the pioneer at Harvard University. There is also Hon. C. G. Morgan, Prof. W. E. Du Bois, Hon. W. H. Lewis, Judge Terrell and R. C. Bruce, and a hundred other men who have met and embraced Opportunity. All we want is a chance.

Since the settlement of America a new and virile type of man whom we call "cosmopolite," for want of a more explicit name, has given impetus to civilization in every part of the globe. Nowhere do we find a corner of the earth that one or many citizens of this Republic are not coloring the social and civil life of the community in which they happen to have cast their lot for the time being. The parent stock from which these "cosmopolitans" have sprung is of every known nationality.

Like the old Negro who claimed to have had every known disease, "Bless de Lord, we've got this replaint, too." There is Lawyer T. McCants Stewart, late of New York, now of Hawaii, figuring conspicuously in the politics of the islands, doing all that he can to break down the growing inclination there to disfranchise the Hawaiians after the style of the South towards the Negroes of that section.

Under our form of government the democratic character of the people has encouraged the development of talent, and the generous nature of wealthy Americans toward a "genius" has made it easy for this peculiar people to shine after their talent is once discovered and acknowledged. It is not at all strange that among those endowed with Nature's richest blessing—genius—we should find some of the brightest wearing the dark line of Africa's sons.

Is it not true that the fate of the Negro is the romance of American history?

It seems so when we have read the pathetic story of this little bootblack with its wonderful ending after twenty short years.

It is predicted, and we must say with every appearance of truth, that in the debatable land between Freedom and Slavery, in the thrilling incidents and escapes and sufferings of the fugitives, and the perils of their friends, the future Walter Scott of America will find the border land of his romance; and that from this source will come the freshest laurels of American literature.

For the sake of argument let us admit that there may be some foundation for the fears of the South that amalgamation will produce a race that will gradually supersede the present dominant factors in the government of this Republic.

It is a daring thought, but not impossible of realization. This reasoning is deduced from a careful philosophical review of the situation.

Who is to say that the type of the future American will not be represented by the descendants of men whose cosmopolitan genius makes them the property of all mankind?

And if amalgamation comes it will not be an illegitimate mingling. The offspring of Samuel Coleridge Taylor, or of Henry Tanner, or of T. McCants Stewart will, in all probability, unite with some one of their social set in the countries of their adoption. Then there are hundreds of Negroes who were born in slavery and settled by their white parents in the English Provinces, after being endowed with wealth. These descendants of Negroes have united with some of the best white families and are living in happiness among their adopted countrymen.

These things are true; and, being true, who can tell when the drop of black blood will inadvertently filter back to the American channels from whence it started, and its possessors be placed by popular vote in the presidential chair?

Anglo-Saxon blood is already hopelessly perverted with that of other races, and in most cases to its great gain. Well, if it is so, what of it? The world moves on; old ideas and silly prejudices disappear in a fog of ridicule. All things are possible, if not probable.[9]

The story of Charles Winter Wood must color the history of the race, and influence its standing in other countries as well as in America.

If we, as men and women, use every honorable means of advancement, none can hold back the tide of prosperity that must inevitably come to us, for "the constant dropping of water wears away the stone."

Here is a thought: Isn't it a strange ordering of events that the greatest wrongs committed against us are by the whites, and our greatest blessings are bestowed by their generosity?

SOURCE J. Shirley Shadrach, "Charles Winter Wood; or, From Bootblack to Professor," *Colored American Magazine* 5.5 (Sept. 1902): 345–348.

9. This passage appears in Hopkins, *A Primer of Facts.*

Rev. John Henry Dorsey

J. Shirley Shadrach

On Saturday, June 21, 1902, in the Baltimore Cathedral, John Henry Dorsey, a Baltimorean, and a graduate of Epiphany Apostolic College, was raised to the priesthood of the Roman Catholic Church, by his eminence Cardinal Gibbons, Archbishop of Baltimore. On Sunday, the day following, Father Dorsey celebrated his first mass at St. Francis Xavier's Catholic Church, Calvert and Pleasant streets, being assisted by Rev. C. R. Uncles, the colored priest of Clayton, Delaware; Rev. J. A. St. Laurent, pastor of St. Francis Xavier's Church, and Rev. Louis Boulden a colored theological student at St. Joseph's Seminary; Rev. Charles Evers, of Brooklyn, master of ceremonies; Rev. John Green and Rev. John Planteville, acolytes.

The sermon was preached by Very Rev. J. R. Slattery, Superior of St. Joseph's Society for Colored Missions.

The church was crowded long before services began, and the aisles and gallery, as well as the steps leading to the gallery, were filled with those who preferred standing to missing the interesting event. The congregation was swelled by about four hundred persons who came over from Washington to witness the ceremony.

The choir had been augmented by additions from among leading singers in Baltimore and Washington, and under the leadership of Prof. Ambrose Briscoe rendered the music of the mass with exquisite taste.

At the end of the religious service, an informal reception was held in the Sunday School hall, and fully two thousand persons pressed forward and tendered Father Dorsey their sincere congratulations on the sacred honor conferred upon him by the Eternal Church.

Later in the day, Mr. Richard Wells gave an elaborate dinner in Rev. Dorsey's honor, and from five to seven P.M. a public reception was held on the veranda of his handsome residence on O street.

Among visitors from Washington were Register Lyons, Judge Terrell, C. Marcellus Dorsey, L. M. Hersham, J. W. Cromwell, Dr. U. S. Lofton, Harry S. Cummings, Willis Smith and Rev. Louis Boulden.

Father Dorsey enjoys the distinction of being the second Negro in the United States ordained to the Roman Catholic ministry. Rev. Charles R. Uncles was the first, at the hands of Cardinal Gibbons, in Baltimore, December 31, 1891. Rev. Father Tolton, who died in Chicago from sunstroke some years ago, was ordained at Rome.

Rev. John Henry Dorsey, son of Daniel and Emma Dorsey, who are descendants of an old Maryland family of Roman Catholics, was born in Baltimore, and received his early education in the public schools of his native city. In 1888, Very Rev. John R. Slattery, then and now a distinguished laborer for the uplifting of the Negro race, began his initial work in the formation of schools and colleges for the education of young white and colored men for missionaries among the Southern colored people in the interest of the Roman Catholic Church.

Rev. Dorsey, then fourteen years of age, made application for admission to this school, and was received. Rev. Dr. Slattery sent young Dorsey to St. Paul, Minn., to study under Archbishop Ireland, where he remained one year. During that time Father Slattery had opened Epiphany College at Walbrook, and he brought his protégé east to become a pupil there.

Father Dorsey graduated with high honors in June, 1893, and matriculated the following September at St. Joseph's Seminary, also established by Father Slattery. His course was then interrupted by ill health, and theological studies were abandoned and Rev. Dorsey taught school in Richmond, Va., and in Baltimore. He resumed his studies in September, 1897, attending the seminary and taking additional courses in philosophy and theology at St. Mary's Sulpician Seminary. At both institutions he did brilliant work, indicating a high degree of intellectual capacity, and the three honorary degrees of the seminary were conferred upon him.

Father Dorsey is a man of athletic build and possessed of great physical strength. His countenance is most benignant, his manners suggestive of poise, reserved strength, social tact and great delicacy of feeling. To the discharge of his sacred duties he brings a mind thoroughly consecrated in the fullest sense to his priestly calling.

Rev. Dorsey has been flooded with invitations to visit almost every section of the country, but he will not accept them prior to entering upon his special field of labor at Montgomery, Ala., next fall. On July 13, 1902, he sang solemn high mass at St. Augustine Roman Catholic Church, Washington, D.C. Once before—during the life of Father Tolton—a colored man celebrated mass in this church. Now, as then, a vast throng crowded the aisles, the doors and portico of this magnificent edifice, listening in silent reverence to the deep, rich, musical tones of a Negro's voice reading in the language of the Caesars, thus filling the most sacred office of a church which has existed in all ages, among all people, in all climes.

Father Slattery is noted for his defense of the colored race, and his devotion to their cause. He preached a forcible sermon, arguing strongly for colored priests in the colored churches. He made a number of brilliant points in favor of the Negro:

The African church of early days was the most glorious part of the Western church. Origen, Tertullian, Cyprian, and Augustine were all Africans.

The foremost western races of to-day furnished the slave marts in those early times. Since then the Aryans have advanced, and the Blacks have become the slaves—hewers of wood and carriers of water.

The Negro, as a free man in our Western world, has not had a long or fair enough trial—only 400 years. A fair show and no favor are all the Negro claims. Has he had them?

The common objection to Negro priests is on the score of morality. We do not think the whites can afford to throw stones at the blacks on this point; mulattoes, quadroons and such folks don't drop from the skies. If the stand of denying orders because some fall away, had been taken from the tenth to the fifteen[th] centuries, Catholicism would have been dead before Luther's time.

The spirit of the political party inimical to the Negro, to which the bulk of Catholics belong, dominates many Catholics. It is this un-Catholic sentiment which looks askance on Negro priests.

The very men who will lynch a Negro will have Negro domestics, and trust the care of their homes to the sable race. The record of the whites in the daily paper gives a pretty poor showing. Are the 99,900 Negroes of Baltimore to be condemned because 100 commit crimes.[10]

Father Slattery spoke like a man, and we honor him and thank him.

Father Slattery's reference to the first spread of Christianity brings out the fact that in addition to its effect on the belief, the lives and conduct of men, it had also important intellectual results. There thus arose a series of theological writers, both in Greek and Latin, who are known as the Christian Fathers, among whom the blacks were most famous:

Tertullian. Born at Carthage, A.D. 160. First of the Latin writers of the Church. His chief work, his *Apology for Christians,* written about A.D. 198.

Origen. Born in Egypt, A.D. 185, editor and commentator of the Scriptures, wrote in Greek.

Cyprian. Archbishop of Carthage, in the middle of the third century. His chief work, *Unity of the Church.* He suffered martyrdom under Valerian.

Augustine. Born in Numidia, Africa, A.D. 354. Bishop of Hippo, known as the Father of Latin Theology. A man of powerful intellect and eloquence. His chief marks are: *On the Grace of Christ, Original Sin,* the *City of God,* and his *Confessions* (an autobiography).

"The common objection to Negro priests is on the score of morality."

Utter nonsense!

Yet how rotten are our politics and religion when it is necessary for a priest to defend a helpless people against malicious outrage at this stage of progressive civilization. Generally, too, there is curb upon every tongue, then the cause of

10. John Richard Slattery (1851–1929) was a regular contributor to *Catholic World.*

the down-trodden and oppressed Negro is under discussion. Wealth, party, and (in some measure) piety are against us.

The immorality of the Negro is a popular fad constantly sounded in the public ear. Says Goethe: "The phrases men are accustomed to repeat incessantly, end in becoming convictions, and ossify the organs of intelligence."

But why this mighty cry rising to heaven against one race alone when all are guilty of the same crime? The wish is father to the thought.

After 250 years of bondage, suddenly the chattel became a man. Ignorant of civilized life, untrained, unintelligent, his ambition and manhood crushed and degraded to the level of the brute, race-womanhood best described by Phillips when he said: "The South is one vast brothel, where half a million of women are flogged to prostitution, or, worse still, are degraded to believe it honorable."[11]

Of this race the highly cultured American Anglo-Saxon exclaims, after only 40 years of partial manhood: "The Negro is hopelessly immoral!" Their judgment is gauged by the most severe moral tests known to man.

The Negro is true to his environment; he is no better and no worse than those whose conduct he copies in living, dress, education, religion and morals. The social evil is everywhere, growing while we sleep. The curse which is a veritable hell to the multitude is common to whites and blacks, yellows, browns and reds throughout the Republic; from the Puritan New Englander who sells her honor for a political position in her own State to the descendant of the F.F.V.'s, who does the same at the magnificent capital of this opulent Union.[12]

The Southern white woman poses in the eyes of the world as the most virtuous of women. We sincerely hope she is. But human nature is the same the world over, and we mark the fact that handsome Negroes cut a wide swath in some communities. And the sin brings its punishment in lynchings and burnings and the torments of the accursed—to the Negro. No guilty woman hesitates one instant to sacrifice her dusky lover to save her reputation.

Let him who is without sin cast the first stone. The Negro meets harsh rebuke, indignant denunciation, scathing sarcasm and pitiless ridicule at every corner. Citizens think it a small matter to ruin a race of men. Father Slattery may well say: "A fair show and no favor are all the Negro claims; but he has not had them."

The influence of the South is everywhere. She does not hesitate to avow her terrible meaning.

We took the Government away. We stuffed ballot boxes. We shot Negroes. We are not ashamed of it. We eliminated all the colored people that we could under the Fourteenth and Fifteenth Amendments.

---

11. Phillips, "Philosophy of the Abolition Movement" (1853), in *Speeches, Lectures, and Letters* (Boston: Lee and Shepard, 1872), 108.

12. F.F.V.'s are First Families of Virginia, a reference to the state's patrician planter class.

I want to call your attention to the remarkable change that has come over the spirit of the dream of the Republicans; to remind you, gentlemen from the North, that your slogans of the past—brotherhood of man and the fatherhood of God—have gone glimmering down the ages. (Tillman.)[13]

These things will not come true as long as the Catholic Church speaks with the true-hearted ring of a Rev. Dr. Slattery.

Once the Negro had many such friends—giant men—Garrisons, Sumners, Phillips and Ben Butlers espoused the lowly Negro's cause.

But in politics it is the dollar that is against us as it is in everything—fraud, bribery, corruption, have destroyed principle.

The Negro, too, has been bullied until he is gradually submitting to all indignities for the sake of a dishonorable peace and the almighty dollar.

> Mammon leads them on.
> Let none admire that riches grow in hell; that soil may best
> Deserve the precious bane.[14]

As Rev. Slattery said, we do not protest against the evil of disfranchisement as we should. We do not stand by our friends as we ought.

No one will deny that our liberties are slowly and surely slipping from our grasp.

Monuments are schools whose lessons sink deep. In General Butler's life was a lesson for the youth of our entire country. But the monument to him was talked down by a Negro![15]

God save us! What are we coming to?

What have we to expect when the spirit of New Orleans regulates the monuments to Massachusetts' sons?

Somewhere there is a subtle force operating against us.

> They work in close design, by fraud or guile,
> What force effected not; that we no less
> At length from them may find, who overcomes
> By force, hath overcome but half his foe.[16]

"No discrimination because of race, color, or previous condition" is the motto of the Catholic Church, and she is fast regaining her old power in the

13. "Pitchfork" Benjamin Tillman, white supremacist South Carolina politician, governor (1890–1894), U.S. senator (1895–1918), delivered this infamous speech on the Senate floor on February 26, 1900. Tillman's remarks were publicized by his supporters and critics alike.

14. Milton, *Paradise Lost*, bk. 1, lines 678, 690–692.

15. Hopkins is referring to William H. Lewis's opposition to a Butler memorial. See Hopkins, "Latest Phases of the Race Problem in America" in this volume for more on Lewis.

16. Milton, *Paradise Lost*, bk. 1, lines 646–649.

world because of her charity towards all. The policy of the Catholic Church, too, is in favor of an educated clergy, upon whose strength the people may confidently lean.

A bit of history.

At the commencement of the period of conquest, the Roman dominion was confined to the peninsular of Italy; at its close it extended over the whole of Southern Europe from the Atlantic to the straits of Constantinople, over a portion of Northern Africa, Egypt, Asia Minor and Syria. Before the conquest she was merely one of the "Great Powers" of the then known world; at its close she was the only Great Power left.

The addition of conquered countries resulted in a new feature of Roman rule called Provincial government, and a vast population of various races and languages were all bound together by the power of Roman rule. The effect of foreign conquest was good and bad; but the evil outweighed the good. Wealth poured into Rome. The political system became corrupt. Great prizes in great offices at home and abroad caused unblushing bribery and corruption.

Vast masses of people ceased from honest industry to subsist upon the price of their votes, the middle class was obliterated and there remained but two extremes—grandee and pauper. The country filled up with a motley parasitic population and the result of intermixture appeared in the degeneracy of the Roman race itself.

The decay of virtue soon became apparent in a great increase of luxury—extravagance in houses, villas, pleasure gardens, dress, food, drink—$5,000 were often paid for an exquisite cook. The lustre of Roman power and glory were then at their height. What a grand thing it then was to be a Roman citizen—followed, feasted, flattered! What a career was opened to them who wished for wealth or aspired to fame! But in the midst of glory the germs of decay were ripening.

All this seems very familiar. History repeats itself. There is nothing new under the sun. Decay stands with tottering limbs and feeble breath, I fear me much, at the doors of the great American Republic, and lisps that we draw near the gates.

Man has always been spiritually little, weak, and, towards a helpless reca-infernal.

Plain words and harsh criticism? Well truth is harsh, and justice uncompromising.

If there is salt in the preaching the galled horse will wince.

But to change public opinion?

That is a difficult problem!

SOURCE J. Shirley Shadrach, "Rev. John Henry Dorsey," *Colored American Magazine* 5.6 (Oct. 1902): 411–417.

Munroe Rogers

Pauline E. Hopkins

$\mathcal{I}$t has been truly said that there is nothing new under the sun.
Who among the rejoicing millions could have been persuaded that in less than forty years from the day they celebrated—Emancipation day—this American people would have turned their backs upon the lessons of humanity learned in the hard school of sanguinary war, and repeated in their entirety the terrible acts exemplified by the surrender of Sims and Burns by a conservative North at the brutal demand of a domineering South!

Alas, that today we must record this fact!

> For mankind are one in spirit, and an instinct bears along,
> Round the earth's electric circle the swift flash of right or wrong,
> Whether conscious or unconscious, yet Humanity's vast frame,
> Through its ocean-sundered fibres feels the gush of joy or shame;—
> *In the gain or loss of one race all the rest have equal claim.*[17]

"Among the problems which the people and government of the United States have to deal with," says Prof. James Bryce,

> there are three which observers from the Old World are apt to think grave beyond all others. These three are the attitude and demands of the labor party, the power which the suffrage rests in recent immigrants from the least civilized parts of Europe, and the position of the colored population at the South. And of these three, the last, if not the most urgent, *is the most serious,* the one whose roots lie deepest, and which is most likely to stand a source of anxiety, perhaps of danger, for generations to come. Compared with it, those tariff questions, and currency questions, and railway questions with which politicians busy themselves sink almost to insignificance.[18]

Such is the intelligent view taken of the situation in our great Republic, by our friends across the water,—views too solemnly true to allow one moment's hesitation in accepting them by all fair-minded people, but to which Americans perversely close their eyes.

---

17. James Russell Lowell, "The Present Crisis" (1884).
18. James Bryce, "Thoughts on the Negro Problem," *North American Review* 153 (Dec. 1891): 641.

The Negro has always been a child of the Republican party, and to that party has given unbounded fealty. Republican rule in order to avoid open rupture with the South, bids fair to shirk a responsibility of its own making. It now wabbles like the fabled ass, between two bundles of hay: Unless it does something for the Negro, and that quickly, it will lose the black vote. On the other hand, if it dares even to hint at this serious matter in the midst of gorging itself with wealth poured into its coffers by gigantic trusts, it will solidify a rupturing Southern Democratic vote.

No, neither politics nor statesmanship can help the black man. The present administration has failed, previous administrations have failed because the Negro question is one of ethics too high for either party to grasp. One does not care to; the other does not dare to.

The Jews when once out of the clutches of the Egyptians, took care not to come in contact with one of the accursed class for years to come. The Negro did not move his dwelling ten miles from the shadow of the old slave pens.

The practice of dynamite bomb throwing which prevails in Russia today, is due to the fact that men ostensibly free are treated by the government like animals. If the colored citizens fired into revolt in this country (and they have plenty of reason), where would the South be? What may not ex-bondsmen dare, who have lost their individuality as they have their owners, who are hovering in a socially comatose condition, between slavery and freedom, who yet are alert to insults? They are not men, for they cannot vote. They are not yet slaves, for they cannot be forced to tasks. They are the missing link between barbarism and citizenship.

A short sojourn in any Southern village of city would supply abundant practical argument against the status quo which no newspaper will supply. Arson, murder and rape are crimes not punished when committed by white men. There is a town in South Carolina where a white man has not been hanged for twenty-five years, and not because he has not committed crimes. The white people of the South are pitiless as is proven by nearly every issue of the daily press. A people who can look with apathy upon horrible scenes of lynching must be pitiless, and without justice, and with no sympathy for fair play. They are not in the Southern blood. In the Negro's case, they do not pity, because they despise; they give him no cardinal help, because they disdain.

There is always a word to be said in extenuation for inherited morals. For the Southern attitude toward the Negro we must blame the grandfathers. These outrages are conducted on a mistaken standard of self-preservation. The South needs nothing less than a new moral code. That does not come in one generation. Yet we cannot wait for time to be their Solon. There are crises in human history which pause not for the manufacture of new laws. The human emergency pits itself against tradition.

The question of disfranchisement has speedily resolved itself into one of serfdom; that means a gradual resumption of all the relations of slavery, with, perhaps, the exception of the auction block, which in the end will also return for short periods, for the punishment of minor offenses.

There are 8,000,000 of the children of Ham, who above all things want manhood—free and expansive—and they mean to have it. They do not want to lord it over white neighbors, though in some states they hold the balance of power; they simply want a fair interpretation of all laws and a share in decent citizenship, and this they are bound to get. They have been patient, more patient than any other nominally free people in the world, but the end is approaching. There is no fierceness, no impulse, but only a steady resolve that is significant. We have our leaders, we are banding together, our clubs are on the increase, our young men's forums are rapidly forming all over the country. These things mean something.

It is a startling fact that, if our prosperity increases in the present ratio, the Negro in 50 years from now will own the greater part of the private landed property in several Southern states. Herein lies the prime cause for Southern antipathy. All the Negro asks is a chance to prove to the world that he is an orderly, capable citizen, and the aristocratic Southerner can pursue his political way in peace. But this they will not do.

If affairs remain as they are now in this unnatural and strained condition, where the manhood of both races is debased, the one by the consciousness of a wrong committed, the other of a wrong endured, there must come a revolution. The air breathes a spirit of restlessness which precedes self-defense. If some Toussaint L'Ouverture should arise!!

The Freedman is a part and parcel of the government. He cannot be deported. He will not seek the malaria of Africa of his own accord. But the sentiment of centralization in this country is a practical one. The Negro must and will be free in deed as well as in effete law. The Afro-American is ready to prove that he is not afraid to put his best intelligence and manhood on a par with that of the Caucasian race.

Contending forces are driving the common people together; the three streams mentioned by Prof. Bryce will form a mighty torrent before which Southern arrogance, trusts, political bossism, and every other abuse waged against God's poor, shall disappear, never to rise again.

The case of Munroe Rogers is apropos to the times, and is another important item in the sum total of inhuman deeds perpetrated against the race.

We have no doubt it will be as interesting to our readers as to us to note the facts in this celebrated case as given to us by Attorney Clement G. Morgan, who was in the forefront of the legal battle, occupying a most conspicuous place; possibly we may except Attorney-General Parker; but naturally the greatest interest centred about the prisoner and Mr. Morgan.

Rogers is a native of North Carolina, and had been employed as a hand in the various tobacco factories for which Durham is noted. Many of these factories are co-operate in their working, and like all monopolies have great influence upon the daily lives of operatives. The foreman in one of the factories was one Mr. Andrews. It is an open secret that the Negro South has no appeal from the will of his employer, and it is a common thing for bosses to kick, whip and otherwise abuse the men and women under them for the most trivial offense. For instance, if one is caught eating an apple during working hours, it is a case for "docking" one's pay at the end of the week.

The pay in the factories is very small, barely enough to keep soul and body together. A man working from 7 A.M. until 9 P.M., deducting one hour for lunch—sixteen hours in all of laborious work—may earn the munificent sum of six dollars per week. And yet the white laborer who rebels has the sympathy of all the laboring fraternity in the country, but the black laborer is lynched on a trumped up charge for daring to leave abuse behind him by seeking new fields of labor, and not one of the labor unions has a word of sympathy for a distressed brother. Thank God, an Almighty hand is being stretched forth to change all this wrong.

Foreman Andrews soon discovered that Rogers was high-tempered and ill-brooked his treatment, and bad feeling was engendered between the men, and Rogers was "docked" repeatedly. Finally he had left the factory; Andrews refusing to give him recommendations, made it impossible for him to obtain work, and for about nine months he did odd jobs about the town.

The first of January, 1902, Rogers returned to his old place in the factory where Andrews was then superintendent and a new man foreman. The new foreman struck young Rogers; they had words, of course, and the colored boy and the friends who took his part, left the factory at once. The news spread through the town, and there was nothing left but to leave the place as soon as possible.

Rogers went around to see his friends and bid them good-by, and among others he went to the house where his sweetheart lived as a domestic. This was with a Mr. Whitaker, and Mr. Andrews happened to reside next door.

Under Mr. Whitaker's house is an opening from which the water supply can be shut off or turned on. Rogers went under the house to turn the water off for the girl and was caught coming out by Andrews, and by him accused of trying to fire Mr. Whitaker's house. In all that followed, Mr. Whitaker and Andrews made no accusation of burning, and the grand jury simply had the boy indicted for *attempt* to burn a place.

Rogers saw his mother that night and told her he was leaving the town; he boarded the train and went to Virginia, working his way from place to place until he reached Brockton, Mass., where he went to work in a shoe factory some time in June. July 22 he was arrested in Brockton; North Carolina officers arrived on the 24th, and Rogers was brought to Boston without a warrant on the 26th.

On the 23rd of July, Mr. Morgan met Rev. W. H. Scott, of Woburn, on the street. He said to Mr. Morgan, "I am going to Brockton to look after Munroe Rogers, I may need the services of an attorney before I get through, will you help me?" Mr. Morgan signified his willingness to render any assistance in his power. The next day word came that Rogers had been brought to Boston by the officers of North Carolina, and that they would ask for his surrender before Governor Crane, on requisition papers. Mr. Morgan went immediately to the Governor's office and inquired about the matter. The requisition papers were faulty—flagrantly inexact—so much so that Attorney-General Parker said the papers did not comply with the statutes, therefore he could not surrender the lad.

From this time on much evidence was collected bearing on the case, all tending to show how extremely dangerous it would be for the Commonwealth of Massachusetts to return Rogers to North Carolina. This evidence cited the cases of two lynchings which recently took place in Salisbury in that State. Governor Aycock himself withdrew the troops just half an hour before the lynchings. The evidence also cited the case of one Wardwell, who set fire to the Manly Brothers' printing establishment, in Wilmington, N.C., in November, 1898, and fired and burned other buildings occupied by Negroes. This man was not indicted. All these happenings created a feeling among New England Negroes, that there could be no justice for an accused Negro in Southern States, and this feeling prompted the citizens of Massachusetts to protest by every means in their power against the return of Rogers.

During this week a very vigorous open letter from the pen of Rev. Mr. Scott was published in the local papers. Lawyer Morgan filed a preliminary brief, Saturday, August 9, and was given ten days for preparation.

On Wednesday, August 20, the protests of leading colored citizens were heard in the judiciary committee rooms at the State House, between 2 and 5 o'clock P.M., before General Parker and his assistant, Frederick B. Greenhalge.

The Attorney-General began his strange tactics in behalf of North Carolina, at this hearing. He said that he wanted it understood that a clear distinction must be drawn between evidence and hearsay or newspaper reports. All evidence would be admitted so as to allow of a proper judgment being formed by the executive, and Mr. Morgan had better give the legal aspect of the case first.

As a precedent, Mr. Morgan cited the case of a colored man arrested in Ohio some years ago for a crime alleged to have been committed in Kentucky. The governor of Ohio refused to give the man up because of lynchings recently happening in Kentucky.

Col. N. P. Hallowell of Civil War fame, was a speaker. He said he had no charge against the people of North Carolina, rather let them speak for themselves. He then read extracts from a paper published at Durham, N.C., in which it was practically acknowledged that no law but lynch law was recognized by numbers of people in dealing with Negroes. In the case of Rogers there was apparently no charge except suspicion.

The Attorney-General asked: "Suppose Massachusetts refused to grant requisition papers in the case of Rogers, would there not be danger that this would be looked upon as a place of refuge for criminals all over the South."

"I should take the chances," replied Col. Hallowell. "But if there is any loophole by which this man can be allowed to remain here, I hope it will be done."

Hon. Archibald Grimké spoke at some length. He said the case should be decided as a specific case. It should stand on its own bottom.

"But how can this be made an isolated case?" asked the Attorney-General. "How can it be otherwise than a precedent?"

"I think that it might be done. I have great faith in the ability and brain power of the legal profession. This man is only charged with arson. The case against him has not been proven," replied Mr. Grimké.

Dr. Henry P. Blackwell, husband of Lucy Stone, said that, in his opinion there was no chance of a black man's getting a fair trial in the South. In the case of Rogers there was no evidence that he had even set a fire, as was charged against him. He was seen in the act of putting fire out, that was all.

Rev. A. N. Shaw followed him with pertinent remarks. Again the Attorney-General showed which way his heart inclined when he said: "This is a profound question we are considering. If it were a question of sympathy, there is no question what the result would be. But the law has no sympathy. This is a question of law."

Lawyer E. P. Benjamin said this case should be tried on its merits. Massachusetts throughout all her history resisted the return of slaves, yet the State was never in danger of being swamped by that class of citizens. Mr. Morgan's argument occupied about half an hour. He said the man under arrest was James Munroe Rogers. The man mentioned in the indictment was Munroe Rogers. His identity was not established. Neither warrant nor indictment charged this man of crime as the Massachusetts statutes required. His guilt must be proved as a criminal before he could be returned. The indictment is not in proper form in that it is not signed by the foreman of the grand jury; and there is no alleging of time or place, city or town where the alleged offence was committed. In 1851, Governor Boutwell refused to grant requisition papers as a precedent. Governor Aycock himself refused to grant requisition papers for an alleged criminal wanted in Tennessee, "Why is North Carolina so anxious to get this man? It seems to me here the ulterior purpose is very clear."

Mr. Morgan's argument was able and exhausting, winning compliments even from the Attorney-General. There was a case in the time of Governor Rice, and one in Governor Butler's time, and, most celebrated of all, the case of Vinal under Governor Brackett. In all of these cases the papers were regular, but from information gleaned at hearings it was decided not to return the prisoners. Attorney-General Parker did not seek to inform himself about these precedents; he made up his mind to return Rogers at the start, and no evidence had the power to move his determination.

Able assistance was rendered Mr. Morgan by Butler R. Wilson, Esq., who was timely with law points pertaining to the occasion.[19]

19. "Attorney General Parker Has the Case," *Boston Guardian*, August 23, 1902, 1, 4. In her essay, Hopkins used the *Guardian*'s coverage of the case. "Attorney General Parker" begins with the August 20 protest.

Tuesday, August 26, the greatest of the series of hearings occurred before the Governor. It is destined to be memorable in the history of extradition cases in Massachusetts and in the annals of Negro history in the North. Aroused by the unfavorable attitude of General Parker, colored men and white men went to the State House in a crowd and filled every approach to the committee room. This hearing was obtained through the persistent efforts of the Boston Ministers' Conference, of which Rev. Mr. Scott is president, and Rev. Johnson Hill, secretary.

Mr. Geo. W. Forbes, of the Public Library force spoke, saying that the extradition was desired not for justice, but to terrorize Negroes everywhere. The Governor asked Mr. Forbes if he meant to say Rogers had committed no crime. Mr. Forbes replied in the affirmative. Mr. Trotter also spoke at some length.[20]

The remonstrants received small comfort from the Governor, and on Wednesday, August 27, he signed the extradition papers and took the train for his home at Dalton. Before going he handed the press the recommendation of Attorney-General Parker, which appeared in the papers on Thursday. On that day the Brockton officers telegraphed the news to Sergeant Crabtree, at Durham, N.C. On Thursday afternoon, Attorney Morgan went to Brockton. He instituted Habeas Corpus proceedings, but before a Federal judge could be found to act, Rogers had been spirited away by the North Carolina officers.[21]

Rogers lies in Durham jail awaiting trial for arson in December. So ends the first lesson in this famous case. What will be the next step? God knows.[22]

What is the chief end of man? The answer used to be, "To glorify God and enjoy him forever." But today times have changed and we have a new catechism.—What is the chief end of man? To put dollars into the hands of our political bosses.

Someone said that Governor Crane would be the next chairman of the Republican National Committee. Therein lies the secret of the executive urbanity to the South.

Black slavery has been abolished, and upon this virtue Republicanism rests, while the great masses are being enslaved by the power of gold, and crushed in the great folds of gigantic monopolies.

The labor question, the question of suffrage rested in the hands of immigrants, the Negro question—all are slowly being merged into one great question envolving the herd of common people of whom the Negro is a recognized factor. The solution of one of these living issues must eventually

20. "Rogers' Case Now Goes to Courts," *Boston Guardian*, August 30, 1902, 1.

21. "They Slipped Rogers Away," *Boston Guardian*, September 6, 1902, 1, 5.

22. A North Carolina judge sentenced Rogers to ten years in prison for arson on Thursday, December 4, 1902. See "Rogers Gets 10 Years," *Boston Guardian*, December 6, 1902, 1.

solve the other two, and no finite power can stay the event. Herein lies our only hope.

The fight is on; neither by the eloquence of the South nor by the wealth of Republicanism can the government hope to escape the iron hand of Destiny, whose fingers relentlessly manipulate the mill machinery of a just God.

Not agitate!

Republics exist only on the tenure of being constantly agitated. We cannot live without the voice crying in the wilderness—troubling the waters that there may be health in the flow.

> We see dimly in the Present what is small and what is great,
> Slow of faith how weak an arm may turn the iron helm of fate,
> But the soul is still oracular; amid the market's din,
> List the ominous stern whisper from Delphic cave within—
> "They enslave their children's children who make compromise with sin."
>
> For Humanity sweeps onward: where today the martyr stands,
> On the morrow crouches Judas with the silver in his hands;
> Far in front the cross stands ready and the crackling fagots burn,
> While the hooting mob of yesterday in silent awe return,
> To glean up the scattered ashes into History's golden urn.[23]

SOURCE "Munroe Rogers," *Colored American Magazine* 6.1 (Nov. 1902): 20–26.

---

23. James Russell Lowell, "The Present Crisis" (1884).

Elijah William Smith:
A Colored Poet Of Early Days

Pauline E. Hopkins

In these early days of the Twentieth century, the complexion and racial characteristics of "the hill," the time-honored West End residence of many a famous family of color in Massachusetts, have changed so greatly in ten years that even the ghosts of our friends of those early days must find it lonely traveling among the present unfamiliar scenes. Yet many familiar landmarks remain to cheer the old inhabitant who still clings to dear associations.

Within a very few years we have had to see many precious buildings broken to bits and carted away to chaos. The old Hayden house and the Cooley house long stood in twin relationship, the beacon lights to many a fugitive from slavery. In the grand words of our poet in a glowing tribute to Lewis Hayden:

> All his thoughts were for his people;
> And for them he toiled; watched while they slept,
> The tyrant foiled; and when the ready hand was
> Called and the strong arm,
> 'Twas his to answer "Here am I,"
> And shield them from all harm.

Hobnobbing with these two families was that of our poet, the Caesars, Rileys, J. J. Smiths, Mitchells, Ruffins, Grays, Wentworths, Bryants, Clarks and a host of other familiar names. But time and tide wait for no man; improvements have crept in and changed the former old-time homes. Many of the present heads of young Boston families helped to form the infant class of Father Grimes's popular church—the present Twelfth Baptist church—on Phillips street, which now seems unrecognizable in its spick-span newness; the old frequenters, too, have died off or dropped away, allured by the welcoming arms of the Episcopal church, whose mission of St. Augustine, near Cedar street, is one of the interesting new features of this neighborhood. Father Grimes's church was the church-home of Elijah Smith and family for many happy years.

On the other side of "the hill," the old St. Paul edifice has done more than change its coat—it has changed religions, too, and now greets us as a Jewish synagogue. If brick and mortar can mourn—even stone possesses life—how many tears that venerable building must have shed over its fall from Christianity. On both sides of the hill, the footsteps of Elijah W. Smith are more compact than elsewhere in Boston, for he was born in 1830, at the corner of West Cedar and Revere streets, obtained his schooling at the old Smith School, now the G.A.R. Hall for colored veterans, on Joy street, and spent his Sabbaths under the voice of his grandfather, Rev. Thomas Paul, in the St. Paul church, founded by him in 1801. But after his marriage to Miss Eliza Riley, Mr. Smith's life became more closely identified with the Phillips street side of the historic hill.

By a happy chance—for they have a trick in Boston now of destroying just the buildings we would select to save—E. W. Smith's successive homes have been spared untouched for our regard. For many years he lived at the corner of Smith court and Phillips street in intimate association with the dearly loved, tried and true leading men of his race, and its white friends, Garrison, Phillips, Sumner, Wilson, Francis Jackson, Gov. Andrew, and all the rest of those stars of the first magnitude, loved Elijah Smith and visited him, finding in his brilliant intellect fit meat for thoughtful minds. Mrs. Smith's library contained the leading writers and most of the books written by colored men. The walls of his house were covered by the pictures of the leading spirits in American history, and one could not but feel the air of culture and refinement pervading his home. The subject of this sketch was the second son of Elijah and Ann Paul Smith. Susan Paul, a sister of Ann Paul Smith, was long associated with William Lloyd Garrison in anti-slavery matters. The Pauls, grand-uncles of Elijah, consisted of five brothers and an only sister. These men were residents of Exeter, N.H., and many of the marriages and births in the family are registered there. The Paul brothers were educated in England and returned to this country to preach. They were all Baptist ministers, very eloquent and forceful in the pulpit. Their descendants are scattered over New York State, throughout New England and in Canada. Elijah Smith inherited his talent from his grandfather Paul; there was another poet in the family, James M. Whitfield, descended from Ann Paul, the only sister of the five brothers Paul, and a second cousin to Elijah Smith. This man published a volume of poems in 1846, which stood the test of criticism. His poem, "How long, O God, how long!" holds an enviable place in American literature. So it will be seen that the law of heredity holds good among all races.[24]

Mr. Smith's immediate family included his wife, two daughters—Mrs. Annie Paul Sims and Miss Hattie Smith—since married to John M. Burrell, Esq., a promising young lawyer of Boston—and Mrs. Susan Paul Vashon, his sister, well and favorably known in the southwest as a public school teacher.

At an early age Mr. Smith was placed in the office of *The Liberator,* to learn the printer's trade under Mr. Garrison's supervision. He soon became an expert typesetter, and afterwards a proof-reader in that office, remaining

24. Elijah Smith was Hopkins's cousin; therefore, the family she details in this article, which includes the poet James Monroe Whitfield and the Paul family, is her own.

there for a number of years, and there he developed the genius of poetry for which he became so celebrated. Ill health demanded a change from the atmosphere of the printing office, and Mr. Smith reluctantly entered new fields of labor.

In those days the colored men of the country earned their bread by barbering, waiting, steamboating, etc. The Howards, Lockleys, Pindells, Charles Rose, Cornelius Lenox and William Jarvis of Lynn (late Governor's messenger at State House, Boston), were all barbers and owned property and made handsome livings. J. B. Smith, Dalton Jacob Moore, were waiters who had amassed a competency. John Spencer, Mr. Woodman, Mr. Boleyn were steamboat stewards, drawing large salaries. Mr. Smith finding himself obliged to change his business, secured the position of steward on one of the steamboats plying between Boston and St. John, N.B., where his financial condition was flourishing. His genial ways, intelligence and refined bearing won the esteem of patrons and employees, and very soon he was offered the position of head-waiter at the famous hostelry known as Young's Hotel, where for twenty-five years he was a leading spirit.

But it is as a poet that we know him best. No one can read his poems without a regret that he could not have written more, could not have enjoyed the life he best loved and that his genius demanded. Few living poets understood better than he did, the elements of true poetry. "The evenness of his numbers," says Dr. Brown, "the polish of his diction, the rich melody of his musically-embodied thoughts, and the variety of his information, show that Nature was not sparing in showering her gifts upon him."[25] Life has been better and brighter for what he has done. Even when he amused he taught, and what light is to the material world, the poet is to the intellectual. Most of his articles have appeared in *The Boston Daily Traveler* and *The Saturday Evening Express*, once well known dailies with a large circulation. The following lines are from the beautiful and soul-stirring poem entitled "Freedom's Jubilee," read at a Ratification Meeting of the Fifteenth Amendment:

> Glory to God! for the struggle is ended,
>   Glory to God! for the victory won,
> Honor to those who the Right have defended,
>   Through the long years since the conflict begun.
>
> O, may the prayers of those ready to perish
>   Guard them from harm like a girdle of fire!
> Deep in our hearts their good deeds we will cherish,
>   And to deserve them we'll ever aspire.

25. William Wells Brown, *The Rising Son; or, The Antecedents and Advancement of the Colored Race* (1874; rev. ed., Boston: A. G. Brown, 1876), 553.

God! at Thine altar in thanksgiving bending,
    Grant that our eyes Thy great goodness may see;
O may Thy light while the temple's veil rending,
    Show, through its portals, the path of the Free.[26]

"Our Lost Leader," written on the death of Charles Sumner, is one of Mr. Smith's best productions. We give the last verse:

Give us the faith to kneel around
    Our country's shrine, and swear
To keep alive the sacred flame
    That Sumner kindled there![27]

The "Song of the Liberators" has in it the snap and fire that shows the author's appreciation of the workers for liberty. We give two verses:

The battle-cry is sounding
    From every hill and vale,
From rock to rock resounding,
    Now shall the tyrants quail.
No more with chain and fetter,
    No more with prison cell,
Shall despots punish heroes
    In the land they love so well.

And thou, O Isle of Beauty,
    Thy plaintive cry is heard;
Throughout our wide dominions,
    The souls of men are stirred;
And rising in their manhood,
    They shout from sea to sea,
"Destruction to the tyrants!
    Fair Cuba shall be free!"[28]

We give the whole of the poem "Robert Morris," read at the Memorial Meeting, held in Boston, at Charles Street church, March 5, 1883:

He sleeps! the faithful sentinel
    On freedom's outer wall;

26. Ibid., 554.
27. Ibid. For the complete poem, see Elijah W. Smith, "Our Lost Leader," in *Sumner Memorial Meeting* (Boston: Committee of Arrangements by Charles L. Mitchell, 1874), 29–31. Hopkins concluded her speech to the Sumner centenary with several lines from Smith's poem.
28. Brown, *Rising Son*, 555.

No more we hear his warning voice,
   No more his bugle call;
But not until the baffled foe
   In dire dismay had fled.
Aye, not until the starry flag
   Waved *spotless* o'er his head.

His boyhood saw grim Prejudice
   Its giant shadow cast
O'er each ennobling dream of youth,
   And every prospect blast.
His early manhood felt the chill
   Of base Proscription's hand;
No refuge for his hunted race
   In freedom's favored land.

For him no bow of promise shone
   Before his eager eyes;
No star of hope lit up the gloom
   Of his o'erclouded skies;
His strife was for equality;
   No honor sought, or fame;
He climbed the adamantine heights
   And chiseled there his name!

And on the summit, all serene,
   What glories met his view!
Oppression's cloud had rolled away,
   And all the world seemed new,
The glorious sun ne'er shone so bright,
   The birds ne'er sang so sweet,
Proscription, with a mortal wound,
   Lay, writhing, at his feet!

And O, how few have seen the bud
   Of youthful hope unfold
Into the perfect flower of joy,
   With leaves of burnished gold!
How few have heard the chorus grand
   Whose first notes caught their ear
Amid the clashing of the chain,
   The sign, the groan, the tear!

We honor him because he stood
   Calm 'mid the raging sea;

True to his God, his race himself,
　　His country, liberty;
And from the polished shield he bore
　　The shafts of malice fell
As billows from the good ship's prow
　　That breasts the ocean's swell.

He serves his race who hears its mark
　　With honor to the end;
And stands equipped, in armor bright,
　　Its manhood to defend;
And he but plays the craven's part
　　Who looked idly on,
While freedom's fight, by other blades,
　　In other hands is won.

Rest thou in peace! thy work is done;
　　How well our lips can tell;
Not with a sorrow without hope
　　We hear thy passing bell:
For with the names of those whose lives
　　Shed lustre on our race,
Unblemished by dishonor's stain,
　　shall Morris take its place.

Rest! for the struggling sun that rose
　　'Mid slavery's gloomy haze
In glory sets; with roseate hues
　　The firmament's ablaze.
Rest! for thy beacon's light shall shine
　　Forth, as one lighthouse more
To warn us of the sunken reefs
　　That guard fair freedom's shore.

And all along our beaten path
　　These bright examples stand:
There Attucks fell, here Morris strove,
　　And Douglass waves his brand;
The martyr, patriot, and sage,
　　The living and the dead,
Still lead our upward march and bear
　　Their banners o'er our head.[29]

29. Elijah W. Smith, "Robert Morris," in *In Memoriam: Robert Morris, Sr.* (Boston, 1883), 46–48.

Though Mr. Smith wrote on various themes, the highest inspiration came to him through the wrongs of his race and the efforts of its friends to right these wrongs. His greatest enthusiasm was aroused by those great men,— Garrison, Sumner, Phillips, Douglass, Nell and other leaders, and his poetic tributes to their valiant leadership have never been surpassed by poet of any race.

Mr. Smith was emphatically a race man; no tale of woe was unheeded by him; his bounty was freely dispensed. Eminently social and domestic, his hospitality was liberal, and though he was a good liver, avoided excesses. It is said that he never lost a friend. Of him it may be truly said:

> He kept
> The whiteness of his soul, and so men o'er him wept.[30]

He was the life and soul of the domestic circle, and in the society of his dear ones at home he passed his happiest hours. No husband and father was ever more truly mourned than Elijah W. Smith. By his daily life he sought to inculcate a comprehensive Christianity. His religious enthusiasm and love for his church, his upright character, and patience during a long illness, all present an example rare and beautiful.

In a simple and sufficient faith he died; in that faith he still speaks to us, although the voice of his muse is hushed. We have learned from his life the value of generosity, purity, kindness, unselfishness, and these are the truest tributes of praise we can give this friend who loved, with a rare and touching love, his friends, his country, and his race.

The veteran writer and poet died October 7, 1895, of a lingering affection of the heart, and the funeral took place from Zion A.M.E. church before a large number of leading and well known citizens. Among those assembled to pay the last tribute of respect to mortality were most of the professional colored men of Boston as well as many leading white citizens; among the latter was Mr. Francis Jackson Garrison, son of the famous abolitionist, with whom Mr. Smith labored for many years. Among the pall-bearers was David T. Oswell, of Worcester, Mass., recently deceased, a life-long friend of Mr. Smith, and one of the greatest musicians the colored race has ever produced, a violin virtuoso of purest genius and most careful culture.

The words of the following poem, written by Mr. Smith in memory of William C. Nell, may well be said of himself:

> Another soldier gone!
>   One of the Spartan band
>   Who fought the fight

---

30. Lord Byron, *Childe Harold*, canto 3 (1816), stanza 57.

With weapons bright
When slavery ruled the land.

God gave thee to behold
Our banner floating free!
Gave thee to hear
The triumph-cheer
That told of liberty!

Dear, faithful friend, farewell!
Our gratitude is thine:
The prayers we breathe
Thy name shall wreathe
With memory's flowers divine!

SOURCE "Elijah William Smith: A Colored Poet of Early Days," *Colored American Magazine* 6.2 (Dec. 1902): 96–100.

Heroes and Heroines in Black 1:
Neil Johnson, America Woodfolk,
Robert Smalls, et al.

Pauline E. Hopkins

*W*e propose in this article to touch upon the noble trait of heroism, in the Negro race, which is defined as gallantry, valor, courage.

The heroic in human affairs is a large topic, deserving of the extended treatment given it by the best thought of all ages. In the literature of heroism we first find Plutarch, to whom we owe the Brasidas, the Dion, the Epaminondas, the Scipio of old. Wordsworth's "Laodamia" and Scott's works have a noble, martial strain of heroic virtue; Robert Burns sings also a song or two. Simon Ockley's *History of the Saracens* tells over the glories of individual courage, while the cool, philosophical reasonings of Carlyle, Emerson, Channing and Thoreau give forth a generous meed of praise and enthusiasm for manly valor.

The heroic spirit in man, we therefore deduce, is the foundation of universal history, history itself being but an account of the deeds of men who have been the models and patterns for the great mass of humanity in past centuries even from the beginning of the world. A man may be in obscurity today,—poor, ignorant, unknown; lo, on the morrow, he may, by one unselfish act, beautiful and sublime, become one of the great men sent into the world as an instrument to accomplish the will of the Father. Such is heroism: a military attribute of the soul; a fine contempt for safety or ease; a mind of such chivalric mold that thoughts of danger cause no disturbance; the highest degree of natural enthusiasm which the world profoundly venerates.

Being then a quality that is God implanted and an attribute of Infinity, it is a most desirable possession. If cultivated, it instills a wild courage, a "stoicism of the blood" that brings to any race undying fame. As a race, we need the stimulus of books and tales of this "cathartic virtue" more than any other literature we can mention.[31]

How strange a thing it is to see a great powerful and prosperous nation, generally fair and impartial to the helpless of other lands and willing to lend them aid and comfort, and boasting of this national trait as of a great and

---

31. Hopkins's introduction to this essay, including the literature references in the second paragraph, are taken from Ralph Waldo Emerson, "Heroism," in *Essays: First and Second Series* (1841–1844; *Making of America*, 2005), 1:233–235.

shining virtue, yet in all questions relating to an unfortunate race brought to their shores by force and treachery, descending to the meanest methods of petty spite because of caste prejudice induced by color and a previous condition of servitude.

The great majority of the Anglo-Saxon race professes to see nothing meritorious in the character of the Negro, and delights to lower his reputation by ridiculing his efforts for advancement, and by holding up in the spirit of intense bitterness, every story of possible guilt, with an unctuous glee most revolting to a spirit of fairness. Thus we have details of hideous crimes attributed to "brutal Negroes," spread upon the columns of the daily press in flaring headlines with a minuteness of account that is sickening, while the thousands of brave and unselfish deeds wrought by these same "brutal Negroes" for the benefit of the Anglo-Saxon, are relegated to an obscure corner, perhaps at the foot of some advertising page, to languish in harmless oblivion away from the knowledge of the common people whose views otherwise might suffer a revolution in favor of that same "brutal Negro." Flung out as a weed upon the waters, the Negro has nothing left but the Almighty arm of Omnipotence.

We append some instances of Negro heroism in the twentieth century:

Louisville, Ky., July 19, 1902.

Through the heroism of Neil Johnson, a Negro, seven persons who were out on the Ohio River in a launch were saved from a horrible death yesterday morning. The party consisted of Mr. and Mrs. J. T. Boyd, W. S. Price, Mrs. Briggs, Miss Fannie Bell and John Whyte of Louisville, and Mrs. Fugitt of Washington, D.C. (all white).

Mr. Boyd and Mr. Price were in the bow of the launch smoking, when a lighted match ignited the gasoline in the escape basin, and flames shot high in the air, threatening an explosion of the main tank. The women became frightened and frenzied with despair, sought to leap from the launch to the river, although none of them could swim. It was then that Neil Johnson, who was employed on the launch, *plunged his arm into the fire and turned the valve,* stopping the flow of oil from the tank! Then he threw himself against the flames wherever they appeared, and succeeded in putting out the fire.

His arm was burned to a crisp, and his body severely burned. The passengers escaped without injury.

A colored man, George Robinson, of 55 Sawyer street, Roxbury, Mass., on September 11, 1902, saved fifteen men, women and children from death by suffocation in a fire in a tenement house.

Passing the house about 11:30 P.M., Robinson's attention was attracted by a loud crackling. On investigating, he found flames pouring from a shed in the rear, which burned like tinder.

Robinson dashed down the street, rang in an alarm and returned to try to awaken the inmates by ringing the bell and pounding on the door. Unable to arouse them in this way he kicked in the door and rushed upstairs.

The house was full of smoke, and many of the sleeping inmates were already overcome. From room to room Robinson hurried, afraid that some would be dead before he reached them. Those who were unable to walk he dragged to a window where there was fresh air.

When the firemen arrived to aid in the work of rescue, Robinson was carrying men and women down stairs in his arms. But for his heroic efforts Chief Grady says that many lives would have been lost.

The colored man slipped away as soon as the danger was over to avoid the praise that was showered upon him.

Louisville, Ky., Aug. 14, 1902.

America Woodfolk, a colored woman who was born a slave in Shelby Co., Kentucky, *seventy years ago,* performed an heroic act in New Albany that would have been remarkable in a young and vigorous man.

The old woman lives in the West Albany suburb, on the Budd road, a short distance west of New Albany. She had driven her buggy to the mouth of Falling Run Creek, a short distance from her home, for the purpose of washing it, and while engaged at that work Jeff Stone, an eleven-year-old colored boy, and a companion went into the river to swim.

Stone stepped into a hole over his head and was swept away by the current. America, who is still active and strong despite her age, swam after the boy, seized him from the bottom of the stream, carried him ashore and worked over him until he was resuscitated.

She says she learned to swim while a slave in Kentucky while a girl, and had not forgotten that accomplishment.

To us who are acquainted with the qualities of the Negro, all this is ancient history, but in these days when a willful blindness—colorphobia, affects the majority of our good citizens because of kinship with the Southern chivalry, we must constantly reiterate these old truths. There is always a class of people who delight to exclaim: "Can any good come out of Nazareth!"

During the War of the Rebellion while the country seemed drifting to destruction, the hearts of loyal men were many times made glad by the bravery of Negroes, who by their valor added treasure to the coffers of a sorely pressed administration.

In June, 1861, the schooner *S. J. Waring,* from New York bound to South America, was captured by the rebel privateer, *Jeff Davis,* a prize crew placed on board, consisting of a captain, mate and four seamen; the vessel set sail for Charleston, S.C. Three of the original crew were retained on board, among them the steward and cook of the schooner, a black man named William Tillman. He was put to work and told that he was the property of the Confederate States and would be sold on arrival at Charleston. No one can possibly imagine what Tillman's feelings were. The Negro thought of his home and happy though lowly past; the future promised nothing but the degradation of slavery. Then, indeed, he must have realized the full meaning of Patrick

Henry's inspired words, "Give me liberty or give me death!" He resolved upon a course of action and proceeded to execute it.

Night came on; the vessel ploughed her way toward the South,

> Regions of sorrow, doleful shades, where peace
> And rest can never dwell, hope never comes,
> That comes to all; but torture without end.[32]

The rebels retired to their berths; the mate, in charge of the vessel, took his handy toddy and lay down upon the deck. Then was Tillman's time. Armed with a club, he proceeded to the captain's room and struck a fatal blow. Yet once again the deadly bludgeon rose and fell in the adjoining cabin and the black man was master. Silently, he ascended to the deck, and struck the mate, who, slightly wounded, drew his revolver and called for help. The crew hastened to his side. Once more Tillman's fatal club did fearful execution; the mate fell dead. The Negro seized the weapon, drove the crew below stairs, put them in irons, and proclaimed himself master of the vessel.

The schooner's course was changed; with the stars and stripes flying, a fair wind blowing, the *Waring* rapidly retraced her steps, and five days later she arrived in port under the command of William Tillman, the Negro patriot.

"To this colored man was the nation indebted for the first vindication of its honor on the high seas." The press spoke of the achievement as an offset to the defeat at Bull Run. Tillman was awarded the sum of six thousand dollars as prize-money for the capture of the schooner.[33]

Hon. Robert Smalls, the pilot and captain of the steamer *Planter*, also *Congressman*, must be remembered for his daring deeds.[34] The *New York Herald* of May, 1862, gave a very full account of Smalls's heroic adventure:—

> One of the most daring acts since the war commenced was undertaken and successfully accomplished by a party of Negroes in Charleston on Monday night last. Nine colored men, comprising the pilot, engineer and crew of the rebel gunboat *Planter*, took the vessel under their exclusive control, passed the batteries and forts in Charleston Harbor, hoisted the white flag, ran out to the blockading squadron, and thence to Port Royal, via St. Helena Sound and Broad River, reaching the flagship *Wabash* shortly after ten o'clock last evening.
>
> The *Planter* is just such a vessel as is needed to navigate the shallow waters between Hilton Head and the adjacent islands, and will prove

---

32. Milton, *Paradise Lost*, bk. 1, lines 65–67.

33. Brown, *The Negro in the American Rebellion*, 74–75. Brown attributes the quotation to the *New York Tribune*.

34. Like her source, William Wells Brown's *The Negro in the American Rebellion* (Boston: Lee and Shepard, 1867), Hopkins misspells Smalls's name as "Small," which I have silently corrected.

almost invaluable to the Government. It is proposed, I hear, by the commodore, to recommend the appropriation of $20,000 as a reward to the plucky Africans who have distinguished themselves by this gallant service, $5,000 to be given to the pilot (Smalls), and the remainder to be divided among his companions.

The *Planter* is a high-pressure, side-wheel steamer, one hundred and forty feet in length, and about fifty feet beam, and draws five feet of water. She was built in Charleston, was formerly used as a cotton boat, and is capable of carrying about 1,400 bales. On the organization of the Confederate army, she was transformed into a gunboat, and was the most valuable war-vessel the Confederates had at Charleston. She was commanded by Captain Relay of the Confederate Navy, all the other employees of the vessel, excepting the first and second mates, being persons of color.

Robert Smalls is an intelligent Negro, born in Charleston, and employed for many years as a pilot in and about that harbor. He entered upon his duties on board the *Planter* some six weeks since, and, as he told me, adopted the idea of running the vessel to sea from a joke which one of his companions perpetrated. He immediately cautioned the crew against alluding to the matter in any way on board the boat; but asked them if they wanted to talk it up in sober earnestness, to meet at his house, where they would devise and determine upon a plan to place themselves under the protection of the Stars and Stripes, instead of the Stars and Bars. Various plans were proposed; but finally the whole arrangement of the escape was left to the discretion and sagacity of Robert, his companions promising to obey him, and be ready at a moment's notice to accompany him. For three days he kept the provisions of the party secreted in the hold, awaiting an opportunity to slip away. At length, on Monday evening, the white officers of the vessel went on shore to spend the night, intending to start the following morning for Fort Ripley, and to be absent from the city for some days. The families of the contrabands were notified, and came stealthily on board. At about three o'clock the fires were lit under the boilers and the vessel steamed quietly away down the harbor. The tide was against her, and Fort Sumter was not reached till broad daylight. However, the boat passed directly under its walls, giving the usual signal—two long pulls and a jerk at the whistle cord—as she passed the sentinel.

Once out of range of the rebel guns the white flag was raised and the *Planter* steamed directly for the blockading steamer *Augusta*. Captain Parrott, of the latter vessel, as you may imagine, received them cordially, heard their report, placed Acting-Master Watson of his ship in charge of the *Planter*, and sent the Confederate gunboat and crew forward to Commodore Dupont.[35]

35. Brown, *The Negro in the American Rebellion*, 79–81.

At daylight one morning at the siege of Washington, N.C., a band of seventeen contrabands came to the shore and hailed the nearest gunboat. They had traveled fifty miles the previous night under the leadership of a Negro whom they called "Big Bob."

A few days after their arrival their services were needed for an expedition into the interior. On being told what was wanted of them, not a man showed a sign of fear, although all knew that the enterprise was fraught with danger. They succeeded in penetrating the enemies' lines, arrested three important rebels, and conveyed them to the fleet. On the march to the vessels, Bob, the captain of the company, urged them along in this style: "March along dar, Massa; no straggling to de r'ar; come, close up dar, close up! We's boss dis time." A week later another expedition was planned of greater difficulty and danger. They had not gone far before they were attacked by a scouting-party from the rebel camp, but the enemy was put to flight, and the Negroes escaped. They then took a somewhat different route, and proceeded on their journey, accomplishing their mission finally: destroying two large salt works, a large tannery, and liberating twenty-three slaves.

But Bob's days were numbered; the next day a flat full of soldiers, with four blacks, including Bob, attempted to land at Rodman's Point, but were repulsed by a terrible fire of rebel bullets, all tumbling into the boat, and lying flat to escape being shot. The boat stuck fast on the sand-bar, while the balls were still whizzing over and around the flat. Seeing that something must be done at once, or all would be lost, Big Bob exclaimed: "Somebody's got to die to git us out of dis, and it may as well be me!" He then deliberately got out, and pushed the boat off and fell into it, pierced by five bullets.[36]

These few incidents we have given are but slight to the testimony that might be given in the case of the Negro. The dawn of the Twentieth century finds the Black race fighting for existence in every quarter of the globe. From over the sea Africa stretches her hands to the American Negro and cries aloud for sympathy in her hour of trial. England, at this late day, begins to doubt the wisdom of her course in acknowledging the equality of the Negro race. In America, caste prejudice has received fresh impetus as the "Southern brother" of the Anglo-Saxon family has arisen from the ashes of secession, and, like the prodigal of old, has been gorged with fatted calf and "fixin's." The remonstrances of the faithful son are met by the answer—old things have passed away and all things have become new.

But the Negro still lives, and while life remains, Hope lifts a smiling face.

SOURCE "Heroes and Heroines in Black: 1. Neil Johnson, America Woodfolk, Robert Smalls, et al," *Colored American Magazine* 6.3 (Jan. 1903): 206–211.

36. Ibid., 212–215.

William Pickens, Yale University

J. Shirley Shadrach

William Pickens, the colored orator of Yale, who sprang into prominence a month ago by winning the Ten Eyck prize, the first time in
the history of the university that a colored student has carried off the highest
honor of the junior class, is a much-talked of man just at present.

Why this great commotion over Pickens? He's not the first, he won't be the
last Negro to sweep the stakes in a fair struggle for first place. Numbers of
brilliant colored men have carried off class honors in great schools of learning, at home and abroad, long years ago; it seems almost time for the community to become accustomed to our way of doing business. It is the duty of
every Negro, blessed with honorable opportunity, to take everything in sight
as his portion of this world's goods. This country owes us compound interest
on the toil of our ancestors invested as capital stock in the upbuilding of this
opulent and powerful Republic. We intend to have our interest in spite of the
insane ravings of malicious enemies.

> The pound of flesh, which we demand . . .
> Is dearly bought; 'tis ours, and we will have it.[37]

Despite the wave of sensationalism that has swept over this young man,
threatening to engulf and destroy his future usefulness among his own people, caused doubtless by the wily schemes of capitalists and unprincipled territory grabbers, we see in his career only the pitiful struggle of a man fighting
against fearful odds to accomplish a clear ambition.

However we may individually resent Mr. Pickens's erroneous conception
of the political and social conditions existing in Hayti, as expressed in his
essay, let us not condemn too severely the fervent zeal of youth. Let us weigh
well the temptations surrounding one who has been the under dog hitherto
in this human struggle with poverty, obscurity and the scorn of the world.

Glittering generalities:

William Pickens, the Yale Negro student who won the Ten Eyck prize in the
leading oratorical contest of the year, has received an offer of financial assistance from Mrs. Douglas Robinson of New York, sister of President Roosevelt.

---

37. Shakespeare, *The Merchant of Venice*, 4.1.99–100.

After he delivered his oration in Newport, Miss Lucy Giles, a millionaire's daughter, was so deeply affected that she stuck a diamond pin in his coat.

On May 29, Mr. Pickens came to Harvard University to deliver his oration. He was met at the Back Bay station by a committee representing the university and the city government of Cambridge. These gentlemen had engaged an open barouche to convey the young hero across the Charles to the "college town." This is a pretty strong dose of adulation.

Concealed impudence; specious flattery:

"Evidently he owes nothing to the Caucasian strain, morally or intellectually. He seems to be a Negro, pure and simple, which gives to the incident a significance it would not otherwise possess. He is not a mulatto—or so it seems—not a quadroon, or an octoroon, or a suggestion. He is straight goods and all the better for it."

What a wonderful delineator of the vagaries of the human character old William Shakespeare was! Iago, unable to surpass Othello's brilliant career, or mar his prestige, at last cut the wonderful Moor down to his own pitiful size by sowing dissension in Othello's family.

> I hate the Moor. He holds me well;
> The better shall my purpose work on him.
> To get his place and to plume up my will
> In double knavery—How, then?—Let's see:—
> The Moor is of a free and open nature,
> That thinks men honest that but seem to be so,
> And will as tenderly be led by the nose as asses are.
> I have 't. It is engendered. Hell and night
> Must bring this monstrous birth to the world's light.[38]

In union there is strength. A house divided against itself cannot stand; neither can a race. Let us consign these rotten and insidious invasions of race unity, to the depths of oblivion. The crafty insinuation—promulgated for our undoing—that white blood elevates or that black blood demeans, is, indeed, "a monstrous birth of hell and night."

Of himself Mr. Pickens says:

In 1881 I was born somewhere in South Carolina. The event called for no careful record. My parents had both been slaves, were both illiterate, but possessed the then rare ability to read the New Testament when printed in large characters. My father derived his name from the old Pickens family of Revolutionary fame.

---

38. Shakespeare, *Othello*, 1.3.347–365.

In 1888, on my seventh birthday, my parents were caught by the great black wave that swept westward from the Southeastern States across the Mississippi River, in search of a better home. In 1891 we moved to Little Rock, Arkansas. There, in that same year, I began school and, strangely, I had gathered sufficient knowledge of reading and numbers to be put into the third or fourth primary grade. At the close of that scholastic year the teacher announced that I was the leader of the class.

I became ambitious, and having a good memory, from that day for seven years, I committed each lesson to memory daily, so as to go through my lessons in history, physiology and geography, verbatim.

My mother's death was the first great blow by which God taught me self-reliance. I had been saving money for my books and clothing, which sum always needed her supplement. But now the whole was left to me. I got a job on the skiff ferry of the Arkansas River, where I could work in days of the school period. Thus I completed the first high school grade, tenth year, in 1897. Then a "free bridge" destroyed my occupation. I had yet two years before high school graduation. I got work at a stave factory by the side of a very cruel man who made repeated attempts to maim me, thus teaching me wariness and giving me an insight into human nature that has served me well since. In June, 1899, having made continuously the highest mark of my class for eight years, I delivered at the high school commencement the enviable valedictory.

The last year of the high school I got through by working Saturdays at a sawmill and being the watchman on Sundays. This is the life that I delight to remember. I lay on warm days (Sundays) on a lumber pile, and wrote beautiful little lyrics and class satires, which I took to school on Mondays for the amusement of my schoolmates and the delight of my teacher of literature.

After graduation came the question of the future. My first idea was to work a year or two and save enough to go to Howard University, Washington, D.C., but by chance I became acquainted with a colored Congregational minister, Rev. Y. B. Sims, of Little Rock, who is a graduate of Talladega College, Alabama. By him I was directed to Talladega. Then began my active preparation for college, viz., hard work on the building of the great Choctaw Railroad through the wilds of Arkansas. By the last of September I had saved about $50 of my earnings, and with this sum I started for Talladega, Ala., paying $15 for railroad fare and giving $30 to the college treasurer. Upon examination I was put into the sophomore class, and by good work easily won the friendship of my teachers and finished the year in 1900 at the head of my classes. In the summer of 1900 I earned expenses for the next year by travelling as the speaker in a troupe sent out by the college to solicit aid for its expenses. I was somewhat successful in my role, and was consequently invited to speak at the annual meeting of the American Missionary Association in October, 1900,

Springfield, Mass. I graduated from Talladega College last June. Through the influence of Dr. G. W. Andrews, President of the institution, and Dr. A. F. Beard, Senior Secretary of the A.M.A., I had received word from Prof. H. P. Wright, of Yale, that I could enter the junior class and have a part of my tuition remitted, till Christmas examination, after which any help received would depend upon scholarship and attendance.

I went to Chicago, got work at once as a machinist's helper for $1.50 per day, worked thirteen weeks and got $80. Two or three days before the opening of Yale's fall term, I quit work, bought a few needed articles, paid for a railroad ticket, and landed in New Haven a stranger, and with the lavish sum of about $15 in my pocket.

After getting straight with the college through the dean's office, I began [to] search for a place to earn my board. With great good fortune, I became acquainted with Mr. Wm. Lotze, Secretary of the New Haven Y.M.C.A., and he secured me a place in the association restaurant, where with three or four hours' work daily, I earned board until a few weeks ago.

I now found myself pressed for time. Many nights I did not go to bed before 3 A.M., having got a job at a banquet hall or private party. I lived so far from the institution that I had no time to think of anything save board-earning and lesson-learning. But after Christmas a room was found me in White Hall where I was nearer my work and the libraries.

The Ten Eyck subjects had been announced in the fall. About the middle of January I stepped into the Dean's office, received a catalogue and noticed that the essays were to be handed in February 25. It required considerable nerve to attempt the seemingly impossible, but having already learned the virtue of hard work and been convinced that genius is only a magniloquent and euphemistic expression for determined effort, I decided to write. I saw "Hayti" on the list. I rolled up my sleeves and went in for a good chance to make a philanthropical and magnificent plea for the non-interference of the outside world in Haytian affairs.

Although I went to study with a "previous" opinion, yet that opinion was held subject to change, and changed it was.

I intend to do Christian educational work, and not law. I am unwilling to narrow my work for my race to the small circle of the average colored lawyer. Although many of my dearly-beloved brothers of color will frown at my saying so, there is a far more important and effective power for the Negro race to gain than the ballot.

I know well how a black often feels; sometimes he is almost persuaded that probably he is not human, after all. He wonders if what everyone seems to think is not really so. But it is by the help of doubts, as well as of faith, that we succeed. And I take this opportunity to say to any black man that, after all, nothing can hurt a black man like a black man can hurt a black man's self.

Mr. Pickens is above the average in height, of rather slender build, and somewhat boyish in appearance. His conversation shows the advantage of close application to books; his proficiency in mathematics is marked, for since beginning the study he has never failed on a problem.

Travel, and intercourse with men of broad culture, under different political environments, will doubtless change in a marked degree Mr. Pickens's low estimate of Hayti and the Haytians. Intellectually, the educated Haytian is to be envied, even by our polished Anglo-Saxons. His perfect manners, his cosmopolitan culture, his unswerving race fealty,—all excite our wonder and call forth admiration.

Let us have no fears for the future of Hayti, or for that of our entire race. We feel with the late Frederick Douglass that, as the north star is eternal in the heavens, so will Hayti remain forever in the firmament of nations.[39]

Young blood and inexperience are responsible for the unpopular opinions expressed in Mr. Pickens's essay. Time and experience will round off the corners of his character, and dampen the ardor of his enthusiasm. Give him time, friends.

But just at this crisis such an avalanche of humiliation emanating from the brain and pen of a Negro, has certainly "jarred" us. Under a republican form of government, without the franchise men might as well be monkeys; the ballot makes the man.

SOURCE J. Shirley Shadrach, "William Pickens, Yale University," *Colored American Magazine* 6.7 (July 1903): 517–521.

39. This same sentence concluded Hopkins's profile of Toussaint L'Ouverture in *Famous Men of the Negro Race*.

Mr. Alan Kirkland Soga

Sarah A. Allen

*A*lan Kirkland Soga, the subject of our brief sketch, grown familiar to the readers of the *Colored American Magazine* as a writer of able papers on racial matters of South Africa, was born in the sixties in Kafirland, South Africa.

At the age of seven years he was sent by his parents to Scotland, with two elder brothers, the Rev. Dr. William Anderson Soga, M.D., of Edinburgh, now of Miller Mission, Bomvanaland, and the Rev. John Henderson Soga, of the Presbyterian Mission, South Africa, to be educated. A younger brother, Jotello Festire Soga, M.R.C.V.S. of Dick's Royal College of Veterinary Surgeons, became a government veterinary and served the Cape Colony with credit.

The father of this interesting Afro-Anglican family was the late Rev. Tiyo Soga, who was deceased in 1871; he was the first ordained native minister to the Kosa Kafirs and a man of grand personality, and from this personality as exhibited by the native African who has lived his life in the full enjoyment of the blessing of perfect manly freedom we are able to realize what must have been the glories of the careers of our ancestors at the zenith of Ethiopian ancient civilization. An interesting volume, *The Life of Tiyo Soga,* by the late Rev. John Chalmers, one of England's most noted divines, who was a colleague in the mission field with Rev. Tiyo Soga, deals with the chief features of frontier life and the earlier history of the Eastern Province, and has been widely read and distributed all over the civilized world.[40]

Tiyo Soga was a son of Soga, a councillor of the Baika Chief Sandilli, and came of a long line of "Amapakati," who exercised a powerful sway in the councils of the chiefs. Old Soga and Tyala were the last of the old line of retainers who had followed the fortunes of the royal houses faithfully throughout the stirring incidents connected with the white invasion, and the inter-tribal wars of the last and preceding century. The ill-fated Chief Sandilli was killed in the war of 1877–78 (Gaika-Gealeka war) having ignored the advice against war of Tyala and Soga in favor of the younger councillors. Tyala died of a broken heart at the loss of their country which extended from the neighborhood of King William's Town to the Great Kei River. Old Soga, disappointed at his chief's conduct, exposed himself to the enemy and met

40. See John Aitken Chalmers, *Tiyo Soga: A Page of South African Mission Work* (Edinburgh: A. Elliot, 1877).

his death like the good old warrior he had been, for he was then old. They had served Baika, Sandilli's father, before him, and Soga had taken his part in all the wars against the British from 1818. In that year his father, Jotella, was killed in the historical battle of the Amalinde, on the Debe plains, when Baika was attacked by a Confederation of his brother chiefs—Ndlambe, Hintsa and the Tembus—who complained of his friendly relations with Lord Charles Somerset, the Governor, and the Cape Government. This event, in which Soga narrowly escaped while assisting his father as a youth, has been commemorated in a brief poem by Mr. A. Kirkland Soga.

The history of the family is closely connected with most of the stirring events of colonial frontier life. It is the intention of Mr. A. Kirkland Soga to review the relations of white and black, at the present time, in a book which is in course of preparation and which has been entered for copyright at the Library of Congress, Washington, D.C., under the title of *The Problem of the Social and Political Regeneration of Africa*. It is hoped that the Colored Co-operative Publishing Company, proprietors of the *Colored American Magazine*, will undertake its publication, and we believe that this book, written by a native of the soil, a college-bred man of the highest mental attainments, thoroughly trained in journalism as well as being versed in the intricacies of colonial politics, will be of special interest to Afro-Americans everywhere.[41]

Mr. Soga is a man who takes large views of the higher politics as they affect the relations of the black man generally as he has demonstrated in these columns to the great satisfaction of our readers. For his articles now running in the magazine under the heading *Call the Black Man to Conference*, we predict a sensation among the whites and blacks in the field of letters before they are ended.[42] The illustrations for this book are now in the hands of the well-known firm of John Haddon & Son, Caxton Type Foundry, London, England.

Mr. Soga was educated at Dollar Academy on the banks of the river Devon, to which he transferred from the Glasgow High School, then under the principalship of Dr. Thomas Muir, now Superintendent General of Education for the Cape Colony. From Dollar he proceeded to Glasgow University, taking the Classes of Law under the late Sheriff-Substitute Berry of Lanarkshire, then Professor there, and the Humanity Classes under Professors Ramsay and Jebb.

Returning to South Africa, he entered the Civil Service (Native Affairs Department), subsequently being transferred to the Labor Department at the suggestion of Cecil John Rhodes, who as Prime Minister, shortly before the

41. I have uncovered no evidence that the Colored Co-operative Publishing Company published Soga's book.

42. Six installments of *Call the Black Man to Conference* appeared in the *Colored American Magazine* from December 1903 to April 1904, with the fourth and fifth installments both published in March 1904. The April 1904 article concluded "To Be Continued," although under the magazine's new ownership, it never was. See Alan Kirkland Soga, "Call the Black Man to Conference VI," *Colored American Magazine* 7.4 (Apr. 1904): 252.

Jameson Raid, had established a Labor Bureau under the supervision of Mr. L. G. Taniton, the Government Labor Agent for the Cape Colony. By successfully passing the law examinations, Mr. Soga had obtained the position of Acting Resident Magistrate, but he suspected that the difficulty of obtaining the T. P-ship and his transference into the Labor Department from the Bench was prompted by back-stairs influence and the "color-line" at the hands of his Chiefs in the service. At any rate, the influences were too powerful for him, and as the Labor Department was a new one, and regarded with jealousy by the other service, added to other difficulties encountered by the hostility of the Kruger regime in their treatment of the laborers sent up by the Cape Colony, he threw up the position in disgust and resigned the service. The Bureau was subsequently abolished.

The country was now in a desperate state, owing to the conduct of the Boers, the Kruger regime having strong supporters in the Cape Parliament. The great elections of 1898 were approaching, and owing to the crafty influences of Jan Hofmeyer, the leader of the Bond, and Messrs. Sauer and Merriman, the native paper *Imo* (Native Opinion) under the editorship of Mr. J. Tengo Iabaon, and the oldest established native organ which had hitherto exercised great influence over the native vote, elected to throw in its lot on the side of the Bond. In 1897, fearing that the natives were being misled, the present Directors (native) established the *Izwi Labantu* (Voice of the People) and invited Mr. Soga to assume the Editorship. This he did in 1898, succeeding Mr. Umhalla in that office. Parties since then have been divided into British and Dutch in Parliament and *Izwi* has consistently supported the British ideal. The defeat of Sir Gordon Spriggs' ministry in 1899 was succeeded by the Anglo-Boer war at the outbreak of which the Editor of *Izwi* proceeded to the front as a trooper in Brabants' Horse, serving for a few months and then returning to resume his duties on the paper having come out unscathed. He was present at the memorable retreat of General Gatacre at Stromberg, and in the taking of Dordrect and other lesser engagements.

The Dutch are still strong in the Cape Parliament and are accused of endeavoring to win back by the ballot what Kruger failed to achieve by the bullet. Hence the interest in the present elections now pending and which, it is believed, should finally decide the relative superiority of Bond and Progressive in the future councils of the country. So far the Legislative Council Elections just over, have resulted in a majority of one for the Progressive party. The important Assembly Elections take place probably in January, 1904. Unfortunately, the higher interests of the natives are suffering by the divisions over politics and the native press, and it is sincerely hoped that for the protection of these larger interests the Native Congress which is a body akin to the Afro-American Council, will be able to draw the most intelligent classes together in unity and social co-operation. On politics there is likely always to be a division, but there is no reason why both Negro in America and Bantu in Africa should not unite on larger questions, for their own safety and progress.

Mr. Soga is Convener of the Queen Victoria Memorial (native) for the erection of a national tribute (scholastic and educational) in honor of Queen Victoria, The Good, whose high character as a sovereign contributed not a little to ameliorate the condition of her Black subjects in South Africa during her reign. He is, too, President of the newly created South African Native Press Association, the originator of which is Mr. F.Z.S. Peregrino, Editor of *The South African Spectator*, Cape Town.

Mr. Soga is much interested in his American cousins and would like to see the Tuskegee system of industrial education introduced into South Africa, being a great admirer of Booker T. Washington, whose book *Up From Slavery*, he has read with great pleasure. His dear old mother died recently, his father having married a Scotch lady, Janet Burnside. She had for many years resided in Glasgow since the death of her husband, supervising the education of the younger members of the family.

Mr. Soga recognizes in the Negro what he takes to be a great coming factor in the regeneration of Africa, and as an Afro-Anglican would like to hasten a Conference of black men from the four worlds, to discuss the black man's future if the Negro can sink his differences sufficiently to combine forces towards that desirable end. Such a conference should be held in America and should include all shades of thought and color.

SOURCE Sarah A. Allen, "Mr. Alan Kirkland Soga," *Colored American Magazine* 7.2 (Feb. 1904): 114–116.

Mrs. Jane E. Sharp's School
for African Girls

J. Shirley Shadrach

Within the past twenty years public attention has been drawn to the wonderful resources of Africa. Now that the New World has been partially drained of its wealth, and has become thickly populated, civilization seeks an outlet in worlds yet unconquered, and so the great mineral wealth, the wonderful natural resources of Africa's desert lands, the haunts of savage tribes, are calling to the pioneers of every land to come and feast upon Africa's virgin charms.

The native African may view with sorrow the devastation of his country, but for the general good, a few must suffer. Africa must be restored, and as a race and country renew its ancient prestige. But how?

We find the prophecy in Psalms: "Princes shall come out of Egypt; Ethiopia shall soon stretch forth her hands unto God."

From the day of Africa's decline, the tide of progress has swept westward from Meroe to Egypt, to Greece, to Rome, to Briton, to the undiscovered lands of the Western World. Still sweeping onward, civilization having now circumnavigated the globe, is returning to its ancient haunts, bearing on its waves hope for the restoration of an ancient race. The refining of Africa must be through blood and tears.

In helping along this restoration and upbuilding, Mrs. Jane Sharp is doing a grand work.

Mrs. Jane E. D. Sharp, a graduate of the Boston Girls' High School (class of '73), is making a tour of the United States, seeking financial aid for her girls' school at Mt. Coffee, West Africa.

Mrs. Sharp was born in Missouri, but educated in Boston. After graduation, actuated by a desire to do something for her own race, she accepted a position under the Boston Board of Donation for Education in Liberia, and began teaching in Monrovia.

Liberia, as we very well know, has been, from its start, an effort of humanity on behalf of the black race. The government was founded in 1822 by American philanthropists for the freedmen of the United States, who wished to return to their native land. In 1847, it became an independent. The Liberians are bright, intelligent, and very proud.

Many of Mrs. Sharp's pupils, among them the president's daughters, are now wives and mothers of the leading families of Liberia.

Her marriage with Mr. Jesse Sharp, a wealthy coffee planter, said to possess some Negro blood in his veins, served to increase her interest in the aboriginal people of the Bush tribes. She finally felt that there was her best field of action, and she threw herself into the work among native children—females. After her husband's death she gave herself up entirely to the work.

Mrs. Sharp brought with her from Africa an infant princess, Djana Ruth Wattah, and the daughter of an African king.

Djana Ruth died on July 13, 1903, in the Woman's Hospital, Philadelphia. She was buried at Pleasantville, and a little marble slab now marks her resting place. The other child is now at Father Field's farm in Foxboro, Mass., having a beautiful time going to school. She is about eight years old.

Mrs. Sharp is brilliant in conversation and well-versed in the literature of all nations. Ideality in her is well developed, and adds a touch of romance to a personality at once queenly, yet touched with deep humility.

Mrs. Sharp's plantation was on the St. Paul's river. Mrs. Sharp removed to Mount Coffee after his death.

Then she set about learning the customs, modes of thought, style of expression, religious observances and superstitions of that interesting tribe, the Golahs. So well did she succeed in reaching the heart of these people, as well as of the adjoining tribes, that she was perfectly safe in her work among them, even during the tribal wars of the last four years. The native African she found to be extremely hospitable, dividing his last spoonful of rice with the stranger, and really carrying out the Gospel command about "entertaining strangers." In her home in the "bush," Mrs. Sharp hopes to establish a school for the industrial training of the girls of these tribes, where they can develop industrial skill, their possession of which is shown by the skill with which they now work with crude tools of their own fashioning. They do fine leather-work, weaving in designs with slender threads of the leather in colors, making ornamental pockets, sheaths for knives, and many other articles. They weave by hand the fine cotton growing in the country, making strong cloth, for the coloring of which they use dyes from the native plants. Palms and grasses are also woven into articles for use.

Although agriculture is in its infancy in Liberia, Mrs. Sharp feels that the native girls could be taught fruit culture and poultry raising, the preserving of pine-apples (which grow wild in great abundance), and of the mango plum. By these various means, the girls would be enabled to provide for themselves, and to have suitable clothing, lack of which, especially during chilly rains, is the cause of great mortality among women.

Mrs. Sharp now has a plantation of six hundred and fifty acres, but no suitable buildings. Her thirty little native girls had to be scattered, because she had no house fit for them; but they are to be again gathered up, and their training resumed upon their return. Much of her hope of what may be done by industrial training is based upon the respect the native African has for anyone who can do good work. An instance of this is seen in the standing among the people of a famous Golah blacksmith. He had great skill in working iron, even with his crude tools, and he became, in consequence, a great leader. To him the members of the tribe carried their "palaver" (the settling of their disputes), and he became the great man of his tribe. When he died, he was buried on a much-frequented path—one of those picturesque little zig-zag paths found everywhere in Africa. A large lamp was brought and placed on his grave, which, to his people meant: "Here is a great light that has gone out!" Every passer-by places a stone on his grave.

Liberian children are very precocious, and learn English rapidly. This they use in their study and work; but at play, Mrs. Sharp encourages them to speak in their native tongue, believing that it weakens a people to take their own language from them. These little ones are much loved by their parents, the maternal instinct being very strong in the native African woman. Young girls are carefully protected in most tribes.

"I feel convinced that the women must have more attention paid to their training, before any material advancement will be made," said Mrs. Sharp, to the writer.

That Africa, so far, has not produced anything that the world really needs, is not caused by lack of talents or skill, if rightly directed. I am trying to start a school where industries may be started, that will give some material support. There is nothing for the women to do, and to see them go through the rain with so little clothing, is pitiful. If industries can be started, the women will have clothing and food.

I had a house full of little native girls, but I had to put them in Liberian families, because the house was quite unfit for occupation. We cooked in the shed outdoors, and washed outdoors. The house was leaking badly. The cracks were large enough for snakes to crawl through, where the planks drew apart. We lived in the most primitive way; but I was there with the natives long enough to realize that they possessed possibilities for higher development. You see that the women of many of the tribes have not come in contact with civilization. They are really highly moral. I do not believe that women are ever cannibals.

"I never knew what pride of descent was," continued Mrs. Sharp,

until I went to Africa. I think that one unfortunate phase of this question of the races is the fact that we do no know enough about our ancestors. Pride of descent has played an important part in the development of all the races. I have seen tribes in Africa that I am only sorry that I cannot claim my descent from, such as the Mandingoes, Ashantees, Zulus, and others. If the colored race in America only knew their African antecedents, instead of regarding themselves as being descended from savages or slaves, they would have more self-respect, and would be encouraged to higher effort. My work is altogether for girls.

Dr. Edward E. Hale describes Mrs. Sharp's African work in the following words:

> The work of Mrs. Sharp in Africa has been providential. She went there at the nomination of the Liberia Education Society, to take charge of that department of the College in the city of Monrovia which trained the daughters of the settlers in their higher education. But as time has gone on, it has been evident that her duty is quite as much with the daughters of the chiefs of the neighboring tribes as with the daughters of emigrants from America. She is so favored as to be of the black race. That is sometimes thought a misfortune in the United States, but it is not so in Africa. There is many a province, and barony, and kingdom, and empire in Africa, where a white man would be killed as soon as he was seen, while a black man is welcomed and made at home. The romantic and extraordinary experience recently of Mr. Sheppard, in the very heart of Africa, is an interesting illustration of this.
>
> . . . We must encourage her, on her return to what is now her own country, with the means of extending its civilization.[43]

In order to enable Mrs. Sharp to make the best of these opportunities, to build the plain house she requires, to carry out and support the young assistants she wants, and to be able to look forward to some future for her work, an association has been formed, and "Jane Sharp Circles" started in connection with it. Members of these circles pay a dollar a year to the work, and do what else they can for it. They will receive reports from Mrs. Sharp herself, and from the Mount Coffee Association. The President of the Association is Dr. Edward E. Hale, and the Treasurer is Dr. George M. Adams, Auburndale, Mass.

SOURCE J. Shirley Shadrach, "Mrs. Jane E. Sharp's School for African Girls," *Colored American Magazine* 7.3 (Mar. 1904): 181–184.

43. Edward Everett Hale (1822–1909) was a Boston author, editor, abolitionist, and Unitarian minister, who served as U.S. Senate chaplain from 1903 to 1908. He solicited funds to help Sharp build a school in Liberia. See, for example, Edward E. Hale, "Wanted, A School-House," *Outlook* 77.16 (Aug. 13, 1904): 912. In 1890, William Henry Sheppard (1865–1927) founded the American Presbyterian Congo Mission, and served in Africa until 1910. His dispatches were regularly featured in the Presbyterian Church's *Missionary* and in Hampton Institute's *Southern Workman*.

PART VII

The Dark Races of the Twentieth Century *(1905)*

The Dark Races of the Twentieth Century was published in five installments in the *Voice of the Negro* between February 1905 and July 1905. No installment appeared in April, presumably due to space limitations since an article by Du Bois that was advertised on the cover was "crowded out" of that issue as well.[1] The fifth and final installment of this series, "The North American Indian.—Conclusion," was mislabeled as "VI."

Hopkins's first article for the *Voice of the Negro* was on the opening of the New York City subway in October 1904, the month after her association with the *Colored American Magazine* ended. That article appeared in the December 1904 issue. In 1905, *The Dark Races of the Twentieth Century* was featured prominently in the magazine. With installments on South Asians, Native Americans, East Asians, and Pacific Islanders, this series represents her broadly internationalist outlook. Of the five installments in the series, only one dealt specifically with Africa. The series suggests that African American attention to Africa was part of a political vision that emphasized worldliness and transnationalism, something different than what recent critics of racial solidarity might deem a narrow "identity politics."

1. "Notice," *Voice of the Negro* 2.4 (Apr. 1905): 248.

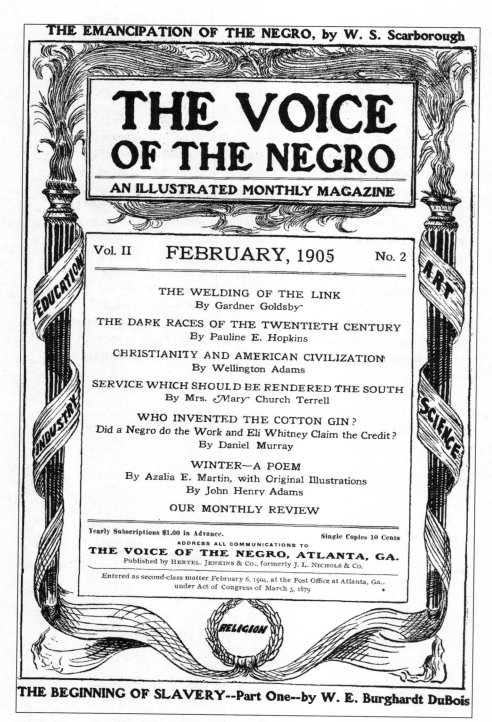

THE EMANCIPATION OF THE NEGRO, by W. S. Scarborough

THE VOICE
OF THE NEGRO
AN ILLUSTRATED MONTHLY MAGAZINE

Vol. II   FEBRUARY, 1905   No. 2

EDUCATION

INDUSTRY

ART

SCIENCE

THE WELDING OF THE LINK
By Gardner Goldsby

THE DARK RACES OF THE TWENTIETH CENTURY
By Pauline E. Hopkins

CHRISTIANITY AND AMERICAN CIVILIZATION
By Wellington Adams

SERVICE WHICH SHOULD BE RENDERED THE SOUTH
By Mrs. Mary Church Terrell

WHO INVENTED THE COTTON GIN?
Did a Negro do the Work and Eli Whitney Claim the Credit?
By Daniel Murray

WINTER—A POEM
By Azalia E. Martin, with Original Illustrations
By John Henry Adams

OUR MONTHLY REVIEW

Yearly Subscriptions $1.00 in Advance.   Single Copies 10 Cents
ADDRESS ALL COMMUNICATIONS TO
THE VOICE OF THE NEGRO, ATLANTA, GA.
Published by HERTEL, JENKINS & CO., formerly J. L. NICHOLS & CO.

Entered as second-class matter February 6, 1904, at the Post Office at Atlanta, Ga.,
under Act of Congress of March 3, 1879

RELIGION

THE BEGINNING OF SLAVERY--Part One--by W. E. Burghardt DuBois

10. The February 1905 cover of the *Voice of the Negro* prominently announced among its offerings Pauline E. Hopkins's *The Dark Races of the Twentieth Century*, a serial that premiered that month.

I.

Oceanica:
The Dark-Hued Inhabitants of New Guinea, the Bismarck Archipelago, New Hebrides, Solomon Islands, Fiji Islands, Polynesia, Samoa, and Hawaii

> Mislike me not for my complexion
> The shadowed livery of the burnished Sun.
> —Shakespeare.[2]

The earnest plea of Portia's somber-hued lover for fair play at her hands despite his "shadowed livery," is but an apt illustration of the firmness with which color-prejudice had fixed itself upon the social life of those distant centuries. It had become in Shakespeare's time an important factor in social science, and has been steadily growing in its proportions to the present date. So important was the quality of color that we find the greatest of all English poets making place for this question in the greatest work of his hands. He had already written *Hamlet* and *Macbeth* and *Lear* was about to follow. There is no such group in the literature of any country or any age as the "four great tragedies"—*Hamlet, Macbeth, Othello* and *Lear*. And of the four great tragedies, many critics assign the foremost place to *Othello*. Wordsworth says: "The tragedy of *Othello*, Plato's records of the last scenes in the career of Socrates, and Izaak Walton's *Life of George Herbert,* are the most pathetic of human compositions."[3] Born with a vision so keen as to pierce the veil swinging between the Present and the Future, Shakespeare left, in perhaps his greatest work, a silent protest against the unjustness of man to man.

So strong is the question of color that all information possible is sought for in reply, and every theory imaginable is advanced by men who should know better. What causes the color of the dark races of the globe? What is it and of what does it consist? Dr. Delany in his eminent work on the *Origin of Races* answers the question explicitly and clearly. He says:

"All coloring matter which enters into the human system is pigment—*pigmentum*—that in the fair race is *red*, that in the tawny being *yellow*, the red

---

2. Shakespeare, *The Merchant of Venice*, 2.1.1–2.

3. William Wordsworth, quoted in Edwin Reed, *Bacon vs. Shakespeare* (7th ed.; Boston: Joseph Knight, 1897), 156n1. Reed's popular work argues that Francis Bacon was the author of Shakespeare's plays.

being modified by elaboration according to the economy of the system of each particular race. In the Caucasian, it is in its most simple elementary constituent; in the Mongolian, in a more compound form. But that which gives complexion to the blackest African, is the *same red matter, concentrated rouge, in its most intensified state.*"[4]

The word of God as given to Paul should settle the question of color origin of the human species beyond a peradventure: "God hath made of one blood all the nations of men for to dwell on all the face of the earth." But the sons of Japheth are a stiff-necked people, prone to improve upon God's work, if possible, and so we have in opening of the twentieth century "perils" yellow and black born alone on an unreasoning insanity on the question of color.

Many causes have lately arisen to augment the desire of thinkers to know all possible of the origin and relationship of the dark-hued races, and the time is ripe for a popular study of the science of ethnology. The rise of new powers and the decline of old powers, the great expansion in the business world or the growth of commercialism, the remarkable development of the imperialistic fever among governments, has caused a searching of the obscure corners of the globe even among untutored savages for world markets and for world conquests. Nor is this new knowledge and insatiable curiosity of little value. It is all in accord with the plan of salvation from the beginning. At the dispersion of the Tower Builders of Babylon the confusion of tongues caused a separation; and so another change is already inaugurated which is compelling a reunion of the scattered members of the great human family. We may always be sure of one fact, "creation had a method." For the benefit of scientific opinion we again quote Dr. Delany:

> The first son of Noah, Shem, was born with a high degree of complexion or color; the second son, Ham, with a higher degree or intensity of the same color, making a different complexion; and the third son, Japheth, with the least of the same color, which gives an entirely different complexion. The three brothers were all of the *same color—rouge—*which being possessed in a different degree gave them different complexions.
>
> Ham was positive, Shem medium, and Japheth negative. And here it may be remarked as a curious fact, that in the order of these degrees of complexion which indicated the ardor and temperament of the races they represented, so was the progress of civilization propagated and carried forward by them.
>
> Physiology classifies the admixture of the races by a cross between the White and Black, as a Mulatto; between the Mulatto and White, a

---

4. Martin Robison Delany, *Principia of Ethnology: The Origin of Races and Color, With an Archeological Compendium of Ethiopian and Egyptian Civilization, from Years of Careful Examination and Enquiry* (1879; repr. as *The Origin of Races and Color*, Baltimore: Black Classic Press, 1991), 30. Hopkins's misspelling of Martin Robison "Delaney" throughout this section has been silently emended.

Quadroon; between a Quadroon and White, a Quintroon; between a Quintroon and White, a Sextaroon; between the Sextaroon and White, a Septaroon; between the Septaroon and White, an Octoroon. The same numerical classifications are given a like number of crosses between the offsprings of the Black and Mulatto, with a prefix of the adjective black; as a Black Quadroon, and so on to Octoroon. A cross between an American Indian and a White, is called a Mustee or Mestizo; and a cross between the Indian and Black, is called a Sambo or Zambo.

Now, what is here to be observed as an exact and with little variation, almost never-failing result, in this law of procreation between the African and Caucasian, or White and Black races is, that these crosses go on with a nicety of reducing and blending the complexion, till it attains its original standard to either pure white or pure black, on the side by which the cross is continued from the first. By this it is seen that each race is equally reproducing, absorbing and enduring, neither of which can be extinguished or destroyed, all admixtures running out into either of the original races, upon the side which preponderates. This is an important truth, worthy the attention and serious consideration of the social scientist, philosopher, and statesman.

"And the Lord said, Behold the people is one, and they have all one language. So the Lord scattered them abroad from thence upon the face of all the earth."[5] And this separation of the three brothers was the origin of races. Each brother headed and led his people with a language, and in all reasonable probability, a complexion similar to his own, each settling the then known three parts of the earth—Asia, Africa and Europe.[6]

The inhabitants of Oceanica form a large proportion of the living dark races, and a curious fact becomes apparent in studying their characteristics: Miscegenation is supposed to destroy a sterling race but this is an *impossible theory*. As stated above, the sterling races when crossed, reproduce themselves in their original purity. The offspring of two sterling races becomes an abnormal or mixed race, and to this abnormal race the Malays and Papuans of Oceanica belong. They are, no doubt, composed of the three original races formed by an intermingling of Egypto-Ethiopian, Persian, Assyrian, Greeko-Macedonian and Tartar conquerors who conquered the original natives. They will, no doubt, become extinct by the resolvent European and Mongolian races settling among them.

The region of Melanesia includes all the islands from New Guinea in the west to Fiji in the east, a region inhabited by the black Papuan race—hence the word *black* describes the people of NEW GUINEA, THE BISMARCK

5. Genesis 11:6, 8.
6. Delany, *Principia of Ethnology*, 24–27.

ARCHIPELAGO, THE SOLOMON ISLANDS, THE NEW HEBRIDES AND NEW CALEDONIA. These people all have frizzly hair. It is a race characteristic, and the whole head of hair has much the appearance of a mop.

The people of New Guinea have been known as Papuans for more than three hundred years. The race is mixed but is very different from its neighbors, the Malays. The average height of a New Guinea native is five feet eight inches. He is strongly built. The skull long, lower jaw prominent, nose large with broad nostrils, lips full, face oval. The dress of a native man is a breech-cloth of bark, while the women wear a fringed girdle of woven grass. Manners and customs vary in the island. Hereditary chiefs are unknown, and there is no recognized form of government, the people having unwritten rules of conduct.

Bismarck Archipelago lies to the east of New Guinea, and belongs to Germany. The inhabitants live in huts similar in shape to bee-hives, small and surrounded by palisades of bamboo. Unmarried men live in a community. Cannibalism is more or less general and polygamy is common. They have the remarkable custom of putting young girls of six or eight years, in cages made of palm leaves, which they can never leave until their wedding day. Old women guard them.

The Solomon group comprises seven large islands which belong to Great Britain. Formerly the natives were so treacherous that Europeans had but little intercourse with them, but now traders come frequently and mission work is spreading rapidly.

The New Hebrides are a group of volcanic islands named by Captain Cook in 1774. They have an area of 5,000 square miles with a population of 70,000, governed by a commission of officers of the British and French warships in the Pacific. In the five Southern islands there are more than forty schools under the patronage of the Presbyterian Church.

South of this group lies the New Caledonia. The people are called Canakas by the French. They wear very little clothing and were cannibals when the French first colonized the island.

Fiji Islands, Polynesians, Samoa, and Sandwich Islands

The inhabitants of Fiji—a group of more than two hundred islands—are Papuans, properly speaking. They have greatly declined in numbers since white men brought them the vices of civilization. They are a fine race, some standing six feet in height. They were cannibals and still practice this horror at intervals. Like most primitive people, they have no fear of death. A missionary was once invited to attend the funeral of the mother of a young Fijian, and great was his surprise upon joining the funeral procession to see the old lady cheerfully walking to her grave. Favorite wives of chiefs cheerfully submit to be strangled at the death of the husband, they believing that in this way they secure happiness and honor after death.

Eastward from Fiji lies Polynesia. Polynesians are supposed to be one of the finest races in the world. One of their games resembles draughts, the same played ages ago by Egyptian Pharaohs and their wives. "Animism," universal animation, or the endowing of all things with a soul is their religion.

The Samoans are a handsome, well-built people, hospitable, courteous, honest and affectionate—a nation of gentlemen. Nominally, they are Christians, the London Missionary Society having over 200 native missionaries in these islands.

The annexation of the Sandwich Islands to the United States is a matter of history and brought the inhabitants prominently before the civilized world. The population is now about 40,000, although at the time of discovery by Captain Cook there were 300,000 inhabitants. The capital is Honolulu. The people have adopted the Christian religion and civilized customs. A melancholy interest is felt in these people because of their misfortunes and the prevalence of that dread disease leprosy among them.

From 1820 to 1860 the Congregationalists held this mission field in Hawaii, and now the Anglican Church has begun work there.

SOURCE "The Dark Races of the Twentieth Century I: Oceanica: The Dark-Hued Inhabitants of New Guinea, the Bismarck Archipelago, New Hebrides, Solomon Islands, Fiji Islands, Polynesia, Samoa, and Hawaii," *Voice of the Negro* 2.2 (Feb. 1905): 108–115.

II.

The Malay Peninsula:
Borneo, Java, Sumatra,
and the Philippines

The Eastern Archipelago which extends westward and northwest from New Guinea, contains among its important islands the Timor group: the Moluccas, Celebes, Flores, the Sunda Islands, and Sumatra, Borneo and the Philippines. The Negritos are found in the Philippines; but the chief race of this vast archipelago is the Malay.

Most of the islands are mountainous, and many of them contain active volcanoes. The climate is very hot, but at an elevation of a few hundred feet, becomes healthful; and, by ascending still higher, we reach a delightful region of perpetual spring. No part of the world is richer in its vegetable productions than these islands. The minerals are also very valuable. All of our spices—cinnamon, cloves, nutmegs and pepper—are raised on these islands. Here also grow the bread-fruit tree, sago, the cocoa-nut palm, bananas and yams. Gutta-percha grows in the forests of Borneo and of other islands in the archipelago. Rice is cultivated in most of the islands. Java exports great quantities of coffee and sugar. Borneo furnishes gold, diamonds and tin. From the Philippines we receive sugar, hemp and tobacco. Many of the animals are among the fiercest and largest upon the earth.

The Malays who inhabit this region are a branch of the great Mongolian or Yellow species of the divisions of mankind. They are described as of medium stature, three or four inches below the European height. Complexion light brown, square face with high cheek bones, black eyes and a short nose quite unlike that of the white man or Negro.

Socially, they are divided into three distinct groups: the "Men of the Soil" or the aborigines, who inhabit Molucca and Sumatra in the accessible wooded highlands, and belong to the Negritos; the "Men of the Sea" or Sea Gypsies, who live by fishing and robbing; and the civilized class, known as "Malay Men," who possess a certain culture and religion. They constitute a section of the race which under the Hindus settled in Sumatra about the fourth century, after which came the Arabs, developing national life and culture and political states.

The chief characteristic of the Malay is his easy-going nature. Generally they are gentle and extremely civil in speech and courteous in manner, and very particular in all matters of etiquette; the upper classes behave with all the dignity of European gentlemen. However, they lack the frankness of Englishmen, being by nature suspicious. The dark side of the Malay character as given by many travelers is not reassuring. Gambling and cock fighting are the greatest amusements.

In the domestic circle we find that the position of woman is not very low, the Moslem Malays treating their womankind much better than the heathen Malays do. One writer says: "The husbands never beat the wives; it is quite the other way." In truth, the woman is highly valued, and a man must pay a heavy price for a wife. These are interesting facts to the student of ethnology, for a hopeful future for a people can generally be determined by the development of its women along the lines of virtue and intelligence.

Borneo

The island of Borneo is not thickly inhabited and is divided into four territories: North British Borneo and the Rajah of Sarawak in the northwest; between these lies the small State of the Sultan of Brunei; the remainder of the island belongs to the Dutch. The entire population may be roughly estimated at 2,000,000.

Numerous ruins of Hindu temples are scattered over the island, reminding one forcibly of the first immigrants to this country. But always predominating, we find the incisive Anglo-Saxon marching along triumphantly toward the sovereignty of the world. An account of the work of Rajah Brooke in Sarawak is interesting and instructive. Mr. Brooke went to Borneo in 1839, and found the country in a chronic state of insurrection. Two years afterward he was made rajah, or king. The personal courage exhibited by Mr. Brooke, and the firmness with which he put down the earlier conspiracies against his rule, won the better class of chiefs to his side. He administered the law with strict justice. A writer says:

> The success of this policy was never better shown than during the Chinese insurrection, when having narrowly escaped with his life, his friends killed or wounded, his house burned and much of the town destroyed, the whole population rallied around the English rajah, driving out and almost exterminating the invaders, and triumphantly brought him back to rule over them. In what country shall we find rulers, alien in race, language and religion, yet so endeared to their subjects? It requires no peculiar legal or diplomatic or legislative doctrine, but chiefly patience and good feeling, and the absence of prejudice. The great thing is not to be in a hurry; to avoid over-legislation, law forms and legal subtleties; to aim first to make the people contented and happy in every way, even if that way should be quite opposite to European theories of how they ought to be happy. On such principles Sir James Brooke's success was founded. True, he spent a fortune instead of making one, but he left behind him a reputation for goodness, wisdom and honor which dignifies the name of Englishmen for generations to come.[7]

7. In 1841, Sir James Brooke (1803–1865) established British control of Sarawak, Borneo (in present-day Malaysia), which his family controlled until 1946. Brooke was the subject of countless popular treatments in the nineteenth and twentieth centuries.

If our powerful American leaders might be brought to emulate the example of Sir James Brooke in dealing with the race question in the United States, how matters would be simplified, and peace take the place of suspicion and hatred. But greed and the desire for high place will eventually override all humane suggestions for the upbuilding of humanity, and we may expect to see the present state of things continue to the end.

Sumatra

The population of Sumatra is about 3,500,000. These people are fairly civilized and cultivate the land. Many of the inhabitants have intermarried with the Arabs, consequently they are mostly Mohammedans and their language is written in Arabic. They are clever craftsmen and build good ships; every man is a soldier.

Philippine Islands

This beautiful group of islands has been destined to bring America, or more properly speaking the United States, prominently before the civilized world in the character of the promoter of human progress. The population of these islands is about 10,000,000, divided among the following tribes: Tagalo, Ilocano, Visayan, Igorrote and Negrito. The Spaniards divided the inhabitants of the Philippines into three classes: Indus or Christians, Infeles or Pagans of the interior, and the Moros or Sulus. They are divided into many tribes speaking different dialects, so that on the island of Luzon we find as many as twenty dialects.

The Tagalo is the leading race and has had the advantages of education and culture. The Ilocano is, however, the hope of the "New Philippines" under the rule of the American Republic, and he will prove a blessing to his countrymen. The Visayan tribe inhabits the Visayas. The Mestizo and Macabebe are interesting. The latter, like the Negrito, is becoming extinct. One is struck with the strong resemblance to the Chinese in all the photographs of the natives. This is accounted for by the fact that the islands have been overrun with Chinese for centuries and they have taken native women as wives. The confusion of types continues and one may trace the Mexican, Peruvian, Japanese and Spaniard. No part of Australasia presents so great a confusion of races.

At the time of Magellan's discovery of these islands lying washed by the Pacific Ocean and the China Sea, the country was peopled by the tribes of Negritos, or descendants of African tribes. Wars and intermarriage have very nearly obliterated the traces of the original stock, and the remaining numbers live in the mountains and cultivate the land. Many interesting theories are offered as to the origin of Negroes in this archipelago. Some scientists say that he was driven from Africa, and others that he came from New Guinea. All we know is that he is there safely housed in the mountains. The Negritos are a most interesting people. Mr. Abraham Hale spent some time among the primitive race and has given much valuable information to the Anthropological Institute of Great Britain. He says that in those districts where the Negritos live to themselves, untouched by the Malays, they are simple-hearted, kind, always anxious to please and are very hospitable.[8]

Professor Keane says of the Sakai, a tribe of Negritos:

Surrounded from time out of mind by Malay peoples, some semi-civilized, some nearly as wild as themselves, but all alike taking from them their land, these aborigines have developed defensive qualities unneeded by the more favored insular Negritos and are doomed to extinction before their time. They have never had a chance in the race of life.

> We suffer yet a little space
> Until we pass away,
> The relics of an ancient race
> That ne'er has had its day.[9]

The cities of the archipelago are beautiful and picturesque; they all have their plazas and churches generally the centers of the respective cities.

Manila, the capital, is the metropolis and the principal port. It is situated on the east of Manila bay, twenty-nine miles from the China Sea, whose breezes make it very pleasant in the afternoon.

New Manila is the home of all commercial enterprise and holds the hotels and places of amusement. The streets are clean and the houses are surrounded by the most beautiful palms, thus presenting a most imposing spectacle to the visitor's eye. The city has improved greatly since its occupation by the Americans. Streets have been widened, driveways repaired and sanitary and water systems perfected.

In this study of the dark races actually living today upon the globe, the reader or student is deeply impressed with the infinite variety of mixture in these races. This very mingling of races proves the theory of "one blood." Indeed, the principle that the human species is *one* cannot be disputed, and all men that inhabit the earth are but varieties of this one species. Next to the curiosity aroused by these so-called "human leopards" comes wonder at the persistent efforts of scientists to separate the dark races endowed with European characteristics, from any possible connection with the Negro, or more properly speaking, African race.

The question is: Was man created in one centre or in several centres of the earth? The consensus of opinion is with those scientists who claim one centre of creation and a triple complexion in the family of Noah.

8. Abraham Hale, "On the Sakais," *The Journal of the Anthropological Institute of Great Britain and Ireland* 15.3 (1886): 285–301.

9. Augustus Henry Keane, *Man, Past and Present* (London: Cambridge University Press, 1900), 162. Keane attributes the poem to Hugh Clifford, "The Song of the Last Semangs." See Hugh Clifford, *In Court and Kampung* (1897; rev. ed., Singapore: Graham Brash, 1989), 133.

The presence of man in all sections is easily explained by migration, and there is nothing to show several distinct nuclei. Man started from one point alone, and by the power of adaptation he has finally covered the entire face of the habitable globe. Therefore we must conclude that the Negritos of the Philippines and the other dark races of Australasia are of the family of Ham.

Buffon supports the theory of three fundamental types of man—white, black and yellow.[10] We believe this theory to be true.

All men, we then conclude, were once upon one plane; hunting and fishing, then herdsmen, and lastly husbandmen. Through these three stages in all countries mankind has passed of necessity before becoming civilized, and why not the Negro or Black?

Says Figuier, "Nations whom we find at the present day but little advanced in civilization, were once superior to other nations" we may point out.[11] The Chinese were civilized long before the inhabitants of Europe, at the very time when the Celts and Aryans, clothed in the skins of wild beasts and tattooed, were living in the woods in the condition of hunters. The Babylonians were occupied with the study of astronomy, and were calculating the orbits of the stars two thousand years before Christ, for the astronomical registers brought by Alexander the Great from Babylon, refer back to celestial observations extending over more than ten centuries. Egyptian civilization dates back to at least four thousand years before Christ, as is proved by the magnificent statue of Gheffrel, which belongs to that period, and which, as it is composed of granite, can only have been cut by the aid of iron and steel tools, in themselves indications of an advanced form of industry.

"This last consideration should make us feel modest. It shows that nations whom we now crush by our intellectual superiority were once far before us in the path of civilization."

Then why not allow that the theory of Ethiopia as the mother of science, art and literature is true? Surely we the descendants of Ham cannot be condemned and ridiculed for claiming that the ancient glory of Ethiopia was the beacon light of all intellectual advancement now enjoyed by mankind. History and the fragments found in buried cities, though meagre, give us a strong claim upon the attention of the world.

SOURCE "The Dark Races of the Twentieth Century II: The Malay Peninsula: Borneo, Java, Sumatra and the Philippines," *Voice of the Negro* 2.3 (Mar. 1905): 187–191.

10. Georges Louis Leclerc Buffon (1707–1788) was a French naturalist and author of the forty-four-volume *Histoire Naturelle, Générale et Particulière* (1749–1804).

11. Louis Figuier (1819–1894) was a French scientific writer, teacher, and author of *The World Before the Deluge* (1872).

The Yellow Race:
Siam, China, Japan, Korea, Thibet

The Yellow race is also known as the Mongol race because of the family characteristics common to both. These characteristics are, high cheek-bones, a lozenge-shaped head, flat nose, flat face, narrow obliquely-set eyes, coarse, black hair, scanty beard and a greenish yellow complexion.

In many of the features which distinguish this race we notice the very objectionable ones supposed to distinguish the black race alone. We find the same flat nose that marks the Guinea Negro and the same peculiar shape of the head—dolichocephalous, elongated cranium from front to rear—which is supposed to be a characteristic also of the same Negro race. But this resemblance to the Negro does not end with the Yellow race, for North Germans of the Caucasian race have the same head development, and we are surprised to note that among the lower classes of the Irish peasantry the flat feet, bent, shapeless body, etc., are seen. Mr. Fred Douglass spoke of this striking likeness among Irishmen to the Negro upon his return from a visit to Ireland. We contend that the characteristics supposed to be peculiar to the Negro are common to all members of the human species under conditions which tend to leave undeveloped the faculties of the mind. From this state of degradation all classes of men may be raised by the cultivation of the intellectual or spiritual part of this body. There alone is the difference; it is the portion of the spirit in every being which raises up to the heights of civilization and eliminates the purely animal, for man is a spirit shining within the body of an animal.

Siam

The kingdom of Siam embraces part of the Indo-Chinese and part of the Malay peninsular. The delta of the Me Nam river is the natural and economic centre of Siam which is flooded every year between June and November. The population of Siam has never been known, but nine millions is a probable fair estimate. France has taken about 80,000 square miles of her territory.

Within the dominion of Siam we find three representatives of the world's races: the Caucasian, Mongolian and the Negro. Ethnologists are puzzled by the mixture of these races. But the most recent investigation seems to show that the modern Indo-Chinese are Malay races sprung from an original tattooing race that occupied the hills of Thibet and drifted down into the plain.

The Siamese are well-formed, of olive complexion, darker than the Chinese but fairer and handsomer than the Malays. Their eyes are well-shaped, lips prominent, noses slightly flattened, a wide face across the cheek-bones, top of the forehead pointed and the chin short. They are very fond of the bath. The men shave the head leaving only a tuft of hair on the top. The preservation of this tuft is a matter of considerable social importance. On a child's head it is knotted and held together by a gold or silver pin. The shaping of the hair tuft of the children is an important event being made a family festival to which friends and relatives are invited. Long nails are considered aristocratic. Opium smoking is indulged but is not on the increase. Marriage takes place at an early age. Marriage for love is rare, and a man may have as many wives as he likes. Education of the females is much neglected, although many girls are taught accomplishments for the amusement of the future husband and his guests. The Siamese are a musical people and possess many wind and string instruments, although they play entirely by ear.

Siam is an absolute monarchy without any limit to right and legislation. There is no army, but in time of war everybody is conscripted. Schools are few and poor but she is sending her boys to Europe and America to be educated. They have telegraph connections established and have begun to build up a good national trade. Siam promises to follow in the wake of Japan in adopting modern civilization, and for this reason, as well as for racial considerations, should be interesting to us.

Socially the government of Siam is a serfdom, and every subject is a slave to the king. The abolishment of slavery did away with caste, but under the corvée system which operates in this government, a free man is a slave still because he has no one to succor him, and finds himself better off under a master. Such conditions may prevail in the United States in a few years under the slavery of caste to which we now seem doomed unless the spirit of humanity is aroused in the nation in behalf of the blacks.

China

The Chinese Empire includes China, Thibet, Korea, Mongolia, Manchuria, Soongaria and Little Bokhara. The last four named divisions are called Chinese Tartary. Thibet and Chinese Tartary are thinly-settled regions.

Lassa the capital of Thibet, is the residence of the Grand Lama who is worshipped as the Supreme Being. His followers believe that he never dies, and that his soul passes into another body—that of some child selected by the priests. This country is of extraordinary interest to all civilized races. No white man living has ever seen Lassa and returned to tell the tale. Thibet is the last land of mystery remaining in the world and is guarded by the highest mountains in the center of which lies the valley which contains Lassa.

In Thibet a woman may have many husbands, but a man may have only one wife.

The general description given of the Mongolian race applies to the Chinese, amongst whom of all the yellow race, civilization was the first to develop itself in former centuries, but in recent years they have remained stationary, and their culture is now second rate compared with the advanced state of civilization reached by Europe and America. The government is a despotic monarchy, the emperor possessing unlimited power over all beneath him. The officers of the government are styled mandarins. Laws are severe, and for trifling offences the bamboo punishment is inflicted, while serious crimes meet with death.

The position of woman in China is a very humble one. Her birth is often regarded as unfortunate. The young girl lives shut up in her father's house. Her place is that of a servant. She is given in marriage without being consulted, and often in ignorance of her future husband's name.

Ancient writers speak of China as the people of the land of Seres. The present area of China is about 4,500,000 square miles, only Great Britain and Russia exceeding it in extent. The early history is obscure; their "Book of History" records events said to have occurred as far back as 2,350 B.C., but gives no account of the origin of the race. A few learned Chinese say that the race now dominating China was not the original race which possessed the land.

The Chinaman is not endowed with much imagination, or it may be that centuries of rigorous training along material lines, have practically so clogged his mental faculties that it is impossible for it now to act under normal conditions.

Education is widely spread in China. The education of the wealthy child commences from the hour of its birth. At six years of age he learns the elementary principles of arithmetic and geography; at seven he is separated from his mother and sisters and takes his meals alone; at eight he is taught the usages of politeness; at nine he is taught the astrological calendar; at ten he is sent to a public school; between thirteen and fifteen he is taught music; at fifteen come gymnastics, the use of arms and riding; at twenty he is often married.

The Chinese have practised the typographical art from time immemorial; but as their alphabet is composed of more than forty thousand letters, they could not use movable type. There are in Pekin several daily papers. There is no country in the world where the walls are so thickly covered with bills and advertisements.

The great movement of the twentieth century is seen in the banding together of all white races as against the darker races, and in the Geary law which excludes Chinese from the United States.[12] It excludes them all and provides a police at an expense of more than $200,000 a year to prevent their coming; yet a considerable number find an entrance each year.

Japan
The Empire of Japan embraces the islands of Nippon, Shikoke, Kiusiu and Yezo besides some of smaller size. The country is aptly described as an empire of islands.

---

12. In 1892, Thomas Geary (1854–1929), Democratic U.S. representative from California (1890–1895), sponsored a bill extending the 1882 Chinese Exclusion Act for an additional term of ten years.

Several different races are blended in the Japanese type of today and this is explained by the geographical situation of the country: it is connected with the Malay group by a chain of islands and by a narrow strait with the Peninsular of Korea and the mainland of Asia. It is also connected with Kamchatka. The Japanese may be considered skilful and daring navigators, and in this way have blended their race with other races.

Political power is divided between an hereditary and despotic governor, the Taicoon, and a spiritual chief, the Mikado. The creed of Buddhism, that of the Kamis, and the doctrines of Confucius equally divide the religious tendencies of the Japanese.

The worship of Buddha and Confucius is carried on in the same manner in China and Japan. The pagodas are similar, the ministers are the same bonzes with shaven heads and long gray robes. The buildings and junks of both nations are identical. Their food is the same—a diet of vegetables, principally rice and fish, washed down by plenty of tea and spirits. Coolies carry their loads in the same way in each country. Japanese women wear their hair in the same style as the Chinese women do, but the resemblance stops there. The Japanese are a warlike, and feudal nation as they have proved in their present war with Russia, surprising the entire world by their endurance and prowess, and they would be indignant at being confounded with the servile and crafty inhabitants of the Celestial Empire, who despise war, and whose sole aim is commerce.

Japanese have but one wife; polygamy is sometimes practiced in China.

Since the war between Russia and Japan began, there has been great talk of the "yellow" peril. As against this gossip Prime-Minister, Count Katsura has made a remarkable statement of Japan's motives:

The struggle is in the interest of justice and humanity, and of the commerce and civilization of the world. Should Japan ever become the leader of the Orient, her influence will be exercised to turn her neighbors' feet into the path she has herself irrevocably chosen—the path of close community with the Occident.

In this struggle, standing as we do for principles, which we believe, are identical with those cherished by all enlightened nations, we look to the United States for that sympathy which we think our cause deserves; and especially do we turn to the people of the universities of America, which have given to so many of us a cordial welcome, and to whose teachers, alumni and students many of us are bound by ties of gratitude and friendship.[13]

13. Katsura Taro (1848–1913) served as prime minister of Japan from 1901 to 1913. For more on Katsura, see Stewart Lone, *Army, Empire and Politics in Meiji Japan: The Three Careers of General Katsura Taro* (New York: St. Martin's, 2000).

Although the Geary law bears on its face an injustice, yet to the student it but marks another mile-stone in the march of human progress.

Japanese prowess has astonished the world. A strike among Russian laborers is no less remarkable.

Cui bono?[14] we ask.

Time will solve the riddle.

Says an eminent writer:

We wage a two-fold struggle: the struggle for bread and the struggle for freedom. We wrestle on the one hand with nature, seemingly niggard; and on the other, with principalities and powers, with laws and systems.

At times the odds appear too great; those who are against us seem stronger than those who are for us. We think to surrender. We are tempted to accept the idler's philosophy and turn over to "Evolution" the task to which we believed God had called us.

Cui bono? Centuries ago the most civilized nations fell a prey to barbarians who overturned dynasty after dynasty and completely changed the character of races and governments, thus placing scientists at fault in the twentieth century in their attempt to classify the living races of their time. Those barbarians were known to the dark races who ruled the world then, as the "white" peril. To those white barbarians the civilized world of today owes the supremacy of the white races.

Silently God demonstrates His power and the truth of His words: "Of one blood have I made all races of men to dwell upon the whole face of the earth."

No amount of scientific reasoning, no strenuous attempts of puerile rulers or leaders can hope to prevail against Omnipotence.

> When a deed is done for freedom,
> Through the broad earth's aching breast
> Runs a thrill of joy prophetic,
> Trembling on from east to west.
> And the slave, where'er he cowers,
> Feels the soul within him climb
> To the awful verge of manhood, as the energy sublime
> Of a century bursts full blossomed on the thorny stem of Time.[15]

SOURCE "The Dark Races of the Twentieth Century III: The Yellow Race: Siam, China, Japan, Korea, Thibet," *Voice of the Negro* 2.4 (Apr. 1905): 330–335.

14. "Good for whom?"
15. James Russell Lowell, "The Present Crisis" (1884).

Africa:
Abyssinians, Egyptians, Nilotic Class, Berbers, Kaffirs, Hottentots, Africans of Northern Tropics (including Negroes of Central, Eastern, and Western Africa), Negroes of the United States

When we consider the fact that there are 1,300,000,000 people in the world and that only about 375,000,000 are white (or one-quarter of the globe's population), we are not surprised that the dominant race dreads a "dark peril," and sees in every movement made by the leading representatives of dark peoples, a menace to his future prosperous existence.

Most of the 1,000,000,000 of dark-skinned brethren are found in Africa, the vast southwestern peninsula of the Old World: No other division of land on the globe has such a compact and rounded outline. Access to the interior is rendered difficult because of the general absence of gulfs and large inlets. With the rapid advance which exploration has made in Africa in recent years, there has followed a great rivalry among European nations for colonies and protectorates; but while great wealth and boundless avenues for commerce have been opened up, civilization has been a mixed blessing to the natives, and today the eyes of Christendom are fastened upon the Congo Free State and its attendant acts of atrocity in the enforcement of slavery within its borders. The regeneration of Africa is upon us, but blood and tears flow in its train.

The characteristics of the people comprising African stock may be described as having heads rather long than broad, hair black and rarely straight, and the skin almost invariably black or very dark.

Abyssinians

The Abyssinians, or Ethiopians, comprise the people of the elevated plateau of Abyssinia. Under this general designation are comprehended many tribes—speaking different languages, but whose origin has long been a puzzle to historians. In stature they are rather below than above six feet, and are fairer than Negroes, with an oval face, a thin, finely-cut nose, good mouth, regular teeth, and frizzled hair. Abyssinia is interesting both in geographical and ethnological features. So striking is the resemblance between the modern Abyssinian and the Hebrews of old that we are compelled to look upon them as branches of one nation in spite of strong evidence to the contrary. As this theory is forbidden us, how are historians to account for the existence of this almost

Israelitish people, and the preservation of a people so nearly approaching to the Hebrewin, inter-tropical Africa? Very recently Abyssinia has become a place of great interest to Americans. A treaty has just been signed between the United States' government and "Menelik II, by the Grace of God King of Kings of Ethiopia." It is a curious fact that the United States authorities maintain friendly relations with all independent black governments, although dealing severely with its own Negro population. To what end is this?

The United States Consul-General gives an interesting description of the military manoeuvres of Menelik's troops. He says in an extended article:

> The escorting troops then wheeled, and moved on in advance. Their numbers increased so rapidly as we approached the city that we were finally preceded by 3,000 men.
>
> Surrounding their chief, the warriors marched in most extraordinary confusion, sometimes performing evolutions, sometimes walking their horses, and sometimes galloping. It was a beautiful spectacle. No two costumes were alike. Saddles and bridles were decorated with gold and silver fringe. Bucklers of burnished gold were carried by soldiers, and from their shoulders flew mantles of leopard and lion skins, of silk, satin and velvet. Only the bright rifle-barrels marked the difference between these Ethiopians and the army of their forbears who followed the Queen of Sheba when she went down into Judea. We were spellbound by the moving mass of color, across which floated the weird music of a band of shawm players—playing as they had played when Jericho fell.
>
> At the farther end of the audience-hall sat the Emperor upon his divan or throne . . . On each side of the throne stood two young princes holding guns, and back of it and extending on both sides until they merged into the crowds waiting in the aisles, stood the ministers, judges, and officers of the Court. A subdued light softened the colors and blended them harmoniously.[16]

The Egyptians, Berbers, and Nilotic People

Egypt, as we all know, was once the scene of a noble civilization. Egypt was in close proximity to Arabia, but the two people have met very different destinies. The Arabian worshipped one god; the Egyptians paid homage to foul deities. Their physical characteristics were also different; the Arabian had a restless visage, lean and active figure. The Egyptians had voluptuous forms,

---

16. In late 1903, Robert Peet Skinner (1866–1960), the U.S. consul-general at Marseilles, France, negotiated a commercial treaty with Menelik II, emperor of Ethiopia. The U.S. Congress and President Roosevelt ratified the agreement in March 1904. Skinner's mission was widely reported at the time. Skinner later recounted the scene in chapter twelve of *Abyssinia of To-day*. See Robert Peet Skinner, *Abyssinia of To-day: An Account of the First Mission Sent by the American Government to the Court of the King of Kings (1903–1904)* (New York: Longmans, Green, 1906), 113–123.

long, almond-shaped eyes, thick lips, large, smiling mouths; complexions dark and coppery—the whole aspect that of the genuine African character, of which the Negro is called an exaggerated type.

The Berbers comprise the native population of the Sahara desert of the country north of it, and the original population of the Canary Islands. This section of African stock is near the Egyptian frontier in Fezzan, Tunis, Algeria, and Morocco. Their language is allied to the Hebrew and Arabic, and hence is called *sub*-Semitic. The tribes bearing this name are very numerous. One very interesting fact in reference to the Berbers is that the extinct aboriginal inhabitants of the Canary Islands owed to them their origin. These were the "fortunate isles" of the early Roman poets, the "Hesperides," or "isles of the blest," of many a song-writer.

The Gallas are spread over eastern inter-tropical Africa and are a formidable and warlike people. In complexion they are brown, their hair worn in tresses over the shoulders. They are of the type which fill up the transition from the Armenian type and the Western and Central African Negro. The Gallas come under the Nilotic class who inhabit the Valley of the Nile.

The Nubians are a most interesting class also. They are of reddish-brown complexion, but of a shade not as deep as the East African Negro. The hair is frizzled and thick. Under the name "Nubian" are comprehended two sections of people alike in physical character, but speaking distinct languages. These are the Eastern Nubians and the Nubians of the Nile. The Eastern Nubians are a handsome people living near the Red Sea. The Nubians of the Nile extend from Egypt to the borders of Sennaar.

Kaffirs

Under this name are comprehended all the South African races. Many tribes and even nationalities, all allied, however, by common customs and similar dialects, come under their name. The word "Kaffir" is considered by them a term of contempt; but as each division of the nation to which it applies has a separate name, their language supplies no substitute, unless the general terms Sechuano, Bantu or Zingian—all of which terms have been applied to the Kaffir race by different ethnologists—be received in its place. The Kaffirs are one of the widest spread of the African families. The Kaffirs are blackish-red in complexion and the hair crisp. The men are a handsome set, very tall with an intellectual cast of countenance. They show much aptitude for civilization, but their origin is a mystery to scientists. The Kaffirs are great warriors.

Hottentots are supposed to be the original inhabitants of South Africa, and were conquered by the Kaffirs. Between the two tribes there exists undying hatred. Bushmen and other allied tribes are found in South Africa. A number of African kingdoms have become famous among civilized peoples: The Kingdoms of Dahomey, Ashanti, etc.

Everyone is familiar with the story of the conquest of Dahomey by General

Dodds.[17] The Amazon warriors of this kingdom are women of prowess who have astounded and amazed the world. General Dodds was himself of Negro descent; he was accorded high honors for his victory upon his return to France.

The Ashantis have been the Spaniards of Southwest Africa, and they have persecuted other tribes assiduously. They are a famous tribe and of a warlike disposition.

Africa is such a wide ethnological region that were we to attempt to describe it even in the most abstract manner, we would need as many volumes at our command as we have had pages in this short sketch. When Africa is mentioned, people instantly associate the tribes as one vast mass of hideous ignorance. Such is far from the case. Some of the tribes are as fine specimens of manhood as one could wish to meet. In proof of the versatility of its people we have but to refer to the great advance of the Negroes of the United States—a heterogeneous mass composed of contributions from nearly all the tribes of the fatherland. In America a great problem has been worked out— the problem of the brotherhood of man, represented by the highest intellectual culture among Negroes, that can be shown by any other race in our cosmopolitan population. "God's image he, too, although made out of ebony."[18] Says Blumenbach: "I am acquainted with no single bodily characteristic which is at once peculiar to the Negro, and cannot be found to exist in many other and distant nations."[19]

Le Maire says in his travels through Senegal and Gambia, that there are Negresses as beautiful as European ladies.[20]

The Negro Freidig was well-known in Vienna as a masterly concertist on viol and violin. The Russian colonel of artillery, Hannibal, and the Negro Lislet of France, who on account of his superior meteorological observations and trigonometrical measurements was appointed correspondent for the *Paris Academy of Sciences.*[21]

---

17. Senegalese-born military commander Alfred-Amédée Dodds (1842–1922) led the 1892–1893 French campaign against King Behanzin of Dahomey that consolidated France's empire in West Africa.

18. In *God's Image in Ebony*, H. G. Adams explains the source of his title: "One word as to the title of this book, to which we anticipate some objections. 'God's Image cut, or carved in Ebony,' was a phrase first used, we believe, by the English Church Historian, [Thomas] Fuller,—a sayer of sententious things; and assuredly this phrase is among the most striking of the graphic sentences which he stamped so deeply into the walls of the republic of letters." See H. G. Adams, *God's Image in Ebony: Being a Series of Biographical Sketches, Facts, Anecdotes, etc., Demonstrative of the Mental Powers and Intellectual Capacities of the Negro Race* (London: Partridge and Oakey, 1854), ii.

19. Johann Friedrich Blumenbach (1752–1840) was a German scientist who devised a system of racial classification.

20. Jacques-Joseph Le Maire, *The Voyages of the Sieur Le Maire, to the Canary Islands, Cape-Verde, Senegal, and Gambia* (1695), in *A Collection of Voyages and Travels, Consisting of Authentic Writers in Our Own Tongue, Which Have Not Before Been Collected in English, or Have Only Been Abridged in Other Collections,* edited by Thomas Osborne (London: T. Osborne, 1745), 2:597–623.

21. Freidig, Hannibal, and Lislet are referenced in Adams, *God's Image in Ebony*, 96–97.

In an able article of the *Southern Quarterly Review*, 1855, we note these facts:

In the whole range of the African continent we discover the same endless variations and gradational blending between the widest extremes, exhibited by all the other people of the earth. In color they vary through every shade from the European that sometimes appear in Egypt, and still exists in the neighborhood of Mount Atlas, to the polished ebony of the thoroughly dyed Negro. In physiognomy, they range between the elegant Grecian outline, and the exaggerated monstrosity of prognathous development. In texture of hair they exhibit every grade from the soft Asiatic and even auburn locks of some Egyptians, to the Auranian Berbers, through the long, plaited ringlets of the Morooran Kaffirs, and short, crisp curls of the Nubian, the thick and frizzled, wolf-like covering of the diffused Gallas and the still more woolly-headed growth of the Fellahs, and the thoroughly developed Negro tufts of the Guinea tribes. In every important part that marks varieties in man, the inhabitants of Africa vary with such indefinite blendings of one grade into another, between the Caucasian standard and the lowest Negro specimen, that it is impossible to draw a line of division at any point of the skull, and affirm that here one type ends and another begins.[22]

SOURCE "The Dark Races of the Twentieth Century IV: Africa: Abyssinians, Egyptians, Nilotic Class, Berbers, Kaffirs, Hottentots, Africans of Northern Tropics (including Negroes of Central, Eastern, and Western Africa), Negroes of the United States," *Voice of the Negro* 2.5 (June 1905): 415–418.[23]

22. "Art. IV. The Human Family," *Southern Quarterly Review* 11.1 (Jan. 1855): 148.
23. *The Dark Races of the Twentieth Century* progresses from installment IV in June 1905 to installment VI in July 1905. There was no installment V.

VI.

The North American Indian— Conclusion

*T*he commonly presented picture of the Indians at the time of the discovery of America by Columbus, is that of a horde of wandering, naked savages whose chief aim of existence was the torturing and killing of each other. Such a picture is totally erroneous, for the Indian had attained some degrees of culture though still living in savagery. He had, indeed, reached the second stage of existence, that of barbarism, and was making progress along the road of civilization.

He was skillful in the practice of many arts. He had possessed himself of the weaver's art, and from the hair of animals, the down of birds and the fibres of plants could weave, spin and color the material for his clothing. Basket making was carried by him to so high a state of perfection that little improvement could be made by his civilized brother. Although his methods were crude, the potter's art was his, and the grace of form and ornamentation, excite the admiration even of this generation. Copper was found and mined and beaten into shape and was used by the Indians of Peru and Mexico; gold was also used and a method of making bronze had been discovered.

We are apt to forget in the enjoyment of the luxuries of our food products, that maize or Indian corn which furnishes a large part of the world's food was the gift of the Indian to civilization. The sweet potato also originated with the Indian, also tobacco.

One would scarcely apply the word architecture to the rude homes of the aborigines; nevertheless, many of their houses were substantial and comfortable. Many Northwest tribes reared dwellings which were capable of accommodating several hundred individuals. The communal houses of mud and stone reared by the people of Arizona, New Mexico and Mexico were pretentious and durable edifices, while in Central and South America, buildings were fashioned out of hewn stone, which from their dimensions, the size of some of the blocks contained in them, and the ornate character of the ornamentation, justly excite the wonder and admiration of the traveler and archaeologist.

Progress had been made in recording events and communicating ideas by picture-writing, which in Mexico and Central America had been so far developed into hieroglyphics as to hint strongly at the invention of a true phonetic alphabet.

The mode of government was organized, rude, to be sure, when compared with civilized nations, but marking a decided advance over the conditions obtaining among most savage peoples. The chieftaincy was transmitted or purely elective. In many sections a considerable advance had been made in political confederation, and neighboring tribes combined for defense and to wage war against a common enemy.

Their advance in religion equalled their progress in other directions. Their medical practice resembled that of the present day faith-cure as its success depended upon the influence over the patient's mind. Roots and herbs were the simple adjuncts to the charms of the medicine man.

Such, briefly, are some of the achievements of the Indian as he was found by civilized man. Whatever value is placed upon them, whatever rank may be assigned them in the scale of human efforts, they were at least his own, and compare favorably with Anglo-Saxon advancement in the scale of progress.

The origin of the red man is still a mystery. Reluctant to classify him with the despised black because of the degrees of higher culture discovered in his crude efforts of advancement, he is held to be a creature solitary in his creation and hard to classify. It has been claimed by some writers that he is of Jewish origin. This belief had a strong hold on the minds of thinkers of the eighteenth century. Some believe America to have been colonized by Phoenicians, others by Carthagenians. Evidences that the Indian came from Scandinavia are as convincing as those that he came from Ireland, or Greenland. Equally convincing are the arguments for a passage by the aborigines across Behring Strait from Asia, across the Northern Pacific from Japan or China in junks, or a across the Southern Pacific in canoes from the Polynesian Islands, or Australia.

Says a well-known writer,

Erroneous hypotheses have, however, been productive of great good in pointing out and emphasizing some of the most useful lessons which the student of anthropology of the present day must learn and keep in mind. Of these perhaps the most important is that the human mind is everywhere practically the same; that in a similar state of culture man in groping his way along will ever seek the same or similar means to a desired end. That, granting the same conditions of environment, man acts upon them and is acted upon by them in the same way the world over. Hence, in large part, arises those similarities of customs, beliefs, religions, and arts which have been appealed to as evidences of genetic connection or of common origin, when, in fact, they are evidences of nothing but a *common humanity*.

But in spite of the conclusions of science, a sharp line of demarcation divides the white from the red-skin, as in the case of the Negro. Driven back to "reserves" and supported by the governments of the United States and Canada, the Indian is steadily decreasing and there is every indication of his ultimate disappearance.

Having viewed the origin, customs and situation of the living dark races, from a scientific view-point, as explicitly as possible in magazine articles, we come to the following conclusions:

The color of the skin, texture of the hair, the development of the cranium and even language, are not infallible indications of race origin.

The African race and its descendants are divergent and undeveloped, ethnically considered, yet stand in close relationship to other races on the broad, indisputable plane of a common origin and a common brotherhood.

The presumption of superiority by the Anglo-Saxon race is insolently arrogant. We mark the insinuating patronage of other races by them, the slogan of social equality, the gospel of racial purity, the dangers of the Ethiopian Movement, as the outcome of a dread fear that is ever present with them and tugging at their very heart-strings. This is caused by the steady uplift of thousands of Blacks, Yellows and Browns. If we let them tell it, the slightest advancement in art, science and government removes all traces of Negro origin; therefore, East Indians, Indians, Japanese, Chinese, Arabs, Abyssinians, Zulus (including Kaffirs), and many others are not classed among the members of the great family of blacks, and we are impressed with the fact that they are all of Aryan descent and claim Japheth as their common father. That the ultimate desire of the Anglo-Saxon is the complete subjugation of all dark races to themselves, there is no doubt; but the persistent rise of the dark men in the social scale and their wonderful increase in numbers is a source of constant menace to the accomplishment of certain designs.

In 1872 a statistician claimed that in the United States and the West Indies and South America there were ten millions of mixed races, today there may be added to this number twenty millions more. As near as can be gleaned from the data of the Eastern world, Africa has about two hundred million of whom we know and this would only include about two-thirds of its inhabitants. In Europe proper about one million are scattered throughout the various countries. Under Turkish rule there are about three and one-half millions, and in the East eight hundred thousand. In the Philippines, Borneo and Oceanica there are probably ten millions, which will make the total Negro population of the world, that is races containing Negro blood, about two hundred and thirty-six millions. This enormous number of men of the future, must yet be reckoned with; and the far-seeing Anglo-American realizes the problem on his hands.

The most serious questions of the hour are the Negro Problem and its fellow—Capital versus Labor. These are the factors which in a future generation will change the current of events and the deductions of science.

Subtle forces have led to the overthrow of republics in the past, and vital reactionary changes have marked the life of the American Republic for the past twenty-five years. How will capital and labor bear upon a question of ethnology? you ask.

Our answer is that sociological conditions have more to do with developing civilization than racial descent. Thus, the white race claims Plato,

Archimedes, Euclid and Aesop; the black claims Hannibal, Pushkin, the Dumas' and Frederick Douglass. Yet, the nine men mentioned were mixed bloods—equal parts of Negro and Caucasian. Archimedes is classed as a white man and Douglass as a black man. Had Douglass lived in Attica with Archimedes, he would have come down to us through the ages as one of the grandest orators of ancient times, and as such would have been classified as a white man. This leads us to the conclusion that few tests for classifying races are more unsatisfactory than that of color. The status of culture is the only true test.

During her first centuries, Egypt had no beggars and no alms-houses. Some were richer, some poorer, but none lived squalidly. By shrewd manipulation, wealth became concentrated in the coffers of the few, and when she fell, two per cent of her population owned ninety-seven per cent of her wealth. During the last years of Babylon, two per cent of her population owned her stupendous wealth. When Persia was expunged from the catalogue of nations, one per cent of her population owned all the land and her people famished. Great estates ruined Greece. Taxes and rent were doubled in Rome. "The Man with the Hoe" became the victim of the man with a "privilege" and an office. The peasant became a vagrant, a beggar, a criminal. The tyranny of concentrated wealth on the one hand, and social, industrial and economic enslavement on the other, caused the ruin of the Roman Empire. When she perished, eighteen hundred men were the virtual owners of the known world. The bloodiest social and political upheaval in the annals of man was caused by sociological problems, and the fruit of that upheaval was the "Reign of Terror." Could we bring ourselves to eliminate the question of franchise, the problem of bread and butter still remains. This brings us on the same plane with the laborer of whatever color or race and would make his interests ours; on the other hand, a Negro is always loyal to the government. There you are. But how could we resist the subtle forces which turn Fortune's wheel and make the beggar of today the ruling magnate of tomorrow?

Six thousand years of isolation in Africa, two hundred and fifty years of slavery in America, savagery, barbarism and semi-civilization in other quarters of the globe give us people burdened with helplessness, melancholy and stifled aspiration to whom the "door of opportunity" is but a fairy tale. But in the great labor contest which will inevitably come to our common country we take a stand with the vast human tide and "sink or swim, live or die, survive or perish" with the great majority. In such circumstances the color of the skin, the curl of the hair, the development of the cranium will not count; we want men with red blood in their veins and not the sluggishness of the cold materialist who scorns the "dreamers" who make up the world's best people. Men of the times and for the times who will serve nobly their day and generation. Men who will teach the Anglo-Saxon that "all men were created equal" and that "*all men*" are not *white* men.

"Though many and diverse are the roads that lead man to the higher life, they all pursue about the same course, and time only is required to unite them into one broad stream of progress.

"Many are the lessons taught by ethnology, but the grandest of them all is the lesson of the unity of mankind, the unity of a common nature and a common destiny."

SOURCE "The Dark Races of the Twentieth Century VI: The North American Indian—Conclusion," *Voice of the Negro* 2.6 (July 1905): 459–463.

PART VIII

Black Classics Series *(1905)*

I n 1905, Hopkins self-published her pamphlet *A Primer of Facts Pertaining to the Early Greatness of the African Race and the Possibility of Restoration by its Descendants* with an imprint from Cambridge: P. E. Hopkins & Co., Publishers. The cover is headed "Black Classics Series . . . . Number One"; however, there is no evidence that any additional titles appeared in this series. As the title page acknowledges, it was "Compiled and Arranged [. . .] by Pauline E. Hopkins," who relied on Martin Delany's *Principia of Ethnology*.[1] Despite her debt to Delany, the volume's only mention of him appears in a list of famous black men and women that recognizes him as "Physician, Ethnologist, Explorer." The same list's most notable omission is Booker T. Washington, whom Hopkins no longer found worthy of mention in this context.

Even though she, like many of her contemporaries, was perceptibly grappling with biological explanations of racial difference, her pamphlet is a clear expression of racial pride. From the first issue of the *Colored American Magazine,* which described her commitment to "uplifting the colored people of America, and through them, the world," Hopkins articulated a vision of transatlantic racial unity that she further develops in *A Primer of Facts*: "the obligation of the descendants of Africans in America" is to become "thoroughly familiar with meagre details of Ethiopian history, by fostering race pride and an international friendship with the Blacks of Africa."[2] *A Primer of Facts* continues the internationalism of *Dark Races* and represents Hopkins's ongoing global concerns.

1. The title page of James T. Haley, *Afro-American Encyclopaedia; or, The Thoughts, Doings, and Sayings of the Race, Embracing Lectures, Biographical Sketches, Sermons, Poems, Names of Universities, Colleges, Seminaries, Newspapers, Books, and a History of the Denominations, Giving the Numerical Strength of Each. In Fact, It Teaches Every Subject of Interest to the Colored People, as Discussed by More Than One Hundred of Their Wisest and Best Men and Women* (Nashville, Tenn.: Haley and Florida, 1895), a work Hopkins knew, provides a similar attribution, "Compiled and Arranged by James T. Haley." As compiler and arranger, Hopkins drew heavily on Martin Robison Delany, *Principia of Ethnology: The Origin of Races and Color, With an Archeological Compendium of Ethiopian and Egyptian Civilization, from Years of Careful Examination and Enquiry* (1879; repr. as *The Origin of Races and Color*, Baltimore: Black Classic Press, 1991), for the first six chapters.

2. "Editorial and Publishers' Announcements" (*CAM*, May 1900), 64.

A PRIMER

of

FACTS

Pertaining to the Early Greatness of the African Race

and

The Possibility of Restoration by its Descendants—with EPILOGUE

Compiled and Arranged from the Works of the best known Ethnologists and Historians

by

PAULINE E. HOPKINS,

Author of "Contending Forces," "Hagar's Daughter," "Winona," "Talma Gordon," "Famous Men of the Negro Race," "Famous Women of the Negro Race," Etc.

Cambridge:
P. E. Hopkins & Co., Publishers.
1905.

11. The title page of *A Primer of Facts* is shown here. Courtesy of General Research & Reference Division, Schomburg Center for Research in Black Culture, The New York Public Library, Astor, Lenox and Tilden Foundations.

A Primer of Facts
Pertaining to the Early Greatness of the African Race and the Possibility of Restoration by its Descendants—with Epilogue.

Compiled and Arranged from the Works of the Best Known Ethnologists and Historians by Pauline E. Hopkins

Preface
Facts versus Theory

> Cities are not great except as men may make them;
> Men are not great except they do and dare;
> Yet cities like men, have destinies that take them—
> That bear them on, not knowing why nor where.[3]

The standing of any race is determined by its mighty works and its men of genius.

A Primer of Facts

Chapter I
Original Man

THE CREATION OF MAN.—Man began his existence in the creation of Adam, therefore all races of mankind were once united and descended from one parentage.

WHO BUILT THE FIRST CITY?—Cain built the first city in the land of Nod, and called it after his first born, Enoch.

HOW WAS THE GOVERNMENT ADMINISTERED?—Probably there was no established government, and the head of the family ruled his own household according to traditional customs.

WHAT WAS THE ORIGINAL MAN?—Until the entry of Noah's family into the ark, all people were of the one race and complexion.

WHAT WAS THE COMPLEXION?—The Hebrew word Adam signifies red. Adam was so called from the color of his skin. His complexion must have been clay color or yellow, resembling that of the North American Indian.

---

3. Eugene Fitch Ware, "John Brown" (1892). Ware's poem was available in several different editions of his popular verse, including *Some of the Rhymes of Ironquill.*

WHAT WAS GOD'S PURPOSE IN THE CREATION OF MAN?—The promotion of his own glory through man's development and improvement in a higher civilization. The progress of civilization was required of man by God.

WHAT AGENCIES PROMOTE CIVILIZATION?—Revolution, conquest and emigration. Of these three, emigration is the most effective. From the Garden of Eden to the building of the Tower, there was but one race of people known as such: "And the Lord said, Behold, the people is one and they have all one language."[4]

Chapter II
Division of Mankind Into Races

WHEN AND HOW DID THE ORIGIN OF RACES BEGIN?—The sons of Noah were three in number: Shem, Ham and Japheth. These were the directors and leaders of the people. They all differed in complexion, and a proportionate number of the people differed in complexion as did the three sons. Shem was the color of Noah, Ham was swarthy, as it is conceded by scholars that Ham means "dark," "swarthy," "sable." Japheth was white.

After the confusion of tongues at Babel, each of the three sons of Noah went in different directions, followed by a proportionate number of the people who spoke the same language as the leader. Shem settled in Asia, Ham went southwest, and Japheth to the northwest, the three grand divisions of the Eastern Hemisphere: Asia, Africa and Europe. Therefore, the confusion of tongues and the scattering abroad of the people, were the beginning and origin of races. All this was according to the authority of the Bible (Gen. chapter xi, v. 6) "And the Lord said, Behold, the people is one, and they all have one language; and this they began to do (the building of the Tower of Babel): and now nothing will be restrained from them which they have imagined to do." "So the Lord scattered them abroad from thence, upon the face of all the earth."

Thus God's design in the creation of races was accomplished, because it roused in the people a desire for race affinity, and also to people the remotest parts of the earth.[5]

Chapter III
The Brotherhood of Man or The Origin of Color

CAN ALL RACES HAVE SPRUNG FROM THE SAME PARENT STOCK?— The answer to this question solves the mystery of the brotherhood of man, showing it is possible for persons of three distinct complexions, as was the case in Noah's family—Yellow, Black and White—to be born of the same father and mother of one race and color. It is an easily understood law of God's all-wise providence.

---

4. Delany, *Principia of Ethnology*, 10–13.
5. Ibid., 13–19.

The human skin consists of three structures: the cuticle or external surface, the middle structure and true skin. The cuticle is a thin, transparent, colorless structure easily rubbed off by abrasion. The second is a jelly-like, colorless substance which throws out clear drops of liquid when the cuticle is rubbed off. The third is the true skin, also colorless or white, naturally. That which gives all races the complexion peculiar to each, lies in the middle skin. It is cellular and each cell is capable of holding whatever enters it in a liquid state. In the white race these cells are empty or partially filled with a colorless substance, clear like water. When color like a flush or blush is seen, it is caused by the red matter entering into the cells of the middle skin.

Elaboration and selection is the first process in the chemistry of all things, animate and inanimate—animal and vegetable and mineral. The coloring matter which enters the cells of the middle skin of the African race is the same red matter, concentrated, which flushes the cheek of the white man under strong emotion. In short, all coloring matter in the human system is pigment; that in a fair face being red, in the tawny being yellow in appearance, the red being modified by elaboration according to the economy of the system of each race.

WHY SHOULD THE SELECTION OF THE SAME COLORING MATTER OPERATE SO DIFFERENTLY IN THE BLACK RACE FROM THAT OF THE OTHER TWO RACES?—or why in the yellow race so differently from the white, if in reality descended from the same common origin of parent stock?—Simply because it is in accordance with the economy of the Creator to give an unerring reproductive system to each race whereby it should always be known by its own peculiar characteristics; the same is true of individuals of a race or family, and the same father and mother produce children of different temperaments, color of eyes and hair. See any family of the white race.

Take any or all fruits known as black; first the color is green, then white, next slight red which deepens daily to a final intense red or blackness in color. The fruit has simply increased in the red color matter until in its intensity we pronounce it black. Prove this fact by immersing a blood-clot in water—you will get a scarlet fluid reflecting the true color, red. The color of the blackest African is then simply concentrated red. The real color of the African is really purple and nothing else. Purple involves a mixture of red and blue, and implies the existence of blue in the blood. This is true, or whence come the blue veins of the white race and its blue eyes? Blue is an element of the blood; hence this purple color of the African. It is a significant fact that purple as a dress color originated in Africa; the Ethiopians and the Egyptians, who had the most delicate perception of color, adopted purple as a royal shade, and it was probably emblematic of the complexion of their kings and queens. Yellow is also a constituent of the blood as seen in the eyes, bile, jaundice and yellow fever. By a regular established law of physiology, an adequate quantity of red blood, blending, forms the purple of the blackest African complexion. The law by which this can be done is well-known to medical men and is beyond controversy. As in the animal kingdom, and in the anatomical structure of all vertebrae from fish to man, the Creator had but one plan; so in human races, running through all shades of complexion, there is but one color, modified and intensified from the purest white to the purest black.[6]

WHAT OTHER CAUSE IS SOMETIMES GIVEN BY WRITERS FOR THE COLOR OF THE AFRICAN AND HIS DESCENDANTS?—CLIMATE. Instances are adduced in which individuals transplanted from one climate to another have changed the color of the skin in a marked degree. Thus people living near the equator and exposed to the intense heat of the sun's rays, are blacker than those living in the northern latitude of temperate zones. The Jews are a good example to illustrate our meaning. Descended from the stock, prohibited from intermarriage with the people of other nations, yet dispersed into every country of the globe, they have the color of every nation; fair in Briton and Germany, brown in France and Turkey, swarthy in Spain and Portugal, olive in Syria, copper-colored in Arabia, and black at Congo in Africa.[7]

Chapter IV
Early Civilization of The Africans

WHICH OF NOAH'S SONS IS MOST INTERESTING HISTORY TO THE PRESENT GENERATION OF HAMITIC ORIGIN?—Of the three sons, the history of the second, Ham, is fraught with more interest than that of either of the others.

HOW MANY SONS HAD HAM?—The sons of Ham were Cush, Mizriam, Phut and Canaan.

HOW MANY SONS HAD CUSH ?—The sons of Cush were six in number: Seba, Havilah, Sabtah, Raamah, Sabtecha and Nimrod.

WHO WAS NIMROD?—The grandson of Ham; son of Cush. Nimrod first arose to national greatness as a monarch so that until this day his name is great among the princes of the earth. He was the founder of the great Assyrian empire.

WHEN WAS THE FIRST PERIOD OF MUNICIPAL LAW?—When the separation took place the entire people began a new process in life as three distinct peoples with entirely different aims and interests. Shem went to Asia, Ham went to Africa and Japheth journeyed to Europe. The different races of the human family began, and at this time also began the period of municipal

---

6. Ibid., 22–35.

7. William Wells Brown, *The Rising Son; or, The Antecedents and Advancement of the Colored Race* (1874; rev. ed., Boston: A. G. Brown, 1876), 79. Brown cites Samuel Stanhope Smith, *An Essay on the Causes of the Variety of Complexion and Figure in the Human Species* (1810; repr., Cambridge, Mass.: Belknap Press of Harvard University Press, 1965) and James Cowles Prichard, *Researches into the Physical History of Mankind* (London: Sherwood, Gilbert, and Piper, 1836–1847) as sources. Prichard's work is among several books under review in "Art. IV. The Human Family," which Hopkins cites in *Dark Races*. While Hopkins's source for this passage was probably Brown, Brown's likely source was Wilson Armistead, *A Tribute For The Negro: Being a Vindication of the Moral, Intellectual, and Religious Capabilities of the Coloured Portion of Mankind; With Particular Reference to the African Race* (Manchester, England: William Irwin, 1848), 63–64. The same passage appears, also probably via Brown, in Haley, *Afro-American Encyclopaedia*, 11–12.

law. Previous to this time the people were governed by patriarchs. Their laws must have been few and simple, each father governing according to tradition or as it seemed best in his judgment.

WERE ETHIOPIA AND EGYPT EVER UNITED KINGDOMS?—From all that we can gather from tradition, Cush went in a south-westerly direction, accompanied by his father, Ham. He settled a colony in Asia, near to Egypt, on the land terminating at the Isthmus of Suez, known to us as "the land of Midian." After remaining here a while, he entered Africa through the Isthmus, Ham settling on the delta or land formed by the mouths of the Nile, while Cush pushed up the Nile into the heart of Africa. Ancient historians agree that Cush left his brother Mizriam, Ham's second son, as ruler of the people in the infant colony, and he was known as the prince of Midian. When the colony at the delta of the Nile—Egypt—had grown in importance, Ham is supposed to have sent for his son Mizriam to assist him in the work of governing Egypt. Mizriam then left Midian in the hands of his brother Phut, joined his father Ham, and became co-ruler with him of the people.

That the rule of Cush extended from the Nilotic borders of Egypt in toward the interior of darkest Africa, and known as Ethiopia, is not to be disputed, all historians of ancient history agreeing on this point. In the early settlement of these countries, Ethiopia and Egypt were united kingdoms under the rule of three princes—father and two sons. Pliny relates that Ethiopia was originally divided into forty-five kingdoms. Diodorus Siculus affirms that the laws of Ethiopia agree with those of Egypt. This was accounted for by the Ethiopians who asserted that Egypt was first colonized by emigrants from their country, and they mention in proof, that the land of Egypt was for a long period entirely covered by water and was afterwards gradually filled in by accessions from the Nile of mud brought every year out of Ethiopia. This theory is confirmed by Herodotus, who designates Egypt as the gift of the Nile, and that the entire region, with the exception of Thebes, was once a vast morass.

The Ethiopians agreed with the Egyptians in most of their laws, their funerals, the deification of their princes, the colleges of their priests, circumcision, in their sacred and civil institutions, in their arts, science, learning and religion. Diodorus Siculus also asserts that not only the same kind of statutes, but also the same characters and hieroglyphics were used in Egypt and Ethiopia, since it is generally allowed that those were the repositories of Egyptian wisdom and literature.

The progress of Cush into the interior of Africa, toward the Niger, was easy because there was no opposition to his entrance. It was virgin soil, an unsettled country, and he was the pioneer in peopling of communities in Africa, and all the Soudan and Nigratia are today filled with the millions of his descendants.[8]

WHAT WERE TWO GREAT CITIES OF THIS UNITED KINGDOM?— Meroe in Ethiopia, and Thebes in Egypt.

8. Delany, *Principia of Ethnology*, 41–45.

WHERE WAS MEROE SITUATED, AND FOR WHAT WAS SHE CELE-BRATED?—Meroe, the queen city of Ethiopia, has been celebrated for more than 2,000 years as the seat of all ancient greatness. It was situated at the junction of the Astaboras river and the Nile in Ethiopia. Flowing through Ethiopia the Nile forms great islands around which it scarcely flows in five days (Pliny). The island of Meroe was one of these great islands 340 miles in length and 115 miles in breadth, and on this island the city of Meroe was built. It is in the province of Atbar and lies between 13 degrees and 18 degrees of north latitude, forming a part of the modern kingdom of Sennaar, the southern part belonging to Abyssinia, a little below the present town of Shendy.

Meroe was the centre of trade between the north and south, east and west, and into the city poured all the caravans of Africa laden with frankincense and gold and fine fabrics. Native products were thus exchanged for foreign luxuries.

Chapter V
Progress in Religion and Government

WHAT WAS THE FORM OF GOVERNMENT IN ETHIOPIA?—A KING-DOM. The rulers were selected from among the priestly caste. There was a custom which appears strange to civilized nations: the electors when weary of their ruler sent him a courier with orders for the ruler to die in any manner most satisfactory to himself. This absurd custom was resisted by Ergamenes, who lived in the reign of the second Ptolemy. He marched against the fortress of the priests and killed many of them. He founded a new religion.

Queens frequently reigned in Ethiopia, and royal women were treated with greater respect in the united kingdom than in any other ancient monarchy. Among the celebrated Ethiopian queens we may mention Candace, Aahmes (wife of Amoris of Egypt), and the queen of Sheba.

HOW FAR DID THE RULE OF CUSH EXTEND?—From the Nilotic borders of Egypt to the interior of the country, the whole of which was called Ethiopia.

WHAT WAS THE RELIGIOUS CHARACTER OF THE ETHIOPIANS AND THE EGYPTIANS?—The religion of the Ethiopians and the Egyptians was a mixture of grand conceptions mingled with superstition. "No other ancient people were so firm in their belief in immortality, or felt its influence so strongly in their daily life; yet no other carried its idolatries to so debasing an extreme," says a writer. This contradiction is not confined to the ancient peoples of earth. We know that such contradictions exist everywhere, even among the professors of the religion of our Lord and Saviour—it is the difference simply which lies between ideal teaching and the personal character of those who receive it. Do we not worship idols today? Inordinate love of money and influence is the rock ahead forecasting the shipwreck of modern civilization.

The sacred books of the Egyptians and the Ethiopians contained the system adopted by the priests. Their fundamental principle was that God is one, unrepresented, invisible. But as God acts upon the world, his various attributes and modes of manifestation were represented in various forms. Some portion of his divine life was supposed to reside in plants and animals, and these were worshiped by the ignorant. To the wise, these animals and plants were merely symbols, but became objects of adoration to the unlearned. The priests perceived the power that this misconception gave their orders and refrained from spreading abroad the light which they possessed. Therefore the common people believed in eight gods of the first order, twelve of the second, and seven of the third; but these were worshiped under many titles, or as connected with different places.

The most interesting article of their mythology is the belief in the appearance of Osiris on the earth for the benefit of mankind under the title of Manifestor of Goodness and Truth; his death by the malice of the evil one; his burial and resurrection, and his office as judge of the dead.

Though many recognized the personality of one true God, they always represented him in three distinct persons, their idea of him being that he was a Three-One-God. This is illustrated in the person of Ham (Rameses I.) deified and worshiped as Jupiter Ammon. He is represented as the body of a man with the head of a ram seated on a great white throne of gold and ivory; in his left hand is a golden wand or sceptre, and in his right a thunder-bolt; at his right side sat a phoenix with extended wings. This representation is symbolical; gold for purity; ivory for durability; the scepter, for authority, and the thunderbolt for power. A ram's head of two-fold significance combining the innocence of the sheep and the caution in the horns not to approach too near, illustrating the biblical declaration that "no man can look upon God's face and live"; and the phoenix illustrating the essential attributes of the Christian conception of God, as a self-created being without beginning and without end.[9]

Chapter VI
Progress in Science, Art and Literature
IN WHAT DID THE ETHIOPIANS EXCEL ALL OTHER NATIONS?—In wisdom and Literature.

WHAT WERE THE PYRAMIDS?—Architectural structures built in Ethiopia and Egypt, begun under Ham, Cush and Mizriam.

WHAT WERE THEIR USES?—They were sacred historical depositories for their bodies after death.

WHAT DO THEY SHOW?—Great advancement in science and the mechanical arts. They show the living reality of Ethiopian knowledge of mathematical accuracy in the science of geometry. No other power could have brought to Egypt's plains the great cubic rocks of thousands of tons weight, and placed them one above the other in regular symmetrical succession to a given height, decreasing from the first surface layer, finishing by a

9. Ibid., 56–59.

cap stone large enough for from twenty to forty persons to stand upon. Doubtless Euclid was induced to pursue his mathematical studies to the discovery of the forty-seventh problem, by dwelling among and studying, in other ages, these stupendous monuments.

HOW IS EACH MONUMENT PLACED?—Each is placed so as to exactly face the cardinal points, and the great pyramid is precisely upon the 30th parallel of latitude.

WHAT MAY BE SAID OF THE TEMPLES OF ETHIOPIA AND EGYPT?—They are the grandest architectural monuments in the world. That of Amun in a rich oasis twenty days' journey from Thebes, was one of the most famous of ancient oracles. Near it in a grove of palms rose a hot spring, the Fountain of the Sun. The oasis was a resting place for caravans which passed between Egypt and the interior regions of Nigritia or Soudan.

The science of medicine was practiced by the priests in even the remotest ages. The universal practice of embalming enabling them to acquaint themselves with the effects of various diseases by examination of the body after death. The Nile valley supplied drugs for all the world.

WHAT MAY BE SAID OF THE ETHIOPIANS IN LITERATURE?—They excelled all other nations in literature. Heliodorus says that the Ethiopians had two sorts of letters, the one called regal, the other vulgar; and that the regal resembled the sacerdotal characters of the Egyptians. The hieroglyphics on the Pyramids show that they understood ancient hieroglyphic characters as well as the Egyptians. Among the Ethiopians a hawk signified quickness or dispatch; the crocodile denoted malice; the eye the maintainer of justice, and the guard of the body; the open right hand represented plenty; and the left, closed, a secure possession of property. Diodorus attributes the invention of these characters to the Egyptians.

According to another writer the Ethiopians invented astronomy and astrology, and communicated these sciences to the Egyptians.[10]

We can believe this because we know that the country of the African is very fit for making celestial observations. The Chaldeans were Hamites.

A learned writer states it as his conviction that the literature of the Israelites, in letters, government and religion, was derived from the Africans, as they must have carried with them the civilization of those peoples in their exodus. We must remember that the highest encomium upon Moses was that he "was skilled in all the wisdom of the Egyptians."[11]

Chapter VII
Restoration
HOW HAVE THE BLACKS OF MODERN TIMES DEMONSTRATED THE FACT THAT THEY ARE DESCENDED FROM THE ONCE POWERFUL

10. Ibid., 46–49.
11. Ibid., 55.

AND LEARNED ETHIOPIANS?—By the number of phenomenally intellectual men produced in Africa and America.

Name a few black men who are famous in science, art, literature, etc.

Scientists
Thomas Fuller, "The Virginia Calculator" (Native African enslaved).
Benjamin Banneka—Astronomer.[12]
Prof. Reason—Mathematician.
Prof. Kelly Miller—Mathematician.
Dr. Martin R. Delany—Physician, Ethnologist, Explorer.

Art
Edmonia Lewis—Sculptor.
Meta Vaux Warrick—Sculptor.
William H. Simpson—Portrait Painter.
Edwin M. Bannister—Landscape Painter.
Henry Tanner—Landscape Painter.
Frederick Hemmings—Landscape Painter.
Samuel Coleridge Taylor—Musician, Composer, Conductor.

Literature
Phillis Wheatley—Poet.
Frederick Douglass—Orator, Editor, Author, Diplomat.
Frances Harper—Poet, Author.
Henry Highland Garnet—Learned Divine (Pure African descent).
Dr. James McCune Smith—Physician, Orator, Author, Graduate of
  Glasgow University.
Dr. Alexander Crummell—Learned Divine, Graduate of Cambridge
  University.
Fanny J. Coppin—Educator, Writer, Orator.
T. McCants Stewart—Orator, Lawyer, Author, Diplomat.
Charles Lenox Remond—Orator.
John M. Langston—Lawyer, Orator, Author, Politician.
Robert Elliott—Lawyer, Politician.
Ebenezer D. Bassett—Educator, Diplomat.
Rev. Tiyo Soga—Learned Divine, Orator, Missionary (Native Kaffir).
Majola Agbebi—Learned Divine, Author (Native West African).
Dr. Blyden—Profound Scholar, Orator, Author (Native West African).[13]

12. Hopkins here uses "Banneka," the African-based spelling of Benjamin Banneker's name. For a consideration of Banneker's possible Dogon ancestry, see Charles Cerami, *Benjamin Banneker: Surveyor, Astronomer, Publisher, Patriot* (New York: John Wiley and Sons, 2002), 7.

13. Edward Wilmot Blyden (1832–1912) was born in St. Thomas, Virgin Islands, and emigrated to Liberia in 1850. He lived in West Africa for most of the remainder of his life, working as an author, journalist, educator, diplomat, and government minister.

Joseph J. Roberts—President Republic of Liberia.
Dr. Spurgeon—Liberian Charge d'Affaires.
Sir Edward Jordan—Editor, Politician (Mayor of Jamaica).
George W. Williams—Historian, Soldier, Minister, Orator.
Prof. W. S. Scarborough—Educator, Author of Greek Text Books.
Robert Morris—Lawyer, Orator.
Clement G. Morgan—Lawyer, Orator, Politician.
Prof. Du Bois—Philosopher, Educator, Author.
Bishops Turner, Coppin, Derrick—Powerful Leaders in the A.M.E.
  Church.

Patriots (Revolutionary War)
Crispus Attucks.
Peter Salem.
Primus Hall.
Prince Whipple.
L. Latham.
James Armistead.

Patriots (Civil War)
Fifty-fourth Massachusetts Regiment—Fort Wagner, Olustee and other
  battles of the Civil War.
Fifty-fifth Massachusetts Regiment—Honey Hill, Olustee and other
  battles of the Civil War.
Eighth U.S. Colored Battery.
First North Carolina Colored Regiment.
Thirty-fifth U.S. Colored Regiment.
Thirty-second U.S. Colored Regiment.
Thirty-fourth U.S. Colored Regiment.
Sixth Regiment U.S. Troops.
Third and fourth U.S. Colored Regiments.

DO WE BELIEVE IT POSSIBLE THAT THE BIBLE PROPHECY CON-
CERNING ETHIOPIA WILL BE FULFILLED?—We do, for even now the
time approaches. What reasons have we for so thinking?—The many significant happenings of the past few years: The establishment of the Liberian
Republic, the Anglo-Boer war in South Africa and the rapid opening up of
the Continent of Africa by civilized powers during the nineteenth century
and the rapid intellectual improvement of Africans and their descendants in
all parts of the world.

What is the obligation of the descendant of Africans in America?—To help
forward the time of restoration.

HOW MAY THIS BE DONE?—By becoming thoroughly familiar with the
meagre details of Ethiopian history, by fostering race pride and an international friendship with the Blacks of Africa.

Are we obliged to emigrate to Africa to do this successfully?—No. Friendly intercourse and mutual aid and comfort are all that are necessary at the present time. The future is in God's hands and will take care of itself.

Epilogue

It is now several years since the first signs of cold indifference on the part of former white friends, towards the social and political condition of the black man, manifested itself openly and aggressively. Nothing is heard from pulpit, press and platform but the growing charity and sympathy on the part of southern whites towards the blacks of their section. Said "charity and sympathy" seem to consist of an overwhelming desire to confine the Black to the cornfield and domestic service. The crux of the position is found in the words of Chas. H. Parkhurst in his sermon of April 28, 1901, after a visit South:

> The less the Negro talks about civic rights under the constitution, particularly the right of suffrage, the better it will be for him and the sooner he will attain to all rights that justly belong to him ... The Northern and Southern friends of the Negro are now counselling him to keep quiet upon the whole suffrage matter, to keep out of politics, not to talk about the constitution, not to insist upon his rights, but to attend industriously to the work of getting himself well ready—which he is not now—for what God and the country and the future have in store for him.[14]

We have been quiet, we have grown so silent that we have become hateful to ourselves. Disfranchisement has been placed in full force at the South while at the North we have watched the narrow radius in which lie employment and advancement for the Black, growing narrower and narrower each month, until, perforce, we must break through the grim walls of ostracism or be crushed to death by want caused from lack of avenues for honest employment. The Propaganda of Silence is in full force. Newspapers and magazines have been subsidized or destroyed if the editors fearlessly advocated the cause of humanity. Every leading intellect has been intimidated while, per contrary, a horde of Southern writers, speakers and politicians are allowed to fill the air with their doleful clamor against a proscribed race, without a protest. Agitation by the black is rigidly barred, but the Southern white is allowed the front of the stage in presenting his grievances to a sympathetic public.

Among the many Southern white ladies engaged in the laudable (?) work of eliminating the black brother and assisting him into the valley of humiliation we find one Mrs. Jeannette Robinson Murphy; her work is an illustration of all the work of Southern whites against the Negro. Since 1898 Mrs. Murphy has diligently canvassed the New England States, proselyting the friends of

---

14. See Charles H. Parkhurst, *The Southland Address Delivered by Rev. C. H. Parkhurst, D.D., before his Madison Square Congregation, New York City, the Sabbath after his Return from the South, April 28th, 1901* (New York, 1901).

the Blacks to the cause of the South, and inducing said friends to view the situation through Southern spectacles. Mrs. Murphy has appeared in the most aristocratic halls of amusement in our Northern cities and is being sustained by the richest and most influential members of our Northern aristocracy. We give an excerpt from Mrs. Murphy's book *Southern Thoughts for Northern Thinkers.*

Had the South been let alone and trusted it would have required but a few years more for the unnatural system of human bondage to have died of itself a natural death, for it was no longer profitable, except in two or three states where the larger plantations could be successfully worked....

Just at the time when there seemed every probability that our Southern men would be able to solve their own problem satisfactorily, there came on the scene a new leader, a stranger to those fair parts. He chanced one glorious summer day to be walking up and down a lovely shaded lane beside a grand ancestral estate in far-famed old Virginia. He looked about him and saw countless broad acres, all gladly yielding their increase. He heard the merry shouts of laughter from hundreds of happy Negroes at work, broken occasionally by joyous religious bursts of song. He saw the courtliest, bravest race of knightly, stalwart men, growing up like their fathers before them, tall and straight and handsome; courteous men who set women up on their rightful pedestals and kept them there. He saw the fairest, tenderest women gladly dependent upon their natural protectors; he travelled all over the lovely Southland, and everywhere as far as his eye could reach were homes which were ruled by love alone, each home a perfect heaven in itself. Enviously he exclaimed,

this will never do; these people love God and are perfectly happy. My power is threatened, and I must change all this and quickly, too, for I see these mothers are proud to possess large families of children to train for God's kingdom, and soon the hosts of good will outnumber my followers, and then I shall be hopelessly lost. I can scarcely credit my senses. If these Southerners have not taken these black savages whom I thought were forever mine, and even gone to Christianizing them, and they in turn are teaching the white babies to love and memorize God's Holy Word. I have never yet seen such noble men and women—I have never before found such stern sense of duty and principle as actuates their every motive.

...So spake his political majesty Satan, as he hurried away to execute his plans. Before leaving the South, however, he had promised large rewards to a few treacherous slaves who would do his bidding.

Arriving at the cold, frozen North he knocked gently at the hearts of a few receptive, sympathetic, credulous souls, and calling himself, "The Voice of the Lord," he gained a royal entrance therein, and straightway those same misguided agents of his were filled with a burning zeal to abolish slavery and carry out, as they now believed, the Lord's will.

These energetic abolitionists did not let the grass grow under their zealous feet, but began to sow the seeds of discontent among the very slaves in whose hearts Satan had already left his poison. They listened with itching ears to the lies of his run-away slaves—how they were beaten mercilessly, starved inhumanly and brutally overworked (as if anyone ever got any hard work out of an old-fashioned, free-from-care "nigger,") and, worst of all, how they were tracked and torn to death by the fiercest of bloodhounds.

Yes, these emissaries of Satan took the South's wealth, but had that great apostle of God, Abraham Lincoln, lived, this wrong would have been righted, for slavery must have been lawful under the constitution, else it would not have been necessary to add that controversial amendment, and so we feel deep down in our inmost hearts that the government of the United States still lawfully owes to the South millions of dollars.

Generous Northerners seek in vain to catch the Southern viewpoint of the vexed Negro question.

The whole trouble and difficulty lie in just one thing and nothing else. We are willing to give the Negro an all-around mental, moral, physical and spiritual education, but we insist upon the utter segregation and social isolation of the colored man. No proposed standing army can ever change the attitude of the white South upon this question. No qualifications or highest education of the Negro could ever make the true Southern man welcome that Negro into his family or hold out to him the tiniest tip of social recognition, for he believes that the mingling of a higher race with a lower one is an abomination unto the Lord. Around this pitiful point future wars and causes of war must lie ...

What often appears as cruelty to human beings is simply an outward expression of an instinctive racial gulf, which we think God fixed unalterably when He Himself first wisely segregated the Negro race in far-off Africa.

As matters stand today the feelings of the Negroes are continually lacerated, because, forsooth, we will not call them "Mr." and "Mrs." and colored "ladies" and "gentlemen."

One's brain sickens and faints at the thought of America's future. There is one righteous solution, and that God alone knows.

For all of the bitter feeling of today on the part of the young Southern Negroes toward their best true friends, their Southern white neighbors, and for all the blood to be shed in the future, we, in our narrow vision, can only thank two sources, that is, the misguided, interfering outsiders since the days before '60, as focused by Harriet Beecher Stowe, who gave the world a false impression of the treatment of slaves by the majority of generous, religious, true-bred gentlemen, their Southern masters, and a few tactless missionaries sent South since the war to lift up (?) the Negro.

I have interviewed all my life great numbers of ex-slaves, and I have yet to find one old slave who will say that he or she was cruelly treated.

Would it not be a good thing, in order to secure to posterity a true knowledge of the situation in those blessed old missionary slave days, to take down, ere it is too late, in the presence of just Northern witnesses, the sworn testimony of every old slave now living? My! what an ever-lasting exoneration our ancestors would have, even at this late day!

Slaves were spoken of always as "our people," and were kept when possible under the same ownership. When colored parents must needs be separated, there were not often such heartbreaking scenes as those blood-curdling tales (to be found in the books and tracts distributed throughout the North) would have us believe. Negro mothers are often unkind and cruel to their own children, though devoted, as a rule, to their white charges, whom they respect. Many a slave mother has said to her master, "Ef you don't sell dat triflin' Jim o' mine 'way frum hyar, I's gwine to kill 'im," and not infrequently the master had to protect children from their savage mothers' rage, and forcibly separate certain dangerous Negro families, for the safety of the lives of their members.

The North does not understand nor love the sure-enough African in his present illiterate, irresponsible, shiftless state, and we of the South do not understand or care for the educated Negro.

As the uneducated as well as the educated colored people are moving North to secure the social and political equality which we will never give them, it may not be many years before the northern section of the United States is overrun by them, and then, since they will not be properly appreciated, the ruptures will be sure to come, and if I were to turn prophet I should say, "in that event it will be God pity the Negro and God pity the North, for a great race war will take place, and the few Negroes who do escape alive will fly back down home to their only friends, and they will long for the blessed old days when their jolly, easy-going fathers held the patient Southerners in bondage."

We lay it to the doors of unwise politicians exclusively for calling Confederates "traitors" in the histories which I am told our Southern children living up North must now read.

Instead of the South wasting any more of its hard-earned money upon the impossible higher education of the Negroes, let us give them as a whole domestic training and sound Bible teaching, employing white ministers to lead them, as in the old regime, and then later on expend all our surplus money and energy in colonizing the race somewhere as Abraham Lincoln suggested, and give it a chance to show if it is really capable of self-government and higher culture.

As a temporary place of colonization we might try New England, since the historic underground railroad has already given the Negro a taste for travel, and the best and most acceptable charity that could be extended to him by the South would be a free ticket one way to such a colony at the welcoming North.

Since writing the above, I have been inquiring into the attitude which Mrs. Harriet Beecher Stowe assumed toward the Negro race after she removed to her Southern home at Mandarin, Florida.

It is said that she gave orders that no Negro was ever to enter her yard. Rumor also avers that shortly before her death she declared that if she had fully understood the Negro nature she would never have written *Uncle Tom's Cabin*, and moreover, that she keenly regretted her part in bringing on the war.[15]

Now is there anything in all this?

There is much in it. As an able white editor has boldly asserted, It means the acceptance of the docile domestic basis, supplemented by a little common school education, or deportation. The idea is to stop the flow of complaints against the white South and to cover its purposes against the Black from the just criticism of the nations of the earth.

Because of the desire and commands of our enemies, shall agitation stop, and shall we sit in silence while our traducers go unanswered? This question answers itself. We cannot cease from agitation while our wrongs are the sport of those who know how to silence our every complaint and plea for justice. NEVER SURRENDER THE BALLOT.

The iron heel of oppression is everywhere; it has reached every section of this country, and every black citizen has a duty to perform. Cultured men and women of color in convention assembled sit in silence while one side of this burning question is discussed—the white side—and we are solemnly impressed with the magnitude of our wickedness and hopeless depravity by partisan white and colored speakers. It has reached the pass where the educated Black will handle any subject in his assemblies but politics. The South and its friends have said: "Not a word of complaint, no talk of lynching, not an offensive word, or it will go hard with you," and the race leaders have bowed to that decree in abject submission.

What are we going to do about it? STICK TO PRINCIPLE.

In replying to Mrs. Murphy's aspersions upon our race, we take first her allusion to the chivalry of Southern men.

---

15. Jeannette Robinson Murphy, *Southern Thoughts for Northern Thinkers* (New York: Bandanna Publishing, 1904), 10–12. A note in *Southern Thoughts* indicates that the eponymous essay originated in the December 16, 1903, *Presbyterian Standard*. Murphy used lower-case *negro*, which Hopkins notably capitalized.

We venture to assert that these gentlemen are responsible for all the evil that slavery wrought in the Southern home. The results of profligacy are the same in any case whether whites or blacks are the aggressors. But if this be true, and pity 'tis, 'tis true, it is but the result of conditions forced upon a helpless people, and not their choice. Tears and heart-burning are the portion of the Southern white woman, and like Sarah of old, she wreaks her vengeance on helpless Hagar.

Chivalrous Southern men desecrated the purity of the Southern home, and, incidentally, opened this question of racial purity.

For the sake of argument, let us admit that there may be some foundation for the fears of the South that amalgamation may produce a race that will gradually supersede the present dominant factors in the government of this Republic. Who is to say that the type of the future American will not be represented by the descendants of men whose cosmopolitan genius makes them the property of all mankind? The offspring of Samuel Coleridge Taylor, or of Henry Tanner, will, in all probability, unite with some one of their social set in the countries of their adoption. There were hundreds of Blacks born in slavery and settled by their white fathers in the English Provinces, after being endowed with wealth. Their descendants have united with some of the best white families and are living in happiness among their countrymen.

These things are true, and, being true, who can tell when the drop of black blood will inadvertently filter back to the American channels from whence it started (especially if Americans continue to unite with Englishmen among whom there is very slight prejudice to color in marriage), and its possessors be placed by popular vote in the Presidential chair.

Anglo-Saxon blood is already hopelessly perverted, with that of other races, and in most cases to its great gain. Well, if it is so, what of it? The world moves on; old ideas and silly prejudices disappear in a fog of ridicule. All things are possible, if not probable.[16]

With regard to the Abolitionists, we as their wards must speak a word in their defence. The present generation little understands the dangers and difficulties which these brave and good men faced. Let us not misunderstand their position; principle alone actuated them. Do not let us flatter ourselves that love for a black skin had anything to do with their acts for us. No; it was love of country and pride in the good name of the Republic simply. With true patriotism they sacrificed their fortunes to their principle in many cases. In penury and want they wrought. Oftentimes their home was an attic, a cot their bed, but withal their treatises on slavery were masterpieces of literature, for the Abolitionists embraced the flower of American intellectual culture. In their lives is a lesson for us in the present crisis of our racial history.

---

16. Hopkins used an earlier version of this passage in "Charles Winter Wood." In the earlier publication, she used *Negro* where *Black* now appears.

In a burst of eloquence as to the future of America, Mrs. Murphy depre-
cates the fact that blood will flow, and seems to take a savage pleasure in the
thought that the Black will be the victim of a race war.

Blood will flow, but not by the seeking of the Black, and he will only participate in the fight when the government places in his hands arms for its protection. Meagre as is our intellectual capacity, we promise not to give the
whites an excuse for the wholesale slaughter of our people which Mrs. Murphy evidently thirsts to behold. Blood will flow! When labor and capital
become contending forces, the Black will float into the full enjoyment of citizenship. Blood will flow, for humanity sweeps onward, and God's purposes
never fail.

The testimony of ex-slaves as to good treatment received during bondage
would be utterly worthless, as the oath of a black man is valueless in our
courts of justice.

When we consider the fact that one of the safe guards of the institution of
slavery lay in obliterating all family ties and in eliminating from the slave's life
all family affection, it would be small cause for wonderment if the black
mother were entirely devoid of feeling for her offspring. Mere vegetation
without consciousness was the plan mapped out for modelling "good
Negroes." Happily the plan failed, for our mothers are the bulwarks of the
race whom we love, revere, and delight to honor.

Parental brutality was on the side of the fathers of the beautiful octoroons
who made the auction sales interesting, and at the same time filled the pockets
of "the courtliest, bravest race of knightly, stalwart men," and also, incidentally
"set women (white) upon their rightful pedestals and kept them there." These
men were totally devoid of the feelings quite common to the brute creation for
its offspring. If the springs of affection had failed sometimes among the blacks,
small wonder when we consider that the master was the slave's god who could
do no wrong, and that the white pastors of the plantations taught the slaves the
duty of master-worship to the exclusion of God-worship.

In conclusion, Mrs. Murphy's arguments appear to the writer puerile and
pointless in whatever light we may view them. As a representative of the most
scholarly of living races she shows lamentable ignorance of the commonest
scientific and historical facts. But more than all else it is borne in upon us by
this attack that the foundation stones of the Republic are tottering. Woman,
gentle, refined woman, who governs the home and whose influence is all
potent with husband and father and brother and son and daughter, whose
thoughts and examples are to rule our future governors and presidents, has
stooped from her high pedestal to the mire of falsehood to crush a proscribed
people lying helpless at the feet of Christendom.

Ethiopia fell because of her arrogance and her stiff-necked idolatry.
Scarcely a sign of her ancient splendor can be found today, and low in the
dust of humiliation lie her suffering children. Egypt fell, and so did Greece.
Rome fell. Why these happenings?

Because Omnipotence was wearied by the injustice of man. History repeats itself. For God will visit us in judgment, and in the last hour when He seems to have left nothing undone that He could do for His vineyard, we still forget justice and judgment; none calling for justice, nor any in the high places of government pleading the cause of the poor, the very poorest of the poor, the despised and humiliated Negro.

Rome conquered the world, and was finally swallowed up by the world which she conquered.[17] NEVER GIVE UP THE BALLOT.

SOURCE *A Primer of Facts Pertaining to the Early Greatness of the African Race and the Possibility of Restoration by its Descendants* (Cambridge, Mass.: P. E. Hopkins, 1905).

17. Hopkins used this passage in the first installment of *Furnace Blasts*.

PART IX

Published Orations (1905–1911)

This section features two orations that Hopkins delivered at Boston centenaries for abolitionists William Lloyd Garrison and Charles Sumner. Both speeches were published shortly after she delivered them. Her 1905 speech at a Garrison centenary appeared in the *Boston Guardian* (the source for this anthology), and in an abbreviated form in a pamphlet whose title, *The Anti-Slavery Cause of Today*, expressed her ongoing belief that the abolitionist struggle was unequivocally germane in the twentieth century. Her 1911 speech at a Sumner centenary organized by Trotter affirms that Hopkins maintained a public persona, and remained active in the Boston progressive community even though she was not employed full-time as a writer or editor. During this period, Hopkins returned to oratory, which she had pursued in the 1890s. Her speeches venerated abolitionists, not out of nostalgia, but to reclaim the relevance of their work to the continuing struggle for equal rights.

Address at the
Citizens' William Lloyd Garrison Centenary Celebration
(December 11, 1905)

I count it, this afternoon, the greatest honor that will ever come to me that I am permitted to stand in this historic hall and say one word for the liberties of my race. I thought to myself how dare I, a weak woman, humble in comparison with these other people. Yesterday I sat in the old Joy street church and you can imagine my emotions as I remembered my great grandfather begged in England the money that helped the Negro cause, that my grandfather on my father's side, signed the papers with Garrison at Philadelphia. I remembered that at Bunker Hill my ancestors on my maternal side poured out their blood. I am a daughter of the Revolution, you do not acknowledge black daughters of the Revolution but we are going to take that right.

The conditions which gave birth to so remarkable a reformer and patriot were peculiar. The entire American Republic had set itself to do evil, and its leading forces, wealth, religion and party, joined the popular side and threatened the death of Liberty in the Republic. But the darkest hour was but a herald of the dawn. No great reform was ever projected or patronized by any powerful organization or influential individual at the outset. Reformation always begins in the heart of a solitary individual; some humble man or woman unknown to fame is lifted up to the level of the Almighty's heartbeats where is unfolded to him what presently must be done. Thus it was that after the imposition of the colonization scheme, the issuing of Walker's *Appeal,* and his own imprisonment at Baltimore, the poor and obscure Newburyport printer's boy, without reputation, social or political influence, or money, inaugurated the greatest reform of the nineteenth century, and within one year of the first issue of the *Liberator,* the entire country knew the name of Garrison. God had heard the prayers of suffering humanity. He said "enough." The hour struck on the horologe of Eternity, and the man was there. Side by side with Martin Luther's "Here I take my stand," is the "I will be heard" of William Lloyd Garrison. (Applause.)

In September, 1834, we are told that the Reformer received the greatest individual help that ever came to him during his life, when he married Miss Eliza Benson, daughter of a venerable philanthropist of Rhode Island, and thereafter woman's subtle, intuitive instinct added another sense to the wonderful powers of this remarkable man. Very shortly after their marriage, this brave woman was called to view the mobbing of her husband by the Boston "Broadcloth Mob." She stepped from a window upon a shed at the moment of his extremest danger, being herself in danger from the rioters. His hat was lost, and brickbats were rained upon his head, while he was hustled along in the direction of the tar-kettle in the next street. The only words that escaped from the white lips of the young wife were: "I think my husband will not deny his principles; I am sure my husband will never deny his principles. I am sure my husband will never deny his principles" The same spirit of encouragement still exists in women. What dangers will not a woman dare for the support and comfort of husband, father or brother? Not so long ago, when a Boston young man of color was hustled and beaten and jailed for upholding free speech and independent thought, he was sustained and comforted by the words of a sister: "Remember, this is not disgrace, but honor. It is for principle—it is for principle." (Applause.)

Mr. Garrison went about his work against slavery with tremendous moral earnestness. At first he advocated gradual emancipation, but after his baptism of injustice in a Baltimore jail his sentiments changed to the startling doctrine of immediate and unconditional emancipation. Gradual emancipation was a popular and inoffensive doctrine, a safe shore from which to view freedom for the Blacks. It is analogous with the startling propaganda of disfranchisement, or gradual enfranchisement after the Afro-American has proved himself fit for the ballot. We remember that history records the broken promises of freedom given by the Southern States to the blacks of Southern regiments in the Revolutionary War. Those men earned their freedom, proved their right to manhood, but at the close of the war were told that, "You have done well, boys, now get home to your masters." The time will never come for the enfranchisement of the black if he depends upon an acknowledgement from the south of his worthiness for the ballot. (Applause.) As if the faithfulness of the black man to this government from the Revolution until this day, the blood freely shed to sustain Republican principles in every war waged against the Republic, the gentle, patient docility with which we have borne every wrong, were not proof of our fitness to enjoy what is right. (Applause.)

Mr. Garrison lived to see his cause triumph in the emancipation of the slave, and died believing that the manhood rights of every citizen of the United States were secured then and forever. But the rise of a younger generation, the influence of an unconquered south, and the acquiescence of an ease-loving north that winks at abuses where commercial relations and manufactures flourish and put money in the purse, have neutralized the effects of the stern policy of these giants of an earlier age.

Great indeed was the battle for the abolition of slavery, but greater far will be the battle for manhood rights.

Let us hope that this timely review of the noble words and deeds of Garrison and his followers, may rekindle within our breasts the love of liberty. Were Mr. Garrison living in this materialistic age, when the price of manhood is a good dinner, a fine position, a smile of approval and a pat on the back from the man of influence, of a fat endowment, again, would he cry aloud, "The apathy of the people is enough to make every statue leap from its pedestal, and to hasten the resurrection of the dead."[1]

Here in Faneuil hall, let us vow, as the greatest tribute we can pay to Mr. Garrison's memory, to keep alive the sacred flame of universal liberty in the Republic for all races and classes, by every legitimate means, petitions to individuals, to associations, to foreign governments, to legislatures, to congress, print and circulate literature, and let the voice of the agent and lecturer be constantly heard. Let us swear to be "as harsh as truth, and as uncompromising as justice." And let us bear in mind the beauty of doing all things for the upbuilding of humanity; persecution and intellectual development have broadened us until we can clearly see that if the blacks are downed in the fight for manhood, no individual or race will be safe within our borders. This government has welded all races into one great nation until now, what is good for the individual member of the body politic is good for all, and vice versa. Here where the south and its sympathizers have so strenuously denied the brotherhood of man, by our mixed population, God has proved his declaration, "Of one blood have I made all races of men to dwell upon the whole face of the earth together." This truth Mr. Garrison and his followers freely acknowledged in the beauty and purity of their lives and deeds.

SOURCE "Colored Woman Makes Chief Address," *Boston Guardian* 5.7 (Dec. 16, 1905): 4. Hopkins delivered her address at Faneuil hall as part of the 3:00 p.m. program on Monday, December 11, 1905. The *Guardian*'s extensive coverage of the program included a photograph of Hopkins above the fold on page one and a bold subheading announcing "Miss Hopkins' Stirring Address." The speech by "Miss P. E. Hopkins, Author Of *Contending Forces*, *Hagar's Daughter*, *Winona*, etc.," was reprinted in *The Anti-Slavery Cause of Today* (Boston: Garrison Centenary Committee of the Boston Suffrage League, 1906; *African American Perspectives: Pamphlets from the Daniel A. P. Murray Collection, 1818–1907*, Library of Congress, http://hdl.loc.gov/loc.rbc/lcrbmrp.t2614, May 11, 2005). The pamphlet excluded Hopkins's powerful first paragraph.

1. This quotation comes from William Lloyd Garrison's editorial in the first issue of *The Liberator* (1831). See Wendell Phillips Garrison and Francis Jackson Garrison, *William Lloyd Garrison, 1805–1879: The Story of His Life, Told by His Children* (New York: Century Company, 1885–1889), 1:225.

Address at *The Two Days of Observance of the One Hundredth Anniversary of the Birth of Charles Sumner* (January 6, 1911)

*M*iss Pauline E. Hopkins of Cambridge, author of *Contending Forces,* who represented the women of the race whom Mr. Sumner championed, said—:

Mr. Chairman, Ladies and Gentlemen:

There have been a few Americans whose characters we, as a race idealize and whose memories we idolize,—Senator Sumner was one of the few.

Centenary celebrations are good for many things: In the lapse of years the heat of passion passes and calm Reason weighs word and act in the balances of eternal justice and thus we are apt to reach the exact amount of good accomplished under certain conditions. The flight of time has but added laurels to Mr. Sumner's fame in spite of his detractors and the student of sociology is thrilled with enthusiasm over the record of this great life which is today's lesson. This man was an intellectual and moral giant with an added divinity that was almost Godlike: Perfect truth in the midst of hideous error, perfect rectitude in the midst of perjury, violence and fraud, perfect patience while encountering every species of gross provocation. But why try to enumerate his virtues,—we cannot detract from his fame; we can add nothing to his glory. Generations yet unborn shall say of him:

> He is gone;
> Gone; but nothing can bereave him
> Of the force he made his own
> Being here;
> And he wears a truer crown
> Than any wreath that man can weave him.[2]

Mr. Sumner was essentially a reformer—a herald of progress, for his aim was to better existing conditions; he hated evil and adored good. Hence arose the antagonism of a conservative North and South. But conservatism is a fundamental principle in social life. In church, state and society, conser-

---

2. Alfred Tennyson, "Ode on the Death of the Duke of Wellington" (1852).

vatism is the ruling force and it is the cause of the unrest and turmoil that has ushered in the twentieth century.

Conservatism protects existing conditions and perpetuates them, and dreads and resists the innovations of the reformer.

All heralds of progress—the men who have been of the most benefit in enlightening the world—have encountered the same difficulties from the materialist. Galileo, seeking the law of gravitation, Columbus sailing for the discovery of a New World, Franklin wresting the thunderbolt from the sky and Benjamin Butler transforming black slaves into contrabands of war—all suffered from the animosity of conservatism.

As a reformer Mr. Sumner was aggressive, looking toward the perfection of the future government—a new Republic without the blemish of slavery. But the conflict and the co-operation of these opposing forces has brought about whatever there may be of present harmony of the material with the ideal.

The stupendous energy of the Twentieth Century is sweeping us onward with frightful velocity we know not where. We believe that now is the psychological moment for the forward movement of the dark races upon the world's arena. Not with hostile intent for the white-souled Sumner taught us "there is nothing in hate, nothing in vengeance," but side by side with all other downtrodden people clasp hands in the good fight of all races up and no race down. Thus, and thus alone the Black man shall come into his own. Were Senator Sumner with us today, he would be in the forefront leading the forces engaged in the uplift of all humanity.

Mr. Sumner said when he pleaded for harmony between the races: "Much better will it be when two political parties compete for your vote, each anxious for your support. Only then will that citizenship by which you are entitled to the equal rights of all have its fruits. Only then will there be that harmony which is essential to a true civilization." Events have justified its prophecy.

Life today is the Negro question, Socialism, the Labor question, Woman Suffrage, New Nationalism, Child Labor, White Slavery, The New Thought, Christian Science—life is the loom, mind and weaver, thought the thread, our good and evil deeds the warp and woof, and the web is the character to posterity as Mr. Sumner bequeathed his to us. Call us then, no longer Negroes, that name so fraught with blood and tears and bitter memories of contemptuous tolerance—but call us Men, mighty factors in the solving of human problems.

The secret of evolution is profound. This American Republic was founded by the Almighty Economist who governs the great seas of progression and retrogression, tossing them hither and thither at his will by unexpected countercurrents. Here all races have found a refuge from persecution; here all races were represented among the Abolitionists; here all races are to be participants in the new order of things slowly evolving out of the present unrest.

> Therefore, not unconsoled, I wait in hope
> To see the moment when our righteous cause

Shall gain defenders zealous and devout
As they who now oppose us.[3]

Men of the National and New England Leagues, it is a charge of honor given into your hands by Mr. Sumner to be handed down from father to son, not to let the Civil Rights bill fail now or ever.

Give us the faith to kneel around
Our country's shrine and swear
To keep alive the sacred flame
    That Sumner kindled there![4]

SOURCE *The Two Days of Observance of the One Hundredth Anniversary of the Birth of Charles Sumner*, ed. Wm. Monroe Trotter (Boston: Boston Sumner Centenary Committee, 1911), 48–49. Hopkins delivered her address at Park Street Church as part of the 2:00 p.m. program on Friday, January 6, 1911.

3. William Wordsworth, "The Excursion. Book Fourth: Despondency Corrected" (1814).
4. Elijah William Smith, "Our Lost Leader," *Sumner Memorial Meeting* (Boston: Committee of Arrangements by Charles L. Mitchell, 1874), 29–31, quoted in William Wells Brown, *The Rising Son; or, The Antecedents and Advancement of the Colored Race* (1874; rev. ed., Boston: A. G. Brown, 1876), 554. Hopkins also quotes "Our Lost Leader" in her biographical essay, "Elijah William Smith: A Colored Poet Of Early Days."

PART X

Men of Vision *(1916)*

M *en of Vision* was published in February and March 1916 in both issues of the short-lived *New Era Magazine* that Hopkins started with Colored Co-operative Publishing Company founder Walter Wallace. The magazine's references to Hopkins's publications in the *Colored American Magazine* in its inaugural prospectus suggest a continuity of its predecessor's work. Even as she maintained her original vision from the early part of the century, she continued to read new works of black history, as evident in her use of William Ferris's *The African Abroad* (1913) in her installment on Mark R. De Mortie. For the second and final installment, she profiles Leonard A. Grimes, using Charles Emery Stevens's 1856 abolitionist account of the Anthony Burns case. As evident by her ongoing admiration of the attempted rescue of Burns (in which a state marshal was killed), Hopkins's commitment to the ideals of the radical abolitionist movement persisted until the end of her literary career. Yet the example of Burns, who was remanded to slavery, cautiously suggests an uncertain, rather than overly optimistic, outlook. Her contributions to the *New Era Magazine* represent her last known writings.

Vol. 1.   MARCH, 1916   No. 2.

NEW ERA MAGAZINE

AN ILLUSTRATED MONTHLY DEVOTED to the
WORLD-WIDE INTERESTS of the COLORED RACE

MISS IRA ALDRIDGE
(See p. 73)   London, England

NEW ERA PUBLISHING CO.
BOSTON, MASSACHUSETTS.

15 Cents a Copy $1.50 a Year

12. The March 1916 cover of the second issue of the *New Era Magazine* featured Amanda Ira Aldridge, the youngest daughter of actor Ira Aldridge, who was an accomplished composer, singer, and teacher in London, England. Courtesy of Moorland-Spingarn Research Center, Howard University.

This series will include the lives of those men of the race who have clearly demonstrated by their achievements that they are really "Men of Vision," and the entire series will be fully illustrated.

"Where there is no vision, the people perish."

—Bible.[1]

NO. 1
Mark Réné De Mortie
Born May 8, 1829, at Norfolk, Va.;
died at Newport, R.I., Sept. 3, 1914

Mark Réné De Mortie was a race man of distinct individuality, generously endowed with the humble virtue called mother wit, and he raised himself to power and wealth by force of character alone, for although born free that was a signal disadvantage; free-born colored men of his time were hampered by every difficulty attending life and only men of signal ability and prophetic insight had the courage to live as becomes free men uncompromising in their allegiance to the doctrine of human rights as set forth in the Declaration of Independence.

It is an unquestionable fact that the colored men who took the liberty denied them and followed the North Star blindly were of the same class as the hardy Puritans—men whose dauntless courage should be inspiring to the young people of the present generation. It is the fashion to ridicule the idealist—call him a dreamer and mock his aspirations but we have yet to realize another fact: Idealism and materialism were twin-born and one does not exist without the other. The fugitive slave dreamed of a paradise where all men were free and his dear ones were his own by right of love divine; did he dare to make these dreams known, death was his portion; nevertheless, the dream was realized. Columbus also dreamed and saw visions under the very shadow of the Spanish Inquisition, and *his* dreams came true; so with Newton and other adventurous visionaries of olden times. The materialistic world owes its colossal modern vigor, its very being to the visions of the dreamers whom it is the fashion to ridicule.

Knowing how to read and write, but practically uneducated and penniless, without the application of this or that elaborate law of eugenics or other scientific training warranted to manufacture men, this man made himself invaluable to his people, and also to the United States Government at a critical period in its history.

1. Proverbs 29:18.

When he was eighteen years of age, Mr. De Mortie became interested in the work of "Dr." Harry Lundy, an uneducated free man, living in Norfolk, whose business was running off slaves by the underground railroad and he took charge of Dr. Lundy's large correspondence with the abolitionists. We give the remarkable story in Mr. De Mortie's own words:

I continued with Dr. Lundy about four years, rescuing a great number of men and women, sending some twenty slaves to Dr. Tobias at Philadelphia, who forwarded them to Canada, and others direct to New Bedford, Mass., by ships. I would conceal one or two men at a time in a vessel bound for the north, paying the captain or steward twenty-five dollars for a man and fifty dollars for a woman disguised as a man; only one woman at a time could be taken as the risk was much greater than with a man. The slaves paid this money with one exception. In 1851, I went to Boston and met Mr. Lewis Hayden; I told him that many more men would run away had they the means and that one man had been trying to save the money for a year. When I returned to Norfolk, Mr. Hayden gave me twenty-five dollars for this man, and I hired Captain Hunt of New Bedford to take the fugitive with him. He was known in slavery as Tom Speatley, locksmith and lamplighter, but he changed his name after he became free.

After this, we helped many more to escape, including Maria Augusta who went to Boston. I also attempted to help Sally Waller, known in New Bedford as Sally Jackson, to reach her brother in Boston, William Dunn, but through a letter written by Dunn to me, which was intercepted by her master, I came very near being imprisoned and was obliged to leave the South myself.

I then went to Boston and opened a shoe store in partnership with William Dunn at No. 127 Cambridge Street. Efforts were made to have Governor Clifford of Massachusetts return me South as a fugitive from justice, my crime being running off slaves or stealing "property," but the governor would not acknowledge property in slaves. My counsel were Lawyers Benjamin F. Hallett, John A. Andrew and Benjamin F. Butler, the latter told me to arm myself with a pistol, go to my store, and attend to my business, keeping near my money drawer, where I must place the pistol, and if a suspicious party entered the store whom I thought might wish to arrest me, to *use it* for it was better to be tried for murder in Massachusetts than for running off slaves in Virginia.

In 1853 I entered politics with the Free Soil Party. In 1854 I allied myself with the Know-Nothing Party in company with the Rev. Leonard A. Grimes, Lewis Hayden, Dr. John S. Rock and Dr. John B. Smith. The colored voters recognized us as the leading colored politicians of the time. The Know-Nothing Party wanted our support for the sake of the colored vote and it succeeded in wiping out all other parties, including the Democrats, Whigs and Free Soilers. Most of the Free Soilers in the State joined the Know-Nothings, which was a secret political party, in order to make it anti-slavery. After the election the executive committee of the Know-Nothings appointed a committee of three members of the legislature (Dr. J. M. Stone, Mr. Charles W. Slack and Mr. John L. Swift, known in the legislature as the three S's) to wait upon the five named colored men (including myself) and ask us what we desired in behalf of the colored people. Our answer was: *Mixed schools*. The committee assured us that they would do all in their power to have our desire gratified. Boston was then the only city in the State that proscribed colored people in the schools. There was but one schoolhouse in Boston which all the colored children in the city, including those in East Boston, were obliged to attend, and that was at the corner of Smith Court and Belknap Street (now Joy Street). William C. Nell, Benjamin F. Roberts and others had been agitating equal school rights for years previously. In January, 1855, when the legislature met, true to the promise made the Rev. L. A. Grimes, Lewis Hayden, Dr. John B. Smith, John S. Rock and myself, a bill was introduced requiring all children to attend the school in the ward where they lived. The bill passed during the session, and in the fall of that year colored children were admitted to all the schools.

Lewis Hayden, Benjamin F. Roberts and I, with others, secured the removal of the abbreviation "Col." (Colored) which was always attached to a colored man's name on the voting lists.

In 1854, when Anthony Burns was arrested in Boston and remanded to slavery, a number of men, including Lewis Hayden, George T. Downing, Deacon James Scott, Nathaniel Butler, T. W. Higginson, stormed the southwest door of the court house in an attempt to rescue the prisoner. We failed, owing to the killing of Deputy Marshall Batchelder, and the crushing of many in the riot.

In 1856 and 1857, Benjamin F. Roberts and I got employment for colored men, by the city of Boston, as laborers.

A political organization, known as the West Boston Wide-Awakes, consisting of 144 uniformed and equipped men of color, John C. Coburn, commander, paraded with similar white organizations in order to arouse the enthusiasm of the voters and secure the election of our loved Lincoln.

About this time events moved rapidly and one stirring episode followed fast upon another until the call came for colored troops. Thus, in 1863, I was asked to accept the position of Sutler of the 54th Massachusetts Colored Troops by Governor John A. Andrew. I accepted and was appointed by Col. R. G. Shaw. It was a position requiring the expenditure of considerable ready money, and not having available funds, I offered an equal partnership to Joseph Paul Whitfield, a New England black man, who had located in Buffalo, New York, and accumulated about sixty thousand dollars in money and real estate. Mr. Whitfield accepted my offer and chartered a ship and stocked it with supplies of all kinds and we sailed with the regiment.

The 54th sailed from Boston on May 28, 1863, and was without pay for eighteen months owing to a law passed by Congress giving the United States Colored Troops seven dollars per month. But the 54th had enlisted as a part of the Massachusetts quota and was not affected by this law, but had been promised thirteen dollars per month, the same amount paid to the white soldiers of the State. When this money was refused the colored men by the United States quartermaster, I told the men in my regiment not to accept the seven dollars and I would give them credit to the amount of two dollars per month if they would stand firm for the amount they had enlisted for. They took this advice and after a wait of eighteen months they received their pay at the rate of thirteen dollars per month, the original amount promised them. They owed us about $14,000, which they paid like men. The 54th had but three pay days during the war; they were mustered out in 1865.

At the close of the war returning to civil life, I opened a tailoring establishment at No. 1 Cambridge Street, Boston, nearly opposite the Revere House. Business was good and I made money.

In January, 1868, the white laborers at the Boston & Albany Railroad struck on a Saturday, and on Sunday morning Judge Russell, a director of the road, called Lewis Hayden and myself into consultation to see if we could get 120 able-bodied colored men to fill the places of the strikers. Up to that time no colored laborers had been employed by that road as freight handlers. We sent notices to all the colored churches asking able-bodied men desiring work to meet us at the rooms of the Union Progressive Association, corner of Cambridge and Chambers Streets at 5 o'clock that afternoon. We enrolled 120 names, the men promising to meet us at the rear of the United States Hotel at 7 o'clock on Monday morning. I reported to Judge Russell, and on Monday morning marched 120 men up the stairs at the depot. Before the men went to work, it was stipulated that they should receive the same pay as had the men who struck and retain their positions as long as they did their work well. The superintendent was willing to agree to this but could make no binding promises until Vice President Chapin arrived from Worcester. He came about noon, agreed to our demands and the men went to work.

Going to Chicago, in 1868, to the Soldiers' National Convention as a delegate when General U. S. Grant was nominated for the presidency, I liked the western metropolis so much that I sold out my investments in Boston and went into the real estate business in Chicago with John Jones of that city. Then becoming interested in the sassafras oil business, I spent my winters in Virginia.

I married Miss Cordelia Downing, a daughter of the Hon. George T. Downing, and located in Virginia, interesting myself in the schools and politics. I was a successful candidate for the Fourth Congressional District, but was deprived of my seat by fraud. I was made deputy collector of internal revenue while there and went as an alternate to the Chicago National Convention in 1880.

When I went to Nottaway County there were but seven colored schools taught by white teachers; when I left there were fourteen colored schools all taught by colored teachers with one exception.

After my oil sassafras factory and saw mill, valued at $6,000, were burned, having no insurance, I sold part of the land and returned to Boston in 1887 and resumed the tailoring business.[2]

The colored leadership had now fallen into other hands, but when a meeting was called at the North Russell Street Church, because of the delay by Governor Ames in signing the $10,000 appropriation bill passed by the legislature for the erection of a monument to Crispus Attucks, I went and was appointed one of a committee to wait upon the governor. The governor finally signed the bill.

About this time the admirers of Wendell Phillips had formed the Wendell Phillips Memorial Building Association. Gen. Benjamin F. Butler was president, Rev. A. A. Miner was the active president, Rev. Jesse H. Jones was the vice-president, Ex-Governor J.Q.A. Brackett was treasurer, Mr. John Latham, secretary, and Mark R. De Mortie was one of the advisory board. At Dr. Miner's death the Rev. Jesse H. Jones succeeded him. Finding that we had not sufficient funds to accomplish the object for which the association was formed the advisory board voted to establish two scholarships—one at Harvard and one at Tufts, to be competed for from the writings of Wendell Phillips. We also placed a bust of Wendell Phillips in Bates Hall of the Boston Public Library. I was the only active colored member and attended all the meetings.

During the period when the Hon. William H. Moody of Haverhill was attorney for the Commonwealth of Massachusetts, Mr. George T. Downing, Mr. Edward E. Brown and I were invited by a committee of Haverhill citizens to go to Haverhill and take part in a public meeting—an anti-lynching meeting—to be held on a Sunday afternoon in the city hall, at which the mayor would preside. Mr. Moody was one of the speakers, and said that were he a congressman he would introduce a bill against lynching. Messrs. Downing, Brown and I immediately got busy and created sentiment that sent Mr. Moody to Congress. Then Mr. Downing wrote him repeatedly, reminding him of his speech at Haverhill. Finally Mr.

2. William Ferris, *The African Abroad; or, His Evolution in Western Civilization, Tracing His Development Under Caucasian Milieu* (1913; repr., New York: Johnson Reprint Corporation, 1968), 2:709–713.

Moody did introduce a bill against lynching, which is the Moody Anti-Lynching Bill, 57th Congress, 1st Session, House Representatives (H.R.) 4572, in the House of Representatives, December 10, 1901.

After the bill had been introduced and before it had been acted upon, President Roosevelt had Mr. Moody resign as congressman in order to accept a position in the Cabinet as one of his secretaries.

I have been spared to be one of the organizers of the Colored National League, to be chairman of the Citizens' Committee of the William Lloyd Garrison Centennial and to preside over the afternoon session of the Centennial at Faneuil Hall. "Mine eyes have seen the glory of the coming of the Lord." My work is done.[3]

So ends this record of an active life of love for humanity.

Mr. De Mortie was paralyzed for a number of years before his death and lived with his wife at the home of his son-in-law, Dr. Marcus Wheatland of Newport, R.I., who married Miss Irene De Mortie.

> O Freedom! thou are not as poets dream,
> A fair young girl with light and delicate limbs,
>
>   . . .
>
> A bearded man,
> Armed to the teeth art thou . . .
> Merciless power has dug thy dungeon deep;
> And his swart armorers, by a thousand fires
> Have forged thy chain; yet, while he deems thee bound,
> The links are shivered, and the prison walls
> Fall outward.[4]
>
> ———
>
> The height by great men reached and kept,
>   Were not attained by sudden flight,
> But they, while their companions slept,
>   Were toiling upward in the night.
>   —Longfellow.[5]

SOURCE "Men of Vision: I. Mark Réné De Mortie," *New Era Magazine* 1.1 (Feb. 1916): 35–39.

3. For Mark De Mortie's speech at the Garrison Centennial, where Hopkins was a speaker, see De Mortie, "Introductory Remarks of Mr. De Mortie," *Boston Guardian*, December 15, 1905, 4.
4. William Cullen Bryant, "The Antiquity of Freedom" (1842). Hopkins uses lines from "The Antiquity of Freedom" as the epigraph to the second chapter of *Contending Forces*.
5. Henry Wadsworth Longfellow, "The Ladder of St. Augustine" (1858).

A Series of Articles on the lives of those men of the race who have clearly demonstrated by their achievements that they are really "Men of Vision."

"Where there is no vision, the people perish."

—Bible.

NO. 2
Rev. Leonard Andrew Grimes

A better subject for a history can scarcely be imagined than the life we are transcribing. It possesses a strong element of romance and is a splendid example of successful individual effort working for the uplift of others as well as of self. The lessons we learn from it are many, not the least of which is being shown how good men may become perverted, deluded and brutalized by the constant violation of the humane laws of Infinity, as outlined in the experiences of Reverend Grimes in the case of Anthony Burns.

It is true slavery is no more, but there are other and as sure ways of ruining a race of people. The modern colored citizen is afflicted by segregation, even as the old-timers were by slavery—ostracism and its attendant evils, the humiliating knowledge that, in general, the public on the highway, in assemblies and employment, shrink from us as from contaminating lepers. It was against just such conditions that Leonard Andrew Grimes fought during an eventful life.

Born in Loudoun County, Virginia, in the midst of slavery, of free parents, Leonard Grimes was subjected to all the disabilities that his race had to endure at the South although only slightly connected by blood with the oppressed race. The Rev. Justin D. Fulton, with whom he was intimately associated during his ministry, loved to tell how puzzled the hotel keepers were as to which of the twain was the colored man and which the white man. When asked to decide the matter themselves, they invariably picked out Reverend Grimes for the white man and Dr. Fulton for the colored man, much to the latter's delight.

Left an orphan at the tender age of ten years, he was placed in the charge of an uncle, but his new home was not a pleasant one. Being taken to his native place on a visit, he refused to return to his uncle and went to reside in Washington, D.C., where he passed several years, first as a butcher's boy in the public market and then as an apothecary's clerk. Finally he attracted the favorable notice of a slaveholder who persuaded him to enter his service for hire. He became this man's confidential servant and a favorite with the entire family. He was offered the post of overseer with a large salary, but refused to have anything to do with the great crime of slavery.

The business of his employer often called for long journeys through the Southern States, and young Grimes accompanied him. On one of these occasions, as they were riding through a patch of North Carolina forest, the screams of a woman was borne to their ears. On reaching the spot, they saw a female slave naked to the waist being lashed by an overseer with a heavy thong. Her back was barred by red stripes from which the blood had collected in a pool beneath her feet. The employer of Grimes was a humane man and drawing his pistol demanded the overseer to stop or he would shoot him on the spot. The man replied that the woman was lazy and would not work. "My baby was dying, and will be dead before I see it again," interposed the wretched mother by way of excuse.

This scene bred an abhorrence of slavery in young Grimes. It was the first time that he had seen any of the atrocities of slavery. His physical system became disordered from dwelling upon the incident and he became sick. Then and there he resolved to fight the institution of slavery.

He soon had an opportunity to practice his purpose. A female slave on a neighboring plantation received thirty lashes for attending a religious meeting, and fled to the plantation of Grimes' employer, who owned her husband. Grimes very speedily put her on the road to Canada, and her husband soon followed her.

Leaving the man who had employed him so long, he went to Washington, D.C., and invested his savings in one or two carriages and horses, and set up in business as a hackman. He prospered and was soon well known in that line of business. His carriages were in demand by the wealthiest people of the Capital and at the same time he was assisting fugitives to the North or to Canada.

At length, the wife and seven children of a free Negro were to be sold to a Southern trader. In his distress, the husband and father applied to Mr. Grimes for aid, and under the cover of night, Mr. Grimes went thirty miles into Virginia and brought the family away and put them on the road to Canada. Three months after, Mr. Grimes was arrested, taken to Virginia and tried for the offence of running off slaves. The jury found him guilty, not according to the evidence, but to save themselves and the prisoner from mob law. The infuriated mob surrounded the Court House and were held back by the military force only. The sentence was hard labor in State prison at Richmond, Va., for two years. There he experienced the change of heart that makes a man new in spirit, and like Paul and Silas, began preaching the Word to all who would listen. Upon returning to Washington he abandoned the livery-stable business and took up humbler employments such as jobbing with a furniture team. Receiving permission to preach by a council of which the President of Columbian College was the moderator, he sought a home in the free North, settling in New Bedford, Massachusetts.[6]

Meanwhile a dispute had arisen among the members of the "First Independent Baptist Church," known to us of these present years as the St. Paul Baptist

6. Charles Emery Stevens, *Anthony Burns: A History* (Boston: John P. Jewett and Company, 1856), 203–207. Although Hopkins knew William Wells Brown's profiles of Grimes in *Black Man* and *Rising Son*, Stevens is her main source. Stevens acknowledges the importance of Grimes to his book: "The Rev. L. A. Grimes bore a large share in the transactions here narrated." See Stevens, *Anthony Burns*, vii.

Church, and about twenty members drew out and formed a mission church. Very soon after this it was whispered about that Mr. Grimes, a very intelligent man, living in New Bedford, could be retained as a leader; accordingly he was invited to visit the small band of worshippers and so well were they pleased with him that he became their pastor, at the small salary of $100 a month.

There were very many fugitive slaves wandering in Boston without a church home, and these Reverend Grimes gathered into the little church until the upper room on Belknap street was too small to hold them, and it became necessary to organize. On the evening of the 24th of November, 1848, the Twelfth Baptist Church was organized with Rev. Leonard A. Grimes as pastor.

Now the business eye of the pastor fell upon a lot on Southac Street; in the early part of 1849 the trustees purchased it.

Reverend Grimes had come to Boston an entire stranger, but he believed in his cause and knew that he would be successful in his desires. He had known Dr. Neale in Washington during his early ministry; they were boys together. When they met it was with mutual pleasure, and the Rev. Mr. Neale vouched for Brother Grimes, and thus he was able to gather about him a host of admirers and munificent gifts came in to him from every direction. A handsome and commodious structure began to rise from the foundation just as the fugitive slave act was passed; the membership of the church was scattered as the frightened fugitives fled to Canada. More than forty fled in this way, among them Shadrach, who finally escaped, but Sims was captured and returned to slavery. After the first fury of the storm had passed, Mr. Grimes set to work; he collected money and bought the members of his church out of slavery that they might return to the United States without fear, and soon, in spite of all these disasters, the church was finished and was dedicated on the very first day that Anthony Burns was put on trial before Commissioner Loring, and the Reverend Grimes immediately distinguished himself by devoting himself to the ransom of this last victim of the oppressor. Mr. Stevens says in his excellent account of the rendition of Anthony Burns:

"The account of Anthony Burns, of his arrest, of his voyage back to Virginia, of his imprisonment and of his sojourn in North Carolina was taken by me from his own lips after his return to Boston.... The Rev. L. A. Grimes bore a large part in the transactions, and I have relied chiefly upon his authority in recounting such matters as came within his personal cognizance...."[7]

In the evening of the 24th of May, 1854, Anthony Burns was arrested as a fugitive slave. He was in the employ of Coffin Pitts, who kept a clothing store on Brattle Street.[8] We cannot imagine the excitement which prevailed when it became known that another man—a fugitive slave—must be returned to bondage. The pursuers of Burns—Colonel Suttle and his allies—were thrown into a state of extreme terror by the angry demonstrations which they had provoked, and to avert the storm offered to sell Burns for $1200 on

7. Ibid., vi-vii.
8. Ibid., 15.

condition that he be first surrendered in order to vindicate the authority of the law for the rendition of fugitive slaves to their owners.[9]

Reverend Grimes was among those who heard the planter's statement. Approaching the counsel, he inquired upon what authority the statement had been made and if Colonel Suttle would not consent to receive the sum named and close a bargain *before* the surrender. The counsel thought not. Mr. Grimes then sought an interview with the marshal who referred him to the slave's owner. After a long parley and many wearisome arguments Suttle agreed to sell his slave *before* the surrender was made. Mr. Grimes responded immediately, "Between this time and ten o'clock to-night, I'll have the money ready for you; have the emancipation papers ready for me at that time."[10]

The morning was well advanced, and before the day closed twelve hundred dollars were to be raised, not one of which had yet been subscribed. Without resources himself, Mr. Grimes had to seek out others who might be disposed to contribute to the enterprise. Among others, he visited Mr. Abbott Lawrence. He found him greatly disturbed in mind. He denounced the Fugitive Slave Law as infamous and declared that he would have nothing to do with it; he would give no money to purchase the freedom of Burns because that would be an implied sanction of the law; but, if Mr. Grimes needed any money for his own use, he might draw on him for the required sum or more. Two gentlemen subscribed $100 each readily and promised to increase the subscription if necessary, another friend gave $50. Mr. Hamilton Willis, a broker on State Street, urged Mr. Grimes to obtain pledges for the amount, which he would honor by advancing the money upon these pledges. Mr. J. M. Williams, a native of Virginia, but then a merchant of Boston, subscribed one hundred dollars and promised to make up whatever the deficiency might be at the end of the day. At seven o'clock in the evening Mr. Grimes had obtained pledges for $800. After several hours more of work the required sum was secured and at half past ten the several parties met to complete the business of the sale. But first one objection and then another was advanced until at the hour of midnight the negotiations were stopped because of the advent of the Sabbath.[11]

It was agreed that negotiations should be resumed again on Monday morning, but when Mr. Grimes arrived at the Commissioner's office eager to complete his agreement, Colonel Suttle refused to sell, and the only thing remaining to be done was to wait until Burns had been returned to Virginia.

Mr. Grimes had been so sure of freeing Burns that a carriage was at the door most of the time in order to take him to his colored friends who anxiously waited his release from the slave power. Nothing was heard of Burns for some months after he was taken from Boston, and all feared that the worst

9. Ibid., 61–62.
10. Ibid., 62–63.
11. Ibid., 63–70.

had happened to the poor victim. At length, by accident, his hiding place was revealed to the anxious pastor and members of the Twelfth Baptist Church.

Rev. G. S. Stockwell, pastor of a Massachusetts church, accidentally got news of the whereabouts of Burns and immediately communicated the fact to Reverend Grimes. They set about getting subscriptions for buying him, intending to make it a joint affair, but eventually the whole business fell upon Mr. Grimes. He opened negotiations with Mr. McDaniel, the new owner of Burns, and it was agreed that for thirteen hundred dollars the master would bring Burns to Baltimore and deliver him to Mr. Grimes. After many fresh trials and many disappointments only overcome through the perseverance of the faithful clergyman, the money was collected and paid, and on February 27, 1855, Anthony Burns commenced his journey to Boston a free man.[12] All honor to Leonard Andrew Grimes!

When President Lincoln called for troops, the members of the Twelfth Baptist Church were willing and anxious to enlist, but an unjust proscription forbade such action. Reverend Grimes set himself to work earnestly to open a way for his young men to become defenders of the Union. He was a trusted and esteemed friend of Governor Andrew as he was of the men in the highest stations of life, and the good Governor heard his prayer, saw the President and finally persuaded him to send forth a colored regiment.

When the time came to enlist colored soldiers, so highly were the services of Leonard Grimes valued that the chaplaincy of the regiment was offered to him, but on account of his church he did not feel warranted in accepting the honor.

From 1865 to 1871, the Twelfth Baptist Church grew rapidly and it became necessary to improve the church building inside and out. This was done at great expense, and a new organ was installed also, at a cost of $2,500. Brother Grimes labored for those he loved and his satisfaction was supreme on the Sunday that the church was reopened, refitted from the basement up—beautiful to behold. He had toiled for that church as a father for a loved child, and no pastor's efforts were ever more supremely blessed. The debts of the church were all removed. The house was absolutely free from every incumbrance; the people owned their church. Still the membership grew and from twenty-three members it had now grown to six hundred. The pastor began to look about for another place to build a larger and more commodious place of worship.

It was then the latter part of 1873. A revival was in progress. Converts were pouring into the church. The heart of the pastor was overflowing with joy. Brother C. G. Swan remarked after the clergyman's death, that on the day he preached for Brother Grimes he never beheld a more heavenly face; it seemed that his soul was ripe for heaven. Those who saw him in the pulpit on the last Sunday that he spent on earth remarked the earnestness and impressiveness of his manner. On Wednesday, March 12, 1874, he took his usual gift of $100

12. Ibid., 202–210.

to the Home Mission Society; this money was to be used in the Freedmen's Fund. On Friday, March 14, 1874, he reached home just in time to breathe his last among his loved ones. The morning papers gave a full account and notice of his death:—

"The Rev. L. A. Grimes, the well-known and universally esteemed colored clergyman, died very suddenly last evening, at his residence on Everett Avenue, East Somerville, Mass. He had just returned from New York, where he had been to attend the meeting of the Baptist Board of Home Missions, of which he was a member. He had walked from the cars to his home and died within fifteen minutes of his arrival. The physicians pronounce it a case of apoplexy."

On the following Monday morning, at the ministers' meeting appropriate remarks were made, and resolutions drawn up. The following appeared in the daily papers:

The Monday-morning meeting of the Baptist ministers of Boston and vicinity was held at ten o'clock Monday, as is the weekly custom. After the devotional exercises, the committee to prepare resolutions on the death of the late Rev. Leonard A. Grimes made their report to the meeting. Pending the acceptance of the report remarks eulogizing the deceased were made by Rev. R. H. Neale, D.D., and others. The resolutions, which were thereupon given a place upon the records of the meeting, are as follows: In the death of Leonard A. Grimes, for twenty-seven years the pastor of the Twelfth Baptist Church of Boston, the city in which he lived, the race for which he labored have sustained an irreparable loss. The confrère of Daniel Sharp, Baron Stow, Phineas Stow, Nathaniel Colver, Rev. Mr. Graves of the *Reflector*, he was one whose coming might always be welcomed with the exclamation of our Saviour concerning Nathanael: "Behold an Israelite indeed in whom there is no guile." His last efforts were put forth for his race. He carried to the Board of the American Baptists Home Mission Society, of which he had been for many years an honored member, a large contribution from his church to help on Christ's work among the freedmen, and, on returning from New York, stopped at New Bedford to comfort a broken-hearted mother whose little child was dying, and then came to the city, and in fifteen minutes after crossing the threshold of his home passed on to God.

His death affected the ministry and churches as when "a standard bearer fainteth." His familiar face was ever welcome. His resolute bearing, his unswerving fidelity to Christ, to truth, to the church at large, and his own denomination in particular, and his life-long service as a philanthropist, his devotion to the interests of the Negro, to whom he was linked by ties of consanguinity and of sympathy, made him a felt power for good in our State and in our entire country. No man among us was more sincerely respected or more truly loved. His departure, while it came none too soon for the tired warrior, impoverishes us with the withdrawal of an all-embracing love, and leaves God's poor to suffer to an extent it is impossible to describe.

Resolved, That the death of this good minister of Jesus Christ imposes heavy responsibilities upon his surviving brethren. The interests of the race of which he was an honored representative are imperilled. Their noble champion has gone up higher; but no waiting Elisha saw the ascent and cried, "My father, my father, the chariot of Israel and the horsemen thereof," so who can hope to wear his mantel and continue his work?

Resolved, That we tender to his afflicted widow and to the church he had so long and faithfully served, this poor expression of our sympathy and this truthful evidence of our love.

Resolved, That the good of his race, just passing from the morning of emancipation into the noonday radiance of a liberty of which they have dreamed, and for which they have prayed, demands that a permanent record be made of this noble man of God.

The ministers' meeting adjourned after the reading of the foregoing resolutions to attend the funeral services which were to take place in Charles-street Church. At an early hour in the morning the body was placed in front of the altar in the church of the deceased, where it lay in state all the forenoon, and where appropriate services were conducted by Drs. Cheney, Fulton and others. Thousands of every grade and hue thronged the church to have a last fond look at the face so full of sunlight in life and so peaceful in death.

At one o'clock the remains were removed to Charles-street Church where the funeral services were conducted with a feeling of solemnity and impressiveness worthy of the sad occasion. The addresses of Drs. Neale and Fulton were full of tenderness and grief. Both of these gentlemen were, for many years, the intimate friends of the deceased. They were all associated together in a noble work for a number of years, and there were no hearts sadder than those of Brothers Neale and Fulton. Clergymen of every denomination were present, and the congregation contained men and women from all the walks of life. The funeral was the largest that ever took place in Boston. On the following Sabbath a number of Boston pulpits gave appropriate discourses upon the "Life and Character of the late L. A. Grimes." The most noticeable were those delivered by Rev. R. H. Neale, D.D., Rev. Justin D. Fulton, D.D., and Rev. Henry A. Cook.

Reverend and Mrs. Grimes had one son, John, who having a fine bass voice, became well-known as a vocalist. John Grimes died quite young. There was also one daughter, Miss Emma Grimes, who married Mr. Giles Robinson. She is survived by one son—Leonard Grimes Robinson of Windsor Street, Cambridge, Mass., who is the grandson of our distinguished subject.

Mr. and Mrs. Leonard Robinson have suffered many trials. They, with many other influential colored families, were victims of the disastrous Chelsea fire in 1908; in it they lost the records and souvenirs of their grandfather's life, together with their property.

The Boston Jamesons are closely allied with Reverend Grimes. The most distinguished member of this branch is Professor Sam Jameson, a musical genius, well-known at home and abroad as a brilliant solo pianist. At one time, Professor Jameson was the greatest educated colored instrumentalist in the race.

Other connections of the Grimes family are Mrs. Charles Henson, New Bedford; Mrs. George Glover, Roxbury; Mrs. George Carter, Mrs. Arnold Washington, Mrs. Gordon, all of Boston, and Dr. Miles Gordon of Springfield, Mass.

SOURCE "Men of Vision: II. Rev. Leonard A. Grimes," *New Era Magazine* 1.2 (Mar. 1916): 99–105.

SELECTED BIBLIOGRAPHY

Works by Pauline E. Hopkins

Allen, Pauline E. "One Scene from the Drama of Early Days." [c. 1870s]. Pauline E. Hopkins Papers, Franklin Library Special Collections, Fisk University, Nashville, Tenn.

Allen, Sarah A. "Converting Fanny." *New Era Magazine* 1.1 (Feb. 1916): 33–34.

———. *Hagar's Daughter. Colored American Magazine* 2.5–4.4 (Mar. 1901–Mar. 1902). Reprint in *The Magazine Novels of Pauline Hopkins*, 1–284.

———. "Latest Phases of the Race Problem in America." *Colored American Magazine* 6.4 (Feb. 1903): 244–251.

———. "Mr. Alan Kirkland Soga." *Colored American Magazine* 7.2 (Feb. 1904): 114–116.

———. "Mr. M. Hamilton Hodges." *Colored American Magazine* 7.3 (Mar. 1904): 167–169.

———. "A New Profession: The First Colored Graduate of the Y.M.C.A. Training School, Springfield, Mass." *Colored American Magazine* 6.9 (Sept. 1903): 661–663.

———. "The Test of Manhood: A Christmas Story." *Colored American Magazine* 6.2 (Dec. 1902): 113–119. Reprint in Ammons, *Short Fiction by Black Women*, 205–217.

Hopkins, Pauline E. Address. In *The Two Days of Observance of the One Hundredth Anniversary of the Birth of Charles Sumner*, edited by Wm. Monroe Trotter, 48–49. Boston: Boston Sumner Centenary Committee of the New England Suffrage League and the Massachusetts Branch of the National Independent Political League, 1911.

———. "'As the Lord Lives, He is One of Our Mother's Children.'" *Colored American Magazine* 6.11 (Nov. 1903): 795–801. Reprint in Ammons, *Short Fiction by Black Women*, 276–286.

———. "Bro'r Abr'm Jimson's Wedding: A Christmas Story." *Colored American Magazine* 4.2 (Dec. 1901): 103–112. Reprint in Ammons, *Short Fiction by Black Women*, 107–125.

———. "By Miss P. E. Hopkins, Author of *Contending Forces, Hagar's Daughter, Winona*, etc." In Moorfield Storey and others, *The Anti-Slavery Cause of Today*, 4–6. Boston: Garrison Centenary Committee of the Boston Suffrage League, 1906. Available online at *African American Perspectives: Pamphlets from the Daniel A. P. Murray Collection, 1818–1907*, Library of Congress. http://hdl.loc.gov/loc.rbc/lcrbmrp.t2614.

———. "Colored Woman Makes Chief Address." *Boston Guardian*, December 16, 1905, 4.

———. *Contending Forces: A Romance Illustrative of Negro Life North and South.* Boston: Colored Co-operative Publishing Company, 1900. A facsimile of the first edition with an introduction by Richard Yarborough. New York: Oxford University Press, 1988.

———. "*The Dark Races of the Twentieth Century* I: Oceanica: The Dark-Hued Inhabitants of New Guinea, the Bismarck Archipelago, New Hebrides, Solomon Islands, Fiji Islands, Polynesia, Samoa, and Hawaii." *Voice of the Negro* 2.2 (Feb. 1905): 108–115.

———. "*The Dark Races of the Twentieth Century* II: The Malay Peninsula: Borneo, Java, Sumatra, and the Philippines." *Voice of the Negro* 2.3 (Mar. 1905): 187–191.

———. "*The Dark Races of the Twentieth Century* III: The Yellow Race: Siam, China, Japan, Korea, Thibet." *Voice of the Negro* 2.5 (May 1905): 330–335.

———. "*The Dark Races of the Twentieth Century* IV: Africa: Abyssinians, Egyptians, Nilotic

Class, Berbers, Kaffirs, Hottentots, Africans of Northern Tropics (including Negroes of Central, Eastern, and Western Africa), Negroes of the United States." *Voice of the Negro* 2.6 (June 1905): 415–418.

———. "*The Dark Races of the Twentieth Century* VI: The North American Indian—Conclusion." *Voice of the Negro* 2.7 (July 1905): 459–463.

———. "A Dash for Liberty." *Colored American Magazine* 3.4 (Aug. 1901): 243–247. Reprint in Ammons, *Short Fiction by Black Women*, 89–98.

———. "Echoes from the Annual Convention of Northeastern Federation of Colored Women's Clubs." *Colored American Magazine* 6.10 (Oct. 1903): 709–713.

———. "Elijah William Smith: A Colored Poet of Early Days." *Colored American Magazine* 6.2 (Dec. 1902): 96–100.

[———.] "The Evils of Intemperance and Their Remedy." [c. 1874]. Pauline E. Hopkins Papers, Franklin Library Special Collections, Fisk University, Nashville, Tenn.

———. "*Famous Men of the Negro Race* I: Toussaint L'Overture [*sic*]." *Colored American Magazine* 2.1 (Nov. 1900): 9–24.

———. "*Famous Men of the Negro Race* II: Hon. Frederick Douglass." *Colored American Magazine* 2.2 (Dec. 1900): 121–132.

———. "*Famous Men of the Negro Race* III: William Wells Brown." *Colored American Magazine* 2.3 (Jan. 1901): 232–236.

———. "*Famous Men of the Negro Race* IV: Robert Browne [*sic*] Elliott." *Colored American Magazine* 2.4 (Feb. 1901): 294–301.

———. "*Famous Men of the Negro Race* V: Edwin Garrison Walker." *Colored American Magazine* 2.5 (Mar. 1901): 358–366.

———. "*Famous Men of the Negro Race* VI: Lewis Hayden." *Colored American Magazine* 2.6 (Apr. 1901): 473–477.

———. "*Famous Men of the Negro Race* VII: Charles Lenox Remond." *Colored American Magazine* 3.1 (May 1901): 34–39.

———. "*Famous Men of the Negro Race* VIII: Sargeant [*sic*] William H. Carney." *Colored American Magazine* 3.2 (June 1901): 84–89.

———. "*Famous Men of the Negro Race* IX: John Mercer Langston." *Colored American Magazine* 3.3 (July 1901): 177–184.

———. "*Famous Men of the Negro Race* X: Senator Blanche K. Bruce." *Colored American Magazine* 3.4 (Aug. 1901): 257–261.

———. "*Famous Men of the Negro Race* XI: Robert Morris." *Colored American Magazine* 3.5 (Sept. 1901): 337–342.

———. "*Famous Men of the Negro Race* XII: Booker T. Washington." *Colored American Magazine* 3.6 (Oct. 1901): 436–441.

———. "*Famous Women of the Negro Race* I: Phenomenal Vocalists." *Colored American Magazine* 4.1 (Nov. 1901): 45–53.

———. "*Famous Women of the Negro Race* II: Sojourner Truth." *Colored American Magazine* 4.2 (Dec. 1901): 124–132.

———. "*Famous Women of the Negro Race* III: Harriet Tubman ('Moses')." *Colored American Magazine* 4.3 (Jan.–Feb. 1902): 210–223.

————. "*Famous Women of the Negro Race* IV: Some Literary Workers." *Colored American Magazine* 4.4 (Mar. 1902): 276–280.

————. "*Famous Women of the Negro Race* V: Literary Workers." *Colored American Magazine* 4.5 (Apr. 1902): 366–371.

————. "*Famous Women of the Negro Race* VI: Educators." *Colored American Magazine* 5.1 (May 1902): 41–46.

————. "*Famous Women of the Negro Race* VII: Educators (Continued)." *Colored American Magazine* 5.2 (June 1902): 125–130.

————. "*Famous Women of the Negro Race* VIII: Educators (Concluded)." *Colored American Magazine* 5.3 (July 1902): 206–213.

————. "*Famous Women of the Negro Race* IX: Club Life among Colored Women." *Colored American Magazine* 5.4 (Aug. 1902): 273–277.

————. "*Famous Women of the Negro Race* X: Artists." *Colored American Magazine* 5.5 (Sept. 1902): 362–367.

————. "*Famous Women of the Negro Race* XII: Higher Education of Colored Women in White Schools and Colleges." *Colored American Magazine* 5.6 (Oct. 1902): 445–450.

————. "General Washington: A Christmas Story." *Colored American Magazine* 2.2 (Dec. 1900): 95–104. Reprint in Ammons, *Short Fiction by Black Women*, 69–82.

————. "Heroes and Heroines in Black: 1. Neil Johnson, America Woodfolk, Robert Small [*sic*], et al." *Colored American Magazine* 6.3 (Jan. 1903): 206–211.

————. "How a New York Newspaper Man Entertained a Number of Colored Ladies and Gentlemen at Dinner in the Revere House, Boston, and How the Colored American League Was Started." *Colored American Magazine* 7.3 (March 1904): 151–160.

————. *The Magazine Novels of Pauline Hopkins.* Edited by Hazel V. Carby. New York: Oxford University Press, 1988.

————. "*Men of Vision* I: Mark Réné De Mortie." *New Era Magazine* 1.1 (Feb. 1916): 35–39.

————. "*Men of Vision* II: Rev. Leonard A. Grimes." *New Era Magazine* 1.2 (Mar. 1916): 99–105.

————. "Munroe Rogers." *Colored American Magazine* 6.1 (Nov. 1902): 20–26.

————. "The Mystery Within Us." *Colored American Magazine* 1.1 (May 1900): 14–18. Reprint in Ammons, *Short Fiction by Black Women*, 21–26.

————. "The New York Subway." *Voice of the Negro* 1.12 (Dec. 1904): 605, 608–612.

————. *Of One Blood; or, The Hidden Self. Colored American Magazine* 6.1–6.11 (Nov. 1902–Nov. 1903). Reprint in *The Magazine Novels of Pauline Hopkins*, 439–621.

————. Pauline E. Hopkins to Cornelia A. Condict. *Colored American Magazine* (Mar. 1903): 399–400. Reprint in *Norton Anthology of African American Literature*, edited by Henry Louis Gates Jr. and Nellie McKay, 593–595. 1st ed. New York: Norton, 1997.

————. Pauline E. Hopkins to John E. Bruce, April 6, 1906. John E. Bruce Papers, Schomburg Center for Research in Black Culture, New York Public Library.

————. Pauline E. Hopkins to William Monroe Trotter, April 16, 1905. Pauline E. Hopkins Papers, Franklin Library Special Collections, Fisk University, Nashville, Tenn.

————. *Peculiar Sam; or, The Underground Railroad.* In Southern, *African American Theater*, 119–205; Hamalian and Hatch, *The Roots of African American Drama*, 100–123.

————. *A Primer of Facts Pertaining to the Early Greatness of the African Race and the Possibility of Restoration by its Descendants.* Cambridge, Mass.: P. E. Hopkins, 1905.

————. "Reminiscences of the Life and Times of Lydia Maria Child." *Colored American Magazine* 6.4 (Feb. 1903): 279–284; 6.5 (Mar. 1903): 353–357; 6.6 (May–June 1903): 454–459.

————. "A Retrospect of the Past." Chap. 1 of *Contending Forces. Colored American Magazine* 2.1 (Nov. 1900): 64–72.

————. "Talma Gordon." *Colored American Magazine* 1.5 (Oct. 1900): 271–290. Reprint in Ammons, *Short Fiction by Black Women,* 49–68.

————. *Topsy Templeton.* Pts. 1 and 2. *New Era Magazine* 1.1 (Feb. 1916): 9–20, 48; 1.2 (Mar. 1916): 75–84.

————. "Whittier, The Friend of the Negro." *Colored American Magazine* 3.5 (Sept. 1901): 324–330.

————. *Winona. Colored American Magazine* 5.1–5.6 (May 1902–Oct. 1902). Reprint in *The Magazine Novels of Pauline Hopkins,* 285–437.

————, ed. "Women's Department." *Colored American Magazine* 1.2 (June 1900): 118–123.

Shadrach, J. Shirley. "Charles Winter Wood; or, From Bootblack to Professor." *Colored American Magazine* 5.5 (Sept. 1902): 345–348.

————. "*Furnace Blasts* I: The Growth of the Social Evil Among All Classes and Races in America." *Colored American Magazine* 6.4 (Feb. 1903): 259–263.

————. "*Furnace Blasts* II: Black or White—Which Should Be the Young Afro-American's Choice in Marriage." *Colored American Magazine* 6.5 (Mar. 1903): 348–352.

————. "Mrs. Jane E. Sharp's School for African Girls." *Colored American Magazine* 7.3 (Mar. 1904): 181–184.

————. "Rev. John Henry Dorsey." *Colored American Magazine* 5.6 (Oct. 1902): 411–417.

————. "William Pickens, Yale University." *Colored American Magazine* 6.7 (July 1903): 517–521.

Works Cited

Adams, H. G. *God's Image in Ebony: Being a Series of Biographical Sketches, Facts, Anecdotes, etc., Demonstrative of the Mental Powers and Intellectual Capacities of the Negro Race.* London: Partridge and Oakey, 1854.

"Aged Writer Dies of Painful Burns." *Chicago Defender,* August 23, 1930, national edition, 1.

American Newspaper Directory. 34th year. New York: George P. Rowell, 1902.

American Newspaper Directory. 36th year. New York: George P. Rowell, 1904.

Ammons, Elizabeth, ed. *Short Fiction by Black Women, 1900–1920.* New York: Oxford University Press, 1991.

Andrews, William L. *The Literary Career of Charles W. Chesnutt.* Baton Rouge: Louisiana State University Press, 1980.

"Announcement." *Colored American Magazine* 1.4 (Sept. 1900): 197.

"Announcement and Prospectus of the *New Era Magazine.*" *New Era Magazine* 1.1 (Feb. 1916): 1–7.

"Annual Convention of the New England Federation of Woman's Clubs at Mt. Olivet Baptist Church, Thames St., Newport, R.I., Aug. 11, 1898." *National Association Notes* 2.4 (Sept. 1898): 4. Available online at *Records of the National Association of Colored Women's*

Clubs, 1895–1992, LexisNexis Primary Sources in African American History, http://www.lexis-nexis.com/histuniv.

Armistead, Wilson. *A Tribute For The Negro: Being a Vindication of the Moral, Intellectual, and Religious Capabilities of the Coloured Portion of Mankind; With Particular Reference to the African Race*. Manchester, England: William Irwin, 1848. Available online at *Documenting the American South*. University Library, University of North Carolina at Chapel Hill, 1999. http://docsouth.unc.edu/armistead/armistead.html.

"Art. IV. The Human Family." *Southern Quarterly Review* 11.1 (Jan. 1855): 116–174.

"Attorney General Parker Has the Case." *Boston Guardian*, August 23, 1902, 1.

Barber, J. Max. "The Morning Cometh." *Voice of the Negro* 1.1 (Jan. 1904): 37–38.

Bergman, Jill. "'Everything we hoped she'd be': Contending Forces in Hopkins Scholarship." *African American Review* 38.2 (2004): 181–199.

Bradford, Sarah H. *Harriet: The Moses of Her People*. New York: Geo. R. Lockwood and Son, 1886. Available online at *Documenting the American South*. University Library, University of North Carolina at Chapel Hill, 1995. http://docsouth.unc.edu/harriet/harriet.html.

———. *Scenes in the Life of Harriet Tubman*. Auburn, N.Y.: W. J. Moses, 1869. Available online at *Documenting the American South*. University Library, University of North Carolina at Chapel Hill, 2000. http://docsouth.unc.edu/neh/bradford/bradford.html.

Brooks, Gwendolyn. Afterword. In *Contending Forces*, by Pauline Hopkins, 403–409. Carbondale: Southern Illinois University Press, 1978.

Brown, Josephine. *Biography of an American Bondman, by his Daughter*. Boston: R. F. Wallcut, 1856. Reprint in *Two Biographies by African American Women*, edited by William L. Andrews. New York: Oxford University Press, 1991.

Brown, William Wells. *The Black Man: His Antecedents, His Genius, and His Achievements*. 2nd ed. New York: Thomas Hamilton, 1863. Available online at *Documenting the American South*. University Library, University of North Carolina at Chapel Hill, 1999. http://docsouth.unc.edu/brownww/brown.html.

———. *The Negro in the American Rebellion: His Heroism and His Fidelity*. Boston: Lee and Shepard, 1867.

———. *The Rising Son; or, The Antecedents and Advancement of the Colored Race*. 1874. Rev. ed. Boston: A. G. Brown, 1876.

Bruce, Blanche Kelso. *The Mississippi Election; Speech in the United States Senate, March 31, 1876*. Washington, 1876.

Bryce, James. "Thoughts on the Negro Problem." *North American Review* 153 (Dec. 1891): 641.

Bullock, Penelope L. *The Afro-American Periodical Press, 1838–1909*. Baton Rouge: Louisiana State University Press, 1981.

Burkett, Randall K., and Nancy Hall Burkett, eds. *Black Biography, 1790–1950: A Cumulative Index*. Alexandria, Va.: Chadwyck-Healey, 1991.

Carby, Hazel V. *Reconstructing Womanhood: The Emergence of the Afro-American Woman Novelist*. New York: Oxford University Press, 1987.

Carlyle, Thomas. *On Heroes, Hero-Worship, and the Heroic in History*. 1840. Project Gutenberg, 1997. http://www.gutenberg.org/dirs/etext97/heros10.txt.

Cerami, Charles. *Benjamin Banneker: Surveyor, Astronomer, Publisher, Patriot*. New York: John Wiley and Sons, 2002.

Chalmers, John Aitken. *Tiyo Soga: A Page of South African Mission Work.* Edinburgh: A. Elliot, 1877.

Child, Lydia Maria. *Letters of Lydia Maria Child.* Boston: Houghton, Mifflin, 1883. Reprint, New York: Negro Universities Press, 1969.

Clarke, James Freeman. *The Rendition of Anthony Burns: Its Causes and Consequences; A Discourse on Christian Politics, Delivered in Williams Hall, Boston, on Whitsunday, June 4, 1854.* Boston: Crosby, Nichols, 1854.

Clifford, Hugh. *In Court and Kampung.* 1897. Rev. ed. Singapore: Graham Brash, 1989.

"Col. William H. Dupree." *Colored American Magazine* 3.3 (July 1901): 228–231.

Combe, George. "To What Extent are the Miseries of Mankind Referable to Infringement of the Laws of Nature?" Chap. 5 in *The Constitution of Man Considered in Relation to External Objects.* 1828. 8th ed. Edinburgh: Maclachlan, Stewart, 1847. 127–330. Available online at *The History of Phrenology on the Web,* edited by John van Wyhe, 2002. http://pages.britishlibrary.net/phrenology/constitution/chapter05.html.

Daniel, Walter C. *Black Journals of the United States.* Westport, Conn.: Greenwood Press, 1982.

De Mortie, Mark R. "Introductory Remarks of Mr. De Mortie." *Boston Guardian,* December 15, 1905, 4.

Delany, Martin Robison. *Principia of Ethnology: The Origin of Races and Color, With an Archeological Compendium of Ethiopian and Egyptian Civilization, from Years of Careful Examination and Enquiry.* Philadelphia: Harper, 1879. Reprint as *The Origin of Races and Color.* Baltimore: Black Classic Press, 1991.

Doreski, C. K. "Inherited Rhetoric and Authentic History: Pauline Hopkins at the *Colored American Magazine.*" In Gruesser, *The Unruly Voice,* 71–97.

Douglass, Frederick. "Haiti and the United States: Inside History and the Negotiations for the Môle St. Nicolas." Pts. 1 and 2. *North American Review* 153 (Sept. 1891): 337–345; 153 (Oct. 1891): 450–459.

[Du Bois, W.E.B.] "The Colored Magazine in America." *Crisis* 5.1 (Nov. 1912): 33–35.

———. "Debit and Credit." *Voice of the Negro* 2.1 (Jan. 1905): 677.

———. W.E.B. Du Bois to William Monroe Trotter, March 15, 1905. In *The Correspondence of W.E.B. Du Bois: Selections, 1877–1934,* edited by Herbert Aptheker, 97–98. Vol. 1. Amherst: University of Massachusetts Press, 1973.

duCille, Ann. "Discourse and Dat Course: Postcoloniality and Afrocentricity." In *Skin Trade,* 120–135. Cambridge, Mass.: Harvard University Press, 1996.

Dunbar, Paul Laurence. "Is Higher Education for the Negro Hopeless?" *Philadelphia Times,* June 10, 1900. Reprint in *The Paul Laurence Dunbar Reader,* edited by Jay Martin and Gossie H. Hudson, 45–47. New York: Dodd, Mead, 1975.

Dworkin, Ira. "American Hearts: African American Writing on the Congo, 1890–1915." PhD diss., City University of New York, 2003.

"Editorial and Publishers' Announcements." *Colored American Magazine* 1.1 (May 1900): 60–64.

"Editorial and Publishers' Announcements." *Colored American Magazine* 4.4 (Mar. 1902): 335–336.

"Editorial and Publisher's Announcements." *New Era Magazine* 1.1 (Feb. 1916): 60.

Elliott, R. S. "The Story of Our Magazine." *Colored American Magazine* 3.1 (May 1901): 43–77.

Emerson, Ralph Waldo. *An Address Delivered in the Court-House in Concord, Massachusetts on 1st August, 1844, on the Anniversary of the Emancipation of the Negroes in the British West Indies.* Boston: J. Munroe, 1844.

———. *Essays: First and Second Series.* 1841; 1844. 2 vols. in 1. Boston: Houghton Mifflin, 1883. Available online at *Making of America.* Ann Arbor: University of Michigan Library, 2005. http://name.umdl.umich.edu/acj8800.0001.001.

Ewing, Quincy. *A Sermon on Lynching by the Rev. Quincy Ewing in St. James Episcopal Church, Greenville, Miss., August 11th, 1901.* New Orleans: Women's Christian Temperance Union of Louisiana, 1901.

Ferris, William. *The African Abroad; or, His Evolution in Western Civilization, Tracing His Development Under Caucasian Milieu.* 2 vols. New Haven, Conn.: Tuttle, Morehouse and Taylor Press, 1913. Reprint, New York: Johnson Reprint Corporation, 1968.

"A Few of the Good Things to be Found in the *Colored American Magazine* During the Year 1901." *Colored American Magazine* 2.1 (Nov. 1900): [ii-v].

Foster, Frances Smith, ed. *A Brighter Coming Day: A Frances Ellen Watkins Harper Reader.* New York: Feminist Press, 1990.

Fox, Stephen. *The Guardian of Boston: William Monroe Trotter.* New York: Atheneum, 1970.

Franklin, John Hope. *George Washington Williams: A Biography.* Chicago: University of Chicago Press, 1985.

Garrison, Wendell Phillips, and Francis Jackson Garrison. *William Lloyd Garrison, 1805–1879: The Story of His Life, Told by His Children.* 4 vols. New York: Century Company, 1885–1889.

Garrison, William Lloyd, Jr. "Industrial Education—Will it Solve the Negro Problem." *Colored American Magazine* 7.4 (Apr. 1904): 247–249.

Gilbert, Olive. *Narrative of Sojourner Truth, a Northern Slave, Emancipated from Bodily Servitude by the State of New York, in 1828.* Boston: J. B. Yerrinton and Son, 1850. Available online at *Documenting the American South.* University Library, University of North Carolina at Chapel Hill, 2000. http://docsouth.unc.edu/neh/truth50/truth50.html

Grady, Henry Woodfin, and Oliver Dyer. *The New South.* New York: Robert Bonner's Sons, 1890.

Gruesser, John Cullen, ed. *The Unruly Voice: Rediscovering Pauline Elizabeth Hopkins.* Urbana: University of Illinois Press, 1996.

Hale, Abraham. "On the Sakais." *The Journal of the Anthropological Institute of Great Britain and Ireland* 15.3 (1886): 285–301. Available online at JSTOR, http://links.jstor.org/sici?sici=0959–5295%281886%2915%3C285%3AOTS%3E2.0.CO%3B2-I.

Hale, Edward Everett. "Wanted, A School-House." *Outlook* 77.16 (Aug. 13, 1904): 912.

Haley, James T. *Afro-American Encyclopaedia; or, The Thoughts, Doings, and Sayings of the Race, Embracing Lectures, Biographical Sketches, Sermons, Poems, Names of Universities, Colleges, Seminaries, Newspapers, Books, and a History of the Denominations, Giving the Numerical Strength of Each. In Fact, It Teaches Every Subject of Interest to the Colored People, as Discussed by More Than One Hundred of Their Wisest and Best Men and Women.* Nashville, Tenn.: Haley and Florida, 1895. Available online at *Documenting the American South.* University Library, University of North Carolina at Chapel Hill, 2000. http://docsouth.unc.edu/church/haley/haley.html.

Hall, Charles Winslow. "The Funeral of Liberty." *Colored American Magazine* 1.1 (May 1900): 48–56.

Hamalian, Leo, and James V. Hatch, eds. *The Roots of African American Drama: An Anthology of Early Plays, 1858–1938.* Detroit: Wayne State University Press, 1991.

Hamedoe, S.E.F.C.C. "El Sr. Don Jose Rizal." *Colored American Magazine* 7.4 (Apr. 1904): 253–257.

Harlan, Louis R. "Booker T. Washington and the *Voice of the Negro,* 1904–1907." *The Journal of Southern History* 45.1 (Feb. 1979): 45–62.

———. *Booker T. Washington: The Wizard of Tuskegee, 1901–1915.* New York: Oxford University Press, 1983.

Harper, Frances Ellen Watkins. "Woman's Political Future." In *The World's Congress of Representative Women: A Historical Résumé for Popular Circulation of the World's Congress of Representative Women, Convened in Chicago on May 15, and Adjourned on May 22, 1893; Under the Auspices of the Woman's Branch of the World's Congress Auxiliary,* edited by May Wright Sewall, 2:433–437. Vol. 2. Chicago: Rand McNally, 1894.

Hawkins, William G. *Lunsford Lane; or, Another Helper from North Carolina.* Boston: Crosby and Nichols, 1863.

Hutchinson, John Wallace. *Story of the Hutchinsons (Tribe of Jesse).* 2 vols. Boston: Lee and Shepard, 1896. Available online at *History of the Hutchinson Family,* edited by Alan Lewis, 2005. http://www.geocities.com/hfsbook/storytofc.htm.

Hux, Roger K. "Lillian Clayton Jewett and the Rescue of the Baker Family, 1899–1900." *Historical Journal of Massachusetts* 19 (Winter 1991): 13–23.

"In Annual Convention." *Boston Guardian,* August 15, 1903, 1.

In Memoriam: Robert Morris, Sr. Boston, 1883.

"In the Editor's Sanctum." *Colored American Magazine* 7.5 (May 1904): 382–383.

"The Inauguration of Mr. Roosevelt." *Voice of the Negro* 2.4 (Apr. 1905): 215–216.

Jefferson, Thomas. Thomas Jefferson to Francois D'Ivernois, 1795. In *The Writings of Thomas Jefferson,* edited by Paul Leicester Ford, 7:5. 7 vols. New York: G. P. Putnam, 1892–1899.

Johnson, Abby Arthur, and Ronald Maberry Johnson. *Propaganda and Aesthetics: The Literary Politics of African-American Magazines in the Twentieth Century.* 1979. Amherst: University of Massachusetts Press, 1991.

Johnson, Edward A. *A School History of the Negro Race in America, from 1619 to 1890.* Raleigh, N.C.: Edwards and Broughton, 1890.

Keane, Augustus Henry. *Man, Past and Present.* London: Cambridge University Press, 1900.

Knight, Alisha. "Furnace Blasts for the Tuskegee Wizard: Revisiting Pauline Elizabeth Hopkins, Booker T. Washington, and the *Colored American Magazine.*" *American Periodicals,* Forthcoming.

Langston, John Mercer. *From Virginia Plantation to the National Capitol; or, The First and Only Negro Representative in Congress from the Old Dominion.* Hartford, Conn.: American Publishing Company, 1894. Reprint, New York: Arno Press, 1969.

Le Maire, Jacques-Joseph. *The Voyages of the Sieur Le Maire, to the Canary Islands, Cape-Verde, Senegal, and Gambia.* 1695. In *A Collection of Voyages and Travels, Consisting of Authentic Writers in Our Own Tongue, Which Have Not Before Been Collected in English, or Have*

Only Been Abridged in Other Collections, edited by Thomas Osborne, 2:597–623. 2 vols. London: T. Osborne, 1745.

Lewis, Leopold. *The Bells.* New York: Samuel French, 1871.

Lone, Stewart. *Army, Empire and Politics in Meiji Japan: The Three Careers of General Katsura Taro.* New York: St. Martin's, 2000.

Martineau, Harriet. *The Hour and the Man.* 3 vols. London: Edward Moxon, 1841. Reprint, New York: AMS Press, 1974.

McElrath, Joseph R., Jr., and Robert C. Leitz III. Introduction to *"To Be an Author": Letters of Charles W. Chesnutt, 1889–1905*, 3–23. Princeton: Princeton University Press, 1997.

McHenry, Elizabeth. *Forgotten Readers: Recovering the Lost History of African American Literary Societies.* Durham, N.C.: Duke University Press, 2002.

"Meeting of the Members of the Suffolk Bar." In *In Memoriam: Robert Morris, Sr.*, 11–23.

Meier, August. "Booker T. Washington and the Negro Press, with Special Reference to the *Colored American Magazine*." *Journal of Negro History* 38.1 (Jan. 1953): 67–90.

Miner, Myrtilla. *The School for Colored Girls, Washington, D.C.* Philadelphia: Merrihew and Thompson's Steam Power Press, 1854. In *Myrtilla Miner: A Memoir*, by Ellen M. O'Connor. Boston: Houghton, Mifflin, 1885. Reprint, New York: Arno Press, 1969.

Moore, Alonzo D. "Memoir of the Author." In William Wells Brown, *The Rising Son; or, The Antecedents and Advancement of the Colored Race*, 9–35.

Moore, Fred R. "Retrospection of a Year." *Colored American Magazine* 8.6 (June 1905): 342–343.

Moore, Thomas. *The Complete Poems of Thomas Moore.* Project Gutenberg, 2005. http://www.gutenberg.org/dirs/etext05/8cptm10.txt.

Murphy, Jeannette Robinson. *Southern Thoughts for Northern Thinkers.* New York: Bandanna Publishing, 1904.

Nell, William Cooper. *The Colored Patriots of the American Revolution, With Sketches of Several Distinguished Colored Persons.* Boston: Robert F. Wallcut, 1855. Available online at *Documenting the American South.* University Library, University of North Carolina at Chapel Hill, 1999. http://docsouth.unc.edu/nell/nell.html.

Nicolay, John G., and John Hay. "Abraham Lincoln: A History. The Attack on Sumner, and the Dred Scott Case." *Century Illustrated Magazine* 34.2 (June 1887): 203–219.

———. *Abraham Lincoln: A History.* New York: Century Company, 1890.

"Notice." *Voice of the Negro* 2.4 (Apr. 1905): 248.

"Our Christmas Number." *Voice of the Negro* 1.11 (Nov. 1904): 501.

Painter, Nell Irvin. *Sojourner Truth: A Life, A Symbol.* New York: Norton, 1996.

Palmer, John Williamson. "Old Maryland Homes and Ways." *Century Illustrated Magazine* 49.2 (Dec. 1894): 244–261.

Palgrave, Francis Turner. *The Golden Treasury of the Best Songs and Lyrical Poems in the English Language.* New York: Thomas Y. Crowell, 1883.

Parkhurst, Charles H. *The Southland Address Delivered by Rev. C. H. Parkhurst, D.D., before his Madison Square Congregation, New York City, the Sabbath after his Return from the South, April 28th, 1901.* New York, 1901.

"Pauline E. Hopkins." *Colored American Magazine* 2.3 (Jan. 1901): 218–219.

Phillips, Wendell. *Speeches, Lectures, and Letters.* Boston: Lee and Shepard, 1872.

Pierson, Emily Catharine. *Jamie Parker, The Fugitive.* Hartford, Conn.: Brockett, Fuller, 1851. Available online at *Documenting the American South.* University Library, University of North Carolina at Chapel Hill, 2000. http://docsouth.unc.edu/neh/pierson/pierson.html.

Pillsbury, Parker. *Acts of the Anti-Slavery Apostles.* Concord, N.H.: Clague, Wegman, Shlicht (Rochester, N.Y.), 1883. Reprint, Freeport, N.Y.: Books for Libraries Press, 1970.

Prichard, James Cowles. *Researches into the Physical History of Mankind.* 3rd ed. 5 vols. London: Sherwood, Gilbert, and Piper, 1836–1847.

"Publishers' Announcements." *Colored American Magazine* 7.11 (Nov. 1904): 700.

Record of Proceedings of a Court of Inquiry in the Case of Rear Admiral Winfield S. Schley, U.S. Navy, Convened at the Navy Yard, Washington, D.C., September 12, 1901. 2 vols. Washington, D.C.: U.S. Government Printing Office, 1901–1902.

Reed, Edwin. *Bacon vs. Shakespeare, Brief for Plaintiff.* 7th ed. Boston: Joseph Knight, 1897.

"Report of the Woman's Era Club for 1899." *National Association Notes* 3.10 (Apr. 1900): 1–2. Available online at *Records of the National Association of Colored Women's Clubs, 1895–1992,* LexisNexis Primary Sources in African American History, http://www.lexis-nexis.com/histuniv.

"Rogers' Case Now Goes to Courts." *Boston Guardian,* August 30, 1902, 1.

"Rogers Gets 10 Years." *Boston Guardian,* December 6, 1902, 1.

Roosevelt, Theodore. Theodore Roosevelt to Hon. ___, Charleston, S.C., November 26, 1902. In *Addresses and Presidential Messages of Theodore Roosevelt, 1902–1904,* 268–269. New York: G. P. Putnam, 1904.

———. Theodore Roosevelt to Mayor Robert Goodwyn Rhett, November 10, 1902. In *Theodore Roosevelt and His Time: Shown in His Own Letters,* edited by Joseph Bucklin Bishop, 1:168–169. 2 vols. New York: Charles Scribner's Sons, 1920.

Schurz, Carl. "Can the South Solve the Negro Problem?" *McClure's Magazine* 22.3 (Jan. 1904): 259–275.

Shockley, Ann Allen. "Pauline Elizabeth Hopkins: A Biographical Excursion into Obscurity." *Phylon* 33.1 (1972): 22–26.

Sienkiewicz, Henryk. *Quo Vadis: A Narrative of the Time of Nero.* Boston: Little, Brown, 1897.

Simmons, William J. *Men of Mark: Eminent, Progressive, Rising.* Cleveland: Geo. M. Rewell, 1887. Available online at *Documenting the American South.* University Library, University of North Carolina at Chapel Hill, 2000. http://docsouth.unc.edu/neh/simmons/simmons.html.

"The Sixth Biennial." *The Clubwoman* 9.9 (June 1902): 321–340.

Skinner, Robert Peet. *Abyssinia of To-day: An Account of the First Mission Sent by the American Government to the Court of the King of Kings (1903–1904).* New York: Longmans, Green, 1906.

Smiles, Samuel. *Self-Help; With Illustrations of Conduct and Perseverance.* 1859. Project Gutenberg, 1997. http://www.gutenberg.org/dirs/etext97/selfh10h.htm.

Smith, Elijah William. "Our Lost Leader." *Sumner Memorial Meeting.* Boston: Committee of Arrangements by Charles L. Mitchell, 1874. 29–31.

———. "Robert Morris." In *In Memoriam: Robert Morris, Sr.,* 46–48.

Smith, Orlando J. *Eternalism: A Theory of Infinite Justice.* Boston: Houghton, Mifflin, 1902.

Smith, Samuel Stanhope. *An Essay on the Causes of the Variety of Complexion and Figure in the Human Species.* 2nd ed. 1810. Reprint, Cambridge, Mass.: Belknap Press of Harvard University Press, 1965.

Soga, Alan Kirkland. "Call the Black Man to Conference VI." *Colored American Magazine* 7.4 (Apr. 1904): 250–252.

Southern, Eileen, ed. *African American Theater.* New York: Garland, 1994.

Spencer, Herbert. *The Principles of Ethics.* Vol. 2. New York: D. Appelton, 1897.

Stevens, Charles Emery. *Anthony Burns: A History.* Boston: John P. Jewett and Company, 1856.

Still, William. *The Underground Railroad: A Record of Facts, Authentic Narratives, Letters, Narrating the Hardships, Hair-Breadth Escapes and Death Struggles of the Slaves in their Efforts for Freedom.* 1871. Rev. ed. Philadelphia: People's Publishing Company, [1878].

Storey, Moorfield, Albert E. Pillsbury, A. A. Berle, Edward H. Clement, P. E. Hopkins, A. B. Hart, and George G. Bradford. *The Anti-Slavery Cause of Today.* Boston: Garrison Centenary Committee of the Boston Suffrage League, 1906. Available online at *African American Perspectives: Pamphlets from the Daniel A. P. Murray Collection, 1818–1907,* Library of Congress. http://hdl.loc.gov/loc.rbc/lcrbmrp.t2614.

Stowe, Harriet Beecher. *Sunny Memories of Foreign Lands.* 2 vols. Boston: Phillips, Sampson, 1854.

Straker, D. Augustus. *Euology [sic] on the Life, Character and Public Services of Robert Browne [sic] Elliott, Ex-Member of Congress and Speaker of the House of Representatives of South Carolina.* Columbia, S.C.: William Sloane, 1884.

———. *Reflections on the Life and Times of Toussaint L'Overture [sic], the Negro Haytien, Commander-in-Chief of the Army, Ruler under the Dominion of France, and Author of the Independence of Hayti.* Columbia, S.C.: Charles A. Calvo Jr., 1886.

Tate, Claudia. "Pauline Hopkins: Our Literary Foremother." In *Conjuring: Black Women, Fiction and Literary Tradition,* edited by Marjorie Pryse and Hortense J. Spillers, 53–66. Bloomington: Indiana University Press, 1985.

Terrell, Robert H. "Theodore Roosevelt." *Colored American Magazine* 7.8 (Aug. 1904): 542–544.

"They Slipped Rogers Away." *Boston Guardian,* September 6, 1902, 1, 5.

Thomas, William Hannibal. "Criminal Instincts." In *The American Negro: What He Was, What He Is, and What He May Become; A Critical and Practical Discussion,* 208–236. New York: Macmillan, 1901.

Thornbrough, Emma Lou. *T. Thomas Fortune: Militant Journalist.* Chicago: University of Chicago Press, 1972.

Trotter, James M. *Music and Some Highly Musical People.* Boston: Lee and Shepard, 1881. Reprint, New York: Johnson Reprint Corporation, 1968.

Trotter, Wm. Monroe, ed. *The Two Days of Observance of the One Hundredth Anniversary of the Birth of Charles Sumner.* Boston: Boston Sumner Centenary Committee of the New England Suffrage League and the Massachusetts Branch of the National Independent Political League, 1911.

"Two Views of *Uncle Tom's Cabin.*" *Outlook* 67.4 (Jan. 26, 1901): 236.

"The *Voice of the Negro* for July 1905." *Voice of the Negro* 2.6 (June 1905): 364.

Walker, Edwin G. "Eulogy of Hon. Edwin G. Walker." In *In Memoriam: Robert Morris, Sr.,* 26–45.

Wallinger, Hanna. *Pauline E. Hopkins: A Literary Biography*. Athens: University of Georgia Press, 2005.

Warner, Charles Dudley. "Education of the Negro." In *Fashions in Literature, and Other Literary and Social Essays and Addresses*, 193–224. New York: Dodd, Mead, 1902.

Washington, Booker T. "Lynch Law and Anarchy." *The Sunday School Times* 43 (Nov. 2, 1901): 713–714. Reprint in *The Booker T. Washington Papers*, edited by Louis R. Harlan and Raymond W. Smock, 13:500–504. Urbana: University of Illinois Press, 1972–1989.

———. *The Story of My Life and Work*. Toronto: J. L. Nichols, 1900. Reprint, New York: Negro Universities Press, 1969.

Washington, Booker T., N. B. Wood, and Fannie Barrier Williams. *A New Negro for a New Century*. Chicago: American Publishing House, 1900.

Washington, Mary Helen, ed. *Invented Lives: Narratives of Black Women, 1860–1960*. Garden City, N.Y.: Anchor, 1987.

Wetherell, Ellen F. *In Free America; or, Tales from North and South*. Boston: Colored Co-operative Publishing Company, 1901.

Whipple, Edwin Percy. *Eulogy on John Albion Andrew*. Boston: Alfred Mudge and Son, 1867.

Whittier, John Greenleaf. John Greenleaf Whittier to William Lloyd Garrison, November 24, 1863. In Garrison and Garrison, *William Lloyd Garrison*, 4:88–90.

———. *Voices of Freedom*. Philadelphia: Thomas S. Cavender, 1846.

———. *The Works of John Greenleaf Whittier*. 7 vols. Boston: Houghton, Mifflin, 1892.

Williams, George Washington. *History of the Negro Race in America, from 1619 to 1880: Negroes as Slaves, as Soldiers, and as Citizens*. 2 vols. New York: G. P. Putnam's Sons, 1882–1883. Reprint, New York: Arno Press, 1968.

Wilson, Henry, and Samuel Hunt. *History of the Rise and Fall of the Slave Power in America*. 3 vols. Boston: James R. Osgood, 1873–1877.

INDEX

Ira Dworkin teaches Africana studies and English at Gettysburg College. He was a Fulbright scholar to the Democratic Republic of the Congo and is writing a manuscript tracing the influence of the Congo on U.S. literary, visual, political, and religious cultures since the late nineteenth century.